HISTORY

OF THE COURT

OF AUGMENTATIONS

1536—1554

THE GREAT SEAL OF THE AUGMENTATIONS

Augmentation Office, E. 329/466, Ancient Deeds, Series B. S.

Walter C. Richardson

HISTORY
OF THE COURT
OF
AUGMENTATIONS
1536–1554

Oh that the kings grace knew of the extorcyon,
oppressyon and brybery that is vsed in his ij.
courtys; that is to say, of the Augmentacyon and
of the Escheker, but specially of the Augmentacyon.
. . . Breake down some of your courtys, for ye haue
to many, being so fylthyly mynystred!

Complaynt of Roderyck Mors

Office and authoritye sheweth what a man is. A
man knoweth not hym selfe, tyl he be tryed. Many
there be that being without office can rebuke magis-
trates, and fynd faut with men that be in office and
preeminence.
Latimer's Fifth Sermon

Louisiana State University Press
Baton Rouge

TO

G. D. R.

Copyright 1961 by
Louisiana State University Press
Library of Congress Catalogue Card Number: 61–7543
Manufactured in the United States of America by
J. H. Furst Company
Designed by Ernst A. Seemann

PREFACE

THIS STUDY HAS BEEN TOO LONG IN THE MAKING, BUT IN one of its kind as much time is consumed in the mere mechanical examination of source materials as in their analysis and evaluation. Over the course of years the very bulk of uncalendared manuscripts to be read has presented an imposing responsibility indeed; nor is the burden entirely removed with the conclusion of the undertaking, for any research investigation must, in a sense, be incomplete. As in all exploratory surveys, no one interpretation can hope to be definitive, so in the *History of the Court of Augmentations* is the final product not one of unqualified satisfaction. Numerous problems regarding Augmentations activities continue unsolved; questions concerning details of procedure, some of vital importance, are still to be answered. Despite the extent and continuity of its archives, many of the records of the Court have been lost or inadvertently destroyed, leaving the unconquerable silence of time hanging over certain aspects of policy and personnel. Did the Augmentations develop a just and efficient administration, one giving as much thought to the good of the nation as to the profits of the crown? Was it regarded as an evil or a boon by the people it served? Were its officials as corrupt as historians of the Reformation have assumed? Unfortunately, lack of proof, either positive or negative, usually renders such queries unanswerable, and historical judgment like the evidence itself must remain tentative and inconclusive.

Because the Augmentations was by inception and growth primarily an administrative institution, the major emphasis has been placed on its fluctuating internal organization and its managerial techniques. Nevertheless, the Court's financial position in relation to the other treasuries of the realm has not been ignored. If scant attention has been given to fines, enclosures, land sales, and the price revolution, it is because they do not form an integral part of the story. These and many other contiguous interests must await the light of further inquiry. It is to be hoped that this study will, in a measure, clear the way for those who seek narrower and more devious trails into the hitherto almost impenetrable Augmentations jungle.

With few exceptions the body of the Court's records are conveniently accessible in the Augmentation Office Division of the Public Record Office and in the Manuscripts Division of the British Museum. It has not, therefore, seemed necessary to specify in each case the location of the document cited. For the benefit of those unfamiliar with certain categories of Augmentations materials, official call numbers currently in use at the former repository have occasionally been added in citations.

For the most part proper nouns have been modernized, but in quotations and transcripts original form and spelling are preserved. Editorial criticism to the contrary notwithstanding, I still adhere to the principle that the faithful reproduction of the text appreciably enhances its value to the specialist.

The prolonged research required for this study has been furthered by grants-in-aid from the American Philosophical Society and the Social Science Research Council and from a generous subvention from the University Council on Research of the Louisiana State University, enabling me to remain in England for an additional summer during my last visit.

To the officials of the Public Record Office, the British Museum, the Institute of Historical Research, the Bodleian and Huntington Libraries, and to the many personal friends who have assisted me in this endeavor, my debt is indeed great. In particular, I wish to express my deepest appreciation to my colleague, Professor Robert A. Pascal of the Louisiana State University Law School, whose criticisms of the legal sections of the book have proved invaluable; and to my old friends Professor Goldwin Smith of Wayne State University and Professor Lacey Baldwin Smith of Northwestern University, who read the entire manuscript, I am especially indebted. Their scholarly advice and helpful suggestions have immeasurably improved the style as well as the accuracy of the text. Finally, acknowledgment must be made to the editor of the *Journal of the Society of Archivists* for permission to use a paper originally published in Volume I of the *Journal*, for October, 1957.

W. C. R.

Louisiana State University
Baton Rouge, Louisiana.
10 June, 1960.

CONTENTS

ILLUSTRATIONS

CHARTS

ABBREVIATIONS

Add. MSS.	Additional Manuscripts in the British Museum.
A. H. R.	*American Historical Review.*
Augm. Office.	Exchequer, Augmentation Office (The records in this office are classified under thirty divisions, E. 301 to E. 330).
B. M.	British Museum.
C. 54	Chancery, Close Rolls.
Cal. of Cecil Manuscripts	(H. M. C.) *Calendar of Cecil Manuscripts Preserved at Hatfield House* (ed. M. S. Giuseppi).
Cal. Pat. Rolls	*Calendar of Patent Rolls.*
Cobbett (ed.), *State Trials*	William Cobbett, T. B. Howell, *et al.* (eds.), *A Complete Collection of State Trials and Proceedings . . .* 42 vols.
Coke, *Reports*	*Reports of Sir Edward Coke.*
Cotton. MSS.	Cottonian Manuscripts in the British Museum.
D. L.	Duchy of Lancaster, records in the Public Record Office.
D. N. B.	*Dictionary of National Biography.*
Dyer, *Reports*	*Reports of Sir James Dyer.*
E. 36	Exchequer, Treasury of Receipt, Miscellaneous Books.
E. 101	Exchequer, Accounts Various.
E. 159	Exchequer, King's Remembrancer, Memoranda Rolls.
E. 163	Exchequer, King's Remembrancer, Miscellanea.
E. 164	Exchequer, King's Remembrancer, Miscellaneous Books.
E. 304	Augm. Office, Conveyances of Crown Lands.
E. 305	Augm. Office, Deeds of Purchase and Exchange.
E. 306	Augm. Office, Duchy of Cornwall records.
E. 313	Augm. Office, Letters Patent, original.
E. 314	Augm. Office, Miscellanea.

E. 315	Augm. Office, Miscellaneous Books.
E. 316-319	Augm. Office, Particulars for Grants.
E. 321	Augm. Office, Proceedings of the Court of Augmentations.
E. 322	Augm. Office, Deeds of Surrender of Monasteries and other religious institutions.
E. 323	Augm. Office, Rolls of Accounts of the Treasurer of the Augmentations.
E. 324	Augm. Office, Warrants for the Delivery of Records.
E. 325	Augm. Office, Accounts of the Sale of Woods in the Court of Augmentations.
E. 329	Augm. Office, Ancient Deeds, Series B. S.
E. 336	Exchequer, Office of First Fruits and Tenths.
E. 351	Exchequer, Lord Treasurer's Remembrancer, Pipe Office, Declared Accounts.
E. 358	Exchequer, Enrolled Accounts.
E. 369	Exchequer, Lord Treasurer's Remembrancer, Miscellaneous Books.
E. 407	Exchequer of Receipt, Miscellanea.
E. H. R.	*English Historical Review.*
Eng. Rep..	*English Reports—Full Reprint.*
Exch.	Exchequer.
G. D.	Gifts and Deposits: Manchester Papers.
H. E. L.	William S. Holdsworth, *History of English Law.*
H. M. C.	Historical Manuscripts Commission.
Harl. MSS.	Harleian Manuscripts in the British Museum.
K. R.	King's Remembrancer's Division of the Exchequer.
Lansd. MSS.	Lansdowne Manuscripts in the British Museum.
L. and P..	*Letters and Papers, Foreign and Domestic of the Reign of Henry VIII*, eds. J. S. Brewer, James Gairdner, and R. H. Brodie.
L. R.	Land Revenue Office.
L. T. R.	Lord Treasurer's Remembrancer (cited as T. R.)
Misc. Books	Miscellaneous Books.
Nichols (ed.), *Literary Remains*	John G. Nichols (ed.), *Literary Remains of King Edward the Sixth.* Volume II contains the King's *Journal.*
P. R. O.	Public Record Office.
Plowden, *Reports*	Edmund Plowden, *An Exact Abridgment in English of the Commentaries or Reports.*
S. C.	Special Collections.
S. P.	State Papers.
S. R.	*Statutes of the Realm.*

CHAPTER ONE

INTRODUCTION

HE YEAR 1536 BROUGHT MOMENTOUS CHANGES TO ENGLISH society, already conditioned by a series of climactic events. Nationally, the Annulment and the Reformation had proceeded hand in hand, as Protestant opinion came to the support of the doctrine of royal supremacy. The death of Catherine of Aragon on January 7 spelt the doom not only of Catholic opposition but also of her successor, though Anne Boleyn escaped the ignominy of repudiation through the more spectacular portals of execution. The king, temporarily placated by a new spouse and the prospect of a male heir, turned his attention to the significant legislation pending in the last two sessions of the Reformation Parliament. Submissive to royal demand, that same parliament added the possessions of the monasteries to the newly found wealth of the crown, while in the north the ferment of economic and religious discontent slowly crystallized into open resistance. But the temper of the northern rebels did not exemplify the spirit of the entire realm, and the rebellion subsided almost as quickly as it had spread. By December the forces of opposition had spent themselves; in fact, the very disunity which led to the failure of the Pilgrimage of Grace strengthened the position of the crown. The king could indeed afford to celebrate Christmas with such a triumphal display of pomp and ceremony that its magnificence " rejoiced every man wondrously." [1]

[1] Edward Hall, *Chronicle*, anno 1536; Madeleine Hope Dodds and Ruth Dodds, *The Pilgrimage of Grace, 1536-1537* (Cambridge, 1915), II, 25.

Wonderful too were the achievements of the vicar-general, Thomas Cromwell, vice-regent of the king in " spirituals," who by the summer of 1536 was at the height of his power. With the dissolution of the monasteries, his grand design for the augmentation of the revenues of the crown, conceived at least two years earlier, was already in operation.[2] The first Act of Dissolution became effective on April 4; thereafter, investigatory activities proceeded rapidly under the fourth of a series of visitation proceedings by royal commission. Simultaneously, parliament passed another measure authorizing the erection of the Court of Augmentations for the receipt and administration of monastic acquisitions. Although the major appointments to the Court were not announced until April 24 of the same year, the machinery of this institution was set into motion several weeks before its final organization was complete. Since the intentions of Cromwell were always suspect, the Augmentations was regarded by many as just another engine of oppression, designed primarily to tap the yet unexploited resources of the clergy. As a cherished project of the king's chief minister, the institution was thus greeted with suspicion from the beginning; yet few men dared openly to criticize a fundamental policy of the government known to be dear to the heart of their sovereign, and fewer still could legitimately accuse the Court's officials of inefficiency or condemn them for any lack of thoroughness. Nor was the new institution, born of administrative necessity and an expanding royal income, to be short-lived. Sovereigns die; ministers rise and fall; domestic problems vary according to circumstances; but once established, bureaucratic institutions perpetuate themselves. For some eighteen years the Augmentations dominated the machinery of central and local government and, for many generations thereafter, colored the financial, judicial, and administrative procedure of the state.

The impact of Augmentations influence was greatest in the field of purely administrative affairs, though the Court itself subsequently came to establish forms and precedents for other revenue departments and legal institutions. Much that was new was developed by it, not the least of which were those judicial and administrative departures which later were acceptable to the officers of the modified Exchequer, while

---

[2] An abbreviated draft of Cromwell's comprehensive ecclesiastical policy was drawn up in 1534: " Things to be moved for the King's highness for an increase and augmentation to be had for maintenance of his most royal estate, and for the defence of the realm, and necessary to be provided for taking away the excess which is the great cause of the abuses in the Church." J. S. Brewer, James Gairdner, and R. H. Brodie (eds.), *Letters and Papers, Foreign and Domestic, of the Reign of Henry VIII* (London, 1862–1910), VII, no. 1355 (hereinafter cited as *L. and P.*). On the details of implementation, see Philip Hughes, *The Reformation in England* (London, 1950), I, 283 ff.

older techniques, adapted and re-established, were preserved. Especially significant was the effect upon administrative procedures within the areas controlled by crown officers of the royal demesne, where innovation was more likely to prove successful. Nevertheless, the Tudor pattern of estate management had already been developing for more than a generation before the system was perfected by the Augmentations.

A marked change in the evolution of crown land administration is perceptible about the time of the erection of the Court, for which it was partly responsible. In fact, the institution was designed to administer the augmented national revenues, already becoming too extensive to be managed properly under the existing machinery. Since the beginning of the reign of Henry VII revenue from the landed estates of the crown had multiplied rapidly, receiving impetus under Henry VIII with the coming of the Reformation. The steady acquisition of attainted property had been going on for a half-century when the suppression of the monasteries brought all the land and property of the dissolved religious houses into the hands of the crown, together with another batch of attainders following the Pilgrimage of Grace in 1536. To this vast demesne were constantly added other royal estates acquired by purchase or exchange, resulting from the calculated policy of rounding out the honorial units of the king's possessions.[3] These factors alone greatly increased the burden of administration and added immeasurably to the problems of revenue collecting and accounting.

The effect of this tremendous increase in revenue is clearly reflected in the accounting procedures used by the office of general surveyors, which prior to 1536 had charge of all crown possessions not under the survey of the ancient Exchequer nor the traditional duchy of Lancaster. Scholars having occasion to use the sixteenth century accounts of the receivers of

---

[3] The royal policy of uniting a number of manors in the traditional land units known as honors was begun in 1531–32 with the creation of the honor of Hunesdon in Hertfordshire, which was formed around the manor and palace of Hunesdon as "the chyef & capytall place" of the enlarged honor. 23 Henry VIII, c. 30, *S. R.*, III, 410. This plan was followed in the erection of the honors of Ewelm or Newelme (Oxfordshire), Hampton Court (Middlesex), Petworth (Sussex), Amphill (Bedfordshire), and Grafton (Northamptonshire). 32 Henry VIII, c. 61 (not printed, 1540) ; 32 Henry VIII, c. 63 (not printed, 1540) ; 32 Henry VIII, c. 64 (not printed, 1540) ; 33 Henry VIII, c. 37 (1541–42) ; and 33 Henry VIII. c. 38 (1541–42), *S. R.*, III, 876–79. In 1545 "An Acte for the ereccion of the Honors of Westminster Kingeston St. Osithes and Donyngton" (37 Henry VIII, c. 18) laid down the general rule for the administration of all such units, a principle which had already been followed. Section vii of the statute provided that in the future all honors should automatically fall within the jurisdiction of the revenue court which had charge of the capital and principal part of the honor at the time of erection. *Ibid.*, 1009–11. Thus the Court of General Surveyors and the Court of Augmentations both benefited by the plan.

crown lands will note a distinct difference between the records for the reign of Henry VII and those of Henry VIII, the accounts for the former period being fewer in number and relatively shorter.[4] Likewise, in the earlier rolls of accounts the crown lands are grouped in large units, for the convenience of receipt and audit, without regard to their geographical location. Indeed, in the case of most of the newer possessions such an arrangement was the natural result of the manner of their acquisition. Though widely scattered, estates were normally acquired piecemeal in large blocks and theoretically retained by the crown in single units, such as the lands of attainted persons which carried the classification of their former owners. Thus, Warwick lands, Salisbury lands, and the Cardinal's lands were listed as belonging to the counties where their capital manors lay. Naturally enough, in accordance with previous monastic practice, a like pattern was at first followed for the possessions that came to the crown through the Dissolution. Although the Augmentations system replaced the earlier monastic administrative units, the county receiver distributed his accounts according to the source of the incoming revenue, so that it was still possible to show the gross receipts of a particular house in his district. More frequently than not, however, the central receiverships of the monasteries were not continued, which meant that local receivers or bailiffs paid their collections directly to the Augmentations receiver and had their accounts audited by the Court auditor of that district. Each parcel of land was then accounted for by the receiver for the county in which the house was located, though in fact the land in question might lie in an area far removed from the original site of the monastery. The property of a monastery was seldom confined to one shire, while some of the larger houses like Abingdon, St. Albans, Furness, or Walsingham owned land in many different counties. The Benedictine abbey of Abingdon in Berkshire not only had vast possessions in that shire but also had holdings scattered throughout ten other English counties, as well as in Wales and the marches thereof.[5] Similarly, the lands of the great St. Albans monastery, valued at £2,102 7s. 1¾d. per annum, lay in several different counties, with an additional dozen cells and hospitals, widely dispersed, subordinate to the monastery proper.[6] Some houses had even acquired possessions beyond the sea,

---

[4] There are 1,880 accounts for Henry VII's reign, usually less than ten membranes each in length, whereas the 7,484 accounts for the reign of Henry VIII are often thirty or more membranes long, the majority of which cover the last decade of the period. *Lists and Indexes*, XXXIV, pt. II, List of Original Ministers' Accounts (1910), Preface, iii–iv.

[5] *L. and P.*, XIII, pt. 1, no. 242. See p. 289, *infra*.

[6] These dependent establishments lay in Hertfordshire, Bedfordshire, Lincolnshire, Norfolk, Berkshire, Essex, and Northumberland. Sir William Dugdale,

as the cell in the Scilly Isles belonging to Tavistock or the affiliations of Furness abbey in Ireland and the Isle of Man. Had the earlier honorial system prevailed in such cases, the accounts of the cells would have been preserved among the records of the county where the parent monastery was located.

In the face of increasing alienations the older usage quickly proved cumbersome and inadequate, and the theory of managerial unity was abandoned as impractical. A chief receiver and an auditor were appointed to each county, while new surveys determined the extent of the crown's holdings therein. Being responsible to the Court for all the revenues in his district, the receiver gathered yearly the rents and duties from the tenants, farmers, and local collectors under him, the debits having been determined by the auditor. By statutory requirement, annual accounts had to be completed before the end of Hilary term, and total receipts paid into the central treasury of the Court prior to March 20, upon pain of forfeiture of office. When tenants were delinquent in their payments, accounts were returned *in super*, to be carried over as unsettled claims, in order that process might be made out against them by the chancellor and council of the Court. In this respect the accounting procedure represented a distinct improvement from the beginning.

Since both the duchy of Lancaster and the office of general surveyors continued to use the medieval pattern, the various changes in the system of crown land supervision were peculiarly identified with the Augmentations. When the organization was complete, it had inaugurated what was, in effect, a county unit plan of revenue administration. Under the new arrangement all crown lands of the Court, irrespective of previous tenure, were included in the accounts for the county of their location. To equalize the administrative burden of receipt and audit, several counties of England and Wales were grouped together according to the extent of holdings in different areas of the country. Ministers' accounts, therefore, were not drawn up under the name of the monastery or family unit but by counties within the circuits, which, with the exception of Yorkshire, included two or more counties. Subclassification of individual manors and particular parcels of larger units in relation to origin was, of course, retained. Under such an arrangement the revenues of a given manor or piece of monastic land were enrolled on the account rolls of the receiver of the circuit in which the county of location was included, and consequently, it was no longer necessary to know the names of both the reciver and the monastery in order to locate its account among the

Monasticon Anglicanum (New ed. by John Caley *et al.*, London, 1817–30), II, 208, 213, 250–55.

Court's records. This system was extended to include all the lands of the Court of Survey, which the second Court of Augmentations acquired in 1547, when the two institutions were amalgamated. While the identity of local units was still preserved in the accounts, all the older land divisions, such as Salisbury lands or the former possessions of Whalley monastery, were broken up; each receiver collected the revenues for all parcels of Salisbury or Whalley lands that lay within the counties of his district.[7]

In years to come many minor improvisations and financial expedients were to be relegated to limbo, but in other aspects of administrative policy the Court's influence was felt long after its more important financial activities had been forgotten. When finally absorbed by the Exchequer in 1554, the Augmentations left an indelible imprint on its practices. In matters of receipt and audit, as well as through the continuation of particular offices, Exchequer procedure was for decades modified by Augmentations precedents.

Considered by historians as a by-product of the Dissolution, it has been customary to dismiss the Court of Augmentations as no more than a temporary organization set up by Cromwell for the control of the monastic wealth as it came into the possession of the crown. Such an interpretation, however, minimizes the evolutionary importance of the Court and ignores its primary position as the central treasury of the realm during the transitional period between the decline of the Tudor chamber and the reconstitution of the Exchequer. At first it was concerned chiefly with taking the surrenders of the suppressed monasteries, the collection and disposition of monastic spoils, land surveys, and the assignment of pensions to the inmates of the late religious houses upon their dismissal. Most of that work, however, was of a temporary character and terminated as soon as the last phases of the Dissolution were over. The sporadic acquisition of additional crown property entrusted to the jurisdiction of the Court rendered such activities as land surveys and inventories of goods occasionally necessary, but within a few years the Court had settled down to the routine of administration. The daily problems of land management and supervision were soon equalled, if not overshadowed, by the mass of complaints of tenants and other altercations concerning crown lands and revenues, both of which became a part of the regular responsibility of the Court. Without intent or statutory prescription, the Court of Augmentations grew into another of those several tribunals which characterized the sixteenth century.

[7] The county unit system is exemplified in the Rolls of Accounts of the treasurer of the Augmentations and in the Ministers' Accounts, General Series (S. C. 6).

Despite its rapid development, its pedestrian character attracted to it little public attention. Methodical and businesslike in all its varied activities, the Court in many respects set the pattern for administrative efficiency. Prior to the general breakdown in all departments of public administration that followed hard upon the death of Henry VIII, it represented the best in Cromwellian standards of speed, reliability, and resourcefulness. Unfettered by tradition and conservatism, it could draw upon the experience of the Courts of General Surveyors and Duchy Chamber to fashion a practical organization adaptable to the changing needs of the government. Considerable care was taken in the selection of reliable officials to head the new institution, and not many mistakes were made in the original appointments. Even among the district and local officers, all but a few proved to be hard-working, loyal servants of the Court, conscientious in furthering the interests of the crown. It was not, however, a feeling of official responsibility that prompted these lesser ministers to serve the Augmentations faithfully, but rather the knowledge that loyalty seldom went unrewarded and an awareness of the vigilance of their superiors. None the less, local influences were strong, and county or manorial officials were often far removed from the restraints of the central office. Some ministers became powerful and domineering, exercising an unwarranted authority over the king's tenants. Within the framework of privilege there was no lack of opportunity for profit.

It is sometimes difficult to characterize a group as heterogeneous and undistinguished as were these Augmentations ministers, whose reputations rest chiefly upon their years of unremitting service. Those like Sir Richard Rich and Sir Robert Southwell who left the Court after a few years went on to higher positions; those who remained contributed unconsciously to the growing respect acquired by the Court in every quarter of the kingdom. None were deliberate intriguers, and few had family influence at court to further their advancement. Most of them were self-made men whose careers in the service of the crown rested ultimately upon their own ability. Ambitious to a fault, they not only entrenched themselves in the good graces of sovereign and council but, as often as not, established family connections profitable to themselves. The system, so prevalent in the Tudor age, of permitting deputies to perform the duties of an office enabled later officials to put sons or brothers under them to be trained for independent posts as soon as opportunity offered. Furthermore, a discreet word to the right person could pave the way for profitable leases or the purchase of coveted manors. Such practices, although sometimes detrimental to administrative efficiency, were not necessarily corrupt. Augmentations officials were simply in a position to anticipate bargains.

Because the greater number of Augmentations ministers profited from the Dissolution, it has been customary to brand them as greedy and unscrupulous. The facts, however, do not altogether support such a hypothesis. As officials of the Augmentations they were resented locally because they represented influence and power in the neighborhood; moreover, they had the authority of the crown behind them, a fact which filled the timid souls around them with awe and envy. It was probably as much jealousy as suspicion of corruption that led to the jokes and insinuations against well-established officials. For example, of the heads of the Court it was said that, not inappropriately, Sir Richard Rich was created baron of lies, instead of Leighs, while Sir Richard Sackville, because of his extensive holdings of monastic property, was popularly referred to as Chancellor Fillsack. Uncomplimentary as were these innocuous puns, there is little concrete proof to support their implications; upon the other hand, all the indirect evidence suggests that the hands of few of the Court's officials were entirely clean. With few exceptions they made the most of their opportunities, while in many cases they deliberately abused their privileges by using government funds and official influence to their own advantage. Nevertheless, in profiting from the generosity of the king, their rewards and emoluments were no more liberal than were those of other civil servants. All the major officers of the Court were recipients of grants of land, but most of it was bought at the standard price fixed by the government and universally applied to all purchasers. The standard price, of course, based upon the annual income of the property as determined by land surveys, was not necessarily the same as the price on the open market.[8] People like Sackville, Rich, Edward North, Thomas Pope, and the Mildmays—Walter and Thomas—all established family fortunes from the profits of monastic acquisitions; but so did the Greshams—John, Richard, and Thomas— William Paulet, Ralph Sadler, Thomas Wriothesley, Charles Brandon, Edmund Peckham, and countless other enterprising individuals who were shrewd enough to make the most of an advantageous market. It was a vigorous, expanding age, and most ministers active in public life were in one way or another carried along with the strong current of national prosperity.

However important in Cromwell's own calculations, the ultimate significance of the Court was not at first apparent. Its later predominance as a financial department lay not so much in the authority granted to it by its original constitution as in the power and influence it subsequently acquired. Initially its duties under statutory regulation were threefold,

---

[8] On the problem of evaluation of crown lands, see Chapter Seven, n. 52.

though in practice it was never strictly limited by constitutional authority. First of all, it was a practical organization, instituted for the express purpose of managing all the lands and properties of the dissolved monasteries and administering the revenues arising therefrom. To these were added from time to time various other possessions and revenues acquired by the crown as a result of the deliberate policy of expanding the royal income. Closely related to this primary function was a second responsibility, that of adjudicating disputes growing out of the Dissolution and settling controversies concerning the personnel and property entrusted to its charge. Of all the litigation actually handled by the Court, however, the greater bulk was in cases of title and possession. As a court of record the Court of Augmentations thus became an important adjunct to the older courts of the realm in the enforcement of the common law. On the other hand, its equitable jurisdiction being extensive, it served the crown as a kind of chancery for people living on the royal demesne. The third duty was more directly an outgrowth of the Dissolution proceedings; claims and pensions of the dispossessed religious were paid and processed by the Court.

A determinant factor in the rapid growth of the Court was the position which it occupied in the administration of the landed revenues of the crown. After 1547, when the Court of General Surveyors was merged with the reconstituted Court of Augmentations, the latter assumed control over the nation's largest single division of crown wealth and was directly responsible to the king for his greatest source of income. Scattered throughout England, Wales, Calais, and the Marches, these hereditary possessions of the crown under the administrative jurisdiction of the Court—lordships, honors, castles, seigniories, manors, chases, parks, and woodlands—constituted a virtually independent kingdom, distinct in status and separate in function from the remainder of the realm. Within this vast feudal demesne the king was still supreme landlord, dispensing justice and collecting revenues according to the traditional custom of *jura regalia*. Tenants, farmers, villagers, and bondmen alike were subject to his jurisdiction, while all tenures, from freehold to knight service, came under the close scrutiny of the royal officials. At the time of his accession Henry VIII's demesne was already considerably greater than that of any of his predecessors. After acquiring all the possessions of the monasteries and chantries, the crown was unrivaled as the chief landowner in the realm; consequently, manorial administration became an integral part of the expanding civil service. Sales and alienations rapidly depleted the crown holdings, but usually not before the royal machinery of local administration had been organized. As lands were acquired by purchase, gift, forfeiture, or prerogative exaction, they were simply added to the Augmentations system.

Except for the ancient duchy of Lancaster no department of administration presented more difficulties nor offered a greater challenge to imaginative officials than did the Court of Augmentations. They were confronted daily with a variety of interesting problems, ranging from local disturbances in remote villages to complicated questions of public relations with other branches of the central government at Westminster. Swarms of monastic pensioners and former officials of the suppressed religious houses besieged the Court for annuities or compensation to cover loss of previous offices or emoluments, while from all quarters of the kingdom informants reported regularly on the conduct of local officials or notified the chancellor and council of crown rents that had been concealed. As such information could not be ignored, the Court was kept busy investigating complaints and checking on reports by means of special commissions of inquiry. Still, all this was routine. In relation to the crown and council the Court had a completely different set of responsibilities. It was expected to collect debts, renew obligations, sell or lease crown lands, make wood sales, and prepare reports to other departments on questions of rents, tithes, and other matters relating to crown possessions. Finally, as a national treasury it made periodic declarations to the council on the state of its revenues and paid its bills as quickly as possible in fulfillment of the innumerable warrants that came to the treasurer's office. Not the least important among the duties of the council of the Court were the official conferences and the annual auditing of revenue accounts.

As crown lands and possessions grew in number and extent, the work of the Augmentations increased proportionately, both locally and centrally, in variety as in volume. As might be expected, it absorbed units that normally would have been put under the Court of General Surveyors or incorporated into the duchy of Lancaster. In addition, as a national treasury it gradually took over much of the revenue formerly assigned to the chamber. Before the end of the Henrician regime it had become the chief paymaster of the state as well as the principal administrative land agency.

To govern this extensive territory the Court maintained a bureaucratic structure which, though controlled through the office at Westminster, spread out over the length and breadth of the land. A half-dozen top officials formed the inner hierarchy of administration, but in the end the most responsible agents were the regional representatives—surveyors, receivers, and auditors—upon whose honesty and integrity the ultimate success of the entire organization depended. Locally, as in any private unit of manorial administration, separate crown officials supervised the individual estates and directed estate management. They numbered several hundred, each of whom was in a position to appropriate a portion, however meager, of the incoming profits and crown revenues. Trustworthiness and efficiency were, therefore, the cardinal prerequisites of a system, the very extent and complexity of which rendered corruption comparatively easy. Strong hands and close supervision were required at all times to keep the machine running smoothly. Like the duchy of Lancaster organization before it, the Augmentations became something of a test case. Then as now, able statesmen were quick to realize that laxity breeds corruption which, once developed, spreads rapidly to all departments of government, and conversely, that an entire officialdom may be inspired by the competence of its leaders. Such were the supervisory roles played by Cardinal Thomas Wolsey and Thomas Cromwell in the broad field of public administration, while in the more restricted sphere of Augmentations activities the able direction of such outstanding ministers as Sir Richard Rich, Sir Edward North, and Sir Thomas Pope had a similar effect. But in public departments as in private business the strength of an institution is determined largely by the character of its entire personnel. With the Court of Augmentations the failure to preserve that high quality of leadership, combined with the absence of an effective centralized control, resulted in the decline and final abolition of a national revenue department that might well have become a permanent feature of Tudor administration.

As everyone expected to share in the economic prosperity of his sovereign, the division of monastic spoils presented an obvious opportunity for peculation and graft; more often than not the acquisition of a few coveted manors simply whetted the appetite for more. Most of the nobles undoubtedly shared the conviction of the impetuous duke of Norfolk, Thomas Howard, that the more persistent they were the greater would be their reward. More outspoken suitors presented their claims frankly, openly offering to pay the king as much as anyone else was prepared to give.[9] Those who sought free grants of land and property or desired to purchase monastic estates at favorable terms " sweetened " their contacts at court. Many sought favors through Augmentations officials obviously in a position to further the interests of their relatives and friends. Others, influential ministers for the most part, approached the king or Cromwell directly, with gifts, promises, bribes, and renewed expressions of loyalty. While some were refused and a few ignored, most of the loyal servants of the crown were rewarded quite generously.

[9] John Vaughan to Thomas Cromwell, *L. and P.*, X, no. 746.

Among the more fortunate recipients were the officials of the Court of Augmentations, whose positions gave them easy access to the more desirable acquisitions. Consequently, all the major posts in the Court were greatly sought, not so much for their own worth, but because each office carried with it liberal opportunities for patronage and profit. Without exception, the leading Augmentations officials rose rapidly, both in affluence and in power.

In addition to material advantages, such positions offered prospects of successful careers in one of the newer branches of administration where traditional barriers of seniority and social prestige were less pronounced. Men fortunate enough to attain those appointments were usually of humble origin, mostly former friends of Cromwell who had risen with him in the royal service. In fact many, like Thomas Pope, John Onley, and the Southwell brothers, Robert and Richard, owed their original patents in the Court to his patronage. For the lesser jobs on the crown estates loyalty and honesty were prime requisites, in many cases being given greater consideration than either training or ability. In the broader reaches of national politics few Augmentations officials attained any particular distinction. Only one officer, the chancellor of the Court, was a regular member of the king's council where governmental policy was determined. For the most part, the remainder were county men of little prominence. Of this larger group only a few, like Sir Walter Mildmay, Sir Richard Southwell, and Sir Thomas Arundell, were ever to achieve more than local distinction. Nevertheless, the indefinite character of the Tudor minister belies his real importance to the state. The strength of the monarchy lay in the co-operative effort of the methodical, undistinguished members of the bureaucracy. Countless obscure, conscientious public servants molded a complex and disunited administration into an efficient system. The ultimate success of the government rested upon their collective achievement.

A characteristic feature of the Tudor bureaucracy was the conciliar principle of centralized control, through which the policies of the independent state agencies were unified. But since the council faithfully expressed the wishes of the crown, its practical supervision of a particular institution was determined largely by the king's demands, which often were of a purely financial nature. When Cromwell was making the decisions, the objectives of national prosperity and a passive public were not lost sight of, but after his downfall the king was more insistent upon having his own way. Money, or the lack of it, became a major concern of the privy council. Henry VIII was not a penurious sovereign, but the growing need for ready capital made him vigilant in all matters relating to revenues and finance. Consequently, the Court of Augmentations, as the principal revenue department, occupied a unique position in the state, gradually replacing the chamber as the dominant treasury. As long as it maintained a high standard of efficiency its position was assured. It was only after the breakdown of conciliar government during the Edwardian period that the Court declined in power and prestige. With the accession of Mary in 1553, the spirit of expansion was over. Retrenchment was the order of the day. The Augmentations revenues were united to the older Exchequer, which once again recovered its former position of ascendancy.

CHAPTER TWO

TUDOR ADMINISTRATION

ESPITE THE CONSTITUTIONAL LIMITATIONS OF MONARCHY, the steady extension of the power of the crown was the most striking feature of the Tudor state. Though parliament and the council were still the two traditional keystones of the government, both were subordinate to the will of the sovereign, whose decisions were influenced, if at all, by only a handful of royal advisers. As an agency of the crown, parliament enacted legislation which it seldom initiated, while in affairs of state the council was expected to deliberate and advise but not to determine royal policies. The functions of the latter body were primarily executive and administrative, although in either capacity it worked through committees, commissions, and separate agencies whose activities it closely controlled. The Tudor sovereigns were not improvisers. They created little that was new. What they did was to adapt the old and established institutions to their own special needs, converting an archaic system into a relatively efficient machinery of government. As the agencies of supervision increased in number, so was the prerogative of the king in council extended to cover the new jurisdiction thrust upon it. Everywhere in the realm authority was basic to the concept of law and order; so in government and administration was unity an essential principle of success. Nationally, executive regulation was increased, step by step, until the strong hand of the state was felt in every aspect of public and private endeavor. No less than the co-ordination of control was the centralization of authority in domestic administration a cardinal achievement.

During the first half of the Tudor period conciliar government developed along lines foreshadowed under Edward IV and laid down by Henry VII, whose reign marked an advance in internal administration. Under the careful scrutiny of a handful of specialized ministers, a small selective council effectively regulated the work of the larger whole. This restricted body of ministers, working in close co-operation with the king, planned a restored national economy and organized the agencies through which the new order was implemented. After the general confusion of the Wars of the Roses the chief problem had been the restoration of law and order, a task which entailed the minute investigation and reorganization of all the major departments of administration. Public officials were bonded and charged with definite responsibilities, among which was a periodic reporting to the king or council. A comprehensive system for auditing accounts was initiated; modern procedures and improvements introduced. Gradually untrained personnel were superseded by professionals experienced in the service of the state. When unsuspected weaknesses were unearthed or hidden evils discovered, they were at once eradicated. Though stricter penalties were imposed, rewards for marked ability were proportionately greater than under previous regimes. By such practices as these the whole structure of the administrative organization of the state was revitalized.[1] Efficiency became the order of the day.

The Court of Augmentations emerged as an integral part of the improved order of government which had been in process of development for more than half a century. Though the ultimate achievement of national centralized monarchy was not realized until Elizabeth's reign, the outlines had been filled in before the death of Henry VIII. Since the Augmentations occupied a key position in the revised system, an understanding of the practical operation of Tudor government is indispensable to any explanation of the role of the Court therein. Before its final dissolution the Augmentations was the principal object of attack by the Edwardian reformers, while afterwards it became the center of a long controversy over revenue procedure between the king's council and Exchequer officials on the respective merits of the old ways as opposed to the new. Even as late as the Restoration the revival of the

---

[1] Best short account of the structure and activities of the early Tudor council is found in William H. Dunham, " Henry VIII's Whole Council and Its Parts," *The Huntington Library Quarterly*, VII (November, 1943), 7–46. For an earlier interpretation, see A. F. Pollard, " Council, Star Chamber, and Privy Council under the Tudors," *E. H. R.*, XXXVII (July, 1922), 337–60. The widespread activities of the Yorkist council are ably presented in J. R. Lander, " Council, Administration and Councillors, 1461–1485," *Bulletin of the Institute of Historical Research*, XXXII (November, 1959), 138–80.

Court could be seriously proposed as a means of re-establishing order in the revenue machinery. At a time when the auditors' books had fallen into confusion, a survey of all crown lands would certainly have served as a convenient guide to the lord treasurer in the granting of crown leases. Indeed, as the author of the project suggested, a departmental service, similar in nature to that rendered by the earlier Augmentations, would have given the government in 1660 a full view of the restored revenues and strengthened the financial position of the crown.[2]

The execution of the original reform program by Henry VII was entrusted to the smaller, more permanent council of the king. Individually or collectively these well-chosen ministers injected new life into a decadent administration that had long been hovering on the brink of complete breakdown. More highly organized under Henry VIII, this body became known as the privy council, with a president, secretary, and a written record of all its proceedings. But like the parent institution from which it emerged, the privy council remained an indeterminate undifferentiated body, composed exclusively of the king's chief ministers and limited in authority only by the exigencies of royal command. The position of councillor was one of privilege rather than right, and not all ministers were so honored, for Henry was cautious in his choice of confidants. Even within the secrecy of its own deliberations the council was not always apprised of the king's true intentions or fully informed on all features of a projected policy. As an executive advisory organ it was required to give counsel and proffer advice but not to oppose or contradict; above all, it was expected to find ways and means for the speedy execution of the broad programs outlined by the sovereign or his chief councillor. Indeed, its daily activities were wide and varied, ranging from important affairs of state to petty details of routine administration. It received petitions, heard complaints, investigated suspicions of disloyalty, delegated authority when authorized to do so, and in general, provided a clearinghouse for the manifold duties of the crown. Judicially, it heard whatever cases the king referred to it, sitting either in council or Star Chamber, according to the nature of the offense, while in financial matters it acted as a consultative committee. In foreign affairs the councillors received embassies, instructed and supervised English ministers abroad, and informally assisted the king in the conduct

---

[2] A proposal of 1660 by John Bowring to settle the revenues which had suffered greatly through embezzlement, by re-erecting the Court of Augmentations. S. P. 29/26, fols. 164–65. This document is calendared in *Cal. State Papers, Domestic, Charles II, 1660–1661*, no. 101, p. 462. Some four years later he was still insisting that a revival of the Augmentations was the best way to improve the national revenue. *Ibid., 1664–1665*, no. 85, p. 147.

of diplomacy. Theoretically their duties were indefinite, but as the business of the expanding government increased, conciliar functions crystallized into more specific spheres of authority.

Historians have long observed the tendency of the medieval council to break up into smaller divisions, each with a separate set of delegated responsibilities. In spite of this fissiparous quality, however, the essential unity of the original institution was not seriously impaired, for the subordinate units retained concurrent jurisdiction and, to a degree at least, common membership. Nominally all those who might conceivably be of some use to the crown were sworn to the council, but most of them attended infrequently, if at all, and under the Tudors only at the king's bidding. Any council of more than a hundred advisers was impractical, though individually the members might offer valuable suggestions. The entire body never sat together at any one time, nor was the majority ever called upon to render a formal decision. In practice, fewer than a dozen men of the older *magnum concilium* directed the main work of the state, sitting with the king *in privatum*. Finally a privy council emerged, but it began as little more than a special group of royal servants meeting together to discharge, in informal deliberation, their collective functions. Whatever its form or composition, the council remained organically unchanged; whether great or small, ordinary or private, it was still to be used for any purpose the monarch desired. In practical operation, therefore, it could divide itself into numerous branches, some of which in their specialized capacities met separately at Westminster; yet always there was retained " about the king's person " an indefinite number of confidential ministers.[3]

Since constitutionally all authority emanated from the crown, the various forms of conciliar administration represented no change in principle nor diminution of royal power but simply a practical division of prerogative jurisdiction. Nominally appointed for life, councillors were shifted among the various conciliar divisions from one branch to another without any loss of prestige or efficiency. Indeed the usefulness of prominent members was increased when they served indiscriminately in whichever council their knowledge and abilities warranted. With the great extension of prerogative functions under the first of the Tudors, the number of council agencies multiplied rapidly. In central and local government alike commissions, courts, crown offices, and regional councils dealt effectively with the problems of sectionalism and the restoration of authority. Frequently headed by representatives of the main council and controlled by it through executive directives, these de-

[3] Kenneth Pickthorn, *Early Tudor Government* (Cambridge, 1934), I, 12–13.

centralized agencies operated independently of each other. A measure of administrative unity was attained through conciliar co-ordination, but the prerogative of the crown was the only centralizing force that ran through the entire system.

When Henry VIII ascended the throne in 1509 these several instruments of government were still in the formative stages of development. In the central council and its embryonic offshoots, the Court of Star Chamber and the Court of Requests, the councillors of the crown dispensed royal justice in the king's name. Similarly, by the extension of conciliar authority, lesser councils ruled over the ancient palatinates of Lancaster and Cornwall, the principality of Wales, and in the northern counties. Improvised offices, such as the mastership of wards and the surveyorship of liveries, supervised special prerogative functions, while, independent of the national Exchequer, the recent territorial acquisitions and newly acquired revenues of the crown were separately administered by the king's general surveyors of crown lands. Financial control over revenue receipts and expenditures had likewise been transferred from the Exchequer to the king's chamber, which was soon to become the principle treasury of the state. All units of administration were directly or indirectly controlled through the council whose meticulous supervision welded them together into an elastic whole.

The effect of such a system was to give to government the same direct authority and personalized responsibility that a feudal lord possessed in his territorial domain or that a modern industrialist can achieve in private business. Translated into terms of personal rule it meant that governmental efficiency was in large part dependent upon a strong executive, one able to visualize the broader needs of the state and unite the miscellaneous agencies under a common policy. Both Henry VII and Henry VIII possessed those businesslike qualities, but neither sovereign had time to give to domestic administration that minute scrutiny so necessary for maximum efficiency. Certainly Henry VIII was temperamentally not disposed to expend his energies in such a tedious manner, although he retained firmer control over the administration than is sometimes accredited to him. Each was shrewd, however, in the choice of ministers capable of directing the entire organization as one organic whole. With the help of a score or more faithful subordinates, Sir Reginald Bray and Sir Thomas Lovell had fashioned the system which Henry VIII inherited. Wolsey and Cromwell perfected it; before the latter's fall, the independent offices had been departmentalized and new institutions erected to take care of the growing revenues. The Court of First Fruits and Tenths was set up in 1535, followed in 1536 by the Court of Augmentations. Six years later the revenue department of general surveyors was expanded into a court of record, with broader powers and wider jurisdiction. At the same time the Court of Wards and the office of liveries were united and the national mint reorganized. By 1543 the structural framework of the chamber system was complete. Cromwell had built well. It remained for later generations to appreciate the true originality of his many achievements.

After the repudiation of Cromwell the king governed the realm through his privy council, which functioned somewhat like a modern cabinet whose responsibility was rather to the crown than to parliament. Composed of the older ministers of state, chief justices, legal advisers, and heads of the various government departments, the council was, in effect, a standing committee of the government whose principle concern was the long agenda of business with which it had to deal at each meeting. Though dominated by no one member it, nevertheless, could find strength in the weight of collective opinion. When at variance with the king on some policy it would suggest and demur, persuasively presenting an alternative point of view without presuming to contradict.

Normally its chief work was administrative, its problems being concerned less with ultimate objectives than with the means to their attainment. Work was parceled out to commissions or divided among the several conciliar offshoots over which the central council exercised a close supervisory control. Regional bodies like the Council of the North, the Council of the West Marches, and the Council of Wales were governed by directives; in the case of the revenue courts the controls were often more direct, though ultimately all orders were embodied in formal instruments of authorization. Since the heads of these courts were also members of the council, many questions were presented to them informally before the final decisions were made. It was of little concern to the king or his councillors who did the work, so long as it was dispatched expeditiously. Conflicting jurisdiction occasionally caused minor quarrels among rival departments, but it offered no difficulty to the central council.

Among its diverse activities the council was occupied principally with two kinds of duties, financial and judicial. The first consisted largely of determining revenue regulations, arranging for the collection of arrears of rents and delinquent crown debts, and issuing warrants for the payment of the ordinary expenses of government. True, certain items of regular expenditure were chargeable upon specific revenues or allocated to particular departments, but generally individual warrants were directed to the court or treasury best equipped to make the payment promptly. After 1539 the chamber was on the decline and seldom able to meet its own recurrent obligations, so it was not often called upon for extraordinary expenditures. In fact, it was usually so short of revenues that ready cash was regularly transferred to it from one of the other departments to cover normal chamber issues. Of the several other national treasuries for the first half of the sixteenth century the Court of Augmentations and the mint were the most reliable, and upon them fell the major share of the financial burden. The profits from those two departments alone enabled the government to meet the expenses of the French and Scottish wars without any undue national hardship.

In a similar manner the privy council allocated the judicial business that came before it. Complaints, requests, and informations that normally instituted investigations or more formal civil trials were often referred to the newer revenue courts under whose jurisdiction the matter quite commonly lay. Bills of complaint or informations relating to disputed lands, debts, or other revenue matters were usually passed on to the Court of General Surveyors or the Court of Augmentations, while prerogative jurisdiction was shared by the Court of Requests or the regional conciliar tribunals. More serious cases, particularly those concerning religion and the safety of the realm, were reserved for the Star Chamber and the council proper. When a supplicant sought justice of the king's council he might find himself pleading before the Court of Augmentations instead, and debtors who appeared before the council were often sent " by the Lords " to argue their cases in one of the revenue courts.

In the light of increasing royal expenditures, rising prices, and expanding costs of government, it is not surprising that so much consideration was given to augmenting the crown income. In the previous reign additional sources of revenue, supplemented by national economies, had enabled Henry VII to amass a large fortune before his death, but the lavish spending and subsequent wars of his son eliminated the possibility of maintaining a permanent surplus. Even Cromwell, with all his resourcefulness, would have found it difficult to do more in devising new ways of raising money than did the council during the last French war. The sale of land was always a sure means of supplementing the revenue, while the sale of movable crown property, particularly lead, bell metal, and timber, provided a steady if small increment. In addition, when the chantries, chapels, and religious colleges were appropriated, a new supply of livestock, jewels, plate, ornaments, and household stuff became available. Likewise the estates and personal property of attainted persons continued as an important source of non-recurrent revenue. By means such as these the king was able to " live of his own " without resorting to parliamentary taxation except in cases of extraordinary need. Revenue institutions like the Court of Augmentations were peculiarly fitted for extending the practical operation of the royal prerogative or supplementing the traditional crown income by methods unsuited to normal parliamentary practice.

In this renaissance age of money economy, when wealth meant power and the mobile resources of the state had to be quickly converted into actual cash, the organization and control of the revenue machinery was a significant feature of public administration. In England land still remained the basic source of crown revenue upon which the ultimate success or failure of national policies so often depended. Parliamentary taxation was unreliable, except in cases of national emergency, and even when war presented such a crisis, parliamentary levies were never quite adequate to meet the situation. War budgets, as well as peacetime estimates, were drawn largely upon the normal incoming revenues; however stable the supply, sudden or unexpected outlays always presented the problems of raising immediate cash. The trouble, of course, lay partially in the fact that no real effort was ever made to forecast required expenditures. Financial crises were met abruptly as they arose; seldom was there any attempt to forestall the danger. Actually, the government always found it extraordinarily difficult to anticipate either the cost of war or the normal expenses of the state. Moreover, the regular expenses of government increased appreciably decade by decade. By frugal economy and ingenious innovations in revenue practices, Henry VII had been able to accumulate a convenient reserve, but his successors were neither so fortunate nor so economical. Henry VIII, opulent in the extreme, was not infrequently hard pressed for funds. Nevertheless, his financial security rested largely upon the efficiency of the administrative machinery, which was chiefly responsible for the augmentation or diminution of the current revenues of the realm. It was natural, therefore, throughout the first half of the sixteenth century that the government should give more attention to the exploitation of crown resources than to the economical administration of them.

Fundamentally the bulk of the revenue came from the land, which multiplied in value as the national prosperity expanded. The first important addition to the ancient demesne had come in 1485, after Bosworth, with the union of the houses of Lancaster and York. The subsequent marriage of Henry VII to Elizabeth of York not only united the two royal families but also brought to the English crown the vast hereditary Yorkist possessions. The second great acquisition was made in 1536 and 1539 when the crown appropriated the land and property of the dissolved monasteries. This immense endowment was sufficient to carry the state through the heavy expenses of the last years of Henry VIII without excessive borrowings, even though the source of royal income was somewhat depleted by the sale of crown lands and timber. Still the national thirst for the treasures of the church remained unquenched. At the beginning of Edward's reign chantries and religious colleges were added to the crown and were the last major increase in demesne holdings. Non-recurrent revenues occasionally were acquired thereafter, but the crown demesne, the permanent source of royal income, was not materially enlarged during the remainder of the Tudor period.

Through successive generations there had grown up in the later Middle Ages an extensive organization for the control of these scattered estates of the crown, consisting of a number of administrative institutions the principal function of which was to assure the sovereign a speedy collection of their revenues. With a few striking exceptions from time to time, all the revenues of the realm flowed through the medieval Exchequer which supervised receipts and expenditures and audited revenue accounts. Older divisions of the ancient demesne, notably the duchies of Cornwall and Lancaster and the principality of Wales, were administered separately, though their revenues were paid into the Exchequer. Thus, prior to the sixteenth century, the Exchequer was normally the only financial department as well as the sole treasury of the nation.[4] Shortly after his accession Henry VII, in an effort to secure greater efficiency in administration, began to modify the older system by introducing more expedient procedures of receipt, disbursement, and audit. By-passing the Exchequer completely, he set up a parallel revenue organization of permanent crown officials known as general surveyors, which developed into an administrative " court of survey " rivaling the exchequer system. Large sections of the older territorial demesne of the crown were transferred to the newer department, which also administered the more recent lands and revenues acquired since 1485. Simultaneously, the king's privy chamber was revived as a personal treasury, soon becoming the chief financial rival of the Exchequer. Since the treasurer of the chamber also acted as the receiver-general for certain specified revenues of the crown and was the ex officio treasurer for the revenue of Wales, for the Court of Wards and Liveries, the office of the general surveyors, and for the duchies of Cornwall and Lancaster, the chamber slowly emerged as the chief

---

[4] Literally this was not true, for household departments had been used as rival treasuries at various times during the Middle Ages, but they had not become integral features of medieval administration. For a comprehensive study of pre-Tudor precedents, see T. F. Tout, *Chapters in the Administrative History of Mediaeval England* (6 vols., Manchester, 1920–33). Cf. also as exampled in G. P. Cuttino, *English Diplomatic Administration, 1259–1339* (Oxford, 1940). Even under the Yorkist sovereigns the chamber was used both as a treasury and as an office of audit. B. P. Wolffe, " The Management of English Royal Estates under the Yorkist Kings," *E. H. R.*, LXXI (January, 1956), 1–27.

treasury of the crown. Traditionally a household department, the chamber was kept under the close scrutiny of the king, who for years used it as a privy purse office. It was not, however, until the profits of the Reformation swelled the revenues to an unprecedented volume that the chamber treasury assumed the proportions of a state department.

The revenue disposition of the Tudors, like the broader governmental administration of which it was a part, represented no significant departure from the practices of earlier English monarchs. The chamber itself was of medieval origin, and its subsequent revival had been projected at least several years earlier by the later Yorkists. Both Edward IV and Richard III were sovereigns of more than average ability, with plans for the renovation of an administrative system grown obsolete through years of neglect. Many of the Tudor innovations in government had been initiated at least a generation earlier, but the stress of internal disturbances had not permitted the development of those reforms. Crown receiverships, royal audits, fines and recognizances, prerogative offices, and administration by commission—all designed to supplement the overburdened Exchequer—were accepted features of personal rule. It was not the novelty of the Tudor program that was so remarkable, but rather the thoroughness with which it was executed. Only in financial matters were the methods employed at all innovatory. That these expedients were profitable as well as practical redounds to the credit of that important group of personally undistinguished crown ministers chiefly responsible for the techniques that gave to the cumbersome system a high degree of efficiency.

In addition to the customs, the revenues of the crown demesne, and the traditional *firma comitatus* of the Exchequer, the profits derived from the deliberate extension of the royal prerogative were immense. Feudal incidents, quite legal but rapidly becoming outmoded by the sixteenth century, were revived and collected. Wardship, marriage, escheat, forfeiture, and primer seizin were exploited by crown agents, sometimes as unscrupulous as they were thorough in the prosecution of their work; simultaneously, penalties for the violation of old statutes were reinvoked and excessive fines for every infringement of prerogative right were compounded.[5] As these and other sources of miscellaneous income were tapped, the proceeds were canalized through the chamber and ancillary revenue agencies organized to receive them. Such were the central offices of general surveyors, wards, liveries, and first

---

[5] See the excellent account of the development of the prerogative royal by Henry VII; Samuel E. Thorne (ed.), *Prerogativa Regis* (New Haven, 1949), Introduction, i–xlvi.

fruits, departmentalized by Henry VIII and put on a statutory basis.
Each administered a division of land and revenues, operating more or
less independently of the others under the general supervision of king
and council. Under Cromwell they became separate crown treasuries
and, in evolution, administrative courts for the enforcement of the
common law.

When in 1536 the Court of Augmentations was erected to complete
the Dissolution and administer the spoils of the monasteries, the last
phase of the Cromwellian financial program was initiated. The additional revenues, now rendered available for immediate expenditure, gave
a strong semblance of reality to Cromwell's proud boast that he would
make his master the wealthiest prince in Christendom.[6] From its beginning the financial work of the Court, at least from the viewpoint of the
king and Cromwell, was its most important function. Although the
youngest of the treasuries to grow up alongside the Exchequer, it soon
overshadowed them all as a financial department of the government.
During its first eight years the Augmentations yielded an income of
about £112,390 per year, with a total of £899,120 16s. net receipts
for the period. Indeed the maximum annual returns seemed unlimited;
for a number of years the revenues increased steadily until a maximum
of over £253,292 was reached by 1544.[7] The other treasuries bore
their proportionate shares in national finance, but individually their total
receipts and expenditures were never comparable to the Augmentations.
The Court of General Surveyors, erected in 1542, seldom exceeded
£38,000 a year, and the Court of First Fruits and Tenths less than
double that amount.[8] Revenues from the Court of Wards and Liveries
were not very great prior to the death of the master of the court William
Cecil, Lord Burghley, but afterward they began to multiply steadily.
In 1542 the total gross revenues from wards amounted to only £10,462
including arrears, with net receipts of but £4,434.[9] Already the chamber

---

[6] Eustace Chapuys to Charles V, December 19, 1534, *L. and P.*, VII, no. 1554.
In February, 1535, Cromwell claimed that he had already increased the revenues
by 500,000 crowns; Henry himself intimated that his revenues were augmented to
the perpetual annual value of 200,000 marks, or about £133,333. *Ibid.*, VIII,
no. 339.

[7] Augm. Office, Treas. Rolls of Accts., Nos. 1–2B, pt. 2.

[8] Add. MS. 32469. An account of the revenues received by the office of general
surveyors for the year 1541–42. *L. and P.*, XVI, no. 352, Declaration of Sir John
Gostwick, treasurer and receiver-general of first fruits and tenths, from January 1,
1535, to Christmas, 1540. During this six-year period £246,321 10s. 7d. was received
from first fruits and tenths and £160,162 2s. from subsidies, fines and other sources
paid into this treasury. From 1542–44 the receipts averaged £77,398 per year, but in
1548 they had dropped to £56,869. Frederick C. Dietz, *English Government Finance,
1485–1558* (Urbana, Ill., 1921), Appendix, Table VI.

[9] H. E. Bell, *An Introduction to the History and Records of the Court of Wards*

was on the verge of decline, while the Exchequer failed to regain its lost ascendancy.[10] Thus the Augmentations was able to retain its position of financial leadership until the end of the reign of Henry VIII, when the reorganized mint became a royal treasury of national importance.

Originally the Tudor system of chamber finance had been initiated to give the king a closer personal control over his revenues. The plan had worked admirably as long as all the principal revenues had been channeled into the office of receiver-general, and the director of that office, the treasurer of the chamber, had remained the king's personal treasurer. But typical of houshold institutional development, the chamber had transcended its initial position. Enlarged, institutionalized, and unchallenged, it drifted "out of court" to become, in its turn, a national treasury. Similarly, the newer revenue courts, once permanently established, soon achieved independent status, freed from the practical control of king and council. Again the king was left without a personal treasury, dependent in his daily transactions upon the slower, more formalized departments of state. For a strong king like Henry VIII such a situation was intolerable. Accordingly, he resorted to a privy-purse office to eliminate the inconvenience of departmental procedure.

By periodically transferring large sums from the several treasuries to the hands of one of the attendants of the privy chamber, Henry VIII was able to circumvent the system by keeping a large supply of cash on hand for personal or extraneous needs. This personal treasury grew in size and importance during the latter years of the reign, as the king depended upon it more and more in cases of emergency to meet the urgent demands of national expenditure, when speed of payment was of vital consequence. Thus by oral command money could be dispatched immediately for the payment of troops, the relief of garrisons, the completion of royal ships, or in personal expenditure, it could be employed without publicity or formal procedure in the payment of royal gaming debts, in the distribution of awards, or in building construction and maintenance on the king's private estates. So convenient did this practice become that the privy purse developed under Edward VI into a permanent institution of considerable responsibility.

When able ministers were in control, the system, complex and haphazard though it was, functioned with remarkable smoothness. Delegated authority from the central council permitted each court or revenue department to perfect its own techniques and to develop procedures along independent lines. As a result of this elasticity each court differed

and *Liveries* (Cambridge, 1953), 47; Appendix II, Table B (hereinafter cited as *The Court of Wards and Liveries*).

[10] Dietz, *English Government Finance, 1485–1558*, 137–38.

appreciably in form and organization from the others, while resembling a common pattern. The prototype was the duchy chamber administration of the palatinate of Lancaster, the oldest and most respected of revenue departments. Honorable and well established, it occupied a prominent place in the Tudor system during the early years of administrative expansion. The renovation of the duchy administration under Henry VII had greatly enhanced the profits of the crown, and Cromwell used it afterwards as a model for the later administrative courts. Nevertheless, the Augmentations was primarily Cromwell's idea, and to it he gave the best of his administrative ingenuity and organizing skill.

Under Cromwell's direction the bureaucracy functioned smoothly, since the weaknesses of decentralization and lack of co-ordination were counteracted by the supervision of a single crown minister responsible to no one save the king himself. During the period 1531–40 Cromwell, virtually singlehanded, directed all departments and agencies of government. No detail was too minute to escape his attention, no aspect of finance too trivial to be neglected. Like Henry VII he had a practical mind, trained to grapple with problems as they arose, yet never allowing significant issues to be obscured by the minutiae of administration. Characteristically thorough in all his undertakings Cromwell had an amazing grasp of everything that came under his supervision. In revenue policy an increase in the profits accruing to the crown meant more power for himself, so the profit motive became the cardinal objective. Nothing was left undone to render revenue operation more efficient. When faithful servants reported corruption or mismanagement, Cromwell was untiring in his efforts to ferret out the truth of the reports. Unhampered by tradition and precedent, such a system was readily adaptable to the needs of expanding administration.

By 1533 Cromwell, with a hand in everything, had secured a firmer grip on internal administration than his predecessor, Thomas Wolsey, had ever achieved.[11] Gradually he extended his influence through the use of patronage as well as by offices acquired for himself, until his position in the state was supreme. In November of 1535 Eustace Chapuys, the imperial ambassador, could describe him as the king's leading minister, " standing above everyone but the Lady." People observed that " there is no one else who does anything "; even the chancellor was " only his minister." [12] Though no one minister was ever

---

[11] In November of that year Chapuys reported categorically that Cromwell ruled everything. *L. and P.*, VI, no. 1445. His rapid rise to power can be traced through his innumerable " Memoranda " and " Remembrances," which begin early in 1531.

[12] Chapuys to Nicholas Perrenot, Sieur de Granville, of the emperor's council, November 21, 1535, *L. and P.*, IX, no. 862.

completely indispensable to the Tudor government, Cromwell came nearer to being irreplaceable than the king cared to admit.

After Cromwell's fall in 1540, Henry VIII ruled without a chief minister, retaining personal control of domestic as well as of foreign policy. Though the stabilizing influence of a strong directing hand was now removed, the results were not at once apparent. Inherently sound, the system of administration continued to develop along the lines laid down by its founders. In practical operation the king formulated the general policies, which in turn were executed by responsible members of the privy council. Since the heads of the various financial courts were also members of that body, a degree of centralization was sustained. Nevertheless, as war and diplomacy came to occupy more and more of the council's attention, it found less time to devote to the daily requirements of administrative routine. During the summer of 1545 warrants were received with recurrent frequency, demanding immediate payment for all kinds of war activities. Additional expenses at Boulogne, Calais, and in the North, large expenditures for defenses at home and for mercenaries abroad, and increased costs for maintenance of the army in France constituted a heavy drain upon the treasury. These burdensome expenses were met by the mint and the revenue courts as promptly as possible, while the council resorted to new shifts, sometimes desperate, for raising extra money.[13] Regular reports on supplies and expenditures were required of the various garrisons; likewise a frequent checking of the financial resources of the several treasuries gave the government a definite picture of the financial situation at any given time. Every Saturday the treasurers were ordered to bring in their declarations to the lord chancellor, " wherby mought appere from tyme to tyme their store of the Kinges treasour, that theruppon the Counsell might the more certeinlye procede in bestoweng the same about his Graces affayres." [14]

Temporarily at least, the financial status of the revenue courts—that is, the actual cash balances they were able to show at a given time— became the chief concern of the council. As long as adequate revenues were forthcoming, internal decay went unobserved. Unchallenged also was the rapid expansion of the courts and their consequent decreased efficiency. Offices and salaries multiplied, discipline relaxed; in the

---

[13] Warrants for the delivery of money or for the payments of bills constituted the principal business of the council during 1545 and 1546. Entries illustrative of the important financial work of the council are far too numerous to cite; they can be followed systematically in the *Acts of the Privy Council.* John R. Dasent (ed.), *Acts of the Privy Council of England* (London, 1890–1930), especially Vols. I and II.

[14] *Ibid.*, I, 356.

absence of proper supervision and safeguards, the individual official went his own way, often unbonded, and not uncommonly encouraged to deception by infrequent audits. Overexpansion of personnel, duplication of functions, neglect of duty, graft, and corruption were the inevitable results. Admittedly these developments were not completely ignored, but reorganization schemes were never entirely successful in restoring the erstwhile efficiency of the Cromwellian administration. In the case of the Court of Augmentations its reformation in 1547 gave it renewed power heretofore unrealized. It retained unquestioned supremacy for another seven years before being swept away in the interest of economy by the zeal of a new reform movement.

The reformers of 1553, led by the veteran administrators, Sir William Paulet, then marquis of Winchester, and Walter Mildmay, the ablest of the former Augmentations officials, envisioned a complete housecleaning in which all departments of revenue administration would be merged into one central institution. According to their scheme the Court of Wards and Liveries and the duchy of Lancaster, as well as the Court of First Fruits and Tenths and the Court of Augmentations, would be combined with the reorganized national Exchequer into a single unified institution. Thus, all the revenues of the nation could be administered uniformly; staffs would be reduced in number and unessential offices and divisions eliminated. Not only would such a reform greatly reduce operational costs but it would automatically ensure uniformity in procedure and practice. For more than a generation ministers had been trained under the rigid disciplines of Henry VII's reign, when singleness of purpose was an abiding feature of policy. During his own lifetime Paulet had watched the administration develop into a complex structure, the success of which was largely dependent upon systematic direction. An assistant architect of the improvement himself, he was as fully aware of its inherent weaknesses as he was of the essential worth of its basic principles. The speedy collection and efficient administration of the non-parliamentary revenues of the kingdom had been the *raison d'être* for the improvisation of the complicated machinery. A practical revenue department of state was as necessary in 1553 as it had ever been, but the forces of conservatism were too powerful to be suddenly overridden. In the end complete renovation gave way to a compromise program.

Admittedly cumbersome and haphazard, in the hands of capable ministers the system had proved to be quite adequate. In actual operation the machinery of government seldom functions in the exact manner prescribed by law or convention. By 1540 all the revenue institutions had become formalized, with powers and functions clearly defined by statutory limitations. In procedure there was infinite possibility of variation, and each department developed its own peculiar techniques—some ingenious and modern, others traditional and cumbersome—but functionally, the machinery was flexible enough to admit of easy and rapid readjustment to the exigencies of change.

The revenue courts were financial expedients, and it was largely as such that they justified their growth. The tremendous increase in Tudor revenue had necessitated additional machinery of collection and audit; likewise, the steady augmentation of crown land had required a new set of administrative offices. To facilitate convenience of expenditure the king's chamber had been revived as an ancillary treasury to assist the Exchequer. In time these separate functions were combined into single institutions, revenue courts which were at once agencies of revenue collection, departments of estate management, and treasuries of their own incomes. Since the growth of the courts was in direct proportion to the extent of the revenues allocated to them, there was considerable rivalry over property recently acquired or for the control of fresh sources of revenue. In fact, the ultimate decline of the chamber was in part attributable to the loss of a large block of the revenues originally assigned to it. During the 1530's and 1540's, when the government was facing a perpetual shortage of money, the resources of all the national treasuries were drawn upon in proportion to their financial balances.

In theory, each court was responsible for specific revenues and fixed payments predetermined by assignment, but in practice, expenditures were conveniently shifted from one to another by warrants of the king or council. Current expenses were met by drawing upon whichever treasury was well supplied at the moment and, as often as not, the reserves of all were exausted by any great national outlay. Functionally perhaps, payments were stereotyped, but all revenue was crown revenue, and it mattered little from whence it came or by whom expended. Under Henry VII the cost of jewels, household deficits, ambassadorial fees, and expenses of the king's ships were nominally paid from the chamber, but such items were commonly borne by the Court of Augmentations during the two ensuing reigns. The change was not one of principle but of simple expediency in using the treasury that had the most money.

Conciliar control broke down when the council was no longer dominated by singleness of leadership and policy. In no other avenue of administration was this more forcibly demonstrated than in the evolution of the Augmentations. The real break came after 1547 when the Court had reached the culmination of its power. The story of its slow decline is the history of the increasing maladministration of the Edwardian period.

CHAPTER THREE

THE RISE OF THE COURT OF AUGMENTATIONS

N LATE APRIL, 1536, THE KING FORMALLY APPROVED TWO
major designs recently conceived by Cromwell as a means
of strengthening his influence over his royal master, an
influence already challenged by developing court opposition.
On the twenty-fourth of the month Henry signed a secret commission for
a special investigation of all kinds of treasonable conduct, which empowered the commissioners to try any and all offenders whom they
found suspect.[1] The same day he affixed his royal signature to the
several patents of appointment for the principal officials of the Court of
Augmentations,[2] whose assistance in the Dissolution proceedings was
already urgently needed. The first of these actions started a series of
stirring events that led to the execution of Queen Anne Boleyn, followed
by Henry's marriage to Jane Seymour and the subsequent birth of a male
heir to the throne;[3] the second instituted a revenue policy, basic to
Cromwell's purpose, which would provide adequate machinery for the
control and supervision of the new wealth resulting from the exploitation
of the monasteries. Acceptable to king and council, these were carried
out with as little delay as possible.

[1] Paul Friedman, *Anne Boleyn, a Chapter of English History, 1527–1536* (London, 1884), II, 243 ff. This action, of course, virtually spelled the doom of Anne
Boleyn.
[2] Augm. Office, Misc. Books 232, pt. 1, fols. 1d–13.
[3] Anne was executed on May 19, 1536; the king's marriage to Jane Seymour
was solemnized the following day.

At the time of its inception the Court of Augmentations created little general interest, either within the limited court circle at Westminster or in the country at large. Overshadowed by the events of the Reformation, the establishment of another revenue institution seemed unimportant to those who surveyed the political scene, except possibly as a potential reservoir of cheap land and more pensions, annuities, gifts, and sinecural appointments. Even the most outspoken critics of the royal policy directed their attacks only against the recent act for the dissolution of the monasteries and what they termed the diabolical work of the visitation commissions. Nevertheless, the Court was obviously in a potentially powerful position to which the initial support and continued cooperation of Cromwell contributed not a little.

When the Reformation Parliament convened at Westminster for its eighth and last session on February 4, 1536, its agenda had been previously determined. In the theory of Tudor government the principal function of parliament was to translate into law the policies of the crown, and this particular session was called upon to validate a series of proposals already projected but not implemented. If the practical gains of the ecclesiastical reformation were to be fully realized, national acceptance could best be assured through parliamentary sanction. The legislative program presented to it, therefore, had been carefully prepared in advance, and Cromwell had made every effort to secure a favorable response to the governmental proposals. Consequently, few of them met with any serious opposition. Among the sixty-three measures enacted into law was the statute effecting the sequestration of the monasteries, which clearly revealed one of the royal motives in attacking the regular clergy.

On Saturday, March 11, the king personally presented to the commons the bill for the dissolution of the lesser houses.[4] By a significant omission the act made no provision for either the administration of the monastic property or for the adjudication of controversies arising therefrom, but it was soon apparent that Cromwell did not intend this new jurisdiction to fall into the hands of the Exchequer. Just before the conclusion of the session the statute establishing the Court of Augmentations was passed,[5] investing the new institution with administrative and jurisdictional authority over all monastic lands and property. As the nationalization of church property proceeded, the Court became closely identified with the crown policy of exploitation. Hence, to the popular mind the Augmentations was little more than an instrument of oppres-

---

[4] Parliament Roll, *L. and P.*, X, no. 243 (18) ; Thomas Wright (ed.), *Letters Relating to the Suppression of Monasteries* (London, 1843), 38–39.
[5] Parliament Poll, *L. and P.*, X, no. 243(61).

sion. Like Cromwell, whose directions they willingly followed, officials of the Court were too often thought of simply as rapacious ministers, determined to advance their own or the king's interest at the expense of the hapless subject.

Whatever the details of the plan, it is clear that the acts of Dissolution and Augmentations were part of a larger project for the secularization of eccleciastical property, the proceeds of which were to be used for the defense of the realm and for the maintenance of the royal estate.[6] Although he was unable to execute completely such a grand design, Cromwell did go far enough to reveal clearly his intention of further strengthening the power of the crown at the expense of the church. Undoubtedly fundamental to the success of the reform program was the reorganization of the revenue administration which followed the first monastic confiscations.[7] It is evident that plans for a new revenue court had crystallized some time before the Dissolution proceedings were completed. Likewise, it is equally apparent that the Augmentations was in actual operation prior to the formal statute of erection.

The act erecting the Court of Augmentations was the penultimate statute of the session, passed just before parliament was dissolved on April 14, 1536. On the first of the month Chapuys wrote to the emperor that the king and council were busy setting up offices for the revenues of the monasteries earmarked for suppression;[8] three days earlier Thomas Warley noted that the principal officials of the Court had been selected and that unusual fees were allotted to them.[9] On April

---

[6] Hughes, *The Reformation in England*, I, 282–83. On documentary evidence, see especially *L. and P.*, VII, no. 1355.

[7] W. C. Richardson, *Tudor Chamber Administration, 1485–1547* (Baton Rouge, 1952), 305–10. Financial independence simply enhanced the Henrician doctrine of royal supremacy. " The dissolution of the smaller monasteries, which followed Cromwell's visitation, was the most drastic expression ever seen in England of the new theory of the secular state." F. M. Powicke, *The Reformation in England* (London, 1941 ; 3rd impression, 1949), 25.

[8] Chapuys to Charles V, April 1, 1536, *L. and P.*, X, no. 601. Commenting on the fact that all the lords were intent on having a share in the church ornaments and movable property, which represented an inestimable amount, he observed that already the dukes of Norfolk and Suffolk had provided themselves with a liberal portion of the spoils. " I am told," he added, " that although Cromwell promoted in the first instance the demolition of the said churches, that nevertheless, seeing the dangers that might arise from it, he was anxious to prevent them, for which reason the King has been somewhat angry with him." If Chapuys' assumption was correct, the royal anger soon subsided in the face of Cromwell's successful machinations.

[9] Thomas Warley to Lady Lisle, March 28, 1536, *ibid.*, no. 573. Warley wrongly surmised that Rich had been selected for a general surveyorship of the Court instead of the chancellorship, which he actually secured. Although the office may have been projected at this time, no such position was in fact created. The

13, 1536, Richard Rich was released from his office of solicitor general for the crown in order to devote his full time to the organization of the new Augmentations.[10] Actually the primary concern of that institution was to supervise the work of the forthcoming visitation. By the end of the month the state program was well under way.

The most immediate problem of the Court was to convert into cash as soon as feasible all the movable property of the condemned monasteries. In fact, so eager was the king to utilize these resources that the work of dissolution proceeded apace. On April 24, 1536, the same day on which the formal appointments to the Augmentations were issued, commissions were set up for a new survey of the religious house.[11] Among the twenty-three items of inquiry forming the instructions for the commissioners were injunctions designed to prevent the leakage of all forms of monastic revenues which could be claimed by the crown. The commissioners for each county, of whom many were future Augmentations officials, consisted of an auditor, a particular receiver, the clerk of the register of the previous visitation, and three appointees of the crown. In accepting the surrender of the monasteries their chief task was to survey and evaluate the land, property, farm stock, ornaments, plate, jewels, household stuff, lead, bells, stone, and miscellaneous articles, and place these movable possessions in safekeeping until such time as they were formally taken over by the Court of Augmentations. As soon as the inquiry was completed, briefs of the survey were presented by the commissioners to the council of the Court. When the visitors encountered any difficulty, the head of the house was sent up to Westminister for a personal examination by the chancellor of the Augmentations.[12]

The problem of greatest urgency for the commissioners was that of the disposition, custody, and safeguard of monastic property. Since the act of dissolution gave the crown possession of all such property as of March 1, 1535, every precaution had to be taken against destruction, fraudulent sale, or even open theft of movable commodities. In an effort to realize as much as possible before surrendering their confiscated houses, many of the abbots and priors had been guilty of flagrant

---

two general surveyors of the Augmentations were not appointed until the reorganization of 1547.

[10] *Ibid.*, no. 775(21). William Whorwood succeeded Rich in the solicitor general's office.

[11] The earlier visitation had been carried out under the general supervision of Cromwell in 1535. *Ibid.*, VIII, nos. 73, 75, 76.

[12] "Instructions to the King's commissioners for a new survey of lands and goods belonging to the religious houses within their commission," *ibid.*, X, no. 721. See also *ibid.*, no. 1191 and XI, Appendix, no. 15. For the original draft of the commission, see Exch., Treasury of Receipt, Misc. Books 116, fols. 50–53.

chicanery. Abundant documentary evidence supports the official charges
contained in the statute itself, that " dyverce of the Chief Governours of
suche Relygyous Houses, determynyng the utter spoyle & dystruccion
of ther Houses, & dreadyng the suppressyng thereof, for the mayntenance
of ther detestable lyves, have lately fraudelently & craftely made feoffa-
mentes estates Gyftes Grauntes and Leasses under ther Covent Seales,
or suffred Recoveres of ther Manors Londes Tenementes and Heredyta-
mentes in fee symple fee tayle for terme of lyf or lyves or for yeres, or
charged the same w^t rentes or corrodyes, to the greate decaye & dymyny-
cion of ther Houses . . ." Such instances of illegal procedure were first
among the earlier cases to be investigated by the Court. Nevertheless,
a bid was made for the better future behavior of the heads of the houses
by the promise of annual pensions, " wherein his Highnes wyll have most
tender respect to suche of the seid chief Governours as well & truly
conserve & kepe the goodes & ornamentes of ther Houses to the use
of his Majestie, w^t out spoyle waste or embesylyng the same." [13]

Until the monastic property was safely in the custody of the king's
officials, a great deal of wholesale exploitation was inevitable. As soon
as rumors of the suppression reached the monasteries a number of the
abbotts and priors sold their movable goods, leased portions of the
monastic demesnes, appropriated relics and plate to their own use, and
in general threatened the safety of much of the newly acquired crown
property. Obviously certain items could be disposed of without too much
difficulty. Lead, stone, and growing timber found an easy market for
those who wished to enrich themselves at the king's expense, and the
observant commissioners were not slow in pointing out to Cromwell that
the best timber of the monastic woodlands was being felled at " a greate
pace." Nor was the pillage of monastic property by any means restricted
to the inmates of the religious houses. The general public was equally
guilty of theft and embezzlement, and not infrequently the king's own
agents or the commissioners themselves were implicated in irregularities
and peculation. The theft of plate, bells, lead, and relics, and the indiscriminate spoliation of monastic buildings was a common complaint
of most of the visitors. Even though constant vigilance was exercised by
Cromwell's agents, few houses were completely safe from local pillage.
There was every reason, therefore, for haste in sending valuable articles,
especially plate and precious jewels, to London, where the jewel house
or the Augmentations treasury offered a safe repository.[14]

---

[13] An act for the dissolution of the lesser monasteries, 27 Henry VIII, c. 28,
S. R., III, 575–78, secs. iv and viii.
[14] *L. and P.*, X, nos. 137, 164, 165, 472, 624; XII, pt. 1, nos. 531, 535; XIII, pt. 1,
nos. 1343, 1433, pt. 2, nos. 367, 377, 526, 840; XIV, pt. 1, nos. 101, 491, 862, 1025,
1189.

The need for the management of monastic property was not the only reason for the erection of still another administrative department. The established financial organization of the realm was completely inadequate for the formidable increase of revenue then expected. Moreover, the office of general surveyors of crown lands and the new treasurership of first fruits and tenths, recently organized to receive the church annates,[15] were both scheduled for enlargement.[16] Since revenue expansion and administrative efficiency were two of Cromwell's principal objectives, the existing system was to be extended as quickly as possible. Thus the Augmentations was only the first of four new revenue courts designed to supplement the work of the Exchequer. Greater efficiency in revenue collection and in the general administration of monastic lands was not the least of the many benefits to accrue from the new institution.

With the organization of the Court of Augmentations, competition for a share, however meager, of the spoils of the monasteries was soon evident among all those who possessed any particular power or influence. The king, Cromwell, and especially the leading officials of the Court were eagerly besieged with requests for purchases, gifts, or exchanges of abbey lands, or for one of the innumerable land offices then available. No award was too trivial to command the respect of the high and mighty, who considered a share in the division of the monastic wealth nothing more than their just deserts. Many a noble doubtless felt, as did the lord treasurer, that he should at least submit a request. With reference to the possessions of Bungay and Woodbridge in Suffolk, he wrote an almost apologetic letter to Cromwell. " If I may have the stewardship of all these lands, so much the better; if not, at least this side Trent. Where others speak I must speak too. Sapienti amico pauca." [17] Few there were indeed who showed any reluctance to speak for an office or a coveted piece of property. And speak they did—not only the nobles of the realm, Oxford, Essex, Rutland, Audley, Wriothesley, Hertford, Suffolk, Shrewsbury, St. John, Russell, Lisle, Wharton, Clinton, Sussex,

---

[15] The office was formally instituted on May 7 1535, with the appointment of John Gostwick as "treasurer and receiver-general" of numerous revenues placed under his charge. As frequently happened in such cases where haste was required, Gostwick had taken over his duties in the receivership a few weeks before his patent was processed. Pat. Rolls, 27 Henry VIII, pt. 1, mems. 8–10. Cf. Richardson, *Tudor Chamber Administration, 1485-1547*, 333–42.

[16] These offices were converted into permanent courts of record in 1540 and 1542, respectively. 32 Henry VIII, c. 45 and 33 Henry VIII, c. 39, *S. R.* III, 798–801, 879–92. During the latter year the office of liveries was joined to the Court of Wards, thus completing the machinery of Cromwell's financial organization. 33 Henry VIII, c. 22, *ibid.*, 860–63.

[17] Thomas Howard, duke of Norfolk, to Cromwell (1536, undated), *L. and P.*, X, no. 599.

and many others—but also members of the gentry and the rising *nouveaux riches*. In one way or another all classes of society came to share a vested interest in the Dissolution. Discerning eyes could soon perceive that the land settlement was to become " the sheet anchor of Henry's reformation." [18]

Some effort was made to preserve the fiction that the monasteries set a high moral standard for the community. The first act of dissolution provided that future grantees of the alienated property should maintain the same levels of hospitality and " Tyllage of husbondry " as the previous occupiers, on penalty of £6 13s. 4d. per month during the period of violation.[19] This vain attempt to placate the popular opposition to the destruction of the religious houses suggests the attention given to public opinion.[20]

The preamble of the act establishing the Augmentations emphasized both the fiscal and administrative functions of the Court. Such a vast nationalization of real property as Cromwell contemplated would undoubtedly require the revamping of the entire revenue machinery if not the addition of several departments of collection and control. Definitively styled " the Courte of Thaugmentacions of the Revenues of the Kinges Crowne," the earliest of the financial courts was erected primarily for the greater security and establishment of the national revenue, " and to thentent that the Kinges Magestie his heires and successours shalbe yerely as well truely and justely aunswered contented and paied of

[18] J. D. Mackie, *The Earlier Tudors, 1495–1558* (the Oxford History of England Series, ed. by G. N. Clark, Vol. VII [Oxford, 1952]), 401. The disposition of monastic lands is fully analyzed in Alexander N. Savine, *The English Monasteries on the Eve of the Dissolution* (Oxford, 1909); Hughes, *The Reformation in England*, I, 328 ff.; Geoffrey Baskerville, *English Monks and the Suppression of the Monasteries* (London, 1937), 54 ff.; and H. A. L. Fisher, *The History of England from the Accession of Henry VII to the Death of Henry VIII, 1485–1547* (the Political History of England Series, ed. by William Hunt and Reginald L. Poole, Vol. V [new impression, London, 1928]), Appendix II, 499–501.

[19] Under the penalty given, holders of the land or property should " kepe or cause to be kept an honest contynewell hous and houshold in the same scyte or precynct, and to occupye yerely asmouche of the same demeanes in plowyng and Tyllage of husbondry, that ys to saye asmouche of the seid demeanes which hath ben commonly usyd to be kept in Tyllage." 27 Henry VIII, c. 28, sec. xvii.

[20] Burnet suggests that Cromwell advised the king to sell the monastic lands to the gentry " at very easy rates " in order to induce them to keep up the wonted hospitality. " This drew in the gentry apace both to be satisfied with what was done, and to assist the crown for ever in the defence of these laws; their own interest being so interwoven with the rights of the crown." Gilbert Burnet, *The History of the Reformation of the Church of England* (a new revised edit. by Nicholas Pocock, Oxford, 1865), I, 358. This earlier notion that monastic lands were given away freely or sold at a low price has been discredited by modern scholarship. As a matter of fact, Henry gave away very little land; most of it was sold on the open market for as much as possible.

the rentes fermes issues revenues and proffittes rising commyng and growyng of the said Manours Landes Tenementes and other Hereditamentes before specified, as of the goode catells plate stuffe of Houshold dettes money stokk store and other what soever profite and commoditie gyven graunted or appoynted to the Kinges Magestie by the same, in suche Courte place fourme maner and condicion as hereafter shalbe limited daclared and appoynted." [21]

Owing to the various forms of citation encountered in documentary references, the name of the Court is rather confusing to the modern reader. However, since it was instituted literally to deal with " thaugmentations " of crown revenues, the official title was accurately descriptive. Nevertheless the full title was seldom used by contemporaries, who ordinarily referred to it as the Court of Augmentation or Augmentations, spelled indiscriminately with or without the " s." The popular terminology was retained after 1547, when the reconstituted Augmentations was erected by letters patent, although the recreated court was then officially styled " the Courte of the Augmentacions and revenues of the Kinges Crowne." [22] This change was, as in the previous case, a literal interpretation of the facts. As the name in fact implied, the second court was simply a union of the first Augmentations and the Court of General Surveyors, which also handled the crown revenues. So similar were the two Courts of Augmentations, both in composition and function, that historians generally have ignored the development of the later institution. [23]

The original Court of Augmentations was designed to fulfill a number of more or less independent functions, each of which constituted a specialized sphere of activity. Having " the order survey and gouvernaunce " of all monastic lands and possessions as well as the control of certain other revenues subsequently put under its jurisdiction, it was by inception fundamentally an administrative department. In this respect it was similar to the office of general surveyors, which had been in process of evolution for half a century. As a financial institution it not only collected but likewise disbursed the revenues allocated to it. In this capacity the Court was an independent treasury equal in status if not in reputation to the Exchequer, with comparable departments of receipt and audit. Pensions of the dispossessed religious constituted a

[21] " An Acte establisshinge the Courte of Augmentacions," 27 Henry VIII, c. 27, *S. R.*, III, 569–74. There are twenty-four sections of the act, with a schedule of revenue annexed. The schedule is not printed in the statutes.

[22] Pat. Rolls, 38 Henry VIII, pt. 5, mem. 15. To avoid needless repetition of the full title, the Court is commonly referred to in this study as simply the Augmentations.

[23] See p. 128, *infra*.

special charge of the Augmentations, although from the very beginning normal expenditures covered a variety of items. Moreover, as custodian of all the records of the dissolved monastic foundations, the Augmentations came to be the storehouse of an invaluable collection of Dissolution documents. When to this vast collection were added the land surveys and documents relating to rentals and land transfers, it soon became one of the greatest depositories in the realm. Finally, as a court of record it was given authority to adjudicate disputes arising from the Dissolution proceedings and to hear cases relating to the land and property under its control. Thus, in effect, it was a composite of estate office, repository, ministry of pensions, treasury, and court of law, all united in a major revenue department of the government.

In organization the Court was modeled upon the ancient administration of the duchy of Lancaster, which had come to represent a high standard in Tudor estate management.[24] Henry VII had indeed taken special pains to improve the duchy administration as well as the duchy revenues and had patterned his chamber department of audit after it. In fact, many of the principles and usages incorporated in the developing office of general surveyors of crown lands were based upon practices of long standing in the duchy. Therefore, when the Augmentations was planned as the culmination of the newer trend toward a less formalized system than the Exchequer afforded, it was natural that the duchy organization should be chosen as the most logical example to follow. Throughout its history, both in structural design and in procedure, the Court showed a marked similarity to the Duchy Chamber. The statute of creation specifically provided that the fees, rewards, and allowances for the clerk and certain other officials should be the same as those allowed there; similarly the expenses of auditors and receivers, including their charges for riding their several circuits, were likewise governed. Even payments for reparations were expeditiously authorized by order of the Court without formal bill or warrant, as was the practice in the duchy administration. Finally, it was empowered to award " suche processe and preceptes with reasonable peynes to be therin lymyted as be nowe commonly used in the Courte of the Kinges Duchie Chambre of Lancastre."

Furthermore, in respect to internal operation, the resemblance of the two courts is too close to be mere coincidence. In the annual declara-

---

[24] Richardson, *Tudor Chamber Administration, 1485–1547,* 26–27, 66, 407–409. For further information on the duchy of Lancaster, see Sir Edward Coke, *Institutes of the Laws of England* (London, 1809), Part Four, 204–10 (hereinafter cited as *Institutes*) ; Robert Somerville, *History of the Duchy of Lancaster* (London, 1953), I. The second volume of this comprehensive study has not yet appeared.

tion of accounts, in local manorial administration, and in the supervision of woods on crown estates the Augmentations also followed the precedent set by the duchy. Both had great seals and privy seals, a chancellor and council as executive heads, " particular " receivers, and " high " stewards, and each of them continued to recognize that ancient administrative division of England into two sectors, the regions north and south of the River Trent. All this notwithstanding, the Augmentations was much more than just a replication of the duchy court. It developed its own precedents and in time initiated new practices and procedures. When the later revenue courts were set up, they in turn followed the duchy pattern already so well established.

As in the duchy, the head of the Court was the chancellor who was assisted by the second, third, and fourth officials, known respectively as treasurer, attorney, and solicitor. These four principal officers in effect constituted a governing board which determined policies and regulated procedures within the broader administrative controls wielded by the king's council. An official clerk, who was also the keeper of the records, an usher, and a messenger completed the central hierarchy, although later additional messengers were appointed [25] as the jurisdiction was expanded. Administrative work in the field was conducted by ten regional auditors and seventeen particular receivers, usually chosen from the county or district which they served. They carried the authority of the Court into every county of England and Wales. Thus, according to its constitution, the Augmentations had an original staff of only thirty-four members, yet as an office for the management of certain prescribed crown estates and crown revenues, it maintained a much larger organization. Including local ministers and the numerous officials found on every royal manor, the total number of the Court's employees ran into hundreds.

Nor is the gradual expansion of the institution at all surprising in view of its peculiar relation to the fiscal prerogative of the crown. Indeed the Court was founded on the assumption that the regular acquisition of crown assets would be further accelerated as the reign progressed. Nevertheless, until such additional property or receipts were assigned to it, the Court was kept busy with the twofold task immediately confronting it, namely the settlement of pensions granted to the dispossessed monks and the adjudication of disputes growing out of the monastic debts and properties. Despite the king's avowal that once he was granted the wealth of the monasteries he would ask for no more money, it was apparent from the beginning that the suppression had

---

[25] See p. 46, *infra*.

only begun. The attack on the Irish monasteries was launched in June, 1536, while in England dissolution by attainder and "voluntary" surrender continued.[26] By 1538 the majority of the larger houses had disappeared, although the process was not completed until the following year.[27] Under the first act of Dissolution 244 monasteries were actually suppressed, with but 47 houses exempted by royal license; by the second act some 184 houses were confiscated. Meanwhile, among the remaining religious institutions, including exempted monasteries, dependent cells and priories, and houses belonging to the order of St. John of Jerusalem, another 209 had been taken into the king's hands by 1540.[28] At the same time, by special act of parliament, all "liberties fraunchises privileges and temporall jurisdictions," formerly exercised by previous owners or tenants, were revived and turned over to the Court; before the end of the reign, the property of certain colleges, free chapels, chantries, hospitals, fraternities, and guilds were acquired in the same manner. To the Augmentations these possessions brought added jurisdiction and greater security.[29] In Tudor administration the significance of any financial agency depended largely on the volume of revenue it controlled. Even before the fall of Cromwell the success of the Augmentations as a supplementary treasury of the government was assured.

In final analysis the Court owed a great deal to that small staff of

[26] Visitations were steady and continuous during 1537 and 1538, during which period many houses were "persuaded" to "submit wholly to the King's mercy" and surrender voluntarily. *L. and P.*, XII, pt. 2, no. 27; XIII, pt. 1, nos. 573, 893.

[27] Brewer was entirely right in his observation that the forms of all free surrenders were carefully maintained: ". . . and in many cases, no doubt, it might be said with truth that the act in itself really was spontaneous. An immediate surrender and retirement on pensions was far better than continued subjection to the harassing restraints imposed by Cromwell's visitors." *Ibid.*, XIII, pt. 1, Preface, vii; see also *ibid.*, XII, pt. 2, nos. 64, 91. At the beginning of 1538 George Rolle could write rather wistfully to his master in Calais: "The abbeys go down as fast as they may and are surrendered to the King. I pray God send you one among them to your part." George Rolle to Lord Lisle, February 8, 1538, *ibid.*, XIII, p. 1, no. 235.

[28] That is, 47 houses exempted by the Act of 1536, some 62 dependent priories, 57 cells, and 43 commanderies. The data in this paragraph is based on Monseigneur Hughes's study, which represents the most recent interpretation of the subject. Hughes, *The Reformation in England*, I, 295, 322, 326–27. See p. 73, *infra*.

[29] An act concerning liberties (1540), 32 Henry VIII, c. 20; "An Acte for dissolucion of Colledges" (1545), 37 Henry VIII, c. 4, *S. R.*, III, 770–73, 988–93. Only a few chantries surrendered under this statute. A new act for the dissolution of the chantries was passed during the first year of the reign of Edward VI, whereby some 2,374 chantries, fraternities, corporations, and minor foundations were confiscated to the use of the crown. "An Acte wherby certaine Chauntries Colleges Free Chapelles and the Possessions of the same be given to the Kinges Mate," (1547), 1 Edward VI, c. 14, *ibid.*, IV, 24–33. J. R. Tanner (ed.), *Tudor Constitutional Documents* (Cambridge, 1940), 103; Hughes, *The Reformation in England*, II, 150 ff.

original officials who formulated its policies and shaped its destinies during those early formative years. Most of them were Cromwell's selections, although a few seem to have been chosen directly by the king. In either case they were generally experienced ministers whose capabilities and loyalty to the crown had been previously tested.

In comparison with other government departments Augmentations salaries, if not exactly liberal, were adequate, though other emoluments considered by most ministers as legitimate supplements to official stipends were always expected. Unless the minister was a complete failure in his job, such rewards were usually forthcoming in the form of wardships, marriages, gifts, annuities, pensions, and royal favors, or as a series of sinecural offices which required little responsibility and no actual service.

On the other hand, there were certain disadvantages to being affiliated with a department so much in the public eye as was the Augmentations. Like the offices of the Court of Wards and Liveries or the earlier prerogative institutions of Henry VII's reign, it was too closely related to the extension of the prerogative royal to be popular; nor did it ever escape censure altogether. Even in an age of disciplined obedience there were still many who believed that the implementation of prerogative jurisdiction or the enforcement of newly acquired royal authority was in some way associated with a policy of exploitation and, in the hand of unscrupulous officials, tantamount to actual extortion. Experience indeed justified such an assumption, and the taint of corruption on the part of the delinquent minister brought suspicion upon the conscientious. Anyone who accepted a post with the Court realized that, to a degree, he had publicly identified himself with the secularization program and stood to rise or fall in proportion to Cromwell's security. Tudor ministers were notoriously apt to be the scapegoats of their sovereign's blunderings; nor was it at all unthinkable that Augmentations personnel might be sacrificed in the event of a reversal of royal policy. In any case they were not in a position to assume full responsibility for the success or failure of the institution so long as the king and council systematically regulated its activities. Still, the mortality rate was never high even among the more responsible ministers; among the lesser officials tenure was dependent chiefly upon patronage, loyal service, and in many cases little more than the ability to keep out of trouble.

Whatever the reason, every position in the Court soon became the object of competition, although the majority of requests for the primary appointments, in all probability, was not considered very seriously. Cromwell and the king were both aware of the importance of the four major positions, particularly the first and second offices. The chancellor, as " chief and principal officer," was the real executive head, with custody of the Court's two seals and was the presiding judge in all matters of litigation. Administratively he was the intermediary link between the Court and privy council, officially responsible only to the king. In the authorization of revenue expenditures the warrants of the chancellor were final, as were his decisions in many other aspects of daily procedure. The treasurer was second in command; responsible for the total revenue assigned to the Court, he was the sole financial officer. In all administrative and judicial deliberations he was an influential member of the executive council and an important judge in any revenue disputes that came before the Court. In either position high qualifications were demanded of him. Implicit honesty, the complete confidence of the king, and the ability to co-operate with Cromwell without alienating political opponents were all prerequisites to the success of the leading ministers of the rising establishment.

The two other posts on the council of Augmentations were held by the attorney and solicitor, respectively the third and fourth officers of the Court. Royal appointees and " learned in the laws of the land " by statutory requirement, they were the Court's chief legal representatives, officiating for the crown in cases where the king was a party. Administratively they had few duties; even on the executive council their principal function was advisory.[30] Except in term time, when the Court was actually in session, the attorney and solicitor were quite free to pursue their profession or to engage in private business. As their salaries would indicate, both offices, in fact, were considered part-time positions, whose occupants sought other and more remunerative posts in order to supplement their official incomes.[31]

These two posts were filled by appointees of Cromwell, who never failed to take care of his own friends and servants. John Onley, attorney for the Augmentations, was already an established lawyer in 1536, and Robert Southwell, solicitor, had just attained a place in Cromwell's service before his appointment to office. Neither of them had previously achieved any marked distinction, but the Augmentations served as an entrée to a successful career for each of them. Onley's career was cut short by his untimely death in November, 1537, only a few months after he entered office. Southwell was immediately advanced to the vacancy, which he retained until March, 1540, when he resigned his office of

---

[30] See pp. 384–85, *infra.*

[31] The original annual salaries of these offices, £40 for the attorneyship and £20 for the solicitorship, were not increased until March, 1540, and then only by £50 each. These appointments to the Court were made in April, 1536. Augm. Office, Misc. Books 232, pt. 1, fols. 2, 2*d*; 235, fols. 2, 2*d*.

solicitor to become master of the rolls.[32] Robert Southwell and his elder brother Richard were members of a county family of great antiquity, whose ancestors derived their surname from the market town and parish of Southwell in Nottinghamshire. The father, a wealthy Norfolk landowner, was connected with the Howards, Cromwells, and other prominent families, a fact which gave opportunities to his sons who enjoyed special royal favor during three successive reigns. Both were active in the proceedings against the monasteries and quite influential in Augmentations affairs.[33] In addition to his work in the Court Sir Robert also served the crown in various other capacities. Knighted in October, 1537, he became a member of the king's ordinary council and before his death served variously as sheriff, commissioner, master of requests, and as a member of the Council of the North. His relationship to the elder Sir Robert Southwell, his uncle, and his marriage to the daughter and heir of Sir Thomas Neville likewise contributed not a little to his professional advancement.[34]

During his early period with the Court Southwell's service as a Dissolution commissioner was of greater value to the crown than was his work as solicitor. A responsible officer of the Augmentations, he was in a position to keep a careful check on the king's revenues and to report to Cromwell and the Court any instances of fraud or deception that came to his attention. In July of 1537, while passing through Yorkshire, he heard many complaints against Lord Cumberland, but he decided not to interfere except in cases of the undervaluation of certain lands which related to his own office; during his short period of royal

[32] Augm. Office, Misc. Books 232, pt. 1, fol. 2; pt. 2, fol. 4. Southwell resigned the solicitor's office on November 23, 1537, and he was succeeded by Walter Henley. Although his formal appointment as attorney did not go through until the following December 16, the treasurer's accounts show both men to have assumed office in the previous November, the month of Onley's death. Southwell held the mastership of the rolls from July 1, 1540, to December, 1550, when he retired to his residence in Kent where he died in November, 1559. *Cal. Pat. Polls, Edward VI.* III, 329.

[33] Richard Southwell, tutor to Cromwell's son, was awarded a receivership in the Augmentations in April, 1538, and a directorship in the Court of Survey as one of the general surveyors in 1542, which office he retained until the court was amalgamated with the Augmentations in 1547. Sheriff of his home county from 1534 to 1535 and afterward member of parliament between 1553 and 1554, Southwell joined the duchy of Lancaster in 1553 for six years service as steward of Norfolk, Suffolk, and Cambridgeshire. He was knighted in 1542.

[34] Brief biographies of Sir Richard Southwell and the younger Sir Robert Southwell are included in the *D. N. B.* On the elder Sir Robert Southwell (d. 1514), friend and councillor of Henry VII, see "Biographical Note" in Richardson, *Tudor Chamber Administration, 1485–1547,* Appendix II. In the *D. N. B.* article and elsewhere Sir Robert Southwell (d. 1559) has been erroneously styled chancellor of the Augmentations, on what authority I have been unable to discover.

service he had wisely learned that it was usually best to remain silent. He once explained that his fee from the Augmentations, including all his extra allowances, was not as much as the salary he gave up in London upon entering his office, adding that he had avoided taking advantage of opportunities for extra bribes and profits.[35] Of course he begged Cromwell's favor and intercession with the king. " I must by the colour of mine office, reside in London the most part of 3 or 4 years," he writes later. " I have as yet no house there but my chamber at the Temple, a good mile from Mr. Chancellor's,[36] so that in going thither and returning I spend a great part of the day." He solicited the aid of friends to help him to procure a small house in London, which he hoped to rent for but £6 per year.[37] While such complaints were usual with ambitious men, always in search of more money, it is certainly true that Southwell was not overpaid. Despite occasional grumblings, his letters show him to have been an officer of great industry and care in all his endeavors. Rich was obviously right in trying to keep at least one trustworthy Augmentations official on every commission survey in order to safeguard the Court's interest.[38]

With the exception of the chancellor who rose rapidly to a position of power and prestige during his incumbency, none of the principal officials of the first Court were outstanding ministers at the time of their appointments.[39] Nor were Rich's successors in the chancellor's office, Edward North and Richard Sackville, in positions of any particular prominence prior to their affiliation with the Court. Likewise, Thomas Pope, the first of the three treasurers, only became wealthy and influential later, primarily as a result of his office in the Augmentations. The more subordinate ministers fell into the same general pattern. As in the

---

[35] Robert Southwell to Cromwell, July 3, 1537, *L. and P.*, XII, pt. 2, no. 206.

[36] Southwell was referring to Rich, chancellor of the Augmentations, who transacted a great deal of the general business of the Court from his house in London or his country house at Leighs, Essex.

[37] *L. and P.*, XII, pt. 2, no. 1338. Certainly Southwell could have afforded a better house, for on £6 rental " a man shall be but slenderly housed in London"; but it must be remembered that he was seeking to enlist sympathy, in the hope of securing either a raise in salary or additional emoluments.

[38] Southwell seems to have been trained as a surveyor as well as in law, for he showed some professional knowledge of technical surveying. At the monastery of Furness in 1537 he reported having surveyed the lands " by eye and measure, and not by credit, as the commissioners for the suppression did." No evaluation of the various parsonages was attempted, however, until a year's profit had been received. Otherwise, any estimate would have been only a guess. He observed soberly, " It is thus that the king who grants and the farmer who receives are deceived." *L. and P.*, XII, pt. 2, nos. 205, 206.

[39] For a list of the principal officials of the Court of Augmentations, see Appendix A.

case of hundreds of other crown employees, a good job in any one of the new revenue courts was virtually a guarantee of a promising future.

That governmental service, even on the lower levels, attracted a superior type of individual is a noteworthy feature of Tudor administration. Doubtless some of these administrators primarily desired power and position for their own sake, while others were lured to the Court by the opportunity for graft, but the majority of them were well-trained, interested in their jobs, and loyal to the institutions they served. In this respect the officials of the Augmentations were no exception. Even at the height of decay during the Edwardian régime, when an attitude of indifference seemed to prevail, the corrupt ministers were always in the minority.

The clerk was the lowest official in the organization, though in technical matters he was not considered as a ranking member of the Court. Nevertheless, the clerkship was in no respect either a petty or nominal post. A junior officer, the clerk also served as archivist and keeper of the records, a position which required some knowledge of the documents that came under his control, as well as a fair understanding of their content. As secretary, he also kept an account of the activities of the council of the Court and a permanent record of its business, both judicial and administrative, enrolling " in a greate boke in parchement " the time, place, and reason for all appearances of persons summoned before the Court and " all actes decrees and orders that shalbe made by the said Chauncellour and Counsaile." [40] Richard Duke was appointed to the office in April, 1536, at a salary of £10 a year, augmented by such regular fees and profits as were customary in the clerkship of the duchy of Lancaster.[41] As indicated in Appendix A, his salary was later increased to £40. The position soon proved to be not only lucrative but exacting.

With the rapid development of the Court the clerical work became too heavy for one person to carry. By 1538 Duke had been given an assistant, Walter Farr, who was authorized to take charge of the " charters and evidences of religious houses suppressed." Thereafter, as clerk of the Court, Duke retained only a nominal supervision over archival activities. From the very inception of his office Farr was, in practice, the " keeper of the records "; in addition to his other duties he acted as a personal secretary to the chancellor when called upon to do so.[42]

An usher and a messenger completed the number serving the Court

---

[40] 27 Henry VIII, c. 27, *S.R.*, III, sec. vii. 572.
[41] April 24, 1536, Augm. Office, Misc. Books 232, pt. 1, fol. 2d.
[42] Appointments in the Court of Augmentations, September 26, 1538, *ibid.*, pt. 2, fol. 60; 249, fol. 36.

in its central offices at Westminster. Neither of these jobs required any special training, yet they were both positions of considerable responsibility and trust. In the sixteenth century a court usher or door-keeper was a more useful official than his modern counterpart. Actually he was a combination janitor, porter, doorman, and general servant, the medieval equivalent of the present day " office boy," who has no fixed duties but, if competent, may be called upon for all kinds of service. In the Augmentations, as in the Court of Wards and Liveries, the usher was the custodian of the premises of the Court. James Johnson, the only official usher the Augmentations ever had, was to serve the Court until its abolition early in 1554, when he was retired on a pension of £6 1s. 8d.[43]

Unlike the usher, the messengers of the Court had a more specific set of functions. They served as dispatch couriers for the chancellor and principal officers of the Court and were responsible for the delivery of court writs and other official documents. While there is no indication that the Augmentations office of messenger ever attained the dignity of " king's messengers," these court attendants occasionally executed charges similar to those performed by the royal pursuivants.[44] They sometimes collected nonrecurrent money due the crown, executed court warrants, and not infrequently took into their custody negligent officials or stubborn debtors. The original constitution provided for but one messenger, though the number was increased to five within a few years, of whom two were pursuivants. The treasurer's accounts indicate that they wore the regular livery of the Court and received a salary double that of the usher. A minimum wage of 4d. per day, plus the various extras they received in the form of gifts, gratuities, and regular allowances for travel, made of the office a fairly lucrative position.[45]

Beyond the central precincts at Westminster the chief representatives of the Court were the receivers and auditors who served locally as executive officers in the counties. In the chain of royal authority they

[43] Johnson was appointed usher of the Court on July 10, 1536, with wages of 2d. per day. Augm. Office, Misc. Books 232, pt. 1, fol. 16. When the Augmentations was remodelled in 1547 he was given a deputy or "under usher" to assist him in the increased duties of his office. *Ibid.* 259, fols. 79, 87d. Shortly after his appointment, when the expanding business of the Court demanded his regular attendance at 4d. per day, Johnson was put on an annual salary of £6 1s. 8d. *Ibid.* (Treasurer's "Books of Payments") 249, fol. 33d.; 256, fols. 72–75d.; 257, fol. 64.

[44] Cf. V. Wheeler-Holohan, *The History of the King's Messengers* (London, 1935), Chap. I, especially p. 7.

[45] See p. 219, *infra.* Walter Skinner, the original messenger, was appointed on July 2, 1536. Augm. Office, Misc. Books 232, pt. 1, fol. 47. The four other messengers of the first Court were John Ward, Jasper Pounte, Henry Atkinson, and Thomas Tyrrell. On the extended activities of the messengers, see Chapter Ten, pp. 335–36.

were, therefore, the connecting links between the central court and local revenue or estate ministers. As supervisory field officers these men became very important members of the Court. In final analysis the ultimate efficiency of the entire administrative machinery depended largely upon their honesty and diligence.

The constitution provided for the particular auditors and receivers, appointed for life or during good behavior by the king and bonded adequately for their proper conduct while in office. They were required to survey woods, determine wood sales, and authorize needful reparations of crown property, certifying their actions to the Court. Thus, the auditors and receivers performed many of the duties later assigned to the county surveyors and county woodwards of the second Court of Augmentations. Normally they worked separately as independent court officials, each having his own prescribed area of jurisdiction; but occasionally they were directed by the chancellor of the Court to hold group conferences for the purpose of united action. In such instances it was deemed advisable that auditors and receivers should " assemble togither aswell for the ordering of the said Religious Houses Manours Landes Tenementes & other the premisses, as of the tenauntes of the same frome tyme to tyme as the case shall require, as for the viewyng & determynacion of the said accomptes to be made therof." [46] Watchdogs of the Court, individually they wielded an unquestioned authority in the local districts.

For administrative purposes England and Wales were divided into seventeen districts, each division comprising a group of counties assigned to a particular receiver. Thus, each receiver had one or more counties under his jurisdiction, the size of the district depending upon the extent of the crown acquisitions expected in that area. The office was a responsible one, carrying as it did a salary of £20 per year, " with profits," plus a liberal allowance for travel and other personal expenses incurred while engaged in official business. Consequently, there were but infrequent changes in personnel; once secured, the office was retained usually until death or advancement to a better position. Of the twenty-nine men who held receiverships in the first Court of Augmentations seven were reappointed in 1547 to the reconstituted Court,[47] and several of the original appointees were still in office when the second Court was organized.[48] Most of them were able officials who served the Court conscientiously during the critical years of its greatest expansion.

[46] For this paragraph, see secs. iii, ix, xiv, and xviii of the statute.
[47] Pp. 49, 282, *infra.*
[48] They were William Bolles, George Gifford, William Green, Francis Jobson, Richard Paulet, John Scudamore, Thomas Spilman, and William Stump. John

Being field officials the receivers never played a conspicuous role in the multiple activities of the Court. They were not judges nor regular members of the executive council but met with that body only when called for particular information or testimony. Actually the receivers seldom appeared at the central office in Westminster, a fact which explains the paucity of evidence concerning their real work. Aside from their official accounts, expense allowances for travel, and recorded payments by the treasurer of the Court for the extended messenger service by which the chancellor and his council kept a close contact with all regional officials, there are only scattered references to their daily activities. Usually a local appointee, the receiver resided in his district, wherein he was widely known, at least by reputation. As a royal official his influence in the county was considerable, although the receiver's office was endowed with neither patronage nor disciplinary authority. Locally his power was subtle and indirect. In revenue collection he could insist upon the immediate payment of a debt to the crown, grant convenient terms, or ignore it altogether; likewise, he could either report or overlook illegalities or infractions of court decrees on the part of the king's tenants. Similarly, in the systematic espionage network developed by Cromwell and his royal master, the receiver, as often as not, was just another loyal governmental agent whose duty it was to scrutinize the actions and general behavior of all who came within his jurisdiction and perhaps to spy upon those who did not. Finally, his was an indirect influence in almost any matter of regional administration, whether it was an appointment, commission investigation, the sale of land or other crown property, or merely a supplication for royal favor which had to be investigated before the decision was made. Augmentations auditors and receivers worked in close co-operation with the central court, and through its officials they were in touch with the leading members of the government or even the king himself.

While the chief work of the receiver was the collection of the king's rents and profits, his duties were by no means confined to these. He was also expected to secure the full and prompt payment of all rents due from the crown tenants in his district. Arrearages always constituted a major problem in any sixteenth century department of revenue, and the Court of Augmentations was no exception to the rule. Periodic drives to collect long-standing arrears were launched, as well as occasional demands from the king's council for the immediate payment of all outstanding debts to the crown. In all such efforts the receiver played

Ailesworth, Richard Bunny, Robert Chester, John Eyre, Robert Goche, Richard Paulet, and Richard Whalley were reappointed as receivers of the second Court. See the list of Augmentations receivers on the opposite page.

PARTICULAR RECEIVERSHIPS IN THE FIRST COURT OF AUGMENTATIONS

All original appointments were dated April 24, 1536. The First Court was dissolved by letters patent on January 1, 1547.

District	Receiver
1 Lincolnshire	John Freeman April 24, 1536–April 20, 1543 Robert Goche April 20, 1543–to the dissolution of the Court.
2 Berkshire, Buckinghamshire, and Oxfordshire	John Danaster April 24, 1536–October 2, 1538 John Carlton October 2, 1538–December 1, 1545 John Doyle December 1, 1545–to the dissolution of the Court.
3 Gloucestershire, Hampshire, Wiltshire, and Bristol	Richard Paulet April 24, 1536–to the dissolution of the Court.
4 Bedfordshire, Essex, and Hertfordshire	Francis Jobson April 24, 1536–to the dissolution of the Court.
5 Leicestershire, Northamptonshire, Rutland, and Warwickshire	George Gifford April 24, 1536–to the dissolution of the Court.
6 Herefordshire, Shropshire, Staffordshire, and Worcestershire	John Scudamore April 24, 1536–to the dissolution of the Court.
7 Cornwall, Devonshire, Dorsetshire, and Somersetshire	Sir Thomas Arundell April 24, 1536–November 1, 1544 John Ailesworth November 1, 1544–to the dissolution of the Court.
8 Diocese of St. David's and the Diocese of Llandaff (South Wales)	Edward Watour (Waters) April 24, 1536–November 24, 1544 George Wall November 24, 1544–to the dissolution of the Court.
9 Kent, London, and Middlesex	Thomas Spilman April 24, 1536–to the dissolution of the Court.
10 Bishopric of Durham and the archdeaconry of Richmond	William Blithman April 24, 1536–February 15, 1544 Thomas Middlemore February 15, 1544–September 20, 1544 William Green * September 20, 1544–October 1, 1544 Cuthbert Horsley October 1, 1544–March 16, 1546 Richard Bunny March 16, 1546–to the dissolution of the Court.

* Temporary appointment of September 20, 1544, upon the death of Middlemore.

District	Receiver
11 Cumberland, Northumberland, and Westmoreland	William Green April 24, 1536–to the dissolution of the Court.
12 Cheshire, Derbyshire, and Nottinghamshire	William Bolles April 24, 1536–to the dissolution of the Court.
13 Surrey and Sussex	John Morice April 24, 1536–July 5, 1540 William Sanders July 5, 1540–to the dissolution of the Court.
14 Cambridgeshire and Huntingdonshire	William Lee (Leigh) April 24, 1536–November 28, 1545 Robert Chester November 28, 1545–to the dissolution of the Court.
15 Yorkshire	Leonard Beckwith April 24, 1536–autumn, 1546 Richard Whalley September, 1546(?)–to the dissolution of the Court.
16 Norfolk and Suffolk	Richard Southwell April 24, 1536–January 17, 1542 John Eyre January 17, 1542–to the dissolution of the Court.
17 Diocese of St. Asaph and the diocese of Bangor (North Wales)	William Stump April 24, 1536–to the dissolution of the Court.

a prominent role. Not only did he receive crown rents and the regular Augmentations revenues, he also acted as a general crown agent for any administrative problem or special investigation within his circuit. He supervised and assisted local officials, determined property evaluations, conducted land surveys, sat on royal or Augmentations commissions, and performed a host of miscellaneous services for the Court upon the advice or direction of the chancellor and council. Included among his special assignments were the supervision and repair of crown property, the sale of stone, lead, and bell metal, and occasional payments for the crown by order of the king, Cromwell, or later, the privy council. As the financial importance of the Court increased, direct payments by the receiver became a regular function of his office.

Until about 1540 all the major officials of the Court were busily engaged in the work of the Dissolution. Since a majority of them also served on the several commissions for taking the surrender of religious houses, their duties as commissioners and Augmentations officials were practically identical. Much of the receivers' time was spent in the annual collection of the revenues within their districts and in the preparation of detailed particulars of accounts, which were presented at the regular audits. Their normal receipts included the ordinary revenues of the suppressed monasteries, debts recovered, and money coming in from the sale of property and movables. The latter item, sometimes classified as *recepta forinseca*, or extraordinary receipts, oftentimes represented an appreciable proportion of the total, since the demand for churches, buildings, timber, stone, lead, and bells was quite constant during the years immediately following the Dissolution, before the market became glutted. Of course the sale of crown lands, and later of timber, was always a major source of Augmentations income, but these special receipts were not within the jurisdiction of the receiver's office. Nevertheless, the total net revenue for any particular district remaining due at the end of the fiscal year was surprisingly small in view of the fact that arrears constituted a not inconsiderable charge on each year's account. Furthermore, annuities, pensions, corodies, rewards, repairs of crown buildings, necessary fees and expenses of both receiver and auditor, and occasional payments by special decree were all a part of the regular expenditure. After the deduction of numerous allowances, the receiver usually found that he had but a few hundred pounds remaining to pay into the Court's treasury.[49]

Irrespective of honesty and ability the field officers were, at all times, under the close supervision of the chancellor and other members of the

---

[49] The accounts of Richard Paulet, receiver in the third district (Gloucestershire, Hampshire, and Wiltshire) for the years ending Michaelmas, 1539 and 1540, show the annual receipts for the three counties, including lead and bells remaining in storage, to have been £10,847 4s. 2d. and £22,543 12s. 1¹¹⁄₂₈d. respectively. Allowances totaled £4,061 17s. 2d. and £8,748 1s. 6½d.; however, long lists of arrears and numerous minor deductions, together with unsold implements, lead, and bell metal, finally reduced the actual amount of cash paid into the treasury of the Court to £295 and £400 odd. Augm. Office, Treas. Rolls of Accts., No. 2A. *L. and P.*, XIV, pt. 2, no. 237; XVI, no. 91. In 1540 the accounts of George Gifford in the fifth district (Leicestershire, Northamptonshire, Rutland, and Warwickshire) carried no less than £5,526 16s. 6¼d. in arrears from the previous year's reckoning. Of the £8,716 19s. 3¾d. due, only £118 5s. 7d. in cash was paid eventually into the Augmentations coffers. The itemized expenditures of this account, as allowed by the auditor, present an interesting analysis of a receiver's ordinary activities. They are grouped under ten headings as follows: (1) fees granted by the late religious and four small fees for the survey of woods, £114 5s.; (2) pensions of late religious persons, £1,910; (3) annuities granted by the late religious houses, £402 18s. 8d.; (4) corodies, £22 12s. 4d.; (5) perpetual pensions, procurations and synodals, and salaries (chiefly salaries of chantry priests)—total, £55 18s. 8d.; (6) debts of houses, paid by decree of the Augmentations, £280 8s. 6½d.; (7) necessary repairs of buildings, etc. £55 15s. 6d.; (8) cost of melting lead, weighing bells, and transportation of the same to storehouses, etc., £93 19s. 7d.; (9) necessary expenses of the auditor and the receiver, £78 2s. 2d.; and (10) money delivered in advance to the treasurer of the Court, £1,049 3s. 7d. Total allowances—£4,063 5s. ½d. *Ibid.*, XVI, no. 92.

council of the Court, who kept in regular touch with them through messenger service.[50] Not infrequently they were called upon for some particular assignment necessitating the services of a royal agent, when no other crown official was locally available. Like all other government ministers the Augmentations receivers and auditors served on the usual county commissions, but as often as not their special work was authorized by the king's council through an informal directive to the Court. In the absence of a clear-cut differentiation of function, the receiver could, when required to do so, serve as general paymaster or financial agent for the crown. John Scudamore, receiver in the sixth district, collected the subsidy of 1540 levied on the pensioners and stipendiaries within his jurisdiction,[51] while in Yorkshire the Augmentations receiver was regularly called upon to send funds for the increasing expenses of Berwick.[52] Normally, however, the extra duties of both the receiver and auditor were administrative in character. In general they were held responsible for supervising local revenue officials and for the regular upkeep of the crown estates.

In addition to the particular Augmentations receivers there were innumerable bailiffs, collectors, and local receivers of revenue for individual manors, lordships, honors, or former monastic land units lying within the seventeen districts; likewise, a few special receiverships had been created by the Court for those lands and revenues which came under its jurisdiction after 1536.[53] Chiefly, these possessions were

---

[50] Fortunately, many of the letters and special directives to a particular receiver, John Scudamore, of the sixth district have been preserved. See the Scudamore Papers, Add. MS. 11041.

[51] *L. and P.*, XVI, Appendix, no. 1.

[52] *Ibid.*, XV, nos. 27, 465, 746; D. L., 42/133, fol. 248; Augm. Office, Treas. Rolls of Accts. No. 1, pt. 2, mem. 3. As a convenience to the crown, receivers were often authorized to make special payments, as when Thomas Spilman purchased crown lands to be enclosed in the king's park of Otford in Kent. *Ibid.*, No. 2B, pt. 1, mems. 10*d.*–14*d.*, sale of goods and chattels of houses.

[53] Typical of such a special unit were the scattered possessions of Henry Algernon Percy, sixth earl of Northumberland, who, dying without issue in 1537, bequeathed his entire estate to the crown. These lands, lying chiefly but not exclusively in Yorkshire and Cumberland, were put under the control of the Court of Augmentations, which incidentally also inherited, as it were, a number of local offices of the late earl that went with the bequest. These lands were administered by the Court as a separate unit, known as "Northumberland's lands," even though the office of general surveyors governed a similar unit, called by the same name, which had come to the crown through the attainder of a previous earl. Michael Stanhope, lieutenant or governor of Hull, was the chief Augmentations officer of the Northumberland lands, for which Henry Whitreason was the receiver. Like many of the local officials, Stanhope held a number of other related positions: chief steward of the Northumberland possessions; master of the hunt in the three parks at Leconfield, Yorkshire; receiver, steward, and bailiff of the lordship of Beverly, Yorkshire, and steward of the court there; keeper of the warren, outwoods, and

acquired either through forfeiture, wardship, or by purchase, and were assigned, more or less arbitrarily, to one of the revenue courts. In the case of the first two of those categories, forfeited lands and wards' lands had been under the direct administration of the offices of wards and of general surveyors since the reign of Henry VII; in 1536, therefore, when the Augmentations was erected, all possessions of persons attainted for treason remained under the control of the Court of Survey.[54] Similarly, lands of wards continued to be administered by the office, and later Court, of Wards. On the other hand, lands acquired by mortgage, exchange, and purchase were always assigned to the Augmentations.[55] From the very beginning special officials were appointed for these separate possessions. Since there was no good excuse for setting up a purely artificial administrative unit for such acquisitions, save perhaps the traditional tendency toward decentralization, the most immediate effect was to add still further to the growing number of superfluous offices.[56]

The administration of exchanged and purchased lands was principally entrusted to three Augmentations officials, a surveyor, an auditor, and a receiver, who had the usual number of local ministers under their general supervision. The first and third offices were combined in the person of Geoffrey Chamber, a gentleman usher of the king's privy chamber, who became surveyor and receiver-general of purchased lands in May, 1536, shortly after the Court was organized.[57] He retained both positions until his death in May, 1544, when he was succeeded by George Wright, who served the Court until its reorganization in 1547.[58] The

---

park of Beverly; and surveyor of the lordship, paler of the park, and coroner and clerk of the market of Beverly. Augm. Office, Misc. Books *236*, fol. 14*d*.

[54] Special offices of general receiver and of auditor of attainted lands were instituted by the department of general surveyors (after 1542 the Court of General Surveyors, or Court of Survey) in 1538, which were filled respectively by Tristram Teshe and Philip Lentall. Richardson, *Tudor Chamber Administration, 1485–1547*, 388.

[55] By the original statute creating the Augmentations, all crown lands acquired by purchase, either before 1536 or thereafter, were put under the control of the Court. 27 Henry VIII, c. 27, sec. vi, *S. R.*, III, 571. Within three years the treasurer of the chamber was complaining to Cromwell that revenues formerly assigned to his office were greatly depleted. Purchased lands had been transferred to the Augmentations, he noted, while "forfeit lands" went mostly to the treasurer of first fruits, who received it under his patent of appointment contrary to parliamentary provision. *L. and P.*, XIV, pt. 2, no. 13.

[56] See p. 134 f., *infra*.

[57] Augm. Office, Misc. Books *232*, pt. 1, fol. 8. Chamber's fee of £20 per year was the same as that received by the seventeen particular receivers, except for the "profits" of office given to the latter officials.

[58] *Ibid.*, *236*, fol. 64. In Wright's patent of appointment, the office was described as that of "surveyor and general receiver of all lands in the King's hands by reason of exchange or gift."

auditorship of these lands was first awarded to John Ashton, already an exchequer auditor as well as a royal auditor of certain purchased and attainted lands remaining under the jurisdiction of the office of general surveyors.[59] Upon his death in August, 1542, he was succeeded by Richard Mody, who had held reversionary rights in the office since July, 1538.[60] Both Wright and Mody were pensioned in 1547 when their offices were absorbed into the reconstituted Court.[61]

Unlike their associates, the particular receivers, the ten auditors of the Augmentations were seldom called upon to perform any duties which were not strictly of a professional character. Nevertheless, along with the receivers and stewards, they exercised in a general way a supervisory control over the crown estates in their respective districts. Moreover, in the accounts that came under their scrutiny, they were expected to detect defaults or concealments of rent and to determine the justice of expenses and allowances demanded by accountants. In the absence of any large body of trained accountants in England, an auditor's office normally required more specialized knowledge than the average administrative post, and any person possessing previous accounting experience might be entrusted with several auditorships simultaneously or find himself serving regularly on numerous commissions of audit. Each auditor was appointed to a particular circuit, wherein he viewed annually the accounts of receivers and local collectors of rent at the yearly audit. Six of the original ten auditors held office for the duration of the first Court, while four of them, John Hanby, Hugh Fuller, Richard Hutchinson, and Thomas Mildmay, continued in the service of the second Court.[62] While all the receivers accounted once a year before the auditors assigned

[59] *Ibid.*, 232, pt. 1, fol. 12. During his tenure in office, from April 29, 1536, until his death on August 14, 1542, Ashton held a number of different auditorships. He was frequently referred to as simply the "king's auditor." *L. and P.*, III, no. 492(12); XII, pt. 2, nos. 260, 1311(26); XIII, pt. 1, no. 889(1); XVIII, pt. 1, no. 623(62).

[60] Augm. Office, Misc. Books 232, pt. 2, fol. 55. Mody was also one of the auditors in the Court of First Fruits and Tenths. *L. and P.*, XIX, pt. 1, no. 1035(153).

[61] See p. 170, *infra.*

[62] Thomas Mildmay, William Berners, John Wiseman, Hugh Fuller, James Rokeby, and Edward Gostwick were all in office when the first Augmentations was reorganized in January, 1547. Augm. Office, Misc. Books 415, fols. 130-130*d*. For the other auditors, see the list on the opposite page. On the case of auditor Thomas Combes, the records are singularly silent. He was definitely numbered among the original ten appointees (Augm. Office, Misc. Books 232, pt. 1, 8*d*-11*d*.) but apparently was appointed as an alternate auditor. I have found no evidence that he ever actually served in the Augmentations office. In fact, the various counties were apportioned among nine rather than ten circuits. (*Ibid.* 415, fols. 130-130*d*.) Neither is there any trace of a pension for him after 1547 nor any records of payments to him by the treasurer of the Court.

AUDITORSHIPS IN THE FIRST COURT OF AUGMENTATIONS

All original appointments, unless otherwise specified, were made on May 12, 1536, at an annual salary of £20, plus the " profits " of the office.

Circuit	Auditor
1 Cambridgeshire, Essex, Hertford-shire, Huntingdonshire, Middle-sex, Norfolk, Suffolk, and London	Thomas Mildmay 1536–June 1, 1545 Brothers { Thomas Mildmay / Walter Mildmay } jointly June 1, 1545–to the dissolution of the Court.
2 Gloucestershire, Hampshire, Wilt-shire, and Bristol	William Berners 1536–to the dissolution of the Court.
3 Cornwall, Devonshire, Dorset-shire, and Somersetshire	William Turner April 23, 1536–October 16, 1539 } William Turner / Mathew Colthurst { jointly October 16, 1539–September 10, 1545 Mathew Colthurst September 10, 1545–to the dissolution of the Court.
4 Bedfordshire, Berkshire, Buck-inghamshire, Kent, Oxfordshire, Surrey, and Sussex	William Cavendish 1536–February 19, 1546 Richard Brasier February 19(?), 1546–to the dissolution of the Court.
5 Herefordshire, Leicestershire, Northamptonshire, Rutland, Staf-fordshire, Shropshire, Warwick-shire, and Worcestershire.	Robert Burgoyne 1536–November 13, 1546 John Hanby November 13, 1546–to the dissolution of the Court.
6 Cheshire, Derbyshire, Lincoln-shire, and Nottinghamshire	John Wiseman 1536–to the dissolution of the Court.
7 Yorkshire	Hugh Fuller 1536–to the dissolution of the Court.
8 Cumberland, Durham, Northum-berland, Westmoreland, and the archdeaconry of Richmond	James Rokeby 1536–August 13, 1542 } James Rokeby / Richard Hutchinson { jointly August 13, 1542–to the dissolution of the Court.
9 North Wales and South Wales	Edward Gostwick 1536–to the dissolution of the Court.
10 Auditor of Queen's lands, Berkeley lands, and the duchy of York.	Thomas Combes * (Combez)

* An alternate auditor. See note 62.

to their districts, the treasurer of the Court, on the other hand, was required to present his yearly account to the chancellor and two or more of the Court auditors.

William Berners, the particular auditor in the second circuit, was the regular choice of the chancellor for the annual audit of the treasurer's account. In this capacity he was assisted, first by the auditor of purchased lands, John Ashton, and after 1538, by either Robert Burgoyne or John Wiseman.[63] In addition to their regular salary of £20 per year, each auditor of the treasurer's accounts received annually not only £15 for diets while in London but also an extra fee of £20 for hearing the treasurer's account, or if the account were unusually long, they might expect a special allowance for materials.[64] This auditorship of the accounts of the treasurer of Augmentations was made a separate office in the second Court; it was awarded to Berners and Wiseman in 1547, and two years thereafter granted to Berners alone.[65] Likewise, for a number of years before the office was created, Berners was, in fact if not in name, serving the Court as a special auditor of the prests.[66]

As the principal field representatives of the Court, the auditors and receivers were brought together in close co-operation. As Dissolution commissioners they had worked side by side in taking surrender of the religious houses; likewise, as field representatives they served as a team in the counties of their districts, assisting each other in their respective duties and laboring diligently in the joint pursuit of the king's rents, debts, and revenues. In this latter capacity they met annually at the regular audits, where indeed mutual assistance was indispensable in determining the final amount due from every farmer and collector in the district. Although not primarily revenue officials the auditors occasionally received and disbursed money.[67] Still, for most of them there was little opportunity for embezzlement; so unlike the receivers, they were not required to furnish bond. However, the bonding of officials was

[63] Augm. Office, Treas. Rolls of Accts., Nos. 1–8.

[64] For the war years, 1544–46, Berners and Wiseman were allowed an additional £13 6s. 8d. annually "for paper and parchment for the engrossing of the said account, more than hath been allowed, by reason of entering of many prests and other the King's warrants concerning his wars." Augm. Office, Misc. Books 249, fol. 35d.; 253, fols. 50, 51, 70; 254, fol. 94; 255, fol. 110.

[65] Grant of October 23, 1549. Appointment for life, from the previous Michaelmas, to the office of auditor of the accounts of the treasurer of Augmentations, at an annual salary of £40, payable half-yearly. Pat. Rolls, 3 Edward VI, pt. 2, mem. 30. Augm. Office, Misc. Books 256, fol. 75; 257, fol. 107d.; 260, fol. 62.

[66] The formal office of an auditorship of the prests was incorporated in the second Court of Augmentations of 1547. See p. 149, *infra*.

[67] See, for example, the receipts of John Wiseman in 1545, *L. and P.*, XX, pt. 2, no. 398.

as much a precaution against malfeasance in office as it was a safeguard against the actual theft of money. In the final determination of the accounts of receivers, collectors, and various local officials the auditors were in an excellent position either to expose or connive at corruption by others.

Now and again minor cases of deception or fraud would develop, but corruption among the rank and file of the officials was not particularly noticeable during the history of the first Court. Nevertheless, in an institution as large as the Court of Augmentations, with as many opportunities for exploitation as its extended revenues presented, dishonesty was bound to crop up from time to time. Receivers were of course particularly vulnerable, being constantly tempted to pocket a portion of their receipts. Here the integrity of the auditors was the chief safeguard, for the revenues due from each unit of property or land were all predetermined. Since receipts had to be presented for all cash expenditures, it was difficult to withhold money without the discrepancy appearing on the final particulars of account. Usually theft occurred in the sale of crown property, which was not reported in the official accounts, or in the withholding of revenues that were reported as arrears. Since in the system of bookkeeping used it was customary to extend arrears from one account to another without any official investigation, it was quite possible for a clever receiver to escape detection for years. More often than not, however, exposure occurred upon the death of the individual or the surrender of the office, when his successor discovered the discrepancy and reported it to the Court or to the king's council.

Usually the offense was no more serious than an unpaid debt to the crown, as in the case of William Blithman of Newcastle-upon-Tyne, the particular receiver for Durham and Richmond, who stood indebted to the Augmentations for " dyvers and sundrye greate somes of money," as indicated by the auditor's views of his accounts at the time of his death in February, 1544. His lands and possessions were promptly seized for the crown until the debt was paid, notwithstanding the widow's claim for her dower rights presented to the Court.[68] Actually the Court was not concerned in the case beyond the recovery of the money due from

[68] Hilary term, January 24, 1545. The bill of Margaret Blithman, filed with the Court of Augmentations, " comprehendyng her tytle to haue dower " of the said lands and tenements was duly considered, but the Court ruled that the title " cannot as yet be defendyd or justlie denyed." The final decree awarded her twenty marks yearly from the revenues of the archdeaconry of Richmond as long as the Court should retain the Blithman property. In addition to the annuity, she was awarded £10 for the arrears due her since her husband's death. Augm. Office, Misc. Books 104, pt. 2, fol. 82d.; Add. MS. 9782, p. 764.

the receiver. Consequently, obligations were taken from his sureties for the payment of the total debt due.[69]

Much more serious were the charges brought against Leonard Beckwith, the receiver of Yorkshire, in January, 1544, just before Sir Richard Rich resigned as chancellor of the Court.[70] Though only a crown receiver, Beckwith was, nevertheless, accused of being " a man of so greate power, aboundaunce of ryches and auctoritie that the kinges officers or baylieffes darre not clayme or yet demaunde such like duties for . . . the king, but taketh and vseth himself as though he were chief lord there which is greatly to the hinderaunce of our said soueraigne lordes royalties and profites there." [71] According to the complaint presented in the Augmentations he was guilty of at least nine violations of the law, ranging from the comparatively minor indiscretions of using two of the king's local barges without royal permission to the actual theft of 12,000 to 13,000 trees which he sold to his own profit, along with lead, timber, and other royal property appropriated to his own use.[72] Possibly aware that all these accusations could not be substanti-

---

[69] Obligations of February 12, 1547. Augm. Office, Misc. Books 327, fol. 2d. The debt, as reported by the auditor Richard Hutchinson, was no less than £2,783 8s. 2d., but woods of Blithman estimated at £528 were " redy to be solde towardes the discharging of þe said deptes." Likewise, debts owed to Blithman totalling over £166 brought the amount due down to £2,089 3s. 6d. Augm. Office, Miscellanea, 35.

[70] Rich surrendered his office in the Augmentations on May 1, 1544, to become *ad hoc* treasurer of the wars against France and Scotland. *L. and P.*, XIX, pt. 1, no. 610 (1, 2).

[71] " An enformation " by John Beverly, esquire, gentleman sewer of the king's chamber, and others against Leonard Beckwith, " of and vppon dyvers and sondrie offences vsurpations, and vntrue actes committed and doon aswell by himself, as by his commaundement, not onely against [the king's] profites and due rightes, but allso against [the king's] . . . veray true and iuste enheritaunce wᵗin his gracees countie of Yorke . . ." Augm. Office, Misc. Books 429, fol. 14 ff. The declaration is signed by Beverly and Oswald Sisson. Separate charges against Beckwith were presented by Robert Heneage, master of woods, concerning certain spoliation of woods in Yorkshire supposedly committed by Beckwith or his deputies.

[72] Although probably an exaggeration in fact, the technical charges against Beckwith did, however, particularize the numerous temptations for personal gain to which the average receiver of the period was subjected. The particular accusations were articled separately: (1) the felling and sale of trees, without authorization, from the crown estates; the cutting of grass and hay in lands not belonging to him; (2) as king's receiver of the revenues of the late monastery of Selby, he and his deputy Robert Walter had appropriated timber and other royal property to their own use and had neglected generally the upkeep and repair of the king's buildings; (3) as royal agent, he had farmed out fishing rights, personally appropriating the profits; (4) he had used, without permission, certain of the royal boats lying within his district; (5) he had refused crown tenants their customary allowances for the carriage of underwood; (6) the theft of the king's lead; (7) the sale, to his own relatives, of buildings and other crown property at prices considerably under the current market value; (8) the personal appropriation of the

ated, Beckwith's enemies proceeded to weaken their case by adding to the original charges until no fewer than thirty-four allegations were lodged against him. In his denial or " answer," presented to the Court, Beckwith refuted most convincingly each article of the indictment, claiming letters patent and other documentary evidence in disproof of his alleged misconduct. In the absence of conclusive evidence by either party the judges of the Court remained undecided.

As was customary in such cases, a special commission was appointed under the great seal of the Augmentations on December 29 to investigate the case against Beckwith and to examine carefully the accounts of his office for the past five years, in order that a " juste tryall of all such articles & matters " might be determined. The commission of five members included three officers of the Court and a master and surveyor of woods.[73] They were instructed to interview the plaintiffs and defendant, check on all the charges presented, examine witnesses, and if necessary enlist the assistance of Hugh Fuller, the auditor of Beckwith's accounts.[74] Neither the report of the commissioners nor the final judgment of the Court has been preserved, but, in the absence of any evidence of a fine or punishment, it is highly probable that Beckwith was finally acquitted. His long service to the crown, moreover, was a point in his favor. On the other hand, if he had been found guilty, the Court would have had to take some action in the matter. While an official might be forgiven a legitimate debt or a public indiscretion, the embezzlement of crown revenues invariably evoked weighty punishment and, ordinarily, dismissal from office.[75]

---

king's " waifs and strays " (i. e., cattle and horses) which had been surrendered to the crown; and (9) the wanton destruction of growing coppice in the king's woods and parks. *Ibid.*, fols. 14–18.

[73] The commission was headed by Sir Ralph Sadler, master of the great wardrobe, and included Michael Stanhope, lieutenant of Hull and chief steward of Northumberland's lands; Robert Heneage, master of woods in the Court of Survey; William Cowper, surveyor of woods in the Augmentations; and John Wiseman, auditor in the Augmentations. *Ibid.*, fol. 1.

[74] *Ibid.*, fols. 24–25. Augm. Office, Miscellanea, 34, contains drafts and copies of informations, depositions, interrogatories, and answers exhibited to the commission. The commissioners, likewise, examined Heneage's books of the survey of woods in connection with the charges of theft and spoliation of timber and consulted Sir William Fairfax of Yorkshire to ascertain what he knew concerning the " concealment," " deceit," and attempts to " defraud " which were " surmysed to be done " against the crown by the defendant. On this case see also *L. and P.*, XX, pt. 1, no. 746 and Exch., K. R., Miscellanea, 11/44, a book of informations and depositions concerning sales of wood and lead in the demesnes of Selby in Yorkshire by Sir Leonard Beckwith, 35 pages.

[75] The Tudor discipline, so thoroughly established by Henry VII, had begun to break down, however, before the end of the ensuing reign. Corruption in governmental administration, which became so prevalent under Edward VI, was

Beckwith seems to have escaped official censure altogether. During the year of his trial he was knighted for his loyal participation in the Scottish expedition.[76] Two years later he was appointed to the Council of the North, and in the autumn of 1546 he was sent to the Continent as controller of Boulogne.[77] Richard Whalley, who had held a survivorship in the office since December, 1545,[78] succeeded to the receivership when his predecessor left for Boulogne, but there is no indication that Beckwith was ever penalized for incompetence or fraud.[79]

In addition to their official duties, the receivers and auditors rendered numerous incidental services to the crown. Many no doubt felt themselves underpaid and questioned the king's appreciation of their industry. A few, like William Green, complained of the heavy expenses incurred while in office, but generally they were all satisfied with their jobs.[80] The crown was sometimes slow in the distribution of rewards, but in the end most of the Augmentations officials were more than fairly compensated for their labors. All of them received grants of land from time to time, and the majority was favored with generous pensions. For the unambitious such rewards were adequate; but for those who judiciously cultivated the right people, a whole array of minor offices and sinecures were forthcoming.

caused in part by the general apathy that had developed in the public civil service. On the official morality of the later period, see pp. 162–68.

[76] Beckwith was knighted in Scotland on May 11, 1544. Harl. MS. 6063, fol. 15. Add. MS. 5482, fol. 9. *L. and P.*, XIX, pt. 1, nos. 561 (3) ; XX, pt. 2, no. 633.

[77] *Ibid.*, XXI, pt. 1, nos. 148 (91–92), 1151, 1334; pt. 2, nos. 22, 232.

[78] Augm. Office, Misc. Books 236, fol. 116*d*. Whalley himself was finally dismissed from office in 1552, after having been convicted of embezzlement charges even more serious than those brought against his predecessors. See pp. 232–33, *infra*.

[79] In 1546 Beckwith had refused an offer of the chancellorship of Ireland, reputed to be worth £400 annually. He returned to England at the end of that year to terminate officially his business in the Augmentations office. *L. and P.*, XXI, pt. 2, nos. 156, 232, 452. He died in May, 1557. *Cat. Pat. Rolls, Philip and Mary*, IV, 97.

[80] Like most Tudor officials, Green was continually seeking extra emoluments or rewards. His complaint of great charges as a result of having " no place to resort to but lie in towns " was unjustified, considering the fact that travel allowances were usually quite generous. His offer to Cromwell in 1539 of £20 for a church preferment was favorably received. *L. and P.*, XIV, pt. 2, nos. 482, 782 (p. 327).

CHAPTER FOUR

DEVELOPMENT AND PERSONNEL

URING THE FIRST DECADE OF DEVELOPMENT THE AUGMEN-tations varied little in either organization or function, yet it gradually extended its influence in both jurisdiction and authority. Revenues multiplied and the crown demesne in-creased in size, but these external factors did not materially affect the continuity of the daily life of the Court; save for a few changes in per-sonnel, the structure remained essentially the same. Only to a minor degree did it broaden administrative operation or enlarge the scope of managerial control. Such improvements as were introduced were largely the result of an imaginative executive board whose members envisioned their own institution as developing into a great financial department and becoming one of the most powerful courts in the land.

In training and fitness the hierarchy of the Court represented a fair selection of ministerial ability. Richard Rich, the man chosen for the chancellorship, was in many respects a typical Tudor careerist, whose success already bore witness to his unusual resilience and tact. A shrewd opportunist whose ambition readily permitted him to support any policy however distasteful, he was able to co-operate remarkably well with superiors and subordinates alike. Though envied by the less for-tunate and criticized by those who condemned the institution he served, contemporary accounts of him were generally not unfavorable. His-torians have maligned him most, with the result that his name is still commonly associated with greed and corruption. Whatever the justice of this estimate, such an interpretation is understandable enough in view of the dearth of information concerning either the personal life or the character of the man. Practically nothing is known of those early years of training prior to his appointment to the Augmentations. Similarly, his later work as treasurer of war and as lord chancellor of England has never been fully investigated. Consequently, historical judgment of him rests largely upon two unfortunate incidents in his life which have colored virtually every account of his public behavior. Testimony at the trial of Sir Thomas More gave rise to a denunciation of Rich by Sir Thomas that has forever branded him as treacherous and unprincipled. Sixteen years later, events incidental to his surrender of the great seal seemed to verify this conclusion.[1] These facts, circumstantial though they were, together with the assumption that anybody high in Augmentations circles was bound to be corrupt, have lent finality to the unsavory reputation accredited to him.

Clouded in obscurity, the chancellor's life will always be something of an enigma. The broader lines of his official activities are clear enough, but the sources are completely silent on matters of individual traits and family relationships. While apparently adequate, little is actually known of his background and education; even the details of his rise in the royal service are uncertain. It was only after his affiliation with the Augmentations that he attained a position of real influence with Cromwell and the council. Neither obsequious nor antagonistic, Rich performed all his assignments with dispatch and without remonstration. During his years with the Court of Augmentations the king, at no time, had occasion to regret Rich's appointment or protest that the royal interests were being neglected. Naturally cautious at first, the chancellor soon acquired those special aptitudes which later became indispensable to his success.

Born about 1496 in the parish of St. Laurence Jewry, London, he was descended from a middle-class Hampshire family which had distinguished itself neither in private enterprise nor in public affairs. His father, also a Richard, was a well-to-do London merchant who had

---

[1] As a result of his leaving the Somerset faction, just before the Lord Protector's final trial and execution, to join the Warwick party, Rich has been accused, as in previous instances, of betrayal of friendship. Therefore his motives for resigning office in December, 1551, have been suspected. His health, age, and desire for retirement from active public life appear to have been the chief motivating factors, rather than fear or base designs. There seems to be no reason to question the truth of his claim to illness; certainly the story of his misdirected letter to Somerset, which was delivered to the wrong " Duke," can be dismissed as ridiculous. On the episode see Edward Foss, *Judges of England* (London, 1848–64), V, 323–25; John Sargeaunt, *A History of Felsted School, with Some Account of the Founder and his Descendants* (London, 1889), 84–86.

encouraged his son, after brief attendance at the university, to embark upon a legal career.[2] While at Middle Temple he undoubtedly pursued his legal studies with some seriousness, for subsequently he was appointed reader there, probably in just recognition of his ability.[3] Having acquired competence in the law, he naturally sought some position where he could profitably employ his newfound talents. His first bid, however, was unsuccessful, for in December of 1526 he was defeated as a candidate for the office of common sergeant of London.[4] Undaunted by this early defeat, Rich began to cultivate influential friendships and to extend his political associations at court. Within two years he had succeeded in bringing himself to the attention of Cardinal Wolsey. Once begun, his career was a long series of rewards and promotions, to some of his contemporaries a source of resentment, to others a model of professional achievement.

Rich's initiative, as well as his knowledge of legal procedure, was demonstrated as early as 1528 when he suggested to Wolsey a program for the reformation of the common law. Although the offer was not accepted, it is to Rich's credit that he felt competent enough in the law to instruct the chancellor in the proposed reforms which Wolsey had projected but had never found time to execute.[5]

The gesture seems to have had the desired effect in bringing him to the attention of the king, for he received his first royal assignment im-

[2] John Stow, *Survey of the Cities of London and Westminster* (London, 1720), Book III, 44; John Campbell, *The Lives of the Lord Chancellors and Keepers of the Great Seal of England* (London, 1845–69), II, 9.

[3] John G. Nichols (ed.), *Autographs of Royal, Noble, Learned, and Remarkable Personages Conspicuous in English History* (London, 1829), no. 20, unpaged; Thomas Wright, *History of the County of Essex* (London, 1836), I, 212.

[4] (November 27 and December 10, 1526.) The report from the Journal of the Court of Common Council of the City of London, Journal 12, fols. 364–65b. The vacancy was created by the transfer of Henry White to the office of undersheriff of the City. His successful opponent, " our trusty & welbiloved subgict William Walsingham Gentilman," father of the more illustrious Sir Francis Walsingham, was elected finally on November 15 as a result of special letters in his favor from the king and queen. As soon as the royal preference became known, Rich, who was the favorite among the seven contesting candidates, was asked to withdraw from the contest in order that the king's choice could be elected. In return for his support of Walsingham, the council pledged itself to "recompence hym with som other condigne amendes & rewardes wherwith the seyd Richard Ryche shall haue cause to be well contentyd & pleasyd." In the end Rich was promised either the office of common sergeant at the time of the next vacancy or the office of undersheriff of the City. He soon went on to higher positions, however, and never attempted to hold the council to its promise.

[5] Richard Rich to Thomas Wolsey, November 16, 1528. Alluding to the various current abuses in the law, Rich indicated that he could provide an adequate solution. *L. and P.*, IV, pt. 2, no. 4937. A. F. Pollard, *Wolsey* (2d impression, London, 1929), 95.

mediately thereafter.[6] From that point forward his rise was progressively rapid. Early in 1529 he served as a commissioner of sewers in Middlesex and in November of the same year took his seat in parliament as a member for Colchester.[7] During succeeding months he was variously employed on a number of general commissions, but his first important opportunity did not come until 1532. In that year he was fortunate enough to receive two major appointments, the clerkship of the recognizances [8] and the office of attorney general for Wales.[9] In October of 1533 he became solicitor general for the crown; on the same day he was awarded knighthood.[10] Though he was at that time only thirty-seven years of age, his reputation for skill and efficiency was already growing.

As solicitor general Rich represented the crown in cases of state prosecution against those who refused to accept the acts of succession and supremacy. In those " non-compliance " trials he frequently had occasion privately to examine prisoners in advance of their public hearings. Such was his implication in the proceedings against Sir Thomas More and John Fisher, the saintly bishop of Rochester, who remain the chief source of criticism for those who have impugned his character. Already Rich had been spotted by Cromwell as an ambitious and useful minister who, if properly rewarded, could be of invaluable service to the crown. Accordingly, he was appointed to the directorship of the office of liveries, where he remained until called upon to launch the Court of Augmentations. Although nominaly a joint director, Rich was never more than a legal adviser to Sir Thomas Neville, the senior head of the office, who continued as the actual overseer or " surveyor " of liveries until 1542 when the office was absorbed by the Court of Wards.[11]

[6] He was appointed to the commission for the peace in Hertfordshire in December of 1528. *L. and P.*, IV, pt. 2, no. 5083(4).

[7] *Ibid.*, pt. 3, nos. 5336(11), 6043(2).

[8] *Ibid.*, V, no. 909(32) ; X, nos. 300, 330, 392(32). Recognizances for debts in London due the crown were taken in the Courts of King's Bench or Common Pleas, or more specifically, drawn up by the merchants of the Fellowship of the Staple; they were leviable by virtue of the recent statute 23 Henry VIII, c. 6, " An Acte concernynge before whome Recognisaunces of Dettes shalbe made & the forme of the obligacion." *S. R.*, III, 372–73. Rich surrendered this office in December, 1548. *Cal. Pat. Rolls, Edward VI*, I, 363.

[9] He was also attorney general for the counties palatine of Flint and Chester. *L. and P.*, V, nos. 1065(21), 418(13).

[10] (October 10, 1533.) *Ibid.*, VI, no. 1383(8,9) ; X, no. 775(21). When he became chancellor of the Augmentations, Rich was succeeded in the solicitor's office by William Whorwood, April 13, 1536.

[11] The dual directorship, so characteristic of Tudor administration, was a device by which a practical administrator and a trained legalist could work together for the better safeguard of the rights of the crown. In such a situation the lawyer invariably acted in an advisory capacity. Rich's appointment to the office came in April, 1535, upon the death of Sir Robert Norwich, serjeant-at-law.

Nevertheless, the brief tenure in that position gave him a firsthand acquaintance with the administrative problems and techniques he was to meet later. During the summer of that year, 1535, he was awarded the additional post of chirographer in the Court of Common Pleas.[12] Already he had proved acceptable to Cromwell, who found in him a sympathetic official, willing to co-operate in the furtherance of any aspect of government policy. A good chance to advance his career came the following year when, as speaker of the house of commons, he was able to enlist its support in the extension of the royal prerogative.

Rich's formal appointment to the Augmentations, at a salary of £200 a year, was not issued until April 24, 1536, although he had assumed the responsibilities of office somewhat prior to that date.[13] About the same time he was sworn to the privy council, which had adopted the policy of bringing to its deliberations the heads of the various departments of revenue administration. Faithful in his attendance from the beginning, he became immediately an influential councillor and continued in the confidence of the king during the remainder of the reign. After the fall of Cromwell Rich transferred his support to the conservative faction led by Stephen Gardiner, an alliance which prompted the martyrologist John Foxe to list him amongst the papists in the deliberations of the king's council.[14] Unquestionably he was a prominent minister, closely in the confidence of Henry VIII; during the latter years of his chancellorship in the Augmentations, he was one of the most powerful officials in the government.

After eight years with the Augmentations, Rich resigned his post in favor of Sir Edward North, who had been joined with him in the chan-

He was succeeded by Sir Thomas Englefield. *L. and P.*, VIII, no. 632(34); XII, pt. 1, no. 795(27). Richardson, *Tudor Chamber Administration, 1485-1547,* 302.

[12] This office was held jointly with John Packington, from July 27, 1535, to July 4, 1537. Pat. Rolls, 27 Henry VIII, pt. 2, mem. 10; 29 Henry VIII, pt. 4, mem. 2.

[13] Augm. Office, Misc. Books 232, pt. 1, fol. 1*d*. Although a salary of £200 is stipulated in the original appointment, the payment by the treasurer of the Court as well as Rich's receipts show him to have received £300 per year in fee and diets. Augm. Office, Treas. Rolls of Accts., No. 1, pt. 1. mem. 8; pt. 2, mem. 17; Exch., Accounts Various, 676/21. (A receipt by Rich for the payment of his fee as chancellor of the Augmentations.)

[14] John Foxe, *Actes and Monuments*, better known as *The Book of Martyrs* (London, 1563; George Townsend edit., London, 1843–49), V, 439. Rich, always a practical person little given to speculative thought, was the type of man who rose above the "pedanticknesse of a scholler, to þ usefulnesse of a statesman." According to a seventeenth century account he had repudiated the contemplative life. "I could never endure those studyes," he is supposed to have observed, "þt furnish me onely wᵗʰ inactive thoughts & uselesse discourse; þt teach me onely to think & speake." In him, as in many a sixteenth century Englishman, renaissance impulses were channeled into practical politics. Sloane MS. 1523, fol. 38.

cellorship on April 24, 1544. At the same time John Williams had been appointed joint treasurer with North, who had succeeded Pope in the treasurership some four years earlier, on March 17, 1540. After North began to take over the chancellor's duties, he resigned the treasurership, and Williams became sole treasurer by an undated patent of appointment. When Rich withdrew from the Court shortly thereafter, the transfer of offices had been effected with a minimum of dislocation.[15] This practice of joining an incoming official with the head of the office before the latter's retirement, in order that he might be adequately trained for the job, was quite common. The procedure had much to recommend it, inasmuch as the departmental confusion resulting from the use of inexperienced personnel was thus avoided.

The change was probably due to the king's desire to take a reliable financier with him on the French expedition of that year, though Rich may indeed have welcomed the arrangement as a relief from his strenuous work of the previous decade. In any event, he was made high treasurer of wars on May 1, with six clerks and a messenger to assist him.[16] His new duties must have required most of his time, but he retained a supervisory control over the Augmentations until shortly before his departure for the Continent in July of that year.[17] His last contribution to the Court came some eighteen months later, when he was called upon to investigate the financial status of the various departments of revenue and report his findings to the privy council.[18]

Rich's later career, while not directly related to this study, is of considerable interest to the student of Tudor administration. Like his friend and contemporary, Sir William Paulet, he represents a class of lesser known English statesmen whose varied contributions to a great

[15] These various appointments and changes are all recorded in Augm. Office, Misc. Books 236, fols. 29, 30, 31, 42, 127. North's formal appointment as sole chancellor was dated July 1, 1545.

[16] Pat. Rolls, 36 Henry VIII, pt. 23, mems. 4, 6. Sir Richard Southwell, Sir Robert Bowes, and Sir John Harrington assisted him as undertreasurers. Rich was allowed 40s. per day for his diets, which was more than the average fee of an English ambassador in the 1540's. Accounts of Rich as treasurer of wars are included in the *L. and P.*, XIX, pt. 2, nos. 366, 419(2), 458(2), 506(2). This was, of course, only a temporary position. See Chapter Three, n. 70. Being the principal paymaster, he was sometimes styled "high treasurer for the wars."

[17] When Henry and his army crossed the Channel to Boulogne on July 14, 1544, Rich accompanied the king and remained to assist in the peace negotiations which followed. *D. N. B.* He was not active, apparently, in the Augmentations office after North's appointment, although I have found no record of his actual resignation. As late as the end of May, 1544, however, he was referred to officially as chancellor of the Court. *L. and P.*, XIX, pt. 1, nos. 610(111), 812(77).

[18] Commission delivered December 14, 1545, for Rich and Sir Ralph Sadler to examine the condition of the revenues and make a declaration of the status of the revenue and revenue courts. Pat. Rolls, 37 Henry VIII, pt. 13, mem. 32.

age of national administration have been neither adequately assessed nor fully appreciated by historians.[19] Both men stand out as model servants of the state—the type that Cromwell loved to discover and advance— each in his own way responsible for the initial success of the two great revenue institutions, the Court of Augmentations and the Court of Wards, the guiding principles and continuity of policy of which they respectively formulated.[20] In spite of the religious changes and political upheavals of the period, they served successively four sovereigns, advancing their fortunes under each monarch. A close confidant of the king, Rich remained active in the privy council during the closing years of the reign, being designated an assistant executor of Henry VIII's will. As a final reward the king had bequeathed to him a legacy of £200 [21] and the promise of a peerage, which was duly bestowed upon him in February, 1547, after the accession of Edward VI.[22] Rich chose the baronial title Leighs, the name of his country estate in Essex, which he had acquired in 1536 shortly after he took over the Augmentations chancellorship.[23]

---

[19] In addition to outstanding statesmen like Reginald Bray, chief minister of Henry VII, and Thomas Cromwell, such a group of Tudor administrators should include others of less spectacular achievement, as Sir Thomas Lovell and Sir Henry Wyatt, treasurers of the chamber and financial ministers of Henry VII; Sir John Baker, chancellor of the Court of First Fruits; Sir Ralph Sadler, master of the great wardrobe, clerk of the hanaper, principal secretary, warden of the east and middle marches, and eventually chancellor of the duchy of Lancaster under Elizabeth; Sir Walter Mildmay, successively auditor, general surveyor, treasurer of the household, and chancellor of the Exchequer; and possibly Sir Edmund Peckham, cofferer of the household, treasurer of the chamber, and high treasurer of the mints. Adequate biographies of these men would add immeasurably to the administrative history of the period.

[20] Created marquis of Winchester in 1551, the first master of the Court of Wards, Sir William Paulet was also a household official, lord president of the council, treasurer, and for a short period lord keeper of the great seal. Thoroughly familiar with the entire revenue machinery, he had become a chief consultant on revenue procedures and techniques. As master of wards, a recent historian of that institution has found in him an archtype of the Court of Wards official. Bell, *The Court of Wards and Liveries*, 33.

[21] Dasent (ed.), *Acts of the Privy Council*, II, 147. This legacy was paid by the treasurer of the Augmentations by warrant from the privy council. Augm. Office, Misc. Books 256, fol. 84*d*.

[22] The king had promised Rich a barony, with £66 13*s*. 4*d*. a year. John G. Nichols (ed.), *Literary Remains of King Edward VI* (Roxburghe Club, 1857), I, Preface, xciv (hereinafter cited as *Literary Remains*). Dasent (ed.), *Acts of the Privy Council*, II, 16, 18.

[23] The charter of creation, along with that of Edward Seymour, William Parr, John Dudley, Thomas Wriothesley, and Thomas Seymour, was issued on February 16, 1547. *Cal. Pat. Rolls, Edward VI*, I, 174. The original grant to Rich of the site and house of the priory of Leighs, in Essex, marked the origin of the family estate, which from the beginning included the local church as well as the manors of Great Leighs, Leighs Parva, Leighs Magna, Felsted, and Fyfield, Essex.

As an influential councillor and friend of Protector Somerset, Rich advanced in both fame and fortune under Edward VI. During the first year of the reign he attained the lord chancellorship, to which high office he was appointed on November 29, 1547.[24] He retained the custody of the great seal after Warwick's advent to power until the end of 1551, when ill health forced his resignation and temporary retirement from public life. By November of the following year, however, he had resumed work in the privy council. Though implicated in the Lady Jane Grey plot, he remained faithful to the Tudors and gave his support to Queen Mary, being sworn to the council immediately upon her accession.[25] He was continued as a member of the council throughout the reign, but recurrent sickness prevented him from playing a prominent part in the government. Under Elizabeth he was recognized as an elder statesman of wisdom and experience, though he appears only intermittently in state affairs during the last period of his life. After some thirty-nine years of almost continuous service to the crown, Rich died at Rochford, Essex, on June 12, 1567. He was buried at Felsted, where earlier he had founded a chaplaincy and a grammar school, just a few miles distant from the magnificent Leighs mansion near Chelmsford, which stands today as an architectural witness to Tudor extravagance and pride.

Since it must be based largely upon conjecture, any characterization of Rich will necessarily be tentative. Neither negligent of his own interests nor reluctant to take advantage of his position when the opportunity presented itself, the very fact of his having accumulated a large personal fortune while in the employment of the state suggests unscrupulousness. Nonetheless, he seems to have escaped official censure altogether; only once [26] was he seriously accused of embezzlement, in which instance the charges appear to have been dropped before the suit came to a final hearing.

(Grants in May, 1536.) Pat. Rolls, 28 Henry VIII, pt. 5, mem. 22. List of lands in Essex granted to Rich, Augm. Office, Misc. Books 339, fols. 42–44*d*.

[24] Pat. Rolls, 1 Edward VI, pt. 3, mem. 34.

[25] Dasent (ed.), *Acts of the Privy Council*, IV, 300, 318, 319, 320, 355.

[26] An earlier accusation of April 7, 1541, against Rich by John Hillary of Keynesham abbey in Somersetshire can be dismissed as being completely unfounded. Hillary claimed that Rich, as chancellor of the Augmentations, had withheld certain information concerning the deception of the late abbot of Keynesham, as a result of which the crown had suffered a loss of 200 marks. After the charges had been heard by the privy council in Rich's presence, it was decided that the informant had manifestly "slanderously and untruely forged the said mattier." Consequently, he was committed to the Marshalsea for his pains. N. H. Nicolas (ed.), *Proceedings and Ordinances of the Privy Council of England, 1386–1542* (London, 1834–37), VII, 169.

The case in question concerned various malfactions in the Augmentations office, which did not come to light until the beginning of Mary's reign, after the Court had been abolished. Several charges were presented against him, some of which were serious in the extreme: namely, that he had profiteered from the sale of lead, had appropriated for himself manors sold by the king to another, had deliberately misrepresented the value of certain lands alienated by the crown, and on numerous occasions had effected exchanges of property without taking indentures or sureties for payment. The total amount involved in the alleged embezzlement is not stated in the accusation but various sums are suggested, including bona fide debts to the crown of over £135 for the purchase of lead and timber for which obligations had been given. It is doubtful if the charges were ever really investigated; but whatever developed there is no indication that Rich was ever bonded for such liabilities or in any way penalized.[27]

The basic problem, of course, remains unsolved. Due to the insufficiency of evidence definite judgment is impossible. Was Rich guilty of the criminal charges of which he was accused? Was he an irresponsible and corrupt minister? And finally, was he the rapacious, objectionable character we have been asked to accept? On the first indictment the records are incomplete. If the case came to trial, no account of the decision has survived, nor is there any indication from other sources that the accusation attracted any attention at the time or that Rich's position was affected by it at all.

On the other counts the verdict must again be relative. Corruption should be evaluated in terms of the mores of the sixteenth century before sentence is pronounced, and ministers should be judged by the standards of their own age. That Rich was guilty of perversion of justice or the misuse of public funds cannot be proved. In all his financial dealings there is no record of the falsification of accounts. As did most public officials he accepted gifts, extra fees, and sinecures without qualms, and like those around him profited from patronage, pluralism, and padded accounts. These were evils of the existing system, but they were not crimes punishable by law. Possibly he abused his power while in public office, or even perjured himself on occasions, as More testified, but it is doubtful if his contemporaries condemned him for these offenses.[28] Per-

---

[27] "Divers causes alleged against the L[ate] Richard Ryche Chauncellour of the Courte of Augmentacions," 28–35 Henry VIII; two documents of five pages each, of which one is a copy and the other the original. Augm. Office, Miscellanea, 37.

[28] In his oft-quoted accusation that Rich was by reputation a man of "little trust" in whom he could find "no commendable fame," More branded his testimony as a fabrication. "In faith, Mr. Rich, I am sorrier for your perjury than I

haps the best explanation of much of the conduct of Tudor ministers was given by Sir Thomas Wyatt at the time of his trial in 1541. What the king ordered, the servant did, regardless of his personal opinion. At one time or another many a public figure had committed his conscience to that rule. He might still mislike or repugn his prince's proceeding, Wyatt maintained, but when "misliking includes disobeying I think him no good subject, but otherwise I know no law to the contrary." [29]

Unofficially Rich had begun the work of the Augmentations before his privy seal of appointment was issued on April 24, 1536, although he did not surrender his office of solicitor general until April 13 of that year.[30] Already he and Thomas Pope, the treasurer of the Court, were immersed in their new duties, which later led them occasionally to participate in the monastic surveys. As early as January 19 of that year Rich had written to the king from Kimbolton, where he was taking an inventory of the late queen's estate, explaining a legal way by which Henry could seize Catherine's property to his own use.[31] The king was probably impressed with such ingenuity; any minister who could prove himself useful in many capacities was invaluable to the crown. Shortly after taking up his duties as chancellor of the Augmentations, Rich was called upon to serve as speaker of the commons in the June-July parliament of 1536. It was in this capacity that he delivered his famous panegyric on the greatness of the king, styling him a Solomon for his justice and prudence, a Samson in strength and fortitude, and an Absalom in comeliness.[32] Despite these and other interruptions, however,

---

am for mine own peril," he said in his refutation. He then went on to declare Rich light of tongue, a great dicer, and a notoriously loose liver, whose evil habits had always been criticized by acquaintances. The original conversation between the two men, as well as the evidence submitted at More's trial, have been variously reported, but essentially the implications are the same in all versions. William Roper, *Life of More*, edited by S. W. Singer (Chiswick, 1817). The case is presented in *L. and P.*, VIII, especially nos. 814, 867(iii), 974(vi), 996.

[29] *L. and P.*, XVI, no. 641 (p. 309). Many, like Wyatt, had erred in their "zeal for the king's service." He was sent to the Tower on January 17, 1541, but was pardoned the following May. *Ibid.*, nos. 640, 678(41).

[30] *Ibid.*, X, no. 775(21).

[31] *Ibid.*, nos. 128, 151; Cotton. MS., Otho. C. x, fol. 220; John Strype, *Ecclesiastical Memorials* (Oxford, 1822), I, pt. 1, 375 (John Strype, *Historical Works* [a new edition, 27 vols., Oxford, 1820–40]). Catherine had died the preceding January 7, but as yet no disposition had been made of her estate. Rich's letter to the king is printed in full by Strype. *Ibid.*, I, pt. 2, 254, no. LXX. Cf. *L. and P.*, X, nos. 128, 151.

[32] This short parliament of less than six weeks duration sat from June 8 to July 18, 1536. Rich as speaker delivered two eulogistic orations on the occasion of the king's visits to parliament on June 10 and July 18. On the second occasion Henry was compared to the sun that nurtures the growing crops so necessary for human existence. For this type of flattery, common in such orations, he has been

he still found time to organize and direct the activities of the institution over whose destiny he was to preside for the next eight years.

Cromwell was the first to realize that in the Dissolution program the usefulness of the Court depended upon the integrity and competence of its directors; it was clear that no sinecures were to be handed out as rewards to those great ministers of state who possessed no particular qualifications for the task at hand. Loyal administrators were needed— men of discretion and judgment who were prepared to give their best in whatever capacity they served—and from that category Cromwell made his final selections. Occasionally in later years mistakes were made in the choice of Augmentations officials, but most of the initial appointees were sound. The three chancellors of the Court were all civil lawyers of considerable repute and, on the basis of previous record, were well suited for their jobs. Rich was the most distinguished of the three, but his successors, Sir Edward North, subsequently first Baron North of Kirtling, and Sir Richard Sackville, were both men of ability.[33] Pope, the youngest of the group, was also the least experienced. Contemporary critics must have considered his background, if not his age, inadequate for such an important job as a major treasurership. Still, in spite of obvious deficiencies in training, Cromwell's confidence in him was quickly justified; a decade of service in the Court proved him a useful minister whose reputation remained untarnished to the end of his life.

Thomas Pope, esquire for the body and former servant of Lord Chancellor Thomas Audley, was only thirty years of age when, in 1536, he assumed the position of treasurer and second ranking officer in the Court of Augmentations.[34] In spite of his friendship with such influential ministers as Audley, More, and Cromwell, he was relatively unknown in court circles at the time of his appointment, his experience in politics having been exceedingly limited. However, the recommendations of his friends, Audley and More, had secured for him an entrée to governmental service by 1532, when he was awarded clerkships in both the Court of Star Chamber and the chancery.[35] Having been brought to the attention of Cromwell, he attained the responsible position of warden

---

branded obsequious and servile. *Journals of the House of Lords* (London, 1767——), I, 86, 101; Foss, *Judges of England*, V, 321. For his work in this parliament Rich was paid £100. *L. and P.*, XI, no. 381.

[33] North, succeeding Rich to the chancellorship in April, 1544, retained that office until the beginning of the reign of Edward VI. In August of 1548 he was persuaded to resign in favor of Sackville, who continued to head the Court until its dissolution under Mary, early in 1554. See pp. 250, 259 and n. 42, *infra*.

[34] Appointments of April 24, 1536. Augm. Office, Misc. Books 232, pt. 1, fol. 1d.

[35] *L. and P.*, V, no. 1499(8). He held the latter office in survivorship until July, 1537, when he succeeded Ralph Pexsall as clerk of the crown in chancery. *Ibid.*, XII, pt. 2, nos. 274, 297; XIII, pt. 1, no. 384(101).

of the mint two years later, a post which he held until the autumn of 1536 when his full time was required in the Augmentations.[36] In May of that year Cromwell procured for him election to parliament from the town of Buckingham.[37] He was knighted in 1537 and shortly thereafter sworn to the privy council. Although he owed his initial appointment in the Augmentations to Cromwell, Pope remained with the Court long after the period of his benefactor's ascendancy. Retiring from the treasurership in favor of North in the spring of 1540, he was transferred to the department of woods in the same administration, where as master of woods he continued until 1549.[38]

Though good friends of Cromwell's, neither Pope nor Rich were quite as subservient to his demands as some writers have supposed. Both men, however, were discreet enough to hold their tongues when the vicar-general differed with them and to move cautiously whenever Augmentations action ran counter to Cromwellian policy. Each in his own way was selfishly politic, willing to take a stand only when his own interests or those of the Court were benefited. Like many versatile ministers they had learned to work successfully with a series of difficult taskmasters.[39]

The hurried activities of the dissolution commissioners continued to enlarge the Court's holdings more rapidly than the monastic property could conveniently be assimilated, despite the efforts of Augmentations officials to keep abreast of the visitation proceedings. With the suppression of each monastery came the practical business of receiving and administering the acquired possessions, which not infrequently were alienated by the crown before they had been fully absorbed into the pattern of estate management set up by the new organization. In any case an entry of each parcel of land had to be provided for the records, and permanent officials appointed to oversee the premises. If not already sold or promised to someone in advance, the lands and monastic sites

[36] Pope retained the wardenship of the mint for two years, from November 13, 1534, until November 9, 1536, being succeeded by John Brown. *Ibid.*, VII, no. 1498 (12) ; XI, no. 1417(1).

[37] He and another Augmentations official, George Gifford, a receiver in the fifth district, were chosen at the same time. Gifford wrote to Cromwell to find out if he should leave his visitation work unfinished in order to attend the parliamentary session. *Ibid.*, X, no. 916.

[38] P. 305 and n. 120, *infra.*

[39] When late in life William Paulet, then marquis of Winchester, was asked to explain how he had weathered the storms of so many reigns, he is said to have replied: " *ortus sum ex salice, non ex quercu,* I was made of the pliable willow, not of the stubborn oak." Robert Naunton, *Fragmenta Regalia: or Observations on the Late Queen Elizabeth, her Times and Favourites,* edited by Edward Arber (London, 1895), 25.

were rented as quickly as possible to suitable tenants. When actually alienated, the estate had to be surveyed, evaluated, and the particulars of sale prepared for final approval. Whatever the disposition, there were the inevitable claims and liabilities to settle before the clear annual revenue of the property could be ascertained.

By the two dissolution measures of 1536 and 1539, " incredible cruelties " notwithstanding, extensive lands spreading over every county in the realm were taken over by the Court; buildings, growing crops, livestock, and other movables were unloaded on a young institution already faced with overrapid development. Nor was this the major burden. In the acquisition of a vast crown demesne the Augmentations also had automatically acquired administrative jurisdiction over the innumerable tenants and villagers living on this land. A total of some 594 houses was suppressed in these confiscations, involving at least 9,000 inmates and a general net revenue of over £136,000. Many times that number, of course, were indirectly affected, though just how many servants and lay personnel were actually deprived of their jobs must remain unknown. For the most part the tenants suffered few inconveniences, except for a change of landlords, while many of the ejected monastic officials—particularly stewards, receivers, auditors, and bailiffs —were continued in the employment of the Augmentations. Likewise, a number of domestics were already provided for by small monastic corodies or annuities, which were recognized by the new Court as legal obligations of the crown. Certainly the myth that thousands of helpless people were cast adrift to swell the tide of vagrancy is no longer tenable.[40]

In the face of rising prices the government program of royal buildings, fortifications for defense, increased expenditures in Ireland, and the normal increase in the annual costs of administration necessitated a new approach to the financial problem. It is true that the king had provided

---

[40] Any definite figures concerning the number of houses dissolved or the total number of their inmates is extremely hazardous in view of the different types of religious establishments involved. Authorities differ as to whether or not their totals include friaries, priories, commanderies, preceptories, and dependent cells. The friaries and the forty-three commanderies of the Order of St. John are not included in the numbers suggested above. See Hughes, *The Reformation in England*, I, 36, 295, 326–27. In the absence of statistical data on the number of domestics and salaried employees, it is to be expected that conjectures should differ quite widely. One Tudor historian has recently estimated a total of 2,000 nuns, 7,000 male religious, and 35,000 " laymen of various kinds." Mackie, *The Earlier Tudors, 1485-1558*, 373. Cf. Savine, *English Monasteries on the Eve of the Dissolution*, Book II, Chaps. I and IV; Baskerville, *English Monks and the Suppression of the Monasteries*, 286–87; S. T. Bindoff, *Tudor England* (London, 1950), 106. The problem of lay personnel is carefully analyzed by Hughes, *The Reformation in England*, I, 45–46.

for temporary emergencies with a backlog of money retained for his
" own use," but that was not enough. Already the recurrent revenue
from the crown demesne had reached a maximum return; furthermore,
the customs revenue was on the decline and the French pensions had
expired. Under the circumstances the confiscation of church property
was an easy way out of the financial difficulties and one which would
obviously lend itself to popular propaganda appeal. Once committed to
the undertaking Cromwell proceeded methodically and with the utmost
dispatch. From the very beginning neither the royal commissioners nor
the Augmentations agents harbored any illusions as to the real motive
of their investigation.[41]

Coincidental with the organization of the Court was the task of taking
over for the crown the confiscated monastic assets. The true annual
value of the lands so acquired, as against the appraised value, is clearly
reflected in the treasurer's receipts, from which the early progress of the
suppression can be traced. Although the briefs of the surveys presented
to the Court by the commissioners of 1536, showing a somewhat higher
evaluation than that of previous surveys, were indispensable to the negotiation of sales and leases, they did not necessarily indicate absolute
value. The total revenue to be derived from rents and the sale of
movable property was a variable, dependent upon unforeseen circumstances of which the extent of cash payments and credit terms were

---

[41] The frequent reports of the commissioners to Cromwell and to the Court of
Augmentations indicate the inordinate attention given to land and property evaluations, detailed inventories of monastic valuables, and zealous searchings for hidden
treasures. " Pleasith it your lordship to be advertysed," the commissioners wrote
to Cromwell, "that wee have ben at saynt Edmondes Bury, where we founde a
riche shryne whiche was very comberous to deface. We have takyn in the seyd
monastery in golde and sylver m.^{l}m.^{l}m.^{l}m.^{l}m.^{l} markes, and above, over and
besydes a well and riche crosse with emereddes, as also dyvers and sundry stones
of great value, and yet we have lefte the churche, abbott, and covent very well
ffurnesshed with plate of sylver necessary for the same." In a similar vein Dr.
John London, on his way to Coventry, reported to Rich: " At Delapray [Delapré
nunnery] I hadde ij. chalyces and a pyxe, and the howse wasse pratily storyd with
catell and corn. Ye schall se me mak yow a praty bank by that tym I com next
uppe." At the same time a watchful eye always spotted the choicest property,
alerting those who were eagerly awaiting a portion of the spoils. " If my lord will
have me do any thing at Colme [Combe abbey]," he concluded, " then I wolde my
lord wold send som oon of hys trusty servantes to me at my being ther, to receyve
the howse with all other rekenynges to my lordes use, the guddes indifferently
praysed. He can nott have a more commodiose howse, and the longer he taryeth
the warsse every thing will be, as universally they mak ther handes all they can
that yet do remayne nott suppressyd. When I am at Coventry, I am but iij. myles
from Colme. And if my lord percase have syns my being ther sett hys mynde
upon any other place, then help M. Gregory or M. Richard may have ytt, ffor
yt ys a thynge to be taken." Cotton. MS., Cleop. E. iv, fols. 229, 207, as included
in Wright (ed.), *Letters relating to the Suppression of Monasteries*, 144, 235–36.

important factors. The practical problem was the actual accrued profit of the crown in any given year, after the expenses of collection and administration had been paid. In this respect the commissioners' reports are not always too helpful. Long inventories of movable goods or glowing accounts of fertile estates and extensive woodlands frequently gave no indication of the liabilities of an institution. Many of the houses were heavily encumbered by debts, corodies, pensions, and annuities to servants and others, which constituted a regular drain upon their estate revenues. To this must be added the costs of administration which have been estimated at about five per cent of the gross total income of the monasteries; [42] likewise there was the property which had been stolen, hidden, or had disappeared before the houses came into the hands of the Court. Promises, leases, preferments, or other commitments made by the priors and abbots on the eve of dissolution committed the Augmentations to complaints and litigation for years to come. Timber was cut and disposed of in spite of the precaution of the commissioners, while other valuables like plate, jewels, and relics, were sometimes given away. Lead and bell metal soon became the most marketable of all the salable items to be disposed of, though, as in the case of land sales, the immediate cash revenue obtained was only a small portion of the sale price. [43]

[42] Savine, *English Monasteries on the Eve of the Dissolution*, 247.

[43] The prior of Tynemouth, a cell of St. Albans, gave away over 200 marks in annuities after the royal visitation, while the head monastery itself was charged over 800 marks yearly besides its outstanding debts. *L. and P.*, XII, pt. 2, no. 256; *ibid.*, Addenda, I, pt. 1, no. 1120. At Lewes, in Sussex, valuables would disappear from one part of the house while possessions were being watched elsewhere. " Here is a great household and stealing nightly," it was reported, " nor will walls nor doors keep them out." *Ibid.*, Addenda, I, pt. 1, no. 1274. Likewise, visitors were often equally appalled at the indebtedness of many monasteries. Particular debts were usually not very large, but the total owed by a house could greatly reduce the cash value of the property. The possessions of St. Osyth's abbey, Essex, amounted to £520 per year, but its liabilities were estimated at £44 in corodies, £200 in pensions, and £560 in total debts. *Ibid.*, pt. 2, no. 1374. If possible, goods and valuables were concealed from the visitors, so that an honest prior who behaved in an exemplary manner tended to attract attention. *Ibid.*, XII, pt. 2, no. 277. Some surveys did not take into account the *novo incremento* not yet levied, nor were various charges on the land always included. The receiver of Augmentations, John Danaster, certified to the Court that, whereas according to the first survey of the parsonage of Nettlebed, Oxfordshire, it was rated for the tenth at £6 13*s.* 4*d.*, at least £6 yearly must be deducted for the serving of the curate, leaving but 13*s.* 4*d.* for the king. *Ibid.*, Addenda, I, pt. 1, nos. 1137, 1185. In many instances, however, the value of the movables more than discounted the monastic obligations. John Freeman, another Augmentations receiver, reported that he had " defaced and pulled down to the ground 5 houses," from which he had collected lead worth £1,332 12*s.* This represented an increase of £462 over the previous inventory. Costs and charges totaled over £116, so that " I have received and must receive £127 17*s.* 5*d.*, which exceeds the cost by £11

The accounts of the treasurer of the Augmentations begin on April 24, 1536, and continue without interruption until January 23, 1554, when the revenues of the Court were absorbed by the Exchequer. During the first twenty-nine months of that period the receivers paid in a total of £27,732 2s. 9⅜d. in land revenue from the dissolved religious houses, which represented the greater portion of the profit derived from retained monastic property. In addition to this sum, £6,987 8s. 11⅛d. was taken in from the sale of monastic movables and goods, such as lead, stone, bells, plate, jewels, ornaments, and " foreign receipts "[44] to the extent of £94 3s. 4d. Compositions for the continuance of certain houses to the extent of £5,948 6s. 8d., fines totaling £1,006 17s. paid for leases, and £29,847 16s. 5d. from land sales[45] complete the total receipts of £71,616 16s. 1½d. Nevertheless, this sum in no wise denotes a real increment of that amount, in view of certain essential expenditures encountered. However careful the Court might have been in curtailing unnecessary expenses, the costs of administration normally were quite heavy, particularly in fees, reparations, and travel allowances. The detailed itemization of all expenditures set forth in the accounts indicates something of the variety and extent of activities during this early period. " Necessaries " for the main office totaled over £413; annuities and pensions, £710; messenger service, £58 15s. 4d.; and payments by Court warrant, more than £1,416, while money advanced by special warrant accounted for another £14,618. Significantly, payments by decree of the Court, which included compensation money awarded to suitors and debts inherited from the dissolved monasteries, aggregated £2,725 6s. 8½d. The remainder of the revenue was spent by royal order or turned over to the king's private coffers.[46]

9s. 10d. For my discharge I have had one of the commissioners' hands at the weighing of the lead and the sales." *Ibid.*, no. 1094. See also *ibid.*, nos. 1218, 1236, 1279; pt. 2, no. 1295; XII, pt. 2, nos. 14, 1083. On practices of embezzlement and fraud consult Francis Aidan Gasquet, *Henry VIII and the English Monasteries* (6th edition, London, 1902), II, 283–86.

[44] These foreign receipts were composed of £25 from wood sales by Rufford abbey in Nottinghamshire and £69 3s. 4d. for household implements sold by William Cavendish and other commissioners from various dissolved monasteries, viz.: Barnwell near Cambridge, Dale (Derbyshire), Dieulacres [Dullakers] beside Leek (Staffordshire), Grace Dieu (Leicestshire), Merevale (Warwickshire), Pipewell or Pipwell (Northamptonshire), Repton or Repington (Derbyshire), and St. Thomas beside Stafford.

[45] From this figure should be deducted £5,702 1s. 11¾d., paid out for land purchased by the king during the period. Likewise, it should be remembered that the sale price listed for movables as well as for land did not usually indicate a cash transaction. Obligations and recognizances always represented a large item of unpaid revenue.

[46] Augm. Office, Treas. Rolls of Accts., No. 1.

If profit derived from the rents and issues of the Dissolution property is considered as true recurrent revenue, the Augmentations took in a total of £415,005 6s. 10d. during the first decade of its existence, or an annual average of over £36,000. On the other hand, the total net receipts for the same period amounted to £1,304,859 3s., which represented an average of approximately £113,466 per year. The peak year for the Court came in 1543–44, when over £253,292 in revenues were collected, of which almost £45,000 came from the land.[47] By far the most important single item of non-recurrent revenue, namely the sale of crown land, was not in the real sense profit at all, but the scope of the alienation of monastic property does suggest the increased attention given to the liquidation of capital assets.[48]

Although not formally in charge of Cromwell's visitations, the Augmentations was closely associated from the beginning with the work of the Dissolution commissions. A few of its officials like William Cavendish, William Blithman, and Richard Southwell had been active in the earlier visitations, while a score of others served on the 1536 commissions and in later investigations. Furthermore, Cromwell drew heavily from the visitation commissions in the selection of the Court's major personnel, the majority of whom had served on one or more of the monastic surveys. Previous service in the Dissolution proceedings was undoubtedly considered as one of the qualifications for an auditorship

---

[47] *Ibid.*, Nos. 1-10. Net receipts are not the same as net income, which can only be arrived at by deducting the regular expenditures of the Court from the gross revenues. Certain expenses, such as fees and diets, travel allowances for messengers and officers, and pensions, were fairly constant, but other categories of payments varied considerably from year to year. Those fluctuating most were payments by decree of the Court and expenditures by royal warrant. It is often difficult, if not impossible, to determine accurately the net profits of the Augmentations, since the total operating costs are not always ascertainable. An analysis of the Court's expenditures is presented in Chapter Ten. The net receipts are derived by deducting the arrears from the gross totals given in the Rolls of Accounts.

Receipts of the Augmentations from April 24, 1536, to September 29, 1547

Land Rents		Total net revenues
1536–38	£27,732 2s. 9⅜d.	£71,616 16s. 1½d.
1538–39	£24,223 7s. 2⅞d.	£108,527 11s. 8½d.
1539–43	£177,806 7s. 4¹³⁄₁₆d.	£465,684 6s. 5⁹⁄₁₆d.
1543–44	£44,945 2s. 11½d.	£253,292 1s. 8⁷⁄₁₆d.
1544–45	£32,739 19s. 8d.	
1545–46	£59,255 6s. 6d.	1544–47 { £405,738 7s.
1546–47	£48,303 3d.	
Totals	£415,005 6s. 10d.	£1,304,859 3s.

The annual averages are calculated on the basis of an eleven-and-one-half-year period.

[48] On the policy for the sale of crown lands see Chapter Seven, pp. 233–35.

or a receivership, since those so experienced would obviously have a better grasp of the peculiar problems inherited by the Court.[49] However, none of the members of the executive council were regular commissioners for the suppression, though they occasionally visited monasteries and took a number of surrenders. Moreover, as dissolution proceeded uninterruptedly through the years 1537, 1538, and 1539, circumstances required the officials of the Augmentations to cooperate more closely than ever with the vicar-general's special commissioners.

Charged with the task of receiving the actual surrender of the monasteries, the 1536 commissioners were concerned less with proving the crown's case for the suppression and more in determining an accurate evaluation of the monastic possessions. Consequently their returns reveal a more tolerant attitude toward the houses visited; likewise, their property estimates were considerably higher than those of the previous commissioners, as presented in the *Valor Ecclesiasticus*. Detailed instructions were given them, including the preparation of complete inventories and an order for a new survey of the monastic demesnes and income. Finally, they were enjoined to send up to the chancellor of the Court of Augmentations a " brief certificate " of all their accounts before proceeding on to another county.[50] These land surveys, known collectively as the " Paper Surveys," of which many are still extant in the Public Record Office, were preserved by the Court as a basis for future rent calculations and for the determination of estate values when parcels of the crown demesne were alienated. As detailed appraisals, made normally by professional surveyors and auditors at the time of the suppression, they present an interesting comparison to the commission returns of 1535.[51]

---

[49] Likewise, administrators trained in the office of general surveyors of crown land rendered invaluable service in the suppression activities. The famous Glastonbury survey, printed in Dugdale, *Monasticon Anglicanum*, I, 10–21, was made by two directors of that office, Richard Pollard and Thomas Moyle, both of whom were outstanding civil servants. The latter minister became a general surveyor in the second Augmentations in 1547, along with Walter Mildmay, another able official of the Court of General Surveyors organized in May, 1542. Had not Pollard died in November of that year, he probably would have gone with Moyle to the new institution at the time of the amalgamation of the two courts. Unlike Moyle, Pollard was never affiliated with the Court of Augmentations as asserted by Savine. Savine, *English Monasteries on the Eve of the Dissolution*, 49 ff.

[50] For instructions to the commissioners of 1536, see *L. and P.*, X, no. 721; the " Mynute of the Commyssion," drafted by Cromwell's chief clerk Wriothesley, suggests that the vicar-general intended to keep a close supervision over all their activities. The text of the instructions is printed in Burnet, *The History of the Reformation of the Church of England*, IV, 304–307.

[51] The " Paper Surveys " are found among the Augmentation Office, Miscellan-

The comprehensive inventories of all the monastic possessions reflect the zeal with which the Augmentations officials went about the business of taking over the property of the surrendered houses. With methodical thoroughness they quizzed the inmates, searched the premises, examined witnesses regarding the whereabouts of missing articles, and patiently recorded the results of their investigations. All salable items of household goods, livestock, grain, hay, and growing crops were appraised and sold as soon as possible, sometimes to a single individual, but more usually " parcelles of implementes or howsehold stuffe corne catell [i. e., chattels] ornamentes of the churche & suche other lyke " were sold separately as the opportunity afforded. After fees, rewards, and expenses were deducted the cash in hand was paid over to the Court, together with an account of the movables remaining unsold.[52]

Since Rich and Cromwell were both working in a common cause there was close co-operation between them, particularly in matters of pensions and recommendations to the king for houses to be allowed to continue. Both men were kept informed of the progress of the commissioners taking the surrenders, not only of the worth of the land and property received, but also of any pertinent information or suggestions that might accrue to the king's profit.[53] Robert Southwell explained to Cromwell in 1537 that dispatching the monks of Furness, their servants, and twelve poor men who had bought their livings from the house required a great deal of time, but that the work there was rapidly nearing completion. The cattle had been sold, since " they could find no other means to rid their train, which was both chargeable and dangerous for stealing." People came from all parts of the south to buy cattle, he noted, though the local inhabitants had been given preference in the sale of milk cows. The lead had been melted down and put into safe keeping, after which the chancellor of Augmentations had been apprised of an improved process used in order that receivers of the Court might be instructed in the latest techniques. All the lands of Furness in Lancashire were already surveyed, except a few in High Furness, which were to be finished later when the church and steeple there are " clear dissolved." His next letters would show values, he added, and how the country was peopled with men fit to serve the king. Annual revenues

---

eous Books, and remain unpublished. The *Valor Ecclesiasticus*, on the contrary, was printed by the Record Commissioners, 1810–34, in six volumes. Savine's detailed comparative study of the two series affords the best analysis yet attempted of the true value of the monastic property. Savine, *English Monasteries on the Eve of the Dissolution*, Book I, Chap. II; Book II, Chap. I.

[52] Augm. Office, Misc. Books 171, 172. Cf. Exch., Treas. of Receipt, Misc. Books 115, 116.

[53] *L. and P.*, Addenda, I, pt. 1, nos. 1079, 1272; pt. 2, nos. 1341, 1350.

would be calculated, save for parsonages, where no particular estimates would be attempted until the first year's returns were in. In this and in other respects he emphasized the accuracy of his reports. For example, at the Cistercian abbey of Boxley in Kent he found that a jewel had been pawned for £40 which he did not redeem because he judged it to be overvalued. In all matters efforts were directed to one end, namely, the protection of the royal interest. In examining the old accounts of the monastery he found that the land revenues had recently declined three hundred marks, " and yett no parte of the possessions clerely alienate from the monastery." This kind of machination was the sort of thing that Southwell enjoyed prying into, always of course, " refferryng our diligence and doynges therin to your jugement." [54]

So the reports ran, as the commissioners journeyed from county to county on the king's business. John Freeman delivered two books of accounts to Cromwell in August, 1538, which he requested should be forwarded to the Augmentations. The house of Leicester had been clearly dissolved, he wrote, and the inmates dispatched " very well content." He had received lead, bells, plate, and ornaments worth £1,506, of which some £170 was already expended in debts and various expenses. Other officials complained bitterly of the untrustworthiness of entire neighborhoods: " What falsehood in the prior and convent, what bribery, spoil and ruin contrived by the inhabitants, it were long to write." At Repton, Derbyshire, the commissioners found the house greatly despoiled and many things " purloined away," though a part of the missing property had been recovered through the perseverence of the agents. Guides were paid for their assistance, servants rewarded, and twenty-five shillings given to five men " that found certain plate." [55] Much attention was given, of course, to the sale of livestock and growing crops and to the proceeds derived from monastic plate, jewels, and other valuables, which the visitors greatly overestimated.[56] Augmentations receipts from these items were never great. The treasurer's accounts show a sale of £23,450 4s. 1⅝d. down to September 29, 1543, and £97,964 8s. for the entire history of the Court.[57]

[54] Robert Southwell to Cromwell, July 3, 1537, *ibid.*, XII, pt. 2, no. 205. *Id.* to *id.*, March 3, 1538, Cotton. MS., Cleop. E. iv, fol. 218. On Southwell's diligence, see also *L. and P.*, XII, pt. 2, nos. 548, 549; XV, nos. 50, 52, 139. He had fully earned Cromwell's commendation to the king for his deserving performance.

[55] *Ibid.*, Addenda, I, pt. 2, no. 1349; XIII, pt. 1, nos. 101, 102; XII, pt. 2, no. 92; XIII, pt. 2, nos. 689, 706, 757, 764, 823, 839, 1059, 1233. See inventories drawn up by Thomas Legh and William Cavendish in 30 Henry VIII, Augm. Office, Misc. Books 172.

[56] S. B. Liljegren, *The Fall of the Monasteries and the Social Changes in England* (Leipzig, 1924), 109.

[57] Augm. Office, Treas. Rolls of Accts., Nos. 1–8. These figures do not, of

Rich L.ᵈ Chancelor.

SIR RICHARD RICH, Chancellor of the Court, 1530–1544

From a drawing by Hans Holbein. Royal Collection (Windsor):
By gracious permission of Her Majesty the Queen.

(Plate 1)

SIR THOMAS POPE, Treasurer of the Court, 1536–1540

From a contemporary portrait by Thomas Stretes (?), at Trinity College, Oxford, England. By permission of the President and Fellows.

(Plate 2)

More serious than the plundering of the houses were the efforts of the abbots to conceal their goods. Articles which had been sold, pilfered, or given away were usually irrecoverable, but hidden property frequently could be retrieved. As reports of concealments multiplied, the Court was enjoined to make a diligent search for such goods in cases where fraud or trickery was suspected. Rumors were not slow in coming in from the visitation commissioners and from informers at large. Usually the concealments were not great, but in some instances they represented appreciable amounts. It was reported by responsible crown ministers that the abbot and monks of Glastonbury had embezzled and stolen enough plate and ornaments to build a new abbey.[58] Fictitious sales and leases were made in anticipation of the approaching disaster, while plate and valuable articles were parceled out among confidants or spirited away to convenient hiding places. The Augmentations did its best to safeguard crown property and to expose undercover activities through continual investigations. Such inquisitions ordinarily were conducted locally by commissioners sent out under the great seal of the Court, but more often than not the district receivers and auditors sat on the commissions as its representatives.[59] The returns of these many commission inquiries, though often indefinite, ably support the evidence presented by the visitation agents that the monks sought to salvage as much as possible by fair means or foul.[60]

Contrary to popular opinion Augmentations officials were anything but ruthless in either the work of suppression or in their later dealings with monastic tenants. William Cavendish, John Danaster, Robert Burgoyne, William Blithman, Edward Gostwick, William Berners, Richard Paulet, Thomas Arundell, Walter Henley, George Gifford, John Carlton, Thomas Spilman, John Scudamore, Thomas Mildmay, John Wiseman, William Green, James Rokeby, John Heneage, Francis Jobson, Leonard Beck-

---

course, represent the total value of the monastic movables acquired by the crown. Some were given away or retained by the king, while large quantities of jewels, plate, and ornaments were sent to the jewel house and the mint.

[58] *L. and P.*, XIV, pt. 2, no. 232. Most of the hidden treasures, secreted in vaults, walls, and elsewhere in the country, were recovered. The French ambassador reported the abbey treasures to be worth 200,000 crowns. *Ibid.*, no. 389.

[59] Instructions, interrogatories, and depositions of these endless Augmentations investigations are found among the records of the Court's proceedings and in the Augm. Office, Misc. Books 108–34.

[60] Notes and comments by the commissioners often embellish the testimony of the deponents. Regarding the spoliation of the late abbey of Hayles in Gloucestershire, the commissioners add: "Item, there be many divers spoils daily done within the said late monastery to a great substance over and above these above written, but by whom as yet it is unknown." It was at this same monastery that the famous counterfeit relic, the "Blood of Hayles" was seized earlier. *L. and P.*, XVII, no. 8; Cotton. MS., Cleop. E. iv, fol. 254.

with, John Freeman, and the Southwell brothers all worked hard in taking the surrender of the monasteries, though they were too far overshadowed by the colorful figures of Drs. Thomas Legh, Richard Layton, and John London to attract much attention. Their official reports as well as personal letters to Rich and Cromwell testify not only to their industry and efficiency but also to a surprising degree of compassion and tolerance for those with whom they had to deal. Their careers still ahead of them, they were little tempted to turn new-found authority to their own advantage, and if they were too scrupulous it was due to zeal in the literal execution of their instructions.

There is "much business to be taken," wrote John Freeman to Cromwell on June 1, 1536, "and I have no encouragement to do more than my fee—for my auditor it will be worth £100 more, to me not twelvepence. I shall bring a profitable inventory to the King, worth £1,000 in one shire, not reckoning Gilbertines nor cells which are ten houses. Of these I reckon a great part in lead and bells, not including woods. For other moveables, they have left their houses meetly bare, nor can we make them bring all things to light." He went on to explain that they pleased the monks by reasonable handling, which made them thereby more diligent to do the king's pleasure, though, he added, "it may be a little unprofitable to the King, I consider he will have enough, and a little thing pleases them. They are people of good nature." [61] Nor was Freeman's boast an idle gesture. During the first six months of the Court's operation, he turned in £8,756 11s. 9¾d.; at the same time rumors were being circulated that he and his fellow agents would soon return to dissolve the larger monasteries. Certainly as early as October, 1538, Freeman had advised Cromwell to suppress all the remaining houses at once, since they were all ready for surrender.[62] As long as he was receiver in the Augmentations he continued to suggest improvements and offer advice, and his comments were usually well founded. He wisely suggested that a general marketing of the lead from the dissolved abbeys would bring in "a great proffite," for which the king could expect at least £4 per fother, adding significantly: "Yt may ples yow to consider that, and yf other owtward prynces wold take apon theym to redres their idell fayned religiouse howses, as the

---

[61] *L. and P.*, X, no. 1026. The Augmentations officials were quite generous in rewarding inmates of the houses they visited. The treasurer's records show, for example, that Richard Hutchinson, auditor of the eighth district, expended £141 2s. 2d. in rewards to the late monks of Westminster, with the servants of the house and the king's "orators" there. Augm. Office, Treas. Rolls of Accts., No. 1, pt. 2, mem. 22d.

[62] Augm. Office, Ministers' Accts., 166, for 27–28 Henry VIII; Fisher, *The History of England, 1485–1547*, 397; *L. and P.*, XIII, pt. 2, no. 528.

kinges highnes hath done, as I mystrust not but and their powers war accordinge as the kinges was and is they wolde so do, and than shall they have suche abundance of lead of suche like howses that they woll than sett litell by ours." His prophecy proved to be correct on both price and demand, as later sales of lead were to indicate. Likewise to the point were his observations concerning excessive fees, which were given out by the dozen where one would have sufficed. " I well parsayve of the gyvyn owte of late, not only there [in Lincolnshire] but also throwghowte the realme," he reported, " thies superfluus ffees gyven by the late surrendered howses. . . . Inded they [the advocates] gave counsel to thabbott to gyve theym a covent seale to robe the kinge of part of his revenues. Wherfore me thinke they [the abbots] might law-fully at this parliament be called in agane, and the kinges highnes shuld resayve therbye within his realme iij. or four thowsand markes by the least yerly." These were bold ideas to present to a superior, but where an increase in revenue could be demonstrated, any minister who was sure of his ground could speak forthrightly.[63]

The major officials of the central office were no less vigilant in their efforts to co-operate with Cromwell and the suppression agents. Busy as they were, they still found time to assist in the visitations and take the surrender of particular houses. Of course as long as Cromwell remained in power their advancement depended largely upon his approval, but there is no reason to assume that co-operation came unwillingly. Pope participated in the visitations of Holywell nunnery and the new hospital of St. Mary, known as St. Mary Spitell at London in 1539, and per-sonally received the surrender of St. Albans in December of the same year. On that occasion he may have been instrumental in saving the beautiful church of St. Albans, which the townspeople purchased from the crown.[64]

[63] John Freeman to Cromwell [undated], Cotton. MS., Titus B. i, fol. 394, printed in Wright, *Letters relating to the Suppression of Monasteries*, 289. Freeman's apology for plain speaking, however, implied no real anticipation of censure. " Besechinge your lordship for my follyshe oppynyon so boldlye to you to write of, that ye wold take with me no displeasure." He concluded, " And thus I remayn your pore man." This letter is abstracted in *L. and P.*, XIV, pt. 1, no. 946 for 1539. When, in 1540, the treasurer of Augmentations informed Freeman that the king was critical of his work in Lincolnshire, Cromwell came to his defense. " I cannot do you service in recompense," he told Cromwell. " I was of your prefer-ment both in that office and in all the rest. Tell his Grace if I have profited 10 *l.* at his expense then let me lose my office and everything, and be turned into my shirt. I dare not come to your lordship, being so far out of quiet." *Ibid.*, XV, no. 1029(23).

[64] Later on, in 1547, Pope bought the " ancient stately mansion house " of Titten-hanger, Hertfordshire, which formerly had been the country seat of the abbots of

Despite occasional misunderstandings Pope's relations with Cromwell were cordial.[65] Among other things special orders for payments from the Augmentations funds often came from his hands, as did warrants for plate and jewels to be turned over to John Gostwick, treasurer of first fruits and tenths, who was acting as personal paymaster for Cromwell. As one who had his hands in everything, Cromwell would intervene in every activity of the Court, ordering pensions, visiting monasteries, advising on appointments, or even personally delivering valuable relics to the king.[66] In one instance when Pope was negligent in writing an acquittance for the Augmentations receiver who delivered over £917 worth of plate to Gostwick, he was reprimanded quite sharply. " I doo sumwhat marvail that you gyve him not a discharge," wrote Cromwell to Pope, " And Therefore thought me to Requyre you that ye shal." As might be expected the release was speedily forthcoming, as was indeed an acknowledgment of receipt from " Maister Gostik." [67]

Similarly, the privy seal interfered in matters where the prerogative of the chancellor of the Court was at stake. In cases wherein Rich's orders differed from those of Cromwell, the latter's always prevailed. Sometimes complaints, which normally would have been directed to the chancellor and council of the Court, were presented personally to Cromwell in the hope of immediate action. In June, 1539, Walter Hungerford, lord of Heytesbury, petitioned Cromwell for compensation as a result of damages claimed for the partial demolition of the late Hinton priory recently purchased by him through one of the visitation commissioners. When the receiver of the Augmentations, Sir Thomas Arundell, had surveyed the property, he had torn down part of the church and other buildings, apparently without knowing that they were already sold.

St. Albans. Subsequently, many improvements were made on the property, which became his favorite country estate.

[65] In July, Pope, having incurred Cromwell's displeasure in the purchase of a piece of land which Cromwell desired, did everything possible to restore himself to the good graces of the vicar-general, even persuading friends to intercede for him. Complaining that he had lost £125 in the transaction, he consoled himself with the thought that he had faithfully carried out an injunction once given him by Cromwell, above all always to keep his word. In the end, however, he credited his patron with continued support. " Next to the king," he wrote to Cromwell, " I am bound to your Lordship, of whom I have received all I have." *L. and P.*, XIII, pt. 1, nos. 1472, 1473, 1488, 1498, 1499; pt. 2, nos. 28, 106, 135.

[66] Manchester Papers, 15/28, 29, 38. For an interpretation of the unique collection of Manchester Papers, see Chapter Fourteen, *infra*. Records of the Court of Augmentations, p. 489, note 44. A typical example of an informal letter from Cromwell to Thomas Pope, ordering payment of £200 granted as an annuity, is printed in full in Roger Bigelow Merriman (ed.), *Life and Letters of Thomas Cromwell* (Oxford, 1902), II, no. 320.

[67] Manchester Papers, 15/100, 101. See Plate 5, facing p. 275.

Furthermore, according to Hungerford, he had evaluated the demesnes at such a high rate " that I cannot pay the rent, unless out of my own hands." The request for compensation from the minister was favorably received and acted upon within a few weeks. Ironically enough the lands procured by Hungerford were soon recovered by the crown, for he was attainted the following year and beheaded on the same day his patron Cromwell was executed. His possessions, however, went to the Court of General Surveyors and not to the Augmentations.[68]

As members of the king's council the chancellor and treasurer sat on royal commissions and executed various special assignments in addition to their normal court duties.[69] Rich in particular played a prominent part in council proceedings where his services as an adviser " learned in the lawes " were frequently required. During the latter years of his chancellorship of the Augmentations he was in regular attendance at the London meetings and on one occasion was required to join the king on a " progress." [70] Considering his manifold activities, it is not surprising that by oversight occasionally an assignment was neglected, " he being very busy." [71] Still, he was not too busy to join in the work of suppression.[72] From Bury St. Edmunds Rich wrote to the king in detail concerning the revenues of the house and the inventoried possessions. Though the plate and ornaments were of less value than expected, the lead and bells on the other hand were estimated at 4,500 marks. While the survey of the lands was in progress, further instructions were required in regard to defacing the buildings.[73]

---

[68] *L. and P.*, XIV, pt. 1, nos. 1154, 1258; XV, nos. 498(59), 939. Augm. Office, Misc. Books 212, fol. 26*d.*

[69] Both Rich and Pope aided in the examination of the Lincolnshire rebels and the subsequent heresy trials of 1537 and participated in the reception of Anne of Cleves in 1539. Rich was likewise later active in the divorce proceedings against her, as well as in the investigation of the misconduct of Catherine Howard in 1541. His special assignments as councillor, particularly in legal matters, are too numerous to detail. *L. and P.*, XIV, pt. 2, no. 572 (3, viii) ; XV, nos. 14(ii), 830, 845, 872, 908, 925, 1027(7) ; XVI, nos. 326, 448, 455, 657, 658, 1394, 1395, 1398, 1400, 1414, 1422, 1433-34, 1461, and 1470.

[70] *Ibid.*, XVI, nos. 68, 112, 168, 326, 1002, 1019, 1063. See Nicolas (ed.), *Proceedings and Ordinances of the Privy Council*, VII, 4, 41 *passim*, 215.

[71] *L. and P.*, XII, pt. 1, no. 4.

[72] Rich, with other commissioners, took the surrender of Bisham, Durford, Bury St. Edmunds, Christchurch, Canterbury, and Rochester, and by special commission Abingdon, Berkshire, and the priories of Binham and Beeston in Norfolk. *Ibid.*, pt. 2, no. 932; XIV, pt. 2, nos. 462, 463, 475, 476, 932; XIII, pt. 1, nos. 625, 1218; XV, nos. 378, 379. Payments for the Court in 31–32 Henry VIII included £165 12*s.* 9*d.* as costs of the chancellor and other officers of the Court riding to receive surrenders of monasteries. Augm. Office, Treas. Rolls of Accts., No. 1, pt. 2, mem. 22.

[73] *L. and P.*, XIV, pt. 2, nos. 475, 476.

A long letter to Cromwell in March, 1538, from Woodrising, Norfolk, gives a clear picture of Rich's extensive operations; his surveys included the manors of Dedham in Essex, Stratford, Nayland, Benhall, Leiston, Henham, and Wykes in Suffolk, and Cawston, Claxton, Stockton, and Costessey in Norfolk. At the " goodly manor " of Benhall he found much land decently emparked, with five hundred deer; Henham was described as having a new house, wholesome air, and two good parks within a mile of a market town. After making this great circuit the commissioners surveyed the late priory of Butley in Suffolk, evaluating it at £80 a year higher than the last appraisal. At Norwich, a " fair city and clean," he inspected the bishop's palace and grounds, with the idea of arranging an exchange for the king.[74] Fourteen days later Rich and the two colleagues assisting him, Richard Pollard and Richard Southwell, were paid £44 for their charges and expenses during the three weeks required for the surveys.[75] If the payment appears excessive, it must be remembered that such allowances always included all expenses for food, lodgings, gratuities, and care of horses for the officials, helpers, and all of their servants. It was probably for this same trip that £17 15s. had been allowed on March 9 to Rich and others for wine and meals, " and for rewards given at places when we lay att our frynds' howses, and for presents." [76] Such payments were common enough during the early development of the Court, when its ministers were all regularly engaged in official travel.

A man in the chancellor's position was bound to encounter a certain amount of criticism. However, considering their vast patronage influence, the Augmentations heads remained singularly free from censure throughout the period of the Court's history. Complaints emerged to be sure, but they were either directed generally against field representatives or else they registered the indignation of some frustrated person in search of a favor. Costs of routine services, delays in the administration of justice, and slowness in the processing of business matters were points of grievance among disgruntled petitioners.

The deviousness sometimes practiced by land-seekers is forceably illustrated in the case of Lord Lisle, who moved heaven and earth to secure a share of the monastic spoils.[77] Having extracted a promise

---

[74] *Ibid.*, Addenda, I, pt. 2, no. 1311.

[75] Manchester Papers, 15/82. Payment by order of the Augmentations, receipted by George Wright, Rich's servant.

[76] *Ibid.*, 15/79. This order is likewise receipted as paid to William Glascok, another of Rich's servants.

[77] Arthur Plantagenet, viscount Lisle, was vice-admiral and deputy of Calais. On the character of Lisle, see *D. N. B.*; Merriman (ed.), *Life and Letters of Thomas Cromwell*, I, 160–64; Richardson, *Tudor Chamber Administration, 1485–*

from the king, he concentrated his energies on the acquisition of Frithelstock priory in Devonshire, with all its possessions and appurtenances
valued at about £92 annually. One of two alternative types of tenure
was requested of the Augmentations, but which it would be no one
could foretell. Various complications developed, including the problem
of raising money. First, Lisle's London agent, John Husee, was informed by the Court that the particulars of the land were not properly
certified; later, that nothing could be done about the grant until the
northern rebellion of 1536 was subdued. Meanwhile, a messenger had
been dispatched to Devon to bring up the accounts of Frithelstock, which
revealed a £10 *de novo incremento* not yet levied. Lisle was advised
to " prick in this book such parcels as you will have," in order that the
agent might do his best " to make friends to obtain them." Husee grew
impatient. " The court is very costly," he wrote to his master, " for it
is new begun, and no men knoweth the order thereof but they." Friends
were recruited who were willing to intercede, including one of the
general surveyors of crown lands. The agent was obviously enjoying his
role in the negotiations. " It is the busiest matter that ever I had in
hand, for there is nothing to be done but at their pleasure "; notwithstanding this, he added encouragingly, " but I think there be not so
few as 500 as well tangled as I am." [78]

Unwilling to act hastily, Rich and his council of the Augmentations
studied the problem, especially in regard to the land value and the terms
of the lease. In the meantime the pertinent question of fees had entered
the picture. Though the fetching of the particulars had cost six angels,[79]
the messenger was still unsatisfied with the fee; likewise, the auditor
and the receiver for Devon demanded £3 6s. 8d., while still others remained unpaid. A few gifts were judiciously distributed, though Rich
assured Lisle that his charges would be no heavier than those normally
borne by other purchasers. In the end, however, the costs of the privy
seal and other miscellaneous expenses for the patent were something
over £14, though what the Court would finally charge " God knoweth."
As the affair progressed, the apparent willingness of the officials of the
Augmentations to co-operate was somewhat vitiated by the difficulty of
getting the executive council together long enough to agree on a definite
policy. Obviously they were feeling their way cautiously, reluctant to
lay down definite principles or to make promises which later might

---

1547, 423, n. 113. A great many of Lisle's machinations were conducted by his
capable, if somewhat gossipy, London agent, John Husee (Hussey or Housee).

[78] *L. and P.*, Addenda, I, pt. 1, nos. 1090, 1092, 1099, 1116, 1123, 1137.

[79] An English gold coin of the period, originally called an angel-noble, varying
in value from 6s. 8d. to 10s.

prove untenable. Besides, members of the council were variously engaged in field work which took them all over England, and when they were assembled at the London headquarters, they were largely occupied with the business of audit or litigation. " It would be as easy to assemble so many of the Privy Council as these four: the Chancellor, Mr. Only, Mr. Pope and Mr. Sowthewell," observed Husee in December, 1536; " Mr. Only was there but once and nothing can be done without him." [80] Despite such obstacles, however, the transaction gradually approached a conclusion. Before the year ended Lord Lisle was promised his coveted estate, not in fee simple as he had hoped but in tail, to him and his wife in survivorship with remainder rights to the heirs. The patent was delivered in September of 1537, although it was some while before the matter was finally terminated, with the new lord of Frithelstock in full possession.[81]

During the course of " his long suit " Husee complained, naturally enough, of unnecessary procrastination as well as charging Rich with duplicity and deception. He told Lady Lisle that Rich was full of dissimulation and " passeth all that ever I sued under." He definitely thought the chancellor to be against Lisle's suit, so it had become necessary, as he bluntly expressed it, to " maugre his head " [82] in order to get acceptable terms from the Court.[83] In relating his difficulty in getting an annuity of £200 for Lord Lisle through the Court of Augmentations he criticized it roundly: " for whoever has ado with that Court shall know what he cometh by or he depart thence." [84] But such comments were not really as sharp as they appear. Rich was responsible to the government for the judicious management of revenues under his charge and was sure to be blamed if corruption developed or blunder occurred, even without his knowledge.[85]

---

[80] John Husee to Lord Lisle, December 11, 1536. Husee was, of course, referring to Rich, Pope the treasurer, attorney John Onley, and Robert Southwell, then solicitor for the Court. *L. and P.*, Addenda, I, pt. 1, no. 1148; XII, pt. 2, no. 555.

[81] *Ibid.*, nos. 1149–54, 1245; Pat. Rolls, 29 Henry VIII, pt. 4, mem. 32. The land, valued at £92 4s. 8d. annually, was granted in tail, with a contingent remainder to the right heirs at a yearly rent of £15 9s. ¾d.

[82] This archaic term, maugre or mauger (modern French *malgré*), was sometimes used in the phrase " maugre a person's teeth or head " to indicate that something had been accomplished in spite of or notwithstanding the resistance of the individual in question.

[83] *L. and P.*, XI, nos. 264, 413–14; XII, pt. 2, nos. 338, 807, 922.

[84] Husee to Lisle, June, 1537. In this letter he expressed the hope that Lisle would write to the treasurer of the Court, inducing him to show more gentleness. *Ibid.*, XV, no. 1030(40), from the Lisle Papers.

[85] Husee's suspicion of Rich's attitude may, indeed, have had some foundation in fact, since Rich had personally promised the Frithelstock parsonage to Walter Farr, who was shortly thereafter given a clerkship in the Augmentations. In this,

Like all the visitation commissioners, ministers of the Court found themselves in a position to profit personally from Augmentations activities. Visitors, surveyors, receivers, and auditors alike had ample opportunity for petty thievery and graft, but excepting the usual minor infractions there is little evidence of widespread malpractice. Ornaments and jewels were occasionally filched, woods despoiled, and movable articles sold without being reported, yet there was never anything approaching a breakdown in discipline. Much more common was the temptation to accept gifts in return for services rendered or even in anticipation of expected favors. Frequently pensions or annuities were awarded to crown officers by the monasteries on the eve of dissolution in the hope of securing preferential treatment.

When visitors like George Gifford or Robert Burgoyne recommended the continuation of monasteries, they may well have been influenced by generous bribes, though more often than not actual proof is wanting. The prioress of the convent of Stixwold wrote John Heneage that the house stood only " by the goodness of my Lord Privy Seal [i. e., Cromwell], and by his only means and suit to the King's Majesty, . . . paying to his Highness 900 mark for a fine, besides our first-fruits; which is 150*l*. and also a pension of 34*l*. by the year for ever." Beseeching his intercession in the convent's behalf, the letter continued: " Good Mr. Heneage, we most humbly pray and desire you in the way of charity, and for God's sake, to be mean to my Lord Privy Seal, . . . for to remit and forgive the said pension of 34*l*. by year; or else we shall never be able to live and pay the King the aforesaid money." [86] Whether Heneage got any reward other than the prayers and charity promised him is not a matter of record; usually, however, when a " trifle " or " a poor token " was received by a minister there was a definite reason for the generosity. Gifford offered Cromwell £20 for his pains in getting for him the farm of St. James in Northamptonshire.[87] A local bailiff promised an auditor of the Court 40*s*. or a nag for helping him to secure an increase in fee and an additional £5 for the assistance of a friend; as if this were not enough, he added: " Also help to the allowance of my portage according

---

as in other cases where his previous commitments conflicted with those of Cromwell or the king, he was forced to yield. In this instance he requested Lisle to lease Farr the property. *Ibid.*, XII, pt. 2, no. 714.

[86] Strype, *Ecclesiastical Memorials*, I, pt. 1, 395. Only a portion of the fine mentioned above, that is, £21 13*s*. 4*d*., was paid into the Augmentations. Other ministers, like Gifford, who favored the monasteries were suspected by the king of having accepted bribes. Wright (ed.), *Letters relating to the Suppression of Monasteries*, No. LXII.

[87] *L. and P.*, XI, nos. 87, 227. He also solicited Rich's favor for the same grant. See the interesting memoranda of Robert Southwell on exploitation and bribery. *Ibid.*, XII, pt. 2, no. 548(2).

to the warrant signed by Mr. Chancellor and the Council. Whereas I promised Mrs. Myldemay 40*s*. a year, pray draw the patent and I will seal it." [88] Similarly, Sir John St. Clair was willing to pay twenty nobles [89] for Mildmay's intercession with the king.[90] William Cavendish and Thomas Legh confessed to accepting a bribe of £18 from the abbot of Merevale, Warwickshire, which they had concealed as plate previously sold to a London goldsmith,[91] while even Rich felt obligated to present Cromwell with a New Year's gift, that his continual suit to the king for a tract of land might not be forgotten.[92] Sometimes, of course, ministers were unjustly accused of withholding revenues that rightfully belonged to the crown. When charged with arrears of rent in the office of the Augmentations auditor for certain lands of Sion abbey, Rich proved to the satisfaction of the Court that the late abbess had remitted the £33 6*s*. 8*d*. in question to him, in consideration of " certain reasonable causes and friendship doon." [93] Significant favors were usually handsomely rewarded.

In routine work the Court was engaged from the beginning in a wide variety of activities: collecting and paying debts, settling claims, examining old leases and issuing new ones, arranging for exchanges of property, supervising reparations, processing pensions, running surveys, and receiving new lands and revenues for the crown. During the early weeks of organization this work was conducted informally at Rich's house or in temporary quarters at Westminster Hall. Permanent offices, however, were soon acquired, which were occupied early in 1537, probably in January. A royal warrant was issued on the thirty-first of that month to the treasurer of the Augmentations to pay Anthony Denny, " kepar of our manour besides Westmenster and payemaister of our buyldinges there," £662 1*d*. for the construction of a house " for the Officers of our augmentations " within the old Palace of Westminster.[94]

[88] Richard Freston to Thomas Mildmay, auditor of the Augmentations, in behalf of Thomas Synger, bailiff, June 26, 1545. *Ibid.*, Addenda, I, pt. 2, no. 1699. The Mildmays of Chelmsford, Essex, were family friends of Rich.

[89] An English gold coin worth about one-third of a pound sterling, or 6*s*. 8*d*.

[90] *L. and P.*, Addenda, I, pt. 2, no. 1663. On Thomas Mildmay's influence in such matters, see *ibid.*, nos. 1554-55, 1562.

[91] *Ibid.*, XIII, pt. 2, nos. 832, 1233.

[92] *Ibid.*, Addenda, I, pt. 2, nos. 1374, 1378. At this time Rich was seeking the possession of St. Osyth's and St. John's in Essex, or if not those, the house and lands of Milton, Dorset, worth without the tenth £400 a year. For the former he was willing to pay £200 in pensions, £44 in corodies, and debts amounting to £560, in addition to 3,000 marks down payment; in the case of the latter, he offered to discharge all the servants' wages, settle for the pensions of the religious, leave all movables for the crown, and give the king 3,000 marks within a year.

[93] Augm. Office, Miscellanea, 15, no. 109.

[94] This warrant was endorsed with the receipt of Denny's deputies; it was ac-

From that point forward accounts were regularly presented by the keeper of the premises, James Johnson, for repairs, new equipment, and the general expenses of the main office. Items of expenditure allowed during the first year included " crepers " for the fireplace, a fire shovel, hinges, bolts, doors, table, stools, a " double plate lock, stock, and spring for the lower house at the stair foot," and five dozen rushes for the " sweetening " of the rooms during Trinity term. Again in 1538 " six cusshyns " were added, while extensive improvements on the buildings and grounds were carried out before the end of the year. The clerk, Richard Duke, was granted a liberal appropriation for " floryng bordyng and celyng with waynscott " the lower rooms of the house, with iron-work and locks for the same, repair of the walls and cleaning of the garden there, and mending of the leads and chimneys of the place. Trained workmen were engaged some four months in this undertaking at a total cost of £168 19s. 8½d. The net result was to give the Court large, well-furnished offices, complete with terraced grounds and garden " yerbes." [95]

Within the premises, too, the necessary office equipment was not long wanting. Green cloth for the accounting board, twelve presses reinforced with iron, strongboxes and bags in which to store the incoming money and valuables, scales, weights, locks, and other essential paraphernalia were purchased as required. Quantities of ink, parchment, and paper were consumed in the making of accounts or tripartite engrossing of official documents; [96] also for court sessions a book called a " jury-

---

companied by a similar order for Pope to pay Denny an additional £2,000 for improving the house of St. James in Westminster Park and other buildings at the royal manors of Westminster, Chelsea, and Hackney. Manchester Papers, 15/19.

[95] *Ibid.*, 15/54, 90, 104. This twelve-page account is replete with detailed data on materials, wages, and prices. Over 13,200 nails were used at a total cost of £6 1s. 9d., thousands of bricks at £8 per thousand, and 400 loads of earth at 3d. each. Wages of workmen varied appreciably, from joiners at 9d. per day to ordinary laborers at 4d. to 6d. Sawyers, carpenters, and bricklayers were worth 8d. per day, while an expert gardener might be able to get as much as 10d. Unfortunately, some of the items are provocatively brief, giving the reader no adequate description of the articles in question, as " baskets," 3s. 4d.; " sprigg nails," 18d.; " three great locks," £1 10s.; and " to John Atkins " for leveling the ground and digging out stones, £2. *Ibid.*, 15/104.

[96] On December 26, 1537, a warrant of the Court authorized the payment of £2 to two of the Augmentations clerks, Walter Farr and George Wright (both men were also servants of Rich), " for writing in paper and for engrossing of the indenture tripartite " made between the king, Giles Leigh, and Sir John Alen, concerning the exchange of the manor of Walton, in the county of Surrey. The document contained twenty-four sheets of paper; the indenture engrossed contained three large skins of vellum; a patent engrossed for Leigh's recompense contained one skin of parchment; and for engrossing a patent for the recompense of such lands as the king secured from the Hospital of Savoy, lying near the royal manor of Hanworth, one skin of parchment. *Ibid.*, 15/61.

book " was procured, " with a silver crucifix fastened upon it." At the same time wax was bought for impressions of the Court's seals which were newly engraved for immediate use. Not the least important among the initial outlays for operational expenses at headquarters were expenditures for gratuities, fuel, and the regular diets for the treasurer's table in London.[97]

The various doings of the Augmentations officials during those formative years which are clearly set forth in the many orders, letters, and miscellaneous accounts for the period, suggest an exceedingly energetic council. Its members, chancellor, treasurer, and two legal officers, appear to have been almost ubiquitous, so numerous and widespread were their activities. During the summer and autumn of 1536 they made repeated journeys to interview the king, make surveys, prepare inventories, execute special royal assignments, or to busy themselves " about the affairs " of the Court. All their expense accounts, which often incorporated insignificant details of expenditure as well as distances covered and time consumed, were duly submitted, to be allowed in full or returned, with items cut down as being excessive or eliminated altogether by the council. The warrants and memoranda speak for themselves: [98]

> [July] . . . the costs and expenses l[aid] out by Sir Richard Riche, knight, and John Onley, esquire, and their servants, riding from London to Dover to the King, and coming home to London by space of eight days, as appeareth particularly by a bill, viz., 4 *l.* 19*s.* 11*d.*

> [September 20; memorandum or warrant] . . . to Mr. Pope, Treasurer of the Court of Augmentations, for the costs of the Attorney and Solicitor for 16 days, 6 *l.* 13*s.* 1*d.*

> For their fees for 16 days at 6*s.* 8*d.* a day, the same journey, 10 *l.* 13*s.* 4*d.* For the Attorney's fees for 16 days in his journey to liver [*sic*] to the King, 5 *l.* 6*s.* 6*d.*

> For the costs and charges of the Solicitor for the survey of Ottford

---

[97] Augm. Office, Treas. Rolls of Accts., No. 1, pt. 1, mem. 10*d.*; pt. 2, mem. 21.

[98] Manchester Papers, 15/3, 6, 7, 12, 17, 18. Quoted as calendared in the *Eighth Report of the Royal Commission on Historical Manuscripts* (London, 1881; reissued, 1910), Appendix, Part II. At the beginning of 1537 Robert Southwell and Walter Henley submitted a bill for surveying the late monastery of Westacre and other crown affairs in Norfolk. Southwell's diets for forty-two days were reckoned at a total of £14, to which item was appended a note by him to " Mr. Chancellor " that, if this item was not allowed, he would refund the money. The sum claimed was stricken out, apparently as disallowed. *Ibid.*, 15/76.

and other lands for the exchange between the King and the Bishop of Canterbury, 4 *l*. 6*s*. 10*d*.

For his fee for 9 days, 3 *l*.

[September 28] . . . the costs of Thomas Pope riding with nine horse to the Court about the affairs of the Court of Augmentationes, the King's Grace then lying at Dunstable, and for the same Thomas at the same time, being 6*s*. 8*d*. per diem by the space of three days, that is to say, for myne expenses 3 *l*. 7*s*. 8*d*., and for my fee 20*s*.; [*summa*] 4 *l*. 7*s*. 8*d*.

[October 3] Item for the costs and expenses of Thomas Pope and Robert Sowthwell the third day of Oct. *anno supradicto* riding to Windsor, by the King's commandment, about the affairs of the Court . . . , and for the fees of the same Thomas and Robert for 5 days; for their expenses, 5 *l*. 17*s*. 1½*d*., and for their fees of 6*s*. 8*d*. by the day, 3 *l*. 6*s*. 8*d*.; summa, 9 *l*. 3*s*. 9½*d*.

[October 12–25] costs of Thomas Pope riding to the Court by the King's commandment, and for hiring of post horses, and for fee for two days, 59*s*. 0½*d*.

For the costs of Thomas Pope the 14th day of October, by the King's commandment, with four men in post, as appeareth by my Lord Privy Seal's letters, and for fee of 6*s*. 8*d*. for one day, 30*s*. 10*d*. For post horses at three other times sent to the Court . . . , 33*s*. 9½*d*.

For the costs of the same Thomas Pope the 25th day of October riding to Windsor about the business of the Court of Augmentations, and for his fee of 6*s*. 8*d*. a day by the space of three days, 54*s*. 7*d*.

[November 16] . . . costs and charges of Thomas Pope, John Onley, Robert Sowthwell and Richard Duke . . . for horse-hire, and for their fees for three days, 6 *l*. 19*s*. 11*d*.

[November 19] . . . costs of John Onley [99] in going to the Court at various times in the year.

For the hire of 6 horses, 4 days at 12*d*. the day, 24*s*.

For horsemete at Windsor, 5 days, 11*s*., and for mansmete, 10*s*.

Travel by the officials implied a variety of undefined services related

---

[99] After Onley's death in December, 1537, his widow secured a royal warrant for the payment of £5 which she claimed to be due to her late husband " for his costs and diet, travelling about the King's affairs." However, she later confessed to the Augmentations that she had already received the money. *Ibid.*, 15/64.

to the general business of the Court. Literally that was the case. Appearance before the privy council or attendance upon the king was accepted as part of their job, since by these interviews explicit instructions were obtained. Memoranda of money paid out by servants of Rich and Pope itemize payments for surveys of land, expenses for the suppression of additional monasteries, special assignments by commission, or simply for " going to the [king's] Court at Westminster at 3 times to speak with the King." [100] Rich conducted a great deal of Augmentations business at his house in Essex, though he too had to travel extensively. When uncertain of his duties he wrote to Cromwell for particulars. Three of the council could transact official business, but oftentimes all members were required to be present. On August 1, 1537, Rich, in acknowledging a receipt of " the book for Bissham " from the treasurer, explained that he would be in London in a few days to " appoint lands to the late Abbot of Chertsey." He requested Pope to appear at the office also if possible, adding that he would like for him and his " good lady " to come to Essex on a personal visit.[101]

Other Augmentations personnel, too, shared in these arduous duties. Richard Duke, the clerk of the council, travelled from Colchester to Hampton Court during the late summer of 1537, to remain there for fifteen days before going on to Windsor for a ten-day period; on the following April 20, he was paid £9 by the Court for " making and writing divers writings concerning the erection and making of Hampton Court Chace " and for drawing up other documents relating to purchased or exchanged lands.[102] The solicitor's clerk at one time spent six days in helping Rich and then went down to Canterbury for four days " to set the Kinges bokys " of exchanges of land, at which time he " rode aswell by nyght as by day and destroyed me a good geldyng." Shortly thereafter he made another six-day trip into Essex.[103] For the

---

[100] *Ibid.*, 15/86–87. Sometimes the officials were out in the field for weeks at a time, but they usually tried to return to the office as soon as possible; e. g., 12s. " for a greate bote, two dayes to the Cowrte at Grenewyche from London, and agayne for Mr. Chancellor and others of the Council of the Cowrte of Augmentations for busynes of the King's." In May, 1538, the attorney's expenses included charges for boat-hire, diets, the hearing of accounts, expenses of servants and attendants, provisions for his horses, and attendance upon the chancellor of the Court, either in London or in riding with him to Oatlands, Hanworth, Hampton Court, and Cuddington " about divers of the King's affairs there." *Ibid.*, 15/96–99; see also nos. 73–77.

[101] *Ibid.*, 15/21, 25, 44, 46, 49, 52, 53, 58, 81, 92. On the general travel expenses of various members of the council, see *ibid.*, 15/21, 23, 25, 35, 36, 39–40, 45–46, 55, 57, 69–70, 79, 81, 85, 89, 90–91.

[102] *Ibid.*, 15/59, 88.

[103] *Ibid.*, 15/70. At the same time solicitor Henley journeyed with six hired horses for eleven days to Otford, Knole, and Maidstone, engaged in making surveys

fiscal year 1539–1540 over £41 was paid out for messenger services, £119 for surveying woods, and a total of £165 12s. 9d. to the chancellor and other members of the Court for riding to receive surrenders of monasteries.[104]

A great deal of this work was, of course, ancillary to the real function of the Court and became less necessary after the force of the Dissolution was spent. Once established, with well-defined spheres of jurisdiction and administration, the Augmentations had more time to devote to judicial affairs and internal problems. Paper work increased as institutionalism developed; writs, grants, warrants, and other similar instruments multiplied. More business was transacted by correspondence and less by personal contact. Ordinarily this procedure was at once cheaper and less time-consuming. However, at the beginning, personal appearances at the Court were not always related to pending litigation. Heads of monasteries and priories, for example, were called in by the council for all sorts of reasons, not the least of which was declaring to them "certain matters for the Kinge's advantage."[105] On the other hand, information might be presented with the intent of furthering the interest of the informer as well as that of the king, in which case it usually came from a receiver or a collector who was having difficulty in the collection of Augmentations revenue.[106]

Indeed obstructionist tactics were often employed by those who shared in the popular resentment against all ministers associated with the suppression. Receivers especially were unpopular in sections where the feeling was strongest. Usually agitation was confined to threats and private denunciations, but once in a while a demonstration would assume violent proportions. The houses and property of receivers like Freeman and Beckwith, themselves subject to biting criticism, occasionally became the objects of attack and pillage.[107]

In 1536 the general reaction to change, so prevalent in the conservative

---

and taking "attornments," i. e., transfers of feudal homage and services from tenants of a former lord to their new lord the king.

[104] Augm. Office, Treas. Rolls of Accts., No. 1, pt. 2, mems. 21d., 22.

[105] Needless to say the Court guaranteed their expenses in such instances. The same kind of payment is implied in the receipt of Lewis Brecknock, late prior of the monastery of Monkton Farleigh, in Wiltshire, who received 20s. from the treasurer in part payment of his costs "journeying from Bath unto London, by commandment of the worshipful Sir Richard Riche Chancellor of the Court of Augmentations." Manchester Papers, 15/34. See also nos. 37, 51, 57.

[106] L. and P., Addenda, I, pt. 2, no. 1850. See informations made by the Augmentations receiver of Yorkshire against John and George Burton, "twoo busy felowes," who refused to pay their rent for two or three years after it was due. Augm. Office, Miscellanea, 18/17; 20.

[107] L. and P., XI, no. 725; XII, pt. 1, nos. 392, 536, 1035, 1163; XII, pt. 2, Appendix, nos. 16–17.

north, found expression in the Pilgrimage of Grace. Social, economic, and legal factors, as well as religious, contributed to the dissatisfaction of the country, but certainly the participants were primarily concerned with the maintenance of accepted Catholic practices and the preservation of the monasteries. Most of the commoners of Lincolnshire were of one opinion in their demands, wrote an observer early in October, 1536; one of them was that the church should retain its old and accustomed privileges without any exactions; another, that the dissolved monasteries should be restored, "except such houses as the king hath suppressed for his pleasure only." Moreover, they demanded that certain of the more unpopular ministers of the crown must either be turned over to the commons or banished from the realm.[108] Among those specifically mentioned were Cromwell and Rich, one because he was considered responsible for the royal policy, the other because he had been a willing tool in the execution of the evil designs. In an earlier list of grievances presented by the Lincolnshire rebels at Horncastle, Cromwell was denounced as a false traitor, while his two "pen clerks," the master of the rolls [109] and the chancellor of the Augmentations, were specifically singled out as the devisers of all the false legislation recently enacted.[110] Certain base-born leaders of the council, "persons of low birth and small reputation," were particularly subject to attack.[111] The seven articles presented at Ancaster Heath on the first Sunday in October specified that the king should take noblemen for his councillors, and either give up Cromwell, Rich, Legh, and Layton to the vengeance of commons or banish them.[112]

The objection to men of low birth dominating the council was due not so much to their non-aristocratic status as to the fact that the king's most unpopular advisers were numbered among the *nouveaux riches*.

---

[108] *Ibid.*, XI, no. 585.

[109] Christopher Hales was master of the rolls at this time, having succeeded Cromwell in that office in July, 1536. Previously, as attorney general, he had been active in the investigation of such personages as More, Fisher, Anne Boleyn, and the holy nun, Elizabeth Barton. Cf. J. M. Rigg, "Sir Christopher Hales," *D. N. B.*

[110] *L. and P.*, XII, pt. 1, no. 70. Dodds, *The Pilgrimage of Grace, 1536–1537*, I, 103. When the commons asked the gentlemen, "Masters, if ye have them [i. e., the specified councillors], would that mend the matter?" they replied, "Yea, for these be the doers of all mischief."

[111] *L. and P.*, XI, no. 705. Articles addressed by the rebels to the king. Cromwell and Rich were specifically charged with using conciliar authority to their own advantage. See also *ibid.*, nos. 1246, 1319.

[112] *Ibid.*, nos. 780(2), 828(5). Although all four men were closely associated with the Dissolution, Thomas Legh (Leigh or Lee) and Richard Layton were not prominent in the council in 1536. Nevertheless, as chief agents of the suppression they had become the most notorious of all of Cromwell's visitors. Biographical sketches of Legh and Layton, by W. A. J. Archbold, are included in the *D. N. B.*

The loyalty of the period was such that to the popular mind these " subverters of the laws," and not the king, were responsible for all the recent unpopular legislation and its attendant evils. The Yorkshire proclamation of Aske was emphatic on this point: " For as muche that shuche symple and evyll dysposyd persones, beynge of the kynges cownsell, hathe nott onely ensensyd hys grace with many and sundry new invencyons, whyche be contrary [to] the faythe of God and honour to the kynges mayeste and the comyn welthe of thys realme, and thereby entendythe to destroy the churche of England . . . : but also the seyd counsell hathe spoylyd and robbid, and farthyr entendynge utterly to spoyle and robbe, the hole body of thys realme and that as well you as us." [113] Again, at Doncaster in West Riding the Yorkshire pilgrims demanded that the unpopular statutes be repealed, that " villein blood " be purged from the council, and that there should be a return to the *status quo* of the old regime when the nobles of the realm " did order under his Highness." [114]

It is hardly to be expected that Henry VIII would permit such implications to remain unchallenged. His lengthy reply, written in his own hand, was as supercilious as it was definitive and to the point. Admitting no error, either in the law or the administration thereof, he reminded his subjects that he had kept them so long in peace and prosperity that they had become unmindful of their many blessings. As for the much criticised legislation, he added, " it shall be duly proved that there were never in any of our predecessors' days so many wholesome, commodious and beneficial acts made for the common wealth, and yet I mean it since their time that would fain have thank without desert." Regarding the lack of aristocratic influence in the government, it was affirmed that there were more nobles, " both of birth and condition," in the council than at the beginning of the reign. In this, as in all the other attacks, the demands of the insurrectionists were contemptuously dismissed: " Now how far be ye abused to reckon that then there were more noblemen in our Privy Council than now? But yet, though I now do declare the truth to pull you from the blindness that you were led in, yet we ensure you we would ye knew that it appertaineth nothing to any of our subjects to appoint us our Council ne we will take it so at your hands. Wherefore henceforth remember better the duties of subjects to your King and sovereign lord, and meddle no more of those nor such like things as ye have nothing to do in." [115]

---

[113] Dodds, *The Pilgrimage of Grace, 1536–1537*, I, 175–76.

[114] Finally, they insisted on the dismissal and punishment of Cromwell, Rich, and the heretical bishops, as subverters of the laws of God and the commonwealth. *Ibid.*, 263. *L. and P.*, XII, pt. 1, no. 1022.

[115] *Ibid.*, XI, nos. 957, 995. Dodds, *The Pilgrimage of Grace, 1536–1537*, I, 275–

The charges against Rich were indefinite. That his name, along with that of the lord chancellor, Thomas Audley, should be associated with Cromwell was natural enough, since the three of them were closely identified with the Dissolution. Rich was popularly believed to be a willing tool of the " hammerer of the monks," Cromwell, whose immediate dismissal, according to the rebels, had become imperative.[116] The appraisal of Rich by a seventeenth century ecclesiastic would probably have represented the feeling of his enemies in 1536. " His staid and solid parts commended him to Cromwell," wrote the canon of St. Asaph in 1665; " Cromwell was the Mawl and Rich the Hammer of Abbeys: He laid open to the Monks their faults and his Master made use of it to force them to a surrendery: For, as he said, when those religious Societies saw they had faults enough discovered to take away their Lands, they had wit enough to give them up." [117] As head of the Court of Augmentations the name of Rich was known to everybody and, consequently, maligned by all those who had a grudge against it. Since this group included most of the regular clergy, disappointed office seekers, and all those others who had failed to secure what they felt to be their just share of the spoils distributed through the Court, it is not surprising that attacks upon him by the radicals were an effective part of the propaganda of the movement.[118]

The seriousness of the northern rebellion had given the government some anxious moments, but there was no deviation in policy as a result

---

78. The " Answer to the petitions of the traitors and rebels in Lincolnshire " was set forth in a similar vein. " First, we begin and make answer to the fourth and sixth articles, because upon them dependeth much of the rest. Concerning choosing of counsaillours, I never have read heard nor known that princes' counsaillours and prelates should be appointed by rude and ignorant common people. . . . How presumptuous then are ye the rude commons of one shire, and that one of the most brute and beastly of the whole realm, and of least experience, to find fault with your prince for the electing of his counsaillours and prelates; and to take upon you, contrary to God's law and man's law, to rule your prince." *L. and P.*, XI, no. 780. Printed in *Cal. State Papers*, I, 463. Quoted in Pickthorn, *Early Tudor Government*, II, 324–25.

[116] Article eight of those demands, on which all were agreed, read: " Lord Cromwell, the Lord Chancellor [Audley], and Sir Richard Riche to have condign punishment, as subvertors of the good laws of the realm and maintainers and inventers of heretics." *L. and P.*, XII, pt. 1, no. 901. These articles of " Aske's Examination " are printed in full in Notes and Documents, in *E. H. R.* (July, 1890), V, 550–73, especially 557. Dodds, *The Pilgrimage of Grace, 1536–1537*, I, 357.

[117] David Lloyd (canon of St. Asaph), *The Statesmen and Favourites of England since the Reformation* (London, 1665), 173.

[118] To counteract governmental propaganda the " pilgrims " distributed verses and couplets against Cromwell, Audley, Rich, " and divers bishops of the new learning which rhymes had been sung abroad by minstrels." *L. and P.*, XI, no. 786; XII, pt. 1, no. 1021 (3).

of the uprising. A taste of easy money had stimulated the desire for more, and the broad lands of the larger abbeys were too desirable to be ignored. " I am so bold as to sue for a greater [monastery]," one of the receivers wrote Cromwell, having " missed the farm of Ormesbie which you meant me to have." However true his ensuing observations might have been, it is a temptation to regard them as justification for the request. All houses might as well be suppressed as a few, he argued, " for they are in a readiness to surrender without any coming, and that doth appear by their acts, for they are in a customed sort all of spoil and bribery, as well the great houses as small, . . . also minisheth the great part of their stock and store. Therefore they should be taken betime." [119] If an excuse were necessary, a good one was found in the treasonable conduct of the larger houses of the north, where the abbots were implicated in the recent uprising. By the end of 1538 Barlings, Bridlington, Fountains, Jervaulx, Kirkstead, and Whalley were acquired by acts of attainder.[120] Since Cromwell proposed to strike while the iron was hot, no time was lost in sending out new commissions to speed up the whole procedure. Beginning with the Lancashire abbey of Furness early in 1537 the larger houses yielded to political pressure without much resistance. In these voluntary surrenders the Augmentations ministers played a prominent role.

The inventories of 1538 show how careful were the commissioners in getting fair and accurate evaluations of all possessions immediately upon surrender. Reliable persons were put in charge to guarantee meticulous supervision of the work by trustworthy officials.[121] Members of the Court were sometimes chosen because, as Norfolk once put it to Henry, like his own servants, " these men look for none of the farms, and there-

---

[119] Freeman, receiver for Lincolnshire, to Cromwell, October, 1538. Accompanying the letter was " A declaration of all such religious houses being of [the order] of Gilberdyns within Lincolnshire lately suppressed," viz., nine abbeys with a revenue of £1,407. Goods to the value of £4,729, various charges deducted, had been sold by Freeman. *Ibid.*, XIII, pt. 2, no. 528.

[120] By a principle contrary to the common law, the property of the corporation over which the abbots ruled was held to be forfeited to the crown. In a similar way it was assumed that the " free and voluntary " surrenders of later abbots were legally binding on their successors. The ensuing act of parliament (31 Henry VIII, c. 13), however, silenced any opposition which might have developed by legalizing that unwarranted assumption. Later, in 1539, the great houses of Glastonbury, Colchester, and Reading were also acquired by the attainder of their abbots.

[121] Augm. Office, Misc. Books 171, 172, 361; on inventories of church goods for the reign of Edward VI, *ibid.* 495–515. M. E. C. Walcott, " Inventories and Valuations of Religious Houses at the Time of the Dissolution," *Archaeologia*, XLIII (1771), 201–49. Instructions for the general visitations of the monasteries and nunneries, 1538–39, are presented in E. M. Goldsmid, *Ten Scarce Books in English Literature* (Edinburgh, 1886).

fore will see to your profit."[122] Already heavy fines had been paid by certain monasteries for the royal privilege of continuation, however short-lived the exemption. Now that the houses were finally dissolved, the unpaid balance due to the Augmentations from these compositions was remitted.[123] Through 1539 and 1540 revenues continued to come in from the larger houses. By March, 1540, only three important prizes remained. Of these, Christchurch at Canterbury and Rochester in Staffordshire were received by special royal commission, on which the chancellor, attorney, and solicitor of the Augmentations, together with two other officials of the Court, sat as the dominant members.[124] With the surrender of Waltham abbey on the twenty-third of the month, the Dissolution was virtually over. A few colleges and hospitals, all of which were acquired by the end of the summer, completed the project.[125]

Meanwhile, the campaign against the friaries and the great national shrines, like those of Canterbury and Winchester, proceeded under special commissions. The former operations were entrusted to the supervision of Richard Ingworth, a prior of the Dominican order of Black Friars of Langley Regis, who had recently been made bishop of Dover. Two facts stand out in his reports: an almost pathetic zeal to please Cromwell and an expressed disappointment that the orders yielded so little revenue to the crown. Great poverty amongst the friars was manifest everywhere he went; even the meticulous concern for selling

---

[122] (May 10, 1537.) *L. and P.*, XII, pt. 1, no. 1172. On the work of the commissioners during 1539, see *ibid.*, XIV, pt. 2, Preface, xxxiii-xxxix. The commissioners included Beckwith, Freeman, Rokeby, Heneage, Cavendish, Wiseman, Moyle, Scudamore, Berners, Arundell, Rich, Robert Southwell, and John Williams. Thirty-two monasteries fell during the last month of the year.

[123] Thirty-three monasteries are enumerated as having given £5,948 6s. 8d. in part payment of "fines or compositions" for "toleration and continuance." The treasurer of the Court explained that there were no arrears due from these fines because the houses had since come into the king's hands by act of parliament and that the residue still unpaid had been canceled. The statute referred to, of course, was the act for the dissolution of the greater monasteries (31 Henry VIII, c. 13, *S.R.*, III, 733-39), which assured to the crown all monastic possessions surrendered by the heads of houses "of their own free and voluntary minds." Augm. Office, Treas. Rolls of Accts., No. 1, pt. 1, mems. 4d., 5. The fines varied from £20 to £400 each. Similar compositions not included in the Augmentations account were entered on the Patent Rolls. A list of these fines is printed in Gasquet, *Henry VIII and the English Monasteries*, II, Appendix, I, 529-30, and in Liljegren, *The Fall of the Monasteries*, 21.

[124] The dean of Rochester, Walter Philips, was paid £20 for his expenses in providing for these commissioners during the dissolution there. Augm. Office, Misc. Books 249, fol. 40. Edward North, as treasurer of the Court, was allowed expenses for taking the surrenders of Christchurch and Waltham, Essex, and for carrying the plate and jewels received to his house in London and thence to the king at Westminster, where they were received by the master of the jewels. *Ibid.* fol. 38.

[125] *L. and P.*, XV, nos. 378, 379, 393, 691, 695, 743, 834.

all articles that could possibly be disposed of brought in but little cash. " The substans in the more parte of the howsys ys very small," he carefully explained, " in dyverse placeys lytyll more than the dettes; and the clamor of pore men to whom the monye ys oweynge ys to tedyus." [126] On the contrary the shrines proved to be more profitable, the richest of them being the fabulous shrine of St. Thomas à Becket, where the booty when picked up by the receiver was reputed to have filled twenty-six carts. However, most of the shrines were much less rewarding and, incidentally, profited the Augmentations but little since a greater part of these spoils went to either the jewel house or the mint. Whatever the total profit, such unwonted measures evoked widespread criticism. After the suppression of the order of St. John in the summer of 1540, the French ambassador was led to remark that the king should reflect that by enriching himself he was impoverishing his people; what he had gained in goods he had lost in renown.[127]

The bill for the suppression of the great Order of the Knights of St. John of Jerusalem was passed in parliament on May 10, 1540, giving to the crown not only all the ancient possessions of the order in England and Ireland but also its movables. Although in part a political measure, the act added revenues to the Augmentations which, in Ireland alone, totaled over £743.[128] In keeping with regular Augmentations practice, an office of receiver-general was set up for the new incoming revenues. Maurice Dennis, a servant of the king, was appointed receiver-general of these lands in England and Wales.[129] The appointment marked the

[126] Visitation of the priories can be traced in *L. and P.*, XIV and XV. Ingworth's letters to Cromwell are included in Wright (ed.), *Letters relating to the Suppression of Monasteries*, especially XCVIII for above quote. The four principal orders of Franciscans, Dominicans, Carmelites, and Augustinians, some of whom had surrendered prior to 1538, numbered 177 houses in 1517. Hughes, *The Reformation in England*, I, 69–70; see also Table, 327. Ingworth was rewarded for his work with the house, site, and lands of the Black Friars of Langley Regis, Hertfordshire, which grant was to be voided if and when he secured ecclesiastical benefices worth £100 or more. Augm. Office, Misc. Books 235, fol. 23d.

[127] Charles de Marillac to Anne de Montmorency, constable of France, August 4, 1540, *L. and P.*, XV, no. 954.

[128] 32 Henry VIII, c. 24, *S. R.*, III, 778–81. Altogether there were forty-three commanderies and preceptories of the order suppressed by the statute. Between April 12 and July 24 this parliament granted the crown these and other concessions, which Suffolk, Norfolk, and others affirmed to be worth £3,000,000 in gold. *L. and P.*, XV, nos. 498(24), 646–47, 697; XVI, nos. 379(57), 778. In addition to a large quantity of plate and jewels, the Augmentations thus acquired revenues amounting to more than £100,000 per year.

[129] Augm. Office, Misc. Books 235, fol. 34d.; 164 (pages unnumbered). Augm. Office, Treas. Rolls of Accts., No. 2B, pt. 1, mem. 10; pt. 2, mem. 5d., show Dennis to have paid £4,399 9s. 11d. and £2,687 14s. 5d. in annual receipts from these lands during the first two years. On October 4, 1545, Dennis surrendered his earlier patent of December 20, 1540, in favor of a joint appointment with Thomas Poley.

beginning of an administrative career that led to the treasurership of Calais in the next reign.

As the treasurer's receipts mounted, the Court assumed a position of growing importance in governmental finance. As early as March, 1540, Cromwell could observe with satisfaction that his revenue program was paying off. After consulting all the treasurers about funds available for the defense program, he noted that the Augmentations had received " great sums," over and above 10,000 marks.[180] For the most part its acquisitions were of a permanent character, consisting of land and property which could easily be converted into cash when need arose. Plate, jewels, relics, ornaments, and precious stones generally passed through the Augmentations to be delivered to the king's use,[181] but lead and bell metal were often retained to await an advantageous market.[182] The last considerable acquisition came from the priory or hospital of St. John, with lands lying in London, Wales, and nineteen different English counties.[133] During the same year a deficiency in the original Dissolution acts was rectified, thereby clarifying an annoying legal ambiguity which had been bothering the Court for some time. The statutes had not expressly stipulated that the franchisal rights of the monasteries were inseparable from the land and hence were also automatically transferable to the crown. The corrective legislation simply provided that all " liberties fraunchises privileges and temporall jurisdictions whiche the said late owners had used and exercised laufully " should henceforth be vested in the Court of Augmentations.[134] After 1540 there were no other

---

Augm. Office, Misc. Books 236, fol. 82. William Rigges, later one of the ten auditors of the second Augmentations, was appointed auditor of these lands. *Ibid.* 235, fol. 43*d.*; D. L. 42/133.

[180] Cromwell's Remembrances, *L. and P.*, XV, nos. 321, 322. The sum of 10,000 marks referred to was probably either the arrears due from the particular receivers or the sum total of obligations then payable at the Augmentations. *Ibid.*, XVI, nos. 93, 617.

[131] Manchester Papers 15/8, 29, 30, 114.

[132] See p. 238 ff., *infra.* At the beginning of October, 1538, the Court had over £3,296 worth of lead and bells from the Gilbertine priories in storage. *L. and P.*, Addenda, I, pt. 1, no. 1361.

[133] S. C. (31–32 Henry VIII) 6/2402. Account of Maurice Dennis, for the revenues of St. John of Jerusalem in Wales, London, Middlesex, Somersetshire, Surrey, Sussex, Cambridgeshire, Suffolk, Yorkshire, Staffordshire, Shropshire, Oxfordshire, Warwickshire, Essex, Hertfordshire, Buckinghamshire, Kent, Lincolnshire, Berkshire, Leicestershire, and Southamptonshire. Dugdale, *Monasticon Anglicanum*, VI, pt. 2, 799 ff.

[134] 32 Henry VIII, c. 20, " The Liberties to be used," *S.R.*, III, 770–73. The same safeguard was set up for franchises and jurisdictions of attainted persons in section ii of the act. Section vi empowered the Court to take acknowledgment of concords of fines of lands, which were to be as acceptable in the Court of Common Pleas as if acknowledged there; also, it was specifically provided that all deeds and obligations must be enrolled in the Augmentations as a matter of record.

large land units transferred to the Court until the second Augmentations was established at the beginning of the next reign. The confiscation of chantry possessions for which provision was made in November, 1545, was not really carried out until after the death of Henry VIII.[185] However, a full survey of the chantry wealth was undertaken early in 1546 by special commissioners in each county under the general direction of Augmentations ministers.[136] Before the first Court was dissolved a number of these endowments already had been taken into the king's hands.[137]

Administratively the task of managing a piece of crown land was the same whether it was retained permanently or alienated within a few weeks after a brief period of possession. By purchase, exchange, or gift, miscellaneous parcels of land were added to the Court's holdings from time to time, usually necessitating fresh surveys and the appointment of additional personnel. Such was the gift of Henry Algernon Percy, " the Unthrifty," earl of Northumberland, who, in 1537, on account of the " debylytery and unnaturalness " of his own kin had decided to bequeath all his property to the king. Since the family fortune had previously suffered from attainder, the gift seems to have resulted from the earl's fears of royal reprisals.[138] Already, as part of a more general attack against private liberties in the north, the king had persuaded him to disinherit his brother and heir, Thomas, in exchange for an annuity of £1,000. The family lands in Yorkshire, Northumberland, and Cumberland, valued at £3,876 per year including wood sales and other perquisites, were surveyed by Robert Southwell, who found a fine estate in a " blemished " condition due to the debts and " folly " of the late earl. But if restored by the king to its original state, he reported, it would add to the glory of the crown " for the honours and castles purporten such a majesty in themselves now being the King's as they are in manner as mirrors or glasses for the inhabitants 20 miles

---

[185] 37 Henry VIII, c. 4, *S. R.*, III, 988–93. The act for the dissolution of colleges, chantries, free chapels, hospitals, fraternities, guilds, and stipendiary priests was ostensibly proposed for the maintenance of the wars against France and Scotland. See p. 293, *infra*.

[136] Names of Augmentations officials sitting on these commissions are given in *L. and P.*, XXI, pt. 1, nos. 69, 302(30).

[137] *Ibid.*, nos. 309, 947, 966–68, 1099. The costs of these chantry surveys were borne by the Augmentations. Augm. Office, Misc. Books 254, fols. 88, 93; 255, fols. 104–10.

[138] Northumberland's brothers and mother were all implicated in the northern rebellion, Sir Thomas Percy being executed less than a month before the earl's death. See *D. N. B.* on the Percy family. At first he granted his land to the king with the proviso that it might descend to his nephew, but after his brother's execution, he made the grant unconditional. F. W. Brooks, *The Council of the North* (London, 1953), 15–16. See Chapter Three, n. 53.

compass every way from them to look in and to direct themselves by." [139]
As the earl was "little monied," no profit was derived from his personal
property; however, the indebtedness of £1,689 charged against the
estate was partially counterbalanced by "gressoming" fines from the
land to the extent of about a thousand marks.[140]

Accessions like the Northumberland lands were assured to the crown
by special acts of parliament. Transcriptions of these acts were made by
the Court's officials, who kept on file an exact record of all annexations.[141] The continuous series of acquisitions can be traced through
these statutes, which enumerate the particular parcels of land in each
successive addition. They include land taken for debts, particular manors
gained by exchange or purchase, and certain temporalities of the church
surrendered to the crown.[142] Most of the exchanges did not, of course,
represent an acreage gain for the Court. If the surveys showed a marked
difference in value, compensation in the form of a cash payment was
made from the Augmentations treasury.

To its officials the ordinary duties of the central office must have
seemed somewhat mechanical, yet in fact they were neither prosaic nor
monotonous. If much of the routine activity was repetitious, it had
the advantage of possessing a human quality which was ever changing.
Primarily dealings were with people rather than with things; even in
such staid matters as receipts and payments the personal equation was
always present, adding interest to an otherwise dull transaction. In
relation to the visitation proceedings the early work of the institution fell
largely into three categories: the assignment of monastic pensions, the
investigation of the status of various smaller dependencies or religious
"cells" affiliated with the larger monasteries, and the receipt of the
dissolution revenues. The first and third of these categories remained
important features of administration throughout the history of the Court,
whereas the second was only temporary in nature.

---

[139] *L. and P.*, XII, pt. 2, no. 548; see also nos. 19, 398, 1311(34).

[140] *Ibid.*, nos. 165, 172, 201, 291, 365, 548. Ingressions (Lat. *ingressus*; commonly called gressoms, gressuns, or gresshams), customarily levied in the north
of England, were payments made by the tenants when a new lord entered into
possession of the land. In this instance Southwell was somewhat exercised about
levying these dues since he had no special commission covering the point.

[141] Augm. Office, Misc. Books 2. Copies of acts of parliament giving lands to
the survey of the Court of Augmentations, beginning with the act establishing it.
All these assurances and exchanges are found in *S. R.*, III.

[142] As in the "Acte concernyng the assuraunce of all the Temporaltyes belonging unto the Bisshoppriche of Norwiche unto the Kinges Highnes and his heires."
When the abbot of St. Benet, William Rugg (Reppes), was appointed to the
bishopric in 1536, all the ancient barony and revenues of the see were transferred
to the crown in exchange for a new endowment. 27 Henry VIII, c. 45, *S. R.*,
III, 608–609.

The commissioners of 1536 were instructed to place all the religious who chose to remain in orders with houses enjoined to receive them and to send others who wished to enter the secular church to the archbishop of Canterbury and the lord chancellor for capacities. Those who thus desired to return to a secular life, " to lyve honestlye and virtuously abrode," were to be accorded " some convenyent Charytie dysposed to them toward ther lyvyng," proportionate to the distance and nature of their new appointments. This " charity," paid usually as a reward or bonus along with the arrears of wages due to most of the inmates, was awarded by the Augmentations. Certainly there was no intention of pensioning all the religious, nor was it necessary. Only the heads of surrendered houses were, in fact, guaranteed pensions allocated to them by the chancellor of the Court, though the monks and nuns actually so awarded were numbered in the thousands. This function of the Court occupied so much time and absorbed such a large proportion of the dissolution revenues that the Augmentations has been referred to, not inappropriately, as a ministry of pensions.[143]

The controversial problem of monastic pensions has been interpreted and reinterpreted many times by Reformation scholars and need not be reconsidered here. The pension lists among the records of the Court of Augmentations show most of the monks and nuns to have been provided for adequately, the compensation being, in many instances, more than generous. From the viewpoint of the Augmentations officials it was not the ethical question of the number deserving compensation or the extent of their rewards that was important, but rather the more practical problem of satisfying all parties concerned.

Under the first Act of Dissolution heads of houses alone were to be assigned pensions upon the recommendation of the visitation commissioners. After the first year, however, when the suppression of the larger monasteries was begun, pensions were promised to the inmates of all houses that submitted voluntarily; usually they were awarded by the royal commissioners themselves as an inducement to surrender.[144] In view of the fact that pensions were granted by various authorities, it is hardly surprising that they varied appreciably in amount. The king's interest in the Augmentations was chiefly financial, so it was naturally the desire of its officials to show as great an annual profit as possible. Nevertheless, the Court seems to have been quite fair in the appraisals.

[143] Baskerville, *English Monks and the Suppression of the Monasteries*, 246.
[144] Gasquet, *Henry VIII and the English Monasteries*, II, 226, 449–51, 454, 456–57; Dietz, *English Government Finance, 1485–1558*, 134. Many individual inmates were provided with some sort of reward or compensation, but in no case were entire communities pensioned.

Whether originally determined by its chancellor or by commissioners, the amount of any pension was always subject to the review of the king or of Cromwell. As a result of this division of authority pension jurisdiction sometimes became a source of controversy between Rich and Cromwell.

All stipends, of course, were supposed to be continued only until such time as the beneficiaries secured preferments or livings or were provided with positions comparable in value to their allowances. In some cases, where the awards were inadequate, individuals were given benefices as well as pensions. With divided responsibility in the awarding of pensions or gifts, cases of graft and deception soon emerged. Continual checking was required to prevent trafficking in pensions and duplication of payments, especially since they could be made quarterly or semi-annually, either by the regional Augmentations receivers or from the central treasury at Westminster.

Processed through the Court, lists of pensions assigned by the commissioners were frequently sent for confirmation to Cromwell; when ratified by him they were forwarded to Rich, who then endorsed them with a scribbled note to Duke to " Pass these pensions." As was customary in all courts, regular fees were paid to scribes and other officials for their labors, including 11s. " of every pentionary " for the chancellor and clerk of the Court. Whatever the validity of the original grants, abuses in the system persisted for years to come. Constituting as they did a heavy burden on the national revenue, state pensions continued to plague the government long after the Augmentations was abolished.[145]

With pensions, as in other business negotiations, most of the Augmentations ministers were just in their dealings with the public, however conscientious they may have been in promoting the king's or the Court's interests. In fact, it was not always easy to maintain a fair balance between the crown's demands on the one hand and those of interested parties on the other, particularly when a minister's reputation for impartiality might well become a determining factor in his future promotions. Some were not firm enough, while others, like Beckwith, became unduly arrogant as they advanced in power. Not all officials had the discretion of Robert Southwell who could write Cromwell with some satisfaction:

---

[145] Bills and payments for pensions are all recorded in the receivers' accounts; those paid by the central office appear on the treasurer's rolls. Likewise, thousands of miscellaneous receipts from pensioners are preserved among the Augmentation Office records. Some of this evidence was used by Gasquet, although the fees demanded by the Court's officials were not usually in excess, as suggested by him. Gasquet, *Henry VIII and the English Monasteries*, II, 464–65.

Sir, we have practysed with the pore men for their pencions as easely to the kynges charge and as moche to his graces honour, as we cowde devyce. The boke wherof we do sende unto your lordeshypp, with the names and summes for the makyng of their patentes, which being sent unto us to be delyvered to the parties afore our departure, shalbe moche to their contentacion, and no lesse to the kynges honour, to imparte with somewhat of his gracyous charyte towarde the maintenaunce of their pore lyvyng.[146]

More involved but no less important than pensions was the question of the actual legal status of many of the smaller monasteries. A number of the lesser houses were dependent units or cells of some larger monastery and, as such, rightfully claimed exemption under the act of 1536. On the other hand, it was possible for a house to cite spurious claims to dependency in order to avoid dissolution. In either case, all such claims had to be investigated thoroughly before exemption could be granted, and it was not expected that the regular visitation commissions would be qualified for such a task. Cromwell had, indeed, envisioned just such petitions when he had organized the Augmentations. As a court of record it was empowered by its own constitution to adjudicate all disputes arising from the Dissolution and to entertain cases directly related to the land or revenues under its jurisdiction. Consequently, the commissioners of 1536 were required not to meddle with any of the dependent or daughter monasteries until the legality of their claims had been investigated by the Augmentations. In such instances the advice of the Court's attorney and solicitor was invaluable. These special cases represent the earliest judicial business that came before the Court for final settlement. While not typical of later suits brought to the Augmentations, the general procedure was similar. Proceedings were initiated by privy seals directed by the commissioners to the heads of the houses claiming exemption, ordering them to appear within a fortnight at Westminster before the chancellor and council of the Court for the examination of evidence.

In policy and organization the Court changed little under the leadership of its first two chancellors. After 1540, with the removal of Cromwell's supervision, it was left largely to its own devices, shaping internal rules and regulations to meet new needs as they arose. Save for financial directives and warrants for expenditures, there was little interference from the king and council in either administrative problems or judicial

---

[146] Robert Southwell to Cromwell from Northampton, March 3, 1538, concerning the dissolution of St. Andrew's there. Cotton. MS., Cleop. E. iv, fol. 218. Printed in Wright (ed.), *Letters relating to the Suppression of Monasteries*, No. LXXXVI.

affairs. A few messengers and assistant clerks were added to the main staff, but most of the increase in personnel was in the regional areas of estate management. Not as highly competitive as those of the central organization, these jobs were mostly filled by county administrators familiar with the problems of particular districts. A knowledge of local manorial customs was still a prerequisite of sound demesne administration, and Augmentations policy made a point of not trying to change established convention. As additional lands were acquired, the manorial officials of the former owners were commonly retained, giving an administrative continuity not otherwise possible. When new appointees were added they were usually stewards or receivers, as supervisory agents of the Court.

At the main office the principal development was in the administration of crown woods. At the time of organization no provision had been made for a special office of woods in the Augmentations, since the execution of the governmental policy regarding the sale of woods and the preservation of growing timber was entrusted primarily to the department of general surveyors of crown lands. As acquired by the Court, woodlands were administered by regular officials, with no special attention being given to either timber preservation or to the systematic sale of growing woods. Wood sales undertaken by the Court were made by special commissions and necessitated no changes in the permanent staff. In the beginning the only additional ministers required were local officials, such as keepers and woodwards, who soon became an integral part of the expanding manorial administration. It was not long, however, before co-ordinating offices were instituted. The earliest of these was a special surveyorship for woods, to be followed a few years later by a general director of the work, who took the title " master of woods."

The surveyorship of all woods, parks, and woodlands within the survey of the Augmentations was given to William Cowper for life in November, 1537, with authority to appoint sufficient deputies under him.[147] Numerous surveys by him and his deputies, as well as regular accounts of wood sales during the 1530's and 1540's, show the job to have been anything but a sinecure. In June, 1544, he was joined in the office by David Clayton,[148] who soon assumed full charge of the work, Cowper's

[147] Exch., Accts. Various, 148/20. A copy of the appointment of William Cowper as general surveyor of all the woods of suppressed monasteries; Augm. Office, Misc. Books 232, pt. 1, fol. 61.

[148] The joint appointment of Cowper and Clayton was dated June 22, 1544, upon the surrender of Cowper's original patent of November 4, 1537. *Ibid.* 236, fol. 71. Clayton was seeking support in securing the office as early as March 14, 1544; he apparently began work some time before his formal appointment. *Ibid.* 253, fols. 49, 70; *L. and P.*, XIX, pt. 1, no. 198; pt. 2, no. 166(20).

services being used increasingly in other Augmentations activities.[149] Clayton died shortly before the reorganization of the Court in January of 1547 and was succeeded by Geoffrey Gates, who continued as a woods official in the reconstituted Court.[150]

Meanwhile, the headship of the new department had been entrusted to Sir Thomas Pope, whose earlier experience as treasurer had fully qualified him for any responsible position in the Court. No record is extant of his official appointment as master of woods, but it was probably in 1543, at which time there was a general expansion in the woods administration. There is, however, some evidence that he may have begun his duties earlier, since he had given up the treasurership almost three years previously.[151] Likewise, it is possible that Pope's resignation in 1540 may have been at the request of the council, in view of his indebtedness to the crown for a large sum upon the determination of his account for the fiscal year ending Michaelmas, 1539. Nevertheless, there is no indication that he came under attack or that he was in any way penalized because of the debt, which he was in a position to assume fully. Indeed one of his original sponsors, Lord Chancellor Audley, referred to his surrender of office as a voluntary " resignation." [152] Moreover, Pope's services were used continually by the crown during the period. In fact, by July, 1543, he had been appointed to membership in the council.[153] It is probable that his promise to settle the account as quickly as possible was entirely satisfactory, for apparently he was not even required to furnish sureties for the debt. By the time he was freed of the encumbrance he was already in the woods office. Receipts for wood sales in the first Augmentations began in 1542–43 when £ 539

---

[149] Augm. Office, Misc. Books 254, fols. 61, 91, 93; 255, fols. 107, 112. Cowper died in the autumn of 1546 and Clayton not long thereafter. *L. and P.*, XXI, pt. 2, nos. 332(91), 476(85), 648(56).

[150] Gates's (Gate) appointment was made on December 14, 1546. At that time it was noted officially that Cowper had resigned the office and that Clayton was dead. Augm. Office, Misc. Books 236, fol. 117.

[151] Although he resigned the treasurership of the Court in March, 1540, Pope continued to hear accounts along with other members of the Augmentations council. Augm. Office, Misc. Books 250, fol. 46. A letter of Pope concerning the Farnham Woods in Buckinghamshire, written some time in the spring of 1542, suggests that he had taken over the woods office earlier, but specific references to him as " master of woods " do not occur until 1543. *L. and P.*, XVII, no. 331; XVIII, pt. 2, no. 406. In the reorganization of 1547 Pope was retained as the principal master of woods in the second Court of Augmentations.

[152] Thomas Audley to Cromwell, March 17, 1540, *L. and P.*, XV, no. 351. He spoke highly of Pope, in whom he had always found " much kindness."

[153] In a grant of July, 1543, Pope was styled " king's councillor." *L. and P.*, XVIII, pt. 1, no. 981(7). At the same time he was paying off his Augmentations debt, he was buying land from the crown. Augm. Office, Misc. Books 249, fol. 51; Augm. Office, Treas. Rolls of Accts., No. 2B, pt. 1, mem. 14*d*. ff.

17*s.* 2*d.* was paid in from that source.[154] From that point forward Pope devoted most of his time to the supervision of wood sales and to the direction of woods officials.

With the Cromwellian policy of augmenting the non-recurrent revenues, increased emphasis was given to the sale of Augmentations timber. By 1543 the receipts from wood sales had become important enough to warrant the addition of two more officers to assist the master and surveyor. Accordingly, an extra auditorship and a special receivership were set up to handle the new revenues and accounts; they were awarded respectively to Griffin Tyndale, then receiver of the lands of the dissolved Tewkesbury monastery, and Walter Farr, the latter having already served the Court since 1538 as keeper of its records.[155] Two years later Tyndale was given an assistant, John Perte, to whom he turned over most of the accounts of his office.[156] About the same time, with the approval of the master of woods, the chancellor of the Court began to appoint individual woodwards for each county.[157] Thus, before the end of the reign, the management of woods and the supervision of wood sales had begun to assume a definite role in Augmentations administration.[158]

Equally important was the movement which led to partial consolidation in 1547. The resultant union of the two youngest land courts was an obvious step in the right direction, but it stopped short of fundamental reform. While most of the apparent evils of the growing bureaucracy could have been eliminated by a unified department for all revenues, conditions being as they were there was little likelihood of establishing a central treasury.

---

[154] *Ibid.*, No. 2B, pt. 1, mems, 46*d.*–47. On Pope's indebtedness for the treasurer's office, see Chapter Ten, pp. 330–31.

[155] Both appointments, made early in 1543, were for life at an annual salary of £20 each: Tyndale's on January 16 and Farr's, as "Receyvour [more often called general receiver] of the woodsales and proufites of woodes bilonging to the Courte of Augmentacions," on the following March 29. D. L. 42/133, fols. 187*d.*, 207; Augm. Office, Misc. Books 235, fols. 127, 128. Farr continued to serve as keeper of the records of the Court, but Tyndale surrendered his receivership of Tewkesbury, Gloucestershire, in favor of James Hunter on May 1, 1543. *Ibid.* 235, fol. 114.

[156] *Ibid.* 236, fol. 46*d.* Joint appointment of April 16, 1545.

[157] *Ibid.*, fols. 43, 90*d.*, *passim.*

[158] Walter Farr was succeeded by his deputy, Richard Tyrrell, near the end of the reign. Upon the dissolution of the first Court of Augmentations he was pensioned as "late general Receyvour of the woodes belonginge to the courte of thaugmentacions," £66 13*s.* 4*d.* Augm. Office, Misc. Books 157, fol. 51*d.* This pension is not to be confused with an annuity of £56 3*s.* 4*d.* granted him during the same year in lieu of several life annuities which he had acquired, payable by the dissolved Court. *Ibid.* 336, fol. 236.

CHAPTER FIVE

REORGANIZATION: THE SECOND COURT OF AUGMENTATIONS

HE REORGANIZATION OF THE COURT OF AUGMENTATIONS IN January, 1547, was not just an isolated effort to bolster up a declining institution, although improvement in the Court's machinery of administration was certainly an objective of reorganization, nor was the action in any sense a repudiation of the existing framework of revenue administration which had developed under Cromwell's supervision. Actually the attainment of more unified control by the amalgamation of two separate revenue departments was a step toward the centralization of governmental functions which Cromwell had always envisioned. Over a number of years general lassitude had developed within the domestic administration, but the government had been too preoccupied with war and foreign affairs to undertake any significant improvements. While the council must certainly have realized that anything less than a thorough reorganization of the revenue structure would in the long run prove inadequate, no real solution to the problem was effected at this time. Even the later Marian reforms proved to be, at best, only an approximation of what was needed.

The change in the system of revenue administration introduced at the end of the reign of Henry VIII simply marked the beginning of a progressive reform movement that culminated in the extended Exchequer reforms of Mary and Elizabeth. The dissolution of the Court of Augmentations and the Court of General Surveyors in 1547 surprised no one, since it was preceded by a public investigation of the state of the national revenues. The resultant examination by the royal commissions revealed the true nature of the problem, which was essentially the same as that presented to the government late in 1552 when a subsequent commission reported the results of its inquiry. In point of fact, if the later developments are to be properly interpreted, they must be studied in the light of the attempts at renovation which had occurred during the two preceding reigns. The preliminary step was taken at the end of the year 1545, when a royal commission was appointed to examine the state of the revenues and to investigate the status of the various financial courts. During the following spring a second commission was set up to consider the problem of reforming the entire revenue administration and to render a report to the crown. The reorganization of the Court of Augmentations and the Court of General Surveyors came as a direct result of the two inquiries.

Ostensibly at least, both surveys were occasioned by the financial embarrassment of the government and were concerned primarily with discovering ways and means of increasing the national revenues. It was not unnatural, therefore, that the main charge of each was that of calling in arrears of revenue and collecting the outstanding debts due the crown. The first commission of mid-December, 1545, was authorized to call before it all the officers of the financial departments of the realm—the Courts of Exchequer, Duchy Chamber of Lancaster, Wards and Liveries, First Fruits and Tenths, General Surveyors, and Augmentations, or any others to which the revenues were appointed—and to survey the procedures of each court. All branches of revenue were investigated in order that a full examination of the crown income might be made and a comprehensive declaration of the financial state of the nation be presented. In addition, the commissioners were empowered to call in all the king's debtors, hear their excuses for non-payment, and when necessary, imprison those who refused to assume responsibility for proved indebtedness. By terms of not more than twenty years' purchase, land was accepted in lieu of cash settlement in cases of debts by individuals who were willing to pay but unable to raise the necessary funds.[1]

Two prominent members of the king's council, Sir Ralph Sadler and Sir Richard Rich, were chosen for the important assignment, at a salary of 20*s.* per day each for as long as they were engaged in the work of the commission. In fact, they had been so employed since the previous November, some three weeks prior to the delivery of the formal com-

---

[1] Signed bill of December 14, 1545. Pat. Rolls, 37 Henry VIII, pt. 13, mem. 32. Abstracted in *L. and P.*, XX, pt. 2, no. 1068(28) ; cf. *ibid.*, no. 1067(38).

mission.[2] Although Rich was more familiar than Sadler with the operation of the revenue system, having only recently resigned from the chancellorship of the Augmentations, both men had become closely identified
with government finance and administration. As war treasurers they
were certainly mindful of the financial needs of the state and were as
acutely aware of the evils of the expanding bureaucracy as they were
cognizant of the difficulties attendant upon attempts at simplification of
the financial structure. Neither minister, however, was imbued with the
zeal of the reformer,[3] as directors or ex-heads of departments seldom
are. Their chief function under the commission was to round up delinquent debtors and bring them to task. Having accomplished this, they
were content, apparently, to postpone the question of administrative reorganization for future investigation. Why should they invite governmental censure or even possibly provoke popular criticism unnecessarily
when they were not explicitly required to do so?

The final report of the commissioners, if indeed they ever made one,
has not survived; nevertheless, there is ample evidence that they were
quite busy in the collection of crown debts. During the ensuing year
they sat for about seven months in continuous session in order to effect
" the more speedy levying of revenues, debts and casualties to the King's
courts." [4] The fact that £32 9s. 2d. was spent by them for messenger
service during the spring of 1546, in addition to an extra £10 for
clerical expenses incurred through " calling in the King's debts and
making books and letters concerning them," suggests that most of their
effort was expended in apprehending debtors.[5] In fact, they had exe-

---

[2] The commission specified that their diets of 20s. a day should be payable from
November 24. Pat. Rolls, 27 Henry VIII, pt. 13, mem. 32.

[3] Rich, who had been general treasurer of the French war since relinquishing
the headship of the Augmentations, was more prominent in 1545 than was his
younger colleague. Both men were privy councillors, Rich especially being in
regular attendance. However Sadler, a former servant of Cromwell, had risen
rapidly in the royal service. To most historians he is best known as a diplomatist,
though he was prominent in domestic politics as principal secretary and chancellor
of the crown duchy of Lancaster and, later, as a trustworthy agent of Burghley
and Elizabeth. As a result of Cromwell's influence he was awarded a number of
lucrative offices under Henry VIII. At the time of his commission appointment
in 1545 he was master of the great wardrobe, clerk of the hanaper, and high
treasurer of wars against Scotland. For his declarations of accounts, see *L. and P.*,
XIX, pt. 1, no. 388(3) ; XX, pt. 2, no. 611. He had served on various administrative commissions including those for the sale of crown lands and for the audit
of special ministers' accounts. *Ibid.*, XXI, pt. 1, nos. 504(33), 970(14, 18), 1166
(12, 53) ; pt. 2, no. 332(43).

[4] Their salaries or " diets " of 20s. per day were paid from the revenues of the
Court of Augmentations by warrant of the king. Rich was allowed 190 days;
Sadler, 218. Augm. Office, Misc. Books 254, fol. 80; 255, fols. 85, 86.

[5] *Ibid.* 255, fols. 105, 106.

cuted their commission so well that it was suggested that they should be sent over to the Continent to organize the administration of Boulogne, which had been captured from France earlier in the war.[6] Practical suggestions for augmenting the revenues were always welcomed, but in the broader reaches of domestic administration extensive proposals for financial renovation were as yet premature. Foreign affairs, government finance, and a successful prosecution of the war were still the paramount concerns of the council during the first half of the year. Financial anxiety, which for several months had overshadowed everything else, was not abated until the conclusion of peace with France in June, 1546.[7] As long as the country was at war there was little likelihood of any serious consideration being given to a comprehensive reform program.

The first significant recommendation for a general review of the administration came from a special committee appointed in the spring of 1546 to continue the work of the earlier commission. It is difficult to understand why Rich and Sadler were not included in the second inquiry, since their own commission had never been officially terminated. Nevertheless, they probably had presented to the council a full declaration of the financial state of the nation, which had been their principal charge in the survey. Perhaps it was felt that, having once made a study of the problem, they had nothing further to contribute or that their services were more valuable in other endeavors.[8] Whatever the reason, their names were omitted from the June commission. Nominally headed by the lord chancellor, Sir Thomas Wriothesley, the commission was composed of five additional members and a professional technician—all outstanding ministers and prominent members of the council.[9] Included were such top-ranking Tudor administrators as Sir William Paulet,[10]

---

[6] Sir Edward Seymour, earl of Hertford, to Henry VIII, June 13, 1546, *L. and P.*, XXI, pt. 1, no. 1055.

[7] Peace with France was concluded by the Treaty of Camp on June 7, 1546, and proclaimed in both countries six days later. However, ratifications were not exchanged until July 17. The final conclusion of the war with Scotland came somewhat later. *Ibid.*, nos. 994, 1014, 1015, 1039, 1083, 1291, 1295; pt. 2, nos. 19, 28, 29, 34, 576.

[8] Both Rich and Sadler were active in conciliar duties during the year 1546. In addition to their regular work on the council they served on numerous important commissions, including the special committee authorizing sale of crown lands. *Ibid.*, XXI, pt. 1, nos. 91, 211, 375, 504(33), 836, 845, 963(158), 970(14, 18, 32), 1166 (12, 53), 1181, 1384(iii), 1433. They were also members of the select committee entrusted with the control of the royal stamp during the busy war months. Pat. Rolls, 38 Henry VIII, pt. 12, mem. 12.

[9] Commission of June 30, 1546, to examine the state of the revenues in the various courts. Signed bill, Pat. Rolls, 38 Henry VIII, pt. 7, mem. 31. This commission is fully abstracted in *L. and P.*, XXI, pt. 1, no. 1166(71).

[10] Paulet, who had been created Lord St. John in 1539 and earl of Wiltshire in 1550, became marquis of Winchester in 1551. A minister of broad administrative

master and steward of the household; Stephen Gardiner, bishop of Winchester; Sir Anthony Browne,[11] master of the horse; and the two principal secretaries, Sir William Paget and Sir William Petre.[12] To assist the commission as legal adviser the king appointed the brilliant young civil servant and administrator, Walter Mildmay, who was just beginning a long and illustrious career in the service of the state.[13] It was his first important assignment, but it led to knighthood and a lucrative office in the reconstituted Court of Augmentations, which he had helped to establish.

Like its predecessor this supplementary commission was to investigate the state of the revenues and arrange for the immediate payment of all debts and arrears in the financial courts, now grown " desperate " as a result of imprudent administration. The commissioners were to examine all the revenue courts, consider the nature and disposition of their revenues, call in debts and arrears due the crown, and command the officials of each court to pay over to the king's use such money as remained in their treasuries. Like Rich and Sadler they were authorized to distrain debtors, determine definite terms of payment, and compound for the collection of outstanding debts, which should be called in during the year. In addition to these charges they were required to investigate and punish officers of the revenue courts who were suspected of malfeasance or official negligence. Finally, they were expected to examine each offense or case of indebtedness on its own merits and report their findings to the crown. Mildmay was appointed to assist them in their

---

experience, he had headed the important office of wards from 1526 to 1540 and, after its departmentalization, became the first master of the Court of Wards and Liveries. As lord treasurer for more than twenty years during his later career, he was to become closely identified with the reform of the Exchequer, which he served from 1550 until his death in 1572.

[11] Browne was also captain of the gentlemen pensioners, or spears of the household, and chief justice in eyre of the forests north of the River Trent. He retained these offices until his death in 1548.

[12] During the last years of the reign Paget was one of the chief advisers of the crown, but his appointment to the chancellorship of the duchy of Lancaster did not come until July of 1547. On the other hand, Petre, as proctor or deputy vicar-general for Cromwell, had acquired some insight into administrative problems. He had been a zealous Dissolution agent and was doubtless quite familiar with the work of the financial courts. Already skilled in finance, Petre was to receive a life appointment as treasurer of the Court of First Fruits and Tenths in October, 1549. The details of his administrative career will soon be available in F. G. Emmison, *Tudor Secretary: Sir William Petre at Court and Home* (1961).

[13] Mildmay's work in the Augmentations and Exchequer is considered in a later chapter. See pp. 117–118, 454 *passim*, *infra*. At this time he had just completed his legal studies and found employment in the Court of Augmentations. His appointment to the commission was doubtless due to the influence of his father, Thomas Mildmay, and his brother, Thomas, Jr., who was an auditor in both the Augmentations and the duchy of Cornwall.

official proceedings; and decisions, either by him or by the commission regarding the payment of debts or the cancellation of recognizances, carried the validity of court warrants. The written commission was not issued until June 30, but by oral appointment its members had been engaged in their activities since the first of the previous April. In effect, therefore, the formal commission was instituted in order to legalize a work that was already some ninety days in progress and probably nearing completion at that time.

Apparently a chief objective of the inquiry had been a thorough investigation of negligence on the part of officials, with the intent of effecting the recovery of old debts and arrears that had accumulated in the several departments of revenue. The preamble of the commission explained that "notable sums" remained unpaid in the Exchequer, Duchy Chamber of Lancaster, Augmentations, General Surveyors, First Fruits and Tenths, and Wards and Liveries, mostly as a result of "the favour or negligence" of officials in those and "divers other courts." The king, being preoccupied with the war, was "enforced somewhat seriously to consider those our causes which might help to th'alleviation of our most weighty burden that ways, and to devise remedy for the speedy collection of the same debts." [14]

The effect of the investigation was quite wholesome. The commissioners were busy during the summer and autumn of 1546 in interviewing crown debtors and in arranging for the subsequent payment of debts. In some instances they themselves decided on the validity of the claims, either exonerating the individuals or assessing days of payment for the debts, but difficult cases were either referred back to the court having jurisdiction over them or passed on to the privy council for final judgment. [15] The debts ranged from a few shillings to over a

---

[14] *L. and P.*, XXI, pt. 1, no. 1166(71).

[15] Typical of the findings of the commissioners was the case of Geoffrey Chamber, for eight years surveyor and receiver-general of exchanged and purchased lands for the Court of Augmentations, 1536–44. He had died in office in May, 1544, indebted to the Court for £2,200 in unpaid receipts. Royal officials were bonded for just such a contingency as this, but the revenue courts had grown remiss in the actual prosecution of delinquent accounts, which were either entered on their records as arrears or ignored altogether. Discovering that the Augmentations had taken no action for the recovery of the debt, the commissioners located Chamber's sureties, called them to task, and arranged terms for suitable payments of their obligations. One of them consented to pay a part of his share in land and "stalle" the remainder of the debt for certain days; another bondman, in consideration of his known poverty, was allowed to pay the crown £20 annually until his share of £150 was paid. The Court of Augmentations was ordered to complete the proceedings, surveying and taking over the land offered and drawing up recognizances for the unpaid balance of the debt. The final settlement for surety by Thomas Barton brought the Court land to the value of £208 and a recognizance for £92,

thousand pounds each, and some of them were of five or six years standing.[16] The long list of debtors submitted to the king's council was drawn largely from the Augmentations, where arrears of revenues had been notoriously slow in coming in.[17] This was not particularly surprising in view of the fact that all departments of administration had grown progressively lax after the strong hand of Cromwell was removed. If Augmentations officials were more often found " negligent " than were those of the other revenue courts, it was because the largest proportion of the crown revenue was under their control.

The commission of 1546 sat from April of that year until January, 1547, and appears to have completed its plans for the reorganization of the revenue administration before the end of the reign. Although the lord chancellor was nominally the chairman of the commission, it is probable that the bulk of the investigation was done by Paulet and Mildmay, who were by far the most competent administrators of the group. Paulet, lord president of the council, was senior in administrative experience, if not in age, and his superior judgment in revenue matters gave him an enviable position in shaping the recommendations of the committee.[18] Nevertheless, like the other members, he was so occupied with other and more pressing affairs of state that he found little time to devote to the work of the commission.[19] Young Mildmay, on the other hand, had all the energy and ambition of the youthful enthusiast, determined to impress his superiors with his industry and knowledge.

As lawyer and civil servant Walter Mildmay had already successfully established himself. His talents lay chiefly in revenue finance, but like

---

payable in three installments, as the remainder of his portion of the debt. Augm. Office, Treas. Rolls of Accts., No. 2B, pt. 2, fol. 2d. *L. and P.*, XXI, pt. 1, nos. 1139, 1236, 1242, 1296. Exch., Accounts Various, 631/35. *Cal. State Papers, Domestic, 1591–1594*, p. 400; *ibid., 1595–1597*, p. 359.

[16] *L. and P.*, XXI, pt. 1, nos. 1032, 1111, 1120, 1128, 1139, 1151–52, 1157, 1165 (25), 1168, 1195, 1223, 1225, 1247, 1249, 1269, 1351, 1387, 1401, 1413, 1417; pt. 2, no. 199 (123, 124). Many of the returns were signed by Walter Mildmay, who played a prominent part in these investigations.

[17] A book of orders taken by the council with the king's debtors, in which the names of debtors, the dates of their appearance, and the final disposition of the debts are given. Most of the debts listed are for arrears of rent in the Augmentations and are for sums under £50. *L. and P.*, XXI, pt. 1, no. 1280. Some debts in the Exchequer were not cleared until 1550. *Cal. Pat. Rolls, Edward VI*, III, 292.

[18] On Paulet's activities, see Index to *L. and P.*, but especially XXI, pt. 1, nos. 359, 643 (65, 67, 68, 71, 74) ; pt. 2, nos. 28, 256, 771 (36).

[19] Paulet succeeded Charles Brandon, duke of Suffolk, as lord president of the council and warden and chief justice of the forests south of the River Trent upon his death in August, 1545. *Ibid.*, XX, pt. 2, no. 1068 (34). At the time of his appointment, Paulet was about sixty-one. Although senior to Petre, Paget and Wriothesley, he was younger than Gardiner and Browne, who were both in their sixties.

so many of his contemporaries he had entered that field through the back door of estate management. As early as 1540 he had secured employment in the Court of Augmentations, doubtless assisting his brother Thomas, who was an auditor in the eastern circuit.[20] His first major appointment came in May, 1543, when he and Francis Southwell were made auditors of all prests and foreign accounts.[21] At the time Southwell was already an auditor in the Exchequer, while Mildmay was in the employment of the crown as a royal auditor.[22] He was still under twenty-five years of age,[23] with a long and active career ahead of him. For the next forty-six years, until his death in 1589, he was one of England's ablest administrators, although he never distinguished himself particularly in general politics.

His rise in the civil service was rapid after 1543. He continued as auditor of the prests and as general auditor of the Court of Survey during the remainder of the reign, and after December, 1545, held one of the three directorships of that court.[24] In June, 1545, over a year prior to the commission appointment, he was made a joint auditor of the Augmentations [25] and, before the end of the year, appointed auditor of crown lands beyond the River Trent in the duchy of Lancaster.[26] Mildmay was probably knighted at the beginning of the new reign, for he was being styled " Sir Walter " by September, 1547.[27] With his appointment to a responsible position in the second Court of Augmentations his future as a civil servant was assured.

If the commissioners tendered a formal report to the government, that document has not been preserved. Since their principal charge was that of raising money by the expedient of forcing crown debtors to pay what they owed immediately, a written declaration of their work was unneces-

---

[20] *Ibid.*, XV, no. 763.

[21] On the origin and development of the auditorship of prests, see pp. 143–50, *infra.*

[22] *L. and P.*, XVII, nos. 267, 1154(63).

[23] The exact date of Mildmay's birth is uncertain; but if the date suggested by his biographer is acceptable, he would have been only twenty-three at the time of his appointment as auditor of the prests. Sidney Lee, " Sir Walter Mildmay," in *D. N. B.*

[24] Mildmay was one of the three general surveyors directing the Court of Survey from December, 1545, until January, 1547, when the court was merged with the Augmentations. Richardson, *Tudor Chamber Administration, 1485–1547*, 366, 368, 369, 489.

[25] Augm. Office, Misc. Books 236, fol. 192. Although Walter did most of the work, he and his brother Thomas held the office jointly until the reorganization the following year.

[26] He succeeded to the duchy office upon the death of Thomas Burgoyne, in September, 1546. *L. and P.*, XXI, pt. 2, no. 199(12). He was, in turn, succeeded in this office by his eldest son, Anthony. Somerville, *History of the Duchy of Lancaster*, I, 437.

[27] *L. and P.*, XXI, pt. 2, no. 754. Augm. Office, Misc. Books 256, fols. 81*d.*, 97.

sary. They collected in cash what debts they could from responsible debtors, authorized recognizances for those who were unable to pay in full, and turned in a list of unpaid debts to the council for further processing if the king so desired.[28] Whatever the recommendations for the reform of the revenue courts were, they must have been presented orally. Certainly the council was more concerned with the financial condition of the country than with anything else during the spring and summer of 1546. War expenses had been mounting steadily, despite every effort at national economy. In early September, 1545, chancellor Wriothesley had complained of the continuous drain on the treasuries, which had disbursed over £560,000 within the past fiscal year.[29] By the middle of the month he was beginning to feel desperate in his efforts to meet the financial demands that were coming in from all quarters and reminded the other councillors that, being fully familiar with the state of affairs, they too were responsible for the raising of additional funds. " This year and last year the King has spent about 300,000*l*.," he informed the council; " his subsidy and benevolence ministering scant 300,000*l*.; and, the lands being consumed and the plate of the realm molten and coined, I lament the danger of the time to come. There is to be repaid in Flanders as much more than all the rest. The scarcity of corn is such that, except in Norfolk, wheat is at 20*s*. the qr., and little of it to be had. Though the King might have a greater grant than the realm could bear, it would do little to the continuance of these charges this winter, most of the subsidy being paid, the revenues received beforehand, and more borrowed from the Mint than will be repaid these four or five months; and yet ' you write to me still pay, pay, prepare for this and that.' " [30] Within a fortnight he confided to Paget that the chamber treasury was empty, though the mint was still " marvellously " serving the government. " God help us," he concluded, " for, for mine own part, it maketh me weary of my life." [31] Still he contrived to pay bills as they came due, though the state of the revenues, as shown by the weekly declarations of the treasurers, was progressively discouraging as the war dragged wearily on to a conclusion.

Though very few proposals for a solution to the problem were forthcoming, except in ingenious schemes for raising additional revenue, some consideration was given to the question of the increasing losses incurred

[28] Most of the debts contained in the book of orders, referred to in note 17, were apparently those presented by the commission. *L. and P.*, XXI, pt. 1, no. 1280.

[29] *Ibid.*, XX, pt. 2, no. 324.

[30] Thomas Wriothesley to the council, September 14, 1545, *ibid.*, no. 336. See also *ibid.*, nos. 211–13, 221, 241, 354, 358, 425, 746, 769.

[31] Wriothesley to Secretary William Paget, September 27, 1545, *ibid.*, no. 453.

through the indebtedness of negligent ministers. Among the " causes for consultation " of the November parliament at least one remedy was projected; all treasurers and receivers of crown revenue should be bound under "a great penalty " to account annually. As a further precaution against those who might die in office before a final reckoning, the heirs and executors would be held fully accountable for all unpaid revenues which normally would be leviable on the estates of the deceased ministers.[32]

Throughout the trying months of 1545–1546 the king was never discouraged, confident that when money was needed it would be forthcoming. Most of the ministers shared his optimism, though they were not quite so sure how large amounts were to be raised in time to meet immediate demands. Actually there was no reason for acute financial embarrassment. The country was prosperous and crown revenues were not all allocated for specific purposes. The problem was not so much the lack as the temporary deficiency of money. Debts and arrears of revenues would bring in a goodly sum, the king argued. The remainder could be raised as required by short-term loans on the Continent. All were agreed that parliamentary taxation should come only as a last resort. " All possible shift shall be made for money," the council in London informed the king early in September, 1546. But the treasuries of the realm had very little surplus, they explained; even their one reliable source, the mint, was dry. " Our daily travail is about the King's debts, and we send out many letters for more debtors." [33] In view of the financial extremities of the moment, it is not difficult to understand why so much time was given to the raising of revenue and so little to the administration of it.

Those, however, who were aware of the financial problems must also have been conscious of the prevailing weaknesses of the revenue administration. The system, while it had the obvious advantage of being thorough, was at the same time bureaucratic, expensive, and top-heavy. Overlapping in jurisdiction and authority, each of the revenue courts had built up its own intricate hierarchy, with little or no consideration for the administrative needs of the nation as a whole. Sinecures developed,

---

[32] *Ibid.*, XXI, pt. 2, no. 344(2).

[33] *Ibid.*, no. 19. Crown debts in Flanders further complicated an awkward situation. " You know the importance of this matter of money and how slowly it comes in," Wriothesley observed at the end of the month. "I would to God the King had a store, as I trust to see him have shortly,—the world is so doubtful and dangerous." *Ibid.*, no. 172. On the success of the government's financial policy at this time, see W. C. Richardson, " Some Financial Expedients of Henry VIII," *Economic History Review*, New Series, VII (August, 1954), 33–48.

offices multiplied, while in the broader ranges of collection, audit, and expenditure, inevitable duplication of ministerial functions was the result. Strong centralized control, so essential to the efficient operation of the Tudor government, was declining during the last years of Henry VIII, and the absence of that co-ordinated direction was the prevailing weakness of the administration during the two ensuing reigns. Chapuys, the imperial ambassador, writing from Louvain upon hearing of Henry's last illness, accurately appraised the situation. " The King's death would be more inopportune for us now than twenty years ago," he commented, "and the Earl and Admiral are the only nobles of age and ability to undertake affairs." [34] Lack of outstanding leadership in the council, as well as division among its members, was a weakness already apparent. Amid the impending affairs of the new regime administrative reform was not likely to assume a significant role.

Such reformation as occasionally was attempted was never thorough. In this, as in other aspects of administration, the government never really came to grips with basic facts. Sometimes it set up new rules, often as ineffectual as the old, to be indifferently enforced, but usually it did no more than modify the structure here and there or, at most, patch a self-perpetuating system. Corrective measures were frequently inspired by a number of reasons, not the least of which was the financial need of the government; perennial abuses, too, called out continually for remedial action: pensions, accumulated debts, delay in the collection of revenue, and operational inefficiency. Periodic investigations by the king's council were the normal reply to the practical reformer whose voice carried enough authority to be heard. A gesture was made, but rarely was much accomplished. Nobody actually wanted reform, and in the end the vested interests of the many triumphed over the reforming zeal of the few. The attitude, like the administration itself, was essentially medieval. Procrastination prevailed, offices multiplied, and the inertia of bureaucracy continued. Perhaps Cromwell's achievements were the exception rather than the rule. Even great statesmen like Winchester and Burghley accepted the situation pretty much as they found it, realizing that fundamental change was, after all, next to impossible.

Such reform schemes as were suggested in 1545 and 1546 were concerned primarily, as might be expected, with effecting either a saving

---

[34] Chapuys to Mary of Hungary, January 29, 1547, *Spanish Calendar*, VIII, no. 386; *L. and P.*, XXI, pt. 2, no. 756. The earl and admiral referred to were Sir Edward Seymour, earl of Hertford, and Sir John Dudley, viscount Lisle, the future dukes of Somerset and Northumberland who, as directors of the state and great "stirrers of heresy," led the religious revolt against the church under Edward VI.

in national expenditure or an increase in the crown revenue. One comprehensive plan for the " diminution " of the king's charges proposed a single revenue department, the Exchequer, for all finances, thus eliminating the expenses of multiple agencies of this type. Intimating that officials of the fiscal courts had grown inefficient, the author recommended the appointment of a few " honest men " to survey all the king's lands.[35] Proposals of this kind, however, were not taken seriously, since their main objective was to enrich the designer rather than to benefit the government. The only major reform of the administration was the complete reorganization of the mints, begun in April, 1545, and continued into the following year.[36] Changes in the administration at this time were not seriously considered simply because they appeared to be unnecessary. The real breakdown in the administrative system came later, when corruption among governmental employees became so prevalent that it could no longer be ignored.

While no systematic checkup on the negligence of public officials was attempted, several measures for improving efficiency were nevertheless undertaken. In recent years the king had been too engrossed in religious and foreign affairs to give adequate attention to all the details of government which formerly had been handled by Cromwell or by responsible ministers thoroughly trained under the earlier regime of Henry VII. Financial officials were not always bonded for their offices, nor were their accounts systematically audited as in the past. In fact, conscientious ministers like Rich, Sadler, Brian Tuke, John Gostwick, or Stephen Vaughan had to petition the council for final reckonings.[37] In the commission of May, 1546, for the survey and public audit of the accounts of the jewel house it was revealed that Sir John Williams, then treasurer

[35] A proposal, " Howe the Kyngs Majestie maye gather a great thesaure without selling or abatyng any parte of his revenuez, but rather augmentyng the same by dymynicion of his charges, the doyng whereof shall redounde to the unyversall welthe of his subjects." Cotton. MS., Titus B. vi, fol. 213.

[36] *L. and P.*, XX, pt. 1, no. 620(11–26, 34, 36–44); XXI, pt. 1, nos. 650(32–35, 37, 48), 716(1–8), 1166(53); pt. 2, no. 476(93). On a scheme for the establishment of another mint at Boulogne or Calais, see *ibid.*, XX, pt. 2, Appendix, no. 16. See p. 25, *supra*.

[37] Special accounts such as those for the jewel house, the wardrobe, the mints, the Merchant Adventurers, the privy purse, Boulogne, Calais, Ireland, treasurers of wars, and accounts of financial agents on the Continent were audited by royal commissions appointed for that purpose. *L. and P.*, XX, pt. 2, no. 910(81); XXI, pt. 1, nos. 504(33), 970(18), 1166(12, 53); pt. 2, nos. 476(39, 41), 648(48). As special paymasters of the crown, ministers like Rich, Sadler, Vaughan, and William Dansell were anxious to have their accounts fully cleared before the interested parties were dead or the transactions in question had been forgotten. Until they had received their *quietus est* they were still legally liable for receipts and expenditures of money for which they may have kept no records.

of the king's jewels, had never been "perfectly charged," no survey of the office having been taken since it was vacated by the attainder of Cromwell six years earlier.[38] Similar commissions to take the accounts of other finance ministers were issued during the year.[39] In the case of the chamber, the treasurer's accounts remained unaudited for almost a dozen years.[40]

Misconduct and waste on the part of public ministers were more often due to remissness and the common disregard for high standards than to wanton neglect of duty. The majority of the offenders hauled before the council or examined privately by the commissioners were guilty of no greater crime than overt negligence or continual procrastination.[41] The bulk of crown debts outstanding in 1546 was either arrears of rents, toward which the revenue courts had long been too lenient, or special obligations, about which under normal circumstances nobody would have worried. The debt of Sir Philip Hoby, gentleman of the privy chamber and master of the ordnance, amounting to £1,172 18s. 6½d., was quite typical of those suddenly called in. Hoby had purchased land through the Court of Augmentations for which he was paying at the rate of £100 per year. When the king needed the money a new settlement was negotiated, under terms more favorable to the crown.[42]

In spite of all the things that were "amiss in the realm" at the conclusion of the reign, there seems to have been no particular opposition to the existing revenue system.[43] As basic treasuries of the realm the financial institutions were under the observation of the council, but otherwise they were left alone, independent of any centralized co-ordina-

[38] Pat. Rolls, 38 Henry VIII, pt. 7, mem. 30; 1 Edward VI, pt. 4, mems. 23d.–24d.

[39] The accounts of the cofferer of the household had not been heard since August 1, 1527, while Sir Martin Bowes, an undertreasurer of the Tower mint, was called on to account for sums received in May, 1532. *Ibid.*, 38 Henry VIII, pt. 7, mem. 29; *Cal. Pat. Rolls, Edward VI*, V, 398.

[40] Under Henry VII the chamber accounts had been subjected to frequent audits, but since John Heron's tenure in that office a general laxity had developed as a part of the pronounced chamber decline. William Cavendish rendered no account for his entire period of office from February, 1546, until just before his death in 1557. Pat. Rolls, 3 and 4 Philip and Mary, pt. 3, mem. 17d.

[41] *L. and P.*, XXI, pt. 1, nos. 150, 993, 1001, 1032, 1157, 1247, 1249; pt. 2, nos. 417, 618.

[42] *Ibid.*, pt. 1, no. 1165(25); pt. 2, no. 647(53). Hoby was appointed master of the ordnance in the north on May 12, 1545. Dasent (ed.), *Acts of the Privy Council*, I, 159. *D. N. B.*

[43] In the famous "Complaynt of Roderyck Mors," written about 1543, the abuses listed include the purely imaginary as well as the legitimate ills of society; "extortion, oppression and bribery" were charges laid at the doors of the courts, which were "too many" and "filthily ministered." The Courts of Exchequer, Marshalsea, Wards and Liveries, and Augmentations were especially criticized but not for the reasons that eventually caused their decay. *L. and P.*, XX, pt. 2, no. 733.

tion. Of the six revenue institutions that came under the review of the commission, the Exchequer and the Duchy Chamber were the least subject to attack. The oldest of the group, supported by the force of tradition and time-honored usage, they were sufficiently entrenched to weather any storm of criticism directed against them. Though neither was free from internal weaknesses, public opinion was more in their favor. Both institutions had been relegated to a secondary role in Tudor administration by the rise of chamber finance and the accelerated development of the Cromwellian system. Whereas, the duchy organization had maintained its former position without too much loss of revenue and prestige,[44] the Exchequer had suffered from the ruthless competition more hardly. With the revival of the king's chamber and the rise of the office, and later Court, of General Surveyors, it had suffered a financial eclipse from which it could not recover as long as its chief competitor, the Court of Augmentations, reigned supreme. The other two courts— Wards and Liveries, and First Fruits and Tenths—were likewise Tudor creations, which had encroached on the older institutions. But they were smaller and, by the very nature of their restricted functions, of a more limited jurisdiction. Furthermore, the problem was chiefly one of unification, not so necessary for the special categories of casual revenue, but fundamental to the most effective administration of the landed revenues of the kingdom. Since between them the Court of Augmentations and the Court of General Surveyors had charge of the major portion of the crown demesne, any scheme of reorganization would involve an extensive alteration of these two pillars of the revenue structure.

Neither of the two courts had changed appreciably in either structure or organization since their original foundation. However, a decade of growth had added considerably to the gross receipts of the Augmentations, particularly through the sale of crown lands and the confiscation of chantries, which was begun in 1545.[45] The fact that the Court was put in charge of the survey and dissolution of these institutions was, in effect, an expression of confidence by the government which favored the Aug-

[44] The duchy administration had been greatly strengthened during the reign of Henry VII by its reorganization under the chancellorship of Sir Reginald Bray. Richardson, *Tudor Chamber Administration, 1485–1547*, 24–27, 278. The augmentation of duchy revenues resulting from Reformation profits was not appreciable, though such increase as appeared was certainly due " less to improvements in existing sources of revenue than to the provision of new." Somerville, *History of the Duchy of Lancaster*, I, 305.

[45] Authorized by act of parliament, 37 Henry VIII, c. 4(1545), for the dissolution of colleges, free chapels, chantries, hospitals, fraternities, brotherhoods, guilds, and stipendiary priests. *L. and P.*, XX, pt. 2, no. 850(4). Surrenders of chantries and hospitals, however, had been coming into the Augmentations since the previous May. *Ibid.*, pt. 1, nos. 718, 762.

mentations in various ways during that year.[46] In January, 1545, the head of the Court was authorized to appoint minor officials in the administration without consulting the crown, perhaps as a guarantee that lesser vacancies would in the future be filled more promptly.[47] About the same time, he was empowered to grant pensions to members of the dissolved colleges, hospitals, free chapels, and chantries. The explanation for such a significant delegation of power, as given in the royal warrant or " byll " of authorization, clearly indicated the king's attitude regarding administrative detail. Unlike his conscientious father who retained a personal control over every aspect of government, Henry VIII was neither systematic nor meticulous in affairs of state. Bored with minutiae, he had little inclination to spend time in routine work which could be done as well by others; moreover, pensions were becoming something of a royal chore. His motive was probably more the avoidance of work that he found undesirable than any consideration for improvement of the system. The warrant provided for the appointment by the chancellor of commissions under the great seal of the Court to " practyce conclude and agree " with the inmates of houses at the time of surrender, or if that were unnecessary, North was given full power to award such pensions at his own discretion as " you shall thinke meate and convenient." As in the case of monastic pensions, all awards were for life or until such time as the recipient was given an office or beneficc equivalent to the clear annual value of his annuity. Speed and increased efficiency in pension procedures were intimated:

> Forasmuche as we considering the causes of our waightye affayres cannot without greate paynes and unquyetnes conuieniently attende and assigne the said annuities and livinges to the said personnes nor to assigne the warrauntes of the patentys thereof to be made and graunted to theym with suche conuenient spede as our pleasure is the same to be don for the spedie dispatche ease and quietnes of the same personnes . . .[48]

[46] The certificates, inventories, and indentures made by the commissioners for the survey of chantries, etc., were returned to the Court of Augmentations. *Ibid.,* XXI, pt. 1, nos. 299, 302(30). The commissioners were assisted in the making of their accounts by the various clerks of the Court.

[47] Pat. Rolls, 36 Henry VIII, pt. 18, mem. 11; Augm. Office, Misc. Books 236, fol. 47*d*. Certain restrictions were attached to the authorization, including the proviso that the king could designate appointees, if action were taken within six weeks after the vacancy occurred.

[48] Undated warrant of 36 Henry VIII. Augm. Office, Misc. Books 236, fols. 58, 58*d*. A copy of this warrant, recited in full, is also included among the decrees and orders of the Augmentations for Hilary term, 1545. *Ibid.* 104, pt. 2, fol. 109. See also special authority granted in May, 1546, *L. and P.,* XXI, pt. 1, no. 970(16).

Not only did the Court grant pensions by letters patent under its own seal but it occasionally provided salary increases for its personnel, when the crown was negligent in providing for cost of living adjustments. In keeping with accepted governmental policy most officials of the Augmentations had, from time to time, been given special pensions or annuities to supplement their regular fees. Some of these indeed were awarded only a short while before the Court's dissolution.[49] However, such salary increases were not out of proportion to the increased cost of living which plagued all crown ministers in the sixteenth century, and in relation to salary adjustments in other government departments, the increments were not unwarranted. Admittedly expenses of administration were high, but there is no indication that costs in the Courts of Augmentations and General Surveyors were proportionately any greater than in other branches of government.

As interpreted by the king and council, efficiency and economy were the keynotes of reform. Commissioners appointed to study the problem were expected to recommend minor technical improvements in the administration rather than anything approximating radical alterations of the revenue system. While they could criticize, interpret, and suggest, they actually had no power to do more. Theirs was the difficult task of submitting a constructive program of reform, which would, at the same time, placate the various conflicting groups involved. Whatever the dictates of pure reason, the practical obstacles to any fundamental change in the revenue system must have been clearly apparent to this and later commissions, the primary function of which was to inject economy measures into a growing bureaucracy. Any significant change would affect countless officials and their friends and families who had gained vested interests in the institutions they served. The most obvious recommendation, and that likely to invoke the least hardship for everyone concerned, was the solution finally hit upon—the incorporation of all newly acquired lands and property under the administration of one department.

In spite of a few difficulties, such a reformation involved little alteration in the machinery of land management and a minimum of dislocation within the existing system. In fact, the ease with which the union of the Courts of Augmentations and General Surveyors was effected was due primarily to the close similarity of the two institutions. Their lands frequently lay side by side; their jurisdiction was comparable; and the various categories of revenue controlled by them were the same, while

---

[49] Among others was an annuity of 40 marks granted to Sir Edward North, chancellor of the Augmentations, in March, 1545. *L. and P.*, XX, pt. 1, no. 465 (90).

structurally both were fashioned after one design. However unlike in origin and development, they were identical in everything else but name. Had the movement toward departmentalism been less pronounced in 1536 the older organization of general surveyors might then have been absorbed by the Augmentations instead of continuing independently.

Since its foundation as a court of record by act of parliament in 1542, the revenue department of general surveyors had expanded rapidly. Originally a government division of audit for accounts of specified revenues withdrawn from the Exchequer, it had emerged under Henry VII an integral part of the chamber system. The sole unit for new acquisitions of crown property, the department in succeeding years became essentially an administrative agency, the revenues of which were paid into the king's chamber instead of the traditional Exchequer. Although departmentally independent, it became a financial adjunct to the chamber treasury, from which the bulk of chamber revenue was derived. Prior to 1542 the general surveyors office had served the state as a centralizing agency for the control of crown lands, woods, and income received from the extension of the royal prerogative, as well as certain blocks of revenue that had been incorporated in the chamber administration. Typical of the latter category were special revenues from wood sales, fines for escaped prisoners, yearly surpluses of certain designated customs, and issues of such offices as royal exchanges, the great wardrobe, the butlerage, and the hanaper of the chancery.[50] However, the greater part of the income of the general surveyors, whether as office or court, came directly from the chamber estates which had increased so remarkably since the accession of Henry VII. Principally they included the county palatinates of Chester and Flint, the principality and marches of Wales, the duchies of Cornwall, Bedford, and York, the earldom of Richmond, and the lands acquired by the crown through escheat and attainder. In addition to this landed revenue, it administered specific categories of extraneous revenues assigned to it from time to time, such as arrears, debts, prizes taken at sea,[51] and profits from land

---

[50] Richardson, *Tudor Chamber Administration, 1485–1547*, Appendix IV. On the organization and early history of the court see especially pp. 248–82, 362–74. Officially it was styled the "Court of General Surveyors of the King's Lands and Revenues," but commonly it was referred to simply as the "Court of Survey."

[51] By commission of October, 1545, all lawful prizes captured at sea and profits resulting from the sale thereof were put under the jurisdiction of the Court of General Surveyors. These revenues were payable in "a grosse summe" to the chamber treasury. Pat. Rolls, 37 Henry VIII, pt. 18, mem. 26. The lands and revenues under the jurisdiction of the general surveyors can be traced through the various commissions, e. g., the commission of February, 1511, *L. and P.*, I, pt. 1, no. 709(14) and acts of parliament regulating the office: 3 Henry VIII, c. 23; 4 Henry VIII, c. 18; 6 Henry VIII, c. 24; 7 Henry VIII, c. 7; 14–15 Henry

sales, wood sales, and the mints. Likewise, all lands acquired by the crown through purchase or exchange prior to 1536 were included within its jurisdiction. During Wolsey's ascendancy the department was the key agency in the reformed administration, representing the maximum of efficiency engendered by the Cardinal. Even later, in the 1530's, until such time as the Augmentations assumed pre-eminence, the office still ranked as one of the great revenue departments of the government, overshadowing the duchy of Lancaster and the national Exchequer; after 1542 the only serious rival of the Court of Survey in the field of land administration was the Augmentations.

With almost identical functions and procedures, the Courts of General Surveyors and Augmentations were no less similar in organization. The council of the General Surveyors, like that of the Augmentations, was composed of the major officers of the court: three general surveyors of crown lands, who collectively constituted "the first and principal officer"; the treasurer of the chamber, who was always treasurer and second officer; an attorney; and a master of woods, with authority to appoint various assistants or deputies under him. An indefinite number of receivers and auditors were authorized by the original act of creation, but at least twenty-seven receivers, five general receivers, four chamberlains, and other farmers were mentioned in the various schedules. Before its dissolution the court had no fewer than twenty-four auditors and sixty receivers, of whom a number also held offices in the Augmentations.[52] As in the Court of Augmentations, the court had a permanent clerk, usher, keeper of the records, and messengers, with fees and salaries simliar to those paid in the Duchy Chamber of Lancaster.

Sir John Daunce, Sir Richard Pollard, and Sir Thomas Moyle, general surveyors, were continued in office as heads of the Court of Survey, though their appointments brought no change in function. Daunce was given priority status as chief director at £200 per year, with special license to be absent from his office without any reduction in salary.[53] Daunce and Pollard were succeeded respectively by Walter Mildmay and Sir Richard Southwell, both of whom retained office until the abolition of the court. After the death of Sir Brian Tuke in November of 1545, the treasurership was held for a short period by Sir Anthony Rous, pending the appointment of Sir William Cavendish, the last incumbent

---

VIII, c. 15; 27 Henry VIII, c. 62; and the final act for the creation of the court, 33 Henry VIII, c. 39.

[52] List of officers of the Court of General Surveyors, *L. and P.*, XX, pt. 2, Appendix no. 13.

[53] Bills under the signet in April, 1542. Duchy of Lancaster Records 42/133, fols. 122, 133, 183, 209 (hereinafter cited as D. L.).

during the period under survey. William Stanford as attorney and John Mynne as master of woods completed the court's roster of principal officials.[54] With the natural increase in business and personnel the old quarters in the Prince's Council Chamber in the palace of Westminster became too small. Shortly before the merger of 1547 new chambers, situated at the upper end of Westminster Hall, were provided for the Court of Survey, together with a separate building to house its growing accumulation of records. As in the Court of Augmentations, original simplicity of organization had given way to bureaucratic expansion. Since both courts were considerably overstaffed, reduction of personnel was obviously a sound reason for the proposed union.

While the government seemed to have been concerned primarily with effecting an economy in administration, it certainly was aware of the growing popular criticism directed against the revenue courts. Confusion and waste as a result of overlapping jurisdiction were both particularly objectionable. Dilatory methods, improper supervision, delay in the consideration of petitions, excessive fees charged for transcripts, privy seals, and other court services, and slowness of litigation were not uncommon complaints. Consolidation alone would not have necessarily eliminated any of these evils, but a single institution designed to perform the work of both courts might have been expected materially to improve the administration.

The 1536 parliament imposed a legal check on the office of general surveyors, by prohibiting further acquisitions of crown property procured either by purchase or exchange. Consequently, all lands acquired in such manner after that date were specifically assigned to the Augmentations.[55] Save for property of attainted persons, the possessions under the jurisdiction of the general surveyors remained fairly constant after the Dissolution. Thus the only monastic spoils awarded to the Court of Survey upon its erection were those houses suppressed by act of attainder, which incidentally included some of the wealthiest monasteries of the north.[56]

---

[54] *L. and P.*, XVII, no. 362(7–10). Upon his death in 1543 Mynne was succeeded in the mastership of woods by Robert Heneage.

[55] Both the proposed legislation of 1531 and the statute actually passed in 1536 failed to assign purchased and exchanged lands to the general surveyors office. Act concerning the King's General Surveyors, 27 Henry VIII, c. 62, sec. vi. These revenues were specifically given to the Augmentations, 27 Henry VIII, c. 27, sec. vi.

[56] See p. 53, *supra*. Lands accruing to the crown by act of attainder had been under the control of the Court of Survey from the very beginning; consequently this particular jurisdiction was guaranteed by the statute creating the Court of Augmentations.

To the revenues derived from these sources should be added the proceeds from the sale of crown lands, a policy inaugurated in 1539. Unfortunately, the declarations of accounts of the court have not been preserved for the period prior to its amalgamation with the Augmentations. However, records for the fiscal year 1541–42, when the office became a court, show the clear annual value of crown lands administered by the general surveyors to have amounted to approximately £38,000.[57] It will be observed that this total included the monastic lands and other properties acquired through process of attainder. Since the miscellaneous revenues, most of which were not derived directly from land, that is, the casual as opposed to the certain revenues, amounted to but a few thousand pounds a year, it would appear that the Augmentations gained something over £40,000 in yearly receipts.

Officialism, conflicting jurisdiction, and unwarranted increases in personnel are normal imperfections of bureaucracy, and the Tudor system was no exception to the rule. Simplicity of organization had been the chief merit of the informal practices of Henry VII before stereotyped procedures and differentiated functions were introduced, but departmentalism had changed all that. Elasticity gave way to set regulations, instituted as often as not by statute authority. Patronage and a cheap labor supply, of course, encouraged the multiplication of offices. A great many of these changes, however, were normal results of over-rapid development. In the expansion of governmental functions more offices were required, resulting in inevitable duplication. When the state was prosperous and everybody office-hungry, jobs were apt to be continued long after the need for them had disappeared. The natural impulse of administrators was not only to create new positions indiscriminately but to avoid the abolition of old ones as long as possible.

All the revenue courts came to be overstaffed, though not so much in the central offices at Westminster as in the counties where the field ministers were often too numerous for effective administration. In this respect the Court of Survey was possibly the worst offender, since it had developed no uniform regional or district organization. When estates were taken over by the court they usually retained their former organization and administrative staffs; whether old lands or new, they were administered as distinct and independent units, with no unified control even on a county basis. Consequently, the number of field ministers was so large—auditors, receivers, chamberlains, stewards, and supervisors, to mention only a few of the more important—that any effective supervision of their activities by the central office was quite impossible.

[57] Add. MS. 32469.

Moreover, there was practically no co-ordination among the many minor officials who served in the local areas where crown lands happened to be situated. In most instances such regional supervisors as there were suffered from a lack of delegated authority. Since Cromwell's death no one had seriously considered the question of administrative integration as a possible approach to ultimate reform. Even in the preamble of the patent of dissolution of the two courts this problem was not mentioned.

Instead, the patent stressed the confusion that had arisen as a result of concurrent jurisdiction between the two institutions. Despite statutory attempts to delimit the respective spheres of authority, no official interpretation had been agreed on. The implication was quite clear:

> We haue latelye perused and seen and by the same do euydently and playnlye vnderstand that hytherto ther haue not been any suche certayne rules and ordinaunces sett forthe in writing wherby our seuerall Officers and ministres of the saide Courtes might perfectlye knowe howe and in what manner our saide honours Castelles manours landes tenementes and hereditamentes beyng within the seuerall surveys of the saide Courte[s] and the proffittes therupon rising ought to be aunswerid to vs, So that suche ambyguytios [*sic*] and doubtes haue rysen amongest our Officers of the saide Courtes forlacke of good rules and orders to theym prescribed that they coulde not by any meanes knowe directlye howe to order the same accordinge to our expectacon and their dueties. By reason meane and occasion wherof our saide honours Castelles manours landes tenementes and heridamentes haue been verye moche and greatlye disorderyd. And the reuenues issues and proffittes of the same very euyll aunswerid to vs wherby hathe ensued great detryment and losse to vs and to the reuenues of our Crowne.[58]

Valid as this criticism undoubtedly was, it overlooked the most obvious reason for bringing the bulk of the demesne lands within a single system, namely, the extension of the principle of county administration to include the possessions formerly under the general surveyors.

Efficiency in land administration and expedition in revenue collection were guaranteed in the Augmentations by the adoption of the county unit in which the regional receivers and auditors worked together to effect co-ordinated control. In contrast to that simplified procedure, the Court of Survey still used the medieval organization, based on the feudal system of independent units, which had been retained by the crown in the management of its landed possessions. As noted earlier, the

[58] Pat. Rolls, 38 Henry VIII, pt. 5, mem. 15.

ancient county palatinates, duchies, and principalities constituted the nucleus of the hereditary royal demesne, which Henry VII had withdrawn from the Exchequer and put under the department of general surveyors of crown lands.[59] As new lands were constantly acquired, chiefly by process of attainder, they continued to be administered as proprietary additions in accordance with the medieval principle that the scattered estates of the magnates of the realm should be regarded feudally as a collection of self-contained units, irrespective of their geographical location. Adhering rigidly to that practice the Court of Survey, consequently, had added a number of such proprietary units to the original chamber possessions, which were named after the families from whom they were acquired. At the time of its dissolution in 1547, the court still retained jurisdiction over some two dozen such groupings, each administered as a separate unit.[60] The Surrey lands, which came to the crown through the attainder of the poet, Henry Howard, earl of Surrey, and his father, the duke of Norfolk, were taken over just after the merger of the two courts, and consequently, broken up into their natural divisions, each administered under the county system.[61] Likewise administered as separate holdings were " purchased lands," " exchanged lands," and the property of those monasteries the surrender of which was effected by the attainder of their respective heads.[62] Despite the particular care given to the management of attainted revenues, leakages were bound to occur; moreover, in some cases years elapsed before such losses were discovered. One of the final efforts of the court in the autumn of 1546 was an attempt to bring in certain uncollected revenues from the former estates of William Holton, attainted.[63]

[59] Pp. 21–22, *supra*.

[60] To those administrative divisions were sometimes attached individual castles, manors, lordships, and honors situated in the same locality. Chief among the historical family units were Abergavenny lands, Beaumont lands, Bedford lands, Berkeley lands, Buckingham lands, Cardinal's (Wolsey) lands, Darcy lands, Exeter lands, Hussey lands, Northumberland lands, Salisbury lands, Somerset lands (called " Coparcioners landes "), Spencer lands, Stanley lands, Richmond lands, and York lands. To this list should be added the property of some of the wealthier persons attainted in the 1530's: Sir Francis Bigod, Sir John Bulmer, Sir Robert Constable, Sir Thomas Cromwell (Essex lands), Lord Leonard Grey, John Hallam, Sir Stephen Hamerton, George Hudswell, George Lumley, John Mantell, Sir Thomas More, Thomas Moigne, Sir John Neville, and John Wyvell.

[61] The earl of Surrey and his father, Thomas, duke of Norfolk, both suffered attainder in January, 1547, although Thomas Howard escaped execution by the death of the king before his sentence was carried out. Surrey was condemned and executed on January 19, 1547, actually a few days before the bill of attainder passed parliament. *L. and P.*, XXI, pt. 2, nos. 697, 702, 753, 759, 770(86).

[62] All purchased and exchanged lands acquired by the crown before the erection of the Court of Augmentations continued under the survey of the general surveyors. On the monastic possessions managed by the Court of Survey, see p. 275, *infra*.

[63] September 10, 1546, Sir Richard Southwell, one of the heads of the Court

In addition to franchisal estates, attainted lands, and monastic property, the Court of Survey, for administrative purposes, had kept intact feudal entities known historically as honors. Of the many feudatories or honors that had come into the possession of the crown by the sixteenth century those controlled by the court still preserved their ancient organization. Although greatly altered during the course of centuries by alienation and annexation, the list of crown honors was still a long one: Amphill, Bolingbroke, Brecknock, Clare, Ewelm or Newelme, Gloucester, Hampton, Kenilworth, Knaresborough, Okehampton, Penreth, Petworth, Pikering, Rayleigh, Richmond, Rochford, Tickhill, Tutbury, Wallingford, and Woodstock. Since the Middle Ages many of the great franchisal estates had been broken up naturally or had disappeared altogether, but under the chamber system, the crown had preserved the ancient practice of regarding an honor as a logical basis for administrative and revenue supervision.

Historically, the " honour," as a seigniory of several manors held under one baron, had played an important role in the evolution of royal administration. Feudally, the honor was an aggregation of separate estates representing the collected holdings of a great lord; in the contractual agreement between the king and his vassals it became the tenurial basis of military service to the crown. Within such estates unified control was achieved through the lord's chief residence or capital on the home manor, which usually became the jurisdictional and administrative center of the organization. As a modern scholar has suggested, " The unity of the honour was expressed in its court, and was so clearly recognized that if a lord acquired more than one honour, by marriage, inheritance, or royal grant, the separate existence of each was usually maintained with care." [64] Furthermore, the capital of these collective estates was not infrequently a castle, which gave its name to the honor and which retained an administrative identity down through the Middle Ages.[65] In a purely geographical sense the honors of the Court of Survey were as greatly dispersed as they had ever been and, like the greater duchies, were scattered over many counties. The administration of these honors, while at one time feasible, had become both expensive and inefficient. What had once been an obvious source of strength to the crown had developed into a serious weakness.

---

of Survey, to Thomas Hall, receiver of attainted possessions. *L. and P.*, XXI, pt. 2, no. 61.

[64] F. M. Stenton, *The First Century of English Feudalism, 1066–1166* (Oxford, 1932), 55. The early organization of the English honor is admirably interpreted by Stenton in Chap. II, " The Honour and the Lord's Household," *ibid.*, 41–82.

[65] Sixteenth century honors like Richmond, Tickhill, Pontefract, and Tutbury, are cases in point.

Just why this administrative technique had not been abandoned is not quite clear. During the earlier centuries of emerging feudalism it had been an advantage to extend baronial influence to those lords who were trustworthy; similarly, through honorial jurisdiction the king had gained valuable administrative agencies in the more remote districts of the kingdom. But those services had been transferred by the Tudors to the council, whose long arm of centralized governmental control gradually reached the newer administrative courts and area councils alike. It is true that the revenue courts of Cromwell, with their directors and councils, fulfilled essentially the same functions which the *dapifer* and baronial council of the lords once performed,[66] but the Court of Augmentations had achieved the same results through the unified county system. It is not surprising that this court, a statutory creation without traditional background and not the older Court of Survey, was the one to introduce fundamental changes in procedure. Sheer apathy, precedent, and the dead weight of tradition all operated against administrative change. It was easier to follow the old pattern than to perfect a new one; certainly the time-honored usage was more popular. But the real reason was one of expediency. Abandonment of the honorial principle would have involved the dismissal of countless officials. Whatever their major intention, reduction in personnel was a factor which prompted the commissioners of 1547 to advocate amalgamation of the two revenue systems.

A principle almost basic to the Tudor concept of civil service was that an employee should not be dismissed without just cause. If and when an individual was deprived of his post through no fault of his own, he was either compensated by a pension or given another position commensurate with the one he had lost. Consequently, when the crown took over a piece of land, it frequently acquired all the administrative jobs in estate management that went with it. On a large honor these offices, as often as not, represented a surplus of unwanted officials, who, with little to do, became a useless element in the governing institution. In the case of the Court of Survey larger land units, when acquired, were usually kept intact, or if annexed to an established division, they at least retained their administrative organization. Under such circumstances there was no reduction of personnel; in fact, additional supervisory officials were sometimes required. When in November, 1539, Richard Whiting, abbot of the monastery of Glastonbury, was attainted, the land, property, and other valuable possessions of this wealthy abbey were seized by the king and turned over to the Court of Survey for

[66] Stenton, *The First Century of English Feudalism, 1066–1166*, 65, 73–74.

processing.[67] Money, plate, ornaments, and other articles "of great value" there were estimated at " £2,000 and above." Richard Pollard and Thomas Moyle, general surveyors of crown lands, assisted by Cromwell's special agent, Richard Layton, surveyed the lands and property of the abbey; "The house is great, goodly, and so princely as we have not seen the like, with four parks adjoining," they told Cromwell, anticipating a subsequent report of Charles de Marillac, the French ambassador, who evaluated the abbey's treasure at 200,000 crowns.[68]

The audit of the accounts and survey of the home lands of the monastery had been completed by early December, 1539, showing a substantial increase in value over earlier surveys.[69] The buildings and chief possessions of the abbey were situated in Somersetshire, but like the honorial units its lands were widely scattered in Wales, London, Berkshire, Dorsetshire, Hampshire, Wiltshire, and elsewhere. Each parcel of this administrative division had its own local hierarchy: stewardships, overseerships, masterships, keeperships, and various minor officials such as bailiffs, gardeners, and collectors, the lowest of which were paid no more than 2*d*. per day. Of the three major coordinating offices for all the Glastonbury lands in England and Wales, one at least was a recent creation. This was the surveyorship of its extensive Glastonbury possessions, wheresoever located, awarded to Sir Hugh Paulet in February, 1540.[70] The other two principal positions, the offices of auditor and general receiver of the unit, were both of ancient standing and con-

[67] Whiting was arrested and thrown into the Tower of London on charges of treason in September, 1539. On the fifteenth of November following he was beheaded and quartered. *L. and P.*, XIV, pt. 2, nos. 206, 272, 530–33, 637. A list of attainders for treason is included in a minute book of the office of general surveyors. Augm. Office, Misc. Books 313B. Glastonbury, Reading, and Colchester, all administered by the court, were three of the wealthiest monasteries in the country.

[68] *L. and P.*, XIV, pt. 2, nos. 232, 389. Cromwell's Remembrances, or personal memoranda, indicate that over 11,000 ounces of gold, plate, rich copes, and furniture of the house, and more than £1,100 "in ready money" were taken from Glastonbury. The prize was offset, however, by more than £2,000 in Glastonbury debts. After current charges had been deducted, the total revenues of the monastery for 31 Henry VIII amounted to £1,860 11*s*. 1*d*. *Ibid.*, nos. 427, 532. Two lay treasurers and two clerks of the house were arrested for embezzlement and "arrant robbery" of Glastonbury church, for which the latter suffered execution. *Ibid.*, no. 530.

[69] *Ibid.*, no. 637. The correction of low appraisals was, of course, one of the principal reasons for the new surveys. On the Glastonbury surveys see Savine, *English Monasteries on the Eve of the Dissolution*, 50–51.

[70] Pat. Rolls, 31 Henry VIII, pt. 5, mem. 33. The fee was £20 per year. Sir Hugh Paulet, son and heir of Sir Amyas Paulet, represented a branch of an ancient Somerset family. He probably secured this appointment through the influence of his brother-in-law, Sir Richard Pollard, general surveyor.

tinued essentially unchanged. John Peppys and Roger Amyce were appointed auditor and general receiver respectively, not only of those lands, but also of the possessions of the abbey of Reading in Berkshire, where the abbot Hugh Cook had recently fallen under the action of attainder.[71] The chief stewardship of the principal lordship went to Sir Thomas Speke of the privy chamber, who as a royal favorite held numerous other offices on the crown lands.[72]

By the autumn of 1546 the commission had finished its work and arrived at a decision to amalgamate the two great land courts into an enlarged Augmentations. Already Mildmay had warned the lord chancellor that the proposed court, soon to be erected, would encroach upon the jurisdiction of the chancery, since all the business of the court would pass under its own seal instead of under the great seal of England. Obviously alarmed at the possible loss of fees, Wriothesley hastened to write to his friend Paget to ask him to intercede for him with the king. Pleading that ancient practices might be followed, he argued that the reputation of the Court of Chancery would not only suffer but that the great seal " will greatly decay, great confusion ensue and many honest men be undone." The better to prove his case, the two chief clerks of chancery, John Hales and John Croke, were sent up to court to explain the situation in further detail.[73]

During late November and early December of 1546 the amalgamation project was gradually implemented. As soon as it became generally known that the two courts were to be united, there was the usual scramble for offices in the new institution. Although the patent of erection for the second Augmentations did not come until the first of the year, some of the major officers were already appointed by December 12, 1546.[74] As the dissolved courts were being liquidated, their re-

---

[71] *Ibid.*, pt. 7, mem. 15. The auditorship carried a salary of £20 a year, but Amyce received a total of £40 annually for the dual receivership, with an additional 20s. per £100 of the revenues collected, a practice later introduced into the Augmentations.

[72] *Ibid.*, 32 Henry VIII, pt. 5, mem. 49. Local offices were awarded to William Gibbs, Edward Rogers, Richard Audley, Andrew Wadham, and Maurice Berkeley. *Ibid.*, 31 Henry VIII, pt. 5, mem. 42; 32 Henry VIII, pt. 3, mem. 43; pt. 5, mem. 50; pt. 8, mems. 17, 48.

[73] Wriothesley to Paget, October 16, 1546, *L. and P.*, XXI, pt. 2, no. 273. Although a member of the commission, Wriothesley apparently did not know the nature of the constitution of the proposed court until apprised by Mildmay. This suggests that the proposal for amalgamation and the plan of organization of the new court came from Mildmay. Actually some protection was accorded the older seals by the provision that leases of Augmentations lands, the annual rental value of which exceeded £6 13s. 4d., should " be passed at thoffices of our signet and priuye seale in mannour and fourme as heretofore hathe ben vsed." Pat. Rolls., 38 Henry VIII, pt. 5, mem. 18.

[74] *L. and P.*, XXI, pt. 2, nos. 338, 475(84), 534, 535. One of the earliest ap-

spective auditors were required to prepare hastily brief books of their revenues for the convenience of the incoming officials. Mildmay seems to have been the guiding spirit of the reorganization, which proceeded without serious interruption despite the fact that as yet there had been no specific patent or statute authorizing the change.

Various difficulties presented themselves almost immediately, not the least of which was the legal problem involved in the status of the Court. Since the revenues from the two dissolved institutions represented an appreciable portion of the entire national income, it was imperative that there should be no serious interruption either in revenue collection or in general administrative business. However, in practical operation the old courts were actually closed down before the letters patent for the erection of the second Court of Augmentations were officially released, though it was necessary to keep one of the institutions in continuous operation during the period of transition. Thus it was that payments by the Augmentations continued without interruption during the entire period of reorganization, with only occasional setbacks. Probably the undated warrant of December, 1546, under the king's sign manual, authorizing the delivery of 2,000 fothers of lead to Sir William Herbert, gentleman of the privy chamber, was typical of the legal obstacles encountered. The warrant, which was addressed to the officials of the second Augmentations, already organized, was rejected as illegal, since in the opinion of Mildmay the new Court of Augmentations was not established by act of parliament and, therefore, " hath not authority to execute the same until the old Court be annuled." The warrant was cancelled and another one for the delivery of the lead issued, this time directed to the original Augmentations which had not been legally abolished.[75]

The desirability of obtaining parliamentary sanction for the amalgamation was based on the objection of legalists that institutions originally erected by statute could only thus be abolished. Accordingly, a bill for the establishment of a renovated Court of Augmentations was prepared for passage in the second session of the last parliament of the reign.[76] It was introduced in the house of lords on the fifteenth of January and

---

pointments was that of John Hanby, an auditor in the first Augmentations, as one of the ten auditors of the reconstituted Court.

[75] Documents signed by stamp in December, 1546. *Ibid.*, no. 647 (13, 14). Many of these documents in December and January of 1546–47 relate to the business of the old Court or to the appointments for the new organization.

[76] This November parliament, which reconvened on January 14, 1547, continued until January 31, three days after the king's death. It was called primarily to effect the ruination of the Howards. The attainder of Norfolk and Surrey was actually the only enactment of the session.

piloted through to the engrossing stage by Paulet and Wriothesley.[77] This
bill may have been based upon a rough draft of a plan for a projected Court
of Augmentations preserved among the records of the Exchequer, which
was never realized. The document is undated and possibly represents
an earlier administrative reform contemplated by Cromwell, but there is
no evidence that such a project was ever seriously considered during the
previous period. Whatever its origin, it bears a close resemblance to the
patent of erection eventually used. The authority and powers of the
first Court were to be reconfirmed in the second, with jurisdiction over
" all Matiers between parties onywise touching ony Lordshippes,
Landes, tenementes," or other properties previously under the control
of the Court, as well as territories and revenues " that hereafter shalbe
within the Surveie and Gouernance of the same according as herafter
ys declared." Likewise, the projected court was to have jurisdiction
over all cases of disputed titles of crown lands.[78] Before the bill had
passed its final reading in the lords, the king was dead. Parliament was
dissolved, and no further attempt was made to legalize the proposed
institution by state authority.

Meanwhile, the two courts had been dissolved and the second Augmentations erected by letters patent dated January 1, 1547.[79] This unprecedented action soon released a controversy regarding the validity of
letters patent when employed to dissolve national institutions originally
erected by act of parliament. Moreover, " sondrie and many ambigui-
ties dowtes and questions " were further raised by legalists as to whether
letters, grants, or other official documents issued under the seal of the
Court were legal, since the second Augmentations had no parliamentary
authorization. This problem was ultimately resolved in the first parliament of Edward VI by an act which validated all the transactions of

---

[77] *Journals of the House of Lords,* I, 284b, 290a; *L. and P.,* XXI, pt. 2, no. 759.
[78] Proposals for an act establishing a Court of Augmentations. Exch., K. R.,
Miscellanea, 11/49. This rough sketch of a project for the Court, apparently
written by Wriothesley, is incorrectly labeled as a plan for a Court of General
Surveyors. The document is undated and the roll mutilated so that the name is
indistinguishable, but internal evidence clearly reveals the court to have been the
Augmentations and not the Court of Survey. Elton adjudged the draft to be
a Cromwellian project for clarifying the constitution of the original Court. G. R.
Elton, *The Tudor Revolution in Government: Administrative Changes in the
Reign of Henry VIII* (Cambridge, 1953), 207.
[79] Pat. Rolls, 38 Henry VIII, pt. 5, mems. 15–28. This patent is very briefly
abstracted in *L. and P.,* XXI, pt. 2, no. 771(1). Two manuscript copies of the
patent are available, one in Harl. MS. 600, fols. 1–19, and the other in Augm.
Office, Misc. Books 17, pp. 1–112. Henry VIII died early in the morning on
Friday, January 28; parliament was dissolved on the thirty-first.

the Court.[80] The former ambiguity, however, was not completely settled until the last year of the reign when the legality of the patent of dissolution was confirmed by statute. The preamble of the act clearly indicates the objections that had been raised:

> And Forasmuche as sens thereccion of the sayd Courte of Augmentacion . . . , stablyshedd and erected by lettres patentes . . . divers ambiguities and doubtes have risin and growen emong suche as be learned in the lawes of the Realme, whether the dissolvinge or extinguishinge and repealinge of the sayd late Courtes erected by aucthoritee of Parleament as ys aforesayd, might by thorder of the lawe bee dissolved extinguished and repealed by lettres patentes, considering that the commencement of them were first hadd and made by aucthorite of Parliament, yea or no. . . . Wheruppon great inconveniences might insue . . .[81]

Although not mentioned in the patent, it is noteworthy to observe that both acts restricted such revenue courts to jurisdiction over cases in which the crown was actually a party; they also specifically prohibited the Court of Augmentations from hearing suits between subjects.

The structure and organization of the second Augmentations are fully set forth in the January patent of 1547, which simultaneously dissolved the two older revenues courts and erected a third one. Negligence in administration was given as a major reason for the reform, though as usual the preamble somewhat overstated the case for the crown. It was true, as alleged, that there was considerable overlapping of jurisdiction and that regulation and supervision had been relaxed, but these were trends apparent throughout the entire administration. None the less, the facts hardly justified the sweeping indictment that the officers of the two courts could not intelligently perform their duties. Nor did it follow as a result of developing maladministration, which to a degree was prevalent in all the revenue departments. More to the point was the allegation that the institutions had become overburdened with superfluous officers, " whereby hathe ensued not onelye a greate and inordinate

---

[80] 1 Edward VI, s. 8, " An Acte for Confirmacion of lettres Patentes," *S. R.,* IV, 13–14.

[81] 7 Edward VI, c. 2, " An Acte for the dissolving uniting or annexing of certayne Courtes latelie erected by the King that deade ys," *S. R.,* IV, 164–65. The act gave the same validity to the letters patent of Henry VIII " as thoughe the same hadd been made and doon by auctoritee of Parliament." Edward VI was also empowered during his lifetime to dissolve, change, or alter any of the existing revenue courts by similar letters patent. Comparable authority was given to Mary during the ensuing year. 1 Mary, St. 2, c. 10, " An Acte for the uniting dissolving or newe erecting of Courtes," *ibid.,* 208–209.

charge and yerelie burden to vs and inquietnes to our ffermours tenauntes and Subiectes but also a greate confusion and mysorder in our
saide reuenewe." [82]

Be that as it may, the real reason for amalgamation, a purely administrative one, was not even mentioned. The obvious solution was a single,
centralized revenue department for all the revenues of the nation, similar
to the original Exchequer administration. Any future revenue department, however, irrespective of size or composition, would need to incorporate the principal features of a decade of progressive Augmentations
administration.

The problem of the permanent status of the two courts was shrewdly
evaded by the legal assumption that they had already become defunct.
"And fyndyng at this present [time]," the patent reads, "the saide
seuerall Courtes voide of officers by whome the reuenues of our saide
honours Castelles manours landes tenementes and hereditamentes seuer-
ally lymyted and appoynted to the survey rule and order of the same
seuerall Courtes shulde be orderyd and vsed to our commodite and
profitte . . . wee be fully resolued . . . that the auctoritie and iurisdiccon
of the same seuerall Courtes shall clerelye frome hensforthe cease and
absolutelye be determyned and extinguisshed and no lenger to contynue.
. . . In consideracon wherof wee by these our lettres patentes de create
erecte make and establisshe . . . a certayne Courte commonly to be
called for euer the Courte of the Augmentacions and reuenues of the
Kinges Crowne and that the same shalbe a Courte of recorde for euer
to endure and shall haue suche iurisdiccions powers and auctorities as
hereafter in these presentes shalbe expressed and declared." The legal
fiction, of course, rested upon the fact that both the courts in question
were "void of officers" and could no longer function. Thus it was unnecessary to dissolve an institution that had already ceased to exist,
so the patent simply recognized a *fait accompli*. As a practical gesture
the court officials concerned had been persuaded technically to resign
their positions in order to lend force to the argument. Therein lies the
explanation for the informal organization of the Court, which had functioned in a practical way for some time before its erection by royal
authority.[83]

---

[82] Pat. Rolls, 38 Henry VIII, pt. 5, mem. 15. The ensuing description of the
organization of the Court is based largely on this long patent of fourteen membranes. Hence, detailed citations to the patent are omitted.

[83] Auditors William Rigges and John Hanby, receiver Robert Goche, and possibly
other field officers of the reorganized court were engaged in Augmentations
business in the summer of 1546. *L. and P.*, XXI, pt. 1, nos. 1249, 1280, 1401; pt. 2,
nos. 561, 601, 749. By mid-December all the auditorships and receiverships had
been filled. In both the old institutions auditors were required to prepare brief

The second Court of the Augmentations and Revenues of the King's crown, to use its full title, was quite similar in organization and structure to the former Augmentations which it replaced. As a court of record it had a great seal and a privy seal under the custody of a court chancellor and council, with as full authority, both judicial and administrative, as its predecessors had possessed. All lands and revenues of the old courts were transferred to the new institution, as well as all such future revenues or possessions which might come to the crown by special act of parliament or otherwise. The latter category included land or property acquired by gift, grant, surrender, purchase, escheat, forfeiture, and attainder and the extensive holdings of all the religious chantries, colleges, guilds, hospitals, fraternities, brotherhoods, and free chapels, appropriated to the crown as a result of the dissolution of the chantries.[84] Consequently, the reconstituted Court was larger and more significant than the earlier Augmentations had ever been, but it represented no striking departure in either authority or jurisdiction. Only in organization and personnel were significant changes effected.

As principal official the chancellor remained head of the Court, with custody of the two seals, to be assisted by two new officers who jointly constituted the second position in the official hierarchy. This office of " general surveyors " had been taken over from the former Court of Survey, the headship of which had been collectively exercised by three officers styled general surveyors, who had served as directors and judges of that court. In order that a continuity of policy might be maintained, the two most important of the three directors, Sir Thomas Moyle and Walter Mildmay, were simply transferred to the Augmentations where they became assistant directors.[85] The office of treasurer of the Court

---

accounts of the past year's revenues within their respective jurisdictions to be turned over to the receivers of the new Court of Augmentations. The directive of July, 1546, from the privy council was specific in its instructions. Augm. Office, Miscellanea, 17; Misc. Books 415, fols. 62, 63, 86, 130–130d. *L. and P.*, XXI, pt. 2, nos. 534–35. Likewise, Richard Goodrich, who was promoted from the attorneyship of the Court of Wards to the attorneyship of Augmentations, seems to have assumed his new duties prior to his formal appointment on January 2, 1547. Although Nicholas Bacon, his successor in the Wards office who was then solicitor in the old Augmentations, ostensibly did not assume office until January, he was paid for his services as of September, 1546. The occasion for these early changes was probably the ill-health of Goodrich's predecessor in the Augmentations office, Walter Henley. In late September it was reported that Henley was seriously ill and almost blind. Augm. Office, Misc. Books 218, fol. 3; *L. and P.*, XXI, pt. 2, nos. 155, 535, 647(24, 41, 42), 771(1, 13).

[84] Special safeguards for all lands and revenues of the Exchequer and the duchy of Lancaster were set forth in the patent. The duchy of Cornwall, however, came under the administration of the new Court. Pat. Rolls, 38 Henry VIII, pt. 5, mems. 21, 22.

[85] Appointment of January 2, 1547, of Sir Thomas Moyle and Walter Mildmay

was thus reduced from second to third position. The attorneyship and solicitorship remained unchanged, but two other positions from the Court of Survey were also added, as fourth and seventh offices. The holders of these latter posts, the mastership of woods and the surveyorship of woods, were given supervisory jurisdiction over all woods and wood sales within the survey of the Court. The geographical areas under the control of each office, however, were divided into two regions, the one north and the other south of the River Trent, in conformity with the ancient administrative divisions of the royal forests. These first seven offices thus formed the executive council, which in comparison with the older Augmentations board was now increased from four to ten members, three of the offices being held jointly each by two persons. A clerk, ten district auditors, eleven particular receivers, and two special auditors of the prests completed the central authority. The usher, keeper of the records, and messengers represented no significant change in the earlier structure.

Externally the county administration was considerably tightened up by the superimposition of three additional categories of field officials, namely, stewards, woodwards,[86] and "particular surveyors." These supervisory officers, one each for every county in England and Wales, directed the local administration, controlled the estate management of crown lands, and generally maintained the operational unity of the county system. Especially important were the county stewards who, assisted by the county surveyors, were responsible for the rent rolls and the periodic sessions of the local manorial courts. They were charged with a series of particularized functions:

And wee further ordeyn and establishe that the sayd Stewardes of the Courtes withe the particuler Surveyours of landes there shall kepe the Courtes of the manours seigniories lordshippes liberties and franchesies within the lymyttes of their offices at suche conuenyent tyme as the surveyours may be present at the same Courtes. And that the same Stewardes shall charge the homage and Jurie to enquyre at the Courtes of all the reparacions of the manours and ffarmes there. And to engrosse the same in the Courte rolles as they

---

to the second office in the Augmentations, at a yearly salary of £200 each. Young Mildmay occupied the senior position of the two surveyorships. Augm. Office, Misc. Books 218, fol. 1*d*.

[86] The local woodwards, like the central masters and surveyors of woods, were really not new developments in Augmentations practice, though these offices had not been authorized by the statutory constitution of the original Court. As noted earlier, they had emerged as by-products of the increased attention given by the government to the administration and sale of woods. See Chapter Four, pp. 108, 110.

shalbe presented by verdict of the homage and certifie thauditours of the same at the next Audite accordinglie. And that the same Stewardes shall cause like inquyre to be made at the Courtes of all wood sales within the manours and whether the copices of the same woodes be well preserued or not and to engrosse the presentmentes and verdicte therof in the Courte Rolles of the sayd manours. And that the same Stewardes shall assesse no fynes nor make any grauntes of copie holde or custumarie landes without thassent of the Surveyour of the landes of the same Countie where the landes lie whiche fyne shalbe assessed by the same Stewarde and Surveyour in open Courte.

In all cases the Augmentations auditor checked on the stewards in his circuit. When found negligent in their duties they were reported by him to the Court and, if guilty, were punished at the discretion of the chancellor and general surveyors. Penalties were likewise imposed upon any steward who failed to deliver his court rolls, " faire engrossed in parchement," to the auditor on the opening day of the annual audit. Particular emphasis was given to the procedure in the local courts:

And we ordeyn . . . that the Courte rolles and all other euydences necessary for the Courtes in euery Countie shalbe collected and brought into one place certayne of the same Countie to be assigned and appoynted for the same where with the Stewardes and Re-ceyvours of the same Countie shalbe charged and shall haue accesse to the same. And thother euydences concernyng the landes in the sayde Countie to remayne lykewise there in the charge of the Audi-tour and Surveyour of the same. And they to make a boke of theym to be delyuered into thys Courte. And we further ordeyne and establishe that the saide Surveyours of the landes for the tyme being shall ride yerelie withe the Stewardes of the Courtes and that the same Surveyours withe the consent of the same Stewardes shall in open Courte assesse fynes and make graunte of copie holde and custumarie landes within the lymyttes of their offices according to the customes of the manours ther.[87]

The most significant departure from earlier usage came, not in the administrative procedures of revenue collection where changes might

[87] Pat. Rolls, 38 Henry VIII, pt. 5, mem. 26. There was no definite number of stewards assigned to each county. The constitution merely required " that there shalbe in euery Countie soche and somany Stewardes of the Courtes to be holden of all the manours lordships and liberties within the same Countie as nowe be or hereafter shalbe appoynted." *Ibid.*, mem. 16.

have been expected, but in the method of impresting governmental money by the Court. This practice, common enough earlier, was borrowed from the general surveyors of crown lands, who had maintained jurisdiction over all such advances by royal warrants, known as prests, since the turn of the century. Accordingly, for the more unified control of these special accounts, together with certain specified revenues originally classified among the " foreign livelihood " withdrawn from the Exchequer, a special Augmentations office was created.

Literally, prests or imprests [88] represented money advanced to an accountant or official charged with some business of the state to enable him to proceed with the undertaking to which he was committed. Money thus paid in advance was in reality no more than a temporary loan, of which definite records had to be kept in order to insure either future repayment or at least a strict accountability, according to the intent of the appropriation. Prests were made for a variety of reasons: advances in salary, public works, reparations and improvements on crown estates, and special funds granted to departments, offices, and institutions for extraordinary or emergency expenditures. Theoretically all such imprests were repayable, but in practice they were usually charged as receipts in the final declarations of account. Payments " by way of prest " or " by way of loan " were common to all departments of government, although they varied greatly in size, ranging from small sums to thousands of pounds. The smaller amounts were usually allotted to ambassadors for their diets upon leaving the country or paid as " prest wages " for as much as a year and a half before they were due.[89] Larger

---

[88] The term prest (*prêt; praestatio,* or emprest) was derived from the Latin *praestitum,* the past participle of *praestare*: to become surety for; "prest money" was money lent or paid in advance, to be accounted for in detail after future expenditure. Occasionally the term was used with reference to national levies or "amicable loans," as in the case of the compulsory "loan" initiated by Wolsey in 1522. "A booke mencionyng all suche sommes of money . . . [as the king's subjects in Berkshire] do prest vnto his highnes by reason of the views taken of their landes and goodes," collected by Sir Richard Weston. The sum of all prests in Berkshire was £3,808 15s. Augm. Office, Misc. Books 465 [Undated]. This and other "prest money" collected by commissioners was paid into the chamber. *L. and P.,* IV, nos. 84, 214, 547.

[89] Lord William Howard, ambassador in France, was paid £240 in advance of his diets at the rate of £2 13s. 4d. daily "by virtue of the King's Privy Council's letter"; Hans Holbein the younger, famous Flemish court portraitist of Henry VIII, was allowed regular advances of his wages; Sir Edward Cobham was granted £10 in prest "upon a reckoning of his wages for the keeping of the King's blockhouse" at Milton, Kent; and £300 was paid to Sir Edward Boughton by order of Cromwell before his attainder to be paid back at Easter, 1544, for which obligations were drawn up and entered in the "book of obligations." The treasurer of the chamber, in explanation of the latter entry, noted that Cromwell had promised him a warrant for the payment but had failed to present it. Such

sums were imprested by warrant for current departmental expenses or upon special plea of the official in charge of an authorized expenditure.[90]

Since the Tudor government was often short of immediate cash, " prests upon warrants," that is, official loans, were used to carry public ministers or agencies over temporary financial embarrassments. Normally funds would be transferred from one of the treasuries possessing a balance at the moment to the borrowing department, with the understanding that repayment should follow the future receipt of assigned revenues. However practicable the expedient was originally, it had become a source of constant irritation to those ministers responsible for repayment. The practice was especially infeasible when applied to departments like the household and chamber, proverbially in debt. As it was always easier to borrow than to repay, most accounts were thus encumbered with outstanding debts of this kind. Even periodic drives for collection were not always successful. Certainly among the financial courts the itemization of money received or paid out in prest figured prominently in the official bookkeeping of the period. In the payments of the first Court of Augmentations issues of prests upon warrants totaled over £321,627 for the first eight and one half years of the Court's existence, or an average of approximately £37,838 10s. annually.[91] The maximum was reached during the French war in 1544–45, when the total payments by royal warrant amounted to £212,527 9s. 5d.[92]

When so many advances on assignments were made before the final allotment became due, it was comparatively easy to forget the earlier payments. Necessary records were not always kept of such detailed transactions, or if payment was by oral command, there was no written evidence to justify the advance. Consequently, it is not surprising that so many accounts of crown paymasters failed to balance.

In September, 1540, when a commission was sent to Ireland to hear the accounts of the vice-treasurer and receiver-general there, it uncovered a good deal of evidence of deception and fraud on the part of the accountant William Brabazon. It was disclosed that he had received many sums of which he had no written record and had made huge payments upon the sole warrant of private letters from the late lord privy

---

negligence explains how advances in cash could easily be " forgotten to be allowed." Payments by the treasurer of the chamber for various years : B. M., Arundel MS., 97, fols. 122, 147, 152d., 179, 185d. ; see also fols. 57 *passim*. Other chamber books are filled with similar entries.

[90] *Ibid.*, fols. 131d., 134d. After 1536 most of the larger prests were made through the Court of Augmentations.

[91] Augm. Office, Treas. Rolls of Accts., Nos. 1–3.

[92] The total payments for this year, from April, 1544, to April, 1545, were only £225,401 19s. 2¼d. Augm. Office, Misc. Books 253, fols. 53–66, 75.

seal which had not been preserved. However, since that kind of informal procedure by Cromwell was familiar enough to all who knew him, the king and council were disposed to accept the accountant's oath as proof of his honesty. None the less, the modern investigator is inclined to suspect undue leniency in the acceptance of an account which showed a deficit of almost £2,000.[93]

No specific attempt had been made to regulate the complex system of prest advances prior to the erection of the Court of General Surveyors in 1542. Even then the delegation of all supervision of prests to that court was no departure from precedent, since the earlier office of general surveyors from the beginning had had jurisdiction over " all manner prestes receyved and sommes of money delyvered from the Kynges Highnes for payment of any manner wages of Capteyns or Soldyours or for any crues of Soldiours and other prestes whatsoever they be frome the Kyng." [94] Section thirty-seven of the statutory constitution of 1542 empowered the directors of the court to sue and process for recovery of loans in any of the other revenue courts to which prests had been made.[95] This provision was undoubtedly designed to expedite the reclamation of prest money under threat of public prosecution. In practice, however, the procedure was difficult to administer because it required periodic surveys of all the treasuries to ascertain what prests were outstanding. The reformers of 1547 sought to eliminate this weakness by creating a special office in the Court of Augmentations which brought the control of prests under a centralized department.

The early history of the office of prests is shrouded in obscurity. Certainly before 1542 the supervision of prest revenues and prest accounts

[93] *L. and P.*, XVI, nos. 103, 656, 775–77. The commission was composed of Sir Anthony St. Leger, lord deputy of Ireland; Thomas Walsh, a baron of the Exchequer; and two professional auditors: John Mynne of the Exchequer and William Cavendish of the Augmentations. The diets and expenses of the commissioners were paid by the chamber. Cavendish remained an extra year in Ireland to perfect the treasurer's account after Walsh and Mynne had returned. *Ibid.*, XV, nos. 978, 988; XVI, nos. 791, 907; XVII, nos. 304, 499. Both auditors were highly commended for their work by St. Leger. Cavendish's duties in the Augmentations during his absence from 1540 to 1542 were performed by his deputy, Gregory Richardson.

[94] Schedule to the act of 14 and 15 Henry VIII, c. 15 of "The Kynges Revenues " that were under the survey of the general surveyors of crown lands in 1523. This statute, which extended the powers of the general surveyors office, also brought within its supervision "all manner personnes which have receyved of the Kyng any somme or sommes of Money by way of prest or lone for any the Kynges newe buyldynges or reparacions made or to be made of or for any provisions made or to be made upon the Kynges Shippes or for newe makyng of Shippes or for any other provisions whatsoever made or to be made for the Kyng or by his commaundement." *S. R.*, III, 228–30.

[95] Statute 33 Henry VIII, c. 39, sec. xxxvii, *ibid.*, 886. All suits for recovery of debts were collectable in the revenue court where the debt originated.

was not co-ordinated but informally delegated to various officials in each department of government. Such centralized control as there was came from the general surveyors office, where all functions and organizations were somewhat indefinite. Prests accounts were audited by appointed commissioners or heard by the general surveyors themselves, who also took the declarations of foreign accounts. Apparently there was no permanent office set up by them, unless it can be assumed that Thomas Tamworth and John Mynne held such a position by oral appointment. The problem is further complicated by the fact that most of the crown officials held numerous offices within the same or different courts, which not infrequently carried identical titles. Consequently, when a surveyor, receiver, or auditor of prests is specifically identified in a document it is usually not possible to determine either which office he represented or in what capacity he was operating.

There is evidence that a definite auditorship of the prests had been set up long before 1543, but no specific appointments have been discovered. When the work of the general surveyors had become too heavy for them in 1514, they enlarged their official staff by the appointment of an additional auditor. The auditorship of certain special accounts was awarded in July of that year to Thomas Tamworth, already an auditor in the Exchequer, who in fact had been exercising the position since the preceding September. The "foreign accounts" as specified were those of the treasurer of Calais, the merchants of the staple of Calais, the keeper of the great wardrobe, the clerk of the hanaper of the chancery, the constable of Windsor Castle, the captain of the Isle of Wight, and the chief butler of England.[96] Actually he was soon assisting with other declarations as well, particularly the accounts of the sergeant of the tents, the ordnance, the navy, and the paymaster of wars, for which in some cases at least he received special remuneration. By 1516 he seems to have been officiating also as an "auditor of works." [97] In May, 1527, he was joined in office by John Mynne, who retained the auditorship

---

[96] (July 7, 1514.) Pat. Rolls, 6 Henry VIII, pt. 1, mem. 18. A life appointment with a salary of £10 per year plus the usual fees for diets suggests that the auditorships of those accounts heretofore had not been consolidated. By the same patent Tamworth was made clerk of the general surveyors and keeper of the records of the office.

[97] It is difficult to ascertain exactly what Tamworth's position was, since he is usually listed without identification or simply as the "king's auditor." On July 24, 1514, he was rewarded £6 13s. 4d. for examining declarations concerning the wars, as presented by paymaster of wars, Sir John Daunce. Many of the sums in this account were prest advances for as much as £4,000 in a single item. *L. and P.,* I, pt. 2, no. 3614 (p. 1517). See also *ibid.,* nos. 2349, 2575, 2900, 3137; II, pt. 2, Appendix, no. 30; IV pt. 1 no. 691.

upon the death of Tamworth in January, 1533.[98] Mynne continued his duties until his own death, late in 1542, a short while after the Court of General Surveyors was organized. Meanwhile, he had been awarded the mastership of woods in this court, which meant that he was temporarily holding two jobs in the same department. He was probably assisted by his brother Nicholas, who assumed the position of auditor of special accounts after John died.

In the latter appointment, made at the end of January, 1543, the explanation of the office was essentially the same as that held by Tamworth and John Mynne, with one exception: to the earlier list of ministers accounting before the auditor was added the keeper of the exchange and money in the Tower and other mints.[99] Thereafter he received several other special auditorships in the court, covering various crown lands under its survey and lands appointed by parliament for the maintenance of the royal garrison at Berwick. Since there is no evidence of his surrendering the position it can be assumed that he occupied the office of auditor of certain foreign accounts until his death in 1546, on the eve of amalgamation with the Augmentations.[100]

No attempt seems to have been made to correlate prests activities until May, 1543, when an audit office for the accounts of works, the king's ships, and all money expended in the king's affairs was created. Whether or not this appointment, given to Francis Southwell and Walter Mildmay, constituted a surveyorship of prests is a matter of conjecture.[101] Certainly many accounts of national expenditures, such as those of the treasurers of wars continued to be viewed by special commissions.[102] From the beginning Mildmay was the dominant auditor, although his activities were by no means confined to prests collections. Periodically he sat on commissions to audit the accounts of the jewel house, the mint, and Boulogne, and occasionally processed the collection of crown debts or the calling in of arrears of revenues as extracted

---

[98] *Ibid.*, IV, pt. 2, no. 3142(5).

[99] Pat. Rolls, 34 Henry VIII, pt. 7, mem. 35; D. L. 42/133, fol. 187*d*. The privy seal was dated January 25, 1543, and delivered on the 29th. Nicholas Mynne was appointed auditor for life of all accounts, views of accounts, and declarations of the offices enumerated. Mynne, a clerk in the Exchequer, had held no important crown offices previously, except to serve the duchy of Lancaster as an attorney in the Exchequer from 1516–28.

[100] *L. and P.*, XIX, pt. 1, no. 610(81, 116); pt. 2, no. 166(2); XX, pt. 1, nos. 620(26), 1081(26); pt. 2, Appendix 13; XXI, pt. 1, no. 884; pt. 2, no. 476(93). *Cal. Pat. Rolls, Edward VI*, I, 313–14.

[101] Privy seal delivered May 10, 1543. The two men were appointed jointly and "severally" in survivorship at a salary of £40 per year. Pat. Rolls, 35 Henry VIII, pt. 5, mem. 12.

[102] *L. and P.*, XIX, pt. 1, no. 267; pt. 2, no. 800(27, 30).

from the accounts of receivers. His partner in office was already an auditor in the Exchequer at the date of his appointment, in itself a time-consuming position.[103] The two men were sometimes referred to as auditors jointly of the king's prests, but individually each was usually styled auditor of the prests or simply king's auditor.

Southwell retained his position in the Exchequer in 1547 but was not continued in the prests office when it was transferred to the Court of Augmentations. Instead, the supervision of both prests and foreign accounts was united in one office, called the auditorship of prests and foreign accounts or " forren reconynges." [104] This responsible post was jointly filled by two obscure but able crown ministers, Gregory Richardson and William Dixe. Both of them, however, had been auditors in the late Court of Survey, Richardson as auditor of accounts of wood sales and Dixe as special auditor of lands of the late Cardinal Wolsey and of the possessions granted to the late queen, Jane Seymour.[105]

As defined by the patent the office was given jurisdiction not only over all prests but also over the foreign accounts that heretofore customarily had been heard in the Court of Survey.[106]

And we ordeyne and establishe that the sayde two Auditours of the prestes shall take the reconynges of the warres build[ing]es shippes ordeynaunces and all other sommes of money delyuered in preste and of the money and reuenues of our hamper [107] the butlerage and

[103] Southwell had succeeded William ap Rice, deceased, in the Exchequer office in November, 1542. *L. and P.*, XVII, no. 1154(63). He also held various other minor offices including the auditorship of Salisbury lands and Fermour lands. *Ibid.*, XIX, pt. 1, no. 610(61) ; XX, pt. 1, no. 134; XXI, pt. 1, no. 1166(11). Southwell was pensioned in 1547, as " late one of thauditours of the prestes " of the dissolved Court of Survey at £53 6s. 8d. per year. Augm. Office, Misc. Books 257 (" Recompences " for offices surrendered), fol. 54d. ; 258, fol. 44.

[104] Pat. Rolls, 38 Henry VIII, pt. 5, mem. 16; 2 Edward VI, pt. 6, mem. 8; 4 Edward VI, pt. 6, mem. 14d.

[105] *L. and P.*, XX, pt. 1, no. 1081(38) ; Augm. Office, Misc. Books 259, fol. 61; 261, fol. 66. As deputy auditor to William Cavendish, Richardson had also done a great deal of Cavendish's work in the original Augmentations. See note 93. Upon the dissolution of the two courts in 1547, Dixe was pensioned, but Richardson was not.

[106] This distinction between prests and foreign accounts was preserved later in the renovated Exchequer. On this point, see Dorothy M. George, " Notes on the Origin of the Declared Account," *E. H. R.*, XXXI (January, 1916), 41–58. Examples of Declared Accounts in the Pipe Office for the reign of Edward VI show such accounts " perused, caste, tried, and examined " by Dixe and Richardson and declared before the chancellor and two general surveyors of the Augmentations. Though certain foreign accounts were still examined by royal commissions especially appointed, they would include in the membership officials of the Augmentations council and usually the auditors of the prests.

[107] The hanaper of the chancery. There was also a hanaper office in the Augmentations which received the profits of the Court's two seals.

the greate wardrobe and to allowe all thinges ordynarelye in the same. And that the same Auditours of the prestes shall ingrosse and declare their bookes of accompte before the sayde Chauncellour and general Surveyours frome tyme to tyme as they shalbe commaunded.[108]

It will be noted that this arrangement consolidated control over all advances of money made in the various financial departments. Monthly certifications of all debts or money delivered in prest were made to the auditors by each of the major treasuries of the realm, namely, the Court of Augmentations, the Court of First Fruits and Tenths, the Court of Wards and Liveries, and the Exchequer in order that proper steps might be taken for prompt repayment. Obviously this procedure was a great improvement over the previous system, which placed the major responsibility for ascertaining the extent of outstanding crown debts at any one time upon the prests auditors who were thus chiefly dependent upon the co-operation of a group of uninterested officials. In contrast, the ministers of the departments concerned were now particularly enjoined to report their loans systematically for regular processing. The auditors of the prests were in turn responsible to the chancellor and general surveyors of the Court of Augmentations, to whom they rendered periodic accounts.

The effect was to achieve a high degree of specialization among the Augmentations auditors. In addition to those of prests and foreign accounts, there were the ten regular auditors who heard only land revenue accounts, two auditors of accounts of woods and wood sales, and two special auditors for Boulogne and Calais. Finally, two auditors were specially appointed to hear the annual accounts of the treasurer of the Augmentations; although by constitutional provision they were to be chosen regularly from among the ten permanent auditors of the Court, as was the practice in the former Augmentations, this stipulation was never actually carried out.[109]

As the senior ranking officers in the Court of Augmentations the chancellor and two general surveyors directed the work of the council and formulated the policy of the Court. Although the entire council officiated as judges in cases that came before them, the first three members constituted an executive committee for administrative orders, court

---

[108] Pat. Rolls, 38 Henry VIII, pt. 5, mem. 24.

[109] See p. 56, *supra*. William Berners and John Wiseman held the office of auditor of the treasurer's accounts until October 23, 1549, at which time Berners was appointed sole auditor, contrary to constitutional provision. This change was effected without royal permission and was considered by the government to have been a usurpation of authority.

decrees, and major decisions of policy. Whereas their oaths of office were administered by the lord chancellor of England, all the others were taken by the chancellor of the Augmentations.[110] They and they alone had full power to award process by writ of *scire facias* under privy seal attachment against crown debtors and were employed, at their sole discretion, to " make orders decrees and iudgementes and . . . devise by all other wayes and meanes suche acte and actes thinge and thinges for the recouery thereof." [111]

In general the Court's jurisdiction was the same as that exercised by the two dissolved institutions, but in order to clarify its exact status definite rules and procedures were stipulated in the patent. The major powers of the central organization, as exercised by the chancellor and general surveyors with the assistance of the remainder of the council, were set forth under seven basic heads: grants under the great seal, warrants, the collection of crown debts, revenues, payments, judicial process, and administrative supervision over court personnel.[112] Appointment of officers, land grants and leases, annuities, pensions, and all charges on the regular revenues of the Court, when authorized by royal warrant, passed under its great seal. Likewise, leases and grants of land for term of twenty-one years could be made by the chancellor, but in cases of the surrender of unexpired leases or leases for reversion the

[110] Corporal oaths, similar in nature, were required of all the Augmentations officials. With the exception of that part relating to the court seals, which were entrusted exclusively to him, the oath of the chancellor was identical to that of the two general surveyors. As presented in the patent the former oath ran as follows: " ye shall swere that ye well and truly shall serue the Kinge in thoffice of the Chauncellourshippe of the Courte of thaugmentacions and reuenues of the Kinges Crowne and shall mynyster equall iustice to riche and poore to the best of your connyng wytte and power. And that ye shall diligentlye procure all thinges whiche maye honestlye and iustely be to the Kinges aduantage and profitt and to thaugmentacon of the rightes and prerogatiues of his Crowne. And truly vse the Kinges seales appoynted to your office. And also indeuour your selfe to the vttermost of the power to see the Kinge truly answeryd of suche rentes reuenues issues and profittes whiche shall or maye arrise or growe in your office. And frome tyme to tyme delyuer with spede suche as shall haue to do before youe. And that ye shall not take nor receyve of any persone any gyfte or rewarde in eny cause or matter depending before youe wherin the Kinges highnes shalbe partie wherby any preiudice hinderaunce losse or disherison shall growe or be to the Kinges highnes so helpe you god and all sayntes." Pat. Rolls, 38 Henry VIII, pt. 5, mem. 16.

[111] *Ibid.*, mem. 18.

[112] " Wee haue thought good to deuyse make ordeyne and establishe," the provision reads, " suche good resonable and conuenyent rules and ordinaunces for the seyde officers and ministers of this Courte and to gyue to theym suche powers and auctorities as hereafter be expressed wherby they maye be the more hable and more certaynly vnderstande and knowe howe to serue vs in the same." *Ibid.*, mem. 18.

special sanction of the crown was required. In most matters, however, the Court had complete authority over its own business. With a minimum of external interference it collected and administered the revenues under its charge, called crown debtors to account, and spent money on its own initiative by ordinary court warrant.[113] Finally, in all normal administration the chancellor and general surveyors had practically unlimited discretion. Upon such considerations as to them seemed convenient, they could institute " suche good rules orders decres iudgementes and direccions for the better aunswering order and gouvernaunce of this Courte and the issues profittes and reuenues of the same."

In purely judicial matters the Court was given wide jurisdiction. It had full authority over all its own personnel and the revenues alloted to it. Cases under the former category were concerned principally with matters of contempt, disobedience, negligence, nonpayment of revenues, or malfeasance in office. In this connection the Court was empowered to commit to ward anyone appearing before the judges " for lacke of payment " of any money due the crown and to assess " fines and penalties " for those found guilty of violation of the Court's decrees. Furthermore, all kinds of civil suits related to and growing out of Augmentations lands or the issues thereof, or disputes arising from " any matter or cause or any other thing assigned or connected, or appoynted " to the Court were delegated to it. In particular these included revenue cases, debts, and disputes over land ownership. Upon the discretion of the Court process was to be duly awarded under the privy seal for rents, arrears, and other matters relating to the revenues thereof, when the crown was a party to the suit, with such attachment and penalties as were commonly awarded in the chancery or in the late Court. In addition, the Court acknowledged concords of fines upon lands within its jurisdiction, submitting them, without fee, for recording in the Court of Common Pleas. Finally, it had power to correct and punish all persons who were brought before the Court " according to the nature qualitie and quantitie " of the offense. In all other matters between party and party, wherein the crown had no tangible interest, cases were remitted to the common law.[114]

Centralization was achieved through the chancellor and general surveyors, who maintained systematic control over all the Court's personnel. As a precaution against theft and corruption various safeguards were established, including regular accounts, close supervision of all

---

[113] Payments by the treasurer were authorized either by warrant of the king, the privy council, or the Court. The chancellor, with the consent of the general surveyors, could decree normal court payments not in excess of £200.

[114] Pat. Rolls, 38 Henry VIII, pt. 5, mem. 21.

activities, periodic inspection of work, and bonding of ministers. Annual declarations of accounts were heard prior to the first of March by the directors, who likewise made yearly reports to the crown on the general state of the revenues under their charge. In order that a permanent record of land leases and grants might be kept, the clerk of the Court was required to enroll all documents passing under its two seals. Likewise he recorded in a separate " boke or registre " a full account of all cases that came before the Court, with a statement of orders and decrees issued. Formal plea rolls were not kept, but informal accounts of court proceedings, together with the supporting documents, have been preserved. As a further guarantee against loss of revenues, the clerk recorded changes in land tenure, as by grants, leases, sales, or other alterations of status which might affect the yearly income, in "a faire boke or legier," and reported such to the auditors three times yearly.

All this attention given to accounts and to the preservation of documents had the effect of making the new institution, in fact as well as in name, a court of record. A keeper of records was now appointed to a full-time position, with a building to house the archives. A clear-cut distinction was made between his office and that of the clerk. Although he was required to give attendance upon the chancellor and general surveyors when requested to do so, the keeper had no jurisdiction over any document until after it had been engrossed, enrolled, and delivered to the Court. " And [he] shall haue the keping of the house where the same recordes shall lie and remayne, prouyded alwaye that the same keper shall not in anywise entermedle to make any copie constathe exemplificacions or other instrument or thing of or oute of the same recordes or eny of theym but that the same copies constathes exemplificacions or other instrumentes . . . shalbe made by the Clerk of this Courte for the tyme beyng or by his deputie or deputies." [115] Walter Farr, who had for a number of years served the previous Augmentations as a practical archivist, was not reappointed. He was replaced by Edward Stradbury at an annual salary of £10 plus the emoluments of his office.[116] Richard Duke was retained as clerk of the Court at no advance in salary.[117]

[115] *Ibid.*, mem. 27. Additional cases and closets were acquired from time to time in order to accommodate the growing volume of records, as in January, 1550, when the keeper was allowed £10 for the construction of ten new presses. Augm. Office, Misc. Books 258, fol. 70*d*.

[116] Stradbury assumed office in 1546 before the old Court was dissolved. Upon the reorganization of the Court his salary was raised from £6 1*s*. 8*d*. to £10. During the last year of Edward VI's reign he was succeeded by Christopher Skevington. Augm. Office, Misc. Books 254, fol. 62; 255, fol. 80; Treas. Rolls of Accts., No. 3, fols. 80*d*., 81; No. 4, fol. 32*d*.; No. 8, fol. 37. On Farr's earlier work as " keeper of evidences," see p. 45, *supra*.

[117] Augm. Office, Misc. Books 218, fol. 3*d*. Duke, like most of the other officers

In order that the Court should be " presentlie furnyshed withe suche officers and Ministers as shall and may furth withe passe the weightie and greatest affairs of the same," the major officials were named in the patent, although the formal appointments were not made until the following day, January 2, 1547. All of them were for life and mostly included the officials who were already serving in corresponding positions in one or the other of the dissolved courts. Those not reappointed were awarded adequate compensation in the form of pensions, assigned by the chancellor and two general surveyors of the Court; but as frequently happened the privy council delayed implementation of the policy. The king, who had been too busy with " other moche more weightie causes," procrastinated so long in signing the warrant for the pensions that the Augmentations finally concluded the matter by court decree. Full compensation, as from the date of the surrender of office, was awarded every official dismissed, irrespective of the time of delivery of the pension grants.[118]

The following table presents a list of officials stationed at the Court's headquarters in Westminster, with their annual salaries at the time of appointment.

In the broader reaches of national administration perhaps the most significant effect of the reforms of 1547 was apparent in the accelerated decline of the king's chamber. Already the chamber had been eclipsed by the newer financial courts of record, and now the fall of the Court of Survey removed all hope of a belated recovery. As a department of state, the position of the chamber depended, obviously, upon its financial status, which was being steadily undermined. Under Cromwell's administration the internal work of the chamber was gradually curtailed, while externally, in the field of financial affairs, the treasurer of the chamber no longer bore the bulk of extraordinary receipts and payments which had come to be more evenly distributed. Chamber decline, if not pronounced, had certainly been accelerated under Sir Brian Tuke, whose period of tenure, nevertheless, marked the last phase of vigorous activity. Sir William Cavendish was in charge of the chamber office in

---

of the Court, had received advances in salary since his original appointment at £10. Of course, the profits of office always enhanced the official salaries.

[118] Augm. Office, Miscellanea, 37; Treas. Rolls of Accts., No. 4. Ablest of the field officers of the dissolved Augmentations who were not reappointed was Mathew Colthurst, auditor in the third district, although his case was warmly supported by Sir Edward Seymour, earl of Hertford. Like many of the other ministers, he had served the old Court for a number of years, and his friends thought he merited a post in the new institution. Nevertheless, there were fewer positions than ministers, and a number of former officials were left unrewarded, save for generous pensions. *L. and P.*, XXI, pt. 1, nos. 100, 156, 171; pt. 2, no. 288. Colthurst was later employed as a commissioner for the dissolution of the chantries.

OFFICERS OF THE REORGANIZED COURT OF AUGMENTATIONS AT WESTMINSTER

	Office	Name	Salary
1.	Chancellor and principal officer	Sir Edward North	£300
2.	General surveyors and second officer	Sir Thomas Moyle Walter Mildmay	£200
3.	Treasurer and third officer	Sir John Williams	£320
4.	Masters of Woods and fourth officer	Sir Thomas Pope, south of River Trent John York Robert Heneage, north of River Trent	£100
5.	Attorney and fifth officer	Richard Goodrich	£100
6.	Solicitor and sixth officer	John Gosnold	£80
7.	Surveyors of woods and seventh officer	Geoffrey Gates, south of River Trent John Arscot, north of River Trent	£100
8.	Clerk of the Court	Richard Duke	£40
9.	Auditors of the prests and foreign accounts	Gregory Richardson £40 William Dixe £40	£80
10.	Keeper of the records	Edward Stradbury Christopher Skevington	£10
11.	Usher of the Court	James Johnson John Grene, deputy (4d. per day)	£6 1s. 8d.
12.	Messengers of the Court	Richard Hall Richard Lyall (4d. per day) Robert Makerell Thomas Tyrrell — plus £1 13s. 4d. for livery	£6 1s. 8d.
13.	Chief mason for the Court	Robert Sylvester Rafe Hilles	£6 1s. 8d.
14.	Chief carpenter for the Court	John Parker	£6 1s. 8d.

1547 when the reorganization scheme went into effect, having been appointed treasurer just before the dissolution of the Court of Survey. Since the treasurer of the chamber was also the receiver-general for that court, most of the revenues formerly flowing through it were then transferred to the second Court of Augmentations.

When Cavendish became treasurer in 1546, he found over £1,848 of back revenues uncollected. During his first two years in office he received but £4,737 12s. 8d., of which £2,400 came from the duchy of Lancaster, £1,000 from wards and liveries, and £1,287 12s. 8d. from obligations. In his annual declaration to the crown on the state of chamber finance in 1548, Cavendish deplored the fact that he was indebted for about £14,000 " or thereabout." He explained that many payments formerly made from the chamber, " nowe of late . . . by want of money in the same office are paied by the Coferer Treasurers and Receyvours of other offices to the greate decaie of the same." Actually he still retained the traditional revenues from the duchy of Lancaster and from the Court of Wards and Liveries, which, along with a few categories of miscellaneous revenues, netted him about £6,000 in 1547. Even so, chamber expenditures always exceeded receipts. While extraordinary payments could be curtailed at the discretion of the privy council or shifted to other treasuries, the chamber was still burdened with " ordinary " charges which, if paid regularly, could have amounted to as much as £25,000 a year. During the following year, 1549, the chamber accounts showed a deficit of £1,167 10s. This was a far cry indeed from the average expenditure of £120,000 per annum during the period 1509–1518, or the maximum of almost £700,000 spent annually during the war years in 1512 and 1513.[119] As a result of the increased competition of the second Court of Augmentations, Cavendish became dependent upon other treasuries for the bulk of his revenues. The heyday of chamber prestige was over.

Although the chamber was slowly reverting to its original status of household department, it continued for another decade as a minor disbursing agency. Whereas, heretofore, the treasurer of the chamber had customarily rendered his accounts to the Court of Survey or to special commissioners designated to examine them, he was now charged to

[119] Excerpts from the receipts and payments of Cavendish during the reign of Edward VI are presented in J. Payne Collier (ed.), *Trevelyan Papers*, (" Camden Society Publications," No. 84 [London, 1863]), pt. 2, pp. 1–38; for a description of the original volumes, see Nichols (ed.), *Literary Remains of Edward VI*, I, Preface, xx(g). The receipts for 1549 were only £16,868 12s., whereas the payments totaled £18,036 2s. 3d. *Ibid.*, pt. 2, pp. 13, 34. On the evolution of the chamber and earlier payments, consult Richardson, *Tudor Chamber Administration, 1485–1547*, especially 219, 221, 240–48.

" accompte yerelie for the same before the Chauncellour and generall surveyours " of the Augmentations, assisted by two of the Court's regular auditors particularly chosen " to fynyshe and determyne the same accompte before the laste daye of Aprill yearlie."

The patent of 1547 also provided that the revenues of the Court of Wards and of the duchy of Lancaster [120] should continue to be paid into the chamber, but revenues of the duchy of Cornwall were transferred to the new court. Anticipating the depletion of chamber revenues, Cavendish was to be supplied for the time being with " suche other sommes of money in grosse as we . . . by our warrauntes appoynte and asigne to and for the ordynarie charges and other paymentes of his office," received regularly from the treasurer of the Augmentations.[121] Actually the chamber accounts show that his principal expenditures after 1547 were borne by large drafts, drawn not only on the Augmentations Court but also on the Exchequer and the mint. These huge transfers of cash by warrant of the king and council represented as much as £1,000 to £2,000 or more per payment.[122] Thus the chamber lost its independent character, becoming completely dependent upon the will of the king and council for the revenues allocated to it.

The expedient of drawing upon the other treasuries for additional funds when short of cash proved to be slow and cumbersome. For the fiscal year closing September 29, 1551, the chamber was accorded no receipts, since it was operating on money received by royal warrant; furthermore, the sum total of expenditures, almost entirely for household wages and related items, amounted to only £16,563 2s. 7d. for the year.[123] In explanation it was recorded that the surplus revenues of the duchy, actually £4,476 19s. 10d. for the year, had been used for other affairs and not paid to the treasurer of the chamber " as it hath been allways heretofore for þe furniture of his Ordinary." Since the very beginning of the reign of Edward VI that " Old Order " or practice had been broken, " whereby the Treasurer of the Chamber hath been

---

[120] A portion of the Lancaster revenues, however, had been assigned to the household.

[121] Pat. Rolls, 38 Henry VIII, pt. 5, mems. 21, 22.

[122] Exch., Accounts Various, 426/5, fols. 6d.–10. By 1550 Cavendish was so " destytut of money for payment of the kinges maiestes workes according to a warraunt dormant that he haith for the same," that the Augmentations was ordered to take over the permanent charge of £100 monthly. At the time, May 14, 1550, the chamber was behind for nine months in those advances, which the Augmentations paid. Augm. Office, Misc. Books 259, fols. 96, 96d. This sort of transference of specific items of payment, formerly a regular assignment on the chamber, was common enough after 1548.

[123] Add. MS. 30198, fols. 30–34. Of this total only £13,041 8s. 2d. were permanent payments to continue, the remainder being " payments to revert and not to continue."

& is unfurnished of his Ordinary receipt." Likewise, the revenues of the Court of Wards and Liveries had not been paid to the chamber since Henry VIII's death as required by its constitution but had been used also for " Extraordinary causes " by orders of the privy council. To make up for this deficiency " Speciall Assignements out of divers Courts " were made regularly for the normal as well as the " most necessary charges," but when the need for money became acute, even that practice had been abandoned in favor of private warrants. It is little wonder, therefore, that such a haphazard system would in the end cause " great Confusion." [124] The final report of the reform commission of 1552 stated the situation concisely :

> And where þe Treasurer of þe Chamber was wont heretofore allways to receive yearly the Revenues of þe whole Court of Wards & Liverys and also abt some Thousand Pounds of þe Revenues of the Dutchy of Lancaster towards the furniture of þe payments in his charge Sithence þe Kings Maties time yt now is (& not afore) the said Revenues of þe Wards & Liveries & of þe Dutchy have been otherwise paid by warraunt for divers Extraordinary affairs of þe Kings & as it appeareth now upon þe view of Beamonts [125] accounts a great part thereof detained from þe King in his hands whereby his Majesties Councill have been constrained to furnish this Treasours Ordinary payments for þe Kings Servants Wages Messengers Posts and others in this Office from þe Mint þe Sales and other uncertain Receipts which hath bread a great confuse [sic] & a great loss to the King as þe Experience hath & will shew if it be not reformed.[126]

The later history of the chamber is uneventful. When Cavendish died in 1557 the treasurership was held in abeyance until the future status of the office could be determined by an investigation of chamber affairs. During this interim necessary payments, totaling £3,032 15s. 9d., were entrusted temporarily to a crown official, Edmund Felton, who directed chamber activities under the general supervision of two of the privy councillors. On October 31, 1558, the office was filled permanently by the appointment of Sir John Mason, councillor, who retained the post until his death in April, 1566.[127] His widow, Elizabeth Mason, exercised

---

[124] *Ibid.*, fols. 49d., 51d.–52.

[125] John Beaumont was receiver-general of the Court of Wards from 1545–51. He admitted to having concealed over £21,000 under cover of arrears in his accounts. No accounts of the court had been presented since 1545, which obviously resulted in " a great unsurety for the King." *Ibid.*, fol. 51.

[126] *Ibid.*, fol. 48.

[127] Pat. Rolls, 5 and 6 Philip and Mary, pt. 3, mem. 38. (*Cal. Pat. Rolls, Philip and Mary*, IV, 429.) The office of the master of the posts, which had been de-

the office for the remainder of the fiscal year, prior to the appointment of vice-chamberlain Sir Francis Knolles as treasurer of the chamber. The accounts of Felton and Mason constitute the first in the series of chamber accounts declared and enrolled in the renovated Exchequer.[128]

veloped by an earlier treasurer, Sir Brian Tuke, was now formally joined with the chamber office.

[128] Accounts of Felton, Mason, Knolles, and Thomas Heneage, as treasurers of the chamber, 225 membranes. Exch., T. R., Declared Accounts, 541, mems. 1–8, 78, 85, 117. Chamber payments were greatly restricted, both in variety and magnitude, being confined to purely court and household expenses.

CHAPTER SIX

BREAKDOWN
OF ADMINISTRATION
UNDER EDWARD VI

HE AMALGAMATION OF 1547 HAD ACCOMPLISHED SOMETHING, but as a reform it was at best only a half measure. The changes introduced affected but two of the six major revenue courts, though it must have been realized that such a step toward centralization was only a beginning. Sooner or later the real question of retrenchment, involving as it would the actual abolition of the least necessary of these financial departments, was bound to arise. While the postponement of any radical departure from established procedures was always popular, eventually the fundamental problem of providing a centralized administration would have to be met. However, during the last years of his reign, Henry VIII was more concerned with a speedy increasing of the national revenue than he was in long-term administrative reformation, and after his death the government was too preoccupied with other matters to give much attention to it. Consequently no further changes were made until the launching of more complete reorganization at the beginning of Mary's reign.

Whatever the inadequacies of the Edwardian administration, the period from 1547 to 1554 was one of growth and prosperity for the Court of Augmentations. Expansion in both power and authority was quite steady, while in the field of finance the Court continued in its role of leading national treasury.[1] The privy council still preserved its super-

---

[1] This financial ascendancy was threatened for a time by the mint, which until 1551 showed a greater clear profit than the Augmentations. For the period from

vision over all the revenue courts, but such conciliar control gradually became more nominal than real. It is true that during the minority of Edward VI both Somerset and Northumberland maintained general direction over the financial business of the various revenue departments, though such centralized authority usually consisted of little more than executive warrants for extraordinary expenditures or series of governmental directives summarily ordering administrative actions or court decrees. For the most part, however, the Augmentations went its own way, unhampered by interference from above.

This institutional independence was a characteristic feature of Edwardian government at a time when the power of the king was weak and the authority of the council divided. It followed that once the close centralized control was removed maladministration was quick to develop. By no means confined to any single institution, corruption in government emerged as a significant fact, but it was not the only flaw in the changing political morality of the day. Increased personnel, advances in official salaries, irregularities in accounting, the accumulation of arrears of revenue, petty dishonesty, and a breakdown of the Court's efficiency appeared before the conclusion of the reign.

Historically the effectiveness of the national administration was inextricably bound up with the power of the central government. When the crown was weak, the absence of commission investigations and disciplinary checks led to carelessness and sloth, if not to downright dishonesty. Such conditions had obtained at times in the fifteenth century, especially during the Wars of the Roses when the public conscience had grown accustomed to official indolence. Still, the Tudor monarchy had put an end to all that, and the country had welcomed the change; whereas ministers had previously viewed laxity as the order of the day, they now accepted external disciplines and meticulous supervision with equal placidity. Conciliar government functioned successfully just so long as there was a forceful sovereign or a competent minister in control of the machinery of state. With the fall of Cromwell Henry VIII himself had supplied the necessary leadership and direction until problems of war and personal ill health had driven questions of purely domestic

the beginning of the reign through 1551, when the disastrous policy was abandoned, £651,500 in profits were derived from debasement. For the same period the net receipts of the Augmentations totaled £457,617. Revenue from the sale of crown land constituted the largest single item of Augmentations income, amounting to over £112,969 in 1548. Frederick C. Dietz, *Finances of Edward VI and Mary* ("Smith College Studies in History," Vol. III, no. 2 [Northampton, Mass., 1918]), 86, 95, 129; Augm. Office. Treas. Rolls of Accts., Nos. 4–7. Cf. C. W. C. Oman, "The Tudors and the Currency, 1526–1560," *Transactions of the Royal Historical Society*, New Series, IX (1895), 167–88.

administration into the background. Just as soon as the guiding hand was withdrawn, the slow process of internal decay set in. Although signs of bureaucratic inefficiency were visible before the end of the second Tudor reign, the greatest deterioration was not to come until after the death of Henry VIII, when there was a general administrative collapse along all fronts—a disintegration that was comparable, for a time at least, to that of the preceding century.

To historians of the reign of Edward VI the events of the Reformation have overshadowed economic and administrative developments. Despite the minority of the young king, the survival of strong monarchy was a fact of the greatest significance, more especially since the royal prerogative could now be exercised in name only. Moreover, undivided sovereignty, centered either in the person of the ruler or in a co-ordinating director acting in his stead, was a prerequisite indispensable to conciliar government. Personal authority and power, at a time when it was the function of a sovereign to rule as well as to govern, had been the keystone to the success of the Tudor monarchy. As illustrated in practically all branches of administration the ultimate efficiency of the governmental machinery depended largely upon the capable and sustained direction of the crown. Likewise, the assistance of the council in maintaining vigilant control over all departments was a fundamental link in the Tudor chain of command. Wolsey and Cromwell in their consistent support of royal policy had contributed not a little within the highly personal government of Henry VIII. Though the privy council supplemented, it could not replace the authority of the crown. With the domination of selfish factions under, first Hertford and later Warwick, the divided council weakened the prestige of the executive and undermined the power of the crown. As internal disorders began to develop, the stability of the entire administration was threatened, and serious disruption was avoided only by a series of Marian reforms which reached a culmination under Elizabeth, after the death of the king and the failure of the Northumberland plot.

Any change in the political consciousness of the people is one of the most difficult phenomena to interpret, particularly in its effect upon the behavior of ministers. Equally elusive is the national reaction to governmental corruption and graft or to distinctions between public and private morality. No doubt much depends upon the moral tone of the age, but in large part the prevailing attitude toward official responsibility and political morality is determined by the government, which sets the standard. During the early sixteenth century devotion to the first two Tudors, deference to authority, loyalty to the state, and respect for the law had combined to instill in most officials a wholesome attitude toward all governmental administration, whether local or central. Under Henry VIII the cult of obedience was strong indeed, in politics as in religion, and those who were tempted to disloyalty were held in check by the knowledge that official inquiries could be penetrating and justice swift. Pronounced as it was, however, this concept was changing in the Edwardian and Marian periods. Complaints of bad government became progressively prevalent, sense of public duty weakened, while in administration, efficiency and pride of attainment were no longer personal incentives. The misappropriation of government funds or even the actual theft of money often carried no stigma. When the leaders of the state could line their own pockets with impunity, lesser officials no doubt considered a portion of the governmental largesse as justly theirs, to be taken as of right.

The frankness with which the whole problem of political morality was approached, not only in the sixteenth century, but also in the seventeenth, indicates a fundamentally different attitude toward the responsibilities of office from that of today. Concepts of graft, embezzlement, corruption, and fraud seem to have been quite unrelated to popular notions of personal shame or public disgrace. A few social reformers harangued against the vices of the administration, but for the most part voices within the government were silent. Occasionally, men like Winchester and Burghley reacted strongly to the system, though they were unable to rise above it. There is no indication, however, that the national conscience was aroused. If the public was then indifferent to what in modern times would be regarded as political dishonesty, it must have been because such practice was commonly accepted as not only normal but customary. That, in addition to salaries, loyal public service should be rewarded in some tangible way by gifts, offices, annuities, or grants of land was an established governmental policy; when awards were not forthcoming as soon as expected, they were asked for, if not openly demanded, by persistent officials, the implication being that they had been discriminated against. Thus Sir John Raynsford of Colchester, Essex, when asking for a piece of monastic property, could expostulate with Cromwell that he had not been properly rewarded for his long years of service to the crown. Was not Cromwell his good lord? Were his services so unacceptable? His own friends remonstrated with him that he had been too unassertive. Why should he not ask for something as well as others, they queried. " Spare to axe and spare to speed," he concluded.[2] If still unsuccessful, what was more logical to a minister than

[2] Sir John Raynsford (Raynesford, Raynsforth, etc.) to Cromwell [Undated letter of 1538]. *L. and P.*, XIII, pt. 2, no. 1262. In the end perseverance prevailed, for Raynsford received several grants of land.

that he should acquire for himself what his government had unjustifiably withheld? On the basis of such psychology only can the inordinate attention given by everybody to getting a share, however small, of the new-found wealth of the state be explained. Nor was this indifference to the welfare of the community, in which public interest was sacrificed to private profit, confined to any particular class of society. It affected all servants of the crown including some of the most trusted and distinguished ministers; yet usually when investigation did occur and guilt was established the punishment was only nominal. Guilty officials not infrequently retained their offices or in some cases were promoted to positions of even greater responsibility. The chief concern of the state, and sometimes it would seem to be its only one, was to recover the money fraudulently appropriated. If imprisoned at all, the individual was treated more as an unfortunate debtor than as a criminal, to be released and pardoned as soon as the payment of the embezzled funds was guaranteed. In view of this attitude on the part of the state it is not surprising that individual behavior was fashioned according to national morality and practice.

Furthermore, other differences in the standards of the age are discernible. Bribes were openly offered and as frankly accepted. With similar candor offices were bought and sold, for as much as five hundred or two thousand pounds, according to Hugh Latimer.[3] Nonetheless, in the prevailing morality actual misappropriation of revenue did not necessarily imply dishonest intent, since financial ministers expected to use whatever public funds they had in their possession until such time as they were called for by the government. This practice was abused when surplus cash was retained for purposes of personal gain instead of being paid into the treasury at the end of the accounting period. When an official pleaded for an extension of time for payment, it might simply mean that he had appropriated goverment money for his own business and was unable to pay it back immediately. Within the complicated

---

[3] Latimer's fifth sermon before Edward VI in April, 1549. In criticizing ministers for the taking of rewards and the acceptance of bribes he pointed out that they were merely compensating themselves for the original cost of their offices. "Ye consyder not the matter to the bottome. Theyr offyces be bought for great sommes, nowe howe shall they receyue theyre money agayne, but by brybynge ye woulde haue them vndone." All things were to be had for a price, he went on to say, adding: "I meruaile the ground gapes not and deuours vs, how be it, we ought not to maruayle, surely it is, the great leuity of god that suffers it. Oh Lorde in what case are we." Edward Arber (ed.), *Seven Sermons before Edward VI, on each Friday in Lent, 1549* (English Reprints, no. 2, London, 1869), 147, 148. Thomas Lever tells the same story of the steady disintegration of morals. Edward Arber (ed.), *Thomas Lever's Sermons, 1550* (English Reprints, no. 25, London, 1871). On contemporary opinion abroad regarding English morality, see Hughes, *The Reformation in England*, II, 163.

system of bookkeeping then in use it is difficult to discover the facts of the case; but the growing volume of accumulated arrears which figures so prominently in all accounts no doubt occasionally represented collections in cash that had been withheld for a period by the collector for private investment. If portions of such withholdings were repaid periodically no questions would be asked. In fact, a receiver of regular revenues might never quite pay out during an entire lifetime, and few of them appear to have died in office without bequeathing to their families modest debts, which the government had been unable to collect.

To the financial officer such irregularities seemed justifiable in view of the fact that his government in turn expected him to meet promptly all payments required of him, whether the money had been collected or not. There are numerous instances where crown ministers, like the treasurers of the chamber or the Augmentations, had used their own money to cover current financial demands when revenues were slow in coming in. Then, too, in comparison with private business the civil servant was underpaid, so that regular " extras " in the form of emoluments and profits were more or less taken for granted. Since salaries were recognized as inadequate, it seems to have been assumed that governmental employees would increase them whenever possible by a certain amount of peculation. To the end of the century the Tudor bureaucrat performed all sorts of free services for the state, not the least of which were espionage activities and various types of commission investigation for which specific compensation was not customary. In part recompense for such services, however, numerous honorific positions, sinecurial posts, and local offices which could be held by deputies were provided. There is some evidence to suggest that superfluous government jobs were perpetuated, or new ones created, in order to compensate underpaid officials and placate the hoard of hungry hangers-on at court who demanded recognition and aid. Patronage represented power and influence to those in a position to dispense it, and their rights had to be considered as much as those of the officials under them whom they protected.

The whole question of the breakdown of law and order and the consequent development of corruption in the government following the death of Henry VIII is in need of special investigation. For years scholars have been conscious of the seriousness of the problem, each adding his own bit to a cumulative indictment of the period, yet no attempt has been made either to explore the extent of exploitation and corruption or to assess their influence on the deterioration of morality within the various departments of government. Much of the contemporary criticism by Thomas More, Robert Crowley, Henry Brinkelow, Thomas Lever, Hugh Latimer, John Hales of Coventry, and others is obviously overstatement for effect, in the same way that the portrayal of the perfect commonwealth was an impossibly idealistic dream. While the contention of writers like James A. Froude that all classes of society were engaged in universal peculation, extravagance, plunder, and fraud is no longer tenable, it is true that the vast amount of evidence pointing toward widespread corruption cannot be ignored.[4] In the best interpretation of the reign of Edward VI that is now available, the author concludes that the desire for wealth became the common mainspring of action, and moral scruples disappeared. " Public interests were sacrificed to private gain, and the welfare of the community counted for little against the temptation to double rents and enclose commons. Malversation became frequent, officials took bribes, and offices were sold. Corruption in high places made the task of government difficult and rendered almost impossible a reformation in any direction." [5] All the financial courts, the Augmentations not excepted, came in for a share of the popular criticism of the times. Corruption among juries and bribery in the administration of justice were especially noticeable according to the critics. " The law is ended as a man is friended " ran a popular proverb; while in both the Exchequer and the Augmentations " wonderos great abuse " of the law was of long standing, observed Brinkelow as early as 1543. Extortion, oppression, and bribery were so pronounced, he declared, that a man was better off in hell than in either of those two courts. As regards the latter, a common saying had sprung up amongst the people: " Christ, for thy bitter passyon, saue me from the court of the Augmentacyon ! " [6]

---

[4] James Anthony Froude, *History of England* (American edition, New York, 1875), V, Chaps. 26, 27. For similar indictments see also Strype, Dixon, and Burnet. An excellent analysis of the Elizabethan problem of corruption is presented in Joel Hurstfield, *The Queen's Wards* (London, 1958), Chap. X.

[5] A. F. Pollard, *England under Protector Somerset* (London, 1900), 54–55. The evils of the existing system continued under Elizabeth, particularly in the Court of Wards where even the great Burghley succumbed to the trend. Joel Hurstfield, "Lord Burghley as Master of the Court of Wards, 1561–98," *Transactions of the Royal Historical Society*, Fourth Series, XXXI (October, 1948), 95–114, especially 98, 107 ff.

[6] Henry Brinkelow, *Complaynt of Roderyck Mors*, ed. by J. M. Cowper (Early English Text Society, Extra Series, no. 22 [London, 1874]), 24–25. Brinkelow presented a similar indictment of the Court of Wards, *ibid.*, 18. Through malversation in the Court of First Fruits and Tenths the king was reported in 1549 to have lost almost £10,000 a year. Patrick Fraser Tytler, *England under the Reigns of Edward VI and Mary* (London, 1839), I, 170. Somewhat later, in 1551 and 1554, similar charges against the revenue courts were presented by the Venetian observers, Daniel Barbaro and Girolamo Soranzo. Reports on England, *Cal. State Papers, Venetian*, V, nos. 703, 934. About the same time the pamphleteer Robert Crowley was writing in like vein of the lack of obedience to the law and the doings of men " without conscience " who were " vtterly voide of Goddes feare."

Exaggerated as was most of the censure, it is noteworthy that allegations of marked decline in public morality were by no means confined to pamphleteers, preachers, and moralizing reformers. In addressing himself to the prevailing evils of society the king noted that " slake execution of the lawes hath bene the chiefest sore of all," while those offenders who were convicted, " either by bribery or foolish pitey," often escaped punishment.[7] Occasionally, however, a guilty conscience would prompt someone to surrender voluntarily a portion of his ill-gotten gains to the state.

In preaching against corruption, Latimer's forthright denunciations brought forward a few repentant listeners to confess their guilt and make restitution. On March 28, 1549, Sir Michael Stanhope, chief gentleman of the privy chamber, was authorized to receive £373 " of suche the Kinges money as came of concelement," which had been received through the " exhortacion " of Latimer. The good doctor's persuasions must have been more effective than modern sermons, for he collected another £104 " conscience money " from one who had deceived the king, which was duly turned over to the council.[8] It is usually impossible to determine the offenses behind the large recognizances through which reprisals were exacted from officials high and low, but certainly those fines represent an important source of state income.[9] Whatever the extent of administrative malpractice official concern was registered in two acts of parliament, the one condemning the sale of offices and the other renouncing the corruption of receivers and revenue collectors who " doo yerely deteine and kepe the same [revenues] to their own gaine profiecte and lucre, contrarie to all right truthe and equitie." [10] In a commission of March 9, 1552, appointed to investigate

---

J. M. Cowper (ed.), *The Select Works of Robert Crowley* (Early English Text Society, Extra Series, no. 15 [London, 1872]), 132, 133, 144, 154 *passim*.

[7] Nichols (ed.), *Literary Remains*, II, 484.

[8] *Ibid.*, I, cxxviii. Latimer was awarded £50 for his efforts. Dasent (ed.), *Acts of the Privy Council*, II, Preface, xvii, 266, 409, 410. Later Sir William Sharington of the Bristol mint was so influenced by Latimer's eloquence that he admitted to charges of embezzlement.

[9] The lord chancellor was bound by recognizance for £4,000 to pay such fine as was later set; Protector Somerset, £10,000; and Lord Arundell stood bound for £12,000, payable at the rate of £1,000 per year. *Ibid.*, II, 103, 384, 398. However, as J. D. Mackie suggests, the use of fines may have been as much a device of party politics as it was an indication of malversation. Mackie, *The Earlier Tudors, 1485-1558*, 501.

[10] 5 and 6 Edward VI, c. 16, " An Acte againste buyinge and sellinge of Offices "; 7 Edward VI, c. 1, " An Acte for the true aunsweringe of the Kinges Majesties Revenues," *S. R.*, IV, 151-52, 161-64. The latter act fixed more rigid requirements for the bonding of officials and the auditing of accounts, as well as for the setting up of new penalties for misdemeanors in office.

law enforcement, it was alleged that although many attempts had been made to guarantee the execution of the laws of the land many evil-disposed persons by their ill-doings had of late " so encoraged and boldenyd others to lyve in suche disorderid sorte without all feare of oure saide lawes as excepte speady remedy be the soner provided verye greate inconveniences are like shortlye to ensue." The commissioners were charged to decide which laws were most necessary for the furtherance of justice and to provide for the proper execution of the same.[11] How-ever, commendable as was the intention of such executive prescription, it had no appreciable effect. A restoration of moral integrity and respect for the law was necessary before any practical improvement could be forthcoming.

Notwithstanding the effect of graft and corruption in high places on the more rigid standards formerly maintained by most departments, there was no general collapse either in the financial machinery or in the broader administrative organization. The established system was too strong for that. However ineffectual they may have been, commission investigations of delinquency, waste, and incompetence were recurrent throughout the reign. Reports from the treasurers and occasional stock-taking of the revenues of the realm show the council to have been aware of the need for closer regulation. Consequently, long-standing accounts of ministers responsible for public funds were called in and examined by professional auditors. In view of the number of them that balanced, it is not surprising that the delinquent accountant stood out as the excep-tion rather than the rule.

As the reign progressed, internal weaknesses in the administrative system came to the surface. Chief among them was the trend toward decentralization which began to emerge with the decrease of conciliar control. Although the council continued to give close and sometimes detailed attention to every phase of government, its regulations were primarily financial. Thus, the revenue courts came in for a fair amount of supervision, especially in the careful oversight of receipts and expen-ditures. In other matters the courts enjoyed remarkable freedom, inde-pendence which led to lethargy rather than to wholesome growth. Under

---

[11] Pat. Rolls, 6 Edward VI, pt. 6, mem. 33*d*. Laxity in administration prompted even the more conscientious ministers to take advantage of the situation. During the Edwardian period the court circle profited immensely, not only from public offices, but also in lavish grants of land. In contrasting such prodigality with later Elizabethan circumspection, William Cecil could declare : " In my whole time I have not for these twenty-six years been beneficed from Her Majesty so much as I was within four years of King Edward." Hurstfield, *The Queen's Wards*, 279. Abuses in the augmentation of fees was also noticeable in Ireland. Dasent (ed.), *Acts of the Privy Council*, II, 76.

the rule of a minor, with ruthless ministers at the top setting an example, the dread fear of reprisal was removed. Officials relaxed, not only in the fulfillment of their duties, but in the maintenance of the discipline which had once brought forth the maximum of effort on the part of their subordinate ministers. Promotions were no longer based upon merit, being more often than not dependent upon personal or political influence. Increased fees, sinecures, and unearned profits were sought, and neither recognition of loyalty and meritorious service nor self-satisfaction in a job well done were any longer found rewarding enough. Heads of departments grew less insistent upon ordinary standards of efficiency. Public audits of accounts were delayed or held not at all. Arrears of revenues mounted, since no pressure was put upon the receivers to require speedy collections. Petty theft, dishonesty, and malfeasance in office passed unnoticed so long as suspicion was allayed by the semblance of honesty. It remained for a new series of commission investigations to reveal the seriousness of the abuses which had crept in.

The assumption of power by Edward Seymour, earl of Hertford and duke of Somerset, in March, 1547, as governor of the king's person and protector of the realm brought few immediate changes in policy. William Paulet, the great master of the household at this time who always managed to retain his influence regardless of political factions, was reappointed director of the Court of Wards and Liveries and made ex officio president of the council. Since he and Lord Rich were the most experienced in the business of administration, they tended to dominate in all matters of conciliar direction. The Lord Protector himself took over the office of lord treasurer, but most of Henry's ministers continued on the council and in their respective offices.[12] In the Augmentations all the appointments of January 2 were confirmed. For a period the chancellor and treasurer of the Court remained the most influential officers, but Sir Walter Mildmay as one of the general surveyors soon became its most important minister.

The first task confronting the new Court was the absorption of the additional lands and revenues acquired from the former Court of Survey. As jointly second officer in the Augmentations, Moyle and Mildmay were responsible for those possessions, though their issues and profits were processed in the same way as the other revenues of the Court. During the late forties greater laxity had developed in the Court of Survey than in the Court of Augmentations, especially in the processing

---

[12] Besides Paulet these directors were Sir Edward North, chancellor of the Augmentations; John Baker, chancellor of First Fruits and Tenths; Sir William Paget, chancellor of the duchy of Lancaster as well as principal secretary; and Sir Edmund Peckham, cofferer of the household and high treasurer of the mint.

of delinquent accounts. In fact, arrearages came dribbling in for years after the Court of Survey was dissolved. Ironically enough the officials of that court, some of whom were still heavily indebted to the crown for unpaid receipts, nevertheless were liberally pensioned in 1547 in compensation for the loss of their offices. Such was the infrequency of earlier audits that many irregularities remained undiscovered until after the Court of Augmentations had taken over the old accounts. In one instance James Morice and William Morice, jointly receivers and surveyors of Richmond lands,[13] owed £1,844 in 1544 as the residue of an original debt to the crown of £2,757 6s. 11d. Land evaluated at £1,133 6s. 8d. was accepted in part payment, although that amount was considered "farre above the valewe" of the property. This concession by the king of "his mere goodnes and most gracyous dysposicion" was granted because James Morice had rendered Henry VIII and his mother "longe trewe and faythefull seruice" for many years. Sureties were taken for the unpaid balance. A year later, £500 of the debt was still due, for which half-yearly payments of fifty marks were required until the debt was paid. Despite the fact that the terms of the agreement were never fulfilled, the receivers continued to draw a life pension of £110 annually after the elimination of their office in 1547, when it was annexed to the Augmentations.[14]

The most important single item of Augmentations business in 1547 and 1548 was the supervision of the dissolution of the chantries and the taking over for the crown of all their scattered lands, revenues, and properties. As the last of the religious endowments to invite exploitation, these institutions had long been earmarked for suppression, though the original act of confiscation in 1545 had never been fully implemented.[15] Commissions for the survey of the possessions of the

---

[13] James Morice, a former servant of Henry VIII's grandmother, the countess of Richmond, had been a receiver of her lands, an office which he held with Hugh Edwards. The office was expanded by the general surveyors to include administrative jurisdiction (surveyorship) and granted to the two men for life or during good conduct. When Edwards died, William Morice, son of James, joined him in the office. The term "Richmond lands" was also used occasionally in referring to the earldom of Richmond or the possessions of Henry Fitzroy, the duke of Richmond, natural son of Henry VIII, who died in 1536. *L. and P.*, I, pt. 1, nos. 94(29), 289(20), 651(2) ; *Addenda*, pt. 1, no. 1248.

[14] Indenture of April 11, 1544. Exch., Accounts Various, 518/29. See also *ibid.*, 76/35 ; Augm. Office, Miscellanea, 24 ; *Ibid.*, Misc. Books 256, fols. 94d., 98, 100d. ; 258, fols. 69, 69d., 71d. ; 260, fol. 68 ; 327, fols. 5d., 38, 38d. ; 342, fol. 31 ; *L. and P.*, XX, pt. 1, no. 1335(14).

[15] Under the first chantry act, primarily an expedient of war finance only, secularized endowments which originally had been founded for religious purposes were brought under attack, although the remainder was subject to investigation. See p. 124, *supra*.

chantries had been appointed early in 1546; however, with the exception of a number of voluntary surrenders, there appears to have been no general acquisition of chantry property until the beginning of the reign of Edward VI.[16] Although the surveys under the auspices of the Augmentations had got well under way before the abolition of the first Court, a fresh beginning had to be made after the death of Henry VIII.[17]

The initial act having expired, Edward's first parliament in the autumn of 1547 enacted a second statute for the confiscation of the chantries.[18] As in the case of the earlier monastic dissolutions the real motive was a pecuniary one. Schools were to be founded from the spoils, and greater benefits made available for the poor, but the real object in the speedy sale of chantry lands was " specially for the relief of the Kinges Majestyes charges and expences, which do dayly growe and encrease." The commons in parliament strongly objected to including all guilds and brotherhoods within the limits of the statute, and only reluctantly were they persuaded to accept the clause " guyldable landes." The commissioners for the investigation surveyed all " lay corporations guilds fraternities companies and fellowships of mysteries or crafts incorporate " and reported what lands and property were vested in the crown by virtue of the act.[19]

In Reformation theory the dissolution of the chantries and collegiate churches was a tacit repudiation of the Catholic doctrine of purgatory. Since the primary function of those institutions was to say masses for the benefit of departed souls, the logic of the reformers was irrefutable. They pointed out that the founding of chantries " argued purgatory to be; so the pulling of them down argueth it not to be"; moreover, " as long as praying for souls departed is suffered, the people will think that

---

[16] *L. and P.*, XXI, pt. 1, nos. 68, 69, 309, 966–68. In appointment of commissioners for chantry surveys, the crown drew heavily on officials in the Court of Augmentations and in the Court of Survey. *Ibid.*, no. 302(30).

[17] Augm. Office, Misc. Books 254, fols. 88, 93; 255, fols. 104–10.

[18] The second chantries act differed slightly from the previous one in setting up various precautions for exemptions. Colleges of the universities of Oxford and Cambridge, St. George's Chapel, Windsor, and a few others were excluded. The act included lands, tenements, rents, hereditaments, and all endowments used for maintaining anniversaries or obits, lights or lamps in any church or chapel. 1 Edward VI, c. 14, " An Acte wherby certaine Chauntries Colleges Free Chapelles and the Possessions of the same be given to the Kinges Ma^te," *S. R.*, IV, 24–33. It can be consulted in convenient form in Tanner (ed.), *Tudor Constitutional Documents*, 103–107.

[19] Dasent (ed.), *Acts of the Privy Council*, II, 184–85, 193-95. The returns of the commissioners are found among the Certificates of Colleges and Chantries in the Augm. Office (E. 301), 121 rolls. Those for Cornwall have been published in Lawrence S. Snell, *Documents Towards a History of the Reformation in Cornwall* (Exeter, 1953), no. 1.

there is a purgatory, and that in process of time will cause many to think that it is [a] pity that houses of Religion should be decayed whose prayers, as they think, profited much to souls departed." [20]   Such rationalizing, of course, strongly justified the action of the government, the straits of which prompted the employment of any measure calculated to yield additional revenues. The profits actually acquired from these foundations proved to be disappointingly meager. Part of the chantry endowments went toward the support of established schools, which were licensed to continue, or for the foundation of grammar schools. Most of the remainder was devoured by rapacious ministers and courtiers who, by gift, purchase, or illegal appropriation, absorbed the greater portion of the chantry revenue before it ever reached the royal coffers. [21]

When in 1547 Somerset's ambition led to war with Scotland and subsequently to a renewal of the periodic conflict with France, every means of raising revenue was utilized in order that enough money be raised " as might serve for this present necessity." [22]   If, as the council hoped, the chantry wealth was to serve as an alternative to parliamentary taxation for war expenditures, no time should be lost in converting it into usable cash. Precedent was not lacking for such an endeavor, though it had met with greater success in the previous reign. The government's need for money was so urgent that the disposal of chantry land and timber began almost before the final surrender of the houses was completed. In mid-January, 1548, the several commissions for the survey of religious colleges and chantries were appointed; by the end of April a royal warrant for the sales had been issued.

The twenty-five commissions set up varied in size from five to thirteen members, the average being eight or nine. Augmentations officials sat on about half of these surveys; among other commissioners the duchy of Lancaster organization was also represented. They were to inquire what colleges and other religious foundations had come to the

[20] Lacey Baldwin Smith, *Tudor Prelates and Politics* (Princeton, N. J., 1953), 168–69.

[21] Dr. Richard Cox, the king's chaplain, warned Paget against the "importune wolves" whose greed threatened to devour all the newly acquired endowment. Unless the king stood strongly against it, "like a hardy and godly lion," he wrote, nothing would be left for the founding of new schools. *L. and P.*, XXI, pt. 2, nos. 260, 282. Writing later in the seventeenth century Fuller voiced a similar indictment: "Now, all scruples removed, chantry-land went down without any regret. Yea, such who mannerly expected till the King carved for them out of abbey-lands, scrambled for themselves out of chantry-revenues, as knowing this was the last dish of the last course, and after chantries as after cheese, nothing to be expected." Thomas Fuller, *The Church History of Britain* (London, 1837), II, 275.

[22] Dietz, *English Government Finance, 1485–1558*, 183.

crown under the recent act and to certify their findings on or before the end of the following May. Returns were made to the Court of Augmentations, which administered all the chantry property save lands which lay within the jurisdiction of the duchy. Thus, a part of the possessions was put under the control of the Duchy Chamber at Westminster. As in the case of the previous inquiry, the commissioners were not empowered to take surrenders. All " costes and charges " for the surveys, as well as miscellaneous expenses " for the makinge and engrossinge faire bookes of the saide Survey and for Reparacions to be done within the same," were borne by the Augmentations.[23]

The wanton destruction of chantries, colleges, and guilds was a serious blow to public education and brought forth a great deal of popular criticism, which Tudor governments were always anxious to avoid. Consequently, it was the intent of the crown in council, as expressed in both acts of suppression, to provide on the one hand for the continuation of worthy educational foundations and on the other to use a generous portion of the appropriated chantry revenues for the endowment of new schools by the crown. Although practical financial embarrassments prevented complete realization of such a policy, the council was perfectly sincere in its intention to preserve and foster education. However, by the time the chantry lands and property had actually come into the king's possession, it was next to impossible to prevent them from being used for other purposes. As the demand for free gifts of land or shares of the spoils spread from the councillors to the greedy harpies at court, the resolution of the government weakened; similarly, when the need for money grew more acute it was easy to spend what was available and justify the action on moral grounds. The execution of such a policy required both tact and firmness; officials were needed who were at once amenable to the council's point of view, sympathetic with the government's financial position, and independent of local pressure. Certainly such independence of action could not be expected of the local commissioners already sitting, who would undoubtedly be prejudiced in favor of preserving educational foundations in their own counties. The delegated power must be wielded by a central authority and by ministers of sound judgment and tact, but such ability is hard to come by in any state. When finally selected, the officials represented

[23] Pat. Rolls, 2 Edward VI, pt. 7, mems. 13*d.*–15. Augm. Office, Miscellanea, 37; Misc. Books 256, 257, 258. Thomas Argall, clerk and keeper of the records of the Court of First Fruits and Tenths, was also paid " for making of all the perticulers of colledges chauntries and free chappelles within the realme and certaine other bokes exhibited into this courte to his no little charges and paines." *Ibid.* 257, fols. 97, 103; 258, fol. 57*d.*; Miscellanea, 23. On the earlier commissions, see p. 33, *supra*.

the revenue courts and functioned through the medium of a temporary commission appointment.

This difficult task fell upon Sir Walter Mildmay, then only recently appointed one of the general surveyors in the Court of Augmentations, and Robert Keilwey, the surveyor of liveries in the Court of Wards and Liveries.[24] Both men were responsible legalists, just emerging into the limelight of public scrutiny. Whatever their personal convictions on the question of the disposition of chantry wealth, they evidently satisfied the council, for they sat on various other commissions during the remainder of the reign. At the time of their appointment they were officially referred to as men " most mete therunto for their tried wisedomes " and " faythefull discrecion in siche mattiers." [25]

In close co-operation with the Augmentations this central executive commission performed a three-fold function. First, the two commissioners investigated the nature and extent of the numerous endowments covered by the act and determined which ones should be continued and which appropriated to the use of the crown; second, they assigned pensions to all those whose offices had been abolished, as well as to the dispossessed inmates of the dissolved institutions, to be granted under the seal of the Augmentations and paid by the receivers of that court; and third, they sold lands, movables, and personal property which had accrued to the crown, paying in the purchase money to the treasury of the Court. Sale price of the chantry possessions was to be based on the certificates of land values determined by the auditor and surveyors of the Augmentations. Messenger fees and all other expenses of the commissioners were to be borne by the Court. An interesting procedure for the auditing of the commissioners' accounts was set forth in their instructions. Those accounts were to be examined by a committee of eight legal experts representing the crown and the revenue courts. When engrossed and subscribed by this committee, they were then to be presented to the king and the council for final approval.[26]

---

[24] Appointment of May 22, 1547. *Cal. Pat. Rolls, Edward VI*, I, 238. Legal reporter and reader at the Inner Temple, Keilwey was one of many reputable lawyers who enjoyed a long service in the Court of Wards and Liveries. He retained his surveyorship in that court until his death in 1581. *D. N. B.*; Bell, *The Court of Wards and Liveries*, 20–21. He was also a commissioner for the survey of chantries in Somerset and Dorset. Augm. Office, Misc. Books 257, fol. 106*d*.

[25] Dasent (ed.), *Acts of the Privy Council*, II, 184–86.

[26] These instructions were incorporated in two separate commissions of April 27 and June 20, 1548. Pat. Rolls, 2 Edward VI, pt. 5, mems, 25*d*.–26*d*.; pt. 4, mems. 23*d*.–25*d*. The patents are inadequately abstracted in *Cal. Pat. Rolls, Edward VI*, II, 57–58; I, 417–18. In the *Calendar* deficiencies in the patents are supplied from the signed bills authorizing them. The committee of audit specified in the

However conscientious, Mildmay and Keilwey were unable to please everybody. Their first duty, of course, was to the Lord Protector and the council whose demands were conditioned by the dire financial necessities of the moment. In theory a fine distinction was drawn between those chantry revenues which had previously been used for pious purposes and those employed in secular pursuits. The latter included "preachings," schools, hospitals, poor relief, and the maintenance of "piers, jutties, or banks against the rage of the sea, havens or creeks "; the former endowments were for the saying of masses perpetually for the benefit of the dead. Thus, theoretically, charitable uses were to be continued, while all superstitious and secular endowments were to be appropriated for war, garrisons, and national defense. When a given project was allowed, the commissioners assigned land or revenues for its support and presented a certificate thereof to the council for approval.

The evidence available indicates this aspect of the work of the commission to have been exceedingly sketchy.[27] Scholars are still not agreed on the extent of Edward's endowment of charitable and educational institutions, although it is now clear that no great number was established by the crown. The burden of pensions for the displaced clergy constituted a first drain on the chantry revenues, after which surplus funds could be employed for other purposes. Some of the former schools were refounded and allowed to continue, while a few were moved to larger centers where they became more serviceable; in other instances new foundations were established, either directly by the king or by private individuals by virtue of royal license. The remainder of the profits accrued to the crown in the form of annual revenues from the lands retained by the Court of Augmentations or through the extensive sale of chantry possessions. Free gifts, as of land, lead, bells, and chattels, were the exception rather than the rule.

Meanwhile, in 1548, a second commission was set up to supervise the distribution of alms, the repair of highways, and various other public

---

commission included the attorney, solicitor, and clerk of the Court of Augmentations. Chancery, Patent Rolls, C. 66/811–12.

[27] The commissioners kept no separate record of their activities, but the mention of their names in connection with controversies arising from chantry endowments or petitions for new corporations suggests that they were busily and conscientiously engaged for a considerable period. The attempt on the part of citizens in Penryn, Cornwall, to secure the conversion of the local college church into a parish church was probably not at all unusual. Walter Midmay and Robert Keilwey to Sir John Thynne, H. M. C., *Cal. of Cecil Manuscripts*, ed. by M. S. Giuseppi, pt. 1, no. 310, p. 74; *Cal. Pat. Rolls, Edward VI*, II, 176–77; III, 13. On the authority of the privy council, crown lands for the support of schools and other endowments were assigned by the chancellor of the Court of Augmentations. Dasent (ed.), *Acts of the Privy Council*, III, 245, 247, 471; IV, 68, 226.

services for which crown lands were appropriated. The commissioners were specifically instructed to call before them the directors of churches, colleges, hospitals, fraternities, and corporations engaged in such work, examine their records of expenditure, order improvements in the use of funds, and deliver all declarations of accounts to the Court of Augmentations.[28] For the most part such control was limited to cathedral and collegiate churches, some of which had been endowed in the previous reign, but more recent corporations were also affected. The new grammar schools were well distributed throughout the country, established in such important towns as Abingdon, Bury St. Edmunds, Bedford, Bath, Chelmsford, Craven, Guildford, Grantham, Ludlow, Maidstone, Stafford, St. Albans, Stourbridge, Southampton, Totnes, and Tonbridge.[29] In some instances the chancellor of the Augmentations or other influential ministers interceded for particular districts; in others prominent officials of the Court like John Williams and the Mildmay brothers were able to found schools in their own home towns.[30] Almshouses, poorhouses, and hospitals for the relief of the poor were also set up, but as in the case of educational foundations, the revenues originally dedicated to the projects were usually insufficient to support them. If appropriated revenues declined appreciably in value, other properties had to be assigned. Consequently, in 1550, the responsibility for the supervision of all crown endowments for schools and poor relief was entrusted to the chancellor of the Augmentations, who was authorized to appoint additional lands to make up the deficit in decayed endowments. From that date onward this control was vested in his office.[31] In June, 1552, he was directed to certify to the council the number of free schools that had been erected.[32]

A major charge in the original commission of Mildmay and Keilwey was the authorization for marketing chantry property; therefore, most

---

[28] *Cal. Pat. Rolls, Edward VI*, I, 232; V, 403. The commission consisted of the chancellor of the Court of Augmentations, a master of requests, the clerk of the hanaper, and Keilwey.

[29] The list is by no means exhaustive. In the grants, schools, almshouses, and hospitals were frequently almost synonymous terms. *Cal. Pat. Rolls, Edward VI*, I, 17, 43–44, 176; II, 176, 211–12, 340; III, 191–92, 192–93, 226, 264–65, 436–37; IV, 21–22, 40–41, 47–48, 97–99, 116–17, 119–22, 251, 293, 303–304, 345–46, 361–62; V, 33–34, 35–36, 68–69, 75, 223–24, 227–28, 278. In general the same policy was continued under Queen Mary. See under licenses to found chantries, schools, hospitals, guilds, poorhouses, etc. *Ibid., Philip and Mary*, I-IV, *passim*. Joan Simon, " A. F. Leach on The Reformation: I and II," *British Journal of Educational Studies*, III (May, 1955), 128–43; IV (November, 1955), 32–48.

[30] *Cal. Pat. Rolls, Edward VI*, I, 176; IV, 11, 116–17.

[31] Pat. Rolls, 4 Edward VI, pt. 2, mems. 9*d*.–10*d*.

[32] Dasent (ed.), *Acts of the Privy Council*, IV, 68.

of their time for several months was devoted to the sale of religious land and movables. Immediately after the surveys had been made, all plate, jewels, and church ornaments were taken over and sent to the king's jewel house in London; at the same time all movable appendages included in the act of dissolution were speedily surveyed and sold as quickly as they could be absorbed on the open market. These included lead, bells, bell metal, ornaments, chattels, superfluous buildings, and various stores of miscellaneous goods. In the case of land the instructions were quite definite. Such possessions were sold " for terme of lyfe lyves yeres or in fee tayle generall or speciall or in fee symple." It was stipulated that larger units should be held in knight's fee or military tenure, " without any rent or tenth to be reservyd for the same," but houses without land and manors with an annual value of less than £4 could be sold in free burgage or free socage tenure, by fealty only and not in chief, at the discretion of the commissioners. At least half the purchase price was demanded in cash payment, with bonds to be taken for the unpaid balance at the rate of £500 for every £200 of the debt so " stalled." [33]

In April, 1548, the council decided to raise money for defense by the general sale of chantry possessions. Sales of land up to the rental value of £5,000 were decided on, and various commissions were issued to process the work.[34] Between April, 1548, and January 23, 1554, over £280,000 had been realized in Augmentations revenues derived from land sales.[35] Most of the proceeds from the sale of land flowed through the Court, but a portion of the purchase money was paid to the king's use, either to Edmund Peckham, high treasurer of the mint, or to Peter Osborne, keeper of the royal privy purse.[36]

---

[33] Pat. Rolls, 2 Edward VI, pt. 5, mem. 25d.

[34] Dasent (ed.), *Acts of the Privy Council*, II, 184–85. The various commissions, set up for the sale of crown lands and chantry possessions, are noted in *Cal. Pat. Rolls, Edward VI*, I, 135, 417–18; II, 57–58, 183; III, 347–48; IV, 354–55, 390–91, 392–93, 397–98; V, 184, 277, 411.

[35] The greater receipts from this item came during the early part of the period, namely, £110,486 for the remainder of the fiscal year 1548; £92,695 14s. for 1549; £47,286 9s. 3d. for 1550; £7,856 4d. for 1551; £5,104 9s. 3d. for 1552; and £16,623 19s. 11d. for 1553 and the following months preceding the dissolution of the Court on January 23, 1554. This total of £280,052 12s. 9d., however, does not include various additional sums for back sales of land, totaling £31,226, 9s. 11d., received by the treasurer, John Williams, since assuming office in 1544 but not recorded until 1553. Augm. Office, Treas. Rolls of Accts., Nos. 4–8.

[36] Beginning in 1552 Peckham regularly received part of the proceeds from chantry sales. During the fiscal year 1552–53 he took in £153,479 from that source. *Cal. Pat. Rolls, Edward VI*, IV, 251 *passim*, 354; V, 184, 411. Dietz, *Finances of Edward VI and Mary*, 99. On Osborne's activities as keeper of the king's privy purse, see pp. 361–65, *infra*.

Meanwhile, in London the Court's officials were kept busy by a variety of extra activities. In order to accommodate the expansion which the recent merger had necessitated, the Augmentations premises were enlarged and considerable alterations undertaken. In June, 1547, John Grene, deputy usher, was paid £76 16s. 4d. for annexing and repairing "the house late called the Court of Survey." During the ensuing months additional payments totaling £18 7s. were "laide owte" in necessaries for the Court.[37]

During the Edwardian period the collection of crown debts and the administration of pensions occupied the major portion of the Court's time. From the viewpoint of its officials the latter offered no particular problem since, once granted and registered in the Court, pension supervision consisted of little more than the authorization of the payment of the pension roll when it came due quarterly or semi-annually. To the government, however, the whole matter of ecclesiastical pensions presented a recurrent issue of some significance. While individually the annuities were not unreasonable, in the aggregate they constituted a heavy charge on the crown revenue. Pensions to the disbanded religious had generally increased under Henry VIII until they had reached a total of £4,463 6s. 8d. at the end of the reign.[38] When to these grants were added the secular pensions and annuities, which took place from time to time, the results were staggering. At the time of the general investigation of the major administrative departments in 1551, the report on the state of the revenues showed the Augmentations outlay for pensions and annuities to have mounted to over £50,000 annually. The total expended on these items by the several revenue courts was £63,288 8s., or about 23 per cent of their aggregate income.[39] As the years passed, however, the normal death toll automatically decreased the original

---

[37] Augm. Office, Misc. Books 256, fols. 94d., 99d., 100. On one occasion William Egerton was paid for 28 days work done for the Court at the rate of 11d. per day. *Ibid.*, 256, fol. 97.

[38] Augm. Office, Misc. Books 255, fol. 39. Additional annuities of £2,605 2s. 9½d. granted by the crown and £918 7s. 6½d. awarded by the monasteries prior to their dissolution brought the total up to £7,986 17s. *Ibid.* 255, fols. 68, 81. Pensions and annuities paid by the Court can be checked conveniently in the fourteen volumes of Books of Payments from 32 Henry VIII to 1 Mary. Augm. Office, Misc. Books 249–262. Giuseppi has incorrectly included Misc. Book 248 in this grouping. M. S. Giuseppi, *A Guide to the Manuscripts preserved in the Public Record Office* (London, 1923), I, 151.

[39] Add. MS. 30198, fols. 36d.–37. There are various errors in the totals given in the report, but they do not materially alter the general picture. The Court of Augmentations spent £50,773 16s. 11d. in pensions and annuities out of the total of £63,288 8s. (The report gives £63,285 8s.) for all the courts. The total receipts of the several revenue courts for all the revenues were £272,913.

number of Dissolution pensioners, a fact which should have appreciably reduced the pension expenditures under Edward VI.

Nevertheless, the theory of anticipated savings was not always supported by hard facts. Early in the reign it was noted by the council, for example, that certain English monks had fled with their " popishe monkery " to Flanders, yet their pensions continued to be paid through friends who collected for them in their absence. Similarly it appeared that monks apparently never really died, since long after their demise friends continued to receive their pensions from the Augmentations. To stop such fraudulent practices it was ordered in June, 1547, that the payment of pensions to all inmates of late religious houses should be transferred from the district receivers to the central treasurer of the Court. Furthermore, he was authorized to investigate each case personally before accepting the claim. Sworn certificates of identification obtained through the local justices of the peace were required as a further check on the true identity of each pensioner.[40] Actual results of this order cannot be determined, but certainly it must have entailed a great deal of extra time on the part of the treasurer. Undoubtedly the plan was originally conceived as a check on the existing pensioners and probably not meant to be permanent. At any rate, the pensions awarded under the chantry act of 1547 were made payable, as previously, by the individual receivers in the counties,[41] although the treasurer continued to pay a certain number of pensions and annuities until the end of the reign, amounting to something over £4,000 per year.[42] As usual the safeguard did little more than highlight an evil which only a thorough investigation could remove. Commission inquiries were instituted, but they merely indicated a situation which everybody knew to be in need of drastic reform. The problem again came up for review at the beginning of the next reign.

Since the Court of Augmentations bore the major burden of pensions and annuities, most of the abuses in pensions' administration had developed there. Many of the annuities granted by the late religious houses were suspected of being " by collusion "; others had been " corruptly granted." Court receivers and their deputies had commonly taken advantage of their offices to buy up pensions from the dispossessed religious, which they continued to pay to themselves long after the

[40] Dasent (ed.), *Acts of the Privy Council*, II, 97-98; III, 315. Pensioners were sometimes required to appear personally, or by representative attorney, before the Augmentations receivers to prove their cases, each bringing with him a certificate from two justices of the peace of his home county testifying that he was " lyvyng & able to receve his pencyon." Augm. Office, Miscellanea, 35.

[41] *Cal. Pat. Rolls, Edward VI*, II, 58.

[42] Add. MS. 30198, fols. 45, 45*d*. (Items 11, 24).

original annuitants were dead. Cases were uncovered where the receivers had been drawing several annuities each, which they had apparently secured from the monasteries at the time of their dissolution. When chicanery was discovered among even a few officials, it naturally gave " occasion of further mistrust in other." A thorough commission investigation was the obvious solution. Pending further inquiry it was recommended that no pension should be paid until the recipient had appeared personally and proved his case or, if collected by deputy, local depositions under the seal of justices of the peace were required. Furthermore, it was suggested that the Court periodically conduct a survey of every county in order to keep a pension list that was complete and up to date. In fact, the charge on the Court was so great, and so many devious practices issued daily therein, that any improvement, however temporary, " cannot be tonarrowly or diligently looked upon." [43]

Accordingly, a systematic checkup was instituted in the autumn of 1552, during which investigation the Court of Augmentations, anxious to strengthen its own position, willingly co-operated. A series of commissions, issued under the great seal of the Court, was appointed in September and October of that year to survey the state of pensions and annuities in the counties of England and Wales. Actually, they had presented their reports before the abolition of the Augmentations, which gave the government ample evidence for the later Marian financial reforms. Among other things, the commissioners were to inquire (1) how many of the pensions of the former religious were still active, (2) how many pensions were unpaid or delinquent, with the reasons therefor, (3) the number of pensioners who were dead, with the dates of their deaths and (4) the names of those who perchance had sold their annuities or pensions, with the identity of the purchaser and the sale price received for each. All recipients were called before the commissioners for examination in order to verify their status. Juries were empaneled to give evidence on the points enumerated, and a complete certificate of return was submitted to the Augmentations. The commissioners employed were mostly local men who personally knew the pensioners involved, although a number of the Court's receivers and auditors were included.

Their reports or " certificates " reveal serious deficiencies in the system employed. Some recipients were neither found nor identified, many were dead " yeres agone," while the pensions of still others had been sold at a profit. One man was believed " to be deade long synce & his patent sold " to one or another of two different suspects. In another

[43] *Ibid.*, fol. 45.

instance fifteen pensioners, " pore and agyd," had been assigned to a hospital at Pontefract, Yorkshire, being paid from the revenues of the late monastery of St. Oscortold. Although the original group had all died, the town took advantage of the receiver's gullibility to secure government aid for the support of its own poor : " and upon any of thir deths an other ys placyd in the dedes roome & is very convenyent to be . . . aswell for the helpe of the pore & agyd people of the towne of Pontfrett where the same standyth as for others." A surprising number of pensioners had changed residence and could not be located ; a few were drawing annuities from more than one receiver. Whenever pensioners had gone unpaid for a number of years, as sometimes happened, it was usually occasioned by restraints imposed by the privy council or because the receivers had no money available with which to pay them. In some cases this delinquency was no doubt due to shortage of revenue in a particular district, such as Yorkshire where the demands for fortifications, garrisons, and other extraordinary royal expenditures were unusually heavy. Nevertheless, the Augmentations officials were sometimes suspect. If the receiver or his deputy pocketed the revenues from which annuities were paid, they had only to tell the complainants that " they had no money in theyr handes to pay them." [44]

A good many of the life annuities had been granted to favorites during Henry VIII's reign or were held by officials who had since been otherwise compensated for offices surrendered. Some were, moreover, believed to have been acquired by fraudulent means. These might be greatly curtailed, the council advised Mary,[45] without seriously affecting the welfare of the displaced ecclesiastics, whose continued support had been guaranteed by the legislation restoring the first fruits and tenths to the church. As a gift to the clergy this act placed about £25,000 per year at the disposal of the church, to be used to supplement the inadequate livings of priests. This gift also provided for the continuation of pen-

[44] Commissions and returns concerning monastic pensions. Exch., Accounts Various, 76/11–36; see especially 76/11, 13, 17, 20, 21, 23, and 25. These reports were formerly classified in the Public Record Office as " Augmentation Bag," Box 154, among the Chapter House Records. Later, however, they were reclassified among the miscellaneous exchequer accounts. See *Forty-Ninth Report of the Deputy Keeper of the Public Records* (London, 1869), Appendix No. 3, 211–12. On the certificates of returns of the commissions see in particular Exchequer of Receipt, Misc. Books 59.

[45] *Cal. State Papers, Domestic, Mary,* I, No. 22. It was noted that certain annuities, including £1,597 in grants to Englishmen and £2,590 to foreigners could be discontinued immediately. For a detailed analysis of restrictions imposed by the government of Northumberland on the payment of pensions, see A. G. Dickens, " The Edwardian Arrears in Augmentations Payments and the Problem of the Ex-Religious," *E. H. R.,* LV (July, 1940), 384–418.

sions and corodies for the late religious personnel.[46] As pensioners died, the annual charge on the government was gradually reduced. New pensions were awarded more sparingly, although there was no abatement on annuities which were commonly nothing more than substitutions for governmental salaries. After the amalgamation of 1554 the greater part of the expenditure for pensions and annuities was borne by the receipt of the Exchequer. As a part of the "ordinary charges," the annual total of fees and annuities under Elizabeth never ran above £35,500 and generally below that figure, the lowest being around £23,000.[47]

During the early years of Edward VI the council was as usual preoccupied with financial problems, many of which were occasioned, in part at least, by the price revolution of the period. The steady rise in prices throughout the century spelled for the state increased costs of administration. Even under normal circumstances the relatively fixed feudal and other revenues were insufficient to meet the ordinary expenses of government, and conditions at this time were anything but normal. Temporary borrowings begun by Henry VIII were continued and increased. By 1551 some £250,000 was owed at home and in Flanders, while the gap between current charges and regular revenue receipts widened.[48] It is not surprising, therefore, to find so much attention given to administrative matters in a rather belated attempt to restore efficiency and to augment the annual flow of revenue. Conciliar action took the form of surveys and commission investigations in which the officials of the Court of Augmentations played an important role.

Sir Walter Mildmay was an active participant in the administrative work of many of these commissions; his legal training stood him in good stead, and in many cases he was doubtless a legal as well as an administrative consultant. Ambition, natural ability, and indefatigable energy combined to give him a reputation well beyond his age; within a few

---

[46] Dietz, *Finances of Edward VI and Mary*, 115. An act abolishing first fruits, etc., 2 and 3 Philip and Mary, c. 4, *S.R.*, IV, 275–79. This revenue was restored to the crown at the beginning of the next reign. An act for the resumption of first fruits and tenths, 1 Elizabeth, c. 4, *S.R.*, IV, 359–64.

[47] Frederick C. Dietz, *The Exchequer in Elizabeth's Reign* ("Smith College Studies in History," Vol. VIII, no. 2 [Northampton, Mass., January, 1923]), 96–104, tables of Exchequer expenditure. There was an appreciable increase in expenditures on pensions and annuities under the early Stuarts. See accounts in *Cal. State Papers, Domestic, Charles I, 1629–1631*, 439, Nos. 16, 18.

[48] The real crisis came under Northumberland, when a bankrupt government found itself unable to meet the interest payments on Antwerp loans without ignoring domestic creditors. Additional loans were negotiated. Despite the economies under Mary, Elizabeth inherited a debt of £227,000 of which some £107,000 represented continental borrowings. G. N. Clark, *The Wealth of England* (London, 1946), 81–82.

years he was easily the most outstanding official in the Augmentations.[49] Through him and numerous other of its officials the Court was in a position to influence most of the recommendations that at length found their way before the council.

The reign opened with a commission for the compounding of fines in distraint of knighthood.[50] The commission was composed of only three members, Sir Richard Rich, Sir Richard Southwell, and Sir Thomas Moyle, the latter representing the Court of Augmentations. There followed several commissions for the hearing of accounts designed to check waste and peculation, of which the complete surveys of the jewel house and ordnance department were the most important.[51] These audits also included long-delayed reckonings for the English agent at Antwerp and the high treasurer of wars. Meanwhile, a small committee of four councillors was delegated to examine fully the state of the revenues and render a comprehensive report to the council. It was required to investigate the five revenue courts of Exchequer, Augmentations, Duchy Chamber of Lancaster, First Fruits and Tenths, and Wards and Liveries, to determine in particular what their annual revenues ought to be and what outstanding debts, goods, or chattels in each were still uncollected. Paulet headed the commission, and he chose as assistants men of previous experience upon whom he could rely, Mildmay of the Augmentations, Petre, principal secretary, and Keilwey. In so far as the Augmentations was concerned its officers had to present a " perfect declaracion " of all lead and bells retained in storage, as well as a full account of all revenue on hand, either as cash or in the form of bonds and obligations payable at some future date. Obviously, a first step toward improving the financial position was to determine the actual extent of the uncollected revenues of the courts. Indeed, the " great and vrgent causes and consideracions " behind this assignment were so pressing that a speedy report was requested.[52]

In 1551 and 1552 the whole field of governmental finance was brought under review by a number of special commission investigations, resulting in a serious attempt to improve the financial position by collecting all outstanding debts. During the previous decade numerous commissions had been set up to call in old debts, but such measures had not been very

[49] During his period of service with the second Court of Augmentations, Mildmay sat on no fewer than thirty-five special commissions. Most of these are included in the *Cal. Pat. Rolls* for the years 1547–1554.

[50] As proclaimed by the sheriffs, all persons who for three years had had a yearly rent or income from land of £40 or more were required to assume knighthood or pay a fine in lieu thereof. *Cal. Pat. Rolls, Edward VI*, I, 185–86.

[51] Society of Antiquaries of London MSS. 129A and 129B.

[52] S. P. 10/2 (No. 9), fols. 24–36; C. 66/801.

successful. In spite of many which could never be collected, each of the revenue departments had a substantial backlog of accumulated rents, fines, and arrears of revenue which, though remaining a potential asset, never really amounted to more than a paper balance. Although no one knew exactly how many of the debts were bona fide and hence collectable, or just what proportion of the annual revenue they represented, the king himself reckoned the total at £100,000.[53] Since the Court of Augmentations was expected to yield the largest portion, a beginning was made there.

Early in March, 1550, Sackville and Williams were summoned to appear before the council with a complete list of all debts and arrears due the king in the Court. On June 12 following, the lord chancellor was directed to present to the council such records of the state of all the revenue courts as remained in his office, and on the ensuing twenty-eighth of September official letters were sent to all the " Courtes of chardge," demanding a perfect declaration of the state of their revenues since April, 1546.[54] The next step was the setting up of commissions for the implementation of the conciliar decrees. Those established for the investigation of the revenue courts represent the practical results of the king's proposals for a division of the council's administrative activity. While the reorganization of the council was never carried out, the scheme, nevertheless, clearly envisioned a real need for some form of delegated executive authority.

The Tudor council under Edward VI continued to retain nominal control of all departments of government; however, in both composition and authority significant changes were plainly discernible. Constitutionally always an advisory body for the crown, the privy council gradually had come to be the principal centralizing force in the government. Under capable leadership, the council was the chief expression of executive power in the state and collectively upheld common purposes in the routine work of administration, but during the minority of young Edward this unity had given way to partisan factions and consequent division of authority. Whether driven by personal ambition or political jealousy, Warwick, who after the fall of Somerset ruled in the name of the king, failed to achieve even that semblance of conciliar harmony maintained by his predecessor. To increase the influence of his own clique new members were added, and functional effectiveness could hardly be expected from an unwieldy body of forty councillors.

[53] A memorial by the king as to ways and means of raising money in 1552 for the payments of debts beyond the seas; from superfluous plate £20,000, the subsidy £80,000, and " my debts owing me " £100,000. Lansd. MS. 1236, fol. 21; Nichols (ed.), *Literary Remains*, II, 550.
[54] Dasent (ed.), *Acts of the Privy Council*, III, 46, 133, 228; IV, xxix, 45.

Edward's plan of reform, presented in March, 1552, was as simple as it was practical. In a council grown inconveniently large the principle of " separation of powers " was, in effect, introduced without any loss of theoretical functions. The work of the council was to be divided among various committees, or commissions, with specific duties assigned to each, the king himself sitting with the commission " for the state." Two of the commissions were charged with revenue matters, acting in a supervisory capacity as committees of the larger council. One was the commission on debts, and the other was a select commission on the revenue courts. Members of the latter commission were expected to examine " the state of all the courtes, specially the new erectid courtes," the Augmentations, the First Fruits and Tenths, and the Wards and Liveries; and they " shal see the revenues aunswered at the hauf yeres ende, and shal consider with what superflouse charges they be burdened, and thereof shal make certificat, which they shal deliver." Even further conciliar reorganization was contemplated as indicated in the later Petre memorandum of January, 1553.[55] The reign closed before the project could be fully carried out, but the two commissions on debts and revenues were duly implemented and in time submitted detailed reports to the council.

In December, 1551, the king noted in his journal that a commission was made out to the bishop of Ely, the lord privy seal, Sir John Gates, Sir William Petre, Sir Robert Bowes, and Sir Walter Mildmay, " for calling in my dettes." This important commission thus contained six prominent councillors representing major departments of state. The actual patent is undated but was delivered on January 2 and authorized its members either to collect or to rearrange all crown debts in the Courts of Exchequer, Duchy Chamber of Lancaster, Wards and Liveries, First Fruits and Tenths, and Augmentations.[56] Fortunately, the full

[55] Nichols (ed.), *Literary Remains*, II, 500–501; see also 403, 406, 409, 498–99. Richardson, *Tudor Chamber Administration, 1485–1547*, 392–93. Cf. F. G. Emmison, " A Plan of Edward VI and Secretary Petre for Reorganizing the Privy Council's Work, 1552–1553," *Bulletin of the Institute of Historical Research*, XXXI (November, 1958), 203–10. The committee on debts was expected to merge with the committee on the state of the revenue when its special commission assignment was completed.

[56] Nichols (ed.), *Literary Remains*, II, 383, 389. Pat. Rolls, 5 Edward VI, pt. 4, mems. 19*d.*, 20*d.*, 21*d.* This commission was to call before it the heads and other officials of the revenue courts and " take order with them " for the levying of the king's debts. The commissioners were well selected. Thomas Goodrich, bishop of Ely, was chancellor and keeper of the great seal; Lord John Russell, earl of Bedford, was not only keeper of the privy seal but also great steward of the household; Sir John Gates (or Gate) was vice-chamberlain and captain of the guard as well as being chancellor of the duchy of Lancaster; Sir William Petre, principal secretary, was treasurer of the Court of First Fruits; and Sir Robert Bowes, lord

report of this commission has been preserved among the miscellanea of the Exchequer. The instructions to the commissioners indicate that the investigation was expected to yield " greate and notable sommes of money," which if not speedily called in would soon " growe desperate." [57] The commissioners were authorized to cancel, alter, or collect, by the usual legal processes, all debts and arrearages due the crown and to call for a full written declaration from each court of all revenues, rents, and casualties within their respective jurisdictions. Accordingly, minutes were sent to all the revenue courts requiring their co-operation and help. Each court submitted a " full and particuler declaracion " of its debts, together with accounts prepared by the auditors of all arrears within its districts. These records were in the hands of the commissioners by the end of January, though the auditors and receivers of the several courts met with them thereafter in London from time to time as the investigation proceeded. As this commission had been set up as one of the select committees of the council recommended by the king, it had already begun its work before being formally recognized.[58]

The names of the debtors investigated, but not the total amount of money collected, are included in this lengthy register. However, payments to the extent of £16,667 were recorded among the Augmentations accounts by the end of the fiscal year 1552. These and later collections were usually turned over to Peter Osborne, who received the cash to " the king's own use." [59]

In 1552 and 1553 there were at least a dozen additional commissions appointed to collect debts and bring in delinquent revenues.[60] Walter Mildmay sat on all of them, as did other members of the original commission on debts. Although varying somewhat in size and authority, their purpose was the same. They were required to investigate the revenue courts and report all debts and arrears that remained due; intending always to pay his own debts, the king thought it only reasonable that those who were indebted to him should without compulsion

warden of the East Marches and master of the rolls, became chancellor of the county palatine of Durham in July, 1553. Mildmay, of course, represented the Court of Augmentations.

[57] A paper register of proceedings of the commissioners appointed for levying the king's debts and perusing the state of the revenue, 256 pages. A copy of the commission is included (fols. 10–12*d*.), and the names of the debtors for each revenue department given. Exch., K. R., Miscellanea, 163/12/14.

[58] A copy of the form letter from the commissioners to the revenue courts is presented in full in the proceedings. It is dated the last day of December, 1551, which shows the commission to have been functioning before its formal appointment. *Ibid.*, 163/12/14, fol. 13*d*.

[59] Augm. Office, Treas. Rolls of Accts., No. 8, fol. 82*d*.

[60] Nichols (ed.), *Literary Remains*, II, 406, 468–71; *Cal. Pat. Rolls, Edward VI*, IV, 355–56, 391–92, 397–98.

" offer the payment of theire dueties " and refrain from drifting further into debt. Accordingly, the commissioners were given plenary powers to call before them any or all treasurers, paymasters, or receivers of revenue for a full declaration of account, examine revenue records for obligations and recognizances, and search the chancery records for old debts. Many such had been accumulating since 1536, when the spoliation of monastic wealth had begun. They were enumerated in the various commissions as being debts for sales and exchanges of land, for increased value of land since the time of alienation, fines, arrearages, and money still due in the form of back payments for crown property, such as lead, stone, plate, bell metal, jewels, buildings, livestock, and other personal goods which had come to the king by acts of attainder or otherwise. Debtors were warned to pay promptly or else to make personal appearances before the commissioners for hearings. In most cases land was accepted in lieu of cash settlement, or debts were " estalled " under bond when future collection seemed possible. In cases of default culprits were arrested and brought in for punishment. At their discretion commissioners were permitted to cancel any debt which appeared to be unjust or reduce the principal in order to induce speedier payment. Cases of debts that appeared hopeless were referred to the " Council for the State " for final settlement.

Nor did the revenue officials themselves escape investigation. The commissions of December 7 and December 12, 1552, compelled all ministers, who at any time had received of the king or his father, Henry VIII, any money, treasure, or revenue and had never rendered a full account of their receipts and expenditures, to do so immediately. Likewise, those who had sold for the government " allame, fustyans, copper, powder, jewelles or other goodes," were required to submit their books for examination and to pay arrears. In all instances acquittances were given for accounts duly passed, and offenders were punished. Those found guilty of embezzlement were usually turned over to the council for special trial, but ordinary ministers who had merely " misused their service," either by making untrue values or passing sales, gifts, or purchases to the loss of the crown, were tried by the commissioners.[61]

There is no complete record of the various sums that must have accrued to the government as a result of these inquiries. Part of the money collected found its way into the various treasuries; the remainder was paid to Peter Osborne, gentleman of the privy chamber, who had

---

[61] *Ibid.*, 391–92, 393, 397–98. Under the commission of July 13, 1552, the investigators were empowered to call before them any officer of the revenue courts and compel him, by distress or otherwise, to pay in the money due the crown. Bonds were taken of those who were unable to pay their arrears. *Ibid.*, 355–56.

been appointed personal treasurer to Edward VI. On May 18, 1553, the Augmentations auditors Thomas Mildmay and William Berners were directed to ascertain what other revenues Osborne had received for the king's " causes " and to audit his accounts. But money kept in the royal palace at Westminster was not always safe. On May 2, 1552, £600 of Osborne's hoard was stolen, which threatened to be his " utter undoing." In the final declaration of his account, presented June 17, 1553, he was exonerated from all responsibility concerning the theft and given discharge for £39,948 ⅛d.[62]

In addition to routine business the chief officers of the Court of Augmentations were expected to serve the crown as special auditors. The former Court of General Surveyors had always been a court of audit, and from it the second Augmentations inherited jurisdiction over the accounts of the chamber, the hanaper, the jewel house, and the mint. Still, the auditing procedure was by no means standardized. Unless a minister was under suspicion no one but himself was particularly interested in his official discharge. Consequently, more often than not the conscientious official was forced to implore the council for a final reckoning. Frequency of audit was not guaranteed by the practice of requiring ministers to account before auditing commissions, which were never regular nor systematic. Usually such commissions would consist of a number of privy councillors, assisted by one or two professional auditors who were really responsible for the technical audit, as in the case of the jewel office in April, 1547. Five councillors, Sir Richard Rich, Sir Ralph Sadler, Sir Richard Southwell, Sir Thomas Pope, and Sir Walter Mildmay were commissioned to survey the plate and jewels remaining in the hands of Sir John Williams and deliver them to Sir Anthony Aucher, who was currently holding the office of master of the king's jewels.[63] Since none of the commissioners, with the possible exception of Mildmay, were trained auditors, William Berners and Thomas Mildmay, regular auditors in the Augmentations, were called in to check the accounts under the general direction of the commission.

Chancellor North and Sir Walter Mildmay sat on a number of special commissions of audit, although occasionally other members of the Court

---

[62] The declaration of Osborne's account " fayre written in parchement and subscribed with your [the commissioners'] handes " was accepted without much probing, since it concerned payments and receipts by special assignment. The commission likewise passed, without charges paid either at the signet, privy, or great seals, all payments made. *Ibid.*, V, 85, 185.

[63] Williams succeeded Cromwell in the jewel house in 1540, and was followed by Sir Anthony Rous in 1545. After a brief tenure of twenty-nine months, Rous was in turn succeeded by Anthony Aucher on September 29, 1545.

were also represented.[64] Since there were so many special receivers, treasurers, and commissioned financial agents who, from time to time, handled large sums of money, a great deal of the council's time was devoted to the supervision of their activities. The logical procedure would have been to channel all such irregular receipts and expenditures into the regular revenue courts, where reliable safeguards were already established. This would have eliminated the endless round of commission inquiries so prevalent under the Edwardian government. But a general distrust of these institutions was developing. The council would neither surrender its control of expenditures nor delegate its financial responsibilities.

A significant change occurred in the headship of the Court in August, 1548, when Sir Edward North surrendered the chancellorship in favor of Sir Richard Sackville.[65] North was only fifty-two years old at the time and at the height of his career.[66] There is little doubt that his resignation was forced upon him by political pressure, although there is no absolute proof of this. It seems that he was offered some compensation for the loss of the office, though the remuneration was granted him by the crown rather than by Sackville.[67] While the evidence is not conclusive, it would seem that Sackville assumed responsibility for North's debt of £2,000 to the crown, which represented the unpaid balance of £3,000 in arrearages incurred earlier by him in the treasurership of the Court. As security for the payment of the debt Sackville transferred lands in Sussex and Huntingdonshire to the king for a period of ten years, then leased the land for a rent of £200 per year.[68] On the fifteenth of the

[64] Some of these public commissions undertook an investigation of all special ministers who had handled government funds, either in receipts or payments. Such accounts included provisions, munitions, artillery, marine affairs, fortifications, public works, war expenses, and money received in prest. After discharge was given, duplicates of the audited accounts as well as copies of the commissions were filed in the Court of Augmentations. *Cal. Pat. Rolls, Edward VI*, I, 417; IV, 391–92. See also *ibid.*, I, 93, 116, 136, 139, 232, 261; III, 214; IV, 352; V, 185, 186.

[65] Pat. Rolls, 2 Edward VI, pt. 2, mem. 4. This privy seal of August 24, 1548, offers no explanation of North's surrender of office. Sackville was granted the office for life at the same salary of £300 per year with arrears from the past midsummer.

[66] There is no definite proof of the date of North's birth, though it is usually given as 1496. Augustus Jessopp, " Edward North," *D. N. B.* There is some evidence that he was only about forty-seven in 1548. Nichols (ed.), *Literary Remains*, I, cviii.

[67] There seems to be no foundation for the story that Edward VI accused North of having cheated the crown of certain Augmentations estates, as told in Dudley North, *Some Notes Concerning the Life of Edward Lord North, Baron of Kirtling* (1658; published with another long essay, London, 1682), 10–11. This account is repeated in Frances Bushby, *Three Men of the Tudor Times* (London, 1911), 15, 18.

[68] Augm. Office, Misc. Books 327, fols. 16*d*., 31*d*. The indenture between the

following February the council issued a warrant to the treasurer of the Augmentations to pay North £1,540 14s. 8d. " for certein consideracions of service, by way of his Majestes reward." [69] The amount involved was certainly too large a reward for ordinary services, and there is no evidence that he was particularly meritorious of the king's largesse at this time. In the absence of positive proof to the contrary it is probable that this " reward " represents the price of North's resignation.[70]

Richard Sackville was forty-one years old when he assumed the headship of the Augmentations. Although he had influential connections at court, he had attained no particular distinction under Henry VIII, save to sit with his father on a number of important commissions. As the eldest son of an upper middle class family, he had studied at Cambridge and Gray's Inn, where he became a reader in 1529.[71] During the same year he was returned to the Reformation Parliament from Arundel, probably through the support of William Fitzalan, the eleventh earl of Arundel, who had already taken young Richard into his service as an estate steward.[72] His father John Sackville of Buckhurst, Sussex, a man of considerable property and high local standing, forwarded the public career of his son as much as possible. His mother was an aunt of Anne Boleyn through whose influence he was brought to the attention of the king, who employed him on numerous minor assignments. Prior to his appointment to the Augmentations he had served the crown as commissioner, army treasurer, and royal escheator in Surrey and Sussex.[73] He began to buy land about 1541, and long before his father's death in

---

king and Sackville, by which certain manors were granted to the king for a ten-year period, was dated August 9, 1548. On the earlier debt of North, see *ibid.* 104, fols. 127–28; 14, p. 127. Add. MS. 9782, p. 135.

[69] Dasent (ed.), *Acts of the Privy Council*, II, 392. The reward was paid in full on March 16, 1549, a month later. Augm. Office, Misc. Books 258, fol. 89.

[70] North retained his position on the privy council. In July, 1550, he was granted an annuity of £100, payable in the Court of Wards and Liveries; he also received annuities of £6 1s. 8d. and £7 from the Court of Augmentations. *Cal. Pat. Rolls, Edward VI*, III, 313. Augm. Office, Misc. Books 260, fol. 37; 262, fol. 36d. He had also received a gift of £300 upon Henry VIII's death. *L. and P.*, XXI, pt. 2, no. 634; Dasent (ed.), *Acts of the Privy Council*, II, 323.

[71] The best brief sketch of Sackville's life is contained in Charles J. Phillips, *A History of the Sackville Family* (London, 1930), I, 126–50. The colorful history of the Sackville estates, acquired by Sir Richard as the founder of the family fortune, is popularly presented in V. Sackville-West, *Knole and the Sackvilles* (London, 1948).

[72] Augm. Office, Misc. Books 101, fols. 55d.–56d. In February, 1541, he was made chief steward of Arundel Castle and of the lordships and manors of the Arundel estates in Sussex. He was also a steward of the manor of Clerkenwell, Middlesex, for the convent of St. Mary the Virgin in London. *Ibid.* 103, fols. 112–112d.

[73] W. A. J. Archbold, " Sir Richard Sackville," in *D. N. B.*

1557 he had added greatly to the family estates. By the beginning of the reign of Elizabeth, Sackville had acquired a fortune. When he became undertreasurer of the Exchequer in 1564, he entered on the last but most important phase of his career, which once again brought him into close association with his old friend, Walter Mildmay.[74]

Sackville was kept busy in his new office, which carried with it membership in the privy council and the usual number of conciliar assignments attendant upon active participation in its meetings. Like his predecessors in office, his activities necessitated considerable travel, although the records available suggest but the barest outlines of his work.[75] Each autumn he and the two surveyors of the Court took the annual accounts of the several auditors, for which they received in addition to their regular salaries a special compensation in the form of allowances for diets.[76] Land grants, collection of debts, manumissions, land surveys, and supervision of the sale of lead and timber constituted the bulk of routine work requiring the chancellor's constant attention when he was not officiating as presiding justice in Augmentations litigation. New lands and property still dribbled in through acts of attainder which entailed extra work for the ministers of the Court. For example, in November of 1549 Sackville, Mildmay, and Moyle all served on a commission to survey the personal assets of Protector Somerset at Sheen and Sion House, for which they were paid extra for special expenses incurred.[77] From that point forward until his second arrest and final execution on January 22, 1552, the officers of the Augmentations assisted the privy council in the payment of the Duke's debts and in the administration of his estate.[78] For the most part, however, the chancellor's work was administrative and confined to the Court's jurisdiction.

Only occasionally was his authority increased by special commission. Such supplementary powers were delegated to Sackville, as chancellor of the Court of Augmentations, by the privy council in February, 1550, with the obvious intent of lightening the administrative duties of that

---

[74] On the later careers in the Exchequer of Sackville and Mildmay, see p. 454 *infra*. Sackville's property in London alone, including the famous Sackville House (later Dorset House), consisted of some twenty-eight shops and tenements.

[75] In February, 1549, he was granted the office of *custos rotulorum* in Sussex, which he was permitted to hold by deputy. *Cal. Pat. Rolls, Edward VI*, II, 181.

[76] Sackville received £40 in diets for such audits and the surveyors, £20 each. Augm. Office, Misc. Books 259, fols. 103*d.*, 104.

[77] An account book for the expenses of Sackville and others for the survey, Exch., Accounts Various, 520/6; also a certificate of the amounts received later from the possessions of the duke of Somerset for 6 Edward VI, *ibid.*, 520/8.

[78] Nichols (ed.), *Literary Remains*, II, 370. Dasent (ed.), *Acts of the Privy Council*, III, 393, 447, 457, 459, 460, 469, 479, 501; IV, 55.

body. Government by commission was a common feature of Tudor administration, but its use was effectively extended by the council during the Edwardian period. In most instances these commissions were composed of a number of men, dealing with particular abuses or problems of a temporary nature. Sackville's commission, however, was directed to the chancellor alone, dealt with general rather than specific matters, and conferred upon him permanent obligations and responsibilities. In fine, it had the effect of amending the constitution of the Court as set forth in the original patent of erection by widening its base of authority.

The new powers conferred upon the chancellor by this special commission were embodied in twelve articles, each constituting a separate category of administration.[79] Most of the provisions dealt with the leasing or alienation of crown lands; the others were concerned primarily with debts to the king, royal revenues, and the manumission of bondmen. As director of the Court, the chancellor was empowered to receive lands for the crown in lieu of debts and, at his discretion, to extend the time of payment, providing that no lands above the rate of twenty years' purchase were involved. Upon the authorization of the privy council he could allocate lands and property in fulfillment of gifts and promised endowments by the crown for the erection of charitable institutions, and assign additional lands or property to the institutions or corporations when the original appropriations were inadequate. In addition, he was authorized to grant lands formerly promised by the king, or land and property paid for and not delivered, and with the consent of the council of the Court, to accept the surrender of land leases, make new leases, and exchange crown land for other property of comparable value. Upon his own discretion he could take the surrender of offices of the defunct Courts of Survey and Augmentations and assess the pensions to be paid the ministers in compensation for their loss. In departure from former policy, Sackville was permitted to make appointments to local administrative offices and, where salaries were not fixed, to determine the fees; in earlier practice, the chancellor of the Court could fill minor vacancies, such as offices of stewards, bailiffs, woodwards, and local revenue collectors only when the king failed to exercise his prerogative right of making crown appointments.

[79] A commission of February 20, 1550, to Sir Richard Sackville, chancellor of the Augmentations ("in consideration of the regard due to gifts and promises by Henry VIII and the king for the erecting of grammar schools, appointment of livings for preachers and the poor, endowment of vicars, payment of debts and like godly acts, and also to the rewarding of good services") conferring on his office certain specified powers. Pat. Rolls, 4 Edward VI, pt. 2, mems. 9d.–10d.; *Cal. Pat. Rolls, Edward VI*, III, 214–16; S. P. 10/4, fol. 96. Cf. above, p. 176, n. 31.

Contrary to customary procedure, the council delegated to the Augmentations certain payments which would normally be exercised by the king or by some responsible minister. Sackville was required to compensate private owners for losses or injury sustained through enclosures [80] and from land purchased and paid for which had not been delivered or had been given up by Court decree. He was further authorized to " take order " for the erection of grammar schools and vicarages as provided by the crown and to make appropriations for poor relief.[81] Likewise, the special responsibility for the manumission of bondmen was for the first time entrusted to the head of the Court. Whereas the king had " diverse vyllaynes and nefes [82] aswell regardant to our honours lordeshippes and mannours as otherwyse in gros not yete manumysed and dyscharged of their bondage," [83] Sackville was to " manumit " them at his discretion, provided always that a third of their property be retained by the Court as the crown's share of their possessions.[84] Finally, a general provision regarding the payment of special crown debts was inserted in the commission. This item was occasioned, apparently, by the debts of Thomas Seymour, baron of Sudeley, which the crown had acquired by virtue of the lord admiral's recent attainder.[85] Not only was the chancellor of Augmentations ordered to pay all debts related to the Seymour property, but he was also commanded to pay any other debts of the crown by warrant of the privy council. Money for the payment of such debts was to be raised through the sale of chantry goods and the possessions of attainted persons. In all these matters special protection was given to the offices of the signet, the privy seal, and the great seal

[80] On the problem of the imparking and enclosing of crown lands see p. 432 f., *infra*.

[81] Sackville was also empowered to commission, under the seal of Augmentations, responsible ministers " to erect and examine the schools and other assignments " entrusted to him. Reasonable fees and allowances were to be allocated for all such persons appointed. *Cal. Pat. Rolls, Edward VI*, III, 215.

[82] The term is a corruption of the feminine *nief* (nativa) or female " vyllayn."

[83] Bondmen or villeins were of two kinds in England; villeins in grosse were immediately bound to the person of the lord and his heirs, whereas villeins regardant were annexed or belonged to a particular manor of which the lord was owner.

[84] The chancellor of the Court of Augmentations had sat on earlier commissions in 1554 which had raised money by the manumission of bondmen and other expedients. *L. and P.*, XIX, pt. 1, nos. 278 (5, 67), 812 (77). Actually, the Court had inherited a large number of bondmen from the dissolved monasteries, most of whom were freed as a result of royal policy. Sackville did manumit a number of villeins regardant for fines paid into the Augmentations treasury. Some of these fines were as much as £10 to £20 for one family. *Cal. Pat. Rolls, Edward VI*, III, 316; IV, 153, 161; V, 78, 407.

[85] A bill of attainder consisting of thirty-three articles of accusation was brought against Seymour on February 25, 1549. *S. R.*, IV, 61–65. He was executed on Tower Hill on March 20 following. The articles of accusation are printed in Dasent (ed.), *Acts of the Privy Council*, II, 248–56.

of England, which retained their respective fees for all documents processed by them.[86]

Apparently Sackville took advantage of his enlarged powers, for his authority was delimited within the year. The commission was issued on February 20; some seven months later, on September 25, 1550, he was called before the king's council at Oatlands to render an account of crown lands which he had leased or sold since the beginning of the reign. He was temporarily forbidden to grant or lease land under the great seal of the Augmentations as authorized by the commission.[87] Nevertheless, his ensuing declaration of account must have proved satisfactory, for the order of curtailment was rescinded the following December. However, on January 10, 1551, his authority in the free use of the Court seal was again curtailed. This time he was permitted to grant leases only by warrant of the privy council. Finally, on August 10, 1551, all these imposed restraints were removed, " forasmuche as it seemeth the advice that was given him here at the Borde for abbridgeng his libertie of graunteng of leases and revercions " was in effect a " defaceng of his aucthoritie and a taking of his office out of his hande." Since " in deede ther appeareth no matter whie he shulde be so prescribed or restraigned," he was completely exonerated by the council, although in the future use of the great seal of the Court he was mildly admonished " to have that respect unto the Kinges Majesties proficte that the duetie of his office requireth, which the Lordes no thinge mistrusted in him." [88]

This check on the chancellor of Augmentations was only a minor phase of a general conciliar investigation of national finances and revenue administration that was initiated in 1550 and continued until the end of the reign. The previous burden of war, the upkeep of numerous garrisons, mounting expenses in Ireland, and increased current expenses in the household had constituted a heavy and continual drain on the attenuated national resources. In addition to these current expenses the

[86] Exchanges of land and gifts in fee tail or fee simple were assured under the great seal; likewise, manumissions were processed under the great seal. Similarly, all leases of over £6 13s. 4d. annual rental were issued under the privy seal and the signet. Articles 1, 11, and 12 of the *Calendar; Cal. Pat. Rolls, Edward VI,* III, 214–16.

[87] Dasent (ed.), *Acts of the Privy Council,* III, 130–31. Sackville was required to present to the council a formal declaration of such leases and grants and ordered to refrain from issuing any further grants for the time being. This may have been the restriction on Sackville's authority referred to in the king's journal of July 9, 1552: " The chauncellour of th'augmentation was willed to surcease his commission, geven him the third yeare of our raigne." Nichols (ed.), *Literary Remains,* II, 432. Since no commission was issued to him during the regnal year, 1549–1550, the one referred to was probably the above commission of February 20, 1550, issued during the fourth rather than the third year of the reign.

[88] Dasent (ed.), *Acts of the Privy Council,* III, 173, 189, 331.

council had to plan for the repayment of the government's debts at home and abroad which, by the end of 1552, were variously estimated at a total of somewhere between £219,686 and £251,000.[89] In an attempt to solve this financial problem, the council resorted to all the old familiar Tudor expedients, including the usual petty economies which tended to emerge during times of crisis. Debasement, the sale of crown land and property, the further despoliation of church lands by the annexation of dioceses, and parliamentary taxation all helped, but they did not solve the fundamental problem.

In October of 1552 the young king presented to the council a summary of "matters to be concluded," which consisted of no fewer than twenty-seven articles, all dealing with major problems of administration and finance. They were intended to reduce governmental expenditures and thereby raise £300,000. It was hoped that the "mass of money" thus secured would not only pay off the current debts but also provide a working surplus of £50,000 for possible emergencies.[90] Appreciable savings were to be achieved by reduction in the Irish army and the English garrisons, by the sale of crown lands and property, and by a speedy collection of the arrears and money owing to the crown. The coinage of church plate was also recommended. The remainder could be acquired by borrowing from English merchants. A few articles, however, offered pertinent suggestions for administrative reform. Among the departments mentioned were the household, the wardrobe, the admiralty, and the revenue courts. Article Twelve provided for the elimination of all superfluous fees in the Court of Wards and Liveries and the Court of the Duchy Chamber of Lancaster, and Article Eleven sought to eliminate excessive allowances in the courts for portage charges. Of all the suggested items, however, Number Ten was the most fruitful. It anticipated the conclusions of a later commission study by recommending the union of the Court of Augmentations and the Court of First Fruits with the Court of Exchequer.[91] Timely though the proposal

---

[89] See pp. 183–84, *supra*. A detailed explanation is presented in Dietz, *English Government Finance, 1485–1553*, Chap. XV, 188–201. Dietz estimates the English debt to have been £108,800 in England and about £132,372 in Flanders. *Ibid.*, 191, n. 9. A brief of all the king's debts with suggested provisions for repayment was drawn up by William Cecil in October, 1552. The domestic debt was given as £108,826 19s. 10d. and the external debt as £110,860. H. M. C., *Cal. of Cecil Manuscripts*, pt. 1, nos. 395, 396.

[90] "Matters for the Council, October 13, 1552": Lansd. MS. 1236, fol. 19; Nichols (ed.), *Literary Remains*, II, 543–46. Strype's version of this document is presented in *Ecclesiastical Memorials*, II, pt. 1, p. 594 ff.

[91] It was assumed that great economy could be achieved by "saving al thos fees that may be spared." Article Sixteen was concerned with the auditing of the accounts of all the crown's treasurers and special receivers of revenue since 1545. A commission for that purpose had been set up the previous January 8, 1552.

may have been, the argument recommending amalgamation was that of economy rather than improved administration.

The gravity of the situation became evident in the late summer of 1552. Every expedient for raising money was tried, but the incoming revenues still proved inadequate to meet the growing demands of the government. Faced with complete bankruptcy the council temporarily suspended all payments in August while the king was on progress, on the dubious assumption that he could not " be troubled with payments " until his return to London. Loans in Antwerp were becoming more difficult to secure and always at a higher rate of interest.

In the midst of these difficulties it is not surprising that any irregularity on the part of a high revenue official would have caused considerable excitement in the council. Such were the circumstances at the time of the investigation and arrest of the treasurer of the Court of Augmentations in the spring of 1552. On April 3 letters were directed to the chancellor and treasurer of the Court ordering them to appear before the council at seven o'clock the next morning with a statement of the money remaining in the treasurer's charge. The next month the Court was directed to call in all the particular receivers in order to ascertain the exact amount of their receipts in every district. In explanation of the order the council said that " his Highnes hath presently occasion to employ monny, and that the Lordes understand that the more part of the tenauntes have allredy paid the sayd Revenues, his Majestie mindeth to have the same employed in suche sorte as he shall think convenient; willing them therefore to put in a redines, so as it be forth cumming when it shalbe called for." [92] The chancellor was then directed to permit no payments from the revenues of the Court by its treasurer without the special warrant of the king or council.[93] On the following day similar restrictions on expenditures were imposed on the duchy of Lancaster, and by the end of the month the restraint was extended to the Exchequer and the Court of Wards and Liveries.[94] Shortly thereafter, on November 14, 1552, payment of pensions and annuities drawn

---

[92] Dasent (ed.), *Acts of the Privy Council,* IV, 12, 37, 43. The special requirement that treasurers and receivers " doo with diligence advertise unto theyr Lordshippes [the council] in writing, aswell what monny is presently in theyr handes of the Revenues of every theyr offices, as what they suppose and doo looke shall cume to theyr handes of the receypt of the same Revenues due at thannunciacion of Our Lady last past," should have been unnecessary. By standing order the courts were supposed to render regularly weekly declarations of their accounts. *Ibid.,* 62.

[93] A postscript to this council letter of May 14 prohibited the Augmentations receivers from paying out their receipts to anyone except the treasurer of the Court. *Ibid.,* 46.

[94] *Ibid.,* 48, 62, 74–75.

on the Augmentations revenues were suspended until such time as the Court's revenues "that ought to cumme clere to the Kinges Majesties coffers be fyrst payed, and then to make payment of the pencions accordingly." [95]

It would appear, however, that these limitations did not result directly from the council's suspicion of the Court's treasurer. Williams, who had been arrested on April 8 for exceeding his authority, was out of prison before the above restrictions were rescinded and back in his office at the Augmentations. Suffering no more than a reprimand from the council, it is unlikely that he had brought upon the Court any penalties or restraint of authority as a result of his indiscretion.[96] In the light of events that followed it is clear that the regulations governing court payments were purely precautionary. The government urgently needed money, and the revenue courts did not have enough left over after their regular monthly expenditures to meet the council's demands. Consequently, the government expected its own payments to come first. In other words, money for the king's "own use" was given priority over ordinary pensions or normal payments by warrant of the chancellor and council of the Court.[97]

Meanwhile, in the autumn of 1552, financial inquiries were made of various other revenue departments and agencies. These surveys, which sought to ascertain how much money was expected to come in by September 29, included the household, the wardrobe, the ordnance, and the offices of the stables and works. At the same time the receiver of the Augmentations in the fourteenth district was ordered to report to the council on how much he had already paid to the garrisons and fortifications in Essex and to certify the total amounts due them at Michaelmas, the end of the fiscal year.[98] Again, at the beginning of December, 1552, the treasury courts were required to submit certificates of the money they had on hand, as well as declarations of all arrearages and debts due but uncollected in their respective institutions.[99] The latter inquiry was possibly an outgrowth of the comprehensive investigation of the entire revenue machinery which was then in progress.

This important commission, issued on March 23, 1552, for the survey

[95] *Ibid.*, 170. By warrant of the chancellor and council of the Court, receivers were permitted to continue payment of small pensions under £10 per year.

[96] On Williams' arrest and trial see Chapter Eight, pp. 265–66.

[97] Dasent (ed.), *Acts of the Privy Council*, IV, 67, 170. The restraining regulations were gradually lifted before the end of the year.

[98] *Ibid.*, 115.

[99] *Ibid.*, 183. Declarations of debts and arrearages were to be presented with full particulars: viz., "to whome and for what; but they may not stay thereupon so muche, but that they must make the certificate of theyr remaynes owt of hande."

of all the courts having custody of the king's lands and revenues, was to investigate " principally the state of suche latter courtes as have bene erected for the revenues in the tyme of our said father of noble memorye." It was composed of nine councillors of whom six had been chosen by the king earlier in the month to constitute a special standing committee on courts and revenues.[100] Collectively, the nine represented a fair proportion of the council's administrative ability, as drawn from the household, the revenue courts, and the church. The chairman, Thomas Lord Darcy, baron of Chiche and lord chamberlain of the household, had risen rapidly under Edward VI to a position of importance in council deliberations.[101] With the exception of two appointees, all the members held responsible positions in the government.[102] They were Thomas Thirlby, bishop of Norwich; Sir John Gates, vice-chamberlain, captain of the guard, and chancellor of the duchy of Lancaster; Sir William Petre, principal secretary and treasurer of the Court of First Fruits and Tenths; Sir Robert Bowes, master of the rolls and warden of the East Marches; Sir Richard Cotton, controller of the household; Sir Walter Mildmay, general surveyor of the Augmentations; John Gosnold, solicitor of the Augmentations; and Sir Thomas Wroth, one of the four principal gentlemen of the privy chamber.[103] Wroth was probably the least able of the commissioners, although he was certainly one of the king's favorites.[104] Thirlby, the only churchman in the group, was an able jurist and administrator and probably took an active part in the work of the commission.

Of the nine members appointed only six actually sat, as indicated in the final report of the commission. Petre, Wroth, and Gosnold were excused from active participation apparently, although for no good reason save perhaps their activity in other affairs during the summer and

---

[100] The original six members represented seven departments, since the two offices of vice-chamberlain of the household and captain of the guard were both held by Sir John Gates. The seven offices were: the lord chamberlain (chairman), the vice-chamberlain, the controller of the household, the master of the rolls, the captain of the guard, the principal general surveyor in the Augmentations, and the bishop of Norwich. Pp. 185–86, *supra*.

[101] On April 5, 1551, Darcy, then vice-chamberlain and gentleman of the privy chamber, was created Lord Darcy of Chiche and advanced to the chamberlainship. John G. Nichols (ed.), *The Diary of Henry Machyn* (London, 1848), xvii.

[102] Pat. Rolls, 6 Edward VI, pt. 6, mem. 33*d*.

[103] Four of the original nine were also members of the council commission on debts, i. e., Gates, Petre, Bowes, and Mildmay.

[104] Wroth, first the ward and later son-in-law of Sir Richard Rich, had risen to prominence through the latter's influence. Although not a privy councillor, Wroth sat in two Edwardian parliaments and was appointed to several commissions, including the one on the king's debts for December, 1552. *Cal. Pat. Rolls, Edward VI*, IV, 352–53, 391; V, 356, 414. A. F. Pollard, " Sir Thomas Wroth," in *D. N. B.*

autumn of 1552. The absence of these men left Mildmay as the only professional administrator and technical expert on the commission. Gates subsequently represented the duchy of Lancaster, but he had not been in the chancellor's office long enough to become skilled in administrative techniques or familiar with problems of revenue procedure.[105]

Presumably the commission began hearings immediately, although detailed evidence of its varied activities is not extant. Each court submitted answers to ten articles of inquiry, which covered the pertinent points later encompassed in the final report. Nor was the council unmindful that a significant investigation was in progress which might modify the entire administrative policy of the government. To this end there was some concern shown in making the results available as soon as possible. Late in September Sir Walter Mildmay was ordered to bring in " the bookes of the survey of the Courtes as sone as he may conveniently fynishe the same." [106] Less than three months later a report was submitted, the scope and particularity of which suggest the fundamental character of the investigation. In essence the commissioners constituted a reform committee whose ultimate task was to suggest a feasible plan of administrative reorganization, though it had been charged more immediately with effecting a savings in the costs of the revenue bureaucracy that had grown out of the Cromwellian organization. Nevertheless, the detailed evidence presented was not entirely acceptable; neither were its findings altogether accurate, nor its final recommendations completely carried out. In spite of these shortcomings, the report remains the most basic and comprehensive contemporary estimate available of the financial situation at the close of the Northumberland administration.

Dated December 10, 1552, it was presented to the council in three distinct sections, each dealing with a separate aspect of the survey. The first part of the certificate consisted of a detailed review of the revenues of the kingdom as administered by the fiscal courts and subsidiary financial departments, such as the chamber, the jewel house, and the mint. This section contained financial estimates for the fifth year of the reign, giving a full analysis of both receipts and expenditures based on the testimony and the declarations of account submitted by the officials of the courts and other financial agencies. Under the heading of " notes

[105] Gates was not appointed chancellor of the duchy of Lancaster until July 4, 1552. However, he still retained his post as vice-chamberlain of the household as well as other sinecurial positions. *D. N. B.*; *Cal. Pat. Rolls, Edward VI*, V, 143–45, 234, 248.

[106] Augm. Office, Misc. Books 476, fol. 28; Dasent (ed.), *Acts of the Privy Council*, IV, 128. On the activities of the commission, see Augm. Office, Misc. Books 476, fols. 46–47.

and remembrances " the second part set forth in considerable detail the weaknesses, abuses, and procedural techniques in the revenue administration, with suggestions for improvement. Finally, the third section offered recommendations for revenue revision whereby the national income might be increased and by which " divers superfluous offices and fees and sundry great yearly [charges] now burdened upon his majesty may be considered and reformed." [107]

The wider implications of this report have been incorporated in other studies and need not be included here.[108] Nevertheless, the portions dealing with the Augmentations contain valuable evidence relating to the Court's decay during the latter period of its history. The terse comments and criticisms offered by the commissioners present a vivid picture of an institution impaired by uncontrolled bureaucratic growth.

A glance at the enumerated revenues for the fiscal year ending at Michaelmas, 1551, will indicate at once the predominant position occupied by the Court of Augmentations as the principal treasury of the nation. Of the total receipts taken in by the five revenue courts, the Augmentations yielded £159,295 10s. 5d., or about 58.56 per cent.[109] All revenues were classified as either " certainties " or " casualties "; the former consisted of regular fixed income derived chiefly from land, and the latter, of variable receipts which fluctuated from year to year. The Augmentations certainties were rents, farms in possession, and reversion of lands granted for term of life, all of which amounted to £144,825 8s. 2d. To this was added £1,475 19s. 11d. which was assigned, for no apparent reason, to the Court yearly out of the Exchequer, to be paid to the great wardrobe. The casual revenues of the Court included such extraneous income as fines for leases, tunnage and customs fees in the duchies of Chester and Cornwall, perquisites of court,

---

[107] The certificate of returns of the commissioners appointed for a survey of the king's courts of revenue, together with two other parchment membranes, which taken collectively constitute the original report. The remainder of the roll appears to have been lost. Three copies, however, are available, from which the full text can be reconstructed. Exch., K. R., Miscellanea, 12/19. Copies of the report are available in Add. MS. 30198; Society of Antiquaries of London MS. 209; and Harl. MS. 7383. The first two of these copies do not contain the last part of the original.

[108] The full significance of the report can be studied in Richardson, *Tudor Chamber Administration, 1485-1547*, 393-95, and in Elton, *Tudor Revolution in Government*, 231-37. The latter work presents a complete analysis of the financial problems involved in the proposed changes suggested by the commissioners.

[109] The distribution among the courts was as follows: the Augmentations £159,295 10s. 5d., the Exchequer £39,348 16s., Wards and Liveries £31,749 2s. 5d., First Fruits and Tenths £23,564 4s. 3d., and the duchy of Lancaster £18,054 18s. 9d. Add. MS. 30198, fol. 35. The Augmentations total would be £100 less if the figure for the Court's casualties as given on fol. 24 is accepted.

commorth rent in Wales,[110] and profits from fairs, wood sales, the butlerage, and the two seals of the Court.

The chief expenditures were the fees of the officers of the Court and the salaries of other state ministers borne by it, which totaled £ 20,551 1s. 2d., and a host of miscellaneous payments classified as " deductions to continue " and " deductions to revert." Those to continue were more or less permanent, such as expenses for fortifications and garrisons, upkeep and repair of crown buildings, diets of ambassadors, costs of the annual audit of accounts, and regular assignments on the Court by royal warrant. In the last category were mostly pensions, annuities, and grants of crown property for life or term of years. These charges constituted a heavy burden on the Court, aggregating no less than £131,333 14s. 8d. annually. The surplus remaining, therefore, was £29,337 15s. 8d., which was listed as " possession." If to this total was added an extra £63,511 12s. 3d. " reversion," which might be expected to revert to the crown when the recipients of annuities and such like payments died, the balance was increased to £92,849 7s. 11d.[111] As compared to the total expenditures of all the departments of revenue, the Court of Augmentations payments amounted to over 55 per cent of the total. Similarly, the surplus of £29,337 was almost four-fifths of the total surplus of all the revenue courts.[112]

The most the commissioners could possibly show, therefore, was a maximum annual balance of £115,037 16s. 7d., over two-thirds of which would probably never be realized. Even accepting the reversionary surplus as legitimate, it was obvious that the finances were in a desperate plight. Moreover, certain items were not amplified in the financial estimates, such as the various sums of money transferred from time to time from the treasuries of the revenue courts to the king's privy purse. This " obscure depository known as the king's coffers," as the report called it, had been instituted by Henry VIII as a safeguard against temporary shortages of cash on the part of the regular departments of revenue. Likewise, there were several major items of national ex-

---

[110] In origin the commorth (*cymmorth* or *commortha*) was an ancient contribution or payment collected from the land at the time of marriage or when young priests said their first masses. It became one of the many local customs in Wales over which there was considerable dispute. The fine or rent commonly due from the tenants every third year was payable to the king over and above the regular rent. The amount and frequency of the fine varied; in some cases it was customarily due every fourth year.

[111] *Ibid.*, fols. 23–25. Compare with figures on fol. 20d.

[112] *Ibid.*, fols. 36, 37. The total national expenditure, as given for the five courts, was £235,398 19s. 4d., with a surplus of only £36,513 17s. 2½d. With a " reversion " of £78,523 19s. 4½d., the ultimate annual surplus was swollen to a total of £115,037 16s. 7d. for all revenue departments.

penditure which were always larger than anticipated. The expenses of Calais and Ireland regularly exceeded the revenues allocated to them, while the annual charges of the admiralty, the ordnance, the great wardrobe, and the household were far greater than their normal appropriations. To these extra expenses should be added such fluctuating variables as New Year's gifts, rewards, and money spent for the king's personal affairs. All these annual charges were suggested but not interpreted by the commission.[113]

After a complete analysis of the current finances of the government, the commissioners proceeded to the main portion of their report, namely an unrestricted criticism of the entire revenue system, together with copious suggestions for improvement. With the English penchant for practical rather than theoretical reform, they subjected all branches of the administration which dealt in any way with the nation's revenues to a thorough examination. To those at all familiar with the operation of the administrative machinery, that review must have been as convincing as it was realistic. In twenty-four folio pages the defects of every department were systematically itemized, each particular abuse being substantiated by facts and figures. Altogether, it was a very imposing indictment of the Tudor bureaucracy initiated by Cromwell. Although inherently sound in principle, its practical success depended largely upon a small core of select administrators who provided the coordination so necessary for effective operation. Under the decentralizing influences of Edwardian government the system had degenerated for lack of just such competent direction.

The " remembrances and notes " [114] set forth all the evils of this young and top-heavy officialdom which the research historian of the period has long suspected but never proved. Graft, waste, petty corruption, and fraud were cited; malfeasance in office or, in numerous cases, actual theft were uncovered. Such glaring abuses as multiplicity of office, delays in rendering accounts, incompetent supervision, use of deputies in important positions, arrears of revenues, careless bookkeeping, and pervading irresponsibility were common to all revenue departments. Nevertheless, some of the disorder was attributable to those in authority. Though remissness undoubtedly existed, under strong central leadership it would not have recurred. Adequate safeguards and checks existed under the law, but they were not properly enforced. In this respect the

---

[113] " Yearly charges to be considered " but which were not deducted from the total revenue. *Ibid.*, fols. 37, 37*d*.

[114] " Remembrances and notes made by the said Commissioners upon Examinacion of the Estate of the Kings Courts of Revenue and conference with the Officers of the same," *ibid.*, fols 39*d.*–52.

valuable lessons of the two preceding reigns had already been forgotten. Elaborate regulations governing the duties and behavior of each of the revenue officials, from the highest to the lowest, were provided in the constitutions of the respective courts, but in the easygoing indifference of Edwardian administration, they had been ignored. Particularly grievous, from the governmental point of view at least, were the evils of salary increases and failure of those in authority to put the more important financial ministers under bond. Need for bonding all revenue officials, especially receivers and collectors, had been repeatedly stressed. Some unbonded ministers actually died while in office without " a just account and payment," while others left their positions with no final audit required. In any event, in addition to sustaining a constant loss of revenue, " the King remaineth in great uncertainty as hath appeared sufficiently before." [115]

In many ways the Court of Augmentations was typical of the other revenue institutions, since it combined the abuses of them all. At once the newest, the largest in personnel, and easily the most important in total receipts and expenditures, it embodied all the weaknesses of a young department in which spirit and discipline had not kept pace with its phenomenal expansion. In continual adjustment to new practices and procedures the Court had not had time to develop that body of convention and tradition which had given a measure of stability to the Exchequer and the duchy of Lancaster. Consequently, under an easy administration, it became a fertile field of exploitation for the unscrupulous, an easy prey for land speculators and irresponsible office seekers. No fewer than fifty separate items were required to list its deficiencies.[116]

The list of indictments begins with a charge of losses of perquisites of local courts sustained on Augmentations lands in the north of England, which were held by leasehold instead of by copyhold as under " the old order." That practice was injurious, not only to the tenants, but also to the crown, since it eliminated the lucrative fines that would otherwise accrue from descent and alienation.[117] Likewise, " a good porcion of the decays " of the Court resulted from the lack of proper land surveys and

---

[115] *Ibid.*, fol. 49*d*.

[116] Notes on the Court of Augmentations, *ibid.*, fols. 44–47, including *dorso* pages. The points of criticism are not numbered in the report, but each is listed as a separate " item."

[117] Tenants would willingly give one year's rent for every alienation or death of tenant, it was explained. The remedy was to grant all crown lands to the value of £3 8*d*. or under only by copyhold tenure, which would give the crown " a years rent at the change of every tenaunt," eliminate all reparations, and be " much more profitable both to the Kings Majestie and to his tenauntes then is now."

carelessness in the certification of crown lands acquired by exchange, attainder, or purchase. Under the latter heading it was noted that sometimes land remained within the jurisdiction of the Court for three or four years before any revenues were collected from it, since the Augmentations auditors and receivers were given " no certain knowledge " of the acquisition. Auditor John Pickerel reported that a manor in Buckinghamshire, which was delivered in exchange by Sir Thomas Heneage four years previously, had never been charged the £11 rent due from it and cited another exchange in the same district which entailed a loss to the crown of £43 per annum. Because of these and several other losses occasioned " for lack of Certificate," it was recommended that a special commission under the jurisdiction of the Court be appointed to search for such uncertified lands.[118]

In the execution of their charge the commissioners were concerned primarily with the problem of discovering ways and means of immediately augmenting the king's revenues. The investigators explored the financial weaknesses of the revenue courts more thoroughly than they did the administrative abuses. In the Court of Augmentations, as in the other departments, questions of arrears, decay of revenues, and decreased profits were the principal subjects of attack. The mise, in Wales, which was due upon the king's first entry into the principality, had not been collected, reversions and entailed estates were not promptly reported to the auditors when they fell due, and their revenues were lost, while further losses were sustained through failure to record all the particulars of land grants in the Augmentations.[119] In the levying of fines the Court had been particularly negligent. Out of sheer carelessness or indifference they were sometimes not levied at all or, if collected, were pocketed by some dishonest official. Fines for leases, for example, were not charged against the treasurer's accounts. This was quite a serious omission; unless extracts were made by the clerk of the Court and presented to the auditors of the treasurer's account, there was no way of determining what fines had actually been paid. Similarly, the treasurer was not required to keep a record of land sales. The only check on such

---

[118] In many cases ministers learned of the acquisition of lands only from the parties concerned. In one instance Richard Bream and wife owed the Court of Augmentations £50 16s. 1d. rent annually, though only £13 6s. 8d. yearly had been collected for over twelve years. Incredible as it may seem " nothing appeareth why the rest should be discharged the certainty whereof is not known [to the Court] for lack of Certificate in time from them which were privy to the Kings grant." *Ibid.*, fol. 44.

[119] It was recommended that a search be made of the letters patent in chancery in order that the crown should be answered of the revenue according to the statutes of 35 Henry VIII and 1 Edward VI.

payments was "his own confession," which the commissioners rightly argued was "a large error to walke in and is much worthy of Examinacion." In fact, few controls of any kind were imposed upon the Court's treasurer. It was noted that John Williams, treasurer of Augmentations since March 31, 1544, had "not yet accompted for any of the years past," although the regulations plainly required a reckoning every year. In view of the fact that he was not even bonded, it is understandable that the government was somewhat disturbed lest the treasurer die without accounting and leave the king "in great unsurety." [120]

Unwarranted expenditures had resulted from the indiscriminate allowance of special payments by officials, without any investigation of the validity of the claims. The receivers were especially guilty in this respect, collecting excessive fees for portage and travel, padding their expense accounts, or even charging twice for the same item.[121] As a precaution against unauthorized and illegitimate charges it was advised that, under no condition, should auditors be permitted to allow extraordinary payments which were not specifically authorized by the chancellor and council of the Court, as provided in the constitution. Other types of payment, while quite legitimate, were nevertheless considered either too large or unnecessary. Too much was allowed for travel, reparations, waterworks, questionable debts, and appropriations for peacetime defenses. In the case of reparations as much as £5,437 had been spent by the Court during one year, none of which had any authorization save by the bills of the local surveyors or their deputies, who affirmed the money to have been spent without previous surveys or examination.

Much of the graft and corruption in the revenue administration was due to delays in accounting. In addition to hearing the accounts of its own officials, the Augmentations audited the accounts of a number of auxiliary departments, all of which were continually behind in their declarations. The treasurer of Berwick had not accounted for two years, nor the chief butler for five years, whereas many special treasurers of buildings, wars, victuals, and other items purchased for the crown had not accounted at all. As already observed, the Court's own treasurer had not declared an account since assuming office. In the case of advances on account, which by 1552 had become a common practice, it was

[120] Add. MS. 30198, fol. 47.
[121] One auditor allowed a receiver, without warrant, £20 for travel charges, another £53 for riding costs in North Wales. In Kent and Surrey the receiver collected £6 13s. 4d. in portage fees which he had sustained in delivering money for defense fortifications, yet he claimed, and secured, the same amount for his expenses in riding with the money to the bulwarks. With typical English understatement, the commissioners suggested that this "double allowance" was excessive. *Ibid.*, fol. 45d.

especially difficult to ensure speedy accounting. Unless the individual were honest, there was no method by which repayment could be assured. The two auditorships of the prests had been set up in the Augmentations for just that purpose, but latterly few ministers had bothered to account for their advances. If they did not voluntarily submit themselves for an audit, apparently no effort was made by the prest auditors to require a declaration. To rectify this alarming situation several safeguards were suggested. Firstly, every treasurer and receiver-general of the realm should be required to present annually to the auditors of the prests ordinary certificates of all money by them delivered in prest in order that the recipients might be called to account. Secondly, auditors of the prests should deliver their own accounts and certificates to the Augmentations at least once a year in order that they might remain there as a matter of record. Thirdly, all persons receiving money in prest should be adequately bonded. This was especially desirable for those ministers who regularly spent large sums of money for the crown, as the paymasters of the victuallers' office, the admiralty, the ordnance, and the surveyor of works. Finally, the best guarantee of all for regularity of accounting was the selection of responsible officers for the important financial positions in the government.

Yet, however qualified the appointees, it could not be assumed that all officials would remain completely trustworthy. Those ministers who were responsible for large sums of money needed to be bonded with ample sureties.[122] Even with lesser offices the Court had no assurance of payment if the incumbent had no sureties.[123] The only reliable rule was to bond everybody who was in any way charged with the collection, spending, or distribution of the national revenue. This was the standard set up by the commissioners.

In other respects, too, the Augmentations had travelled a long way from the rigid disciplines established by Cromwell. The greatest change, probably, was in the creation of sinecural positions and in the augmentation of the fees and salaries of its own personnel. Since the beginning of the Court in 1547 the salaries of the chancellor and general surveyors had each been increased by £40, those of the attorney and solicitor by 20 marks each, and that of the clerk by £13 6s. 8d. Together the court auditors had added over £537 to their annual salaries; the receivers,

[122] The treasurer of Berwick remained unbonded though his receipts were well over £3,000 annually; with the treasurer of the Court of Augmentations in charge of revenues that totaled £100,000 or more per year, it was ridiculous to permit him to continue in office without submitting an adequate bond.

[123] In at least one instance a receiver in the northern district, Sir Thomas Newnham, not only was unbonded but held office entirely without sureties or even patent of appointment.

more than £622. The fees of various officers' clerks had been raised £131 10s. per year, while expenses of the annual audit had risen from £1,052 3s. 4d. to £1,976 8s. 4d. Though individually not very important, these " divers incroachments & increase of allowance " totaled £2,336, which the commissioners correctly deemed " worthy of Consideracion." Certain offices that had been given significant salary increases might well have been eliminated altogether. These included especially the two masters and the two surveyors of woods, forty-four particular surveyors, and thirty-six woodwards, at varying rates of pay, to which should be added travelling expenses for the two latter categories. The discontinuance of those eighty-four officials, it was estimated, would save the Court £1,172 8d. plus riding charges of an indefinite amount.[124]

In all fairness to the Court, however, it should be noted that the commissioners were unduly critical of this particular problem. No doubt a number of individual increases were unwarranted, but the rising cost of living made some adjustment inevitable. The government itself refused to face the situation squarely and with some justification, since all costs of administration were prone to rise more rapidly than the national revenue. Prolonged by conservative leadership and sheer public inertia, official salaries tended to remain stationary, in spite of spiraling prices. Consequently, institutions were forced to seek their own remedy. This they did. In one way or another most officials contrived to augment their salaries in an effort to offset the hardships of inflation. In this respect the courts were no more culpable than other departments of the government.

In the field as well as in the central office a ruthless program of retrenchment was proposed. Drastic reductions in the number of local officers, such as clerks, keepers, bailiffs, collectors, and stewards, it was thought would not materially impair the operational efficiency of the Court.[125] In the duchy of Cornwall the office of attorney could well be eliminated, while in Wales the chancellor, chamberlain, and justices were all unnecessary, since the council of Wales had completely taken over the administration of justice in that area. Moreover, savings could be effected in other quarters. It was noted that the clerk of Windsor Castle, whose sole duty was the oversight of reparations, received £24

---

[124] Items Ten and Eleven of " notes and remembrances " on the Court of the Augmentations. *Ibid.*, fols. 44d., 45; Harl. MS. 7383, fol. 62d.

[125] Many of these local officials had also secured significant increases in salary and fees. For example, it was decided to apportion the fees of bailiffs and collectors according to the amount of money collected, in no case to exceed 6d. to 8d. in the pound.

yearly for services that could easily be done by warrant, that the salary
of the chief butler of England had recently been tripled, and that it was
believed that the profits of his department could be increased 100 per
cent by closer supervision. Under recent administration, when many
sought to line their own pockets, bureaucratic offices multiplied with
alarming rapidity. Two posts in the Court illustrate the trend. When
set up in 1547 it had single receiverships and auditorships for north and
south Wales; since that date, the duke of Somerset had separated the
work into two offices, at a cost to the crown of £100 in fees and
allowances. In like manner the Augmentations had created new posts
without royal warrant. By constitutional provision the treasurer originally accounted annually before two of the court auditors. This regulation
necessitated no separate office, since the two who heard the account were
selected in rotation from among the regular ten regional auditors and
received no extra compensation for this service. Subsequently, however,
William Berners, auditor in the Court, had procured an appointment
for life as special auditor of the treasurer's accounts. Thus another
office was created, a fee added, and " the Order of the Court broken
both to þe Kings loss & overcharge & to his unsurety in service." [126]

Even in the minor details of administration the indictment subjected
the Augmentations, from top to bottom, to inexorable scrutiny. Local
courts were held infrequently, audits postponed, records imperfectly
kept, and rents not promptly collected, if at all. Debts to the king
remaining unpaid grew daily more hopeless. In the counties woods were
despoiled, timber sold with neither record nor warrant, and unauthorized
payments made to the great detriment of the crown. Receivers had
fallen into the habit of paying local fees and annuities out of their regular
revenues before forwarding their collections to the treasurer of the
Court. As a result their surpluses were all spent before the demands of
the crown were met. This was deemed an intolerable situation, since the
king's payments should be given priority. Therefore, all surplus revenues
of the receivers and collectors should be paid " wholly " and immediately
into the central treasury. This procedure would enable charges for
the household, ambassadors, defense, and important affairs to be met
promptly, " rather then the King should tarry for his part." The same
principle applied to the issues by the treasurer of the Augmentations,
for experience had proved " that those which ought to be ffirst paid are
faine to tarry last & the same groweth by Occasion aforesaid."

Strangely enough, the chancellor and general surveyors were practically the only officers of the Court who escaped censure, although it

---

[126] Add. MS. 30198, fol. 46. See p. 150 and n. 109, *supra*.

might have been assumed that they were responsible for the situation which prevailed. With no restraints imposed upon their own conduct they had subjected subordinate officials to none. The report gives the general impression that court rules and regulations were enforced only when it was convenient for everybody to do so. Even in such minor matters as archival procedures, official indifference prevailed. Whereas all court rolls and local records by law were to be stored in some fixed place, usually the capital of the shire, they had been permitted to "lye very confusedly dispersed"; since stewards were paid before their records were turned in, there was no incentive to be either honest or efficient. Even auditors were permitted to retain their own accounts indefinitely rather than to deliver them to the Court's keeper of the records at Westminster. Still it is well to remember that the institution was no worse an offender in these matters than other departments and agencies.[127] The notes conclude with a statement concerning the need for general declarations of accounts from the various independent agents of the crown. The item clearly revealed a current defect in the administration which was to remain uncorrected long after the Augmentations was abolished:

Finally among other things upon the perusing this Court it seemeth very necessary to the Commissioners that a perfect accompt were made of the Kings Lead Bell mettall goods plate and Jewells of Abbys and attainted persons the Records whereof as it is informed were never perfectly Examined nor declared and the matter being of so great Importance it is the more worthy to be called on in time.[128]

[127] The Council of the Marches of Wales and the Council of the North had each increased the diets and fees of its membership since the beginning of Edward's reign. In the former council the increase was £578 6s. 6d., but members of the Council of the North had more than doubled their collective salaries, the total being raised from £666 6s. 8d. to £1,400 6s. 8d., or by £734. Proportionately these increases were far greater than those of the revenue courts. Since the salaries of these councils were paid from Augmentations revenues, the item is included among the notes on that Court. Of course, extenuating circumstances, such as the debasement of the currency and the rise of living costs, were not taken into consideration. The item was concluded by a compromise proposal which avoided the necessity of arriving at a judgment. The combined salaries of both councils of over £2,842 was "to be diminished in part or in all as shall be thought good." *Ibid.*, fol. 45d.

[128] *Ibid.*, fol. 47. This recommendation and various other suggestions of the commission were carried out before the end of the reign. On December 12, 1552, a commission of eleven members, including Walter and Thomas Mildmay and Richard Goodrich of the Court of Augmentations, was appointed to investigate those "great and notable" quantities of such items and compel those who had not accounted to submit to an official audit. The commissioners were also authorized to check on losses incurred by the exportation, without license, of gold, silver,

By the time the commission had completed its investigation the accumulated evidence in favor of reorganization was overwhelming. The reduction of overhead expenses, cutting of salaries, and abolition of superfluous offices, however relentlessly carried out, was not enough. Petty economies only served to emphasize the more basic problem of redundancy, with too many similar institutions performing identical functions. It was not just a question of general retrenchment and the internal reform of several departments of revenue; if the maximum of efficiency at the lowest possible cost was to be achieved, a complete reorganization of the whole revenue machinery was required. But such a radical departure from the old order was, at that time, impossible. In the end all the vested interest groups were protected. It is doubtful if the commissioners themselves had any hope that the more extreme proposals incorporated in the third and final portion of their report would be adopted.

The last part of the report presented a brief declaration of the principal charges on the national revenues for the fiscal year ending Michaelmas, 1552, with detailed recommendations as to how the total revenue could be increased by adequate improvements and reforms. The principal charge on which a major saving might be effected was in the total annual expenditure of £18,532 11*s.* 11*d.* on salaries, but by the most rigid paring this item could not be reduced to less than £12,104.[129] As a major economy measure such a meager saving was obviously inconsequential. A more fundamental solution was sought in an alternative scheme of reconstruction which, if accepted, would revolutionize the existing revenue system.

The proposed plan called for the complete abolition of all five financial courts and for the organization of two new revenue departments, to which all governmental receipts and expenditures would be entrusted. Actually, the change was more in the nature of a consolidation than a general overhauling of the existing structure, for one of the departments, a reformed Exchequer, would have absorbed the revenues formerly administered by the Court of Wards and Liveries, the Court of First Fruits and Tenths, and the older Exchequer; the other, to be called "the Courte of the Kinges Revenue," would have taken over all the duties and functions of the erstwhile Augmentations and duchy of Lan-

---

jewels, bullion, and other rich wares. Pat. Rolls, 6 Edward VI, pt. 7, mem. 10*d.* S. P. 10/16, fol. 156.

[129] The third section of this copy of the report (seventy-two folios) presents the final recommendations of the committee, identified as "A Briefe Declaracion of the chardge . . . at this yeare with thofficers of his graces Revenue wth certeyn divises for the diminishment of the same, As shall stand withe his highness pleasure." Harl. MS. 7383, fols. 61–72. Cf. Exch., K. R. Miscellanea, 163/12/19.

caster. The design was as logical as it was expedient. Under the proposed pattern all the revenue would be divided into two major categories based on the source from which it was derived. Revenues from land, with all the issues and profits pertaining thereto, were to be administered by a single department, the Court of the King's Revenues; all other revenues, whatsoever their origin, were to come under an expanded, reconverted Exchequer.

Among other significant changes the Exchequer under this plan would annex the bulk of the revenues of the king's chamber, which would virtually be reduced to its pre-Tudor status. As clearly indicated in the report, it was apparent that the chamber was no longer an integral part of the administration. There was ample justification therefore for reducing it to " thold forme," as a subsidiary household department. This recommendation probably met with little opposition, save from the treasurer himself, since it merely recognized in theory a situation which in fact had existed for a number of years. The head of the chamber, William Cavendish, a privy councillor and favorite of Edward VI, successfully withstood the attack, however, and remained the treasurer of the unreformed chamber until his death in October, 1557.[130]

A final alternative proposal put forward by the commission was even more radical than the first choice and, consequently, had less chance of adoption. It would have consolidated the entire revenue administration into one major department, a national Exchequer court, but with the addition of several new offices designed in part to take care of the extra work which the fusion of the five courts would entail.[131] It was estimated that such a consolidation would effect an economy of £10,242 10s. 7d. annually. Probably the soundest of the recommendations, it carried the support of the numerous Exchequer officials, entrenched in traditional positions of authority and prestige, and a small conservative group in the council who, while criticizing the innovations of the newer revenue courts, advocated a return to the " ancient course " of medieval administration. Whatever the plan adopted, there were many who sensed the dangerous opportunities for power and the abuse of the royal prerogative

[130] Harl. MS. 7383, fols. *62d., 65d., 69.* Chamber reforms recommended by the commissioners included reduction of fees, elimination of superfluous offices and other unnecessary expenses, bonding of the chamber treasurer, and a regular audit of accounts. The master of the posts, Sir John Mason, was particularly remiss in his failure to render an account, although his office was responsible for over £4,000 of the issues of the king's chamber. Sir William Cavendish was chamber treasurer at this time, the office of the master of posts having been separated from the chamber in 1544 upon the death of Sir Brian Tuke who held both positions. On the general decline of the chamber, see Chapter Five, pp. 154–59.

[131] Notably, two general surveyors, two auditors of the prests, five more regular auditors, and regional feodaries would be added. Harl. MS. 7383, fols. 64–64d.

inherent in a structure as flexible and versatile as that created by Henry VII. One thing was certain. The bureaucrats in charge of the system would accept no such radical reform without a fight. Nevertheless, the odds were in favor of those moderates willing to accept a degree of compromise rather than the die-hards, who merely wanted a return to the status quo without the fruits of a half century of progress. It was the old story of the danger of untried ideas; there was safety in the old ways.[132]

Thus by the end of 1552 the stage was fully set for immediate reform, but actually nothing of a concrete nature had been accomplished. The evils of the administration had been clearly set forth in the reports of innumerable commissions of investigation; various suggestions for improvements had been made, yet no definite action had been taken. The government was too preoccupied with religious and financial matters during the last few months of the reign to launch a major reform program. As usual, financial difficulties continued as the chief concern of the council. Revenues were slow in coming in and always inadequate to meet the growing demands of the state. Proceeds from the sale of crown lands seem to have been the principal internal source of revenue, though due to a serious glut in the land market the final results were rather disappointing. The sale of church plate and goods, as well as other crown possessions, proceeded apace, but there again the government was faced with leakages and concealments which greatly reduced the anticipated profit. With insufficient cash on hand to meet ordinary payments, the treasurer of the Court of Augmentations, who usually bore the brunt of the financial burden, was forced to borrow from himself in order to honor the council's warrants. When in May, 1552, Williams was called upon to pay £534 immediately to the English ambassador in France for his diets and other allowances due him from the Augmentations, he was instructed " to make shift for so muche as [he] shall want, and repay hym sellf againe of the fyrst monny he shall receyve of the Kinges Majesties revenues." [133] Ten days later he was ordered to pay the ambassador in Germany some £600 " and upwardes " in back diets, " or yf the sayd Treasourer have not so muche in his handes as will aunswer the sayd debt, then to treat with sume of the Receyvours of that Courte to prepare so muche monny as may discharge the same, and to make aunswer of that he shall have don herein as sone as he conveniently may." [134]

---

[132] Elton, *Tudor Revolution in Government*, 237.

[133] Dasent (ed.), *Acts of the Privy Council*, IV, 32.

[134] *Ibid.*, 41. The item forcibly illustrates two significant facts which show the disorganized condition of the Court: (1) that the Court could be behind as

In a practical way the findings of the recent survey as submitted at the end of that year were being borne out by actual experience. The Court was sadly in need of some sort of reorganization, but the reign was to end before anything constructive could be completed. Edward died on July 6, 1553. The enabling act of parliament for the dissolution of the Court of Augmentations was not implemented until the beginning of the new reign.

---

much as £600 in an ordinary payment, and (2) that the treasurer should not have such a small amount in ready cash. The communication was directed to the chancellor of the Court, either because of the urgency of the situation or, more probably, because Williams was then in prison.

CHAPTER SEVEN

PROBLEMS AND PERSONNEL

HE DECAY IN ADMINISTRATION UNDER EDWARD VI HAD been due more to a decline in public morality than to operational inefficiency. The recognition of this fact occasioned, in part at least, the sporadic attempts to check local mismanagement and to stop recurrent leakages in revenue collection. The latter problem, particularly in view of the government's need for more money, led to repeated efforts to call in arrears of rents and outstanding debts to the crown. With reference to the Court of Augmentations such measures were usually effective; in any case, the principal officials, if not always the regional ministers, were fully co-operative. Through council support the institution had expanded and prospered; if decline had set in, no fundamental changes were as yet apparent. Indeed, since the evidence available is scattered, it is difficult to determine how much the Court was affected by the lassitude that prevailed throughout the country. For the most part the taint of scandal passed it by. Within the central office at London business seems to have proceeded as usual, and beyond negligence in requiring regular accounting, no particular slackness is noticeable. Among the numerous field officers and local personnel, however, efficiency was less easily maintained, though no major complications developed. Most of the problems that emerged were strictly administrative in character, only a few being inherent in the structural organization of the Court. Otherwise the situation was a normal one, common to all large institutions in which many personnel factors and widely scattered areas of jurisdiction are involved.

Though in competition with the other statutory courts, the Augmentations was able to avoid most of the friction that might be expected to have developed among rival departments. Even with the common-law courts, with which possibilities for discord were the greatest, her relations were completely cordial. Moreover, the supervisory authority of the council had never presented any real difficulty, nor had the overlapping jurisdiction of the Court of Survey offered more than a passing involvement, which was of course eliminated by the amalgamation of the two courts in 1547.

During the earlier years the Court had faced a series of altercations with the duchy of Lancaster concerning their respective claims to monastic possessions, but in the end a satisfactory solution had been effected, albeit the compromise for the most part favored the Augmentations.[1] Of the ten houses in Lancashire eight came under the first Act of Dissolution, the two largest monasteries being Furness and Whalley.[2] Two of these, Lytham priory and Penwortham priory were lost to the Augmentations because they were cells of Durham and Evesham respectively, and thus were adjudged as not under duchy jurisdiction. Others, like Alcester in Warwickshire and Tutbury in Staffordshire, which were claimed by the duchy as earlier foundations of the Lancastrian dukes, were eventually awarded to the Augmentations. Of the two abbeys, Whalley and Furness, the possessions of the former went to the office of general surveyors of crown lands after the attainder of its abbot in 1537; the latter was given to the Augmentations, which retained the lands of Furness until 1540, when they were annexed to the duchy by special act of parliament.[3] In any event, the revenues involved were not particularly significant, especially since the gross income realized was greatly reduced by salaries, debts, and pensions to the inmates.[4]

Nevertheless, the duchy officials strongly begrudged the loss of lands and revenues to the newer institution, though their resentment never

[1] Pp. 273–74, *infra.* D. L. 41/29/13; 29/8836; 29/2313.
[2] Savine, *English Monasteries on the Eve of the Dissolution,* 275. The other eight were the houses of Burscough and Cockersand, and the priories of Cartmell, Conishead, Holland, Hornby, Lytham, and Penwortham.
[3] Annexation to the duchy of Lancaster of the possessions of the late abbey of Furness, 32 Henry VIII, c. 57 (1540), not printed. See also sec. viii of 32 Henry VIII, c. 20, "The Liberties to be used." On the division of the suppressed monasteries between the Augmentations and the duchy, consult *L. and P.,* X, no. 1191; XII, pt. 1, nos. 1, 896, 903; XIII, pt. 2, no. 1195; D. L. 43/5/14.
[4] Furness was more valuable than any of the other monasteries, yielding the duchy over £754 in 1540–41. The total revenue from all the monastic possessions under the jurisdiction of the duchy was only £1,292 in 1546–47. Originally the duchy could claim connection with twenty-five houses. Somerville, *History of the Duchy of Lancaster,* I, 287, 293.

caused an open rupture. Uniformity in dissolution procedures was demanded, and the duchy officials were forced to follow the advice of the Court of Augmentations in that respect. It was thus Richard Rich and his council who set the standard of regulations, and not the duchy. They were repeatedly consulted on matters great and small. Nor did they refuse co-operation but gave advice on such important aspects of administration as the type of land leases preferred, the payment of monastic debts, and the pensioning procedures to be employed. Even in purely local problems, questions of antagonizing local custom or dispositions of monastic valuables such as bells, lead, tile, and slate, the duchy conformed to Augmentations practices.[5]

If protracted dispute between the two organizations developed, it was not a matter of record. Only in Lincolnshire and Yorkshire did the question of conflicting jurisdiction become very serious, and there again the Augmentations won a significant victory. In both cases rents due from the lands of suppressed monasteries were involved. In Lincolnshire the Court persistently refused to turn over to the duchy those revenues formerly collected from the dissolved monasteries, nor would it suffer court fines to be paid from the duchy honor of Bolingbroke or allow tenants to sue in the duchy courts. Similarly, the arrears of rent of two of the larger abbeys of Yorkshire, St. Mary's and Byland, which regularly had been denied the duchy by Augmentations ministers, grew to appreciable proportions before the Court was abolished.[6]

In the case of the large Premonstratensian abbey of Cockersand in Lancashire, clearly recognized as a duchy monastery and surveyed by a duchy commission, the house was lost because its dissolution was postponed until 1539. Passed by in the first suppression because its value was accorded more than the £200 limit fixed by the statute, Cockersand later bought exemption at a cost of £1,333 6s. 8d.[7] This sum, as well as fines for permission to continue from various other houses, was paid into the Augmentations. When it finally surrendered in January, 1539, the land and property of Cockersand became a part of the Augmentations rather than of the duchy.[8] The Court also took over the valuable muni-

---

[5] D. L. 5/6, fols. 204d.–205; 41/12/11–12. An interesting controversy arose in 1543 concerning disputed jurisdiction between the two courts in the lordship of Walles. The land in question in Walles parish, Yorkshire, was a parcel of the late priory of Bradenstock in Wiltshire. When duchy officials distrained goods of felons, waifs, and strays in the lordship, an Augmentations investigation proved, by sworn witnesses, the duchy claim to be false. Augm. Office, Miscellanea, 34.

[6] D. L. 41/29/13; 29/556/8836.

[7] *Ibid.* 29/147/2313 (Ministers' Accounts). *L. and P.*, X, nos. 364, 1191(5).

[8] *Ibid.*, XIV, pt. 1, no. 163. By sec. iii of the second Act of Dissolution, 31 Henry VIII, c. 13, all monastic possessions were put under the survey of the Court of Augmentations.

ments acquired from the monasteries; for years such records served as significant sources for legal disputes in which judgment might have sometimes hinged upon particular monastic documents.[9]

In these controversies as in other matters the Court had the support of the privy council, which always retained considerable control over its activities. Sometimes that control was purely nominal, but not infrequently the council intervened in judicial causes and in internal administrative affairs. Informal routine supervision was maintained in part through oral communication with the chancellor, who was also an ex officio privy councillor, but more usually the council's will was expressed through written directives. In addition to innumerable warrants ordering the expenditure of money, literally hundreds of letters are extant covering almost every aspect of Augmentations business. Ordinary warrants embraced such things as transfers of land, appointments, annuities, reparations, evaluations, surveys, or the delivery of lead, timber, stone, bell metal, and other materials commonly disposed of by the king and council. These requests usually entailed no urgency, but the Court was also called upon to produce specific information of all kinds, as often as not " ymmedyatly and without stay." Reports of debts, arrears, rents concealed, enclosures, particular revenues, and lists of suppressed monasteries came under this category, as did information concerning suspected officials, or records and extracts from documents needed by the council. Likewise, the chancellor of the Court was further burdened with specific orders, often accompanied by minute instructions relating to their execution. Certain lands were to be enclosed, payment of debts deferred, rents remitted, recognizances drawn up, property seized for the crown, revenue assigned for schools and other beneficences, or discretionary action taken according to equity and justice as " for the kynges most suertie shall seme convenient." While ordinarily conciliar directions, however detailed they might be, did not interfere with the constitutional rights and privileges of the Court, they might occasionally influence policy or limit authority. Such was the temporary restriction regarding the granting of leases and reversions imposed upon the chancellor in September, 1550, whereby " he was advised not to suffer any moo leases or grauntes to passe his handes untill the Kinges further pleasour were knowen." [10]

<hr/>

[9] E. 321/45/55. Report of the Charles Buller Commission presented on August 15, 1836. *Report of the Select Committee of the House of Commons on the Record Commission* (London, 1836), 438.

[10] Dasent (ed.), *Acts of the Privy Council*, III, 130–31. See p. 194, *supra*. The directives and letters of instruction to the chancellor and other principal officers of the Court are widely scattered. The bulk of them, however, is found in the collection of Augm. Office, Miscellanea, and among the records of the privy council.

During the early years of operation success depended largely on three factors, which continually occupied the attention of the central officials. The first two were problems of external relations involving a dual responsibility of the Court: on the one hand, an endeavor to satisfy the government and, on the other, to gain the respect and approval of the vast body of crown tenants brought under its jurisdiction. The third was purely internal, being a question of personnel relations. The entire staff of field ministers and local officials, many of whom previously had served monastic or private landlords, had to be won over to new allegiance. If a high degree of morality was to be realized their loyalty and co-operation were indispensable. No one was more conscious of the implications of these responsibilities than the original directors of the Court; in fact, the cordial relations established between it and the council, as with the other revenue institutions, were due as much to reasonableness and tact as to the standard of efficiency maintained. The king was satisfied, the council continued its support, and internally friction among personnel was reduced to a minimum. Nor is there any reason to suppose that the tenantry was ill-disposed toward its new lord. While the evidence is quite vague on the point, there is some indication that estate management under the Augmentations was equal if not superior to that of the monasteries on the eve of the Dissolution. Reports that Court officials had been well-behaved were not uncommon. There was a strong element of truth involved in the kind of flattery accorded chancellor Rich by the tenants of Abingdon who agreed that he had treated them in such " good facion " that they were all ' gladd of theyr new landlord." [11]

In personnel management the Court faced a major problem of salary adjustment. As in all branches of public employment the absence of any system of periodic wage increases led many officials to feel that their services were not sufficiently appreciated. Moreover, while prices were going up their own incomes remained fixed. As might be expected, complaints of the rising cost of living were more prevalent among those ministers whose duties necessitated prolonged travel, especially the messengers and field officers. The hundreds of extant travel accounts present lists of detailed expenditures covering a wide variety of items: meals, lodgings, wines and beer, wages for servants, the hire and care of horses, boat hire, rewards, outlays for local courts and audits, and special riding expenses which oftentimes emerged under conditions of great urgency.[12] Letters, injunctions, privy seals, and decrees had to be de-

---

[11] Report from Abingdon in 1538. S. P. 1/129, fols. 126–27, 193–94; abstracted in *L. and P.*, XIII, pt. 1, nos. 359, 403.

[12] Many accounts were itemized in great detail, the cost of each particular outlay being faithfully recorded, as in Exch., Accounts Various, 518/22, 519/25,

livered at all costs if the prestige of the Court were to be upheld. Commenting on the difficulty of serving process on crown debtors, one messenger " moste humblye " observed in 1549, " that the serving of thes lettres was muche more paynefull and chargeabill than other ordinarye prosses," since oftentimes his search took him through several counties. If he found the principal dead, he was then compelled to locate the heirs and executors of the deceased, which extended his travels still farther. Sometimes he was forced to remain two or three days in a place and " for sparing of his owne gelding was dryven to hyere other horsses and guides to retorne the same." Since all expenses were " duble the price accustomed," such informative clarifications usually ended in requests for additional allowances, in this case an extra £2 7s. 6d.[13]

The current increase in prices alluded to was a common grievance of the messengers, who insisted that their fees were inadequate. If prices had doubled, and some said that they had tripled, ministers were loth to travel at all for they lost money on each journey. One messenger explained that he had been on the road continuously for fourteen months for which service he was compelled to keep two or three horses in constant readiness. In such cases, if a request for an extra allowance was not presented to the Court, a generous reward at least was expected. In presenting his bill another messenger pointed out to the chancellor that it had cost him eight pounds to earn the amount stipulated in the account; although asking for no particular sum in compensation he put himself at the mercy of his superiors, beseeching them to allow him as much as to them seemed just and charitable. Such pleas, if not exaggerated, seldom went unheeded. Compensation was often accorded in other ways, either by annuities, special rewards, or through grants of land and additional offices. Eventually the travel rate was raised from one penny to two pennies per mile which, in addition to the fee of four pence per day plus ordinary allowances, seems to have satisfied the ministers.[14]

674/36; in these cases it was comparatively easy to judge the accuracy of the total expenditure. On the other hand, claims were often couched in the most general terms, the exactness of which it was usually impossible to determine unless the accountant was called in for questioning, as indeed not infrequently happened. A receiver's " briefe booke " would simply enumerate a series of estimates, indicating such expenses as " Riding abowte w[th]in the said shire abowte the keping of Severall Courtes by the space of xiiij dayes " for himself and three men at 6s. 8d. per day, £4 13s. 4d. (L. R. 12) Exch., Receivers' Accounts, Ser. III, 28/989.

[13] A file of unnumbered miscellaneous papers connected with the administration of the Augmentations, containing numerous travel accounts. Augm. Office, Miscellanea, E. 314/24.

[14] Bills and receipts for money expended by the messengers of the Court. E. 314/19. Augm. Office, Misc. Books 252, fols. 61, 65d. 68, 72d.; 259, fol. 78

Operational efficiency was always more difficult to maintain in county administration, especially in areas far removed from the watchful eye of the central office. Plurality, absenteeism, inadequate sureties, and the use of deputies in office were all current evils of the Court; yet these were practices which the Augmentations sought to correct and for which ordinarily it was not responsible. Despite official attempts at consolidation in the interest of administrative efficiency, superfluous offices remained a prevailing weakness of the Tudor bureaucratic system. So long as sinecures were given out as rewards, all efforts to reduce personnel within the administration were of little avail. Furthermore, the practice of employing deputies to perform the actual work of an office increased the number of office seekers. No position was too insignificant nor its stipend too small to be ignored by all the eager petitioners, alert for an opportunity to further their own interests. In some instances where professional standards were maintained, plurality was not necessarily undesirable, but ethical principles were seldom the sole consideration. Minor offices were sought for their fees alone, and appointments commonly awarded to people of influence or bestowed indiscriminately on the basis of the market price. The sovereign entertained no dislike for those who contrived to secure office; Sir William Cecil told Ralph Sadler on the eve of his appointment to the chancellorship of the duchy of Lancaster, "as fishees are gotten with baytes so ar officees caught with sekyng." [15] Not infrequently such requests were accompanied by gifts or promises of future payment. While there were few cases of actual bribery in the Augmentations, pluralism was never effectively curtailed.

As noted in an earlier chapter, the majority of the principal officials of the Court were from time to time engaged in outside activities and regularly supplemented their basic incomes by additional stipends and offices. While a general surveyor in the Augmentations, Walter Mildmay was also an auditor for life in the duchy of Lancaster, both offices being highly responsible positions; nevertheless, he found time during his tenure in the Augmentations to sit in parliament, execute exacting special assignments, and serve on innumerable commissions for the crown. The surveyor of woods, John Arscot, though a barrister by profession, likewise served the duchy as a surveyor, while Sir John York, master of woods, was also undertreasurer of the mint in the Tower

---

passim. By the following century the travel rate for the four messengers in the renovated Exchequer had been increased to fourpence per mile. S. P. 16/520/10. It might be noted that in Cromwell's time fivepence per day was considered sufficient for a traveling purveyor. *L. and P.,* VI, no. 1609.

[15] William Cecil to Ralph Sadler, April 27, 1568. *Cal. State Papers, Domestic, 1547–1580,* 309.

and on various occasions employed in secret missions abroad.[16] Among the Court's auditors, Hugh Fuller and Thomas Notte were both auditors in the Court of Survey, and William Cavendish may have continued as auditor in the first Augmentations after he was appointed as treasurer of the chamber.[17] More conspicuous was auditor William Berners, who besides his auditorship held at least four other posts, all of which should have required a resident officer.[18]

Being more time-consuming than an auditorship, the duties of receiver required, during most of the year, either regular attendance to the office or a degree of close personal supervision. Nevertheless, minor offices within and without the Augmentations were acquired by a number of them. While receiver, Sir Thomas Arundell was bailiff of the lordship of Marshwood Vale in Dorsetshire, keeper of the parks there, high bailiff for the bishop of Salisbury, and chancellor to Queen Catherine Parr. Similarly, Sir Anthony Aucher held several offices in addition to his receivership. He was a victualler of works at Dover, chief victualler of Boulogne, joint master of tents, marshal of Calais, and after November, 1545, master of the jewel house. The receivers were also in a position to secure local offices controlled by the Court, especially in their home counties. As an example, John Carlton gained the office of steward and woodward of the close of Hampton Court only a few months after obtaining his receivership.[19]

The most outstanding pluralists were found among the great ministers of state, whose political positions and influence at court enabled them to grab for themselves the more desirable plums. When the major offices had been filled there still remained for their consideration that countless number of lesser jobs scattered throughout the realm, of which the greater revenue courts in particular offered a wide variety of choice.

[16] In June, 1552, York was pardoned for offenses in the mint office, though required to repay the £9,523 6s. 2¼d. which he owed the crown upon the determination of his account. *Cal. Pat. Rolls, Edwards VI*, IV, 301.

[17] Cavendish's duties in the Augmentations office were either performed by his deputy Gregory Richardson or by his successor, Richard Brasier, whose appointment has not been found. Nevertheless, in the treasurer's accounts for the last year of the reign he was listed as auditor for the fourth district. Brasier probably assumed office sometime during the latter part of 1546. Cavendish was pensioned £200 per year for the audit office. Augm. Office, Misc. Books 259, fol. 70; 260, fol. 56d.

[18] Berners was a special auditor of the treasurer's accounts as well as a regular auditor in the first Augmentations. At the same time he was the holder of four additional offices: auditor of Warwick and Spencer lands, auditor of Bedford lands in Nottinghamshire and Derbyshire, auditor of woods in the Court of General Surveyors, and keeper of Horsefrethe Park in Essex. Furthermore, he served under commission as auditor in Ireland and Boulogne. *L. and P.*, XII, pt. 2, no. 382; XIX, pt. 1, no. 1035(153); XXI, pt. 2, no. 201.

[19] Augm. Office, Misc. Books 233, fols. 328, 328d.

Individually the salaries of these minor offices were unimportant, but in the aggregate they help to explain the great wealth amassed by many of the more energetic officials. While the Augmentations came in for its share of political appointments, they were for the most part minor offices in rural areas where the principals were less open to criticism. Most of the great officers of state sooner or later secured a few of these appointments. Cromwell, Winchester, Somerset, and Paget all held local offices in the Court, though the actual work performed by them was nominal. Such duties as the office required were relegated to their underpaid deputies.

Cromwell was more interested in power than he was in money, so he chose for himself those key positions which gave him control of government policy. However, he was not one to spurn an easy penny nor, once entrenched, to surrender willingly any portion of his various sinecures and emoluments. Among the many petty offices acquired by him before his downfall were several in the Court of Augmentations and in the Court of Survey. In addition to his major state positions he was steward of the queen's lands and high steward of Northumberland lands north of the River Trent; his minor preferments also included receiverships, stewardships, bailiwicks, and keeperships of crown lands in Cheshire, Essex, Hertfordshire, Kent, Middlesex, London, and the Isle of Wight.[20] Some of the latter were, in fact, well worth the seeking. The stewardship and receivership of Writtle manor, Essex, with the keepership of the park there netted him £15 2s. 2d., while seven offices in the lordship of Havering-at-Bower in the same county totaled over £28 annually.[21] Undoubtedly a great number of such appointments could have been eliminated without jeopardizing administrative efficiency. Their retention for patronage purposes was due to government policy rather than to Augmentations needs.

Cromwell's most lucrative position in the Court was the high stewardship of all Augmentations lands lying north of the River Trent, for which he received a fee of £100 annually. Not only was the actual work of this office done by his servant, Henry Polsted, but the deputy's fee of £20 yearly was also borne by the Court.[22] Upon his attainder in 1540

---

[20] *L. and P.*, XIII, pt. 1, no. 505; pt. 2, nos. 967(2), 1051, 1199; XIV, pt. 1, nos. 639, 646; pt. 2, no. 264(19); XV, nos. 942(25), 1027(1). S. C. 6/5974, 5975. Cromwell also held a few offices in the duchy. Somerville, *History of the Duchy of Lancaster*, I, 448, 606, 614. Merriman's list of nineteen minor offices of Cromwell is by no means exhaustive. Merriman (ed.), *Life and Letters of Thomas Cromwell*, II, 283–84.

[21] *L. and P.*, XII, pt. 2, no. 1311(6); XV, no. 1027(1).

[22] Cromwell's appointment was dated May 25, 1538. Augm. Office, Misc. Books 232, pt. 2, fols. 4d. 32, 72d.; 249, fols. 33, 34.

this office was awarded to the lord chancellor Thomas Audley, lord of Walden, who also held the office by deputy.[23] A comparable stewardship for lands south of the River Trent had been set up in 1536 for Thomas Howard, duke of Norfolk, who retained the office until the dissolution of the first Court.[24] Apparently both these offices had been sinecures from the very beginning; no trace has been found among the records of the Court of any activity in either stewardship. If actual duties were involved, they must have been largely nominal. Neither office was continued after 1547 in the reconstituted Augmentations.

Cromwell was by no means the only high official carried on the payroll of the Court. The two principal secretaries, Wriothesley and Sadler, Winchester, Somerset,[25] Northumberland, and a host of lesser officials in the household served on the crown estates in minor capacities. Likewise, instances of plurality among Augmentations personnel were not uncommon. In principle, no opprobrium was attached to the holding of more than one position in the same institution; on the contrary, it was considered a legitimate means of augmenting official salaries which carried no regular increases. Other conditions being equal, the less important jobs were given to the first petitioners, unless of course their requests

[23] Appointment of September 20, 1540. John Lucas served as deputy in the office. Augm. Office, Misc. Books 235, fol. 40*d.*; 249, fol. 34*d.*; 251, fols. 70–72*d.* Upon Lord Audley's death in April, 1544, Charles Brandon, duke of Suffolk, took over the stewardship, which he held by deputy until his own death in August, 1545. George St. Pole (St. Pol, Sayntpole) served as Suffolk's deputy or understeward. The office appears to have lapsed after the death of Brandon. Augm. Office, Misc. Books 236, fol. 43; 254, fol. 62; 255, fol. 80.

[24] Appointment of May 26, 1536, with £100 per year salary; his deputy, Sir Nicholas Hare, received £20 per year. Augm. Office, Misc. Books 232, fol. 12; 249, fols. 33, 35. On the various offices held by Norfolk, netting him over £750 annually, see *L. and P.*, XXI, pt. 2, no. 556. Before the second Court of Augmentations had been erected it was already rumored that these stewardships were to be discontinued. *Ibid.*, nos. 601, 665.

[25] Seymour in particular, as confidant of the king and finally Protector, took every advantage of his high position to enrich himself by the steady acquisition of both offices and property. At the time of his attainder lands to the total value of over £7,000 were forfeited to the crown by special act of parliament. Under Henry VIII he was advanced through a succession of state offices—governor and captain of Jersey, warden of the Scottish marches, lord high admiral, great chamberlain, lieutenant-general in the north, and lieutenant and captain-general of Boulogne— and upon the accession of Edward VI he was appointed high steward and granted the positions of earl marshal and treasurer of the Exchequer. In the Court of Augmentations he secured for himself the offices of chancellor and chamberlain of North Wales, which he had held jointly in survivorship with Sir John Salisbury, together with the receivership in the principality. In addition to extra fees these offices alone paid salaries of £20 and £30 respectively. At Bristol he was not only steward of the city but also constable and keeper of Bristol Castle. From July, 1547, onward he received an annuity of 8,000 marks from the revenues of the Augmentations. Augm. Office, Misc. Books 257, fol. 61; *Cal. Pat. Rolls, Edward VI*, I, 163, 180, 184; III, 177–78, 186, 329; *D. N. B.*

were unsupported by records of past loyalty and demonstrable diligence in office. Members of the Court's council, being in a position to anticipate changes in district offices, were able to put in their bids for appointment before vacancies actually occurred. The chancellors, treasurers, and general surveyors all held minor positions in the Court for which they drew extra compensation.

Perhaps the best example in the Augmentations of plurality was the case of the last treasurer, Sir John Williams. During his ten years in the treasurership Williams acquired at least a dozen minor sinecures, though he possibly may have also held other local offices of which no records are extant. A number of these had been secured, however, before he became treasurer, appointments due largely to the support of his kinsman Cromwell, who brought him to the attention of the king. He began his administrative career in 1531 as general receiver of Buckingham lands, then under the office of general surveyors.[26] Upon the attainder of the abbot of Woburn monastery in Bedfordshire, he was made receiver of the lands and possessions of the dissolved abbey in July of 1538. Two years later he was awarded a number of related offices in Buckinghamshire and Northamptonshire: namely, chief stewardships and bailiwicks of the manors of Grafton, Hartwell, Aston, Pury, Alderton, and other lands in those counties, together with the local keeperships attached to them. At the same time he was made bailiff of the lands and keeper of the park of Pottersbury manor in Northamptonshire, at a salary of £1 a year for the bailiwick and 2*d.* per day for the keepership.[27] During the year 1542 he became chief steward and bailiff of Paulers Pury manor in Northamptonshire and keeper of the park there; he was also made keeper of the manor and garden of Notley, Buckinghamshire, and general receiver of all the attainted lands of the late Richard Fermor. With the latter appointment went the chief stewardship of Easton Neston manor in Northamptonshire and the keepership of the park and manor house there.[28] Holding office jointly

---

[26] The Buckingham possessions were absorbed by the Augmentations in 1547; after the office of general surveyors was elevated to the dignity of a court in 1542, Williams paid those revenues to the treasurer of the chamber. He had succeeded Thomas Magnus, archdeacon of East Riding, in that office. Morgan Wolf acted as his deputy receiver. Augm. Office, Misc. Books 257, fol. 51*d.*

[27] Augm. Office, Misc. Books 235, fol. 24. *L. and P.,* XIII, pt. 1, no. 1519(57); XV, no. 282(42). Later Grafton was made a royal honor, when Pottersbury manor and other crown lands were annexed to it by act of parliament, though it still remained under the administration of the Augmentations. *Ibid.,* XVII, no. 28(22); Augm. Office, Misc. Books 250, fols. 51, 52, 53.

[28] Augm. Office, Misc. Books 235, fol. 62*d; L. and P.,* XVII, no. 220(58, 78). During March of the same year, 1542, Williams was awarded the mastership of the royal cygnets in the River Thames and the keepership of the king's swans in

with his son, Henry Williams, he was steward of cathedral lands in Oxfordshire; still later he became ranger of Witney Chase in the bishopric of Winchester, steward of Grafton honor, warden of the forests of Salcey and Whittlewood, and master of the game within the honor, with the right of appointment of minor officials.[29] Most of these offices were either in or near his home county of Buckinghamshire. Under Edward VI, Williams was likewise the recipient of an annuity of £40 from the Augmentations, in addition to numerous grants of land from the crown in token of continued service.[30] Although he took advantage of his position to augment his income, he appears to have made no attempt to exploit these various offices. Neither in the charges presented against him in 1554 nor in the official investigation that ensued was there any suggestion of corruption outside the treasurership of the Court.[31]

So long as all appointments were made by the crown, Augmentations officials could do little to check the abuse of patronage. The king's candidates usually took precedence over their own nominees, and once in office it was difficult to get rid of royal favorites who might be unqualified or incompetent. Only occasionally, when complaints against dishonest or negligent officials came to the attention of the privy council, was the system brought under review. Such was the investigation of 1540 when the lord chancellor and the heads of all revenue departments were required to submit complete lists of administrative offices under them, together with their respective fees and the names of incumbents.[32] Periodic inquiries of this kind may have prompted the change introduced five years later in the Augmentations, when certain appointive privileges were conferred upon the chancellor of the Court.[33] That he took advantage of his enlarged powers is attested to by the long list of appointments made by him during the ensuing months. Since many crown appointees retained their offices " at will without eny lettres patentes or other like graunte therof," North ordered the auditors to

---

all the waters of England, the duchy of Lancaster excepted. D. L. 42/133, fols. 56d., 106d. The Fermor lands, as attainted possessions, were under the jurisdiction of the Court of Survey until 1547.

[29] Augm. Office, Misc. Books 104, pt. 2, fols. 167–68; 236, fol. 73; *Cal. Pat. Rolls, Edward VI*, III, 370; IV, 149–50, 179; *Mary*, I, 195; *Philip and Mary*, II, 157, 179.

[30] Augm. Office, Misc. Books 260, fol. 36d. Upon his surrender of the receivership of Woburn lands he was paid a compensation for that office. E. 358/22, mem. 17.

[31] Williams may have held other minor positions in the revenue administration, but the evidence is inconclusive. There were other officials of the same name, as for example the Welshman, John Williams, who was bailiff and collector of Old Sleaford and New Sleaford manors in Lincolnshire. On Williams' trial under Mary, see Chapter Eight, pp. 267–69.

[32] *L. and P.*, XVI, nos. 140, 146, 147, 169; Nicolas (ed.), *Proceedings and Ordinances of the Privy Council*, VII, 58, 59, 60–61.

[33] P. 125, *supra*.

investigate the situation in their circuits and submit a full report on the status of local offices in each county. In this way the Court was apprised of the number of minor officers, their fees, qualifications, length of service, the nature of their tenure, and their value to the administration.

The returns were quite revealing. Some officials, old and incompetent, were unable to travel; others were in debt to the crown or behind in their accounts through " lak of delygence "; a number officiated through unworthy deputies, while a few were absentees. In many cases salaries were inconsistent; some fees were too high, others not paid at all. When stewards were given no allowances for manorial courts, it is presumed none were held. Numerous bailiffs were reported as unbonded; a few were considered neither " mete nor substanciall " enough to discharge their offices effectively.[34] In general, the Court carried out the recommendations of the field officials in filling vacancies. New appointees were more carefully chosen. Incompetence was reduced by better supervision, forced retirement, and partial equalization of fees. Unnecessary jobs were not all eliminated, to be sure, nor all indolent officials removed, but the situation was temporarily improved.

In the management of the royal demesne the primary objective of the Court was to bring in the revenues with as little cost as possible; but as a national treasury it also had a secondary responsibility, the safeguard ing of that revenue against loss and needless dissipation. The crown and privy council for the most part determined the policy of the Court, but economy in administration depended largely on the chancellor and legal advisers. In their daily routine of revenue supervision, however, few difficulties were encountered, save in the vexing problem of unauthorized disbursements and the ever-recurrent question of delayed collections. Unless he exceeded his delegated authority, all payments of the treasurer were made by warrant of the king or council, warrant of the Court, and by Court decree. Occasionally he might pay out money on his own initiative or by word of mouth, without written authorization, but such procedure was quite exceptional. It is true that Cromwell sometimes had used the informal device of an oral command in order to speed up financial transactions; nevertheless, the practice was recognized as unsound and one to be discouraged. Verbal understandings with the king or council, if acceptable as emergency measures, were normally followed up by written directives as a necessary protection to the treasurer. Likewise, written receipts for even the most insignificant disbursements were always an indispensable precaution; otherwise the treasurer would ultimately face the auditors of his account with no

[34] Particulars for Grants of Offices. Augm. Office, Misc. Books 157 and 158.

positive proof of either authority for an uncertified expenditure or evidence of the actual payment. In case a warrant was lost inadvertently and a second one was required, the Court was careful to provide for the cancellation of the original if it ever turned up, so as to avoid " double charge " on the crown.[35] When the government was short of cash and every available item of revenue was important, negligence in complying promptly with orders, either for the receipt or the payment of moneys by Augmentations officials, might easily slow down the broader administrative program or jeopardize particular operations. It was not uncommon for the treasurer of a court to be advised in a warrant that the payment in question was to be made immediately and without undue delay. In fact, many of the Augmentations disbursements by order of the council were completed the same day the warrants were received.

While it was relatively easy to control the receipts and expenditures of the treasurer, it was much harder to regulate the work of the more distant district officials. Far removed from the central offices at Westminster they could be contacted normally only by court messenger, and knowledge of ministerial negligence or dishonesty ultimately reached the chancellor and council only through the devious channels of local complaints or the semi-official reports of other royal agents. Carelessness, imprudent extension of authority, or deliberate neglect of duty were serious failings in an officer. None the less, mounting arrears of rent were not necessarily the fault of ministers, nor in all cases were uncollected debts due to neglect. Similarly, enlarged expense accounts were not always proof of intention to swindle. Most of the Augmentations offices were permanent posts in which incumbents were retained throughout the Edwardian period when corruption was evidenced in all branches of government. Except among local officials on the manor, where administration was weakest, there was comparatively little turnover in personnel.

As a safeguard against duplicate payments the district surveyors and receivers were prohibited from spending money on their own initiative. As a result most expenditures were authorized through the main office where disbursements under specific warrant could be conveniently checked. Furthermore, this procedure greatly simplified the auditors' responsibility in determining which local payments should be honored

---

[35] Frequently the chancellor of the Augmentations would add to the later warrant a memorandum informing the treasurer of the circumstances in the case and request him to return the original document for cancellation, if and when it came in. Exch., Accounts Various, 76/36, fol. 18. In 1540 the vice-treasurer of Ireland, upon the determination of his account, testified that he had received a great deal of money and made many payments by warrant, but only in the form of personal letters of Cromwell. *L. and P.*, XVI, no. 103.

and which ones disallowed. Thus the intent was to channel all major payments of the Court through the treasurer's office, where close supervision was more easily maintained. There were, however, two exceptions to this rule, both of which led to numerous complications and, in the end, encouraged embezzlement. One was the payment of pensions locally; the other concerned the transfer of funds from the Augmentations to special treasurers for the support of castles and garrisons in the north.

The constitution of 1547 specifically provided that all pensions of former religious persons should be paid by the receivers but only after the recipients had personally appeared before them or otherwise had given proof of their identity.[36] However sound in principle, the regulation never worked well in practice. Monastic pensions remained a continual drain on the central treasury, while other pensions and annuities were frequently drawn on particular revenues and thus payable locally. In fact no clear-cut division between central and local expenditures was ever worked out, although the bulk of Augmentations revenue flowed through the treasury office. Disbursements by receivers, on the authority of royal warrant or Court order, included payments for debts, reparations, fees of local officers, compensations, costs of local courts and audits, as well as larger expenditures for exceptional purposes. Payments to the Council of the North and outlays for defense came under the latter category. Expenses for fortifications and the upkeep of castles were particularly heavy in certain counties. All this extra work must have tempted the receivers to impose additional fees for special services. Subject to fixed penalties, excessive charges were limited by law, but there is little indication that these restrictions were ever effectively enforced.[37] Such abuses as developed were probably not widespread; at any rate they were not reported.

Authorization for special payments by local Augmentations officials came from the chancellor of the Court or directly from the king, sometimes by warrants dormant. Since huge sums, amounting to hundreds or thousands of pounds, had to be sent regularly into the north parts

---

[36] Pat. Rolls, 38 Henry VIII, pt. 5, mem. 25. Conversely, the treasurer of the Court was explicitly charged not to "medle" with the payment of the same. *Ibid.*, pt. 5, mem. 22. Similar restraints on the payment of uninvestigated annuities were sometimes imposed by the first Augmentations, as when receivers were warned against allowing pensions and annuities without proof or paying those not exemplified by the Court. *L. and P.*, XVI, nos. 91, 92.

[37] An award of 1*d.* in the pound was allowable as a portage fee for the delivery of a pension or annuity; the maximum charge for the writing of a receipt, 4*d.* However, when the recipient presented his acquittance "redy made," the receiver could take nothing. Pat. Rolls, 38 Henry VIII, pt. 5, mem. 25.

for the upkeep of garrisons and bulwarks, it seemed rather ridiculous to assume the hazards and expenses of transporting bullion from London when it could be sent by the northern receivers out of their own collections. Thus orders for payments to Hull, Berwick, and Carlisle were drawn upon the Augmentations, to be paid from the revenues collected in the northern districts. As an assurance against fraud it was provided that an indenture should be entered into between the treasurer receiving the money and the receiver delivering it, of which " thone part wherof shalbe presented in that our Courte of thaugmentacons," as a discharge for payment.[38] Moreover, in other spheres, as in the case of payments to the ordnance division, it was found convenient to regularize certain recurrent disbursements. A royal warrant of January 24, 1542, ordered the Court to pay not only £1,403 13s. 10d. to the master of the ordnance for the captain and soldiers of new fortresses but also " tallowe receyvours where suche fortresses be negh for the payement of ther wages quarterly fromhensforth." [39] More commonly, such warrants came through the Court, though not infrequently they were sent directly to the minister ultimately responsible for the payment. Before, as well as after, the Augmentations was annexed to the Exchequer, the receiver of the seventh district sent money for the expenses of the garrison on the Scilly Isles by direct warrant of the council. In some instances when a local receiver paid out funds for a specific purpose by order of the king's council, he was reimbursed later from the Augmentations.[40]

Under normal circumstances the regular auditing of accounts was a sufficient deterrent against deception or possibly more serious forms of fraudulent action. Opportunity for graft, petty theft, or other deliberate methods of embezzlement, however, was certainly available to those who sought easy money. Special revenues, such as those derived from old debts, outstanding arrears of rent, and sale of lead, stone, timber, or other crown property could be pocketed by the recipient without recording such items in his formal declaration of account; similarly, payments might be claimed for which no receipts were forthcoming, or claims for travel expenses so expanded as to allow a neat, personal profit for the minister. Of course, subterfuge might be detected by the auditor and the items disallowed, but unless the accountant was under

[38] Exch., Accounts Various, 60/14.

[39] Warrant to the Court of Augmentations to pay Sir Christopher Morris, master of the ordnance, for wages due the soldiers of the fortress. D. L. 42/133, fol. 93.

[40] Warrant of September 3, 1549, to the treasurer of the Augmentations to reimburse Robert Goche, receiver, for £100 delivered to the royal minister, Lord William Willoughby, later lieutenant-governor of Calais, to be employed about "the kinges highnes affaires at his Town of Lynne." Exch., Accounts Various, 76/35, fol. 117.

definite suspicion he was usually given the benefit of the doubt. Sometimes these petty malpractices continued for years without discovery, being uncovered eventually by general investigating commissions. Such a case was that of the regular portage fees for money delivered to Berwick which were paid to the receiver in the northern district, despite the fact that the treasurer of the town received a duplicate allowance for the same service.[41]

On the basis of fragmentary evidence it is impossible to estimate the prevalence of such deception. Undoubtedly in an organization as large as the Court of Augmentations there were always minor cases of malfeasance, but the records are surprisingly free from instances of proved corruption. Complaints and accusations against ministers were common enough, but more often than not they grew out of jealousy or spite. Seldom did such charges stand the test of official investigation. On the other hand, despite regularity of audit, ministers were frequently indebted to the crown. When the Courts of General Surveyors and Augmentations were united in 1547, the receiver of Buckingham lands in Gloucestershire and Somersetshire entered into an obligation with the crown for £119 11s. 2d. due from his office; at the same time John Carlton was bonded for £288 14s. 1d. in accumulated arrears.[42] Upon the accession of Edward VI, Richard Southwell, an executive official of the former Court of Survey and receiver in the Augmentations, was indebted for his various offices to the extent of almost £1,900, which he agreed to pay within ten years.[43] A few years later, in January, 1551, Anthony Aucher was found to be behind £2,455 19s. 6d. upon the determination of his account as receiver of the ninth district, a part of which was later discharged as having been legitimately expended. He was, therefore, bound in obligation for the remainder to pay £300 per year for six years.[44] Yet none of these ministers suffered any public discredit.

Cases of actual dismissal from office were quite rare and then only

---

[41] Add. MS. 30198, fol. 46.

[42] Augm. Office, Misc. Books 327, fols. 8, 29; Miscellanea, 15/109, p. 184. Exch., Accounts Various, 613/3.

[43] "The accompt and declaracion of the debtes of Sir Richard Southwell," taken June 20, 1 Edward VI, by Sir Edward North, chancellor, and the council of the Court of Augmentations. Southwell was allowed certain payments for which he had no receipts; furthermore, he was discharged of sums involved in the delivery and sale of lead for which he had overcharged himself due to errors and negligence on the part of his servants. Until further proof was forthcoming the Court accepted "Mr. Southwelles allegacion" on questionable points. Augm. Office, Miscellanea, 13/1. On Southwell's indebtedness see also Augm. Office, Miscellanea, 16; Misc. Books 327, fols. 25d., 26; 339, fols. 130, 131. Petitions for allowances by Southwell, late receiver in Norfolk and Suffolk. Exch., Accounts Various, 676/35.

[44] Augm. Office, Misc. Books 327, fol. 39d.; Dasent (ed.), *Acts of the Privy Council*, III, 195, 356; Exch., Accounts Various, 613/3.

after definite proof of guilt had been established. With but few exceptions the Augmentations officials were neither great officers of state nor influential councillors and, consequently, were unlikely to be mixed up in political disturbances. In the case of Sir Thomas Newnham, however, his arrest and ultimate discharge seem to have been due entirely to his political machinations. A northern receiver of the Augmentations in the seventh district, Newnham was arrested in July, 1551, for a riot in Coventry on the complaint of a man named Wilkes. Having been examined by the privy council and " founde faultie," he was committed to the Fleet, only to be released a few days later under bond of £500 to appear for trial in the Court of Star Chamber during the ensuing Easter session. Meanwhile the district auditor had been directed to take his account in order that the king's council might know exactly what his charge to the crown was. The succeeding events in the case are by no means clear, but it appears that both he and his deputy, Richard Ashton, were suspended from office pending his trial in Star Chamber. The details of the ensuing investigation have not been preserved, though his guilt seems to have been accepted as conclusive. On the fourth of September, 1552, the chancellor of the Augmentations was notified that Newnham had been dismissed from office because of " the disordre by hym in the same." The Court was informed that the deputy receiver was authorized to collect the next half-year's revenues and that the auditor should take his recognizance for £8,000, thus binding Ashton for full payment of the whole year's revenues of the office.[45] The recognizance indicated that since Newnham had made no payments to the Court in performance of his office, it was " thought convenient to discharge " him. Ashton was permitted, therefore, to continue in the office to which he had been informally appointed by the receiver.[46]

Minor thievery might sometimes have escaped detection for several years, but sooner or later the truth came to the attention of the authorities. When the Augmentations was dissolved in 1554, the auditors presented books of arrears in that court to the Exchequer, in order that due process for collection might be awarded against all delinquents. It was discovered that certain collectors in the ninth district had been reported as owing some £100 or " thereabouts," though they exonerated themselves in the Exchequer by producing a *quietus est* for each of their payments, signed by the former Augmentations auditor. The auditor in question, Henry Leak, admitted that he had pocketed the money,

[45] Newnham's bond for this office, as preserved in seven obligations of February, 1550, was £700. Augm. Office, Misc. Books 327, fol. 53*d*.
[46] Dasent (ed.), *Acts of the Privy Council*, III, 312, 316, 470, 478; IV, 30, 96, 112, 121–22, 207.

recording the several payments as arrears, as though the money " had remayned in their handes unpaid." After having cooled his heels in the Fleet for three months, Leak was sentenced by the Star Chamber to a threefold punishment. First, he was assessed a " grete fyne," which was subsequently " in respecte of his penaltie remytted "; second, he was paraded before all the courts at Westminster during term time, wearing on his head, like a dunce's cap, an open statement of his crime; and finally, in ignominy and shame, he was forced to stand in the public pillory and advertise the evidence of his guilt to the world.[47] By such means as this did the administration seek to shame erring officials into a renewed sense of responsibility.

In Yorkshire charges of peculation were twice directed against Augmentations officials, which in the second instance developed into the only major scandal in the Court's history. In the first case, the accusation proved to be unfounded; certainly the episode in no way jeopardized the career of the accused, who continued to serve the crown until his death.[48] In contrast, the conduct of Richard Whalley was far more serious because of political implications. As a court favorite, Whalley had risen to a position of prominence under Cromwell and, later, Somerset, becoming an ardent supporter of the latter during the early Edwardian period. He had succeeded to the receivership of Yorkshire in 1546 when Beckwith was sent to the Continent as controller of Boulogne; he retained this office until surrendered to John Fisher in June, 1552. A born intriguer, Whalley tried to retain the favor of both parties in the Somerset-Warwick rivalry, with the result that he was faithful to neither. When his intrigues came to the forefront early in 1551, he was arrested and sent to the Fleet but obtained a release under bond within a few weeks. Upon Somerset's second arrest in October, Whalley was also imprisoned; although he obligingly gave evidence against the duke, he was retained in the Tower until June of the following year. At this point he was fined heavily and forced to give up his lucrative Yorkshire receivership, which was immediately bestowed on Fisher.

In the following September he was again committed to the Tower, but this time for a more willful offense, malfeasance in office. Examined by the chancellor of the Augmentations and others, he confessed to the various items of the indictment. If committed as alleged, his crimes certainly demanded more than a nominal punishment. He had used the

[47] Articles concerning the misbehavior of Henry Leak, auditor. Lansd. MS. 106(No. 9), fol. 61; Nichols (ed.), *The Diary of Henry Machyn*, 105. Leak had served the first Augmentations as deputy auditor to Mathew Colthurst.

[48] For the case against Sir Leonard Beckwith, see p. 58, *supra*.

Court's revenues for his personal profit, had speculated on the inflation of the currency to the extent of £500 gain "at one crying," and had met the Augmentations revenues due from his office by taking the money from the collected arrears of the previous year. As if this were not enough, he admitted to falsifying his accounts, citing certain crown lands which he had purchased from government funds. All this totaled an embezzlement of over £2,000, which he presumably repaid, though there is no record of subsequent negotiation for payment. He was retained in prison for the remainder of Edward's reign but was liberated on August 6, 1553, just as soon as Mary succeeded to the throne. Since Whalley seems to have suffered no stigma from this condemnation, the circumstances surrounding the whole affair suggest that the crown had a greater interest in the receiver's political involvement than in the enforcement of justice. Whalley died in 1583, an esteemed and wealthy man. Though he sat in three successive parliaments and obtained other public recognition, he failed in a final attempt to regain the Yorkshire receivership.[49]

Essentially unrelated to internal administration were certain special assignments in which the Court served as a direct agent of the crown. Among such, the disposition of crown lands and property under its jurisdiction was the most important. As shown by the treasurer's accounts this was, from the very beginning, a permanent feature of the regular work of the chancellor and council. Procedural practices as laid down by the original act of 1536 were modified very little in the Court's second constitution of 1547, and for the most part the regulations were followed literally. While all new leases were limited to twenty-one years, existing contracts of the monasteries for longer terms were honored, unless the grants had been made within a year prior to the Dissolution. As in cases of previous monastic obligations the Court was particularly generous in allowing claims of pensions, corodies, annuities, and unsettled debts, and in usually not passing on those charges to the purchasers.

Persons negotiating for the purchase of crown property were first required to petition the Augmentations for a certificate of evaluation of the premises desired. Furthermore, the written request had to be accompanied by an official survey of the property in question, prepared by the auditor or his deputy in whose district the land lay. These

---

[49] Dasent (ed.), *Acts of the Privy Council*, II, 372; IV, 31, 82, 90, 126, 176, 201, 234, 254, 312, 337; V, 238. Nichols (ed.), *Literary Remains*, I, 241, 303, 355, 423. Strype, *Ecclesiastical Memorials*, II, pt. 1, 390, 497; pt. 2, 44–45. A. F. Pollard, "Richard Whalley," *D. N. B.* Nichols (ed.), *The Diary of Henry Machyn*, 10, 25, 327.

detailed surveys, known as "particulars," were carefully examined by the officers of the Court for adjustment and approval before being sent to the commissioners appointed to conduct land sales.[50] Further inquiry or even new surveys might be forthcoming in support of the final decision. Fines, fees, and other details of the transaction were added, together with the name of the original owner and a statement of the annual value of the land. The number of years' purchase, terms of sale, the amount of the down payment, and such like particulars were determined by the commissioners, who forwarded the necessary recognizances to the Court for enrollment and future collection. In all instances the sale price was based on the calculations of the auditors, although there was an appreciable variation in the standard of rating.[51] Normally a prominent member of the sales commissions, the chancellor of the Court played a leading part in both the preliminary and final stages of negotiation.

Recent studies of alienations of crown property in particular counties have greatly clarified the problem of Tudor land values and ratings, but until further investigation in that direction has been made, no definitive conclusions are possible.[52] Nevertheless, older assumptions regarding land speculation and bargain prices far below the market level have already been discarded. Abuses there probably were, including bribery and exorbitant fees, but evidence of such seldom found its way into the official records. However, there is no doubt that all the principal Augmentations officials took advantage of their positions to secure coveted possessions of their own choosing.

Prior to 1536 alienation of crown land was chiefly in the hands of the general surveyors, but the total acreage sold was not large. In the

---

[50] These Particulars for Grants of crown lands form an important continuous series of land records of the Court of General Surveyors and the Court of Augmentations (E. 318), from their beginning under Henry VIII to the reign of Elizabeth. See the *Inventory* as printed in the *Ninth Report of the Deputy Keeper of the Public Records*, Appendix II, 148–309. The grants are arranged alphabetically under the names of grantees.

[51] The basic rating was arrived at by multiplying the annual value of the property, as certified by the auditor, by the number of years' purchase. The standard in the 1540's was twenty years' purchase, but it rose to twenty-four years' under Mary. By Elizabeth's reign the general rate was thirty years' purchase. H. J. Habakkuk, "The Market for Monastic Property, 1539–1603," *Economic History Review*, Second Series, X (April, 1958) 362, 366.

[52] See especially *ibid.*, 362–80, and Joyce A. Youings (ed.), *Devon Monastic Lands: Calendar of Particulars for Grants, 1536–1558* (Devon and Cornwall Records Society, New Series, I[1955]); "The Disposal of Monastic Property in Land in the County of Devon," a thesis summary, *Bulletin of the Institute of Historical Research* (November, 1951), xxiv, 198–202; "The Terms of the Disposal of the Devon Monastic Lands, 1536–1558," *E. H. R.*, LXIX (January, 1954), 18–38.

case of Dissolution property, there was a fair number of sales from the start, although not all of them are enrolled among the Augmentations receipts. The Court's proceeds from land sales were only £29,847 16s. 5d. during the first eighteen months of operation but jumped to £80,622 for the fiscal year 1538–1539.[53] The latter figure included £36,572 16s. 10d. for lands sold by Rich and Cromwell under special commission; this resulted from the shortsighted policy, begun in 1539, of supplementing the current revenue by the temporary expedient of disposing of a portion of the crown demesne. Lands so alienated were " rated and ordered alwey by the Chauncellor & Counsell " of the Augmentations, according to the particular values determined and certified by the auditors, receivers, and surveyors of the Court.[54] It is significant that land to the total value of over £2,840 was purchased by the crown during the same year.[55]

In accordance with instructions receipts from lands sold by the royal commissioners were distributed among the various revenue courts having jurisdiction over them. Since the declarations of the receipts for the Court of General Surveyors are incomplete for the entire period, it is not possible to estimate the total revenue derived from that source; nevertheless, between 1536 and 1552 most of the purchase money flowed into the Augmentations. The peak was reached in 1545 when £165,459 17s. 1d. was taken in during the fiscal year. When the Court was abolished in 1554, it had received no less than £1,103,239 1s. 10d. from the sale of crown lands.[56] If the treasurer's accounts show a decrease in the receipts from this item during the last years of the Court's history, it is because collections from commission sales were paid into the hands of Sir Edmund Peckham for the king's own use.[57]

Among other expedients employed to meet the increasing expenses of

[53] Augm. Office, Treas. Rolls of Accts., No. 1, pt. 1, mem. 7; No. 1, pt. 2, mems. 7–15d.

[54] The commission of December 14, 1539, authorized Cromwell and Rich to sell crown lands at twenty years' purchase to the clear annual value of £6,000. However, the Augmentations accounts show them to have been selling monastic lands by special assignment before receiving the formal commission. Pat. Rolls, 31 Henry VIII, pt. 6, mem. 38d. Copies of this commission are found in Augm. Office, Miscellanea, 18 and Royal MS., 14B, xvij. The following March Cromwell associated himself with the general surveyors for the sale of lands under their administration to the clear annual value of £1,000. Pat. Rolls, 31 Henry VIII, pt. 5, mem. 1. After Cromwell's downfall special commissions for land sales became a regular feature of government policy.

[55] Augm. Office, Treas. Rolls of Accts., No. 1, pt. 2, mem. 22.

[56] *Ibid.*, Nos. 1–8.

[57] *Cal. Pat. Rolls, Edward VI*, IV, 354; V, 184, 277, 411. During the fiscal year 1552–53, Peckham received £153,479 from land sales. Declared Accounts, Pipe Office, 2080.

the government was the novel project for selling the surplus of the "king's lead" which had accumulated from the dissolved religious houses. Initiated in the summer of 1544 when financial resources were continually strained, the plan called for the exportation of large quantities of the metal to the Continent, where supposedly it could be sold at favorable terms for ready cash. The idea may have originated with the king, but it seems to have been received by the council as another welcome device for raising money. In March of the same year two commissions were issued to secure money for the defense of the realm by the sale of the king's possessions. These commissions, both of which included the chancellor of the Augmentations were authorized to sell wards, crown land, lead, and prizes of war, as well as to compound for fines and incomes from leases and the manumission of bondmen.[58]

Somewhat later, on the eve of the projected French invasion, Wriothesley drew up a memorandum of the estimated expenses for the next three months, which included £40,000 from the sale of land and £50,000 derived from lead, "to be sold or laid to gage." [59] The phrase "laid to gage" plainly suggests that the lead was either to be sold outright or deposited somewhere as a pledge or security for the fulfillment of an obligation, presumably the repayment of a loan. The key to this item of the estimate is found in the correspondence of Stephen Vaughan, the English financial agent in the Low Countries, to whom had been delegated the difficult task of borrowing money from the Antwerp merchants. As the English need for cash had become more urgent, the possibility of contracting large loans on the Antwerp Bourse had receded. Faced with the dual task of establishing sound English credit and of exchanging, to the king's advantage, large amounts of sterling into national currency expendible in Europe, Vaughan had hit on the idea of offering lead as a tangible bond for the repayment of the king's contracted loans. Such an enterprise, however, would have necessitated the transportation to Antwerp and storage there of a substantial stock of lead which could have been disposed of gradually after the loans, for which it had served as security, had been repaid. Vaughan naturally reasoned that such a step would materially strengthen the credit of his sovereign with the

---

[58] *L. and P.*, XIX, pt. 1, nos. 278(4, 5, 67), 812(77). Grants in March, 1544. The preamble of each of these commissions sets forth the need for preparing a "mass of money" for the "great surety" of the commonwealth and for the enterprise of the invasion of France. These sales were justified on the grounds that the king was unwilling further to "molest his loving subjects for money" unless absolutely necessary.

[59] *Ibid.*, no. 272. In the sixteenth century the term "gage" commonly signified a pledge or deposit; it was used here to mean a security for the performance of some future action.

European bankers. Nothing could be more advantageous, he argued, "than that the King's Majesty might please to send hither some great quantity of lead to remain here, the sight whereof only would get us credit . . . , for where we now seek credence by that means credence would seek us." [60]

Although he had advised the use of lead as a means of strengthening Henry VIII's credit in the Low Countries, Vaughan had never envisioned the possibility of such a large-scale enterprise as eventually materialized. On the other hand, the king and council, captivated by the idea of procuring immediate cash by what appeared to be such a simple expedient, determined to market as much lead as possible. Despite the protests of the Antwerp agent that lead could be sold on the Continent in limited quantities only and that an oversupply of the metal would glut the market, force the price down, and thus defeat the very purpose of the venture, they decided to experiment with a trial shipment of 12,000 fothers, to be followed by further consignments when that was sold. When Vaughan learned the full details of the project he was completely taken aback by the lack of foresight on the part of his superiors, for he was convinced that he would never be able to dispose of more than 3,000 fothers a year and that, only by the most judicious marketing. While dismayed at having to cope with " so great a trowpe of lead," he, nevertheless, accepted the situation as inevitable and set about to salvage as much as possible from this misguided enterprise. [61]

However interesting the lead episode, it was only indirectly related to Augmentations administration. It is sufficient to note that after many delays and miscalculations the lead was finally exchanged for Spanish alum which was disposed of in England during the ensuing reign at a loss to the crown of some £8,000. [62]

The king's council bore the full responsibility for the lead transaction, but it was upon the Augmentations that fell the task of collection, transference to the ports of embarkation, and preparation of lead for shipment. Most of the surplus supply in England had come from the buildings of the confiscated religious institutions and, as part of the spoils of the Dissolution, had remained in the hands of the Court. Always in constant demand for ordnance, buildings, and fortifications, lead and bell metal were the most salable of all the marketable commodities, and the Court continued to conduct a profitable business in them throughout its

---

[60] S. P. 1/189, fols. 159–62d. The financial situation in Antwerp at this time is presented in some detail in W. C. Richardson, *Stephen Vaughan: Financial Agent of Henry VIII* (Baton Rouge, 1953), especially Chap. V.

[61] S. P. 1/190, fols. 31–32; 1/195, fol. 221.

[62] Richardson, " Some Financial Expedients of Henry VIII," *Economic History Review*, New Series, VII, 45 ff.

history. From the very beginning lead and bell metal were sold advantageously, either by direct order of the king in council or by warrant from the chancellor of the Court, who in this instance was given authority to dispose of such commodities at his own discretion. Usually the sales were negotiated by the latter, who notified the Court receiver of the nearest district where the lead was available to arrange for delivery and receive payment for the sale.[63] As the spoliation progressed, the supply soon exceeded the market demand, and the lead and bells were melted down and stored at convenient towns or castles. Although the crown had drawn heavily on this reservoir for current governmental needs, the reserve continued to grow. Occasionally monastic buildings were sold before being stripped, but usually the lead and bells were disposed of separately. In many instances lead was the most valuable of the salable items, as at Butley priory in Suffolk where it was worth, by estimation, £1,000.[64]

As a part of his regular duties, the chancellor of the Augmentations directed the sale of lead and bell metal and countersigned royal licenses for their exportation from the realm.[65] Such exports were fairly constant during normal years and give some indication of the extent and profit from this trade. Exporters included both English and foreign merchants, of whom John White, Thomas Walker, John Core, John Dymock, Anthony Dunryche, Bartholomew Compagni, and Anthony Guidotti were the most important.[66] Despite the inconsistencies of governmental policy the lead market remained steady. During the period when Vaughan was trying desperately to sell lead abroad, private sales

---

[63] The voluminous correspondence of Sir John Scudamore, receiver in Yorkshire, indicates the extent to which such business occupied the attention of Augmentations officials. See Add. MS. 11041.

[64] The house had practically no other wealth, except cattle. *L. and P.*, XIII, pt. 1, no. 393. Lead and bell metal were such valuable items that in sales and leases of crown property they were normally reserved for the crown.

[65] The tedious business of closing accounts for lead purchases made at the time of the Dissolution continued long after the Court of Augmentations was abolished. An interesting case developed in the Exchequer Chamber in 1558 concerning the legal responsibility of the chancellor for bonds, which through fraud had never been enrolled in the Augmentations. Sir Edward North, as chancellor of the Court, had sold and delivered by royal warrant four hundred fothers of lead at £4 6s. 8d. per fother, but his clerk Thomas Benger, who took the bond for the sale, failed to deliver it to the Court. Instead, he connived with the purchaser to cancel the bond, for which he received a bribe of £400. Consequently, when the crown sued North for the debt of £2,000 he was held to be technically responsible for the payment; but in equity North was adjudged guiltless, unaware of the false practices of his subordinate, and fully exonerated. Benger and his accomplice were charged with the entire sum of the bond. Sir James Dyer, *Reports of Cases* (Dublin, 1794), II, 2–3.

[66] Indentures of sale were retained by the Augmentations and are today widely dispersed among the Miscellanea and Misc. Books.

in England were curtailed. In general, exportation of lead was restricted in late 1544 and in the spring of 1545, but small quantities were sold regularly by special warrants from the king or council directed to the chancellor of the Court. When the restraint was lifted in the summer of 1545, moderate exportation was resumed by royal license.[67] At home the Augmentations officials continued to gather in the lead, supervise local surveys, and finance costs of transportation to storage depots scattered along the English coast.[68] Under royal warrant the chancellor delivered lead regularly to the king's agents or to cash purchasers in lots varying from a few hundred to three thousand fothers at a time. In one instance at least a hundred fothers was delivered to a Bristol merchant as part of the purchase money for an addition to the royal navy.[69]

About a year before the Court of Augmentations was joined to the Exchequer, a general commission was appointed to investigate the status of church movables which had come to the crown since February 4, 1536. A distinguished group of eleven ministers, headed by the master of the household, John Dudley, duke of Northumberland, was to take cognizance of " a great and notable quantity of lead, bell metal, plate, jewels, ornaments, stock and store, goods and chattles " which the king had acquired from the religious houses, as well as forfeitures of gold, silver, jewels, plate, bullion, and " other rich wares " which had come to the crown by virtue of attainder and other penal statutes. They were ordered to find out how much lead and bell metal had been gained, what part of it had been sold and under what authority, how much of the metal still remained unsold, and where it was stored; also to find out how much bullion, both coined and uncoined, had been exported without license; and finally, to call before them for examination all royal officers or commissioners who had received payment for goods sold. Those who had not previously accounted were to do so and, if found indebted to the crown, proceedings were to be instituted against them. The Augmentations, which was more concerned with the disposal of such crown

[67] Lead shipments from Newcastle were restricted until the end of July. Merchants there were holding large quantities " to be conveyed Eastward " as soon as the restraint was lifted. *L. and P.*, XX, pt. 1, nos. 544, 707, 732, 879, 926, 1076, 1260, 1275, 1285, 1302.

[68] In addition to regular storage centers at Boston, Bristol, Grimsby, Hartlepool, Hull, Lynn, Newcastle, Scarborough, and Whitby, lead was stored at Lincoln, York, and Worcester Castle.

[69] An order from chancellor North to receiver Scudamore, dated April 22, 1546, to deliver one hundred fothers of lead to John Smith of Bristol, in exchange for his ship, the *Trinity Smythe*, and £200 in cash. *L. and P.*, XXI, pt. 1, nos. 650(52), 652. A copy of the royal warrant for the transaction was enclosed. Augm. Office, Misc. Books 472, fols. 13–14.

possessions than the other revenue courts, was represented on the commission by three of its officials, the Mildmay brothers and Richard Goodrich, the attorney of the Court.[70] In November of 1555, a select commission of three former auditors of the Augmentations was appointed by Mary to conduct a similar inquiry; to its duties was added an investigation of previous wood sales and exchanges of land wherein the crown might have been cheated. In case valuations had not been made, the commissioners were required to have special surveys run in order that a true value might be determined and the necessary payments collected.[71]

Full returns of these commissions would have undoubtedly yielded valuable evidence on the breakdown of administration during the Edwardian period, but all their reports, if ever presented in written form, have not been preserved.[72] The investigation must have done something, however, to resolve the complicated question of outstanding crown accounts which for so long had remained a perennial burden on the whole revenue administration. In the Augmentations, where the issue had always been more or less acute, it had become progressively pronounced. Not only had arrears mounted year by year, but to its own roster of uncollected debts had been added from time to time bonds and recognizances turned over to it by the council for processing. The lists of crown debtors, obligations, recognizances, and books of arrears and debts

---

[70] December 12, 1552, commission to Northumberland, great master of the household, the lord keeper of the privy seal, the king's chamberlain, the high admiral of England, the controller of the household, and the earl of Huntingdon; Sir Ralph Sadler, Sir Philip Hoby, Sir Walter Mildmay, Thomas Mildmay, and Richard Goodrich. *Cal. Pat. Rolls, Edward VI*, IV, 391. At the same time a similar commission was appointed to take the accounts of all persons handling such commodities in order to render a full account of their receipts and deliveries and collect arrears. Upon an examination of the " leager boke or bokes " of the clerks of the privy council, it was to inquire of all council warrants since the beginning of the reign as to what payments had been authorized, how the money had been spent, and to award acquittances or punishments to those investigated. *Ibid.*, 391–92.

[71] *Ibid., Philip and Mary*, III, 25–26, 116. This commission to auditors William Berners, Thomas Mildmay, and John Wiseman was reissued in a slightly modified form on June 18 of the following year. They were further empowered to assess fines for the spoliation of woods and commit offenders to the Fleet prison. *Ibid.*, 114–15.

[72] The returns which are available give a clear picture of the difficulties encountered in the collection of long-standing debts, especially where the original circumstances had in many cases been forgotten. Nevertheless, a considerable number of old debts were brought under review to be canceled, refinanced, or paid in full. Report and proceedings of the commissioners concerning the disposal of lead and bells during the reigns of Henry VIII and Edward VI. Exch., K. R., Miscellanea, 24/21 (ten documents). Other documents relating to the work of the commissioners are scattered among the Augm. Office, Miscellanea and Misc. Books.

preserved among the records of the Court bear witness to the magnitude of the problem.

The procedure was simple enough in most cases. Debtors investigated by the privy council or special commissions were ordered to report to the Augmentations to pay a portion of their debts and arrange terms for future settlement. Recognizances enrolled in the Court thus became legal records, subject to collection according to the provisions of agreement. After 1547 chamber obligations were also processed there in the same manner; upon the satisfactory adjustment of an account the treasurer of the chamber would be ordered to cancel the original recognizance and deliver it to the debtor. Since the party seldom had enough money to pay more than an installment or so of the debt, the king was usually compelled to take land or personal property in lieu of cash payment. Thus every year the crown acquired an appreciable amount of land through the collection of debts. Usually, preliminary negotiations having been completed, the Court was ordered to evaluate the property and make the necessary transfer. When faced with a shortage of cash it was always easier for the government to call in unpaid obligations than to devise new sources of revenue. Consequently, most reform measures were accompanied by special commission examinations of crown debts and delinquent accounts.[73]

Registers of money due the crown for any given period reveal a miscellaneous assortment of obligations which had been allowed to accumulate through the years without any action having been taken on them. The amounts varied greatly depending on the nature of the debts as originally contracted. Most of them were political fines imposed by the privy council or Star Chamber, balances remaining unpaid upon the determination of accounts, and legitimate debts contracted for the purchase of lead, timber, land, and other crown possessions. Less important but more suggestive of administrative disorder were the innumerable small debts of crown tenants and minor officials for prest money, arrears of rent, and odd items of incoming revenue for which no accounts had been rendered. Oftentimes, where accounts had remained for years unaudited, it was exceedingly difficult to determine if a deficit indicated actual embezzlement or merely unrecorded expenditures. In many instances, irregularities which normally would have been reported currently by the auditor were not discovered until after the death of the

---

[73] The council proposals for a general financial reform, presented to both Edward VI and Mary, included checks on such things as unpaid accounts for purchases of land, timber, lead, bell metal, and other crown commodities, as well as demands for immediate declarations of account by royal agents and those who had received money in prest. "A remembraunce of thinges worthie examinacion," S. P. 10/5, fol. 154; 11/1, fol. 57.

minister when the circumstances of the case had become even more elusive.

Ordinarily, neither political fines nor bona fide debts to the crown were ever collected in full. Upon a petition for leniency a portion of the total would often be remitted by royal warrant, or if the debtor had given long service, small debts might be canceled altogether.[74] Even after the debt had been reduced, it was usually " stalled " by the substitution of installment payments favorable to the payee. When Sir Anthony Kingston was called on to settle his account totaling £2,181 18s. 11d., he transferred certain property in Herefordshire to the crown at twenty years' purchase; for the remainder of the debt the Court was ordered " to estall and geve daye for payment " at £50 per year until the entire amount was paid.[75] Likewise, obligations of foreign merchants were enrolled in the Augmentations, where renewals, installment payments, and the final settlement of debts were made.[76]

More difficult to cope with was another type of debt, known officially as arrearages, which represented either revenue unpaid at the date due by tenants and collectors or the remainder due on an account at the time of audit. Delays encountered in the collection of rent were a never-ending source of annoyance to the receiver, although he was seldom able to alter the situation. Some tenants had no money and could not pay their rents; others refused to settle " withoute compulsion." Property was sometimes arbitrarily vacated or, as frequently happened, it had deteriorated to such an extent that the collector was forced to petition the Court for an adjustment to cover the " decayed rents " under his

[74] The long-standing debt of £3,000 owed by Ralph Rowlett, master of the mint under Henry VIII, contracted in 1530, was not canceled until 1551. The Court of Augmentations, apparently unnotified of the pardon, issued a privy seal against the son, Ralph Rowlett, in 1553. Augm. Office, Miscellanea, 39.

[75] Augm. Office, Misc. Books 472, fol. 31. In a similar case the countess of Rutland, widow and executrix of Thomas Manners, earl of Rutland and favorite of Henry VIII, delivered parcels of land claimed to be worth £34 15s. 9d. per year in part payment of her husband's debt of £1,748 18s. 11d. The chancellor of the Court of Augmentations took assurance of the property, binding her to warranty the value for six years. The settlement for the remainder of the debt was deferred until the son, the second earl of Rutland, returned from France. (August 1, 1546.) *Ibid.* 479, fol. 85; 104, fols. 45–48d.; Add. MS. 9782, p. 755.

[76] Many of these bonds were quite large. For example, the Court of Augmentations held obligations of the Florentine merchants, Dominico Erizo, Marco Antonio Erizo, and Guido Cavalcanti, for £500 and £1,894 7s. 11d. A part of the debt was paid in " fyne salt peter of Naples," and new bonds " of good substanciall Englyshemen " were drawn up in April, 1552, for the payment of the remainder. Augm. Office, Miscellanea, 39/85; Misc. Books 327, fol. 17d.; Dasent (ed.), *Acts of the Privy Council*, IV, 11.

jurisdiction.[77] As shown by the ministers' accounts, all classes of officials, woodwards, stewards, collectors, and receivers alike were behind in their payments. Whatever the reason, arrears mounted steadily throughout the years, the total for the Augmentations reaching £125,486 18s. 3d. before its dissolution.[78]

On the other hand, the collectors were not always blameless. With the less conscientious, arrears represented indolence or indifference to responsibility. Receivers themselves were sometimes defaulters, and people dependent on them suffered. Those more hardly affected were pensioners and annuitants who not infrequently were at their mercy. Despite the fact that receivers were often hard pressed for money to meet required expenditures, few arrears of pension payments seem to have been due to lack of funds. When restriction of payment was not imposed by the government, the local receiver was usually at fault. Influential recipients were doubtless favored, but in some instances pensions were deliberately refused or at least withheld until appropriate bribes were forthcoming.[79]

Among those heavily indebted to the crown were many of the Augmentations ministers, particularly the receivers, some of whom, upon the determination of their accounts, were faced with heavy deficits.[80] In few cases, however, were charges of embezzlement involved. Unless the honesty of the accountant was questioned, reasonable arrears in office brought neither reproof nor penalty to the accountant.[81] All collectors and receivers were supposed to be bonded; in most cases, therefore, if a properly bonded official died before his debt was paid, legal responsibility was simply shifted to his sureties. When the debts were only a few hundred pounds, the majority of Augmentations ministers was able to

[77] Decays in rents and " vacacions " of tenements and cottages were always a large item in the receivers' accounts. As much as £1,000 in Yorkshire, these two deductions totaled £5,234 15s. 1d. for all the districts. Add. MS. 30198, fols. 17, 25. Sometimes a half or a whole year's rent was allowed for repair of houses.

[78] Augm. Office, Treas. Rolls of Accts., No. 8, fol. 116d. On arrears in the earlier Court of Augmentations, see Chapter Ten.

[79] Dickens, " The Edwardian Arrears in Augmentations Payments and the Problem of the Ex-Religious," *E. H. R.*, LV, 401–403.

[80] The names of most of the crown debtors are found in the Ledger Books of Receipt kept by the treasurer of the Court of Augmentations. Augm. Office, Misc. Books 336–49.

[81] See the interesting case of Sir Robert Chester, Augmentations receiver in the fourth district, concerning the question of forfeiture of office for failure to pay arrears at the date due. By judicial decree under Mary it was decided that his office was not forfeited without a writ of *scire facias*, because he was an officer of record. Later, in 1562, the court ruled that the receivership had become extinct by virtue of the letters patent dissolving the Court of Augmentations. Dyer, *Reports*, II, 210–11, 216. On December 14, 1553, Edward Hastings was appointed to succeed Chester in the renovated Exchequer. *Cal. Pat. Rolls, Mary*, I, 56.

settle them promptly, either by land or cash payments. But the breach between good and bad debts was constantly widening. By the beginning of Mary's reign the reserve of potential revenue derived from collectible debts in the Augmentations had been virtually exhausted.

Arrears of accounts and other forms of maladministration in the Augmentations were too far removed from the public eye to arouse more than passing criticism. Such popular resentment as was manifest seems to have been directed against excessive fees, especially for the use of the Court's seals and for the drafting, engrossing, and enrolling of official instruments by the various clerks. Among all the officers the chancellor and the clerk of the Court profited most from these emoluments. Instruments passing under the great seal of the Court were numerous: leases, surrenders, commissions, fees, annuities, pensions, appointments, indentures, and grants of land, tenements, liberties, and franchises; for each document the fee was 13s. 4d., of which the chancellor was allowed half. The remainder was paid into the Augmentations treasury. In addition he received commensurate fees for the sealing of commissions and processes.[82] While there is no way of calculating total charges, annual profits must have been considerable, even if privileges were not abused. It was probably extra fees rather than the regular salary which kept Richard Duke in the clerk's office for the entire span of the Court, to retire in 1554 with a liberal pension.[83] The special allowances scattered throughout the treasurer's accounts illustrate the nature of such fees. During the fiscal year 1543–1544 Duke earned £14 8s. by enrolling indentures and £53 6s. 8d. in writing privy seals of summons; in December, 1546, he received £14 2s. for the enrollment of deeds.[84] When the second Augmentations was organized he was paid £40 extra for office supplies, enrollments, and for copies of " the boke of the erection of the courte," three on parchment and seven on paper. Among other fees during the following year, 1549, he collected £597 4s. for drafting and enrolling 2,991 patents at 4d. each, by virtue of the king's warrant.[85] All these payments were, of course, entirely legitimate,

---

[82] Pat. Rolls, 38 Henry VIII, pt. 5, mem. 18. The commission of 1552 recommended that all grants pass under the great seal of England, which would double the profits of the crown. At that time the Augmentations seal was earning £314 6s. 8d. per year. Harl. MS. 7383, fol. 72.

[83] His salary was increased significantly from £10 to £40 per year, plus an extra 20 marks in fees and allowances, indicating the growing importance of his office. Add. MS. 30198, fols. 21, 45. The extra £13 6s. 8d. was for ink, paper, parchment, and wax. Augm. Office, Misc. Books 259, fol. 61. Duke was also the recipient of several annuities paid from the revenues of monastic lands. He made enough from the Augmentations office to invest heavily in Dissolution property.

[84] Augm. Office, Misc. Books 253, fols. 73, 74d.; 255, fol. 102.

[85] *Ibid.* 257, fol. 101; 258, fol. 108; 251, fol. 69d. In the sixth year of Edward

part of the ordinary business of his office. Heavy enough under normal circumstances, clerical work was greatly increased when special campaigns were instituted for the sale of land or the collection of debts. Instances of excessive fees there probably were among the principal ministers of the Court, but they never constituted an administrative problem at the central office. Unreasonable charges for official services, such as the drawing up of accounts or the issuing of receipts, were more likely to develop within the local groups of Augmentations officials in the counties.

The inflationary cycle served to augment the prevailing trend, and many ministers indeed appear to have assumed that moderate exploitation of government positions was justifiable. Throughout the period the public accepted the fact that it had to pay for all government services, whatever their nature. In this sense, the whole nation was guilty of perpetuating corruption. So strongly was this notion implanted in the popular mind that the government was never able to combat it effectively. Attempts were made to prevent such common practices as the acceptance of gifts and speculation with crown funds retained by ministers for that purpose, but these efforts were never wholly successful. The amusing reflection offered by Hugh Audley early in the next century regarding the value of his lucrative clerkship in the Court of Wards probably had considerable validity. The worth of a government position, he suggested, depended as much on the character of the official as on the manner in which the office was used: " It might be worth some thousands of pounds to him who would go, after his death, instantly to heaven; twice as much to him who would go to purgatory; and nobody knows what to him who would adventure to go to hell." [86]

VI's reign he earned at least £79 from the enrollment of annuities alone. *Ibid.* 261, fol. 69d.

[86] *D. N. B.*; quoted in Bell, *The Court of Wards and Liveries,* 35.

CHAPTER EIGHT

THE DISSOLUTION OF
THE COURT

ARY'S FIRST PARLIAMENT OF OCTOBER, 1553, PROVIDED FOR the abolition of the Court of Augmentations by an enabling act authorizing the union, dissolution, or re-establishment of courts. This legislation was enacted, however, only after a definite course of action had been agreed on. It was accordingly specified that " if her Highnes hereafter shall annexe any of the said Courtes unto her Courte of thexchequer, That then all thinges within the surveye of the sayd Courte so annexed shalbe ordredd in lyke maner to all intentes as the said Courte of thexchequer ys or ought to bee by the common Lawes and Statutes of this Realme." [1] Despite the plenary powers conferred on the queen by this statute, only three courts were directly affected. By letters patent the Augmentations and the First Fruits and Tenths were dissolved and immediately thereafter annexed to the renovated Exchequer. The reformers had secured results at last, but only after numerous attempts had been made to bolster the decadent organization.

Near the end of the late reign a comprehensive schedule of various administrative matters to be investigated had included a reminder for the elimination of the " faultes " and a redress of the " superfluous

[1] 1 Mary, St. 2, c. 10, sec. iii, *S. R.*, IV, 208–209. This act was similar to an earlier statute of 1553 (7 Edward VI, c. 2): "An Acte for the dissolving uniting or annexing of certayne Courtes latelie erected by the King that deade ys." *Ibid.*, 164–65. A copy of Mary's statute is found in Cotton. MS., Titus B. iv, fols. 62–62d.

charge " in the several revenue courts, as advocated by the recent commission.[2] This memorandum and other economy measures suggest that a real program of retrenchment had been contemplated. A reduction in the complements of various garrisons was ordered; in the Scilly Isles construction was brought to an abrupt standstill, and the superintendent of works commanded to dismiss all workmen immediately. During the autumn of 1552 the government decided on a drastic reduction in the postal service; whereas it had recently been ordered " that the postes thourough owt the realme " should be discharged, it was now resolved to let those messengers who " wilbe content with twelve pence by the day " remain; all those who refused were to be discharged and others hired in their stead.[3]

Upon the accession of Mary similar economies were proposed, though none of them were fully realized. Among those considered were lower salaries, restriction of land sales, reduction of pensions and annuities, and curtailment of household expenditures. The limited expense program was expected to be continued; furthermore, it was hoped that improved rents would yield an increase in crown land revenue. As usual the treasuries were low and the need for money constant, but immediately public approval of government policy was more important than reform. Undoubtedly the general pardon of 1553–1554 was proclaimed, in part at least, as a bid for popular support.[4] In London the national goodwill was expressed by a loan of £10,000 from the City.[5] Meanwhile, the council was debating the problem of cutting expenses wherever possible. Already the initial step had been taken when the Court of Augmentations was relieved of one of its legal officers. In accordance with the recommendation of the reform commission of 1552 the solicitorship was eliminated, the duties of the office being henceforth taken over by the solicitor general for the crown. When Gosnold was advanced to that position in May, 1552, it was agreed that there should be " no more sollicitours " appointed for the Court.[6]

When it was finally decided to amalgamate the Augmentations, the Exchequer, and the First Fruits and Tenths, the fundamental question of ways and means was raised by the legalists. Since the reconstruction

<hr />

[2] In a slightly modified form this memorandum and other similar " remembrances " for financial revision were drawn up for Mary in the turbulent early weeks of the new reign. S. P. 10/5, fol. 154 ff.; 11/1, fols. 5, 56 ff.

[3] Dasent (ed.), *Acts of the Privy Council*, IV, 33–34, 104, 151.

[4] *Cal. Pat. Rolls, Philip and Mary*, I, 164–65, 388–90, 410–69. This pardon roll contained the names of the members of the council and other officials of the Court.

[5] Dasent (ed.), *Acts of the Privy Council*, IV, 343, 353; see also 297, 368, 369. 387.

[6] Harl. MS. 7383, fol. 62d. Edward Griffin (Griffith) was promoted to the position of attorney general for the crown in all the courts of record on September

of the Court of Augmentations in 1547, its legality had been questioned on the grounds that an institution established by statute could not be abolished by letters patent without special authorization by parliament. This confirmation was accordingly granted by the March parliament of 1553, which validated the original patents and empowered Edward to combine, alter, unite, or abolish any of the revenue courts by letters patent. The act passed the Commons on the thirtieth but only after adequate guarantee had been given that all officials of any court or courts that might in the future be dissolved would be awarded annuities commensurate with their former salaries.[7] At the same time an act " for the true aunsweringe of the Kinges Majesties Revenues" was passed, which required receivers and treasurers to be bonded. Regular periods of accounting were provided for and certain dates of payment established when the king's revenues should " be justly and truly answered " by all accountants.[8] The reformers were then ready to proceed with the final steps of reorganization.

Nothing was changed by the death of the king in July, 1553. In the minutes for his last will, drawn up by Secretary Petre, the executors were reminded that " they shall consider to bee discharged all superfluous charges, bothe in th'excessive expenses of our howshold and chamber, and in the overgreatt number of cowrtes, by uniting the same according to the statute provided in thatt behalf, and such other superflous charges." [9] Mary's first parliament convened on October 5; about the same time the chancellor of the Court of Augmentations, Sackville, was required to tender his resignation. A commission of seven, headed by the lord treasurer, Sir William Paulet, marquis of Winchester, was speedily appointed to take over the seals of the Court and manage Augmentations affairs during the period of transition.[10] Presumably there

---

30, 1553. Gosnold, former solicitor of the Court of Augmentations, succeeded him in the office of general solicitor for the crown. *Cal. Pat. Rolls, Edward VI,* IV, 336; *Philip and Mary,* I, 71; Nichols (ed.), *Literary Remains,* II, 415. The Court of Wards had had but one legal officer, an attorney.

[7] *S. R.,* IV, 164–65; *Journal of the House of Lords,* I, 435a; *Journal of the House of Commons,* I, 25a, 26a.

[8] 7 Edward VI, c. 1, *S. R.,* IV, 161–64.

[9] Nichols (ed.), *Literary Remains,* II, 574.

[10] Commission of October 17, 1553, *Cal. Pat. Rolls, Mary,* I, 67, 300. The commissioners, of whom three formed a quorum, were empowered to abolish offices which they considered superfluous, when the offices became vacant, and to hear all judicial cases that came before the Court. On the administrative work of this commission see Augm. Office, Misc. Books 462: A certificate of wood sales in Leicestershire, by Thomas Cocke, woodward. This and other surveys during the first year of Mary's reign were under the direction of the Winchester commission " appointed for the governaunce of hir Highnes Courte of Augmentacon." See also Exch., Accounts Various, 63/18; *Cal. State Papers, Domestic, 1547–1580,* pp. 51,

was still doubt as to whether or not the Court of First Fruits and Tenths was to be dissolved, for no mention was made of it in this commission. During its first session Mary's parliament was chiefly engaged in effecting the ecclesiastical settlement; therefore it was not until late November that it found time to deal with the problem of the revenue courts. In its final form the second act for the union, dissolution, " or newe erecting of Courtes " was essentially a repetition of the previous act of the same year which had expired with the death of the king. Under it Mary was authorized at her discretion to dispose of the courts by letters patent in such manner as to her seemed expedient. What followed was the work of the council since the queen was at the time fundamentally interested in but one thing, the repeal of the religious legislation of the Reformation. The abolition of the Court of Augmentations was meaningful to her only if it meant a step toward the re-endowment of the church. But however much she might appeal to parliament and complain to her council, she could not force upon her people an acquiescence to any material loss of property already acquired. Officially Mary could restore the Roman faith, but she could not restore to the church lands and property which Catholics and Protestants alike had shared. The most she was ever able to accomplish was the restoration of a few houses which were immediately reannexed to the crown by Elizabeth.[11] Among them was the famous order and hospital of St. John of Jerusalem which was re-established for a short time both in England and Ireland.[12]

Meanwhile, on November 16, 1553, the treasurer of the mint, Sir Edmund Peckham, had been appointed special treasurer to receive the revenues of the realm during the interim of reorganization.[13] In the succeeding months, while the revenue courts were in the throes of dissolution, Peckham acted as central paymaster and receiver-general for the government. The amalgamation was finally accomplished in January, 1554. Under writs of *certiorari* the Court of First Fruits and Tenths and the Court of Augmentations surrendered all their records into the

---

55. Local activities of the Court continued without interruption under the direction of its two general surveyors, Mildmay and Moyle, who were also members of the commission.

[11] A half dozen monasteries were restored by Mary: the Benedictines of Westminster Abbey, the Carthusians of Sheen, the Franciscan Observants at Greenwich, the Dominican friars at Smithfield, the Bridgettine nuns and brethren at Sion, and the Dominican nuns at Dartford. All their property was annexed to the crown when the houses were dissolved in 1559.

[12] This grant included the capital house and site of the late hospital or priory of Clerkenwell, near London. *Cal. Pat. Rolls, Philip and Mary*, IV, 43–44, 313-21; *Elizabeth*, I, 29, 72; II, 507.

[13] *Ibid., Mary*, I, 72. The commission is dated December 5, but it appears from internal evidence that Peckham began work on November 16.

chancery, which subsequently delivered them by writs of *mittimus* to the renovated Exchequer. At the same time the lord chancellor was directed to proceed with letters patent for the dissolution of the two courts and their annexation to the Court of the Exchequer. These orders were issued in the form of a commission on the nineteenth. The following day Sackville was temporarily reappointed head of the Augmentations in order that he might officially supervise its closing.[14] Accordingly, the necessary letters patent, dated January 23 and 24, were issued, which completed the transaction by the end of the month.

During the first few months of Mary's reign, preceding the dissolution, business at the central offices of the Augmentations was reduced to a minimum. A few grants of land were made under the Court's seal, but practically all payments were received by the treasurer of the mint, Peckham, in his capacity of commission director in charge of all finance. Council warrants directed to the treasurer of the Augmentations for all kinds of payments, normally so recurrent throughout the pages of the *Acts of the Privy Council*, are singularly lacking after the accession of Mary. The same is true for the general business of the Court, as revealed in the numerous official directives to the chancellor and council [15] which are found in earlier volumes. Several important payments were made in October and November of 1553, including £4,526 6s. 4d. to the great wardrobe, but Williams was already under suspicion.[16] On December 17 he was ordered to appear before the privy council with a memorandum of all the money and revenues which had come into the Augmentations treasury since the close of the previous fiscal year at Michaelmas. This is the last official entry for Williams in the council records. His latest recorded payment was for December 2, when he paid, after some delay, the traveling expenses of the crown auditor for Ireland.[17] Otherwise, the Winchester commission of October, 1553, worked with the Augmentations ministers in a supervisory capacity. On December 22 they were directed to investigate a debt of £800 due the Court and take obligations for its payment. Several vacancies in the Court were filled during this period, but they were positions in the field which would continue after the annexation by the Exchequer. If the commissioners

---

[14] *Ibid.*, 67, 73.

[15] When need arose, executive functions of the Court could always be performed by specially appointed crown commissions.

[16] Dasent (ed.), *Acts of the Privy Council*, IV, 359, 362, 368.

[17] *Ibid.*, 375, 379. Having delayed in executing an earlier warrant for this payment Williams was reprimanded for his delay, the council " marvailing muche why he refuseth to pay him." The last entry in this volume on the Augmentations Court itself is for December 22, 1553, and concerns bonds taken for debts due from the queen's woods. *Ibid.*, 381. Cf. *Cal. Pat. Rolls, Mary*, I, 60, 140, 170, 217, 282, 332.

found unnecessary offices that might be eliminated, as originally suggested in their instructions, there is no indication that any formal action was taken.[18]

The actual mechanics of amalgamation were worked out between the twenty-third and twenty-sixth of January, 1554, by a series of legal enactments which, taken collectively, constitute a valuable précis of the organization of the three courts at the time of their union. By letters patent the Courts of Augmentations and First Fruits and Tenths were dissolved on the twenty-third and annexed to the Exchequer on the twenty-fourth. Accompanying schedules set forth the rules and regulations governing the administration of the revenues under the new system, but all this was only a preliminary to the physical transfer of the countless number of documents, rolls, and manuscripts that made up the body of official records of each court.[19] Writs of authorization were directed to the Exchequer, where the lord chancellor in a public ritual presented the various instruments for acceptance and subsequent enrollment.[20] Curiously enough the patents are not enrolled on the patent rolls but on the back of the close rolls, although the patent of annexation for the Augmentations is found among the Miscellanea of the Exchequer.[21]

The economic motive was offered as the reason for amalgamation, which was thought to be conducive to " the better suerer and more spedy aunswering of our yerely revenues casualties or profittes nowe aunswerable in thesaid Courtes." However, in the case of the Augmentations a more pertinent justification was suggested among " dyvers other greate and weightie consideracions." Since 1536, the date of the original foundation, the Court had lost " a greate parte of the possessions and hereditamentes " under its survey; " And yet neverthelesse the yerely allowaunces fees dyettis [diets] rewardes and other superfluous charges . . . appeare vnto vs to remayne and rather to be augmented then dymynysshed

---

[18] In the Court of First Fruits and Tenths William Dansell was reappointed receiver-general on January 17, 1554, at his original fee of £66 13s. 4d. per year. *Cal. Pat. Rolls, Edward VI*, III, 311. A curious proviso was included in the grant that in case the court were " at any time altered, determined or anew erected," he should still retain his office. *Ibid., Mary*, I, 49.

[19] The bulk of the Augmentations records was not delivered into the Exchequer until the twelfth of the next month.

[20] Exch., K. R., Memoranda Rolls, 333, mems. 75, 80.

[21] Close Rolls, 1 Mary, pt. 7, (C. 54/500), mems. 3–6 inclusive; Exch., K. R., Miscellanea, 13/2. An abbreviate of the letters patent for the Augmentations is contained in Lansd. MS. 168, fols. 348–49; see also incomplete copies in Cotton. MS., Titus B. iv, fols. 63–67. The various documents are likewise enrolled on the memoranda rolls. Copies were made in 1775 by Henry Rooke, clerk of the rolls, for the duchy of Lancaster, which include the lengthy articles of the schedule for the Court of Augmentations. D. L., Miscellanea, 41/12/26. The Close Roll copy is complete and easily accessible; it is the manuscript used in the following analysis.

to our greate and excessive charges." A decrease in crown lands was certainly an important factor in determining the number of revenue courts actually needed, although the Augmentations still administered far more revenue than any other department. In point of argument it would have been more logical to preserve that institution and consolidate the Exchequer and the First Fruits and Tenths under its jurisdiction.

The schedules of annexation were concerned exclusively with the reorganization of the Exchequer and throw no further light on the subsequent Augmentations developments of 1554. The obvious intent of the Exchequer officials was to effect a return to the older procedures used before the Tudor innovations had been introduced—in other words, to revert to " thauncient lawes and customes of thesaid Exchequier." That this course was not eventually followed is more a tribute to the effectiveness of Augmentations methods than a criticism of Exchequer efficiency; nevertheless, the administration benefited greatly by the new forms, despite the continued opposition of many die-hards. The settlement finally accepted was at best a bad compromise, with little logic or merit to recommend it. Of two alternatives, only one offered a real solution to the problem: either a single centralized revenue department with jurisdiction over all types of revenue or two independent agencies, one for the traditional landed revenues of the kingdom and the other for residual revenues and parliamentary levies. Neither possibility, however, was politically expedient, since each would have involved too great a displacement of interested personnel. The Duchy Chamber and the Exchequer were too firmly entrenched in court circles to be easily overthrown, the Court of Wards too close to the personal prerogative of the Crown. None the less, the government was expected to benefit from the union, especially in lower operational costs resulting from reduction in personnel.[22]

In the report of 1552 the commissioners had given a great deal of attention to the dual problem of excessive salaries and superfluous personnel, but in proportion to their revenue the amounts involved in these two categories were not very significant. Total annual expenditures on salaries in the Court of First Fruits and Tenths were only £956 15s. 1d., of which £490 14s. 8d. represented increases that had been made without royal license.[23] In fact, the court's payments for 1551 total but £3,699

---

[22] The records are silent on the significant exclusion of the Court of Wards. The problem is fully surveyed in Hurstfield, *The Queen's Wards*, 211–14. On the organization and operation of the renovated Exchequer, see Chapter Thirteen, *infra*.

[23] In contrast Peter Vane, Latin Secretary, received 40s. per day in fees and diets as ambassador to Venice, which item alone cost the Court of First Fruits and Tenths £730 yearly. Add. MS. 30198, fols. 28, 34d–35, 50.

10*s.* 1*d.*, which was only a small portion of its annual receipts.[24] Augmentations officials, on the other hand, had been somewhat more liberal in providing themselves with fees and allowances. The report of 1552 listed ten offices the salaries of which had been substantially increased since the reorganization of 1547.[25] The chancellor and general surveyors had been the worst offenders in that respect, having added £40 and £20 respectively to their regular annual fees and allowances. It is only fair to point out, however—which incidentally the report did not indicate—that these extra allowances to the head officers of the Court were granted for diets and not, strictly speaking, as advances in fees. Even so, assuming that diets and travel allowances could be curtailed, it soon became apparent that no major saving could be achieved by the abolition of a few unnecessary positions. A careful selection of trained personnel, designed to improve morale and increase efficiency, might have been more beneficial.[26] It is interesting to note that reforms in local administration, where much economy was possible, were ignored altogether.

It will be remembered that both statutes authorizing the dissolution of the revenue courts had guaranteed adequate compensation for loss of offices to all ministers affected by such a procedure.[27] Consequently, the reforms of 1554 saddled the administration with a whole new batch of government pensioners whose cost to the state was far more than the savings from the amalgamation. The list of displaced persons who by law had to be compensated included about a dozen top officials of the Court of First Fruits and Tenths and thirty-one ministers of the Augmentations. Most of them fared quite well, receiving in recompense as much as or more than their former salaries. Early in February, 1554, Sir John Baker and Sir William Petre, formerly chancellor and treasurer of the First Fruits and Tenths, were pensioned for the full amount of their official fees and emoluments. Both annuities were paid from December 25, 1553, presumably the day they surrendered their patents of office.[28]

[24] The total year's receipts were just over £23,564. The balance, or £19,864 13*s.* 9*d.* remaining, "be it more or less," was yearly assigned to the household. *Ibid.*, fol. 28. There is a slight discrepancy in the totals given on fol. 28 and fol. 35.

[25] This list does not include the £40 fee of William Berners, who had secured appointment as special auditor of the treasurer's annual accounts. Several clerkships had been added which had increased the expenses of the yearly audit from £1,052 3*s.* 4*d.* to £1,976 8*s.* 4*d.*, or more than £924. *Ibid.*, fol. 45.

[26] In many instances the laxity of court officials was chiefly responsible for the long-standing arrears of accounts. Because of such habitual negligence in the Court of First Fruits and Tenths, many uncollected debts had accumulated: " also þe good Order be taken for calling in of þe debts of this Court because many remain due long time past unpaid & divers of them for lack of calling on in time grow utterly desperate." Add. MS. 30198, fol. 50.

[27] See p. 248, *supra.*

[28] Baker's salary was only £133 6*s.* 8*d.*, but the lucrative issues and profits of the

Petre immediately petitioned for an auditing of his accounts, which was granted on the following seventeenth of February.[29] Some of the pensions were actually greater than the basic salaries of the officers had been, since supplementary allowances and emoluments by the court were quite liberal. For example, the office of messenger had paid only £2 10s. yearly, though special allowances brought the annual stipend up to almost £16. The two auditors, John Wroth and Thomas Leigh, were awarded annuities of £60 each for life, which was three times the fee set up for the surrendered office; the £133 6s. 11d. listed as salary included all their extra allowances. As shown by the following table,[30] the clerk and the keeper of the records received no compensations. Instead, they were awarded the newly created Office of Remembrancer of First Fruits and Tenths in the Exchequer at a joint salary of £80.[31]

The displaced Augmentations officials were treated just as handsomely. On May 4, 1554, Mary directed a warrant to the lord chancellor, commanding him to receive the surrender of their offices and grant to them " reasonable recompenses for their ffees and commodities." [32] Their annuities, payable out of the Exchequer, ranged from £200 in the case of the chancellor to £6 1s. 8d. awarded to the usher, James Johnson. As the following table shows, the pensions were generally the same as the Court's salaries in 1547 before the less justifiable increases of the next reign. There were, however, certain discrepancies, notably in the case of the clerks and the messengers, whose compensation included allowances for liveries. The former official, Richard Duke, was generously awarded a life pension of £133 6s. 8d., almost a threefold increase over the salary he had given up. While no evidence is available on the exact annual profits of the clerkship, fees for copying documents, ab-

---

court seal to which he was entitled added another £100 to his fee; similarly Petre had received but £120 per year as salary; the remainder of his fee, an additional £159 6s. 8d., was in allowances for chests, boxes, bags, paper, ink, green wax, cloth, boat and carriage hire, diets for himself and his clerks, and " other necessaries " of the office. Presumably, a portion of this sum had gone to his clerks. Actually Petre's pension was £266 13s. 4d. Add. MS. 30198, fol. 28; *Cal. Pat. Rolls, Mary,* I, 5, 164.

[29] *Ibid.,* 78.

[30] The list of fees for the officers of the Court is given in the commissioners' report of 1552. Add. MS. 30198, fol. 28. Basic salaries can be determined from the original patents of appointments to office. Grants of compensation are abstracted in the *Cal. Pat. Rolls, Philip and Mary, 1553–54.* The pensions were all for life and retroactive, being payable from Christmas, 1553.

[31] February 12, 1554. Pat. Rolls, 1 Mary, pt. 1, mems. 16–17. *Cal. Pat. Rolls, Mary,* I, 6. Grant jointly, in survivorship, to Thomas Godfrey and Thomas Argall, respectively clerk and keeper of the records of the dissolved court.

[32] Cotton. MS., Titus B. iv, fols. 139–40. It was dated May 4 but not processed until May 30. A copy of the queen's warrant, with the accompanying list of pensioners, is found in a hanaper register in Add. MS. 38136, fols. 16d.–17d.

stracts, and the use of the court seals, the amount of the compensation would suggest a figure of approximately £80 to £95.[33] Because of the discontinuance of the office of prests for a few years, the two incumbents, Gregory Richardson and William Dixe, who had been so active during the Edwardian period, were retired on full salary. More difficult

FEES AND ALLOWANCES IN THE
COURT OF FIRST FRUITS AND TENTHS

Official	Salary	Pension
Chancellor	£233 6s. 8d.	£233 6s. 8d.
Treasurer	£279 6s. 8d.	£266 13s. 4d.
Attorney	£ 26 13s. 4d.	£ 26 13s. 4d.
Two auditors	£266 13s. 10d. (£133 6s. 11d. each)	£120 (£60 each)
Clerk	£ 40	None
Keeper of the records	£ 20 (plus an additional £9 in rental fees for a house to keep the records in and for the use of the chancellor of the court)	"
Deputy to the treasurer	£ 40	"
Pursuivant	£ 15 17s. 3d.	£7
Usher	£ 5 7s. 3d.	None
Treasurer's clerk	£ 6 13s. 4d.	"
Auditors' clerks	£ 13 6s. 8d.	"
TOTAL	£956 15s. 1d.	

to justify, however, is the compensation awarded to William Berners, who as special auditor of the treasurer's accounts had suffered a recent public indictment for unethical conduct in procuring his position.[34] Perhaps the explanation lies in the political influence which officials like him could exert at court.

Wages of district receivers and auditors had constituted a major item of operational cost, but as in other salary categories any saving in fees was eaten up by comparable expenditure in pensions. The twelve receivers of the Court were given no compensation since they were con-

---

[33] *Ibid.*, fol. 17. P. 244, *supra*.
[34] Exch. of Receipt, Miscellanea, 407/71. On the case of Berners, see p. 208.

FEES AND ALLOWANCES IN THE SECOND COURT OF AUGMENTATIONS

Central Officials	Salary in 1547	Salary in 1551	Increase in Salary	Pension Awarded
1 Chancellor	£300	£340	£40	£300
2 Two general surveyors (at £200 each)	£400	£440	£40	£200 each
3 Treasurer	£320	£320		£320
4 Two masters of woods (at £100 each)	£200	£200		£100 each
5 Attorney	£100	£113 6s. 8d.	£13 6s. 8d.	£100
6 Solicitor	£80	£93 6s. 8d.	£13 6s. 8d.	£80
7 Two surveyors of woods (at £100 each)	£200	£200		£100 each
8 Clerk of the Court	£40	£53 6s. 8d.	£13 6s. 8d.	£133 6s. 8d.
9 Keeper of the records	£6 1s. 8d.	£10	£3 18s. 4d.	
10 Usher	£6 1s. 8d.	£6 1s. 8d.		£6 1s. 8d.
11 Chief carpenter	£6	£6		
12 Chief mason	£6	£6		
13 Three messengers (at £6 1s. 8d. each)	£18 5s. or with livery £23 5s.	(33s. 4d. each for livery) £23 5s.		£7 15s. each
14 Two auditors of the prests (at £40 each)	£80	£80		£40 each
15 Auditor of the treasurer's accounts		£40		£40

FEES AND ALLOWANCES IN THE SECOND COURT OF AUGMENTATIONS

Central Officials	Salary in 1547	Salary in 1551	Increase in Salary	Pension Awarded
16 Attorney in the Exchequer Master of the Rolls		£100		None
17 Assistant to the Court Justice of the King's Bench		£6 13s. 4d.		"
18 Assistant to the Court Justice of Common Pleas		£6 13s. 4d.		"
19 Assistant to the Court		£6 13s. 4d.		"
20 Clerks of chancellor and general surveyors at time of declaration of accounts		£121 10s.	£121 10s.	"
21 Clerk of the master of the woods South of the River Trent		£10	£10	"
Expenses for the annual audit	£1,052 3s. 4d.	£1,976 8s. 4d.	£924 5s.	"
Field Officers				
Ten district auditors	£1,588 9s. 4d.	£2,126 8s.	£537 18s. 8d.	£50 to £200 ea.
Eleven district receivers	£1,188 3s.	£1,810 9s. 6d.	£622 6s. 6d.	None
Forty-four county surveyors	£622 6s. 8d.	£622 6s. 8d.	None recorded	"
Thirty-six local woodwards	£149 14s.	£149 14s.	"	"
Stewards and keepers of courts		£2,328 16s. 1d.	"	"
Bailiffs and collectors		£3,904 12s. 6d.	"	"
Keepers of woods, parks, chases, etc.		£2,589 9s. 10d.	"	"
Officials in Wales		£642 1s. 5d.	"	"
Exchequer officials at Chester		£284 13s. 1d.	"	"

tinued in office under the new Exchequer organization.[35] The auditors, on the other hand, lost their positions, though in all cases they received fair compensation. At the time of dissolution there were twelve auditors' circuits but only eleven auditors, one auditor, Thomas Mildmay, having done double duty in two circuits. Furthermore, the number had recently been increased in Wales, where Protector Somerset had added extra offices to the payroll by dividing the principality into two districts.[36] In the case of Mildmay his pension of £200 was somewhat larger than any of the others because of his holding, in effect, two offices. With the exception of two men, William Hamerton and Thomas Tyndall, the remainder of the group received annuities of 200 marks or £133 6s. 8d. each. This represented £1,400 [37] as against the £2,126 8s. per year previously spent by the Court, which had included all fees and extra allowances.

After 1554 the bulk of public pensions was carried by the Exchequer, which had inherited pensions, annuities, and corodies to a total of £50,766 16s. 8d. from the Augmentations.[38] Interestingly enough, £2,933 4s. of this went to pay ex-personnel of the earlier Court of Survey and the first Court of Augmentations, which were dissolved in 1547.

Most of the stipends were for life, though in the case of displaced officials the annuities were ostensibly justifiable only so long as the government failed to provide comparable employment elsewhere. As a matter of fact, most of the abler ministers found other jobs almost immediately. When the £90 pension of William Stanford, formerly attorney of the Court of Survey, was taken over by the Exchequer in

[35] The original constitution of the Augmentations provided for eleven receiverships, but an extra office had been created in Wales by dividing the district. Actually there were thirteen, if the receiver-general of Cornwall is included. In 1554 this office was held by Henry Gates, who succeeded Sir Thomas Arundell, executed for attainder on February 26, 1552. *Cal. Pat. Rolls, Edward VI*, IV, 386.

[36] Among the recommendations of the investigating commission of 1552 was the following item: " Also the Office of Thauditor & Receiver of Northwales and Southwales by the Kings Ordnance upon the Ereccion of this Court were ffirst appointed to be one and after the Duke of Somersett divided [it] into Two Offices by reason whereof þe King is charged wᵗʰ £100 ffee and allowance more than else he should and the same may well enough be served by one Auditor and one Receiver." Add. MS. 30198, fol. 45d.

[37] Mathew Colthurst and Henry Leak, holding office jointly, were pensioned 100 marks each. The other auditors were Thomas Mildmay (£200), John Wiseman (200 marks), William Rigges (200 marks), John Hanby (200 marks), Richard Hutchinson (200 marks), Thomas Notte (200 marks), Thomas Mathew (200 marks), John Pickerel (200 marks), William Hamerton (£83 6s. 8d.), and Thomas Tyndall (£50). Add. MS. 38126, fol. 17d.

[38] The total expenditure in pensions and annuities for all revenue departments was £63,285 8s. in 1551. *Ibid.* 30198, fols. 24d. 25, 36d., 37.

May, 1554, he had already found other work. Although successively serjeant-at-law, queen's serjeant, and justice of the common pleas, he continued to draw his compensation until his death in 1558.[39] Nor is Stanford's case at all exceptional. In spite of later advancements the Mildmay brothers continued to draw pensions of £200 each until they died.[40] Two of the auditors, John Hanby and Thomas Mathew, soon attained auditorships in the Exchequer,[41] while chancellor of the Court Sackville certainly earned as much as his pension of £300 after he became undertreasurer of the Exchequer.[42]

From the very beginning Mary's financial problem was a serious one, at a time when the normal expenses of government and administration were increasing rapidly. Retrenchment and reform were in the air, and the council was resolved that the economic disasters of the past regime should be avoided at all costs. Her ordinary expenses ought to be moderate enough for the crown to bear, the queen was reminded, and at the same time enable her to accumulate a reserve in case of war. "And for this cause all such superfluous new charges as have of late crept in are to be taken away," she was admonished, "and the size of the household, the admiralty, ordinance, mint, Ireland, Calais, Berwick and other places reduced near the same charges that they were in the latter end of King Henry VIII." [43] Needless to say, this goal was not easily attained, but at least something was done to cut down expenses. Throughout the government a definite effort was made to eliminate the waste of Edwardian corruption. On such matters the queen was wise enough to accept the advice of her experienced treasurer, the marquis of

---

[39] *Cal. Pat. Rolls*, Mary, I, 10; see also *D. N. B.*

[40] Walter Mildmay served as treasurer of the army in Calais in 1557–58, under Mary, and became auditor of the duchy of Lancaster, treasurer of the household, and undertreasurer and chancellor of the Exchequer under Elizabeth. Lansd. MS. 171, fol. 344. Thomas Mildmay at the time of the closing of the Augmentations was auditor of the duchy of Cornwall; he later sat on numerous commissions but held no major office afterwards.

[41] Mathew obtained his auditorship in December, 1556; Hanby, at the beginning of 1560. *Cal. Pat. Rolls, Mary*, I, 199; *Philip and Mary*, III, 457; *Elizabeth*, I, 250, 295. Another auditor, William Rigges (Ridge), held auditorships in both courts in 1554 and continued his office in the Exchequer. *L. and P.*, XIV, pt. 2, no. 780(25); *Cal. Pat. Rolls, Edward VI*, II, 163; *Mary*, I, 495.

[42] Pensioned on May 30, 1554, Sackville continued to draw his compensation until his death in April, 1566. At that time he was receiving fees of over £804 per year from the Exchequer, including the £300 pension for the chancellorship of Augmentations and an additional £180 per year for his office of undertreasurer. *Cal. Pat. Rolls, Elizabeth*, I, 144; S. P. 12/39, fols. 163–163d. There is no foundation for the oft-repeated assertion that Sackville held the office of chancellor as well as undertreasurer of the Exchequer.

[43] A memorandum of August 4, 1553, of things to be done, *Cal. State Papers, Domestic, 1547–1580*, 54. See also the interesting proposals for further economy presented in 1555. Cotton. MS., Titus B. iv., fols. 129–31d.

Winchester, who "like a good husband for the crown, shewed her belike how low her treasure was, and therefore prayed her to be sparing of giving away her lands, especially in his absence, . . . at least, not before he had advice of it." Grateful for his kindness and vigilance she promised to consult him in the future before sanctioning grants of land. She even refused to reward her trusted minister Peckham, if Strype can be believed, until the lord treasurer had signified his approval.[44]

Since Mary's chief interest was always in religious reform, the early work of the government was directed mainly toward that end, and any solution of the revenue problem depended largely on the ingenuity of her financial ministers, especially Lord Winchester and Walter Mildmay. The situation was further complicated by the royal policy for the restitution of church property, which only served to accelerate the revenue shortage. That the queen was serious in her intention of restoring all those ecclesiastical goods which still remained in the hands of the crown is indicated by the governmental investigation instituted in the autumn of 1553. Already, in the final spoliative action, officials of the Augmentations had assisted in collection of church plate and other valuables during the last months of the preceding reign. To facilitate the Marian inquiry the last two chancellors of the Court, North and Sackville, were directed to make available all the Augmentations records of the former church movables. A part of this "mine of wealth" was recovered and redelivered to the churches. Most of the defaced plate that remained was sent to the jewel house in the Tower of London.[45]

However widespread the various economies of the reign, they were not enough to offset the rise in prices and the increasing costs of administration. Additional crown revenue was the obvious solution, yet there were no new sources of income available. Nevertheless, remedial measures, for the most part old and well tried, were duly instituted.

[44] When Peckham's request for a grant of land was received, Mary consulted Winchester, recommending the transaction (*Cal. Pat. Rolls, Philip and Mary*, II, 294–95). A postscript in her own hand added: "My Lord, I most heartily thank you for your daily painfulness taken in my service." Strype, *Ecclesiastical Memorials*, III, pt. 1, 195. The *Calendar of Patent Rolls* shows leases to have been made by the treasurer's advice.

[45] Dasent (ed.), *Acts of the Privy Council*, III, 228; V, Preface, xiii, xxi, 45, 70, 71, 104, 112, 128, 132, 176, 201, 249. Nichols (ed.), *Literary Remains*, II, 409–10. *Cal. Pat. Rolls, Edward VI*, IV, 392–93; V, 413–17, 417–19; *Philip and Mary*, III, 25–26, 114–15, 116. The Edwardian inventories particularly included bells and valuable plate. Special attention was given to investigating the widespread private embezzlement of church property that had developed. A comparative study of the Edwardian inventories of church goods and the Marian returns for Cornwall is available in Snell (ed.), *The Edwardian Inventories of Church Goods for Cornwall: No. 2 of Documents Towards a History of the Reformation in Cornwall* (Exeter, 1955).

Customs rates were raised, rent adjustments made, and fines for entry gradually augmented. More affecting the subject, heavy payments were extracted from persons implicated in the late Wyatt rebellion; at the same time commissions were set up to compound for denization and knighthood. Outstanding debts to the crown were scrupulously collected, and before the reign was over a forced loan was finally initiated. As might be expected, the sale of crown lands was continued according to the policy previously established.[46] Despite various checks on administrative efficiency, however, money was slow coming in. Although very little could be done to speed up the Exchequer process of revenue collection, orders for prompter payment by receivers were issued. Each effort yielded an appreciable return, but of them all the government stood to gain most from crown debts. In fact a great deal of the council's effort at this time was directed toward the apprehension of debtors and the examination of charges against them.[47]

Of the many who for various reasons were indebted to the state, only the more influential came under the special investigation of the council. The majority came before commissions of inquiry or were prosecuted under ordinary court procedure. Only about a score of ministers were examined by the council, most of them facing serious charges of embezzlement with intent to defraud. Some of the arrests grew out of declarations of accounts which more recently had been required of all financial ministers, in many instances years after the irregularities had occurred. Edwardian procedure for processing " suche debtes plate sommes of money and other thinges " due to the king or his father was a long and continuous business, which not infrequently revealed serious default on the part of crown ministers. Many obligations were collected in part or in full, but a great number were either " estalled " or refinanced, while unusual or more desperate debts were certified to the " Council for the State " for special investigation.[48] To expedite the work various commissions of audit were appointed under Mary as part of the general plan to inject greater efficiency into the administration.[49]

---

[46] *Cal. Pat. Rolls, Mary*, I, 265, 301, 304, 332; *Philip and Mary*, II, 103, 205; III, 314–15, 554–55; *Edward VI*, V, 184, 277, 411.

[47] Dasent (ed.), *Acts of the Privy Council*, V, 329, 335, 350, 351. Necessity led to new extremities. A permanent committee of four councillors was finally set up, including Walter Mildmay, with instructions to sit daily until some means of raising money had been determined. Froude, *History of England*, VI, 476.

[48] Commissions of 1551–53 for the survey of crown debts and the enforcement of payment. Pat. Rolls, 5 Edward VI, pt. 4, mems. 19d.–21d.; 6 Edward VI, pt. 6, mems. 36d.–37d.; pt. 7, mems. 16d.–18d.

[49] *Ibid.*, 1 Mary, pt. 2, mems. 42d.–43d., 45d.; pt. 7, mems. 1d.–4d.; pt. 10, mem. 35; pt. 11, mems. 36d.–39d.; 2 Mary, pt. 2, mem. 30d.; 1 and 2 Philip and Mary, pt. 5, mem. 5d.; pt. 15, mems. 8d.–10d.; 2 and 3 Philip and Mary, pt. 1, mem. 19d.;

Yorkshire seemed particularly susceptible to graft, due partly to the large number of crown ministers located there and to their remoteness from the capital, but also in part to the size of the expenditures involved in that area. Before the Augmentations had been dissolved, Richard Whalley, the Court's receiver for that county, had been dismissed from office for the falsification of accounts and the theft of crown revenues.[50] Somewhat later, in early November, 1553, the treasurer of Berwick-on-Tweed, Richard Bunny, formerly a receiver in the Augmentations, was committed to the Fleet for "misbehaviour both in using the Quenes Majesties treasure in his charge and in trifling before the Lordes of the Counsaill." Upon conciliar examination he was found to be indebted to the crown for £2,800 on his account in Berwick, having "medled with paymentes" there. This was on the seventh; on the fifteenth he was released from prison and sent back to Berwick in order to declare the state of the debts there and make restitution to his creditors. Again in March of the following year he was remanded to the Fleet for "mysdemeanour" in office. During the course of subsequent examination, Bunny was found guilty not only of theft but also of forgery. In punishment he was dismissed from office and forced to give bond for his debts. Legal recognizances for £2,000 were duly drawn up and land to the annual value of £53 was accepted by the crown in satisfaction of the remainder of his obligation.[51]

The zeal with which debtors were investigated reveals a number of unusual situations that need not have developed had safeguards been established earlier. The fact that large government debts could remain inactive for years without question was a serious indictment of the administration. In one case over half of a debt of £1,400 by Sir Edmund Carew, contracted in February, 1515, remained outstanding until the end of the year 1556, when his grandson, Sir Peter Carew, was called to account. In addition to that amount Sir Peter owed a personal debt of £986 13s. 4d. for 230 fothers of lead which he had bought from the Court of Augmentations in 1547 and for various arrears of rent payable there, a part of which still remained due.[52] In the light of such negli-

---

pt. 4, mems. 4d.–7d.; 3 and 4 Philip and Mary, pt. 3, mems. 15d.–17d., 19d.–20d.; 4 and 5 Philip and Mary, pt. 1, mems. 1d., 6d.; pt. 3, mems. 3d.–4d., 6d.–7d.; pt. 9, mem. 22d.

[50] Before him, Leonard Beckwith had become involved in a similar scandal. On these two receivers, see pp. 58, 232–33.

[51] Dasent (ed.), *Acts of the Privy Council*, IV, 362, 366; V, 3, 43–44, 77. Giles Heron replaced Bunny at Berwick at midsummer, 1554, although the patent of appointment was not issued until the following September 19. *Cal. Pat. Rolls, Philip and Mary*, II, 199. He was pardoned by Elizabeth at the beginning of the next reign. *Ibid., Elizabeth*, I, 194.

[52] *Ibid., Edward VI*, IV, 398–400; Dasent (ed.), *Acts of the Privy Council*, VI,

gence on the part of the government it is little wonder that careless officials postponed the settlement of their accounts as long as possible. Some men died before the auditors caught up with them, leaving the burden of their obligation on their families; some doubtless escaped altogether, while still others spent years in paying off old debts which they hoped might eventually be remitted. Such a debtor was Sir Maurice Dennis, treasurer of Calais, who, upon the determination of his account in 1552, was found to owe the crown £7,486. Three years later he was still paying on over £2,500.[53]

In the autumn of 1554 the undertreasurer of the mint, Thomas Egerton, was summoned by the council to answer for £20,000 in Spanish money received from Thomas Gresham in Flanders for which he had not accounted.[54] Sir Walter Mildmay and Sir Nicholas Hare were deputized to investigate the charges against him and certify their findings to the council. Apparently their report was unfavorable, for Egerton was lodged in the Tower to cool his heels pending further investigation. In June, 1556, a second commission was appointed to examine him and determine how much he still owed the crown.[55] The commissioners were instructed " to use the best meanes and waies they can in travayling with him to cause him to paye all suche sommes of moneye and other thinges valuable as he could possiblie make during thexaminacion of his accompte into the Receipte of theschequier." The sum involved was £1,020 10s. which Egerton, still in the Tower, promised to pay. The records are vague on later developments in the case, but it seems that in order to raise such a large sum, Egerton was compelled to sacrifice his house in London.[56] Debts of such " greate sommes of money " were not too unusual among ministers who handled large receipts. The late

---

27. The Augmentations had been concerned with many of these cases of debt and corruption, especially when the debtor's property was confiscated.

[53] Dennis had presented no declaration since his appointment in 1548. His account was taken by Thomas Mildmay and other commissioners in June, 1552. *Cal. Pat. Rolls, Edward VI*, I, 298; IV, 352; *Philip and Mary*, II, 118–19.

[54] Egerton had been a treasurer of the mint and exchange in the Tower of London under Edward VI since June, 1552 (*Cal. Pat. Rolls, Edward VI*, IV, 322), the appointment as " undertreasurer " being confirmed by Mary on January 22, 1554. *Ibid.*, Mary, I, 61. His accounts, along with those of the undertreasurer of the mint at York, were audited by a commission in March, 1554, which apparently reported Egerton to the privy council. *Ibid.*, 195–96.

[55] The commission was headed by the master of the horse, Sir Edward Hastings, and composed of some of Mary's ablest financiers: Sir Francis Englefield, master of wards; Sir John Baker, chancellor of the Exchequer; and the Mildmay brothers, Walter and Thomas. *Ibid., Philip and Mary*, III, 23–24.

[56] Dasent (ed.), *Acts of the Privy Council*, V, 73, 210, 233, 284, 300, 302, 331, 334. After 1556 Egerton's name disappears from the records, although his embezzlement caused a reform of the mint. *Ibid.*, 348. He is not to be confused with the later Thomas Egerton (Baron Ellesmere) who was lord chancellor under Elizabeth.

receiver of the Augmentations for London, Middlesex, Hertfordshire, and Essex owed the crown £1,412 upon vacating his office,[57] while the treasurer of the chamber confessed to a deficit of £5,237 5s. when his accounts were finally audited in 1557.[58] This must have been noted by the council as being quite in keeping with the precedent set by the chamber office in 1546. When Sir Anthony Rous died in that year, he was found indebted to the crown for a total of £6,089 12s. Even after a claim by his son for £1,737 16s. 10d. was allowed by the Court of Augmentations, the debt stood at over £4,351.[59]

After 1554 many of these unpaid accounts were acquired by the Exchequer from the dissolved Court of Augmentations, which in a similar manner had earlier inherited the chamber obligations. Especially numerous were arrears of rent and old recognizances, often long overdue, representing large sums still uncollected for previous purchases of crown land and lead.

Process in the Exchequer brought to task such influential officials as Lord William Grey of Wilton, Lord Cobham (George Broke), William Herbert earl of Pembroke, William Somerset earl of Worcester, Lord Clinton (Edward Fynes), and Lord Williams of Thame, formerly treasurer of the Augmentations.[60] Privy council examinations disclosed unpaid Augmentations recognizances for debts varying from a few hundred to over two thousand pounds.[61] When the offender could present a reasonable excuse the council was usually lenient, but it could be severe if the debtor was recalcitrant. Edward Pease of London, unable to settle his debt of £2,310, was committed to the Fleet with a time limit to make a token payment of £500. If he ignored the first

---

[57] *Ibid.*, 41, 42, 336.

[58] *Ibid.*, VI, 182; a report of the debt of Sir William Cavendish, late treasurer of the chamber, Exch., Accounts Various, 224/10.

[59] The "bill of peticion" of the son, Thomas Rous, was presented to the Court with the claim that certain payments for fortifications had been made for which no written allowance was given. The question was turned over to William Dixe and Gregory Richardson, auditors of the prests, for further examination. After investigation by the Court, the facts of the petition were substantiated, and the claim allowed in full. Add. MS. 9782, fol. 864; Augm. Office, Misc. Books 15, p. 147d.; 105, fols. 147d.–50; Proceedings of the Court of Augmentations, E. 321/44, Package IV, no. 12.

[60] Dasent (ed.), *Acts of the Privy Council*, V, 279, 343, 345. See also pardons for debts as abstracted in the *Cal. Pat. Rolls, Philip and Mary.* In 1558 William Somerset, earl of Worcester, was released from crown debts totaling £1,602. *Ibid., Philip and Mary*, IV, 432–33. Many of these old accounts were brought to light by the commission of November 14, 1555, appointed to investigate all sums still due the crown for sales of plate, jewels, lead, bell metal, and timber that were made since February, 1536. *Ibid.*, III, 25–26, 114–15, 116.

[61] Dasent (ed.), *Acts of the Privy Council*, V, 278–79, 292–93, 306, 332; VI, 14, 191.

warning, he was " thenne to be committed to suche more streight prison as shall cause him to be wery thereof." [62] Nevertheless, malicious intent could seldom be proved. Unless the procrastination was obvious and deliberate, the guilty official might be permitted to absolve himself by a pledge of repayment and given ultimate pardon. Seldom was he punished beyond a fine and temporary imprisonment; usually he was not even suspended from office. Quite frequently exposure came as a result of attack by political enemies or court factions; in such instances the minister, temporarily in disgrace, could always bide his time in the hope of finding favor with a new monarch.

As in England, so also in Ireland, was the administration open to abuse by irresponsible officials. However, a single negligent or dishonest minister was enough to give a department a bad reputation, and it is only fair to point out that those who fleeced the government were in a decided minority. Such was the situation in 1554 which ultimately led to a full investigation of Irish finance. The accounts of Andrew Wise, late undertreasurer and general receiver for Ireland, were found to be in such hopeless confusion that a special commission was appointed to investigate them. Later it was proved that other accountants were far behind in their payments, that arrears were mounting, and that " no perfect account of the revenues of the realm " had been made for a long time past. The Irish auditor, Thomas Genyson, who was partially responsible for this state of affairs, had already been dismissed for " misdomeanours " in office.[63] Meanwhile, Wise had been arrested and confined to the Fleet to await his trial. On September 20, 1555, Wise was condemned in a Star Chamber hearing and required to give surety for over £10,000, but not before another committee of the council on Irish affairs had been set up.[64]

Isolated cases of course prove nothing, but it is impossible to ignore the numberless instances of minor defalcations. The low tone of public morality had borne fruit. Whether at Berwick, Calais, Dover, or in the Isles of Scilly, the same story of misappropriations and petty fraud is registered. Local and central officials alike were found guilty of major or minor misdeeds.[65] In 1552 the treasurer of the Court of Augmenta-

---

[62] *Ibid.*, 281, 297–99.

[63] Commission of February 24, 1555, to the new auditor of Ireland, Valentine Brown, to receive and determine the accounts of all the accountants in Ireland. When duly allowed, they were to be formally drawn up and delivered to the Exchequer as a matter of record. *Cal. Pat. Rolls, Philip and Mary*, II, 104. Sir Richard Sackville was one of the commissioners appointed to audit the accounts of Wise.

[64] Dasent (ed.), *Acts of the Privy Council*, V, 4–5, 18, 59, 182, 196, 261, 262, 267.

[65] *Ibid.*, 24, 43, 44, 74, 296, 301, 325, 355, 357. In 1556 Sir Edmund Peckham,

tions could be committed to prison for no greater crime than disobeying an order of the privy council. A few years later, after he had been found guilty of malfeasance in office, he was pensioned by Mary and awarded a baronage. The vicissitudes of Tudor ministers were remarkable.

Unless new evidence is discovered, the treasurer's case will remain unsolved. As a servant and kinsman of Cromwell, John Williams' fortunes had prospered with those of his master. Successively clerk of the king's jewels, master of the jewel house, treasurer of the Augmentations, and member of parliament, he had played an important role in national politics. His significance during the two earlier reigns, at least as far as the crown was concerned, was purely financial, for as treasurer of the Augmentations from 1544 until its dissolution he was the chief paymaster of the nation. In such an office the opportunities for peculation were considerable, particularly when years might elapse before an incumbent would be called on to render an account of his stewardship. Despite an earlier investigation, it was revealed by the commission of April, 1547, appointed to determine his account, that Williams had presented no declaration for his eight years in the jewel office.[66] The findings of this commission, if indeed a report were presented, are not known, but an item among the Augmentations payments for the first year of Mary's reign suggests that he had not settled his final account until forced to do so by a royal commission for the collection of crown debts. Williams is recorded as having paid £826 in arrearages for the jewel office.[67] It is unlikely, however, that this debt was anything more than the result of personal neglect. Far more serious were the charges against him in the Augmentations office, where his accounts were still incomplete and unaudited in 1554.

---

as high treasurer of the mint, was ordered to cease payment of £104 per year to officials of the mint for their diets; " forasmouche as there have not byn of long tyme any coynage," he was required " to take indelaied ordre accordingly." *Ibid.*, 348.

[66] Pp. 188, 196–97, *supra.* Williams' tenure in office was from about 1536–44, since he had in fact served as master of the jewels for several years during Cromwell's nominal headship. Richardson, *Tudor Chamber Administration, 1485–1547,* 485. Strype, without stating his authority, gives the arrears in the jewel house at £16,667 7s. 11¾d. Strype, *Ecclesiastical Memorials,* II, pt. 2, 76, 257.

[67] Undated payments made to Peter Osborne, special treasurer of the king, that had grown out "of suche debtes and arrerages as was presented before certeyn commissions appoynted for the calling in of the same besides £826 11s. 10d. paide by Sir John Williams for the Arrerages of his office in the Mᵣ of the Jewelhowse." Augm. Office, Misc. Books 262, fol. 67. This item was canceled as authorized by Sackville and Walter Mildmay. Ledger Book of Receipts: 6 and 7 Edward VI, *ibid.* 348, fol. 20. The commission referred to was probably that of July 13, 1552. Pat. Rolls, 6 Edward VI, pt. 6, mem. *36d.–37d.*

Despite a court regulation that the treasurer should account yearly, Williams had been permitted to continue in office for almost ten years without a final reckoning. The investigation of 1552 showed that at that time he had not been called to task, although his clerk testified that the court auditor had all of his records and unfinished accounts up to Michaelmas, 1549. Incredible as this may seem, such culpable remissness is all the more incomprehensible when it is remembered that the treasurer of the most important financial department of the realm, at any given time responsible for thousands of pounds in national revenue, should have remained unbonded for his entire tenure of office.[68] Nor was a commission appointed to hear his accounts until March, 1554, seven weeks after the dissolution of the Court.

The six commission auditors were instructed that all bonds and specialties remaining in his hands were to be delivered to the queen's remembrancer in the Exchequer. Whether or not the commission discharged its duties is not known, but eight months later it was renewed with fuller instructions, which included the inspection of his entire receipts in office since his original appointment to the first Augmentations in 1544.[69] The investigation revealed the usual arrearages, but it seems that Williams over the course of years had kept back either intentionally or from negligence various sums in receipt of land sales, which had not been recorded in the treasurer's accounts. The payments involved totaled some £31,226; they were entered in the account as a lump sum for the penultimate year of the Court's receipts, that is, from September 29, 1552 to September 28, 1553.[70] The facts of the case strongly suggest a deliberate intention to defraud the government, but under the plea of extenuating circumstances Williams could have claimed that the omission resulted from carelessness and oversight. Whatever the evidence of the hearing, the details are not a matter of record. As a man of property, however, he must have been in a position to assume responsibility for the debt charged against him. He probably paid a part of it in cash, with convenient terms granted him for the payment of the remainder.

There is definite evidence at least that he was gradually paying off

---

[68] Pp. 196, 200, 225, *supra*.

[69] Commissions of March 16 and November 24, 1554. The commission of six contained three privy councillors, but only one professional auditor, John Wiseman. All of them were former officials of the Augmentations. They were Sir Edward North, Sir Thomas Pope, Sir Thomas Moyle, John Wiseman, John Arscot, and Richard Duke. The latter commission is enrolled on the Treas. Rolls of Accts., No. 8, fols. 1–1*d*. Pat. Rolls, 1 Mary, pt. 10, mem. 35; 1 and 2 Philip and Mary, pt. 15, mem. 9*d*. Incomplete abstracts are found in *Cal. Pat. Rolls, Philip and Mary*, I, 265–66; II, 343. Augm. Office, Misc. Books 261, fol. 1.

[70] Augm. Office, Treas. Rolls of Accts., No. 8, fols. 28*d*.–31.

the obligation during the years preceding his final pardon. In May, 1555, an indenture between him and Thomas Sanders, the queen's remembrancer in the Exchequer, shows £534 19s. to have been paid over as a part of the Augmentations debt.[71] On June 5, 1556, just a few days before his final release by the crown, Williams, then baron of Thame, was summoned to the council "taunswere his debte" of £2,100 which he pledged to pay by the twentieth of the month.[72] Presumably this sum was to make up the deficiency in his account which he had been paying on since the date of declaration. There is no reason to assume that the money was not paid as promised. His pardon and release were granted on June 10, in consideration of his service to three sovereigns; "all debts, bonds, arrears, accounts and actions against him" were then closed, long after the initial charges had been presented.[73] He had already been accepted by Mary as a trusted councillor. The pardon came, therefore, not so much as a justification of his honesty but as a reward for political loyalty. The Northumberland rebellion and the circumstances attendant upon Mary's accession enabled many ministers who had been tainted by the fraudulence of the previous reign to start afresh.

There seems to be no connection between Williams' indebtedness to the crown and the earlier episode of his arrest and temporary imprisonment for willful negligence in the Augmentations office under Edward VI.[74] Actually that brief imprisonment in 1552 was occasioned by his open disobedience rather than by deliberate neglect of duty, for he always took his responsibilities seriously. As treasurer of the Court and principal paymaster of the realm he naturally came under the close surveillance of the council, which periodically undertook a systematic check of all revenue expenditures. Suddenly and without warning Williams was summoned before the council on April 3, 1552, under suspicion of having paid pensions to dispossessed monks and chantry priests without special authorization.[75] This action was taken as a result of his having

---

[71] Thirteen separate obligations, some of them dating as far back as Henry VIII's reign, were delivered into the Exchequer. An accompanying memorandum explains that Williams agreed to answer for the obligations if any of them could not be collected. Augm. Office, Miscellanea, 24.

[72] Dasent (ed.), *Acts of the Privy Council*, V, 279.

[73] *Cal. Pat. Rolls, Philip and Mary*, III, 72. As late as May, 1558, Williams was required "to make hys indelayed repayre" to the privy council and show his pardon granted upon his accounts as treasurer of the late Augmentations. Dasent (ed.), *Acts of the Privy Council*, VI, 319; see also S. P. 12/8 (27).

[74] I have found the circumstances of the arrest in no way related to the later charges against him. See p. 197, *supra*.

[75] Young Edward recorded in his *Journal* that Williams had been committed to the Fleet for "disobeying a commaundment gevin to him for not paying any pensions without making my counsel prevy." Nichols (ed.), *Literary Remains*,

ignored an order to the Augmentations to cease temporarily payment of all religious pensions except by order of the council. Such punishment was unduly severe, especially since the fault lay partly with the head of the Court for not having insisted on strict obedience to instructions. On the eighth Williams was committed to the Fleet where he was kept in close custody, being allowed to see no one. It was during this confinement that the chancellor of the Augmentations came to the prison to confer with him concerning the Court's payments. However, the severity of Williams' sentence was soon relaxed, and he was allowed to walk in the prison gardens where his wife and children visited him.[76] He was finally brought before the council on May 22, at which time he made his " humble submission " to the formal charge of negligence in office. Subject to recall at any time, he was then provisionally released, but obtained full liberty on June 2 following.[77]

All formal restrictions originally imposed on his official payments seem to have been removed at that time, although later there is some indication of further carelessness.[78] In the absence of council records, however, the precise nature of the indictment brought against Williams can only be conjectured. If the motives of the council were political, then the issue was considerably graver than the " lack of doing his dutie in his office layed to his chardge." For the remainder of the reign Williams confined himself exclusively to the work of the Augmentations and escaped further punishment. Seizing the chance to redeem his lost prestige upon Edward's death, he immediately espoused the cause of Mary and raised a large army in Northamptonshire in her support. His actions were as fruitful as they were timely, and his motives could not have been completely ulterior. Religiously he was what Froude called one of those " bigoted Catholics "[79] and as such probably welcomed the return to Catholicism expected from Mary. Moreover, his adherence to the queen went beyond the mere anticipation of royal favor. He had been trained by Cromwell and North, to whom unqualified allegiance to the state was a cardinal virtue. Loyalty was in his blood. Nor did his services go unrewarded. For the loss of the Augmentations office he was given an annuity of £320 in April, 1554;

421–22. His clerk had suffered a similar fate the previous September for possessing a loose tongue. He had publicly stated that if he were in his master's position he would rather accept imprisonment than meet the large payments required of him by the council. Dasent (ed.), *Acts of the Privy Council*, III, 371.

[76] *Ibid.*, IV, 16, 17, 20, 26. This leniency of permitting him " to take the ayre " was granted in order to insure " the better recovery of his helth."

[77] *Ibid.*, 54. See also pp. 75, 76, 91.

[78] *Ibid.*, 188, 375.

[79] Froude, *History of England*, VI, 279.

he was created baron of Thame, and shortly thereafter, upon the queen's marriage, was made lord chamberlain to Philip of Spain. As sheriff of Oxfordshire he presided for the crown at the trial and execution of the three Protestant martyrs, Cranmer, Latimer, and Ridley, and in various ways served the queen as friend and councillor. He had also befriended young Elizabeth before and after her accession and, as lord president of the council of Wales, retained her favor until his death in October, 1559, as a distinguished son of Oxfordshire.[80]

Other officers of the dissolved Court likewise remained active ministers, to render valuable service to the state after 1554. Several of them, in fact, held permanent positions in the Exchequer, where their intimate knowledge of Augmentations methods proved particularly useful. Undoubtedly the persistence with which those practices and procedures continued was in large part due to their influence.

---

[80] To many, Williams is best remembered for the free school and small almshouse founded by him at Thame, where he and his wife are both buried.

CHAPTER NINE

THE AUGMENTATIONS AS AN ADMINISTRATIVE AGENCY

HE COURT OF AUGMENTATIONS WAS SET UP PRIMARILY AS A court for the administration of crown land and property acquired from the church, and it remained so to the end. Originally its jurisdiction was exclusively over the possessions of the dissolved monasteries, and added later were those of the chantries and other religious institutions appropriated by the acts of 1545 and 1547. As enumerated in the statute of erection these possessions included " all the Manours Meases [1] Landes Tenementes Rentes services Tithes Pensions Porcions advousions patronages and all hereditamentes apperteynyng or belongyng to any the said Monasteries Priories or other Religious Houses," as well as " the good catells [chattels] plate stuffe of Household dettes money stokk store and other what soever profite and commoditie gyven graunted or appoynted to the Kinges Magestie." [2] These initial properties were supplemented from time to

---

[1] A messuage was that portion of land used as a site for the dwelling house and its various appurtenances. In general usage the term messuage would include a curtilage and possibly an orchard, garden, and adjacent buildings, such as a mill or dovecot.

[2] 27 Henry VIII, c. 27, " An Acte establisshinge the Courte of Augmentacions," secs. i and v, S. R., III, 570, 571. The second Act of Dissolution enumerated thirty-three specific properties of the religious houses which were turned over to the Augmentations: manors, lordships, granges, lands, tenements, meadows, pastures, rents, reversions, services, woods, tithes, portions, pensions, parsonages, appropriate vicarages (i. e., a benefice annexed to a religious corporation), churches, chapels, advowsons, nominations, patronages, annuities, rights, interests, entries, conditions,

time by other categories of crown estates or revenues, such as queen's lands, purchased lands, exchanged lands, attainted lands, and various miscellaneous revenues arbitrarily assigned to the Court. The latter group included debts, fines, money prested, profits from the butlerage, and other similar items. Finally, the whole problem of compensating the displaced monastic personnel was dumped into the lap of the Augmentations. In the performance of this function the Court became an important governmental bureau of pensions as well as an administrative revenue department.

Administratively the Court was an admixture of duchy and Exchequer principles and practices already conventionalized by usage. Sprung from the need of the overburdened administrative system unable to adapt itself to the demands of the rapidly expanding national revenue, it was actually something of an innovation. Prior to 1536 the landed revenues of the crown were all paid into either the Exchequer, the Duchy Chamber of Lancaster, or the office of general surveyors. Historically those three departments had been responsible for "the order, survey and governance" of all the revenue of the nation, particularly that which was derived from land. The oldest of the three, the Exchequer, was chiefly concerned with the ancient farm of the shire, the *firma comitatus* of the sheriff, and the customs and parliamentary levies which had always been paid into it. Almost as time-honored, but not nearly as old, was the duchy, charged with administering only the Lancastrian revenues and possessions of the crown. When the monasteries were dissolved, a practical compromise between the Lancastrian palatinate and the Augmentations had been agreed on, by which control of monastic lands was divided according to the geographical location of the houses. Monasteries lying within the county palatine were to remain under the jurisdiction of the duchy.[3] All other houses were assigned to the Court of Augmentations, with the exception of those founded by the earlier dukes of Lancaster, which by royal discretion could be awarded to either one department or the other. This, of course, was an impossible situation, in view of the fact that the twenty-five monasteries originally so founded had acquired during the course of years possessions that were scattered throughout the realm.[4] It was apparent from the beginning that the two administrations would

---

commons, leets, courts, liberties, privileges, franchises, and other hereditaments. "An Acte for dissolucion of Abbeys," sec. iii, *S. R.*, III, 734.

[3] The statute erecting the first Court of Augmentations, sec. xxiv, *S. R.*, III, 574.

[4] The duchy had also acquired certain rights of appointment of corodians and of patronage over other houses. A few of this original group had been dissolved prior to 1536. Somerville, *History of the Duchy of Lancaster*, I, 287–88, 289.

WARRANT to the treasurer of the Augmentations for money paid to the keeper of the privy purse for the king's own use, 1537.
Manchester Papers, G. D., 15/19.

(Plate 3)

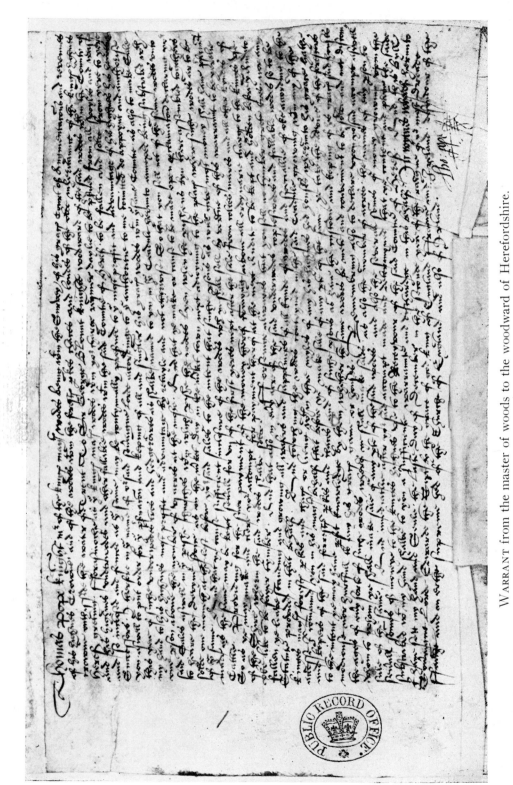

WARRANT from the master of woods to the woodward of Herefordshire.

Augm. Office Misc. Books 461 fols. 1 1d

(Plate 4a)

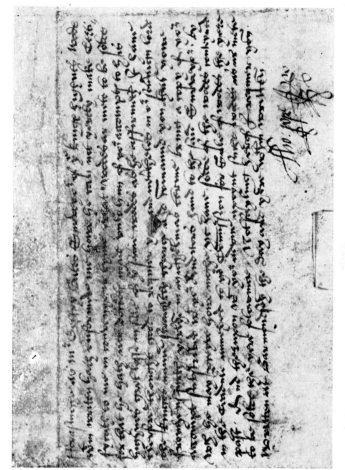

Note on dorso of the warrant.

(Plate 4b)

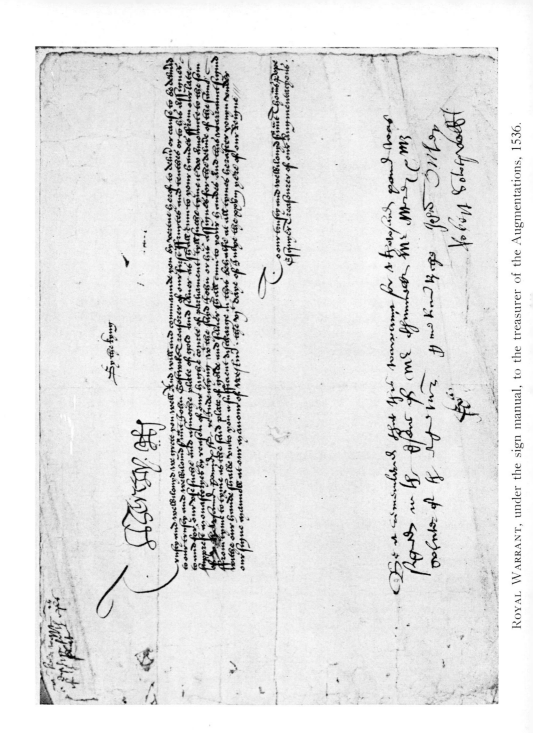

ROYAL WARRANT, under the sign manual, to the treasurer of the Augmentations, 1536.

(Plate 5)

soon conflict under such a complicated arrangement. Only mutual agreement could settle the controversy satisfactorily.

A settlement was finally arrived at in 1536, but not before considerable friction had arisen. During that year the chancellor of the duchy, Sir William Fitzwilliam, was authorized to assume charge of all the suppressed monasteries which owed their foundations to the dukes of Lancaster, in accordance with the statutory plan of division of Dissolution property.[5] However, it was the Augmentations rather than the duchy which apparently supervised the division.[6] That, of course, was eminently practical, since the latter institution had taken no part in the Dissolution proceedings outside its own jurisdiction of Lancashire.[7] According to the directions to the chancellor and council of the duchy, a new schedule of houses to be dissolved was authorized, which would be signed by the king; in other words, it was the king and not the chancellor who was to have the ultimate decision as to which houses were to be dissolved and which continued. Likewise, detailed provisions concerning livings, pensions, and disposition of the movable property of the monasteries were set forth.[8] These articles, twenty-one in number, were submitted to John Onley, the attorney of the Court of Augmentations, for comment and advice before being implemented. Onley's interpretations were entirely satisfactory, it seems, for the duchy decided to adopt the same order and procedure as that being used by the Augmentations.[9]

[5] D. L., Miscellanea, 41/12/10. A draft commission, undated, directing the chancellor of the duchy to take over the possessions of all the dissolved religious houses in the palatinate of Lancaster and of such houses founded by the dukes of Lancaster in the duchy. Four sheets. On the duchy of Lancaster records, see (P. R. O.), *Lists and Indexes*, No. XIV. Among the thirty-six bundles of documents in this " Miscellanea" are many items for the reign of Henry VIII.

[6] D. L., Miscellanea, 41/12/11. Articles concerning the dissolution of religious houses in the county palatine of Lancaster. This paper of four pages was prepared by the clerk of the duchy, under the supervision of the Augmentations.

[7] Meanwhile, duchy commissions were organized for the survey and suppression of religious foundations in that county. Disputed questions regarding the confiscation and disposal of controversial monastic property were frequently referred to the officials of the Augmentations, since their court was considered to be the higher authority on all Dissolution problems. Monastic possessions thus acquired in Lancashire were designated as "the augmentations of the Duchy." Somerville, *History of the Duchy of Lancaster*, I, 292.

[8] Signal fires and warning bells formerly maintained by the monasteries as a means of alerting the population of the marches " during troublesome times " were to be continued. D. L., Miscellanea, 41/12/11.

[9] *Ibid.*, 41/12/12, 13. " The Answers & advyse of John Onley esquyer the kynges attorney of his Courte of Augmentacions to certeyn artycles & doubtes concernyng thorder of matters & causes for the dissolucion of certeyn religious houses w'in the countie palatyne of Lanc." The document is undated but was probably presented during the first half of 1537, since Onley died in November of that year and was succeeded in the attorney's office by Robert Southwell.

Thus the question of control of monastic lands within the county palatine was settled. The real problem was to determine what lands came under duchy administration by virtue of their original charters of foundation.

This question was eventually resolved in a conference of the representatives of the two courts held at Westminster on July 5, 1536. It was agreed that the duchy should suppress and administer all houses within the county palatine, including " thorderyng bothe of their landes & tenementes goodes & cattalles," whereas the Augmentations would control all monasteries on other duchy lands even if they had been founded by the dukes of Lancaster.[10] Full responsibility for monastic debts, pensions, and property leases was accorded to the duchy officials, and special safeguards were set up to guarantee uniformity of administration. In general, the practices already established in the Court of Augmentations prevailed. In order that the records of the two courts might be kept intact, the Augmentations officials agreed to certify the true value of all duchy foundations dissolved and to turn over to the duchy auditors all such rentals, books, and accounts, and other records and writings relating directly or indirectly to the monasteries in question.[11] Crown approval was given to the unofficial conference on the following July 11, when a special royal warrant confirmed the conclusions of the meeting.[12] With the general support of the crown the Augmentations seems to have won most of the arguments in the controversy, with the duchy actually securing only five houses, of which Furness, acquired in 1540, was the most valuable.[13] Chantry possessions lying within the palatinate were administered by the duchy court, but proceeds from the sale of such lands went to the Augmentations until 1552, and afterwards to Sir Edmund Peckham as special crown treasurer.[14]

In other ways, too, the Augmentations was soon calling the tune before it was piped. From its very inception the Court had come into conflict with the department of general surveyors, whose constantly

[10] " A Remembraunce of the Articles agreed betwene the Chauncellors of the Duche of Lancaster & of the Augmentacions at a metyng to gether at the Whythall at Westm. in the Kinges Court ther." Sir Richard Rich, chancellor; Sir Thomas Pope, treasurer; and John Onley, attorney, represented the Augmentations; Sir William Fitzwilliam, chancellor; John Coningsby, receiver-general; William Coningsby, attorney; John and Thomas Burgoyne and Robert Heneage, auditors; and William Heydon, clerk, sat for the duchy. D. L., 5/6, fols. 204*d.*–205.

[11] All the evidence suggests that the agreement was strictly observed, both in the appointment of commission surveys and in the transference of monastic records. Cf. the case of the abbeys of Furness and Whalley, *L. and P.*, XII, pt. 1, no. 896.

[12] D. L., Miscellanea, 12/7, no. 39. Warrant from the king to the chancellor of the duchy confirming the principles agreed on at the conference.

[13] On particular aspects of the controversy, see p. 215 ff., *supra*.

[14] *Cal. Pat. Rolls, Edward VI*, II, 57; IV, 354, 390; V, 184, 411.

growing jurisdiction was bound to encroach upon its own. Although the general surveyors had not been given any monastic land or property per se, it, nevertheless, had acquired a considerable amount under the principle of attainder. All lands and property accruing to the crown by the feudal prerogative right of attainder had been brought under its control. These " attainted lands " came to include numerous monastic estates, since attainder of the heads of important religious houses was one of the more successful instruments of suppression.[15] About a dozen of the larger monasteries fell into this category, of which Jervaulx and Bridlington in Yorkshire, Barlings and Kirkstead in Lincolnshire, Reading in Berkshire with its dependent cell of Leominster priory, Herefordshire, and the ancient abbey of Glastonbury in Somersetshire were the most important.[16] The net revenue from all such possessions, however, was not very much, totaling only about £8,282 annually.[17] Complete surveys of them, comparable to those of the Augmentations, were made by the general surveyors, but the older monastic unit of administration was retained rather than the county unit plan adopted by the former court.[18] In addition to these lands, they also, from time to time, gained portions of Dissolution property from the subsequent attainder of ministers and nobles who had been awarded extensive holdings from the church property. Before his execution in 1540 Cromwell, for example, obtained possession of the abbeys of Lewes, St. Osyth, Launde, Michelham, Modenham, and Alcester, which reverted to the crown upon his attainder.[19]

The Dissolution surveys under the direction of Cromwell were conducted independently, more or less free from the interference of the

[15] The general surveyors got independent jurisdiction over attainders by 14 and 15 Henry VIII, c. 15 and 33 Henry VIII, c. 39. *S. R.*, III, 228–30, 879–92.

[16] Most of these monastic estates in the north were acquired as a result of the attainders following the Pilgrimage of Grace. To the list of houses under the administration of the general surveyors' office should be added Lenton priory, Nottinghamshire, St. John's monastery, Colchester, Essex, Whalley in Lancashire, Woburn abbey, Bedfordshire, and the Cistercian abbey of Sawley (or Salley) in Yorkshire.

[17] Savine, *English Monasteries on the Eve of the Dissolution*, Appendix, 270–88 (Table of Monastic Income).

[18] See, for example, the declaration of the lands belonging to the late attainted abbey of St. John's at Colchester in 1539. Egerton MS. 2164; *L. and P.*, XIV, pt. 2, no. 778; XV, no. 939.

[19] John Rither was receiver-general for the attainted lands of Cromwell, paying his receipts into the king's chamber. Some of the properties were quite valuable, Lewes in Sussex and St. Osyth in Essex being worth £922 and £677 net respectively. One scholar has estimated that Cromwell and his nephew together received monastic lands representing a total revenue of almost £200,000 in modern values. Hughes, *The Reformation in England*, I, 328, n. 2. A list of the lands of Cromwell is given in the Ministers' Accounts, S. C. 6 (Henry VIII)/923.

revenue courts, although an attempt was made to have a court representative on the commissions that took the surrender of houses referred to their charge. Thus Richard Pollard, one of the general surveyors of crown lands, was a prominent commissioner for the survey of Bridlington, Glastonbury, Jervaulx, Reading, and other abbeys which fell under the jurisdiction of the Court of Survey.[20] In both institutions, however, the administrative procedure was similar, with the striking exception of the unit system of estate management perpetuated by the Court of Survey until 1547. Nevertheless, this difference was fundamental, based as it was on the older feudal concept of honorial unity. Tenurial groups of land acquired since 1485 had never been broken up, so that such ancient entities as Cornwall, Chester, Wales, and attainted lands were each still considered, for administrative purposes, as unbroken wholes, even though they might be geographically dispersed.[21] When the monastic possessions were added to this latter category they were retained as separate groups of " attainted lands," managed as distinct monastic units. Revenue from the scattered estates of each dissolved monastery was collected by local officials who paid in to the receiver of that particular unit. These particular receivers sent their revenues to one of the general receivers of attainted lands who sent all collections to the treasurer of the king's chamber, as receiver-general for the entire court.[22]

As conceived by Cromwell, there was to be in the future a clear-cut distinction between the original revenues of the crown and those occasioned by the Reformation. According to his plan the Exchequer would continue to look after the accustomed revenues of the shires, along with the parliamentary levies, while the widely dispersed hereditary estates of the crown—the ancient demesne lands of England and the revenues resulting therefrom—would be divided between the duchy of Lancaster and the office of general surveyors. Fundamentally both agencies were administrative crown land departments and ill-equipped to handle the great influx of supplementary revenue that constantly flowed in. The Court of First Fruits and Tenths and the Court of Wards and Liveries were erected for separate sections of these revenues, primarily the non-

---

[20] *L. and P.*, XII, pt. 2, nos. 92, 144, 234, 432, 1083; XIV, pt. 1, no. 324; pt. 2, nos. 171, 531.

[21] Preserved among the State Papers is an interesting document for the 1530's describing the subordinate agents who were held responsible for the lands under the administration of the Court of General Surveyors. S. P. 1/67, fols. 32–36. Cf. Stowe MS. 554, pt. 1, Receipts of the Treasurer of the Chamber.

[22] Tristram Teshe and Thomas Hall were receivers-general of attainted lands in Yorkshire and Lincolnshire respectively. Teshe was succeeded by James Nedeham in June, 1544, who surrendered the office to Thomas Sternhold the following year.

landed. All the more recent land acquisitions, including even lands acquired by purchase and exchange which had heretofore been under the general surveyors, were allocated to the Augmentations. In contrast to the older departments it was unhampered by tradition and bureaucratic ways. Mobile in form and organization, it was easily the most adaptable of the revenue courts. There is every evidence that Cromwell intended it as a departure from the ancient pattern, at once a model for other institutions to follow and an experimental laboratory in which different procedures and techniques might be reviewed and tested.

As observed earlier, the most radical departure in Augmentations practice was the adoption of the county unit system which broke up the original feudal and ecclesiastical land groupings. Under such a plan, however, local estates were frequently still kept intact, each with its own particular set of ministers. Since the Augmentations lands were by no means evenly distributed geographically, the number of field supervisors required varied from area to area. Of these the county auditors and receivers were the most important in safeguarding the royal interests. Consequently, their work was apportioned according to regional or sectional districts, set up arbitrarily as groups of counties, to each of which were asigned an auditor and a receiver. Thus, the officials in these seventeen administrative districts, fifteen in England and two in Wales, constituted the regional bureaucracy of the Court.

This arrangement was an improvement over the honorial system, being at once simple and practical. Moreover, it eliminated the duplication of offices which already had become a major weakness of the expanding government. Finally, it increased the efficiency of central control from Westminster. Selection of honest, capable receivers and auditors practically guaranteed a smoothly running machine in each district. Nevertheless, however significant the change, the basic evils of concurrent jurisdiction in local administration remained unremedied. There were still too many crown officials. In addition to Augmentations ministers each district had a number of other administrative agencies performing similar services and duties. Prior to 1547, for example, there were royal auditors and receivers for the Exchequer, the duchy of Lancaster, the office and later Court of General Surveyors, and the Court of Wards. In Yorkshire, which alone constituted an Augmentations district, there were several other auditors and receivers, not to mention innumerable collectors of purely local rents and revenues. Hugh Fuller and Leonard Beckwith were respectivaly particular Augmentations auditor and receiver for the Yorkshire district; overlapping their jurisdiction were the Court's auditor and receiver of purchased lands and the queen's officials for the revenues of her lands lying in that county.[23]

The Court of Wards was organized along similar lines under a system of county feodaries, though it had but one auditor and one receiver-general for the entire realm.[24] The office, and later Court, of General Surveyors, however, maintained a number of special financial ministers in the north of England. As supervisory ministers, Philip Lentall, auditor, and Tristram Teshe, receiver-general, had general oversight over all attainted lands in the north, but each administrative unit also had its own Yorkshire representative. Thus there was an auditor and receiver for that county representing Buckingham lands,[25] Stanley lands, Richmond lands, March lands, Cromwell's or Essex lands, Exeter lands, Beaumont lands, Suffolk lands, Spencer lands, Bridgewater lands, Berkeley lands, Northumberland lands, Wolsey's lands, Fermor lands, Bedford lands, and Salisbury lands. In the case of special lands and property in Yorkshire, acquired as a result of the Dissolution (besides those houses situated in the county), most of the larger monasteries in the country had property there.[26] In some instances special auditors and receivers were maintained for former monastic units in the county.[27] Finally, both the General Surveyors and the Augmentations kept separate ministers for the general revenues accruing from wood sales in the northern districts.

After the merger of 1547 receivers and auditors of the Augmentations were confronted with greater responsibility as a result of the additional lands and revenues committed to their charge. According to the letters patent of erection the second Court of Augmentations was to be provided with eleven receivers and ten auditors, the limits of whose

---

[23] P. 53, *supra.* John Ashton, who died in 1542, was then auditor of purchased lands of which Geoffrey Chamber was receiver; Richard Mody and Richard Dove, jointly, succeeded Ashton as auditors of exchanged and purchased lands. Thomas Twisell, followed by Thomas Bourchier, held the auditorship of queen's lands. A valor of queen's lands for 1542 gives the following receivers (named in the order of their tenure): George Taylor, Wymond Carew, and John Smith. *L. and P.,* XVII, no. 135. Later Carew and Anthony Bourchier were respectively receiver-general and auditor to Catherine Parr. *Ibid.,* XIX, pt. 2, nos. 551, 688, 722.

[24] Two auditorships in the Court of Wards were provided for by statute, but Sir John Peryent remained the sole auditor until near the end of the century. Philip Paris, John Beaumont, and William Dansell were the first three receivers-general of the court. Bell, *Court of Wards and Liveries,* 24–25, 38–43.

[25] Usually these ministers had several counties under their jurisdiction, as in the case of the auditor and receiver of the attainted lands of the duke of Buckingham in Yorkshire, Buckinghamshire, and other counties in England and Wales.

[26] A list of the officers is presented in Augm. Office, Misc. Books 256 and 257. Sixty-six of the dissolved houses were in Yorkshire.

[27] These were especially Barking, Evesham, Glastonbury, Kirkstead, Reading, St. Albans, Sheen, Tewkesbury, Waltham, and Whalley.

circuits were to be set forth in their official appointments.[28] Even before it was fully organized in early January, the auditors were selected in order that they should have time to call in all the revenue records from the ministers of the dissolved courts, and from their accounts draw up new declarations for each district, to be delivered to the incoming receivers.[29] As actually set up the country was divided into twelve districts rather than the ten originally planned, of which ten were in England and two in Wales. Since the lands and revenues of the duchy of Cornwall were taken over intact, the full complement of district officials for the Court consisted of eleven auditors and thirteen receivers.[30]

AUDITORSHIPS IN THE SECOND COURT OF AUGMENTATIONS

Circuit	Auditor
1. Bedfordshire, Berkshire, Buckinghamshire, and Oxfordshire	John Pickerel (Pickerell, Pikerell, Pykarall)
	John Thompson (Thomson)
2. Cheshire, Derbyshire, Lincolnshire, and Nottinghamshire	William Rigges (Ridge, Rigge)
3. Gloucestershire, Hampshire, and Wiltshire	Richard Mille (Milles, Myllys)
	Thomas Mathew
	John Hornyold (Hornolde, Hornewolde)
	William Kenyet (Kyneat)
	Thomas Mathew
4. Essex, Hertfordshire, Middlesex, and London	*Thomas Mildmay
	Brian Taylor

[28] Pat. Rolls, 38 Henry VIII, pt. 5, mems. 16, 24. "And to thentent that the lymyttes of euery of the offices of the saide tenne Auditours of the reuenues of this Courte and the landes tenementes and reuenues to be appoynted to euery of thofficers of the same offices maye be the more perfectly and certenlye knowen. We haue thought good to deuyde the same offices into tenne circuites the lymyttes Counties and places of whiche circuites shalbe expresed . . . in the lettres patentes of the same Auditours." *Ibid.*, mem. 23.

[29] *L. and P.*, XXI, pt. 2, nos. 534–35, 749. The forthcoming appointments of the auditors and receivers to the Court were not made formally until the summer and autumn of 1547.

[30] There were, of course, twelve auditors' circuits, but Thomas Mildmay held two of them as well as being auditor for the duchy of Cornwall. See the accompanying lists of auditors and receivers. For the auditors pensioned in 1554, see Cotton. MS., Titus. B. iv, fols. 139–40. As an economy measure the privy council in 1551 advised curtailing the number of Augmentations auditors, but the recommendation was never implemented. Dasent (ed.), *Acts of the Privy Council*, III, 316.

Auditorships in the Second Court of Augmentations (*cont'd.*)

Circuit	Auditor
5. South Wales	William Hamerton John Thompson
6. North Wales	John Perte Thomas Tyndall John Thompson
7. Cumberland, Lancashire, Northumberland, Westmoreland, the bishopric of Durham, the archdeaconry of Richmond, and the Isle of Man	*Richard Hutchinson (Huchenson, Hucheson, Hochenson) Jointly { Anthony Rone (Rouen, Roue) / John Swift
8. Herefordshire, Leicestershire, Northamptonshire, Rutland, Staffordshire, Shropshire, Warwickshire, and Worcestershire	*John Hanby Jointly { John Hanby / John Swift John Swift
9. Cornwall, Devonshire, Dorsetshire, and Somersetshire	Henry Leak (Leek, Leeke, Leke) John Hornyold
10. Yorkshire	*Hugh Fuller [William Fuller, deputy] Anthony Rone
11. Cambridgeshire, Huntingdonshire, Norfolk, and Suffolk	Thomas Mildmay Brian Taylor
12. Kent, Surrey, and Sussex	Thomas Everard Thomas Wiseman Jointly { Thomas Wiseman / John Thompson John Thompson
Duchy of Cornwall	Thomas Mildmay

Note: Thomas Mildmay held two circuits, Four and Eleven, for most of the period. At the date of annexation to the Exchequer there were but eight auditors—namely, Anthony Rone, John Swift, John Hornyold, Brian Taylor, John Pickerel, William Rigges, Thomas Everard, and John Thompson (possibly William Kenyet in Third Circuit); Thomas Mathew was reappointed auditor in the Third Circuit after midsummer, 1553.

* Auditors who had served in the first Court of Augmentations.

PARTICULAR RECEIVERSHIPS IN THE SECOND COURT OF AUGMENTATIONS

District	Receiver
1. Bedfordshire, Berkshire, Buckinghamshire, and Oxfordshire	George Wright
2. Cheshire, Derbyshire, Lincolnshire, and Nottinghamshire	*Robert Goche
3. Gloucestershire, Hampshire, Wiltshire, and the Isle of Wight	*Richard Paulet Chidiock Paulet
4. Essex, Hertfordshire, Middlesex, and London	*Robert Chester Edward Hastings
5. South Wales	Mather Herbert Jointly { Mather Herbert / John Perte Jointly { John Perte / William Wrightman William Wrightman
6. North Wales	John Salisbury
7. Cumberland, Lancashire, Northumberland, Westmoreland, the bishopric of Durham, the archdeaconry of Richmond, and the Isle of Man	*Richard Bunny (Bunney, Buny) Thomas Newnham (Newneham) Richard Allerton
8. Herefordshire, Leicestershire, Northamptonshire, Rutland, Staffordshire, Shropshire, Warwickshire, and Worcestshire	William Sheldon
9. Cornwall, Devonshire, Dorsetshire, and Somersetshire	*John Ailesworth
10. Yorkshire	*Richard Whalley Jointly { Richard Whalley / John Fisher John Fisher
11. Cambridgeshire, Huntingdonshire, Norfolk, and Suffolk	*John Eyre
12. Kent, Surrey, and Sussex	Anthony Aucher Jointly { Anthony Aucher / John Garraway (Garrawey) John Garraway

PARTICULAR RECEIVERSHIPS IN THE SECOND COURT OF AUGMENTATIONS
(*continued*)

District	Receiver
Duchy of Cornwall	*Sir Thomas Arundell
	Henry Gates
	Jointly { Edward Waldegrave, John Cosworth (Goseworth)

NOTE: By constitutional provision there were eleven districts in the second Court, but Wales was divided, thus making twelve districts. In 1547 the duchy of Cornwall was taken from the Court of Survey and continued to be administered as a separate honorial unit. It did not constitute a thirteenth district.

* Receivers who had served in the first Court of Augmentations. Sir Thomas Arundell's services with the first Court had been in the seventh district.

The duchy of Cornwall was the only unit of the former Court of General Surveyors to retain honorial organization under the renovated Augmentations; therefore, the revenues from its scattered lands and properties, lying both within and without the county of Cornwall, were not collected by the county receivers but paid to a receiver-general for the duchy in continuation of past practice. No reason was given for this exception. The constitution of the Court simply ordained that all the revenues of the duchy would be " aunswered accompted and payed in the sayde Courte . . . by suche speciall Officers and Ministers thereof as heretofore hathe been or hereafter shalbe appoynted for the same so long as they shall remayne and be in thandes or gouernaunce of vs our heires or successours." [31] Accordingly, the whole hierarchy of duchy officials, of whom the most important in relation to the new administration were the receiver-general and the auditor, was brought under the control of the Augmentations.

Like the duchy of Lancaster, it held an entrenched position at court, its officials being influential royal favorites who probably held out stoutly against any attempt to eliminate their jobs. Chief among them was the Catholic Sir Thomas Arundell, second son of Sir John Arundell of Lanherne, who was the most important person in all Cornwall at that time.[32] Sir Thomas had been receiver-general of the duchy since 1533,

[31] Pat. Rolls, 38 Henry VIII, pt. 5, mem. 21. However, the treasurer of the chamber continued to receive the revenues of the duchy of Lancaster and the Court of Wards. *Ibid.*, mem. 22.

[32] On the great Arundell family, "the chief mainstay" of Catholicism in Cornwall, see *D. N. B.* and A. L. Rowse, *Tudor Cornwall, Portrait of a Society*

having succeeded his father in a life appointment.[33] Upon his attainder in 1552, Sir Henry Gates, a gentleman of the privy chamber rising rapidly in the royal service, was appointed to the receivership, which he retained until his own attainder in 1553. He was followed by Edward Waldegrave and John Cosworth, who held the office jointly until the dissolution of the Court.[34] During this entire period the auditorship of the duchy was held by Thomas Mildmay, who by combining three offices in one person became the most important auditor in the administration.[35]

With a concentration of lands in Devon and Cornwall the duchy unit of crown estates constituted an important segment of Augmentations possessions. In addition to such large areas as the manor of Kennington in Surrey, the honor of Wallingford [36] in Berkshire, and the Scilly Isles, parcels of the duchy were also found in other counties, principally Essex, Dorsetshire, Hertfordshire, Lincolnshire, Norfolk, Northamptonshire, Oxfordshire, Somersetshire, Warwickshire, and Wiltshire.[37] The

---

(London, 1941), 83, 219–22, 342. The elder Sir John Arundell and his two sons, John, who as the elder succeeded him, and Thomas, were all influential ministers of the crown. However, Sir Thomas Arundell was never chancellor of the Augmentations as Rowse states. *Ibid.*, 86.

[33] *L. and P.*, I, pt. 1, no. 54(81); II, pt. 2, no. 756; VI, no. 300(14). John Caplin was his deputy receiver. Augm. Office, Misc. Books 346, fol. 42*d.* Arundell also had held a receivership in the southwest counties under the first Augmentations for eight years. See p. 49, *supra.*

[34] Arundell was executed on February 26, 1552, and Gates was appointed the following day. Sir Henry escaped execution through a royal pardon. *Cal. Pat. Rolls, Edward VI*, IV, 386; *Philip and Mary*, I, 55, 85, 206. Augm. Office, Misc. Books 349, fol. 15*d.*

[35] The auditorship carried a fee of £71 8*d.* plus allowances of £37 8*s.* 8*d.*; the receivership paid £41 in addition to £40 in portage fees and £8 14*s.* for extra allowances. The salaries of local officials in the duchy were paid by the receiver-general. A book of all the offices under the crown, S. P. 12/221, pp. 5*d.*–7.

[36] The honors of Wallingford and St. Valery were detached from the duchy by Henry VIII, but lands of equal or greater value were given in compensation, particularly the Cornish estates of the attainted marquis of Exeter and numerous possessions of the dissolved priories of Launceston and Tywardreath. 32 Henry VIII, c. 53, abstracted in *L. and P.*, XV, no. 498(34).

[37] A thorough study of the administrative history of the duchy is badly needed. Its entire development is sketched in Sir John Doddridge, *The History of the Ancient and Modern Estate of the Principality of Wales, Duchy of Cornwall and Earldom of Chester* (London, 1630), but with the exception of Rowse's *Tudor Cornwall* and his brief article, "The Duchy of Cornwall," *Nineteenth Century*, CXXI (January, 1937), 43–56, little information on the changes in the duchy during the sixteenth century is available. There are a number of records, accession books, acquittances, and miscellaneous manuscripts relating to the duchy preserved among the Augmentations records in the Augmentation Office of the Exchequer. The administrative history of the duchy for a part of the seventeenth century is briefly presented in Mary Coate, "The Duchy of Cornwall: Its History and Administration, 1640–1660," *Transactions of the Royal Historical Society*, Fourth Series, X (April, 1927), 135–69.

annual receipts from these properties as paid into the treasury of the Court averaged over £2,500 under Edward VI, a fair proportion of Augmentations revenues.[38]

Except for this single discrepancy, the general pattern of Augmentations organization was the same in all parts of the country. So similar, in fact, was the development in each county that a few examples of different historical " types " of crown property will illustrate the general procedure. Unlike other revenue departments, a striking uniformity in land administration was maintained, however great the historical differences. In the management of monastic and chantry lands the earlier patterns of church administration were similar, if not practically identical. In other cases, however, previous organizational procedures influenced Augmentations practices. Particularly interesting is the distinct organization apparent in the administration of the revenues of the Scilly Isles.

The ancient islands of Scilly just off the coast of Land's End were historically part of the earldom of Cornwall,[39] although the Blanchminster family had been in possession of the earldom lands in the Isles since the beginning of the fourteenth century. The church lands and revenues which came to the crown after 1536 included at least one priory on Tresco Island, formerly a dependent cell of Tavistock abbey in Devonshire.[40] In 1547, when the duchy administration was taken over by the Augmentations, the temporal control of the islands was in the hands of Sir Thomas Seymour who was later charged with having acquired these " strong and dangerous Isles of Scilly, bought of diverse Men." [41] When, as lord high admiral, he was sent to suppress privateer-

---

[38] Under the second Court the receipts were £3,177 13s., £2,178 2s. 7d., £1,847 18s. 7d., £3,203 8s. 11d., £3,745 3s. 7d., and £866 1s. 8d. Augm. Office, Treas. Rolls of Accts., Nos. 4–8. Rowse estimated the salaries of duchy officials at £138 3s. 4d. within Cornwall. Rowse, *Tudor Cornwall*, 82. As I understand it, Dietz infers that the receipts from the duchy continued to flow into the king's chamber during this entire period, instead of being transferred to the Augmentations. Dietz, *English Public Finance, 1558–1641*, 408.

[39] An extension of the promontory of Land's End, this chain of some forty small islands is situated about twenty-five miles west by south from the Cornish coast. Altogether they have a total area of about 6.3 square miles, but only five of the larger islands are habitable, namely, St. Mary's, Tresco, St. Martin's, St. Agnes, and Bryher.

[40] The churches and lands in Scilly had been granted to Tavistock abbey by Henry I. The priory of St. Nicholas had been maintained there in order to oversee the distant possessions of the monastery. H. P. R. Finberg, *Tavistock Abbey* (Cambridge, 1951), 15, 220.

[41] William Borlase, *Observations on the Ancient and Present State of the Islands of Scilly* (Oxford, 1756), 110. The islands represented little economic value to the crown at the time. Ralph de Blanchminster as proprietor had held them under the duchy in the mid-fourteenth century, as of the honor of Launceston, at an annual rent of 300 puffins. Under Henry VI the rent had declined to but 50

ing in the Scillies he came to terms with the pirates there in a manner mutually advantageous to all parties concerned. He seems to have retained possession of the islands with a share of the spoils of the pirates in return for which he conveniently ignored their illegal operations. At any rate, the Scillies reverted to the crown, along with his other possessions, when he was attainted and executed in 1549.[42] Thus civil power and ecclesiastical jurisdiction, as well as lands and revenues, were reunited in the Augmentations under duchy administration. By this time definite steps had been taken toward the fortification of the Isles, for which purpose lead from dissolved monasteries and chantries in Cornwall had been furnished by the Augmentations. As in all defense measures, new garrisons brought additional expenses, and usually it was the Augmentations treasurer who was called on to furnish the extra money.

In February, 1549, Thomas Godolphin was appointed " chieftain " of the people and captain of the garrison of the Isles of Scilly where certain fortifications were to be erected for the protection of the inhabitants and " all others tradeng and passing that waye." [43] On November 9 of the same year the Augmentations set up a commission of three to survey the islands, with the intent of leasing the land to farmers who would be encouraged to establish permanent homes there and develop their holdings. As might be expected, however, the primary objective was to strengthen defenses rather than to promote agriculture. Although the land at that time lay " waste and voide of habitacion of people," it might be made " very mete for husbandmen ffisshermen and mayners to Inhabite," the preamble of the commission reads, " wherby the Commen Welthe shulde be advaunced and the Countrey there muche

---

puffins, or about 6s. 8d. In 1484 their annual value was estimated at 40s. in time of peace, "in time of war nothing." Seymour bought them, apparently, from the descendants of the earlier Blanchminster family. C. C. Vyvyan, *The Scilly Isles* (London, 1953), 25. The authority for Seymour's control of the islands comes from the manuscript copy of the articles against him. Cf. Froude, *History of England*, V, 137; Nichols (ed.), *Literary Remains*, II, 370 ff.

[42] The control of the lands and revenues of the Scillies during this period is difficult to determine. If Thomas Seymour held a formal grant of the islands I have been unable to discover it. However, the tithes and certain rights in the Scilly Isles, formerly belonging to Tavistock monastery, were leased to the receiver-general of the duchy, Sir Thomas Arundell, in June, 1545. These, of course, reverted to the crown upon his attainder. Augm. Office, Misc. Books 217, fol. 68d. H. M. C., *Cal. of Cecil Manuscripts*, pt. 1, no. 184.

[43] *Cal. Pat. Rolls, Edward VI*, II, 250. An accompanying commission gave to him and two others certain rights of jurisdiction over the inhabitants in civil and criminal causes, with treason cases reserved for the privy council. Shortly thereafter Godolphin was ordered to report on conditions in the Scillies to two of the council, Sir Richard Southwell and Sir Edward North, and abide by their directions. *Cal. State Papers, Domestic, 1547–1580*, no. 49, p. 26.

better defended agayne fforren enemyes attempting to arryve there at any tyme." Small farms leased for life or for term of years at favorable rents were the inducements offered.[44] These efforts having met with some success, it was decided to continue the policy along the same lines already established. Some nineteen months later a similar commission was authorized to divide the land into small portions for convenient settlement, each household to be given sufficient land for tillage and pasturage of cattle; the holdings were to be let for twenty-one years at variable rates, the rent being determined by the extent of improvement expected. In this case the commissioners themselves were empowered to lease the land, certifying their grants to the Augmentations, whereas leases under the earlier commission could be made only by the Court.[45]

Meanwhile, the defenses of St. Mary's Isle and the construction of a fort and two blockhouses on Tresco proceeded according to schedule. In June of 1551 one of the commissioners, John Killigrew, was delegated to provide workmen and sufficient materials for the completion of the new fortifications. A later Elizabethan inquiry of 1579 estimated the charge of the Scillies under Edward VI to have been £6,000, with but two of the islands inhabited. Although laborious enclosures of rough land had been made, it was observed that only eighty tenements had been erected. Even so, the tillable ground available did not nearly provide sufficient food for the population which consisted at that time of about a hundred men and their famiiles.[46] An interesting declaration of payments to the Scilly garrison in January, 1554, reveals the size of the military establishment maintained there and the major costs of operation. Thomas Godolphin had just been reappointed captain of St. Mary's by order of the council to serve until further notice, with a house in the old castle, twenty acres of ground rent free, and an annuity of £40. At Tresco John Beauchamp was in charge, commanding seven " good souldiers," with daily compensation plus the profits of the island. Recommendations for improvement emphasized the need for more ordnance " for that is the thing that putteth strangeres in feare." For

[44] Augm. Office, Miscellanea, 34/320.

[45] *Cal. Pat. Rolls, Edward VI*, IV, 142–43. John Godolphin and John Killigrew of Cornwall sat on both commissions. Sir William Godolphin joined them in the latter survey. All rents were paid to the receiver of the Augmentations. Strype misdates this commission as being of May, 1551. Strype, *Ecclesiastical Memorials*, II, pt. 1, 466; pt. 2, 203.

[46] *Cal. State Papers, Elizabeth, Addenda, 1566–1579*, p. 559. This report refers to Thomas Seymour as having bought the interest of other holders in not only the lands of the former abbey of Tavistock but also all the islands. As late as the reign of Charles I only four islands were inhabited. An undated parliamentary survey states that the Scillies were then in lease of the crown for thirty-eight years at £40 per year. S. P. 16/520, fols. 53–57.

more than two continuous months during the previous year French and German ships had lain side by side in the harbor, thus creating a situation in which there was " no little a doo to kepe peace by twene them." Pirates from the Barbary coast as well as Spaniards were threatening, and the government was warned that the latter " may ill spare Sullie." [47] These and similar accounts of payments explain why so many early efforts were directed towards the construction of additional fortifications in view of the vulnerability of these and other islands in the event of war.[48]

However interesting, the later history of the Scillies is beyond the province of this study. The Godolphins, members of that ancient Cornish family that figured so prominently in the profitable tin mining of the west country, continued in the administration of the islands, maintaining a connection which, with but few interruptions, was successfully preserved for over two and a half centuries. In 1570 Elizabeth leased the Scillies to Francis Godolphin (later Sir Francis and lord lieutenant of Cornwall for thirty-eight years),[49] after which the increased Spanish menace accelerated the demand for greater protection of such a strategic outpost. It was during this period that the ramparts and Star Castle of St. Mary's, now a hotel, were constructed; likewise, " Harry's Walls," popularly attributed to the reign of Henry VIII, were built about the same time, 1593, as a further protection to the harbor. The parliamentary surveys of the seventeenth century give a full description of the later development of the islands. During the period of the Civil War when the Cavaliers sought refuge there, the attention of the country was again focused on the Scillies as a significant naval base.[50]

[47] " A Declaracion of the paymentes made to the old Garrison of Sullie " for 252 days ending January 31, 1554, together with "a Certificat of theestablishing of the new orders made by the honerable Councell for quallifyng of the . . . former charges and a certificat of the Artillarie and ordenance there, and of thinges other necessaries to be provided." Exch., Accounts Various, 63/8 (twelve pages).

[48] At the same time similar efforts were being made to strengthen the defenses of Jersey, the largest of the Channel Islands, and the Isle of Wight. On the accounts for the Scillies, see Augm. Office, Misc. Books 259, fols. 90–101; S. P. 10/13, no. 41; and Add. MS. 25300, fols. 1–8 for the reign of Mary. After the dissolution of the Augmentations such expenses were chiefly defrayed by the Exchequer.

[49] Indenture of a lease of the Scilly Isles to Francis Godolphin dated December 14, 1570, *Cal. State Papers, Domestic, 1547–1580,* p. 397.

[50] No research history of the Scillies has ever been attempted. The dozen or more longer accounts that exist are drawn mostly from legend and fiction as recorded by the earlier chroniclers. Among the better known are Borlase, *Observations on the Ancient and Present State of the Islands of Scilly*; John Troutbeck, *A Survey of the Ancient and Present State of the Scilly Islands* (London, 1794); Alexander G. Gibson and Herbert J. Gibson, *The Isles of Scilly* (London, 1925); E. L. Bowley, *The Fortunate Islands* (St. Mary's, Isles of Scilly, 1945); Geoffrey Grigson, *The Scilly Isles* (London, 1949); and Vyvyan, *The Scilly Isles.*

In contrast to the Scilly Isles, the monasteries and chantries under the control of the Court fell into a conventional pattern. Normally the lands and properties were sold, given away, or leased for term of years to the king's profit, but occasionally one of the houses was kept intact and its lands administered as a unit by the Augmentations. Such was the ancient Benedictine abbey of Abingdon in Berkshire, which for almost sixteen years remained a problem child of the crown. Although possessed of a venerable history, this great abbey, like so many of the larger monasteries, had declined greatly in importance during the period immediately preceding the Dissolution. Economically it was certainly not very prosperous, its net income being reckoned at about £1,876 10s. per year.[51] The visitation of the monastery had been made by one of Cromwell's commissions under the direction of the gossipy archdeacon of Buckingham, Dr. Richard Layton, although the actual survey of Abingdon was made by the Augmentations officials. Together the two reports offer a fairly clear view of the status of the abbey on the eve of its surrender.

The abbey was earmarked by Cromwell for suppression as early as 1537, though no definite action seems to have been taken during that year. However, on the seventh of February following, the royal commissioners John Tregonwell and William Petre were advanced over £600 by the Court to be spent by them on bringing about its dissolution.[52] On the ninth it surrendered, and before the end of the month the Augmentations officials had completed their survey and tendered a full report to the crown.[53] Though usually optimistic in his reports and predisposed towards the preservation of monastic houses, Rich's detailed description of the abbey's condition was anything but encouraging. The buildings were run down and in need of repair, he noted; even the abbot's lodgings were uninhabitable. The king had considered the possibility of converting the property into a royal residence, so the report

[51] Savine, *English Monasteries on the Eve of the Dissolution*, 288. According to Gasquet, the house had been beset with financial difficulties, expensive litigation, and annoying interferences from the crown and Cromwell. Gasquet, *Henry VIII and the English Monasteries*, II, 293-94. A sketch of the earlier history of the abbey is given in Dugdale. According to Speed, its gross income was £2,042 2s. 8¾d. Dugdale, *Monasticon Anglicanum*, I, 505-30.

[52] Augm. Office, Treas. Rolls of Accts., No. I, pt. 1, mem. 12d. Petre and Tregonwell were among the more active visitors of the larger monasteries, procuring the surrender of twenty houses in 1538. *D. N. B.* Philip Paris was also associated with them in the dissolution of the abbey.

[53] Report of February 22, 1538, by Sir Richard Rich, chancellor of the Augmentations, to Cromwell. S. P. 36/41. This report is abstracted in *L. and P.*, XIII, pt. 1, no. 332. The commission was composed of Rich and the solicitor of the Augmentations, assisted by the Court's auditor and receiver for Berkshire, William Cavendish and John Danaster.

was written with that prospect in view. This idea, however, was definitely rejected, as requiring a far greater outlay than Henry had anticipated. Rich pointed out that there was no land really suitable for an adequate park and that, if one were to be set up among the more fertile fields on the south side of the Thames, the town itself would likewise decay. With an eye to the royal profit he advised spoliation, concluding that a " great part may be defaced and yet sufficient left for his graces contentation."

Well might Henry have viewed with satisfaction the valuable lands and possessions of the monastery lying not only in Berkshire but also in Oxfordshire, Buckinghamshire, Wiltshire, Dorsetshire, Somersetshire, Gloucestershire, Hertfordshire, Worcestershire, Middlesex, Northumberland, and elsewhere in England, Wales, and the marches.[54] A further survey of all the woods belonging to Abingdon listed a total acreage of 1,197, with 12,712 trees valued at £2,948 15s. 4d.[55] Ten years later the lead remaining on the buildings after the church and cloister had already been stripped clean was estimated as amounting to forty-seven fothers.[56] At the then current price in England of about £4 per fother, the lead alone had a salable value of £188.

All the evidence indicates that the officials of the monastery offered no resistance to surrender, which perhaps explains the liberality accorded the inmates. The abbot and prior both fared quite handsomely, as did the subprior and the twenty-four monks. The abbot, Thomas Rowland,[57] was awarded a pension of £200 per year, in addition to a lifetime residence at the manor house on the Cumnor estate, where he lived in as great if not greater comfort than formerly. The prior, Richard Eynsham, received £22 and the rectorship of Sunningwell; the subprior, £20; the other pensions varied from £5 6s. 8d. to £8.[58]

At the time of surrender, Sir Edward Seymour was steward of the monastery and Edmund Ashfield was receiver.[59] As soon as the monas-

---

[54] See *Eighth Report of the Deputy Keeper of the Public Records,* Appendix II, 7; *L. and P.,* XIII, pt. 1, no. 242.

[55] (March 18, 1538.) The woods of Abingdon monastery. *Ibid.,* XIII, p. 1. no. 544.

[56] P. H. Ditchfield and William Page (eds.), *A History of Berkshire* (London, 1906–24), II, 59.

[57] Rowland was the abbot's family name, but he was known to the church as Pentecost.

[58] Agnes C. Baker, *Abingdon Abbey* (published by Friends of Abingdon, 1949), 5; see *First Report* and *Second Report* of the Historical Manuscripts Commission on the town of Abingdon. Four of the monks received £8, seven £7, two £6 13s. 4d., two £6, and five £5 6s. 8d. Augm. Office, Misc. Books 210, fol. 22; 232, pt. 2, fols. 7–11, 136.

[59] Seymour apparently succeeded the duke of Norfolk, who had assumed the stewardship upon the death of John Audelett of Barton in November, 1536.

tery came into the king's hands, John Welsborne, a gentleman of the privy chamber, was appointed Augmentations steward of the Abingdon lands, with a fee of £20 a year, and Oliver Welsborne became bailiff and woodward.[60] John Welsborne had been a member of the commission which took the surrender of the abbey and was appointed keeper of the property until such time as new administration could be set up. His reports to Cromwell and Wriothesley indicate that the king's ministers proceeded with " good forwardness " and that the people of the town were well satisfied with the work of " such wise discreet honest men." Like Rich and others he testified to the poverty of the house, complaining that there was no household stuff left and no place to lodge the Augmentations surveyors upon their arrival. Even the household furniture allocated for his own accommodations had been borrowed. He was able to keep the plate safely in his possession, but a representative of the abbey, William Button,[61] had absconded to London taking with him not only the keys to the exchequer but also the court rolls, rentals account books, and other records of the monastery. Yet, despite such obstacles, Rich and his surveyors discharged their commission with greater dispatch than might have been expected. Welsborne praised the work of the chancellor, adding that he found more honesty in him than was accredited by the common belief of the country. Finally, he observed that he had heard of no one being grieved over the dissolution of the abbey.[62]

Rich found everything at Abingdon in bad condition except the church, which he described as " a great and goodly thing well repaired." After a general view of the possessions of the monastery, which had " the slenderest rentals and accounts ever seen," Rich departed for London with the plate and ornaments, leaving John Danaster and William Cavendish to complete the survey.[63] Meanwhile a Burford merchant by the name of Tucker had asked Rich for permission to establish

---

[60] The appointments are dated December 17, 1539, and October 26, 1538, respectively. Oliver Welsborne was also keeper of the chief messuage, called Manor Place, at Cumnor, parcel of Abingdon lands. Augm. Office, Misc. Books 233, fols. 43, 252; 235, fols. 36, 72. Add. MS. 35818, fol. 19*d*. Thomas Denton was appointed understeward or deputy to John Welsborne. Augm. Office, Misc. Books 235, fol. 11*d*. Welsborne had been serving as keeper of the monastery and site of Abingdon since its dissolution, as well as keeper of Culham manor in Oxfordshire. His formal appointment to those offices is dated January 24, 1539. *Ibid.*, 233, fol. 340.

[61] Button was apprehended in London and lodged in the Tower. He claimed that the possessions of Abingdon were worth 3,500 marks. *L. and P.*, XIII, pt. 1, nos. 332, 379.

[62] *Ibid.*, nos. 260, 268, 284, 285, 305, 325, 359, 403.

[63] *Ibid.*, nos. 332, 341. Some of the ornaments from Abingdon were probably transferred to Wallingford Castle at the request of Dr. John London.

not one but two fulling mills at Abingdon. Tucker, who was said to have employed as many as five hundred workers, was but one of several wealthy English clothiers who were flourishing in the 1530's and 1540's. His petition for the rental of sufficient crown land for the site for his factories was under the circumstances reasonable enough.[64] The records are silent on the future activities of Tucker and the success of his Abingdon project, although a later grant of Edward VI to one of the townsmen suggests that the clothing industry had been encouraged. In March, 1550, a Breton, Francis Owderey, described in the patent as "our cheif workeman of weving of our poldavies and oleroundes [65] in Abingdon," was awarded a life annuity of 8*d*. per day out of the revenues of the Augmentations on the condition that he not only practice the art himself but instruct such people as the crown should appoint in the new craft.

Despite feeble attempts to bolster the town's economy after the Dissolution, Abingdon continued to decline. The truth of the prediction of the Court's surveyor that it was "sore decayed and lyke dayley more to decaye" was soon demonstrated.[66] Breakup of the monastic community proved a serious blow to the townspeople; buildings were torn down, stone and lead shipped away, while locally both trade and markets suffered considerably. The locks and mills were reported so dilapidated by July, 1538, that workmen estimated the cost of repairs to exceed £100. In fact, they advised that if reparations were long postponed the costs would increase and the king's rents remain unpaid.[67] The suppression must have greatly furthered decline, both in industry and in education.[68] The town continued under the rule of ministers appointed by the Court until its incorporation in 1556, but the evidence concerning Augmentations administration there is extremely fragmentary. In November, 1551, a special commission of oyer and terminer was ap-

[64] *Ibid.*, nos. 332, 415. Ephraim Lipson, *The Economic History of England* (London, 1929–31), I, 459, 478, 479.

[65] Breton fabrics which were introduced into England. Poldavy or poldavis was a coarse canvas or sacking, used extensively for sailcloth, and originally woven in Brittany. Oleroundes may have been a corruption of the French rondelettes, which was also an early sailcloth of Brittany. Owderey's grant was dated March 22, 1550, at Leighs, the home of Baron Rich, then lord chancellor. *Cal. Pat. Rolls, Edward VI*, III, 310.

[66] Add. MS. 28666, fol. 152.

[67] In the spring of that year the town was also beset by an attack of the plague, which took a death toll of twenty-six within the month. *L. and P.*, XIII, pt. 1, nos. 444, 484, 1466.

[68] The local abbey school was continued under its former head, a monk, by the voluntary contributions of the townspeople. A. L. Rowse, *The England of Elizabeth* (London, 1950), 493; Arthur E. Preston, *The Church and Parish of St. Nicholas, Abingdon* (Oxford Historical Society Publications, V. 99 [Oxford, 1935]), 290 ff.

pointed to investigate " a treason or commocion " which had developed around Abingdon. On the same day a warrant was directed to the treasurer of the Court to reimburse Sir John Mason, privy councillor and master of the posts, for money paid to certain men of Abingdon who had given evidence in support of the inquiry.[69] The seven members of this commission were all associated with the government of the town.

In March of the following year the chancellor of Augmentations was ordered by the privy council to restore to the town all such lands as had formerly been appointed for the maintenance of two bridges and for the support of certain poor men. This property had only been acquired by the crown a short time before " uppon coullour that the same were within the compasse of thact of Chaunteries." [70] Two years later a further concession was granted to the inhabitants, at the request of their friend and benefactor, Sir John, a loyal native son of the town. A grant of crown land to the annual value of £65 11s. 10d. was appropriated for the repair of a local road and four bridges and for the perpetual endowment of a hospital. Thus was founded Christ's Hospital at Abingdon, with a corporation of twelve governors, of which Mason was appointed master governor for life.[71]

A number of individuals, including some of the Augmentations officials, obtained a share of the abbey's spoils. Of the Abingdon ornaments the king retained three pontifical rings, while two mitres were bought by Thomas Pope,[72] then treasurer of the Court. Much of the land was acquired either through gift or purchase by favorites and courtiers.[73] The site, buildings, and lands of the abbey in Berkshire were granted to Thomas Seymour in 1547, but upon his subsequent attainder were given to Sir John Mason and Sir Thomas Wroth.[74]

In addition to the abbey lands remaining under its control, the Aug-

---

[69] Both commission and warrant emanated from the council and are dated November 21, 1551. The seven members of the commission were Richard Bridges, Thomas Denton, Thomas Vachell, Roger Yong, John Yate, Alen Fetiplace, and Oliver Welsborne. John Welsborne had died in 1550 and was succeeded as steward by his deputy, Denton. Dasent (ed.), *Acts of the Privy Council*, III, 421, 423.

[70] *Ibid.*, IV, 226–27.

[71] Grant of May 18, 1553. The land was held by the corporation by fealty only, in free and common socage and not in chief. *Cal. Pat. Rolls, Edward VI*, V, 142–43.

[72] Augm. Office, Treas. Rolls of Accts., No. I, pt. 1, mem. 3. Later, in 1543, chancellor Audley and Pope were granted various Abingdon lands lying in Gloucestershire and Oxfordshire. *L. and P.*, XVIII, pt. 1, no. 100(10).

[73] In addition to chamber officials, the list included the lord chancellor, Sir Thomas Audley, the duke of Suffolk, and Williams, Pope, North, and John and Oliver Welsborne of the Augmentations. As usual, Cromwell and Rich were besieged with requests for coveted portions of the abbey lands. *Ibid.*, XIII, pt. 1, no. 415; pt. 2, no. 633.

[74] *Cal. Pat. Rolls, Edward VI*, IV, 188; V, 18–19.

mentations gained some chantry property in Abingdon when, in 1547, Edward VI seized the revenues of Holy Cross.

On November 24, 1556, some three years after Abingdon had passed from under the jurisdiction of the Court, the town received its charter of incorporation. Nor had this " ancient and populous town " recovered appreciably from its earlier collapse, if the preamble of the patent can be believed. Still the capital of the county, the town is described as inhabited by a number of poor people; moreover, it had sunk to " such ruin and decay in default of repair of the houses and buildings within it as it is like to come to extreme calamity unless remedy be provided." [75]

With the dissolution of over two thousand chantries and other small religious foundations in 1547, large isolated sections of church property were added to the Augmentations management. This act, however, did not dissolve all chapels, but only chantry chapels, which excluded many that were simply places of public worship dependent on a parish or cathedral church. Chantry chapels were endowed foundations maintaining a priest to chant masses for the repose of some soul, usually that of the original founder.[76] Since the royal commissioners appointed for the survey of all these religious institutions were often over zealous in their pursuit of the crown's interest, numerous disputes arose over chantries claiming exemption under the act. Whether inadvertently or by intent, the commissioners sometimes seized property to which the king had no claim under the law. Such was the situation in the case of the picturesque little chapel of Oakwood, Surrey, originally a chapel of ease to Wotton Church for " þe inhabitants of þe outborders of þe parysshes of Wotton, Okley, Abinger, Rydgewyke, Warnham and Ewhurst in þe county of Surr: and Sussex . . . . whiche dwell very ffar dystant from þe parryshe churches," which came into the possession of the crown in 1547.[77] At the end of the following year the property was sold to Henry Polsted of Chilworth and William More of Loseley, both of Surrey; included in the grant were various closes, woods, and lands formerly belonging to the chantry, together with the chapel and chapel house, wherein had lived some priest to serve as curé " tyme out of mynd." [78]

---

[75] *Cal. Pat. Rolls, Philip and Mary,* III, 380–86. A translation of the charter is printed in full in Bromley Challenor (ed.), *Selections from the Municipal Chronicles of the Borough of Abingdon, 1555–1897* (London, 1898), 1–36.

[76] Free chapels—that is, those founded by the king—were included in the statute and, therefore, became confiscatable.

[77] Oscar Stanway, *The Story of Okewood Church* (Dorking, 1940), 3–4. The earlier spelling " Okewood " was always used in the sixteenth century records. In 1547 the advowson of Wotton Church, including Oakwood Chapel, was in the hands of Henry Owen and his wife, Dorothea.

[78] *Cal. Pat. Rolls, Edward VI,* I, 280–84.

The Augmentations records show the priest at that time to have been Hamlet Slynge, who for the loss of his office was awarded a pension for life of five marks or £3 6s. 8d.[79] After the sale of the chantry land and property the chapel was automatically closed, though the building was neither defaced nor torn down. In renovated form it still stands to serve the rural Surrey community and grace the beautiful countryside.

Deprived of their convenient place of worship the people of the local community appealed for restoration of the chapel. The petition to the Augmentations was presented in 1552 by thirteen of the leading yeomen of the village in the name of all other inhabitants to the number of three-score householders. The case for the restitution was strongly set forth; undoubtedly the loss of the priest had been a blow to them:

> Syns wch tyme there hath bene no servyce vsed ne Celebrate in thesaide Chappell wherby thesaide Inhabytantes w^t ther yougth & ffamylyes ar lyke to growe into an intollerable ignorance of almyghty god & of his holy worde & of the dutye to our soueraign lorde the kynge booth to the great daunger & perell of ther Sowles & hynderance of Cyvyll order to be vsed emong all good Subiectes. In Consideracion wherof hit may therfore please your good Mastershipes thpremisses considered to awarde order & decree somme certen yerely pencion as by your Masterships shalbe thought convenyent . . . towards the ffyndynge of a preest to celebrate in thesaide chapple for the ease of thesaide inhabitantes . . . & your saide Orators shall dayly pray for the preservacion of your good Mastershippes longe to contynewe w^t increas of moche Worship.[80]

Upon the receipt of the petition, presented " humble wyse " in obvious good faith, the chancellor of the Court proceeded to appoint a special commission to investigate the situation locally and report on the facts of the case.[81] Some weeks later, on April 26 of the same year, an inquiry was held, at which time a number of local witnesses were

[79] The pension was assigned by Walter Mildmay and Robert Keilwey, executive commissioners appointed for the implementation of the act. P. 174, *supra*. Slynge died four years later just before the Augmentations was annexed to the Exchequer. Augm. Office, Proceedings of the Court of Augmentations, E. 321/45.

[80] Undated petition of the yeomen of Oakwood to the Augmentations. Augm. Office, Misc. Books 128, fol. 9.

[81] The commission conformed to the general pattern of Augmentations practice in that it consisted of only a few members, one of whom represented the Court. John Carell, Henry Polsted, and Nicholas Leigh were local citizens; William Goodwin, the county surveyor of Surrey, was chosen because of his official position. He probably acted as chairman of the commission.

examined and depositions taken by the commissioners.[82] As leader and spokesman for the group the sixty-year-old yeoman, Thomas Hill, submitted full testimony on all the controversial points involved in the case, the other witnesses simply verifying the evidence presented by him. It was shown that there was from the beginning a churchyard of about half an acre attached to the chapel which had always been kept as a burial ground, the local priest, appointed by church wardens, receiving a yearly stipend from the issues and profits of certain lands as " assured by dyvers good people in olde tyme towardes þe fyndynge of þe saide preest." Furthermore, no fewer than sixty-eight neighboring householders and villagers living within a radius of six miles from the church were dependent on the curate for all their spiritual needs. In view of the complete agreement of the evidence, the decree of the Augmentations was in full support of the original petition.[83]

The decision was rendered during the Easter term of 1552. By court order of May 28 the chapel, churchyard, and " litell house with a Gardeyne adioynyng," were restored, together with an appropriation to be used for the employment of a new curate. Accordingly, five marks per year were assigned to the chapel as a pension for the endowment of a community priest who was to receive the arrears of that sum since the death of Slynge, the last incumbent. The church wardens were given jurisdiction over the priest and his annuity, the stipend being turned over to them twice yearly by the Augmentations receiver for Sussex.[84] It should be observed, however, that this decree did not restore any of the chantry lands which had already passed from the crown by alienation. Nor was the decree immediately implemented. Within a few months the Court was incorporated into the Exchequer, where the Oakwood decision and related evidence became buried in the mass of records transferred to the Exchequer Court. If not actually lost, the decision was conveniently forgotten during the rush of events of the new reign.

The reaction of the inhabitants of Oakwood to the failure of the Exchequer to execute the Augmentations decision is unknown. Nevertheless, hope was not abandoned, for they renewed their efforts in 1560

[82] Nine questions were submitted: (1) What was the chapel called and where was it situated? (2) Was it a chapel of ease? (3) Did it have a churchyard and a cemetery? (4) Was there a priest for the conduct of religious services? (5) Was he furnished with a house? (6) If there were such a curate, who appointed him? (7) What lands or pension had been appropriated for his support? (8) Who was the last incumbent, and when did he die? (9) How many householders " do resorte comanly to þe saide Chappell for dyvyne service " and how far away from their own parishes do they live? " Interrogatoryes towchinge the byll of Okewode Chappell in the Countye of Surrey." Augm. Office., Misc. Books 128, fol. 9.

[83] *Ibid.*, 105, fols. 231–32.

[84] Augm. Office, Proceedings of the Court of Augmentations, E. 321/45.

with a second petition requesting that the original order be complied with. This was eight years after the case had first been settled, a fact which suggests that some action may have been taken earlier, especially since Queen Mary was anxious to restore as much church property as possible. However, if complaints of Exchequer negligence or inefficiency were made the records have not survived. The Elizabethan petition was presented by a local Oakwood citizen who had been one of the six witnesses to testify before the Augmentations in 1552. His deposition explained that the annuity provided for had not been paid nor had a chapel curate been maintained; consequently, the community had suffered accordingly, with no one " to celebrate Divine Service and Sacrament to the excessive damage detriment and grievance of the subjects of the Lady the Queen dwelling near the said Chapel." Being favorably received, the petition was given prompt action. A search of the Augmentations " Rolls and Accounts " unearthed the earlier decree which, however belatedly, was finally fulfilled. The regular services under the much emphasized " honest pryeste," which were duly established in 1560, have continued without interruption down to the present day.[85]

However important to the local communities, most of the questions that came under the review of the council of the Augmentations were not of a challenging nature. The normal administrative work of the Court was chiefly concerned with such routine business as hearing petitions, answering inquiries, leasing or selling crown lands, collection of debts or arrears, sale of lead and timber, and supervision of the activities of local officials. Usually the chancellor of the Augmentations was in constant attendance at the meetings of the privy council, where he sometimes received personal orders or instructions regarding the business of the Court. Under normal procedure, however, instructions were transmitted by messenger. The council always kept close oversight of all the administrative work throughout the kingdom, exercising particular watch over each of the revenue institutions.[86] More formal directives were

---

[85] Interestingly enough, the original annuity of £3 6s. 8d. established by the Augmentations decree is still a constituent part of the church's income. For some unknown reason, however, the original sum has been reduced to £2 17s. 8d. In 1853 the chantry was reorganized as a consolidated chapelry, which converted it into a parish church. At that time the patronage of the benefice was vested in the Evelyn family of Wotton, Essex, in whose hands it still remains. Stanway, *The Story of Okewood Church*, 8–9.

[86] Originally Henry VIII had taken a personal interest in the Dissolution, assigning " with his owne hande in the bryeff certyfycat whiche houses shalbe dissolved & whiche not," but in most later instances royal instructions were received through the privy council. D. L., Miscellanea, 41/12/12. Informal instructions concerning the disposal of lands were frequently received by the Court. Harl. MS. 283, fol. 326.

presented in written form, either as warrants or official orders explaining the extent and nature of assignments, and usually addressed to the chancellor and council of the Court. Warrants from the king or council covered all types of command, from purely routine appointments and court procedure to such important matters as reparations, defense, or the payment of the king's troops at Berwick and other garrisons. Hundreds of these warrants are preserved among the miscellanea of its records.[87] A few examples will illustrate the varied nature of Augmentations activities.

[May 29, 1543] A warraunt aswell to the Chauncellour of the augmentacions to make furth [*sic*] such l[ett]res and writinges as shalbe expedient for thestablishing of a perpetuall lecture of dyvinitie to be reade in Oxforde, erected and founded by the ladye Margarete late Countisse of Richemonde & Derbie. As also to the Treasaurer of the same for the tyme being to paye yerely to the Reader of the same xiij^{li} vj$s$. viij$d$. for his stipende together w^t tharrerages nowe due.[88]

Sometimes the warrants were in the form of commissions, as in the warrant of April 12, 1547, directed to the chancellor and chief officials of the Court:

Whereas Sir Martin Bowes, knight, one of the undertreasurers of the Mint in the Tower, by command of Henry VIII received money, plate and jewels from Sir John Williams, knight, and others, to be paid out in the king's affairs, and also received money out of the treasures of the Courts of Augmentations and First Fruits and other sums " due him of the Mint " as appears by indenture dated 16 May 24 Henry VIII, of which money, plate and jewels Sir Martin has heretofore declared no account:

To call Sir Martin Bowes or his executors to make account for all money, plate and jewels received by him as above since 1 April 24 Henry VIII (the account due for the said Mint since 28 May 36 Henry VIII when he was appointed one of the undertreasurers and anything concerning the Mint since Sir Edmund Peckham,

---

[87] A change in procedure was instituted in May, 1547, when the general warrant " conteigning the hole of the saide summes to be made furth in parchement " was authorized as a substitute for a series of individual warrants for specific payments. It was thought that such general warrants, " passed under his Graces Signet in fourme accustomed," would be " a more ample and effectual warraunte and discharge " for the treasurer of the Court. Dasent (ed.), *Acts of the Privy Council*, II, 88–89.

[88] D. L., Miscellanea, 42/133, fol. 231.

knight, has been high treasurer of the mints only) and to deliver any surplus to the Treasurer of Augmentations; and to give the said Martin or his executors his discharge and a duplicate of his account signed with their hands.[89]

Or, in the case of ordinary directives, the records of the privy council are filled with such items as the following:

[Windsor, November 15, 1540] Lettres wer sent to the Treasourer of thaugmentacions for the dispeche of suche diett money as was appoynted to the Bishop of Wynchestre et Sir Henry Knyvet [90] Knyght by a warrant directed unto them for that purpose, et also to delyver to the sayd Bishop such money as was to be sent over now at this present to Calais for the payment of the garrison there.

[Hampton Court, January 15, 1541] A lettre was sent to the Chauncellour of the augmentacions aunswering to his lettre sent unto the Counsail and requyring him to set at libertye such of Pates servauntes as he and Mr Pollard had before examyned.[91]

[Greenwich, April 5, 1541] A lettre was sent to Mr Chancelo^r of thaugmentacions signifyeng unto him that the Kinges Ma^te had appointed Sr Richard Engist prist to be one of the prebendaries at Rochestre, and therfor willed him to take such ordre therin as the said prist might enjoye his Highnes graunt accordingly.[92]

[December 2, 1552] A lettre to the Chauncellour of the Augmenta- cions to certefy hither what annuitie James Morrys and William Morris have had owt of that Courte,[93] wherefore it was payed unto them, and why they had not a patent thereof as other at that tyme had.[94]

[June 11, 1553] A lettre to the Chauncellour of thaugmentacions to examine a byll therewith sent hym, exhibited by Sir John Rus-

[89] *Cal. of Chancery Warrants, 1547–1553,* 398; cf. *Cal. Pat. Rolls, Edward VI,* I, 138–39. Bowes original appointment was dated May 27, 1544. Pat. Rolls, 36 Henry VIII, pt. 7, mem. 22.

[90] Stephen Gardiner, bishop of Winchester and chancellor of the university of Cambridge, was appointed ambassador extraordinary to Charles V in November, 1540. He was accompanied on this mission by Sir Henry Knyvett (Knevet or Ganvet), a gentleman of the privy chamber.

[91] Nicholas (ed.), *Proceedings and Ordinances,* VII, 83, 116. The men referred to were Edmund Dokery, Robert Gifford, William Langland, and other servants of Richard Pate, bishop of Worcester; they were examined by Rich of the Aug- mentations and Richard Pollard of the Court of Survey, on January 12, 1541.

[92] *Ibid.,* 168.

[93] On the case of James and William Morice see Chapter Six, p. 170.

[94] Dasent (ed.), *Acts of the Privy Council,* IV, 183.

sell,[95] touching certaine landes concealed from the Kinges Majestie, and to cause justice to be ministred therein, so as his Highnes may be restored to that is his right [*sic*].[96]

Conversely, the chancellor and council of the Augmentations transmitted their own orders by warrant of the Court:

[1536] Maister Treasorer—I praye you to deliu[er] vnto Sir Roger Wheler & Sir Richarde Stanfilde late canons of the Monasterye of Derford late desolvyd—ffifte thre shillinges and foure pens by waye of Reward and this bill signyd w^t my hand shalbe ¬nto you a sufficient discharge in this behalfe at all tymes herafter. At London the xj^th daye of Nouember [97]

> Your lovyng frendes
> Robert Southwell
> Richard Riche
> John Onley

Similarly, at the beginning of Edward's reign the treasurer of Augmentations was authorized by warrant of the Court to advance whatever money was necessary to provide for the adequate storage of its records and to appoint a supervisor for the execution of the project:

[August 16, 1547] Forasmuche as we have appoynted this bearer Mighell Robert Jaynour w^t all possible diligence to make and sett up at Westm[inster] certeyn presses chestes boxes and other thinges of waynescott for the saufgarde sure keping and a bestowing of the kinges ma^ties evydences and recordes whiche nowe dispersidlie remayne in sundrye places of the realme and shall forthewith be conveyed thether . . .[98]

Hugh Losse, already a royal surveyor, was appointed overseer of the project, and within a few months the "evydence howse" at Westminster was completed. All receipts for Losse's various expenditures on the building may not have been preserved, but those which are

[95] At that time Lord Russell was keeper of the privy seal. He was reappointed to that office by Mary on November 3, 1553.

[96] Dasent (ed.), *Acts of the Privy Council*, IV, 286.

[97] This order is attached to the receipt of Wheeler and Stanfield for the payment. Manchester Papers 15/14–15. At the time of its visitation in October, 1535, Commissioner Layton described Durford in Sussex, which he called "Dirtyford," as being deeply in debt and in great decay. Gasquet, *Henry VIII and the English Monasteries*, I, 268.

[98] Augm. Office, Miscellanea, 314/19. Robert Jenour was probably a relative of Richard Jenour, formerly clerk of the Court of General Surveyors and sometime "generall clerke" of the first Court of Augmentations.

extant show him to have spent a total of at least £50 on the Augmentations recordhouse.[99]

Not least of the Court's contributions to later generations was the preservation of land surveys of the royal demesne. Beginning with the Dissolution all lands and property assigned to it were systematically surveyed, and these surveys, filed with the clerk of the Court, came to constitute the most important permanent land evaluation records of the period. The chief object of the original surveys was to determine the exact amount of revenue available from each unit of property, but a great deal of miscellaneous data was also included in them. Although they were neither as elaborate nor as uniform as the parliamentary surveys of the seventeenth century, the comprehensive reports of the Tudor surveyors included essentially the same material. The most complete " books of survey " usually gave not only the full boundaries, extent, and value of the premises but also the worth and location of growing timber, perquisites and profits or other particulars relating to the various estates, and miscellaneous data pertaining to customs and rentals of the manors or lands examined.[100] After 1547, when the records of the Court of General Surveyors were acquired, the Augmentations possessed full and accurate descriptions of most crown possessions. To these were added, from time to time, extra surveys by special warrant, such as the certificate required in 1541 " of all honors, castles, manors, mansions, sites of houses, forests, parks, chaces, and lodges " within the jurisdiction of Anthony Bourchier, auditor of the Court of General Surveyors, together with the names and fees of all their keepers, their allowances for repairs, and such profits as might be gained by selling superfluous houses or by enclosing and renting some of the parks.[101] Sometimes, however,

---

[99] On the back of the warrant is a receipt for £20, dated August 18, 1547, for the construction of the storehouse. On November 7 and 15, Losse receipted payments of £20 and £10 to be used for the same purposes. *Ibid.*, 314/19.

[100] Some of the sixteenth century surveys are almost as complete as those described by S. J. Madge in his study of the land surveys of the next century. The typical parliamentary survey contained seven distinct sections: (1) perquisites and profits of the manor surveyed; (2) particulars of all premises, either in possession or known to be demised; (3) calculations of the value of timber on the estates; (4) enumeration of patents, leases, and especially reprises; (5) memoranda relating to manorial customs, commons, boundaries, and waste lands; (6) rentals of manorial tenants with an indication of their premises; and (7) a comprehensive abstract of the values of the whole survey, summarizing its characteristic features. Sidney J. Madge, *The Domesday of Crown Lands* (London, 1938), 141. The Tudor surveyor was seldom as thorough, but he frequently presented as much information without formally organizing it into such precise categories. The comprehensive abstracts were usually omitted.

[101] *L. and P.*, XVII, nos. 116, 223. Sometimes pressure had to be exerted to induce obdurate tenants to yield the desired information. *Ibid.*, XIV, pt. 2, no. 108.

the surveys were no more than mere " certificates of value," designed simply to state the annual income or current rental of a particular piece of land.

The surveys were usually made by the local officials of the Court,[102] but the chancellor and members of the council might assist in special assignments. Such was the case in 1538, when Rich and Pope, assisted by Richard Pollard of the Court of Survey and Richard Southwell, a receiver for the Augmentations, spent a full three weeks in surveying lands in Essex, Suffolk, and Norfolk [103] or when required surveys were taken by Augmentations officers of newly attainted property. In fact, council directives to the chancellor requesting immediate surveys of this or that constituted a normal part of executive routine. In these special assignments both the attorney and solicitor of the Court assisted, being allowed extra remuneration for such labor.[104] Some of these surveys are of special interest, as the unique *Liber Valorum Particularium* which gives the only complete record of crown lands under control of the Court of Survey in 1542 on the eve of its erection,[105] and the minute description of all the lands and revenues in the town and marches of Calais as administered by the Augmentations.[106] Most surveys, however, were made for a specific purpose, usually to determine exact boundaries and measurements or to ascertain the increased value of particular pieces of land at the time of alienation.

Some of the confiscated property remained in royal hands for only a short while, though officials seldom knew in advance which portions of the crown estates were to be alienated. In 1540 Henry VIII's decision to implement the Bishoprics Act of the previous year [107] brought to the

[102] Normally this work was done by the county surveyors, but not infrequently the auditors and receivers were ordered to certify annual values or other particulars.

[103] The lands in question were those of Danby, the duke of Suffolk, and the priory of Butley. Cecilie Goff, *A Woman of the Tudor Age* (London, 1930), 48, 110–11.

[104] The fifteen volumes of Books of Payments for the Augmentations, Misc. Books 248–262, contain numerous references to such surveys. In 1541 the attorney, Walter Henley, spent forty-two days in surveying Augmentations lands and property. *Ibid.* 250, fol. 47.

[105] The value of the court's revenue in each town and county is listed, the highest being Yorkshire with an annual revenue of £5,235. The total revenue for the fifty-one counties and cities was £38,080 6s. 1d. Add. MS. 32469.

[106] A survey of Calais and the Marches, made shortly after the Augmentations was annexed to the Exchequer, recorded in two large volumes entitled: " The description of the limytes, waves, rivers, watergangs, and perambulacions and particions of parisshes of the same, by measure from pointe to pointe directed by compas maryne by the Low Countrie measure." Augm. Office, Misc. Books 371 and 372.

[107] An Acte for the King to make Bisshopps, 31 Henry VIII, c. 9, *S. R.*, III, 728. The king was authorized by this act to establish by letters patent as many bishoprics

Court the task of surveying and evaluating the possessions assigned to the newly created sees. Between December, 1540, and August, 1542, six bishoprics were organized around the new cathedral centers of Westminster, Chester, Gloucester, Peterborough, Bristol, and Oxford, with Augmentations lands and revenues assigned to them from the circuits of various auditors.[108] At the beginning there was some dispute over the collection of the tenths from these lands, which by the original patents had been allocated to the Augmentations instead of the Court of First Fruits and Tenths. The bishops were "double chardged," it was argued, "for that the Paimentes therof in oone of the saide Courtes is no dischardge in thother, contrarye to the true entente and meaning of the Kinges Hieghnes." This controversy was terminated in 1543, however, when these revenues were transferred permanently to the latter court.[109] Nevertheless, no appreciable portion of the confiscated monastic property was rededicated to either religious or educational purposes. Only one further appropriation deserves mention—the endowment of Christ Church, Oxford, and Trinity College, Cambridge. Revenues to the clear annual value of £3,840 were assigned for the support of these institutions, together with back revenues paid by the treasurer of the Augmentations.[110] Appointments of scholars for the two colleges were made either by the university authorities or by the chancellor of the Augmentations.[111]

Periodic surveys likewise played a significant role in the administration of woods and forests. Prior to the erection of the Augmentations the supervision of the chases, parks, and woodlands on the royal estates

---

or collegiate and cathedral churches as should be considered necessary. Unfortunately for the church only a third of the number of sees contemplated were ever founded. See *L. and P.*, XIV, pt. 2, nos. 428–30.

[108] Erected by letters patent of December 17, 1540, August 4, 1541, September 3, 1541, September 4, 1541, June 4, 1542, and August 30, 1542. *Ibid.*, XVI, nos. 333(2), 379(30), 1135(4–5), 1226(2, 4–5, 6–8, 10); XVII, nos. 443(9), 881(3, 25–26), 1154(60). The Westminster bishopric, the first of these creations, was annexed to the diocese of London on April 1, 1550. *Cal. Pat. Rolls, Edward VI,* III, 171.

[109] An act requiring these bishops to pay their tenths into the Court of First Fruits and not into the Court of Augmentations. 34 and 35 Henry VIII, c. 17, *S. R.*, III, 916.

[110] Augm. Office, Misc. Books 415, fols. 87–105. The evaluations were made by auditors of the Court: £2,200 for the college of Oxford and £1,640 for Trinity at Cambridge. *Ibid.*, fols. 118, 119–20, 123. On the original foundations of these colleges in December, 1546, see *L. and P.*, XXI, pt. 2, nos. 475(65), 476(9), 647(25, 26), 648(25, 43, 51), 770(12).

[111] It is interesting to note that Christ Church, Oxford, grew out of Cardinal Wolsey's college which had been reconstructed as "King Henry the Eight's College." This ecclesiastical foundation was in turn suppressed in 1545 to help endow the new college. When originally suppressed, Cardinal College lands and property had been taken over by the Augmentations.

was in the hands of special " surveyors of woods," officials closely associated with the development of, first, the department and, later, the Court of General Surveyors. Organized in 1521 and reconstituted two years later as a separate office under the general surveyors of crown lands, the surveyorship of woods became a major agency, the chief function of which was evaluating timber lands in order that wood sales might be made to the king's profit. This work was soon important enough to warrant the introduction of special auditors of wood sales, as under Cromwell's competent guidance profits from the sale of timber became a regular source of crown revenue.[112] After the acquisition of the monastic property by the crown, an office of general surveyor of woods was also set up by the Augmentations to oversee the vast woodlands of the dissolved houses.[113] From that point forward the increase in the sale of timber was more pronounced, while in both courts wood sales constituted a regular item of revenue.

The amalgamation of the two institutions in 1547 brought a general expansion in administration and with it the enlargement of the woods office. The traditional forest division of lands north and south of the River Trent was adopted, with two Court officials, a master of woods and a surveyor of woods, assigned to each district. The masters of woods, " masters of the woodes of the fforestes parkes chaces and landes of the olde inheritaunce of our Crowne," were empowered to determine " what woodes are mete to be solde " and, upon certification of the surveyors of woods and by the advice of the chancellor and general surveyors, to conclude all sales of " vnderwoodes and coppice woodes " within the survey of the Court. However, before any wood could be sold, the local woodwards were required to advertise the sale by " open proclamacion " in the parish wherein the woods lay and in the nearest market town adjoining in order to guarantee full publicity to the proceedings, " Prouyded alway that they make no sales of any Oke likely to serue for tymbre without our specyall warraunt." [114] Similarly, wood sales

---

[112] These profits, as were all the revenues of the Court of General Surveyors, were paid into the chamber. On the evaluation of the earlier office of master or surveyor of the king's woods, see Richardson, *Tudor Chamber Administration, 1485–1547, 259–73.*

[113] Most of the monasteries had large sections of wooded areas, a great number of which included valuable timber. The suppression accounts show many individual houses to have been in possession of several hundred acres of woods, evaluated according to acreage or in terms of the age and number of salable trees. For example, Peterborough abbey had over 800 acres of timber land, while a number of other monasteries held over 400 acres each. On the woods officials in the first Augmentations, see Chapter Four, p. 108 ff.

[114] The constitution of the second Court of Augmentations. Receipts from the sale of timber were collected by the local woodwards and paid directly to the

in the royal forests could be made only with the approval of the justices of the forests, notice being given to the local keepers.

The masters of woods were the formal heads of the office, determining policy and directing the sale of timber; under them the surveyors of woods, assisted by the local woodwards, were responsible for the routine forest administration. They made periodic surveys of all the woods lying within their respective jurisdictions, filing "perfect bookes" thereof with the Court to remain as a future record.[115] Likewise, they investigated cases of spoliation, trespass, and similar misdemeanors, assessing fines up to the value of forty shillings for petty violations. Fines and punishment for damages in excess of that amount were reported to the masters of woods, who by the authority of the chancellor and general surveyors of the Court were permitted to adjudicate such cases.

A great deal of the surveyors' time was occupied in making surveys of woodlands as they came into the king's hands and in running special surveys whenever parts of the timber or wooded areas were sold. The surveyor of woods for the first Augmentations was steadily engaged in surveying the woods of dissolved monasteries, for which work he received 10*s.* per day for riding costs and other expenses in addition to his regular salary of £20 per year.[116] Under the second Court the surveyors' salaries were increased, but they still received liberal allowances for their "charges and travaile."

Since the southern region of England was far more heavily wooded than the northern, the woods administrators south of the River Trent were given priority ranking in the Court and considered senior to the officials in charge of the north. When the second Augmentations was organized Thomas Pope and Geoffrey Gates were appointed respectively master and surveyor of woods in the south, while the corresponding positions north of the Trent were awarded to Robert Heneage and John Arscot. Superior in both training and experience to his colleagues, Pope immediately became the responsible head of the organization. Heneage was likewise an able civil servant, having served the crown as auditor in the duchy of Lancaster and as master of woods in the Court of

---

county receivers of the Court. The masters of woods were required to keep yearly books of all wood sales and to certify the same to the county auditors that they "maye be the better hable to charge the woodwardes accordinglie." Pat. Rolls, 38 Henry VIII, pt. 5, mems. 22–23.

[115] It was particularly stressed that no wood sales should be permitted under any conditions until the timber was "well and perfitlie surveied." *Ibid.*, mem. 23.

[116] Regular payments to the surveyor of woods for routine surveys varied from a few pounds up to £119. Augm. Office, Treas. Rolls of Accts., No. 1, pt. 2, mem. 22; Misc. Books 249, fols. 33, 35, 39, 40, 41; 250, fols. 37, 39, 44, 46; 251, fols. 71, 77, 78; 252, fols. 49, 61–62; 253, fol. 49; 254, fols. 61, 91, 93; 255, fol. 79.

General Surveyors.[117] On the other hand the two surveyors of woods were less experienced. Although a barrister of some note, Arscot seems to have held no office prior to 1547. Shortly after his appointment to the Augmentations he was made a surveyor of the north parts for the duchy of Lancaster, which position he held until his death in 1558. Gates, a professional surveyor but with no social prestige, was carried over from the earlier Court. Upon his death in 1550 he was replaced by Sir Francis Jobson of Colchester, formerly a particular receiver.[118] Meanwhile, Pope continued in office until 1549 when he resigned in favor of Sir John York,[119] who was shortly to become undertreasurer and later master of the mint in the Tower. As the principal master of woods Pope had headed the woods department for some six or seven years, having served the first Augmentations since 1543 as sole director of timber sales and woods management.[120] It was he rather than his successor who first introduced an orderly system of centralized control for all the woods and forests that came under the Court's jurisdiction.

Augmentations records show Pope to have kept in close contact with the surveyors of woods and the local woodwards under them, over whom he exercised rigid supervision. After 1543, when some protection of the national supply of timber was afforded by law,[121] surveys were

---

[117] Heneage resigned his auditorship of the duchy in 1546 in favor of his deputy, John Purvey. He served the Court continuously as master of woods until the abolition of the office, when the Augmentations was merged with the Exchequer. Arscot likewise continued in the surveyorship of the north for the same period.

[118] Jobson's patent was dated September 4, 1550, at which time he was still receiving a pension of £83 6s. 8d. for the loss of his receivership in the first Court. Under Edward VI he was knighted and made keeper of the crown jewels. At the beginning of Mary's reign he was pardoned for implication in the Lady Jane Grey plot. He remained in the woods office until the abolition of the Augmentations. This Sir Francis should not be confused with the Francis Jobson of Ireland, who surveyed the forfeited Desmond estates in Munster. *D. N. B.*; *Cal. Pat. Rolls, Edward VI* (see index); *Philip and Mary*, I, 224, 412. Augm. Office, Misc. Books 257, fol. 48d.; 260, fol. 45d.; 261, fol. 55d.; Exch., Accounts Various, 76/36, fols. 73, 74.

[119] The original appointments of the two masters and two surveyors were made on January 2, 1547, with fees of £100 each. Augm. Office, Misc. Books 218, fols. 2–3d. Most of the later patents of appointment, however, are neither extant nor recorded in the enrollment books of the Augmentations. York had certainly assumed office by October 1, 1549, by which time he was directing the felling of timber in the temporalities of the bishopric of London that came into the possession of the crown when Edmund Bonner was deprived of the see. *Ibid.* 260, fol. 45d.; 261, fol. 55d.; Dasent (ed.), *Acts of the Privy Council*, II, 400, 405; III, 49 *passim*. York's work in the woods office was overshadowed by his secret missions abroad and by his financial activities as merchant and master of the mint. *D. N. B.*

[120] Pope was first mentioned officially as master of woods in the treasurer's payments for 35 Henry VIII (1543–44). Augm. Office, Misc. Books 252, fol. 62. The master's clerk received a salary of £10 per year. *Ibid.* 259, fol. 55.

[121] "An Acte for the preservacion of Woodes," 35 Henry VIII, c. 17, *S. R.*, III,

systematically conducted, of which detailed accounts were presented to the central office at Westminster to remain as a permanent record.[122] Memoranda, attachments, receipts, lists of purchasers of wood or underwood, expense accounts, certificates of trees felled, petitions for allowance of fees, and warrants of authorization for the sale of particular timber were carefully preserved by the county woodwards as pertinent evidence to be submitted at their annual audits.

Complaints of tenants were forwarded to the Court by the local officials to determine the pleasure of the council before answers were given; surveyors endorsed woodwards' requests for payment of their fees; bailiffs wrote for enough lumber to repair mills on the king's manors; and woodwards tendered specific reports on woods that might profitably be marketed: " Please it your lordship to be aduertised that in little Okeley hall in Essex there is a parcell of wood . . . mete to be felled and solde this yere, whiche is of xxij yeres grow^t and conteyneth by estimacion viij acres." [123] Instructions to the woodwards included such important items as regulations for timber preservation, precautions to be taken against plundering, enclosures, perambulations, proclamations for sales, and information concerning the final declaration of their accounts. The masters seem to have been given a free hand in their administration, subject only to the execution of orders for the sale or delivery of timber by the chancellor and council of the Court.[124] Pope received regular orders for the delivery of timber for reparations, new constructions, fortifications, brick kilns, and other miscellaneous purposes; many of the bills under the signet contain warrants like the following:

[May 4, 1543] A warrant to Sir Thomas Pope to deliuer to Alexander Zenzano oon of the ryders twentie oakes w^t loppes toppes and berkes out of the parc of Benston and Newburie besides St. Albanes.[125]

977–80. Under the statute, restrictions were imposed on promiscuous cutting of timber by private owners, except by special license. On this act, see Richardson, *Tudor Chamber Administration, 1485–1547*, 273.

[122] Typical of such " fayre bokes " was the survey of woods in Devon and Cornwall made by Geoffrey Gates in 3 Edward VI(1549–50). It is a beautiful account book of forty-seven folios, detailing the extent of each wood, with a description of the age, quality, and value of the timber. Augm. Office, Misc. Books 431.

[123] Augm. Office, Misc. Books 157, fol. 32; 158, fol. 56; 462, fol. 35; *ibid.*, Miscellanea, 314/24.

[124] Similarly, commissions of inquiry concerning disputes over woods or woodlands claimed by the crown were not infrequently referred to the Augmentations and generally included the chancellor, one of the masters of woods, and either the attorney or solicitor. A typical example of such a commission is found in Augm. Office, Misc. Books 458, fols. 21–21*d*.

[125] D. L. 42/133, fol. 235. The Court regularly furnished lumber for public

Doubtless the king's interest in woods was chiefly financial, but Augmentations officials were equally concerned with preserving the timber on the crown estates, if for no other reason than to be able to meet the constant demands for special deliveries of lumber. Local ministers were instructed to " preserve woods from all spoyles and wastes," to take special care of the great oaks, and to fence in all areas where the larger timber had been cut in order to protect the undergrowth from destruction by wandering horses and cattle. Regular schedules of " falleable woodes," which contained specific directions as to the size and nature of the trees to be sold, were submitted to the woodwards, as well as instructions for the issuance of proclamations of sales, to be announced in the nearest churches and market towns at least thirty days prior to the sales. However, care was taken lest the hunting preserves on the royal demesne be jeopardized. No wood within three miles of the king's castles or manor houses was sold until the local crown officials had been consulted to determine if such action would be " hurtfull of any of his graces gayme." [126]

As in the case of the other administrative courts, a serious problem was presented by the negligence of officials in rendering their accounts. Woods were not infrequently sold without authorization, a practice which only the constant vigilance of the Court auditors could prevent. Writing to John Hanby, the auditor of the fifth circuit, in 1543, Pope charged him not only to forbear to take any of the woodwards' accounts until they had presented " a docket subscribed w^t my hand, wherby they may be charged," but also to submit immediately to the woods office additional dockets of their accounts, subscribed by him. The latter injunction was designed to facilitate Pope's own annual accounting, for without such abstracts " I shall not be hable nether to make a declaracion what wodes haue byn solde, nor yet certenly appoynt the sales for the next yere." Moreover, the auditor was enjoined to notify, just before the annual audit, all the surveyors within his district " willinge them . . . to aduertise yow what tymber hath byn appoynted for reparacions, to the ende the loppes, toppes and berke of the same may be charged accordingly." [127] Memoranda by Augmentations officials on the margins

---

works, fortifications, the king's ships, and reparation of crown buildings on the royal lands.

[126] Augm. Office, Misc. Books 458, fols. 14–20. Pope's warrant to Sir George Blount of Herefordshire, as given on the opposite page, presents a striking illustration of the type of work required of woodwards. The necessity of rendering prompt and full reports of wood sales is clearly shown in the note sent to Blount regarding his yearly accounts to the surveyor of woods. See Plate 4, following p. 274. *Ibid.* 461, fols. 1–1*d*.

[127] Hanby was also required further " w^t as convenient spede as ye can to make

of accounts of wood sales relating to the difficulty of securing accurate and systematic accounting indicate that not all the blame rested upon the accountants. The auditors and receivers also had to be spurred on to greate diligence in regular collections and audits.[128]

After the abolition of the Court, woods and wood sales came under the control of the Exchequer. Sale of timber continued; the exploitation of forests was somewhat accelerated, but on the demesne lands the administration of woods was generally less systematic than under the Augmentations. In December, 1557, a general commission was issued for a complete survey of all the royal forests, parks, and chases, and upon the return of their report to the Exchequer, the commissioners were directed " to cause such of them as they shall think most convenient to be disafforested and disparked and converted to the best profit of the crown." The reason for the survey was obvious. Such lands as were disafforested, that is, removed from the legal status of forest and freed from the operation of the forest laws, were to be leased by the commissioners for such rent as they deemed advisable.[129] Meanwhile, under the new system, the earlier woods organization had been considerably modified. The office of county woodward was retained, but the Augmentations masterships of woods were discontinued. Arscot was pensioned by Mary in May, 1554, for the surrender of the surveyorship in the north, at which time the office seems to have been abolished. On the other hand, the surveyorship of woods south of the River Trent was retained by Jobson, whose duties in that capacity were performed by his deputy, Roger Taverner. In 1572, John Taverner, the son of Roger, obtained the reversion of the office at a fee of £50 per year.[130] The executive functions formerly exercised by the masters of woods were mostly taken over by the chancellor and treasurer of the Exchequer.

Tudor policy of exploiting the woodlands of the royal demesne, begun by Cromwell, eventually led to a serious depletion of the nation's timber supply, but there is little evidence of any attempt at wholesale destruc-

---

me out dockettes subscribed wᵗ your handes of Þᵉ woodwardes accomptes for thes ij yeres past." *Ibid.* 458, fol. 13*d*. See also *ibid.* 461, fol. 1.

[128] Exch., Accounts Various, 149/26.

[129] *Cal. Pat. Rolls, Philip and Mary*, IV, 73. All deer, both red and fallow, remaining in the forests were to be surveyed and sold " to the most profit of the crown."

[130] Augm. Office, Misc. Books 262, fol. 76*d*.; *Cal. State Papers, Domestic, Elizabeth, Addenda 1566–1579,* p. 380. After 1625, or perhaps earlier, the northern office appears to have been reconstituted, the surveyors of woods on either side of Trent both working under Thomas Fanshawe, general surveyor of crown lands. F. S. Thomas, *Note of Materials for the History of Public Departments* (London, 1846), 85.

tion of woods during the first half of the sixteenth century. Nevertheless, the continual acquisition of extensive timber holdings, combined with the growing demand for lumber, prompted the government to utilize this excellent opportunity for profit. Once under way the movement was gradually accelerated as the financial needs of the state became more acute. Since the constant supply of " standard " oaks was always conveniently marketable, their sale provided a tempting way to augment the crown revenue. Consequently, wood sales became a regular part of the Augmentations administration, although the preservation of young timber and the replanting of cleared areas was also an important function of the woods officials. Nationally the institution of special Augmentations offices of auditor and receiver of woods suggests the extent of the timber sales throughout the country.[131] However, it must be remembered that much of the timber felled was used for practical purposes and not sold for profit. Lumber was constantly in demand for building, reparations, fortifications, public works, and ship construction, and it was a function of the Court to supply local requirements from the nearest woods within its jurisdiction. Frequently the availability of timber was a determinant factor in the purchase or exchange of land by the crown.[132] In fact, one of the reasons for appointing, in the first Augmentations, a special receiver for revenues derived from woods was to collect money owing to the monasteries for woods sold on the eve of the Dissolution. So hastily had many of these sales been negotiated that full payments had not been made when the Augmentations took over the property. Thomas Pope estimated that over £2,400 was due the king in revenue from this source alone.[133] Since easy profit was the chief concern of the crown, little was done to curtail the cutting or sale of timber except when

---

[131] There were also surveyors of woods in the outlying possessions, such as Guisnes and Boulogne, whose work was largely confined to preserving timber and supplying wood for local building needs. The surveyor, or overseer of woods, at Boulogne and New Haven (Ambleteuse in Boulonnais) also had authority to sell woods to the king's profit. *L. and P.*, XII, pt. 1, no. 474; *Cal. Pat. Rolls, Edward VI*, I, 249.

[132] The king sought to acquire the manor of Knell in Sussex in 1537 in order to have a convenient supply of available timber for Calais. Whereas the manor was worth but £48 yearly, the wood sales had been averaging 40 marks to £40—never under £20 per year, except latterly when the restraint on exporting wood had caused a decline in the amount sold. The owner had refused an offer of £1,500 for the timber, holding it to be worth £2,000. *L. and P.*, XII, pt. 1, no. 739.

[133] Pope to Anthony Denny of the privy chamber, keeper of the royal palace at Westminster, February 10, 1543. Urging the appointment of " a discreet man in woods " to act as a receiver of all revenues from woods on the Augmentations lands, he recommended David Clayton for the position. Clayton, who at this time was serving as a clerk to William Cowper, was passed over in favor of John Perte. As noted earlier, he was finally awarded the office of surveyor of woods which he held jointly with Cowper. *Ibid.*, *Addenda*, I, pt. 2, no. 1584.

certain woods were reserved by it for particular purposes. By Edward VI's reign local shortages of timber were already developing in certain areas. In 1550 the surveyor of woods was ordered to prohibit any further felling of trees within a radius of four or five miles of Deptford, Kent, because no other timber for the king's navy or buildings was available for twenty miles "thereaboutes." A few months later he was required by the council to stop the sale of all woods from the manor of Bevington in Surrey until further notice.[134]

Most of the timber taken from the crown estates prior to 1536 was felled either on the authority of special commissions or under the direction of the office of general surveyors. There was, of course, the usual destruction by petty thieves and marauders, common enough throughout the century, but despite the complaints of local officials losses sustained from such "spoils of woods" were never very great. More important perhaps was the unauthorized sale or misappropriation of the best trees from royal manors, which oftentimes took place openly with the connivance of irresponsible ministers. From its inception one of the primary functions of the woods administration was to check just such abuses as these.

During the period from 1542 to 1547, therefore, two separate and distinct agencies, the Court of General Surveyors and the Court of Augmentations, were in charge of woods administration, both supervising wood sales under the general direction of the crown. Without warrant, the chancellor of the Augmentations was empowered by statute to authorize such sales only on the advice of two of his council.[135] Two types were usual: selected cuttings of underwood and of larger timber trees. The former was wood actually cut as distinct from that gathered by hand; it included coppices consisting of young trees fifteen to thirty years old, enclosed as protection from marauding animals and rights of common and subject to periodic cutting. Among the larger trees were the valuable oaks which were used for shipbuilding. Sales were normally made upon warrant from the master of woods by the county woodward, according to a definite schedule of instructions received by him. Thus, strict limitations were imposed on the number, age, and location of the trees to be sold, and safeguards were set up for the protection of

---

[134] Dasent (ed.), *Acts of the Privy Council,* III, 49, 470.

[135] Section vij of the first constitution of the Court, 27 Henry VIII, c. 27, *S. R.,* III, 571–72. Receivers and auditors jointly made reparations, conducted surveys of woods, and sold such timber as the Court authorized. The master of woods in the Court of General Surveyors could sell wood from the forests with the assent of the justices of the forest, but "greate tymber" could be sold only as warranted by the crown. *Ibid.,* 883–84 (sec. xviij). Similar authority was given to the Court of Wards by its own constitution. 32 Henry VIII, c. 46, *ibid.,* 803 (sec. x).

the growth left standing. Fellable areas were enclosed and fenced in order that " the same may be contynually preserved to the moste profyte & advauntage " of the crown. In districts where prized crown estates or royal game might be jeopardized, the advice of local keepers, stewards, and foresters was required. When select timber was cut for the use of the crown the undergrowth that remained was sold separately. Usually the needs of crown tenants were first taken care of, the scrub oak and less desirable trees being used to fulfill such demands. In the case of major annual sales the utmost publicity of procedure was demanded. Competitive bidding and public advertising prior to the actual auction usually assured a fair price, " to thentent that suche persons as will give moste money shall haue preferment of the same." [136] In January, 1551, John Lawrence, woodward of Hertfordshire, was warranted by York to sell three acres of twelve years growth and four acres of fourteen years growth, as certified by the surveyor. It was suggested that he consult a few honest and substantial men in the community in determining the price to be charged and to " make sale of the same [woods] to such persons as wyll geue moste mony therfore." He was further advised to take all necessary precaution for the protection of the new growth as set forth in his previous orders. In this and in other similar warrants he was ordered to pay his receipts to the particular receiver and account with the circuit auditor at the next audit.[137]

Commissions issued under the great seal of the Court illustrate the same general procedure. When, in November, 1541, commissioners were appointed to sell, " as well by the acre as otherwayes to our vse and moost advauntage," woods and underwoods from the royal manor of Sees Court in Kent, they were instructed to advertise the sale and sell to the highest bidder. Moreover, according to the customs of the county young trees and undergrowth were to be preserved. Money, bonds, covenants of sale, and indentures for future payments were to be delivered to the county receiver, from whose hands they reached the Court treasurer. A full report was required within thirty days after the sale, at which time the commissioners certified to the Court in writing an itemized account of all timber sold and the price received.[138]

---

[136] Augm. Office, Misc. Books 267, fols. 1, 10; 458, fols. 15, 15d. Exch., Accounts Various 150/31, fol. 1 *passim*; 674/37.

[137] Nine warrants to John Lawrence, woodward of Hertfordshire, for the year 1551–52. Exch., Accounts Various, 694/7, fols. 1–10. By decision of the council of the Augmentations, woodwards were allowed 1s. 8d. per day for travel expenses. Augm. Office, Misc. Books 415, fol. 6 ff.

[138] Drafts of commissions for wood sales. Augm. Office, Miscellanea, 314/18. The twenty acres of woods to be sold were part of the former possessions of Dartford priory, which was used as a private residence by both Henry VIII and Anne

The problem of estimating the amount of timber felled by the Augmentations and the Court of General Surveyors is baffling, for no complete set of records is available either of the extent of the cuttings or of the total revenue derived from the sale of woods on the royal demesne. Literally hundreds of wood sales are extant for the period, but frequently they are imperfect and unfinished, or if complete they fail to yield all the data required for an accurate calculation. Furthermore, it is not always possible to determine whether or not the sales authorized were ever made or what proportion of the total records has survived. There is ample evidence to indicate that there was considerable destruction of valuable larger timber, such as beech, elm, birch, ash, and giant oak on both private estates and royal properties, but complete accounts of such plundering are not available. As early as 1484 proposed reforms in crown land administration had called attention to the prevalent waste of the king's woods by which revenue had been " lost to his gret hurt," and offered suggestions for more systematic control of woods and parks. In the honor of Tutbury the royal steward was instructed " that there be noo wood fallen . . . for paleyng but such as is moost mete and convenient for the same, and the coppies of the said pailling wood with the brewsing that is metely for thexpenses of the kinges houshold or his reparacions be kept therfore, the residue to be praysed and sold to the kinges most advauntages." [139] At the time of the Dissolution many abbots sold marketable timber from their land before it was confiscated, but on the basis of random examples the total acreage involved can easily be exaggerated.[140] Likewise, private sales of timber, either for domestic consumption or for exportation by royal license, were not uncommon.[141] Such conditions presented an administrative problem, but there is no indication that there was cause for any serious alarm.

During short periods where the records are plentiful and continuous the extent of wood sales is measurable by the accounts of woods officials

---

of Cleves. Other Augmentations commissions for wood sales are found in E. 314/20–21.

[139] Harl. MS. 433, fol. 270 ff.

[140] The problem of illegal sale and destruction of woods was undoubtedly serious enough to be given special attention by the administration. In the case of Vale Royal in Cheshire, where the earl of Shrewsbury was steward, some 5,000 oaks were reported to have been cut before the surrender of the monastery in September, 1538. *L. and P.*, XIV, pt. 2, nos. 49, 814; XIII, pt. 1, no. 477; pt. 2, nos. 315, 726, 1263; XIV, pt. 2, Appendix no. 49.

[141] In 1540 an informer alleged that merchants of York, daily practising the " feat of malt making," had almost destroyed the city and consumed all the woods within twenty miles of it. *L. and P.*, XV, no. 515. On private felling and sale of timber, see *L. and P.*, Indexes: e. g., XIV, pt. 2, nos. 105, 191, 814; XV, nos. 65–67, 205, 515; XVII, no. 71 (33).

and the receipts paid in to their respective institutions. In the case of both the office and the Court of General Surveyors, however, the records are disappointingly meager. Scattered among those of the Exchequer and the Augmentation Office, these accounts are seldom comprehensive and frequently incomplete. Trees were cut regularly for the use of the crown and occasionally a minister alluded to " great sums " for trees felled at the king's charge, but sales for profit appear to have been casual and the final payments made to the chamber seem to have been small.[142] The greatest profits came during the reign of Edward VI through the reorganized Augmentations, which then had charge of most of the timber sales for the crown lands.

Until 1547 the receipts from wood sales were paid into the treasury of the Court by the receiver-general of woods, whereas under the second Augmentations the county woodwards turned over their surplus revenues directly to the district receivers. Consequently, in the treasurer's annual accounts they are included among the receipts for each county and are not separately recorded. There seems to have been a gradual increase in the amount of timber sold after 1543, but in proportion to the total revenue of the Court the annual income from this source was not exceptional. Individual sales by the woodwards were seldom over fifty acres each, though the purchase price rather than the acreage is usually given.[143] As in the receipts of the office of master of woods in the Court of Survey, the payments from the receiver-general varied from £1,000 to £1,500 per year, reaching £1,820 in 1544.[144] In the second Court of Augmentations gross receipts from the county woodwards ranged from £50 to £100 annually with only occasional larger sales reported. Receipts of over £200 for any one county were quite exceptional.

In all cases local fees and expenses of sales were heavy, eating away the clear profit eventually realized. The case of the woodward of Yorkshire in 1545, who had only £56 7s. 9d. left " in redie money " after his costs of £10 4s. 4d. were allowed, was not at all unusual.[145] During

[142] Accounts of wood sales are numerous, but see especially Augm. Office, Misc. Books 457–462; E. 325, accounts of the sale of woods. Exch., Accounts Various, 148/20; 149/7, 17, 19, 25, 26A, 31–32, 39, 41.

[143] Examples at random for 33–34 Henry VIII show £7 paid for 3 acres of woods, £20 for 7 acres, £63 6s. 8d. for 25 acres, and £20 received for coppices. Sir John Baker bought 2½ acres of St. John's Wood for £3 15s., and Henry Hodgkins paid £53 6s. 8d. for 40 acres of underwoods in Gloucestershire, while an unrecorded quantity from the manor of Long Ditton in Surrey was sold to Sir Thomas Heneage for £120. Occasionally small sums were collected for vandalism, as £4 for " certyne pettye spoyles and wastes made in the kinges woodes " at Otford, Kent. Augm. Office, Misc. Books 336, fols. 4d., 18, 33, 37d., 45d., 55d.

[144] *Ibid.* 337, fol. 124; 338, fol. 109; 339, fol. 132d. Exch., Accounts Various, 148/38–39.

[145] Augm. Office, Misc. Books 460, fols. 16–19d. In Northamptonshire fees and

the transitional period in the early months of Mary's reign, surveys and sales of woods were authorized by the special commission appointed for the liquidation of the Court. For a time, when the records and revenues were being transferred to the Exchequer, considerable confusion prevailed.[146] Administrative neglect produced delays in accounting, while in a few counties sales were abandoned altogether. In other counties unlicensed cutting was reported, and instances were uncovered where woodwards, by their own confession, had sold crown timber without warrant.[147] This situation, however, was soon remedied under the efficient Exchequer administration of Paulet and Baker.[148]

Despite the assertion of the investigating commissioners of 1552 that "the King is much unsuredly served and his woods much spoyled," the department of woods in the Augmentations was better organized and conducted than comparable agencies in the other courts. None the less negligence had crept in there as in other departments. Reformation of evil practices was also recommended for the duchy of Lancaster, the Court of Wards and Liveries, and the office of the justices of the forests. Timber on wards' lands was sold by feodaries without warrant, for which no systematic accounts were rendered, while in the duchy the ancient custom of selling woods only on the authority of commissions had been abandoned. In the latter it was recommended that the office of surveyor of woods, "new begun" in 1532, be discontinued altogether. In these criticisms economy was the primary consideration. Actually the total revenue derived from wood sales by all these institutions was only £1,709 4s. 6d. at this time.[149] Of this amount over £800, or

expenses of the woodward reduced his receipts from £206 17s. 7d. to £172 14s.; in Wiltshire £1 13s. 4d. was spent in the sale of £5 19s. 8d. worth of timber, or just under 28 per cent; in other counties the revenue received for the woods sold scarcely sufficed for the cost of reparations required. *Ibid.* 458, fols. 2, 23 ff.; Exch., Accounts Various, 150/16.

[146] On wood sales during the reigns of Mary and Elizabeth, see the interesting article, G. Hammersley, "The Crown Woods and their Exploitation in the Sixteenth and Seventeenth Centuries," *Bulletin of the Institute of Historical Research,* XXX (November, 1957), 136–61. Unfortunately contemporary allegations of large wood sales are seldom accompanied by positive evidence, as the assertion of Henry Percy, the Elizabethan earl of Northumberland, that he had taken in £20,000 from wood sales on his estates, yet his accounts for 1585–1600 reveal a total of only £3,862 from such receipts. A. R. Batho, "The Finances of an Elizabethan Nobleman: Henry Percy, Ninth Earl of Northumberland," *Economic History Review,* Second Series, IX (April, 1957), 436.

[147] Augm. Office, Misc. Books 460, 462.

[148] Under the renovated Exchequer, wood sales had to be commissioned by the lord treasurer and two officers of that court. During Mary's reign Paulet (Marquis of Winchester) was treasurer and Sir John Baker was chancellor and undertreasurer. Exch., K. R., Miscellanea, 13/2(3).

[149] Add. MS. 30198, fols. 23d., 24, 26, 29, 46d., 49, 51d. The respective revenues

slightly more than 50 per cent of the total, came from the Augmentations. The highest receipts of the year were in the tenth and twelfth districts, where woods to the value of £433 11s. were sold. Thus over half the total sales by the Court were made in four counties.[150] Though in many respects not a typical year, nevertheless, wood sales amounting to but 5.57 per cent of the gross casual revenues of the Court could not have evoked much criticism of Augmentations policy.[151]

In the management of woods as in other spheres, the close co-operation of receivers and auditors with the county officials was essential. Small payments were, therefore, never too insignificant to merit scrutiny by Court overseers in regional administration where much depended upon close supervision of local affairs. In this respect the most important control was the annual audit, provided for by the second constitution of the Court. It required that the county audit should be held yearly, sometime between Michaelmas and Christmas, although the final reckoning of the auditor was not due until some months afterwards, on or before the first of August.[152] Meanwhile, by the first of the previous March particulars of accounts had been submitted and a complete

from wood sales are: Court of Wards and Liveries, £189 10s.; duchy of Lancaster, £718 11s. 1d.; and the Court of Augmentations, £801 3s. 5d. Harl. MS. 7383, fol. 71.

[150] Receipts from wood sales as paid in by the Augmentations receivers for the year ending Michaelmas, 1551. For the counties represented in each district, consult chart, p. 281. The distribution is as follows: first district, £140 7s. 3d.; second district, £16; third district, £67 16s. 8d.; fourth district, £39 12s. 8d.; fifth district, no sales recorded; sixth district, no sales recorded; seventh district, no sales recorded; eighth district, £93 5s. 9d.; tenth district, £105 1s. 8d.; eleventh district, £8 16s.; twelfth district, £328 9s. 4d.; and the duchy of Cornwall, £3 8s. 9d. The casualties for the same year, of which wood sales formed a minor part only, are classified as perquisites of court, wood sales, coal mines, customs, fines for leases, and profits from tin, fairs, the butlerage, the great seal of England, and the hanaper of the Augmentations. Add. MS. 30198, fols. 14–19, 24.

[151] The records of wood sales under the early Tudors are widely dispersed among various classes of documents, including a few manuscripts in the British Museum. With the exception of scattered records, the bulk of this material is distributed as follows: (a) ledgers of receipts by the treasurer of Augmentations, 11 vols., Augm. Office, Misc. Books 336–349 (an earlier volume in this series is found in Exch., K. R., Misc. Books (Series I), 68); (b) warrants, accounts, certificates, and other miscellaneous documents pertaining to the sale of crown woods, Augm. Office, Misc. Books 457–462; (c) accounts of wood sales, Exch., Treasury of Receipt, Misc. Books 96–97; (d) accounts of wood sales by the Augmentations and general surveyors, Exch., Accounts Various, especially E. 101/146, 148, 149, 150; (e) wood sales, Augm. Office, Miscellanea, Bundles 18, 20–21; (f) accounts of the sale of woods from Henry VIII to the Commonwealth, E. 325; and (g) miscellaneous volumes among the rentals and surveys, Augm. Office, Misc. Books 357–435 (described in *Lists and Indexes*, No. XXV).

[152] The account must be declared before the "feaste of Seynt peter thadvincula yearly." Thus, the date was that of the feast of St. Peter *ad vincula* and not that of St. Peter and St. Paul, which latter would have fixed the last date for the audit at June 29.

list of arrearages placed in the hands of the chancellor and general surveyors. At the time of the final accounting the auditor appeared before the council, presented his " books " engrossed in parchment, and declared his account in person. The declaration was then delivered " by indenture " into the Court where it was kept as a permanent record, a copy of the account being retained by the auditor for future reference.

Since the county audit was the only effective check on local accountants, certain safeguards were set up to maintain high standards of proficiency and uniform proceedings. As indicated earlier, notices of the meeting were posted in the four most important market towns of the county, in which the time, place, and duration of the session were indicated. In addition to public announcements, each accountant received an individual notification from the auditor, which had to be delivered to him at least twelve days in advance. This " precept," as it was called, summoned the accountant to the forthcoming audit and provided him with the necessary preliminary instructions for his declaration of account. After the audit was held, names of all delinquent officers and accountants who either failed to appear or refused to render an account were turned in to the central office in order that due process for collection might be directed against them. As a further precaution the auditor was required each year to submit to the Court a list of all ministers who were not bonded. Finally, before the end of March he had to deliver the book of arrears for his entire circuit, indicating all debts and unpaid revenues within his jurisdiction for the past fiscal year.

Provisions for the enforcement of these regulations were also stipulated in the constitution. Any auditor who failed to submit the names of delinquent accountants before the tenth of January was himself held accountable for the revenue not reported. He could " receyue it agayne of the partie or parties owing the same," which implied that he was expected to reimburse himself later for the amount involved if he could. Such a condition protected the crown but did not penalize the defaulter, unless subsequently he became subject to legal action. Thus the responsibility for instituting charges was shifted from the auditor to the council of the Court or, more particularly, to the chancellor and general surveyors. If by their negligence they failed to award process against the offenders within twenty days after the delinquents were reported to them, then they themselves were held responsible for the debts involved. Properly enforced, these measures should have insured speedy collection of revenue at all times, but under Edwardian administration the penalties were seldom if ever invoked. However, local tenants and ministers were less influential than the major officers of the Court and not uncommonly suffered the full penalties of the law. In the case of accountants refusing to pay the revenues found due upon their accounts, the auditors were empowered to commit them to ward and hold them in custody until they had made satisfactory settlements or until such time as the Court itself had begun prosecution against them. Attendance at the audit was enforceable by discretionary punishment, though reasonable excuses were usually acceptable:

And by cause the saide Auditors muste ryde to diuers Shires and must therefore of necessitie appoynt a certayne lymytt of tyme for their seuerall Audittes length then Whiche tyme they may not conuenyentlye tarye therfor We ordeyne and establishe that if eny accomptaunt faile the daye appoynted in the precepte of eny of the sayde Auditors and come neuerthelesse before thende of the Audite Wherby the Auditors shall not be hable to dispatche the same Within the tyme there appoynted if eny man kepe not his certeyne daye then euery of the sayde Auditors shall and maye punyshe the disobediencie of euery suche accomptaunt by imprisonament or fyne to our vse by his discrecyon hauynge respecte to thobstynacye of the person so offendyng fforseying also that the same accomptaunt make his accompte and paye his money to the Receyuour before his departure thence.[153]

In all instances the full expenses of the audit were borne by the Court. Paid by the receiver, a statement of the costs incurred was recorded in " a particuler booke indented betwene the Receyvour and the Auditour," which was presented as evidence upon the annual declaration of accounts at Westminster. For the accountant the final *quietus est* of the auditor was the only discharge honored by the Court. Ultimately this rule led to considerable confusion as well as to occasional injustice. If the original discharge could not be produced, the tenant might be called on for a second payment of his rent.[154]

The many surviving proclamations of audits and special summonses to accountants requiring their attendance suggest that the auditors, at least, were faithful in their compliance with the law. Advertisements were mostly well in advance of the audits, which were by custom generally held during the same month each year. Length of sessions varied appreciably according to the extent of Augmentations property in the county and the number of accountants involved, but they seldom lasted more than ten or fifteen days. The same form of proclamation was used apparently by all the auditors. The introduction always explained

[153] Pat. Rolls, 38 Henry VIII, pt. 5, mems. 23–24.
[154] *Ibid.*, mem. 24. The auditor could charge the accountant not more than a shilling for each discharge.

that public advertisement was required by the Court, to the intent that all accountants should stand " in a redines about their receipte . . . and so to make their accomptes and paie their money accordinglye." A typical advertisement of August 21, 1547, for an audit in Herefordshire explains the general procedure:

> Theis shalbe to signyfie vnto you that thauditt for all his highnes Revenues w^{th}in the countie of Herefford is appointed to be kept at Hereford the xxiiij^{th} of Nouember nexte, and so to contynew and make and ende the xxx^{th} daie of the same monethe willing and comaunding in the name of of [sic] our said soueraigne lorde the kinges maiestie all bailliffes, ffermers, Collectours, Revis, wood-wardes and all others accomptauntes and suche other persons as haue occasion to repaire to the said Audite vpon eny accompte to be made or for paymente of eny Rentes to the kinges highnes vse of and for eny landes or Tenementes lieng w^{th}in the said countie and w^{th}in the Jurisdiccion of the said courte to repaire to the said place w^{th}in the tyme above lymyted and appointed at your further perrill. Written at London the xxj^{th} daie of August in the furste yere of the Raigne of our most drade and gracious soueraigne lorde Edwarde the sixte by the grace of god, king of Inglande, ffraunce, and Irelande defendour of the faithe and in erthe supreme hedde of the churche of Ingland and Irelande.
>
> God saue the Kyng
> by me Johon Hanbie Audit.[155]

Although there were slight variations in detail during the previous reign, the procedure for the district audits was practically the same. Receivers co-operated with the auditors in the view of county accounts within their districts, but the responsibility for the advance proclamations of the meeting and for the individual notifications sent to the accountants rested with the latter. Every year between Michaelmas and Christmas the auditor journeyed to some appointed place within his circuit to hold the required audit. For the previous year, ending Michaelmas, 1546, Hanby and the receiver, John Scudamore, had held the joint audit for Herefordshire and Worcestershire at Worcester, each county being allotted five days. The receiver and auditor had just come

---

[155] This proclamation is prefaced by the usual explanation stating the purpose of the advertisement. Augm. Office, Miscellanea, 314/17. Two years later Hanby held the audit at the town of Bowdley in Worcestershire, from November 14 to 22. Annuitants and pensioners were requested, however, not to appear before the twenty-first, after the main audit was over. Augm. Office, Misc. Books 461, fols. 2, 14.

from Bridgnorth, Shropshire, where from October 29 to November 10, they had viewed the accounts of all local receivers, bailiffs, reeves, collectors, and farmers within the adjacent counties of Shropshire and Staffordshire.[156] The precepts sent out to each accountant guaranteed a maximum of attendance at the audit:

In the kinges ma^ties name I require you tappere before me at weschester the xxix^th day of October next coming ther to yelde y^or accomptes of thissues and profetes of your office for the yere to be ended at michaelmas next ensuing the date herof bringing wth you all your Rentalles extractes Comtrolles and all other thinges necessarie touching yor said accompt together wth somuch money as shalbe determined then to be due not failing of all the premisses and circumstaunces of the same at your perell from london the last day of august anno R Rex. E. vj^th quinto.[157]

Nevertheless, many accountants failed to appear at the audit or, having duly rendered their accounts, " stole away " without making payment. The certificates of the auditors reporting such cases to the Court reveal an alarming number of irresponsible collectors. Some of them were merely negligent officials who eventually paid their debts before legal action was taken, but many were seasoned evaders, stubbornly refusing to pay " withoute compulsion." In exceptional cases repeated citations for appearance in court were ignored, and writs of attachment had to be levied. Oftentimes, too, local ministers took advantage of easy-going auditors to pocket profits of courts and other incidental revenues and postpone payment of collected rents as long as possible. Such was the perverseness of a bailiff of the hundred of Dytton, Surrey, who though he

[156] As required by law, the proclamation for the Shropshire audit was read in the open markets by the bailiffs and mayors of the following towns: at Drayton on September 29, Shrewsbury on October 6, Bridgnorth on October 9, and at Newport on October 16. For the sake of still greater publicity it was likewise proclaimed outside the county at Chester, Cheshire, on October 4. This particular announcement began: " To all people to whom this present proclamacion shall come vnto be harde redde or sene John hanby on of the kinges ma^tes auditors . . . sendith greting . . . these shall be to signifie and give knowlege vnto you and euery of you that god willinge I haue appointed . . ." etc., etc. Dated London, August 20, 1546. Augm. Office, Miscellanea, 29/8. The expenses for this audit were £19 9d., and the one at Worcester £39 12s. *Ibid.*, 29/21. The proclamation for Shropshire is abstracted in *L. and P.*, XXI, pt. 2, no. 272. Similar proclamations and audits were held for the other counties in Hanby's district.

[157] Summons to an audit by William Rigges, auditor of the second circuit of the later Court of Augmentations to John Ghegge, farmer of the grange of Wirrihall, Cheshire. Augm. Office, Misc. Books 115, fol. 151. The general procedure for local audits in the Court of General Surveyors was similar. See, for example, summonses to collectors of attainted lands in the north, *ibid.* 382, fol. 98 ff.

" hathe hadde diuerse privie Seales and hathe nott accompted this iij yeres," he still remained " the moste vntowarde baylie in this Shyre." [158] Still, the vigilance of auditors was not enough. Though lists of those in default were submitted to the main office more or less regularly, arrears continued to multiply in every district.

In addition to the regular reports of the auditors and receivers information supplied by manorial officials was indispensable. Sometimes special assignments to the Court could not be fulfilled without their cooperation, as in the regulations for the government of Beccles Fen, Suffolk, drawn up by the chancellor in 1543.[159] In fact, many of the cases that came before the Augmentations were related to the work of local ministers, being either charges against them by crown tenants or their own complaints of " wronges done vnto the kinges maiestie " or to themselves. They were charged with such offenses as favoritism, embezzlement, intimidation of tenants, failure to hold court, negligence in accounting, withholding revenues, and demanding payment of rents before the date due. In their dealings with tenants the ministers, in turn, were beset with numerous problems. Precautions taken by them against unscrupulous people in the protection of the king's interest constituted a normal part of manorial supervision. Minor infractions of regulations were dealt with locally, but intractable offenders were referred to the Court for investigation and trial. More serious misdemeanors included pillage, trespass, petty theft, open defiance of authority, the appropriation of stray livestock claimed by the crown under prerogative right, devastation of woods, and wanton destruction of crown property. Among other high " persumpcions," repeated violation of manorial custom could be very detrimental to a crown minister, while the continued refusal of occupiers to pay their rents might lead to his " vtter vndoing." [160] Even when paid to an unauthorized agent, the official collector was responsible for all rents and profits within his jurisdiction. If collected

---

[158] Augm. Office, Miscellanea, 23/19; 39/21, 45; see also various letters and items concerning rents in Miscellanea, bundle 17.

[159] When Beccles in Suffolk was incorporated in 1543, the marsh and pasture of Beccles Common and Beccles Fen, containing about 1,400 acres formerly belonging to the monastery of Bury St. Edmunds, were granted to the town. The lease reserved certain rights for the crown, however, including waifs, strays, and sedges sufficient for the repair of the king's houses in Beccles. Richard Rich, as chancellor of the Augmentations, was ordered to assist the inhabitants of the town in drawing up ordinances for the good rule of the marsh. Grants in March, 1543, *L. and P.,* XVIII, pt. 1, no. 346 (20). Rich's draft of the statute of government is preserved among the Exch., K. R., Miscellanea, 11/4. See also the report on the administration of crown lands in Gloucestershire, *ibid.,* 11/13.

[160] Proceedings in the Court of Augmentations. Augm. Office, Miscellanea, 37–40, and E. 321.

under false pretenses by an imposter, his only recourse lay in an appeal to the Augmentations for justice.[161]

The duties of bailiffs, keepers, collectors, and receivers of special revenues were similar to those of minor officials in any private manorial unit; consequently this group of local officials, important enough in provincial affairs, had little if any contact with the institution they served, save through the yearly ordeal of the county audit. Singularly free from restrictive regulations, they remained for the most part obscure figures whose unknown names appear on manorial rolls. Much more important to the Court were the intermediary officers, the woodwards, stewards, and county surveyors who supervised the routine work of the manor. The woodwards, appointed by the masters and surveyors of woods, were much more directly under their control, whereas stewards and surveyors worked together as the principal executives of the county unit, chiefly responsible to the chancellor and general surveyors at Westminster. The surveyors were bonded and sworn to the honest execution of their offices. As surveyors of land their chief duty, of course, was to make surveys, but they also returned rent schedules, inspected enclosures of woods, and generally assisted the stewards in all sessions of manorial courts held within their respective counties. Furthermore, they annually examined sea walls, fences, weirs, mills, dovecotes, and other buildings in order to provide for necessary reparations. Construction and repairs not exceeding £10 could be provided for by them, but for appropriations over that amount the authorization of the Court was required. Timber requested for such purposes was delivered by the appropriate woodward upon warrant from the surveyor and steward, who regularly certified to the auditor the number of trees requisitioned. As a further check on the work, the whole proceeding was entered as of record on the court roll of the steward, the reparations having been " viewed by the hole homage [162] of the manour whether they be done accordinglie." [163]

---

[161] Situations of this kind actually did develop occasionally, as in *Thomas Pope, bailiff*. v. *John Bager*. Pope (not to be confused with Sir Thomas Pope, treasurer of the Augmentations) suffered a protracted illness while bailiff of the crown lordship of Great Malvern in Worcestershire, during which period certain revenues from the lordship were collected by Bager, under the pretence of having been chosen to succeed to the office in the event of Pope's death. Upon his recovery, Pope was obliged to pay these rents, amounting to over £7, out of his own pocket. Failing to secure redress by personal action, he sued Bager, whom he claimed had acted without authority, for restitution and damages. Augm. Office, Misc. Books 516, fols. 3–24.

[162] The homage of the manor was that body of tenants or other persons owing allegiance and attendance at the manorial court.

[163] Pat. Rolls, 38 Henry VIII, pt. 5, mems. 16, 17, 27. On the work of the stewards and surveyors in the manorial courts, see Chapter Five.

As one who " dylygently and paynefully travayled in and aboute the kinges majesties affayres wthin his offyce," the county surveyor was frequently called on to execute special commissions or assignments which, though not strictly related to his regular work, were exacting enough to require professional training. In March, 1550, John Grenville, surveyor of Cornwall, was sent out of the county to deliver jewels and ornaments collected from colleges and chantries. Also " he did moche travaile in a commissyon " concerning a doubtful pension paid to a stipendiary priest from local crown revenues.[164] As king's agent, he served regularly as informer to the crown, reporting all manner of transgression and destruction of property committed within his jurisdiction by " evill and disordred persons." In many instances he was able to retrieve stolen property without the aid of the Court. Undeniably the surveyor was an important instrument for the protection of the crown's interest in remote areas. In the course of ordinary routine surveys a vigilant surveyor could render immeasurable service to the Augmentations in uncovering concealments, losses of revenue, thefts, or in the revaluation of rents and salable property.[165] In fact he was an estate agent, accountant, overseer, and general representative of the crown, all combined in one person.[166] An able and conscientious surveyor easily justified his salary and emoluments.

The local steward was also an important crown agent with diverse duties, the chief of which was that of holding court. Nevertheless, he

[164] Augm. Office, Miscellanea, 23; Misc. Books 259, fol. 86. Usually the surveyors' work was quite heavy and their expense allowances considerable. The surveyor of Warwickshire was allowed over £262 for expenses during one year in surveying lands, for riding costs, and for the purchase of paper, ink, canvas bags, and other paraphernalia connected with his office. *Ibid.* 459, fols. 54–54d. An interesting survey by the same surveyor, Clement Throckmorton, made in 1553, has been published. W. B. Bickley (trans.), *Survey of the Borough and Manor or Demesne Foreign of Birmingham* (undated; notes and introduction by Joseph Hill).

[165] Augm. Office, Miscellanea, 23, 24, 37; Misc. Books 258, fol. 72d.; 259, fols. 86d., 87; 521, fols. 12, 18, 36–38. Exch., Accounts Various, 76/35, fol. 134.

[166] The work of a surveyor, or supervisor, is fully explained in a contemporary manuscript in the British Museum, in which the duties of the office are described. With but few reservations the description would apply to the county surveyorship of the Augmentations. Cotton. MS., Titus. B. iv, fol. 111 ff. In 1549 the surveyor of North Wales had " of newe Revived & Increased " the revenues within his circuit £20, exactly the amount of his salary. Exch., Accounts Various, 76/36, fol. 18. However, the salaries for local ministers of the Court were not fixed but varied according to circumstances. The £20 per year earned by William Cecil in 1550 as surveyor to Princess Elizabeth was not at all exceptional, and as Professor Read infers, the duties of such an office were usually quite exacting. Conyers Read, *Mr. Secretary Cecil and Queen Elizabeth* (London, 1955), 65. The Augmentations land surveyors received fees from £6–8 up to £20 a year, £13 6s. 8d. being common. In almost all instances the stipulated fees were regularly augmented by liberal allowances and extra payments.

shared so much work with other officials, especially the county wood-wards and surveyors, that it is sometimes difficult to isolate his own functions. This was true even in judicial activities, since the manorial courts were declining in significance during the sixteenth century and consequently played a less prominent role in demesne administration than formerly. In the Augmentations organization the offices of chief stewards, or high stewards as they were often called, were commonly held by influential persons as sinecures, the actual duties of the office being performed by deputies or understewards. Some of these steward-ships were primarily administrative positions, as the high stewards north and south of the River Trent, but most of them were estate supervisors whose principal concern was the manor, lordship, or honorial units under their jurisdictions. Their reports covered not only petty prob-lems but also such miscellaneous items as leases, disputed bills, decayed rents, fines, wood sales, the employment of local workmen, the theft of woods, lead, stone, and other materials available for reparations, and the general condition of arable lands, woods, and buildings in the bailiwick.[167]

The manorial jurisdiction of the steward normally included the view of the frankpledge and the holding of the court-leet, as well as matters pertaining to ordinary demesne administration. Presentments of the homage revealed concealments of lands and rents, disputed boundaries, refusal of tenants to pay their duties or conform to " the custom of the manor," heriots overdue, and the unauthorized felling of timber. Profits of the courts, while varying greatly according to local circum-stances, were annually paid into the treasury of the Augmentations, which also bore the costs of the court sessions and other miscellaneous expenses of all the stewards. Likewise, the central office occasionally was called on to support them against unco-operative tenants, or to assist them in upholding the rights of the crown against the encroachment of aggressive lords. Not infrequently these altercations were referred to the chancellor and council when local officials were unable to cope with the situation.[168]

In spite of the numerous checks on crown ministers maintained by

---

[167] A declaration of certain matters connected with the administration of crown lands in Gloucestershire, by Thomas Watson, steward, Exch., K. R., Miscellanea, 11/13; the certificate of John Pygott, steward-general of Hertfordshire, Augm. Office, Miscellanea, 24.

[168] Numerous controversies arose as to exactly what franchisal rights, among which were perquisites and profits of court, were included in Augmentations grants of land. Such was the dispute at Waterwell, Norfolk, in June, 1552, con-cerning a leet and the view of the frankpledge. *Rex* v. *Edmund Beaupre*, Augm. Office, Proceedings, E. 321/45; Miscellanea, 35; Misc. Books 105, fols. 232d.–33; see also Proceedings, E. 321/5/52.

the Court, it was not always easy to eliminate waste and maladministration in remote districts. Oftentimes the fault lay rather with the tenant or occupier than with the official whose greatest crime might only have been undue leniency in his treatment of delinquents. Even when guilty of wilfull neglect of duty or downright dishonesty, it took time to prove the charges against him. If the culprit was a person of standing in the community, commission investigations were instituted, and before final action was taken the suspect given a chance to defend himself. Frequently collectors of revenue had to be prompted to pay in their receipts at the appointed time; conversely, if their complaints are any criteria, they were constantly faced with the problem of " decayd rentes." In some cases the decay was real; in others it merely indicated land or property which through negligence had not been leased or rents that remained uncollected because the tenant was too poor to pay. Less reprehensible perhaps, but as much of a problem, was the guilty minister or his deputy who was pardoned by the king because of previous loyal service. In the formal declarations of accounts presented to the Court it was difficult to distinguish between technical arrears and revenues which were simply not collected or, if received, not paid into the treasury. Furthermore, the practice of using deputies in office only made conditions worse. Under such a system accountants might easily get far behind in their payments, even inadvertently, before the auditor caught up with them. When ultimately faced with specific charges, ministerial excuses could be very convincing. If the official's attitude was not one of defiance, he was usually absolved by the Court. Sometimes he was warned and given a chance to redeem himself. Only in extreme circumstances was he dismissed from office.

In conclusion it can be observed that the administrative policy of the Augmentations, if indeed it had one, was not always clear. If lower standards and inefficiency were more prevalent in the second Court than in the first, it was largely because of changing circumstances during the Edwardian period. Decay had already set in; likewise, the increase in land, revenues, and personnel after 1547 made effective operation more difficult to maintain. Standards were not deliberately lowered but, when less was being demanded from the executives of the Court, they themselves ceased to exact the same high performance from their subordinates.

CHAPTER TEN

THE AUGMENTATIONS AS A FINANCIAL DEPARTMENT

LTHOUGH IN CONCEPT AND ORIGIN AN ADMINISTRATIVE court and only secondarily a financial one, the Augmentations found its financial work more often than not exceeding in importance its other activities. Its bureaucratic independence as a revenue department was due in part to Cromwell's intention to channel all the new revenues into a few central institutions, of which the Augmentations was to be the most important; within a decade it was overshadowing the chamber as the supreme treasury of the realm. Gross receipts of the Court for the last three years of the reign of Henry VIII amounted to £507,935 15s. 11d., with a total expenditure of £482,867 11s. 6d., whereas the declarations of the chamber show it to have been in a state of growing decay.[1] The volume of financial business handled by the Augmentations declined after 1544, but in aggregate net receipts, it still averaged over £116,000 per year. Net receipts for the entire history of the Court totaled £1,947,376.[2]

The ordinary receipts of the Court were derived, directly or indirectly, from the demesne lands within its jurisdiction. Normally they fell into six divisions: (1) receipts from the issues of the lands, as collected by the receivers-general and particular receivers; (2) receipts from the sale of buildings and movable possessions, such as plate, jewels, bells,

---

[1] Richardson, *Tudor Chamber Administration, 1485-1547*, 245-46; Augm. Office, Treas. Rolls of Accts., No. 3.

[2] That is, £1,304,859 3s. for the first Augmentations and £642,516 17s. 1d. for the second. *Ibid.*, Nos. 1-8.

lead, stone, livestock, and other chattels from the dissolved religious houses; (3) money received from the sale of land, either by the officials of the Court upon authorization of the crown or by royal commission; (4) wood sales; (5) fines paid for leases; and (6) miscellaneous receipts, particularly profits from the Court's seals and special fines imposed by the privy council.

The first category included rents from regular monastic land, purchased land, land of St. John of Jerusalem, and after 1547, attainted land as well as the revenues from the duchy of Cornwall. The total revenue under this heading varied appreciably from year to year, depending on the amount of land that had been sold and on the sum collected from wood sales, which was sometimes incorporated in this category since it was paid into the treasury by the receiver of woods. To these should be added various extraordinary revenues which were, from time to time, directed into the Augmentations treasury. Proceeds from the sale of mortgages to the citizens of London, loans, aids, the subsidy levied on monks' pensions, fines paid by monasteries for exemption from the acts of dissolution, *grati oneris* from rents reserved on certain grants of lands and from the enhancement of the coinage, debts collected, fines for exemptions from accompanying the king on the French expedition, and unexpended balances from royal treasurers or financial agents which were occasionally turned in to the Court were among those special items. Such nonrecurrent revenues were never very large in any one year, but together they constituted a significant portion of the total receipts of the Court. In 1544 compositions for exemption from going on the king's continental expedition aggregated £5,776 7s. 8½d.; during the same year £12,970 16s. 8d. was received from aids and £22,616 13s. 4d. from mortgages of land to the citizens of London.[3] During the ensuing three years almost £5,000 was collected from back debts which were due the monastic houses at the time of their dissolution.

Under the second Augmentations the receipts were similar in nature, with still more lands under its jurisdiction, which then included the income from the chantry possessions as well as the revenues of the earlier Court of General Surveyors. Land sales fluctuated under Edward VI but remained a constant item, while fines for leases reached a new peak of £1,968 13s. 8d. in 1551. Recovered debts and fines imposed by the privy council, sometimes as much as £2,000 each, found their way into the Court's treasury; likewise, unexpended balances remaining in the possession of royal treasurers and financial agents of the crown after the final determination of their accounts were paid to the

___

[3] *Ibid.*, No. 2B, pt. 2, fols. 30d., 31d., 33.

Augmentations. Foreign receipts varied, but they included such regular items as the surplus from the hanaper of the chancery and profits from the Court's two seals. Unusual items were fairly rare, as the £629 18s. received in 1548 from Sir Richard Gresham for the sale of arms and armor on the Continent.[4]

In accordance with ancient medieval practice, Augmentations revenues were classified as either "certainties" or "casualties," depending on the nature of their source. The certain or fixed revenues were by far the greater, consisting as they did of all the rents and issues from the crown possessions. In addition to these, however, profits from the sale of land, as well as assignments from the Exchequer to the great wardrobe which were paid through the Augmentations Court, were regarded as certain, since they came in every year. In contrast, the casualties were sporadic and uncertain, like fines, customs, or the prisage of wines which, although regular, varied appreciably in amount, "some years more some less." For the fiscal year 1550–1551, some two years before the dissolution of the Court, the certain revenues were more than ten times the casual receipts, which amounted to only £14,370 2s. 3d. They were divided into eleven categories, of which fines for leases were sometimes considered as special receipts. As a group they present a fair picture of the Court's diverse profits. In descending order they were: profits from the hanaper of the chancery, which heretofore were normally paid into the chamber—£3,910 2d.; perquisites of courts—£3,544 17s. 2d.; tunnage of tin, customs duties on other merchandise in the duchy of Cornwall, and the "gestment" of cattle[5] there—£2,925 16s. 7d.; fines for leases—£2,012 16s. 4d.; wood sales—£801 3s. 5d.; profits of the butlerage—£647 5s. 2d.; profits from the hanaper of the Augmentations—£314 6s. 8d.; profits from coal mines—£101 13s. 4d.; customs duties on wines in Cheshire—£50 15s. 11d.; commorth rent[6] in Wales—£42 6s. 8d.; and profits of fairs—£19 8d.[7]

---

[4] Dasent (ed.), *Acts of the Privy Council*, II, 267. In 1547 the surplus of money, plate, and jewels remaining in the mint was turned over to the treasurer of the Augmentations, after the mint accounts had been audited. *Cal. Pat. Rolls, Edward VI*, V, 398.

[5] Agistment (gestment or gistment from *agistamentum*; O. F. *gist, agistement*) was the ancient right to the herbage of the forest, or pasturage of other lands. Special officers, called agisters, agistators, gist-takers, were sometimes appointed to collect the profits from herbage, pannage, and pasture. Agistment tithes for animals were quite common at the time of the Dissolution, but decay of agistments on crown lands had already set in before the Augmentations was dissolved. The total profits from that source during this year were only £39 11s. 5d. There were also agistments of seabanks, where lands were charged with a tribute to keep out the sea.

[6] On commorth rent, see p. 201 and n. 110, *supra*.

[7] Add. MS. 30198, fols. 21, 24. There is a manuscript addition error for the

In view of the peculiarities of sixteenth-century bookkeeping, the treasurer's record of receipts and payments requires some explanation. These financial accounts are classified among the Augmentations records as the Treasurer's Rolls of Accounts and are complete for the entire life span of the Court.[8] As *compoti*, or annual declarations of account, they are based on the particular accounts of the receivers and collectors and contain a detailed itemization of receipts, as well as a record of all disbursements, including special allowances and extraordinary expenditures authorized by warrant of king or council. With the exception of three rolls which cover longer periods, each account is for a twelve-month period covering the fiscal year from Michaelmas to Michaelmas. The accounts are written in Latin and standardized in form, each consisting of two parts, the traditional " charge " and " discharge." This system was a convenient method of determining the liability of the accountant, the *debita* indicating the surplus or the amount owed the crown and payable to the Court treasury.

The arrangement served the purpose for which it was intended, but the method is confusing to the modern scholar, interested only in the clear profits for the period. The arrears, for example, are listed as part of the charge, while fees of officers, special allowances, and moneys delivered to the royal coffers are included among the various items of discharge. Under such a division the first part of the account, the charge, represents all the revenues or money for which the Court was responsible to the sovereign; the second part consists of all the various expenditures paid out during the year, listed in ten or twelve categories as " payments." The account concludes with a statement of the balance due from the treasurer, ostensibly being the difference between the total receipts and the total expenditures, or the net profit for the year. However, the very simplicity of the form is as deceiving as the figures themselves are misleading. Special " allowances," granted by the king from time to time and sometimes presented as a third section of the account, included arrears of revenue as well as exemptions from payment by Court officials of money due upon the determination of the account. As a result, it is rather difficult to determine exactly just how much money the Court had on hand at any one time, especially since not all of the paper balance shown on the books was necessarily in actual cash.

---

total of the itemized casualties of the duchy of Cornwall, which is given as £2,924 16*s.* 7*d.* instead of £2,925 16*s.* 7*d. Ibid.,* fol. 24.

[8] Augm. Office, Treas. Rolls of Accts., 10 rolls. These are numbered 1 to 8, but Nos. 1 and 2 have two parts each, making ten rolls altogether. The " rolls " consist of large parchment folios stitched together at one end. The receipts of the particular receivers are preserved among the Ministers' Accounts. Some of John Scudamore's accounts for Yorkshire are found in Tanner MS. 334.

Receipts and expenditures of receivers constituted a fairly stable element in Augmentations finance, although the total amounts depended on the size of their districts and the revenues allotted to their care. Under the second Court the highest receipts were from the Eighth District, followed by the Second, Twelfth, and Tenth Districts. The Seventh, in the north, was the lowest. For the duchy of Cornwall the revenues were fairly constant for the period, rising to well over £3,000 in peak years.[9] To a great extent the nature of payments by the receivers was standardized in both Courts and, with few exceptions, was similar for all districts. Ordinary expenditures included fees and allowances for themselves, the auditors, and other local officials, traveling expenses, expenses of the stewards' courts and the annual audit, reparations, and the payment of certain pensions, corodies, annuities, and " other perpetual charges." Rewards, expenses of melting or transportation of lead, storage, haulage, weighing costs for bell metal, and payments for the upkeep of barracks and fortifications were local items which, although not necessarily recurrent, were by no means uncommon. Finally, to suit the convenience of the Court, receivers were frequently ordered to pay debts, make advances, or send money to the Council of the North, sometimes by warrant dormant.

As in all revenue courts, the biggest problem was getting the revenues paid at the time due. However vigilant the officials, they were never completely successful in dealing with this; consequently tenants remained behind in their rent, and unpaid money or revenue, although long overdue, was still carried in the accounts under " arrearages " as if it were already received. These items of arrears, with which each account always began, usually denoted the revenue or back rent remaining unpaid from the previous year, but they might also have included the amount of money in the hands of the treasurer of the Court at the date of the conclusion of the account—that is, the cash balance carried over from the last declaration. Likewise, the term was often used to indicate debts or overdue payments collected during the current year. Thus arrears were carried from year to year, growing progressively as the period advanced. In his second declaration of September, 1539, Pope began his account with £23,308 14s. 1½d. in arrears. By 1544 the figure stood at £74,365 15⁄16d. and increased to £123,694 17s. 8d. in 1548, when the revenues of the Court of General Surveyors were added to the Court's income.

In addition to the arrears there were always the special allowances to be deducted from the final balance. Normally these covered regular

[9] The chart of receivers districts is given above, p. 281. Augm. Office, Treas. Rolls of Accts., Nos. 7, 8.

expenses of the annual audit, rewards, and unpaid sums due from purchasers of land. Less common deductions embraced losses sustained through debasement of the currency and necessary adjustments in the estimate value of jewels, plate, and ornaments taken from the dissolved monasteries. More essential to the security of the treasurer was the allowance for money paid out by him on the sole authority of the oral command of the chancellor of the Court, " who sayeth he hath the Kinges warraunt for the same." [10]

As given in the accounts, the total receipts at the end of the fiscal year thus included the sum total of accumulated arrears to date, which artificially swelled the final balance given. The actual income for the year is obtained by deducting the amount of the arrears as presented in the first item from the figure given as " total receipts." For example, in the account of Thomas Pope for the fiscal year ending in 1539, the total receipts of £131,836 5s. 10d. are reduced to £108,527 11s. 8½d. when arrears are deducted. Payments for the year aggregated £63,008 12s. 6¼d., which left a remainder of £68,827 13s. 3¾d. due the crown as indicated in the account. This balance, of course, included over £23,000 arrears. Moreover, it did not represent either the real balance or the amount actually paid by Pope to his successor, Sir Edward North, who had assumed the duties of the treasurer's office on March 17, 1540. The balance was reduced to £7,801 17s. 2d. by rewards of £42 given to the auditors and their clerks for auditing the account and by some £37,675 in arrears from land sales which had been accredited as receipts, despite the fact that it represented only promised payments.[11]

Of course a large part of the uncollected revenue was received later by the treasurer as payments came due, but it was not again entered into the account since the full purchase price of the land had already been recorded in the original entry of the sale. True, these later payments were included in the particulars of accounts from which the declaration was drawn up, but it was difficult to uncover a defalcation when an accountant deliberately concealed the cash payments and carried the amount in the arrears as unpaid debts. The effectiveness of the system depended largely on the integrity of officials, since it was not too difficult for dishonest ministers to cheat the king systematically over a period of years before being discovered. It appears to have been taken for granted

[10] Augm. Office, Misc. Books 249, fol. 51.
[11] Augm. Office, Treas. Rolls of Accts., No. 1, pt. 2. Abstracted in *L. and P.*, XIV, pt. 2, no. 236, p. 75. The arrears of land sales here referred to were detailed under receipts in 196 items, but the total was not given. In all cases land purchasers who still owed a part of the purchase price were bound by recognizances. Ordinarily a buyer made a substantial down payment for his land and was granted terms for the remainder.

that a public official would appropriate to his own use a certain portion of the revenue passing through his hands as a justifiable supplement to his salary, which was frequently inadequate. Otherwise, it is difficult to explain why so many accountants were exonerated from paying the full amount due on their accounts. In a great number of cases officials must intentionally have pocketed some of the money they received, with the assurance that the king would eventually excuse them from paying the deficit.[12]

It is not surprising, therefore, to discover that Pope did not pay the full amount specified in the above account. His loyalty and honesty were beyond question, and what was more important, he stood high in the estimation of Cromwell and the king. During the next four years he paid the new treasurer all of his debt except £534 2s. 6d. Finally, he received an acquittal for that sum by royal warrant, dated December, 1543, which he had obviously expected all along.[13] Presumably Pope had stalled payment as long as possible, hoping in the end to keep as much of it as his sovereign would tolerate.

North had been in office almost four years before he was called on to render an account, the period covered being from Michaelmas 1539 to Michaelmas 1543. After the usual allowances had been granted, including £52,036 11s. 3d. arrears from purchasers of land, his account showed a balance of £24,925 13s. 10$^{13}\!/_{16}d$. On April 10, 1544, following the close of the account, North was ordered " henceforth to surcease meddling in the said office " and to hand over his books and treasure to his successor, John Williams. He forthwith paid the new treasurer £22,328 8s. 9$^{15}\!/_{16}d$., which left £2,597 5s. $^{7}\!/_{8}d$. remaining unpaid. Meanwhile, North had succeeded Rich as chancellor of the Court, though he did not settle his debt as former treasurer until May of the following year. Even then the king permitted him to clear the debt by an exchange of land favorable to the crown.[14]

As principal treasury of the nation, the financial significance of the Court is indicated by the scope and magnitude of its expenditures

---

[12] The political morality of the Tudor official is discussed at some length at the beginning of Chapter Six.

[13] Addressed to the chancellor and other officials of the Augmentations, the warrant recognized Pope's new assignment by referring to him as " Cheiff Master of our Woodes " within the Court. The document is attached to Pope's original account. Augm. Office, Treas. Rolls of Accts., No. 1, pt. 2, mem. 41; see also Augm. Office, Misc. Books 1, fol. 28d.

[14] North deeded the king land worth some £425 a year in return for land valued at approximately £289 annually, chosen from lands under the administration of the Augmentations. The exchange is recorded in a warrant, attached to the foot of the account, discharging North of his debt. Augm. Office, Treas. Rolls of Accts., No. 2B, pt. 1, mems. 110–110d.

through the central office. Most of the issues were recurrent, varying but little from year to year; in the treasurer's accounts they were normally recorded under twelve general headings. Ordinarily the several groupings of payments were presented in the same order, although items three and four were sometimes combined: (1) " payments of fees," chiefly to Augmentations officials; (2) annuities; (3) pensions for term of life; (4) annual and perpetual pensions, mostly paid out of revenue from suppressed religious houses; (5) necessary expenses of the Court, including fuel, diets, and rewards; (6) costs for messenger service; (7) payments for land purchased or exchanged; (8) necessary payments by warrant of the Court; (9) payments by Court decree; (10) payments by royal warrant; (11) prests made upon the king's warrant; and (12) money delivered to the royal coffers for the king's personal use. The majority of these items are self-explanatory, but some categories require analysis. The detailed yearly expenditures of the Court show it to have taken over much of the financial business of the older revenue departments, especially the wardrobe, the chamber, and the Exchequer.

With the exception of pensions and annuities, the Court's expenses were not heavy during its early years. Consequently, the greater part of its revenue was spent on national items, such as land, armaments, defense, fortifications, and public works, or turned over to the king in cash for his personal disbursement. Fees for the central officials of the Court amounted to only £916 in 1539, though they rose to £1,567 five years later, to level off at slightly over £1,000 per year. The total of this item varied appreciably, depending on the number of quarterly or semi-annual salaries paid during the year and on how many extra " fees and diets " were included. Furthermore, as the Court itself was sometimes not prompt in meeting salaries as they came due, the official payroll for any given period was not always the same. A great many fees were paid as annuities and listed under that category, frequently concealing their true nature. Salaries and allowances of receivers and auditors, as well as the greater number of local officials, were normally paid directly from district revenues, but there were a great many exceptions to this rule. Fees of the attorney for the Augmentations in the Exchequer, the attorney for the duchy of Cornwall, legal assistants of the Court, the auditors of the prests, and the high stewards on either side of the River Trent and their deputies were all borne by the central treasury. Likewise, fees of clerks and other expenses for the auditing of the treasurer's account were paid from his office; these costs included diets and fees for the two auditors appointed to hear his annual declaration of account.

In addition to fees for the leading officials of the Court, those of the two principal secretaries, the great admiral of England, certain justices and clerks of courts, and numerous readers at the universities were regularly included among Augmentations payments. More surprising, however, were the fees paid to an indefinite number of minor officials, especially keepers of castles, forests, parks, chases, and royal houses. The chief of these keeperships were Sherwood Forest, Waltham Forest, Marylebone Park, Hyde Park, Westminster Palace, the gardens at Hampton Court, and the lieutenancy of forests in Northamptonshire, which the treasurer, Sir John Williams, held at a salary of £40 per year. Royal officers of less significance, who previously would have been paid from the household or chamber treasuries, are also found in this grouping: the keeper of the baths, the king's shipwright, the king's cutler, and certain servants such as those responsible for the " stilling of sweet water." [15]

Owing to the long list of fees and allowances by the Augmentations, there is a wide discrepancy among contemporary estimates of official expenditure for salaries. Numerous manuscript accounts of the comparative salaries for the several revenue courts are extant, but no two of them agree as to total charges. Even the treasurer's Books of Payments and Rolls of Accounts are often at variance in this respect because of inconsistency in the grouping of various items of payment. As far as actual salaries were concerned, the amount clearly depended on what fees, diets, and allowances were listed in this category. Fees of only the major officials of the Court at Westminster produced one total, but when all the innumerable field ministers and local officers were added to the list, the result was quite different. In other instances the totals arrived at might include either certain annuitants or a number of salaried ministers who were in no sense officers of the Court.

There was considerable increase in personnel after 1547, much of which was justifiable, but each expansion had the effect of extending the salary budget. At the time of its final dissolution the Augmentations lists forty-one officials at the Westminster office, with a total annual charge of £1,998 11s. 8d.[16] The commission study of 1552, however, gives £1,964 15s. per year paid out in fees and allowances to " the head Officers and Ministers." This list of twenty-four officers is not complete, but it includes diets and certain allowances. In a different summary the same commission report presents a total of £2,126 5s. for the charges of " The Chancellor Generall Surveyor and head Officers of this Court with their Ministers & attendants." If the salaries of

---

[15] In the case of some of the state officials, payment of their fees was authorized by warrant dormant.
[16] Augm. Office, Misc. Books 262, fols. 48–53.

receivers, auditors, surveyors, and woodwards are added, the total is increased to £6,835 3s. 2d. Expenditures on salaries are further augmented by the inclusion of local officers, officials in Wales, the justices and barons of the exchequer at Chester, the keepers of the king's bakehouse and brewhouse at Portsmouth, and the yeoman of the royal studs at Bury. Under this classification the grand total was swelled to £10,801 3s. 10d.[17] A later Elizabethan estimate suggests a total of £7,248 16s. 11d. paid in fees and allowances to officers of the Court, in which portage fees and numerous other charges that were ordinarily paid separately are added.[18]

Diets, rewards, travel allowances, and special expenses might sometimes be included among the regular fees, but only when such items were regularly recurrent, as diets for the annual accounts. Normally, however, these extras would be presented in other divisions of the treasurer's account, usually as payments by warrant of the chancellor and general surveyors. While individually of little moment, in the aggregate they represented a sizable expenditure. For the fiscal year 1543 charges for the " diets and pains " of the chancellor and others of the council in taking the annual accounts amounted to £80; for determining the treasurer's account the auditors and their clerks received another £40; and during the same period the treasurer was allowed £12 for storage bags, parchment, ink, and other materials, his clerks rewarded £13 6s. 8d. for their assistance, and the clerks of the chancellor paid an additional £2 for " casting and trying of the charge and discharge " of the same account.[19] Meals for the council sessions of the Court constituted a regular charge, as did expenses of special sittings, like the £2 1s. 11½d. paid to John Gemme for providing the council's dinner at Westminster on the opening day of parliament, January 16, 1542. When work was especially heavy, diets of the chief officers could become a problem. In 1540, for an accumulated half-year's diets, the treasurer was reimbursed £100. He had been " lying in London contynually

[17] Add. MS. 30198, fols. 21, 23d.–24. In a still different classification of fees and allowances it was estimated that salaries had increased from a total of £4,748 15s. 8d. in 1547 to £7,084 15s. 10d. in 1552. In this grouping were included auditors, receivers, various clerks, and expenses of the yearly audit. *Ibid.*, fols. 44d.–45.

[18] S. P. 12/221, p. 2 ff.

[19] Augm. Office, Misc. Books 252, fol. 62–63. Payments for " diets and travails " during accounting periods varied little from year to year, increasing only when accounts were particularly long. Such payments as warranted by the Augmentations council are conveniently accessible in the series of fifteen Books of Payments by the treasurer of the Court. Misc. Books 248–262 inclusive. For the year ending on March 20, 1547, the expenses of the treasurer's office increased to £16. An unusual number of prests and royal warrants had added to the general costs of audit. *Ibid.* 255, fols. 109–10.

aswell for the receipt of all suche sommes of moneye as dothe apperteyne to the Treasorers office as for the examynaccion of the accomptes perteynyng to the same Court." [20] By 1551 the holding of local courts was costing £761 18s. 6d. per year, and the expenses of annual audits were amounting to over £1,976.[21]

Innumerable expense accounts also imposed a continual drain on the revenues. Sooner or later everyone in the Court had occasion to travel on official business, either for surveys, other necessary work, or by special order. Journeying to London " about the Kinges busines " or going to Leighs in Essex to see the chancellor of the Court were extra burdens to officials. For such additional labor, however, they were granted a liberal fee of 6s. 8d. per day, plus regular allowances usually itemized as riding costs. Numerous accounts, receipts, warrants, and memoranda present detailed evidence on this aspect of Augmentations activity. In December, 1537, the solicitor was paid £4 6s. 8d. for seven days of continuous travel with four servants. Like his associates, Walter Henley himself was responsible for the wages of such domestics, but his clerks were awarded an extra £1 6s. 8d. in writing fees. During May of the following year the council of the Court was allowed £1 17s. 5d. for surveying a commons in Surrey which was to be enclosed as a part of the royal manor of Cullington.[22] At least some travel during the course of the year was accepted by most ministers as a normal part of their official routine.

Field officials or other informants also expected to be reimbursed for their costs in bringing valuable information to the Augmentations which could be used " to the Kynges advantage." [23] while at headquarters, some at least of the council's time was spent in field supervisory activities. Accounts by the chancellor for various trips during May, June, and July of 1537 detail expenditures for meals for himself and four or five servants, plus boat hire, cost for the care and feeding of his horses, and 1s. 8d. spent for ink, paper, and parchment.[24] Since the messengers were the connecting links between the central office and the county districts, much of their time was spent in travel beyond London. Mileages are not usually specified in expense statements, but in one

[20] *Ibid.* 250, fols. 47, 47d.; 249, fol. 32d.
[21] The estimate of the commissioners in 1552. Add. MS. 30198, fol. 25.
[22] Manchester Papers, 15/55, 93.
[23] *Ibid.*, 15/37.
[24] This memorandum by Richard Hutchinson, a servant of Sir Richard Rich, is entitled: " Money laid outt by me Richard Hochonson at dyverce tymes by the commaundment of my M^r [master] he beyng abowtt the Kynges besynes as here after ensuyth." *Ibid.*, 15/47. Other accounts of Rich are also included among these manuscripts.

account, warrants for payment mention that two of the three messengers had ridden 6,476 miles during the year with orders from the Court.[25]

Besides fees and diets, normal expenses of the Augmentations ranged from such prosaic items as livery for the Court's personnel, rewards, servants' dinners, gifts, and fuel for heating the office buildings to more significant expenditures on pensions and annuities, surveys, evaluations, bookkeeping, transcripts of records, and special investigations. For example, in May, 1538, the surveyor of woods was paid £30 for sixty days spent by him and his attendants on a previous survey of various Abingdon lands and Suffolk lands, at the rate of 10*s*. per day.[26] At the same time Richard Southwell was allowed £5 16*s*. 8*d*. spent in the suppression of two Norfolk monasteries. The no less industrious but more influential solicitor received £18 13*s*. 4*d*. as a reward for fifty-six days of constant attention to the Court's affairs, chiefly in travel to collect rents and conduct surveys.[27] Normal charges also covered indentures, acknowledgments of deeds of purchase or exchange, payment of individuals called in for information or consultation, and costs for copying statutes or taking excerpts from those acts of parliament which pertained to Augmentations lands or procedures.

Occasionally, brief entries reveal the varied character of the Court's business. During the fiscal year 1538–1539 diets for the treasurer's table cost £100, while payments for messenger services, including red cloth for liveries, totaled £41 7*s*. 6*d*.; the sum of £500 was allowed to the office of the lord treasurer in full satisfaction of fees due for " the signing of all those instruments under the Great Seal of England by which all late religious [persons] and friars were made *personas capaces*." In order to accommodate the increasing revenues for that year, a huge iron chest was bought for £22 10*s*. in which was stored the money derived from the sale of crown lands by special commission.[28] Apparently the proceeds from land sales made under the royal commission issued to Rich and Cromwell in 1539 were kept separate from the remainder of the revenues.[29]

Most current expenses were met as standard payments in the annual budget, but certain types of expenditure required special authorization,

[25] Treasurer's payments for 34 Henry VIII, Augm. Office, Misc. Books 251, fols. 76, 79–80.

[26] Manchester Papers, 15/94.

[27] *Ibid.*, 15/69, 85.

[28] Augm. Office, Treas. Rolls of Accts., No. 1, pt. 2, mems. 21, 21*d*., 23.

[29] See p. 235, *supra*. The commission was not issued formally until December 14, 1539, but Pope's accounts show the commissioners at work long before that date, having returned £36,572 16*s*. 10*d*. in land sales by Michaelmas of that year. *Ibid.*, mem. 15*d*.

usually in the form of irregular Court orders or written warrants: fees paid to the king's solicitor general or attorney general for legal sevices; legitimate debts that had been inherited from monasteries or arrears of annuities and pensions, both of which represented liabilities and outlays incurred in receiving the surrender of monasteries or chantries. Common also were recurrent costs for the upkeep, reparation, and maintenance of buildings and properties on crown demesne lands, rewards given by royal command, costs for routine administrative work,[30] and fees for the collection of rents and revenues. Occasionally, however, curious outlays are recorded Compensations for enclosures were awarded by warrants, new seals for the Court were purchased, and witnesses or officials were paid for their time and effort in the investigation of cases of embezzlement of the king's revenues. On May 4, 1539, the treasurer spent £30 "for the making of one stronge and newe Treasoure house for the sure keping of the Kinges treasure and for dyverse stronge iron chestes bought by him for the better suertie and sauf keping of the said treasure as by a warraunt thereof made more playnly apperyth." [31]

In the supervision of payments the chancellor and council of the Court exercised wide discretionary powers. They disallowed particular items in expense accounts that appeared to have been padded and approved or rejected a great variety of miscellaneous claims presented for consideration. Fees, wages, expenses of commissioners, and diets of certain

---

[30] Travel expenses were usually generous without being excessive. The sum involved more often than not indicated wide travel rather than exceptional fees. On April 5, 1542, Clement Throckmorton (Throgmerton), as surveyor of Warwickshire, was allowed £100 in advance "towards costs in riding" to inspect certain royal castles and manor houses "with a view to their speedy repair." In four previous payments, between June, 1541, and the following February, he had received £533 6s. 8d. for the same purpose. The royal manors in question were those where the king intended to stay during one of his progresses. Augm. Office, Misc. Books 251, fol. 75; *L. and P.*, XVIII, pt. 2, no. 231, pp. 128–29.

[31] Augm. Office, Misc. Books 249, fol. 38d. This item may have included the great storage chest referred to above, p. 336. For the same period two auditors were allowed £15 each for their "lying at London for takinge the Treasorers accompte as the same is to them allowed in other former yeres." Particular payments were often small sums expended on all kinds of minor or even petty affairs: £1 10s. for "oil and candle" and for "singing bread" due from the Augustine friars to two Londoners,. 17s. 4d. to a local carpenter for making a seat in the privy garden at Southwark, £4 for cages for fowls at the king's house there, £15 19s. to the chancellor's servant for conveying money to the court, and £15 to the treasurer for his expenses in taking the surrender at Waltham, Essex, and Christchurch, Canterbury, and for carrying plate and jewels of the latter monastery to his own house, then to the king at Westminster, and finally for deposit in the jewel house at the Tower. The latter payment also included incidental expenses at Sittingbourne, Kent, where the privy council sometimes met. *Ibid.* 249, fols. 37, 38, 41, 42.

crown agents, ambassadors, and councils were standard obligations.[32] However, many ordinary allowances rested on the judgment of the chancellor. The Court sometimes charged itself for special entertainment of councillors or distinguished guests, as the £2 8*d.* paid by a November 25, 1552, warrant for a dinner at which " other Justices and certein of the Kinges Learned Cowncell " were in attendance.[33] The Court even paid the charges of the principal justices of the Court of Common Pleas during the assizes at Bury St. Edmunds, Suffolk, and Ramsey, Huntingdonshire, in Michaelmas term, 1540,[34] and nine years later allowed the chancellor and others of the Augmentations full expenses for surveying and inventorying the goods and property of Protector Somerset at the time of his first arrest and overthrow in 1549.[35] Later, after Somerset's execution in 1551, Chancellor Sackville was paid £39 11*s.* 8*d.* for costs sustained in the delivery of personal property from Sion and Sheen.[36]

Usually requests for reimbursement of expenses incurred in regular Augmentations business were honored and paid in full. When in 1547 the auditor of the attainted duke of Norfolk was called on by the chancellor to bring in for examination the accounts of the duke's lands, he was allowed six days for the trip, with coverage for himself, two servants, and three geldings. Similarly, a searcher of Milford Haven, Fulk Pigott, was reimbursed £13 6*s.* 8*d.* for his charges in " being sent w^t diuers and sondrie persones for calling in the kinges dettes." [37] Sir John Baker, chancellor of the Court of First Fruits and Tenths, earned £20 for his pains in assisting the council of the Augmentations during the parliamentary session of 1542. During the same month Mrs. George Stoner was allowed £1 13*s.* 4*d.* for dinners and other charges of the chancellor and commissioners of the Court while they were engaged in enclosing

[32] Diets to councils included the Council of the North, the Council of the West Marches, and the Council of the Marches of Wales. Sometimes the diets, including " forreine expences," were quite high. Paid by warrants dormant of the king, the diets in 1551 for the Council of the North were £1,407 6*s.* 8*d.*, for the president and the Council of the Marches of Wales £1,422 9*s.* 2*d.*, and for ambassadors a total of £3,710 16*s.* 8*d.* Add. MS. 30198, fol. 25.

[33] Augm. Office, Misc. Books 261, fols. 81, 84.

[34] Add. MS. 9781, p. 369; Augm. Office, Misc. Books 8, p. 46*d.*

[35] Exch., Accounts Various, 520/6. For their work at Sheen, Surrey, and Sion House, Middlesex, Sackville, Thomas Moyle, and Walter Mildmay received £81 17*s.* 2*d.* During a fourteen-day period 112 horses were hired at 8*d.* per day each. The warrant is dated November 11, 1549. Three days later a clerk in the jewel house was paid £1 11*s.* 8*d.* for costs in transporting several chests of valuables to the Tower, having been summoned by Mildmay " to come in hast to Shene." Such expense accounts as these yield valuable data on prices and wages. On this occasion a barge and nine bargemen were hired for three days, at 1*s.* per day each for the men and 3*s.* rental for the barge. Augm. Office, Misc. Books 258, fol. 67*d.*

[36] *Ibid.* 260, fol. 68.

[37] *Ibid.* 256, fol. 93*d.*; Augm. Office, Miscellanea, 23.

land for the new royal park of Fair Meade in Waltham Forest, Essex.[38] On the following May 4 the steward of the Star Chamber was reimbursed £4 12*s.* 5*d.* for the expenses of the council's dinner at Westminster and on October 30, 1543, he was allowed £50 10*s.* 9½*d.* for the council's diets at the Rolls' Office. In that year payments by warrant of the Court reached £2,442 14*s.* 3¾*d.*, excluding £13 6*s.* 8*d.* paid to William Berners and John Wiseman for ink, paper, parchment, and other necessary paraphernalia connected with the treasurer's account, "more than the charges hath grown unto in times past." [39]

Frequently, however, extraneous evidence reveals that payments, often unidentified, to Augmentations officials were for work done by order of the privy council or for missions performed for the king which bore no relation to their official duties. Typical of such payments was the £126 paid by the Court to its chancellor, Sackville, on February 10, 1552, for the housing of Henry Fitzalan (Lord Maltravers) and his entourage by previous order of the council in November, 1551. This was during the period of his father's imprisonment under accusations of treasonable conduct in plotting with Somerset and others. Sackville was asked to take custody of young Maltravers, then about fourteen years old, "for a tyme," so that he could be kept nearby and sent for if desired. The short period turned out to be sixty-three weeks, during which time the boy, two schoolmasters, and four servants lived at Sackville's house in London.[40] Further complicating the accounts was the practice of ordering money to be delivered to an Augmentations minister or some other trusted crown official who was then instructed to turn it over to somebody else.

For the first few years payments authorized by decree of the Court sitting in judicial session were almost entirely for debts, arrears of pensions, or damages concerning which judgment had been awarded. Some were compensations paid in the name of the crown for previous illegal or unjustifiable collections of money or revenues, but the greater number were bona fide obligations contracted earlier by attainted persons or by the heads of religious houses prior to the Dissolution. While

---

[38] Augm. Office, Misc. Books 251, fols. 75, 76. In this and subsequent accounts recurrent payments relate to expenses incurred in improving the king's new park of Fair Meade.

[39] These and other similar sums for diets were paid to Richard Brown of Whitby, servant of the king and steward of the Star Chamber. *Ibid.* 252, fol. 60; 253, fol. 69 ff.

[40] Sackville was allowed £2 per week for all seven people, or somewhat less than 6*s.* each. Exch., Accounts Various, 76/36, fols. 108, 121; Augm. Office., Misc. Books 261, fol. 85*d.* On Henry Fitzalan, see article on the twelfth earl of Arundel, *D. N. B.*

individual debts were not usually very large, together they became a continual drain on the treasury, indicating rather forceably the extent to which crown possessions were encumbered by the time they came under the jurisdiction of the Augmentations.

Down to 1540 the decree payments averaged well over £1,000 per year, but by 1543 they had declined to almost £400. The next year they jumped to £2,379 5s. 1¼d. and in 1545–1546 reached over £11,,000.[41] As the debts of the encumbered estates had gradually been paid off, however, this larger figure covers other types of Court judgments, more especially recovered arrears of annuities and payments due from crown exchanges or purchases of land. Likewise, many individuals had bought estates or timber from the king which, for one reason or another, had never actually been delivered, despite the fact that substantial down payments had been made. The phrase " recompence of a purchase," regularly used in the accounts, usually meant the return of an original payment or compensation for breach of conduct. Otherwise, decrees for " recompences " were court orders for compensation to be paid clients for offices surrendered, lands enclosed by royal command, or interests in land or rents given up in order that the property might be alienated by the crown.

Nevertheless, all payments by decree under the seal of the Augmentations did not necessarily grow out of formal court judgments. Some of them were no more than ordinary expenditures which had received the definite sanction of a decree instead of the more common authorization by warrant of the chancellor. For example, in 1546–1547 the lord chancellor was refunded £34 6s. 5d. in consequence of an overevaluation of certain land bought from the king. Richard Devereux, son of

---

[41] Annual payments by decree for the first Court of Augmentations were as follows:

28–30 Henry VIII	£2,725 6s. 8½d.
31 Henry VIII	£1,032 6s. 8½d.
32 Henry VIII	£1,559 9s. 1d.
33 Henry VIII	£892 3s. 4d.
34 Henry VIII	£493 6s. 8d.
35 Henry VIII	£404 13s. 4d.
36 Henry VIII	£2,379 5s. 1¼d.
37 Henry VIII	£11,033 10s. 5d.
38 Henry VIII	£6,755 15s. 7d.

Extracted from the Treasurer's Rolls of Accounts and the Treasurer's Books of Payments. Similar payments under the second Court declined in volume as expenditures by royal warrant multiplied. For example, in 6 Edward VI payments by decree of the Court totaled but £136 6s. 2d., as compared to £25,821 5s. 11d. paid out by warrant of king and council. For the last year of the Court's existence, the totals were £772 16s. 1d. and £7,367 14s. 7d. respectively. Exch., Enrolled Accounts, Misc. Roll 22, mems. 18d., 19–21, 22–23d.; Augm. Office, Treas. Rolls of Accts., No. 8.

Lord Ferrers, was allowed £100 due on an obligation, and £599 7s. 6d. more was paid to various people for land redelivered to the king. The cost of the enrollment of deeds for the year totaled £14 2s.[42] In April, 1544, the receiver of North Wales was awarded £200 for costs incurred in " suing out a lease of certain wood in the lordship of Wynnoweshedge within the lordship of Muchenhampton which he enjoyed not for that it was sold to the lord Wyndesore," and in October Thomas Barnardeston was reimbursed for having been overcharged for certain land which he had purchased from the crown. By a curious decree of June 5, 1543, the archbishop of Canterbury was recompensed £183 4s. 6d. for certain woodland " which he could not enjoy." More definite were the decree payments of February 20 and March 20, 1544, of £46 13s. 4d. to Richard Duke, clerk of the Court, for his " pains and great charges " in making process for the collection of arrears and other debts due the crown.[43]

With the decline of the king's chamber the treasurer of the Augmentations expended money for all kinds of outlays which earlier would have been assumed by the chamber treasury. Such a development, however, was more accidental than intentional. There was nothing particularly novel in the practice of using whatever funds were at hand to meet current expenses as they arose, nor did the government make any attempt to differentiate between the numerous types of payments when distributing expenditures among the various departments. A new pension or annuity might be assigned indiscriminately to any one of the financial courts. All revenue, irrespective of its source or nature, was the king's money to be distributed as suited the government's needs or the royal convenience. That the Augmentations was more commonly used than the other treasuries of the realm was purely a matter of expedience. The treasurer of the Augmentations, as had the treasurer of the chamber and the treasurer of first fruits and tenths before him, acted as paymaster for the crown only because he was custodian of the greater bulk of national revenues and, hence, apt to have enough cash at any one time to meet even the extraordinary demands of the king. Instead of transferring more funds to the chamber, the king chose to draw on the financial courts for all kinds of national as well as personal expenses. Payments by royal warrant, therefore, became a major expenditure of the Court.

Authorization by warrant of the king or privy council was necessary for payments which ordinarily did not fall within the jurisdiction of the Augmentations; as a general rule it covered all outlays which were in

[42] Augm. Office, Misc. Books 255, fols. 101–102.
[43] *Ibid.*, 253, fols. 73–74.

no sense related to the Court's administration as provided by law. Varied in amount and divergent in character, these extraneous payments can be divided conveniently into two types of issues, ordinary and extraordinary. Together they cover the wide range of crown expenditures and clearly illustrate the extent to which a particularized revenue court could develop into a national finance department of the first magnitude. Within the category of ordinary payments occur all sorts of miscellaneous items that, heretofore, had been relegated to either the jewel house, the household, or the chamber. Expenses of English ambassadors, royal rewards, gifts, personal loans, materials for the wardrobe, plate, jewels " necessaries " for Lady Anne of Cleves, or reparatations for the royal kitchen were not customary expenditures for a department whose primary function was land revenue administration. Payments to coopers, brewers, cutlers, tailors, skinners, the king's goldsmith, or the king's printer were strictly household expenditures; neither the cost of engraving seals for the courts of common law nor allowances to special merchants for stuff bought for the king were in any way related to Augmentations activity. Conversely, regular disbursements by the Court for such things as fortifications, national defense, public works, the army, the navy, ordnance, and general war purposes involved sums of such size as only a major state treasury could handle.

A detailed breakdown of these diverse categories would reveal more clearly than lengthy exposition the full range of Augmentations finance, but such an analysis would necessitate the actual reproduction of major sections of the accounts themselves, which is not possible in this study. A few examples, however, selected from among the innumerable articles set forth in the treasurer's " particulars " of accounts, will suggest the nature and purpose of these warrants which largely determined the true financial character of the Court.

Ordinary payments by royal warrant were often recurrent, as allowances for diets of the king's various ministers, for " coat and conduct money " in the local musters, or for reimbursement of the king's personal attendants or other servants for money spent in miscellaneous purchases for the crown. The amount specified in any one warrant was seldom over a few hundred pounds and usually stipulated the exact nature of the payment. Household officials who bought supplies more or less regularly, as the cofferer, yeomen of the tents, and gentlemen of the privy chamber, were reimbursed periodically for money spent out of their own personal funds. Since the various government departments were frequently short of cash or behind in their necessary current payments, the king drew heavily upon the Augmentations. The diets and fees for the Council of the West and the Council of the North were generally paid from the Court, as were the expenses incurred by John and Richard Gresham who, as agents for the crown, were constantly engaged in local or continental transactions. On warrant of October 25, 1539, Morgan Wolf, the king's goldsmith, was paid £392 5¼d. for plate delivered to the king and distributed as rewards among various agents and messengers of foreign nobles, notably the duke of Saxony and the duke of Cleves. In February of the same year Mary Fitzroy, the duchess of Richmond,[44] was paid £90 from the Augmentations as a royal reward.[45] Thomas Bartlett, the king's printer, was regularly reimbursed for books and proclamations delivered to the king, though individual warrants seldom ran over £100. In January, 1542, Sir Francis Brian, as master of the toils,[46] received £40 for transferring 240 deer from the royal parks at Greenwich, Eltham, and Itchingham, Kent, to Otford Park, in the same county. A year later he was assisted by the Augmentations receiver, John Scudamore, in stocking the king's new park at Waltham, Essex, with deer.[47]

In 1541 Sir John Baker, chancellor of the Court of First Fruits and Tenths, was reimbursed from the Augmentations for outlay on improvements to the royal park and mansion at Halden, Kent, instead of being paid from the revenues of his own institution.[48] Similarly, reparations for property not under its supervision were financed from the Court's revenues, as for example, the construction of an ordnance house in the Tower of London, the repair of the banqueting house at Greenwich, a kitchen at Hatfield, and the parliament house at Windsor.[49] Other warrants authorized payments for a variety of miscellaneous matters:

[44] The duchess, Mary Howard, was the daughter of the duke of Norfolk and widow of the king's illegitimate son, Henry Fitzroy, who was created duke of Richmond and Somerset in 1533. Fitzroy died in 1536.

[45] Augm. Office, Treas. Rolls of Accts., No. 1, pt. 2, mem. 23. During the same year, by prests made upon warrants, the master of the king's works, Robert Lord, was paid £5,600 for fortresses and castles at Dover, the Downs, Hampton Court, and Oatlands, £1,548 for the manors of Hampton Court, Nonsuch, Esher, Hanworth, and elsewhere, and £2,000 for Dover Castle and the Green Fortress upon the Downs, with the necessary provisions for the same. *Ibid.*, mem. 23d.

[46] The household office of toils, "le Toile," had charge of the netting of deer, which was prohibited to the ordinary citizen under penalty of a heavy fine. Brian was also chief butler of England, vice admiral in January, 1543, and ambassador to Charles V from October 6 to December 28, 1543.

[47] Augm. Office, Treas. Rolls of Accts., No. 2B, pt. 1, for 31–35 Henry VIII. They were paid 3s. 4d. each for the transportation of 600 fallow deer and 10s. each for 12 stags caller "redd dere." There are numerous examples in the treasurer's accounts of similar payments for the transfer of deer from one royal park or forest to another.

[48] Augm. Office, Misc. Books 250, fols. 43, 47.

[49] Henry Williams was paid £100 " to be employed upon repairing the higher and lower house of Parliament at Windesore." *Ibid.* 254, fol. 72.

charges for the transportation of lead from Ireland to England; for the embroidering of coats for the royal servants; "spangles" of silver and silver gilt for the uniforms of the king's footmen and the yeomen of the guard; postage fees; royal messenger service; provisions for Boulogne, and periodic payments on the Flanders debt. Not infrequently the expenses of a minister were more than the amount allocated to him. In such cases he was paid for the "surplusage" of his account by royal warrant drawn upon any one of the treasuries of the realm.[50] On the other hand, when the audit of a minister's accounts showed a balance remaining in his hands, he was required to pay over the surplus [51] or "overplus" to the king's use. Thus, in the Augmentations Rolls of Accounts a "surplusage" of accounts might represent either a receipt or a disbursement.

The Books of Payments of the Augmentations present not only a cross-sectional view of national expenditures for any given year but also a fair sampling of the great variety of court expenses. During the Edwardian period these incidental items became more frequent, ranging in size from trivial sums for alms, livery, and wages of royal servants, attendance at council meetings, and charges for political prisoners at the Tower, to large amounts for victuals, revels, dower rights, or appropriations to be spent as directed by the privy council. During the first year of operation the £45,782 19s. 4d. spent by the second Augmentations on the authority of royal warrant included such diverse items as the following: "necessaries" for the council chamber, furniture for Lady Mary's household, charges for the king's colts and mares, fruit trees imported from Rome at 2s. each., £88 for the repair of Henry VIII's tomb, £300 spent on a ship for the admiralty, and £2,000 "towardes the satisfaccion" of creditors of the great wardrobe.[52]

Detailed as monthly payments, these accounts show the degree to which the council relied on the Court in the normal business of the state. Expenditures on Christmas "pastymes" or charges for the introduction of hops on a royal manor were just as much a part of Augmentations

---

[50] Numerous warrants for "surplusages of accounts" were directed to the treasurer of the Augmentations. In September, 1545, Richard Hartlepole, one of the paymasters for the army was allowed £67 4s. 3d. in full payment of the "superplusage" of his account. In December of the same year the king's fishmonger, John Hopkins, was paid £91 15s. 4½d. for surplusage spent by him in providing fish for the navy. *Ibid.*, fols. 72, 76. Both warrants are recorded among the actions of the privy council. *L. and P.*, XX, pt. 2, nos. 428, 1010.

[51] The term "surplusage" was usually used in the sixteenth century to signify a deficit due to the disbursement of more money than the charge of the accountant warranted. However, in a different sense, the term was also used to indicate the remainder of money still unspent, or the "overplus" of an account.

[52] Augm. Office, Misc. Books 256, fols. 78d. 79, 82. 83, 83d., 90, 91.

finance as was the £2,153 paid for the burial expenses of the king.[53] Victualer, purveyor, musician, tailor, coffer maker, master of the horse, lord of misrule, principal secretary, surveyor of works, warden of the marches, treasurer of the chamber, deputy of Ireland, and a host of other agents shared alike in spending the profits of the Court. Obviously the ratio of expenditure by warrant of the crown to the total expenditure for any one year varied greatly. For 1548–1549, however, the charges under this category were unusually high, being £162,176 out of a total of £184,581.[54]

The range of greater payments covered by the treasurer's accounts indicates more clearly the peculiar nature of Tudor finance. When called on, the council turned to whichever treasury happened to have funds available at that moment. Beyond the normal expenses of its own department, no treasury had a monopoly of any one type of expenditure. Current governmental expenses were met as they came in, without favor or preference, by royal warrants drawn indiscriminately upon the chamber, the mint, the Exchequer, or any one of the newer revenue courts. Thus each department bore its proportionate share of the financial burden without the need to earmark particular revenues in advance. In fact, certain standard payments were apportioned by standing warrants among the several courts. The expenses of national defense, the army, navy, Ireland, and Calais were all in part borne by each treasury, while both the jewel house and the chamber were from time to time assisted by special funds transferred from other departments. In the case of the royal household the Augmentations by warrant dormant paid £10,000 annually toward its support.[55] By a similar arrangement £3000 per year was allocated to the household of Prince Edward.[56]

[53] *Ibid.* 258, fol. 78*d.*; 262, fol. 66.

[54] Payments from March, 1548, to March, 1549. *Ibid.* 257, fol. 91. Payments by royal warrant had run high during the war years of the previous reign, reaching a peak of £212,527 for 36 Henry VIII. *Ibid.* 253, fol. 65. The Books of Payments for the reign of Edward VI are found in *ibid.* 256–262. Payments by royal warrant are always listed as a separate category. Many of these originals are preserved among the documents subsidiary to the accounts of the treasurer of the Augmentations. Augm. Office, Miscellanea, 314/19.

[55] This was in addition to the fees of household officials. The annual assignment was apportioned among the various treasuries as follows: the Augmentations £10,000, the mint £10,000, the duchy of Lancaster £6,000, the Exchequer £6,000 (often paid in tallies rather than cash), and the First Fruits and Tenths "suche money as remayneth in their office from tyme to tyme, saving such other ordynary warrauntes as be alredy addressed unto them." Dasent (ed.), *Acts of the Privy Council,* II, 281–82; III, 424; IV, 190; Augm. Office, Misc. Books 250, fol. 51; Add. MS. 30198, fols. 35*d.*, 36. The chamber, already in marked decline, was not included in this assignment; nor was the Court of Wards and Liveries mentioned, for it paid its revenues annually to the chamber. Later, under Elizabeth, the Wards and Liveries bore a regular statutory assignment of £10,000 for the cofferer of the household. Bell, *The Court of Wards and Liveries,* 46.

[56] D. L. 42/133, fol. 76; Augm. Office, Misc. Books 250, fol. 55.

This extreme mobility of organization proved a godsend whenever the state was beset with serious financial difficulties. During the French War in 1544–1546, when all sources of current revenue were exhausted, the practical problem of raising enough cash from week to week to take care of bills as they came in overshadowed all other concerns. When it was needed so desperately, all the treasuries were called on to furnish whatever money they happened to have on hand. Thus, a warrant from the privy council could process a direct payment from any department regardless of its nature. Under such conditions the periodic declarations and informal reports by the treasurers on the state of the revenues obviously proved invaluable to the council in determining just where money was available and how much of it was likely to be unencumbered. However, under the press of circumstances even a cursory check was not always possible, and warrants were issued for indeterminate sums, leaving blank the amount and the name of the paymaster until it was determined on which treasury the order should be drawn.[57] When all the treasuries were low, the amount needed was divided among them in proportion to their ability to pay. In cases of urgency, prior claims were not acceptable as excuse for delayed delivery. When the treasurers of wars were called on in January, 1546, to advance £1,000 " for the maryne causes," they were ordered to take steps for immediate payment, any other warrants heretofore received to be dispatched notwithstanding.[58]

During this period when revenue departments were frequently drained dry, the mint and the Augmentations proved to be the most inexhaustible. As the war burden grew progressively heavier, complaints by governmental agencies of mounting charges and insufficient appropriations became increasingly frequent; only the distressed council seemed aware of the extreme gravity of the situation as they anxiously studied the incoming reports of the state of the revenue. These monthly declarations, however, might be of little avail, since the revenue courts were often empty or in debt and knew not what they could furnish if unexpectedly called on. Nevertheless, the Augmentations bore more than a fair share of war expenses, its monthly payments being exceeded only by those of the mint, which was favored, of course, by the profits of

[57] Usually these warrants were for large amounts, varying from £1,000 to £7,000, earmarked either for specific purposes or delivered to a paymaster to be used generally " towardes the necessary defraymentes within his chardge." Dasent (ed.), *Acts of the Privy Council*, III, 121, 122. See also *ibid.*, I, 335, 336, 349, 361.

[58] As the three warrants of January, 1546, issued by the council sitting at Hampton Court for £1,000 towards naval expenses to be delivered immediately to Robert Legge, treasurer of the king's ships. Payments of £500, £300, and £200 were accordingly assigned respectively to the Augmentations, Exchequer, and First Fruits and Tenths. *Ibid.*, 319, 323. Sir Richard Rich was general treasurer of the war in France and Sir Ralph Sadler high treasurer of the Scottish war.

debasement. Writing to Secretary Paget on November 5, 1545, Wriothesley promised the king to have ready £20,000 in cash within the
week, explaining that in addition to £3,000 recently sent to Boulogne,
the mint—" our holy anchor "— would be able to raise another £15,000.
The declarations of the treasurers showed the Augmentations to have
£3,000, the duchy of Lancaster £1,000, and the Wards and Liveries
£1,000. The Court of First Fruits and Tenths and the Court of
General Surveyors had no funds at all, while the chamber, which had
contributed practically nothing toward the support of the garrisons for
over a year, now found itself heavily in debt with not " one groat
remaining " to contribute to the war effort. The £1,000 balance in
the Exchequer was already earmarked and could not be included in the
total.[59] This fairly accurately represented the normal situation, although
by the autumn of 1546 the pressure was somewhat relieved. However,
the true state of national finance can only be arrived at in relation to the
indeterminate privy-purse reserves which could be used in cases of
emergency.[60]

If the Augmentations carried a large proportion of the national expenditure, it was in part at least because the council had come to rely
on it more than on other departments. In the summer of 1541, when
the king had ordered £4,000 sent to Calais and Guisnes, the council
was at a loss to know where to address the warrant, since it had been
received without direction. It was finally sent to Sir Edward North,
treasurer of the Augmentations, who complained that all warrants were
addressed to him. Since he had but £3,000 left in the Court's treasury,
North made up the difference of £1,000 from his own pocket, thus ful-
fulling the king's command.[61] While such conscientiousness might not
be personally rewarding, it was apt to win an increase in financial business for the Court.

Individually the greatest Augmentations payments were for military
purposes, varying in amount from a few hundred to £10,000 or £20,000
at a time. Extraordinary expenditures included large sums for mercenary
troops, munitions in Ireland, marine causes, provisions for the army

---

[59] *L. and P.*, XX, pt. 2, no. 729.

[60] See p. 201 f. In September, 1546, the mint and the Augmentations were ordered
to pay £2,000 each to Nicholas Bristow, the king's clerk, for construction of a
" banqueting house " for the forthcoming reception of the admiral of France, with
the council's promise that they would not be troubled again for a long while.
Ibid., XXI, pt. 2, no. 82. The payment by the Augmentations is recorded in the
Treasurer's Books of Payments for 38 Henry VIII. Augm. Office, Misc. Books
255, fol. 90.

[61] July 24, 1541, the council in London to the council with the king. *L. and P.*,
XVI, no. 1028.

and the navy, ordnance, " furniture " for the Tower, money exchanged in Flanders to be distributed by Stephen Vaughan about " the Kynges affayres," and for strengthening fortifications and garrisons. Among defense items the total annual costs for strategic garrisons, overseas posts, and coastal blockhouses and forts were always heavy, especially at Calais, Boulogne, Portsmouth, the Isle of Wight, Berwick, and Carlisle. By the time Boulogne was given up in 1550 it had cost the state some £ 1,342,550 during five and a half years of occupation. Likewise in Ireland, always a drain on the English treasury, yearly charges had mounted to £ 42,609 by the end of the reign of Edward VI.[62] The Court usually assumed the lion's share of these heavy expenditures, with payments ranging from nominal sums for the upkeep of the Black Bulwark at Dover or Carmarthen Castle in Wales to some £ 3,000 annually for Berwick. In most inland areas the charges were negligible, but the receivers of some coastal counties like Hampshire faced a drain of over £ 1,000 per year out of their revenues.[63] In addition, huge sums were spent on royal palaces, public works, and general affairs of state. During one day in October, 1548, treasurer John Williams was in receipt of royal warrants for a total of £ 5,000 to be distributed as follows: £ 1,000 for the household, £ 1,000 " for the seas," £ 1,000 for marine causes, £ 1,000 for ordnance,[64] and £ 1,000 advanced to the king's chamber.[65]

The latter payment illustrates a practice that had become common by the end of the Henrician period when the chamber was no longer a

---

[62] Dietz, *Finances of Edward VI and Mary*, 88–89, 91, 104. For details of such payments from the Augmentations, see the Books of Payments series, as for example Misc. Books 254, fols. 64–85; Manchester Papers, 15/28, 30–32, 38, 43, 62, 78.

[63] The total charge in the Augmentations for garrisons, fortresses, and bulwarks at the time of its dissolution was £9,394 per year. Add. MS. 30198, fols. 14d. seq., 24d. This total, of course, did not include reparations and other special payments. Already a reduction in defense spending had been urged on the government, since the charges were considered too great for a permanent peacetime budget. *Ibid.*, fol. 45d. However, retrenchment, although considered by Northumberland, was not really implemented until after the accession of Mary.

[64] The warrant authorized the delivery of £1,000 to Anthony Anthony " for payments under his charge," which probably related to the ordnance office or to the victualing of Boulogne. Anthony was formally appointed master surveyor of the ordnance in the Tower and elsewhere, including the towns and marches of Calais and Boulogne, on January 23, 1549. However, he had been officiating in a similar capacity for some time before his patent of appointment. *Cal. Pat. Rolls, Edward VI*, I, 353; *ibid., Elizabeth*, I, 282.

[65] Dasent (ed.), *Acts of the Privy Council*, II, 225. In December and January following, an additional £1,000 was paid out to creditors of the great wardrobe, £1,000 for the navy, and £5,000 more to the treasurer of the north. *Ibid.*, 232, 234.

major financial department. Having lost the revenues of the Court of General Surveyors upon its dissolution in 1547, the chamber experienced a drastic decline that was almost automatic; [66] consequently, in order that the office might meet its current responsibilities, funds were regularly transferred to it from the financial courts, though they never became routine allotments. The amounts involved were usually just enough to enable the chamber treasurer to muddle along by postponing his larger payments until an advance from another department was forthcoming. Sometimes the money was paid to John Dawes, deputy to the treasurer, "for thinges occurrent," and sometimes delivered in large sums "to be emploied about the kinges maiestes affaires within his office." [67] Usually the deliveries were simply directed to the chamber treasurer or to his deputy, in sums of £500 or £1,000, to be used for any type of expenditure "in his chardge," but not infrequently the particular nature of the payment authorized was specified in the warrant. Less commonly the treasurer of the Augmentations paid the recipient directly, as in the case of a pension payable from the chamber, and deducted the amount from the gross sum assigned to the chamber from the Court's revenues. [68]

During the reign of Henry VIII large amounts were often expended on public works and on crown buildings, especially on the royal residences of Esher, Oatlands, Otford, Mortlake, Hanworth, Nonsuch, Enfield, and Greenwich in Middlesex, Surrey, and Kent. These advances were made either through the local receivers under order of the Court or delivered by the treasurer upon warrant from the council to the overseer of works or paymaster of works. In most cases building materials such as stone, lead, and lumber, as well as costs of construction, were furnished by the Augmentations.

More interesting to the student of administration, however, are the numberless warrants from the privy council ordering payment of small sums relating to miscellaneous items of business that daily came under

---

[66] The treasurer of the chamber was ex officio treasurer of the Court of General Surveyors, so that formerly all the revenues of that court had flowed into his office.

[67] *L. and P.*, XXI, pt. 1, nos. 113, 116, 156, 1167. Augm. Office, Misc. Books 254, fol. 78. Dasent (ed.), *Acts of the Privy Council*, I, 323, 324. Augm. Office, Misc. Books 257, fols. 75*d.*, 88, 90; 258, fols. 84*d.*, 113.

[68] When Williams was commanded to pay Jean de Fontenay, Sieur de Bretteville, a Norman in the English service pensioned by the king, he was authorized to deduct the sum from the total assigned to the chamber by prest. Dasent (ed.), *Acts of the Privy Council*, II, 110. See also *ibid.*, 213, for an advance of £1,000 "to be taken out of the sale money and restored again herafter by the money of the revenues." Exch., Accounts Various, 76/35, fol. 41. On Augmentations payments to the chamber, see also the account book of Sir William Cavendish, treasurer of the chamber, for 1–2 Edward VI. Augm. Office, Misc. Books 439.

conciliar review. Gifts were judiciously distributed for the apprehension of pirates, felons, counterfeiters, and promoters of sedition, or for bringing " certene lewde persones " before the council for questioning.[69] If payments had not been channeled in advance through a particular office, compensation for such ordinary services as the collection of debts, fines, and arrears, for valuable information presented to the council, the retention of prisoners, or for any special expenses incurred in the interests of the king were allowed by royal or conciliar warrant. In May, 1550, when the French ambassadors arrived at the mouth of the Thames, they were met by the king's galley and escorted to London. On this occasion special appointments for the royal vessel were borrowed from the jewel house and £40 in prest was delivered to the clerk of ships by the treasurer of the Augmentations to be used in the furnishing of the galley.[70] Occasionally the details of prest allowances are not divulged, but more often the nature of the payment is specified in the warrant. In consideration of his services to the king and in partial satisfaction of a debt, in December, 1552, Sir William Stafford was paid £900 in cash for the surrender of an annuity of £100 granted him two years previously.[71] In the following January, Armigal Wade, clerk of the council of Calais, was sent £40 to be spent according to the wishes of the king's council.[72]

Personal loans to the king were repaid by royal warrant, sometimes drawn upon the Augmentations, as were the foreign loans contracted in Antwerp by the king's agents. Not infrequently land was accepted in part or full satisfaction of a personal debt to the crown, in which case the Court was called on to evaluate the property, cancel the original recognizance, and draw up a new agreement for future payments. As might be expected, a great number of the ordinary as well as the extraordinary payments were in the form of prests; for the most part expenditures for war, fortifications, the king's works, the household, or allowances in advance of wages and diets fell under this category. Typical of such prests made upon warrant is the council's authorization to the treasurer of Augmentations for the payment of £100 to the surveyor of works, Lawrence Bradshaw, who was continually receiving money for construction projects before the work was completed or even begun.

[69] Augm. Office, Misc. Books 258, fols. 74–89 *passim*.

[70] Nichols (ed.), *Literary Remains*, II, 271; Dasent (ed.), *Acts of the Privy Council*, III, 33.

[71] Augm. Office, Misc. Books 261, fol. 75*d*. Stafford's annuity had been awarded in June, 1550. *Cal. Pat. Rolls, Edward VI*, III, 306.

[72] Augm. Office, Misc. Books 261, fol. 77.

After our right harty commendacions. The Kinges Ma^tes pleasure by aduise of his highness pryve counsail personally attending on his most royal person is that you shal delyv. in prest vnto Lawrence Bradshaw to be employed vppon reparacions of Wyndesor the somme of oone hundred poundes sterl. Thus faire you hartely wel. ffrom Hampton Court the xii^th of September 1547

Your Loving ffrendes [73]

Among the special funds prested by royal warrant were those deliveries made directly to the crown which, in effect, soon came to create a personal treasury. Under Henry VII the treasurer of the chamber and the keeper of the jewels had both acted as special custodians of the royal hoard, but Henry VIII demanded a more definite reserve of money at his command than these offices afforded. As "keeper of the kinges money" he chose his friend and confidant, Sir William Compton, a gentleman of the privy chamber, who informally took charge of privy-purse receipts and disbursements. Although undoubtedly a royal favorite, there is no evidence to justify the assumption of earlier historians that he enriched himself at the expense of the state.[74] From the very beginning of the reign money was withdrawn from regular channels to be paid into Compton's hands for the special use of the king.[75]

Wherever the physical repository of the royal treasure was located, the controling office was one of considerable responsibility and trust, a position awarded only to the most discreet royal servants. It is not entirely accidental, therefore, that the future keepers of the privy purse were drawn from among the gentlemen of the privy chamber. Upon

[73] The signatures of eight of the privy councillors follow, including those of Sir Edward North, chancellor of the Augmentations; Sir William Petre, principal secretary; Sir Anthony Denny, gentleman of the privy chamber; and Thomas Seymour, admiral of England. Exch., Accounts Various, 76/35, fol. 9; see also *ibid.*, fols. 13, 104; D. L. 42/133, fols. 248d., 265.

[74] In the following century it was said of him that "he was too narrow for his Fortune, and more attentive to his private advantage, than to the publick affairs." Compton's wealth was acquired through marriage, his various offices, and as a recipient of the king's bounty. On the other hand, it was probably true that he "studied the King's nature, rather than his business; and humoured rather than advised him." Lloyd, *The Statesmen and Favourites of England since the Reformation*, 110–11.

[75] The earliest recorded instance of these payments "to the kinges own use" is found in the accounts of the hanaper of the chancery by Roger Lupton, from July 12, 1509, to September 29, 1510. The first of five payments of the surplus of the hanaper, totaling £2,787, was delivered to the king's private coffers on December 1, 1509. Exch., Accounts Various, 220/1; abstracted in *L. and P.*, I, pt. 1 (2nd edition), no. 579. Compton was pardoned and released as collector in the port of London, sheriff of Worcester, the king's "pursebearer," and keeper of the king's moneys and jewels, in February, 1526. *Ibid.*, IV, pt. 1, no. 2002(22).

Compton's death in 1528 he was succeeded by Anthony Denny, another gentleman of the privy chamber, who took over the direction of the personal finances of the sovereign in the same way that his predecessor had done. During the latter part of the reign he was ably assisted by his servant, John Gates, who had already risen to a position of influence in the privy chamber before his master's death in 1549.[76] Closely associated with Denny in the privy-purse office was a less prominent minister of the crown, Sir Thomas Heneage. Another gentleman of the privy chamber, Heneage profited personally from his connections with Wolsey and Cromwell but failed to attain the political distinction of either his brothers or his nephew.[77] When, in October, 1549, four " principal gentlemen " of the privy chamber were designated as constant attendants upon the young king, the control of the personal finances of the crown was divided. Nevertheless, early in 1551 a degree of unity was secured again when certain special funds were set aside " to the king's use." Peter Osborne, who was appointed to receive such money, was the last important director of the privy purse during this period, though possibly he was not the actual custodian of the royal treasure.

Privy-purse development in the sixteenth century was neither new nor singular in English administrative history. So long as no distinction was made between the king's money and the nation's money, it was natural that the sovereign should expect to retain some personal control over at least the portion of his finances devoted to private spending. This was the more easily accomplished by designating a trusted person to receive some of his revenue, to be administered as a special fund separate from the finances of the regularly constituted treasuries and employed only for his personal use. Earlier the king's chamber had fulfilled just such a need, but as it increased in power and prestige its keeper gradually outgrew the status of personal treasurer to the king. Henry VII had relied heavily on such responsible ministers as Sir Reginald Bray and Sir Henry Wyatt for control of his personal finances, but no separate institution for crown money had developed. Under Henry VIII privy-purse development was different in degree only. By the end of the reign large reserves of cash, controlled by royal command,

[76] Before Denny's death in 1549 Gates had already begun his steady rise at court. However, his major advances were made during the reign of Edward VI, when he became successively councillor, knight of the bath, sheriff of Essex, vice-chamberlain, captain of the guard, and in July, 1552, chancellor of the duchy of Lancaster. He was executed in 1553 for active participation in the Lady Jane Grey plot. See article, " Sir John Gates " by Gordon Goodwin in *D. N. B.*

[77] His brother, Robert, was master of woods in the second Augmentations. His nephew and namesake, Sir Thomas Heneage, with whom he is sometimes confused, was the most distinguished member of the family. The latter Sir Thomas was courtier and vice-chamberlain of Queen Elizabeth.

were regularly set aside for special necessities, though the purpose for which they were to be used was often cloaked in considerable secrecy. When the national treasuries were running dry and the need for more revenue seemed apparent, the public was not aware that the king still had ample funds available in his private coffers.

As early as 1519 Henry had devised a plan for setting up a reserve fund under the control of his confidential servant, William Compton, to which the treasurer of the chamber would be expected to contribute £10,000 annually. That this project was not carried out was due, in part perhaps, to Compton's rival, Wolsey, to whom the king had entrusted the execution of this and other contemplated reforms.[78] Nevertheless, significant reserves of cash were accumulated by Henry in possibly several informal depositories. Not only were payments from this special treasury made by gentlemen from the privy chamber, but Cromwell, too, tapped this royal financial reservoir.[79] Some of the total was diverted from the chamber and other treasuries, of which revenues of vacant sees formed an appreciable part.[80] As might be expected, this highly personalized finance contributed to both the speed and informality of all forms of business transaction. Thus when the English agent, Stephen Vaughan, was sent on a diplomatic mission to Denmark in the autumn of 1535, he was advanced £5,000 in cash by Anthony Denny, with instructions from Cromwell that whatever amount he did not use should " be repayed into the kinges coffres " upon his return.[81]

The " keeper of the kinges money," being a personal servant of the crown, made no formal declarations of accounts as did other treasurers of the realm, nor was he forced to comply with the usual requirements of written warrants, receipts, and periodic audits. Consequently, it is not always possible to determine exactly either the precise source or the ultimate destination of all the money that flowed through the privy purse. Certain it is, however, that from about 1535 onward

---

[78] See p. 63, *supra*. These reforms of Wolsey are given in Cotton. MS., Titus. B. i, fol. 188 ff.

[79] The most recent Cromwellian study reveals that Cromwell's vast expenditures were drawn as much from the royal coffers as from new sources of revenue. Elton, *The Tudor Revolution in Government*, 143–49.

[80] Some of the ministers who paid their receipts directly to Cromwell were not exonerated until long after his death. For example, the privy council issued a warrant to the Exchequer in January, 1546, requiring the discharge of William Cavendish, auditor, who had paid " the late Lord Crumwell, attainted, to your Majesty's use " £2,033 1s. 4d., which he had collected some twelve years earlier from the temporalities of the vacant see of Ely. The see remained vacant for almost a year after the death of Nicholas West, bishop of Ely, on April 28, 1533, before his successor, Thomas Goodrich, was appointed. Documents signed by stamp, *L. and P.*, XXI, pt. 1, no. 148(29).

[81] Merriman (ed.), *Life and Letters of Thomas Cromwell*, II, no. 177.

Henry began to amass a large surplus of ready money in his own coffers, upon which he could draw at will without recourse to regular channels. If the various treasuries of the realm were frequently dry, it was in part because they were constantly being sapped by the demands of the privy purse.[82] Between 1535 and 1540 the Exchequer contributed £15,533 6s. 8d., and the Court of First Fruits and Tenths £59,139 18s. 4d.[83] The greatest burden, however, was borne by the Augmentations, which delivered over £131,157 for the king's own use during its first five years.[84]

These deliveries to the privy purse varied greatly in amount, though they were seldom less than £1,000 for each payment. Usually, however, they were far in excess of that amount, in one instance being as much as £20,000.[85] Such payments were made to the king's personal servants, Denny, Heneage, and James Joskyn.[86] Strangely enough, the advances by the Augmentations were, with recurrent frequency, for the same amounts, £3,333 6s. 8d. or £6,666 13s. 4d., suggesting that the Court had a standing order to pay 10,000 or 20,000 marks annually to the royal coffers.[87] After the downfall of Cromwell when Henry more and more interested himself in financial matters, he periodically

---

[82] Dietz maintains, and I think with considerable validity, that prior to 1540 claims of financial stringency were entirely simulated. He concludes that not only were the revenues quite adequate "for all the purposes of the government, but a new surplus was rapidly being gathered." Dietz, *English Government Finance, 1485–1558*, 143.

[83] *Ibid.*, 142. Dietz assumes that the subsidy and the fifteenth and tenth collected during 1535–37, which yielded an approximate £77,000, was also probably paid directly to the crown. *Ibid.*, 143. *L. and P.*, XVI, no. 352.

[84] For the period April, 1536, to April, 1541. Augm. Office, Treas. Rolls of Accts., No. 1, pts. 1, 2; Augm. Office, Misc. Books 249, fols. 46, 47, 49, 50, 51, 52, 53. These various items are abstracted in *L. and P.*, XIII, pt. 2, no. 457; XIV, pt. 2, no. 236; XVI, no. 745.

[85] D. L. 42/133, fol. 44. Payment from Sir John Gostwick, treasurer of the Court of First Fruits and Tenths. Warrants for payments by the treasurer of the chamber "for his Grace's own affairs to the hands of Mr. Deny" were usually for £1,000 each, but occasionally for larger amounts. Arundel MS. 87, fols. 70d., 116, 139d.

[86] In 1538 Joskyn was described as "servant" of Sir Thomas Heneage. At that time he was already serving the king in the privy chamber as clerk of the wardrobe of robes and clerk of the king's beds. However, in January, 1541, he surrendered these offices to become a teller in the receipt division of the Exchequer. During the 1530's and 1540's Joskyn not infrequently served as personal receiver and paymaster for money delivered to "the king's hands." He and Denny were both dead by 1550. Heneage continued in royal service, however, until about 1553. *L. and P.*, XII, pt. 2, nos. 191 (48), 796(6); XIV, pt. 2, nos. 236 (p. 75), 782 (p. 338); XVI, nos. 745 (p. 359), 503 (19, 20); XVIII, pt. 2, no. 231 (p. 131); XX, pt. 2, nos. 268, 270; XXI, pt. 1, no. 643 (p. 314); pt. 2, no. 201. *Cal. Pat. Rolls, Edward VI*, III, 178.

[87] The mark was calculated at two-thirds of a pound sterling or 13s. 4d. Sometimes the warrants were issued for the payment of 10,000 or 20,000 marks.

called in whatever surpluses the several treasuries had on hand in order to retain an accumulating reserve fund in his own hands. This cash could be used for purely personal items or employed in affairs of state. Under Edward VI the need for such a reserve was even more apparent, since the charges of various departments of government had gradually increased. This was particular true of pensions, annuities, garrisons, Calais, and the household. By the end of the fiscal year 1551 costs of Calais and the marches exceeded receipts by £5,286. Similarly, expenses of the great wardrobe had increased from £3,910 to £6,875 during the Edwardian period.[88] On the other hand, the device of developing still another treasury to meet the contingency of a national deficit would have solved nothing. To the financial advisers the use of the royal privy purse for either emergency outlays or for extraordinary national expenditures must have seemed strangely like borrowing from Peter to pay Paul. At best it was but a royal convenience, with the only advantage lying in the greater ease and informality of receipts and payments. Indeed, this may have been an additional reason for diverting certain incoming revenues directly to the king's coffers, which practice was begun long before the creation of the special fund administered by Osborne. As early as 1540 a part of the " lay fee " granted by parliament in that year was received by Denny and retained as part of the royal hoard.[89]

By far the greatest number of royal warrants and receipts preserved fail completely to divulge the ultimate objective of the payments to the king's use. If the purpose was suggested at all, it was stated simply that the money was to be employed about " the kinges maiestes secret affayres." [90] The chief repository for this private fund seems to have been the royal palace at Westminster, or more particularly the king's secret jewel house there. Thus the keepers or custodians of Westminster Palace acted simultaneously as the principal receivers and paymasters of the king's money. This office was in the hands of Sir Anthony Denny until his death in 1549, when he was succeeded on October 28 of that year by Sir Andrew Dudley, the king's servant and gentleman of the

---

[88] Add. MS. 30198, fols. 20, 39.

[89] D. L. 42/133; *L. and P.*, XV, no. 600. In the spring of 1542 it was noted that the king had disbursed far more than was expected in revenues that year; in fact, fortifications of the realm were in such a bad state that £100,000 would not meet the expenses for that item alone. Moreover, if the king were to use the money available in his own treasury, some thought he would be ill-provided against any sudden event " either by outward parts or otherwise." *L. and P.*, XVII, no. 194; see also Augm. Office, Misc. Books 250, fol. 50.

[90] *Ibid.* 262, fol. 64d. The payment of £1,800 by the treasurer of Augmentations to John Gates in April, 1554.

privy chamber.[91] Records of their expenditures show money to have been drawn from the king's private treasury for royal buildings and repairs, for the king's "privy alms," [92] for public works,[93] for the payment of troops stationed in English garrisons, and for body armor and horse "harness" used at court tournaments and jousts. Since Denny and his successors were officially in charge of the royal palace at Westminster, a portion of their receipts was expended on jewels, plate, and sundry household items, but certainly the bulk of the money entrusted to them was spent on more important affairs. An extant account book for money charged by the king's commandment to Anthony Denny as keeper of the palace at Westminster, "which shalbe by him received to his said Highness use," itemized £243,423 ¼d. turned over to him during the period 1542–1548.[94] These receipts included large transfers to Denny from the customs, the mint, the household, the Exchequer, the chamber, and the revenue courts. In addition, sums varying in amount from £57 to £30,000 were paid to the privy purse from the privy chamber, the "secret jewel house at Westminster Palace," or various other private royal depositories. Such deliveries were made by some official in the privy chamber or even "by his Highness' own hands." [95]

[91] On the following November 4, Dudley and Francis Everard, a gentleman usher of the privy chamber, were granted in survivorship the office of keeper of the royal household within the Palace of Westminster from the time of the death of Denny, as late occupant of that office. *Cal. Pat. Rolls, Edward VI*, II, 245–46, 368.

[92] Receipts by Richard Cox, the king's chaplain and almoner to Prince Edward, show that money was advanced to him regularly by Denny or Heneage "to be employed upon the King's privy alms." *L. and P.*, XXI, pt. 2, no. 202.

[93] As £3,600 paid to Robert Lord, paymaster of the king's works, by the treasurer of the Court of Augmentations in September, 1540, upon a warrant for £6,600—"whereof £3,000 were aduanced oute of the Kinges treasure at his palice at Westm." From "Payments by the Kinges Warrauntes," Augm. Office, Misc. Books 249, fol 47d. In 1537 Denny was paid £2,662 by the same court for buildings at Westminster, Chelsea, Hackney, St. James's in the Fields, and for the construction of the house of the Augmentations. Augm. Office, Treas. Rolls of Accts., No. 1, pt. 1, mem. 12d.

[94] The recorded entries begin with April 24, 1542, and close with 1548, the last amount being received upon the warrant of February 6, 2 Edward VI. Lansd. Rolls, no. 14, especially fols. 264–72. The first part of this account book contains an inventory of money, jewels, plate, tapestry, and other goods in the custody of Denny. This is entered for 1542 in *L. and P.*, XVII, no. 267.

[95] In this connection "his Highness' own secret jewel house" and "his said Majesty's removing coffers within his said Majesty's withdrawing chamber at his palace at Westminster" are both specified. Money received of the king was delivered to Denny by the hands of Sir Thomas Cawarden (or Carden), a groom of the privy chamber and master of revels, and John Gates, also a groom of the privy chamber. Cawarden held several minor offices in the Augmentations, including the stewardship of various important royal manors. Augm. Office, Misc. Books 236, fols. 2d., 20d.

Occasionally the money advanced to Denny for the use of the king was earmarked for a definite state need, as the payment of December, 1540, which was set forth in an accompanying schedule of particulars. The £640 in prest by a royal warrant on the Augmentations was turned over to Denny and Charles Gold [96] " to be payed and ymployed by them vnto certeyn Capitaynes deputies porters gonners and souldyours of dyverse the Kinges Castelles bulwarkes and fortresses named in a certeyne scedule annexed " for wages of these men during October, November, and December. Upon the completion of the assignment Denny and Gold " shall not onely at their commyng home delyver a just doble by indenture of their indentures for a playne declaracion of their paymentes at euery fortresse but also shall delyver all suche surplusage of money as shall then remayne in their handes by occasion of deathe of any of the saide personnes sithens the first daye of Octobre last past aforesaid/ and further at their accompte to allowe vnto euery of them for their allowaunce ijs. by the daye for their costes during all suche tyme as they shallbe aboute in traveyling for the payment thereof." [97]

Denny apparently held a number of minor household offices, some of which may have been used as private royal treasuries.[98] His accounts certainly show him to have received money within the groomship of the stole; and later another of the privy chamber officials, James Rufforth, a former servant of Denny, was exonerated for having spent, by the king's command, all the money and plate entrusted to his charge.[99]

After Henry VIII's death in January, 1547, the council began to check on such informal practices in an attempt to call in all money remaining in the hands of certain crown agents. A series of commissions were appointed to examine the accounts of those household servants who had been entrusted with the receipt and expenditure of the king's money during the past reign. Two of them examined Denny's accounts, one to check all " goodes, catelles, plate, juelles, apperrell, wardrobbes stuffe, munycons and ordenaunces " and everything else received since his last discharge, and the other to audit the account of " moneys received to the

---

[96] Charles Gold of the privy chamber was also a gunner in the Tower.

[97] Augm. Office, Misc. Books 249, fol. 50d.

[98] Denny was not only keeper of the royal palace at Westminster and custodian of the secret jewel house therein, king's remembrancer, and groom of the stole, but he was also the recipient of a number of other administrative positions. He held several stewardships and keeperships, including the keepership of the important mansion of the late priory or hospital of St. John of Jerusalem, near London. Augm. Office, Proceedings, E. 321/44/45.

[99] Pardon of March 24, 1551, to Rufforth and his executors for having " paid away " and disposed of the king's money, plate, jewels, silks, ornaments, etc., for which they had no written authorization or receipt. *Cal. Pat. Rolls, Edward VI*, IV, 76–77.

use of " the late king. Both commissions were dated July 2, 1547, and appear to have been practically identical in scope and jurisdiction. However, a differentiation seems to have been made between Denny's account as custodian of the palace at Westminster and as keeper of the privy purse.[100]

The commission of audit was reissued in a slightly modified form the following autumn so as to include an inventory of " stuff " remaining in the hands of the keepers. The commissioners were ordered to repair to the king's " mansion houses " of Westminster, Greenwich, Hampton Court, Windsor, Oatlands, Richmond, the Tower of London, and elsewhere and view " all ready money," plate, jewels, apparel, silks, household supplies, stable equipment, munitions, artillery, tents, and other stuff remaining in those palaces upon the death of the king. After an inventory was made of all such goods, they were parceled out to the several keepers of the royal residences, together with " one fayre and entyer boke or inventorye " of all the matériel surveyed. From this comprehensive " lygear," particular ledger books were prepared for each individual keeper, specifying the items received by him. Instructions to the commissioners definitely alluded to the financial activities of the keeper of the privy purse and his assistant:

> And whereas the king's councillor Sir Anthony Denny and servant Sir John Gate have at sundry times between 22 April 32 Henry VIII, and 28 Jan. last received money, plate, jewels, etc., to Henry VIII.'s use, and Denny has since the said 28 Jan. received money to be employed about " certeyn our affayres in his charge," the commissioners are to take their account of such as has come to their hands and declare the said account before the Protector and Council so that they may obtain the king's discharge.[101]

---

[100] The first commission was headed by the lord chamberlain of the household, Henry Fitzalan, twelfth earl of Arundel, and composed of nine members, in addition to the directors and other officials of the jewel house and wardrobe who sat with them. The second commission of audit was a smaller body, headed by Sir William Paulet, already Lord St. John, who held four important offices of state: lord treasurer, great master of the household, master of the Court of Wards and Liveries, and president of the council. Sir Walter Mildmay represented the Augmentations on both commissions, being joined by his fellow auditor, William Berners, in the former body. Only four names are mentioned in the Paulet commission, the fifth appointee being unnamed. Denny's accounts, however, disclose it to have been Nicholas Bristow, who sat with Mildmay as a professional auditor. *Ibid.*, I, 261. Certain jewels, plate, and other valuables remaining were removed to the " secrete treasury house " in the Tower of London for safekeeping. *Ibid., Elizabeth,* I, 443.

[101] Commission of September 14, 1547, to Paulet; Lord John Russell, keeper of the privy seal; John Dudley, earl of Warwick and great chamberlain; and Sir Walter Mildmay, then a general surveyor in the reorganized Court of Augmen-

Finally appearing before Paulet and Mildmay some four years later, Gates rendered " a good and reasonable account " and received his *quietus est* from the commissioners. At that time he was also acquitted for money and goods received from the estates of Norfolk and Surrey, attainted just before the close of the reign of Henry VIII, and for plate from the dissolved college of Pleshey, Essex, for which he had previously accounted at the Augmentations and received an honorable discharge.[102]

Meanwhile the administration of the privy purse was somewhat modified by a reorganization of the privy chamber in mid-October, 1549. During the period of the young king's minority the council decided that " it should be requisite to have some noblemen appointed to be ordinarily attendant about his majesties person in his privy chamber, to give order for the good government of his most royall person, and for the honourable education of his highness in these his tender yeres in learning and vertue, . . . the same six, or at the least two of them, to be always attendant on his majesties person." [103] At the same time " four principall gentlemen " from the privy chamber were selected for special attendance upon the king, whereof at least two should be with him at all times. Thus, these " four principal knights," as they were commonly called, were elevated immediately to a superior position in the chamber hierarchy. In consideration of their new status of confidential trust and honor their salaries were doubled, in partial compensation for " the singular care and travell they should have about his majesties person." [104] Sir Edward Rogers, Sir Thomas Darcy, Sir Andrew Dudley, and Sir Thomas Wroth were promoted to this new office immediately. Later, Sir Henry Sidney and Sir Henry Neville seem to have achieved the same rank. As favorites of the king these men were influential at court, but none of them had attained any particular prominence at the time of his appointment.

The evidence is inconclusive on the length of service of these men,

---

tations. *Ibid., Edward VI,* I, 139. The " Inventory of Effects of Henry VIII " at the Society of Antiquaries of London, MS. 129A. See also the declaration of account by Denny, temp. Edward VI, Exch., Accounts Various, 427/2.

[102] This pardon and release from all claims, reckonings, debts, and arrears for the past reign was granted to Gates on March 4, 1552. He was then styled king's councillor, vice-chamberlain of the household, captain of the guard, and one of the four principal knights of the privy chamber. *Cal. Pat. Rolls, Edward VI,* IV, 381–82.

[103] Deference to social rank was preserved by the requirement that of the six chosen there must be one marquis, two earls, and three barons. William Parr, marquis of Northampton; Henry Fitzalan, earl of Arundel; John Dudley, earl of Warwick; William Paulet, Lord St. John; Lord John Russell, and Lord Thomas Wentworth were appointed.

[104] The accustomed fee was raised from £50 to £100 per year. Nichols (ed.), *Literary Remains,* cxxxiii, as quoted from the Privy Council Register.

but it is fairly certain that there were never more than four " principal knights " at any one time, although there were numerous other " gentlemen " of the chamber. It is also clear that Sir Thomas Audley and possibly Sir Richard Blount, as well as Sidney, attained that distinction before the end of the reign. As under Henry VIII money continued to be delivered to the king's privy chamber to be used by the " chief " gentlemen " towardes the kinges necessarie defraymentes about his person." [105] Sometimes the payments were directed to a particular one of the four, for ordinary or extraordinary charges,[106] but generally the principal gentlemen were not named:

> [December 7, 1550] A warrant to —————— to deliver to the bearer therof m^l li., to be broughte by him to the thandes [*sic*] of the Chief Gentlemen of the Kinges Majesties Privie Chamber, to be disbursed by them in suche paymentes as hathe been accustomed to passe oute of his Majesties pursse.[107]

The accustomed payments alluded to included rewards, reparations, current expenses of the king, the upkeep of the palace gardens and royal parks, and money delivered " otherwise as they [the four principal gentlemen of the privy chamber] shalbe commaunded." [108] As might be expected, the rewards embraced occasional payments to Protestant preachers, as the £40 paid to John Knox on October 27, 1552.[109] The gentlemen of the privy chamber rendered accounts to the government for the money that passed through their hands, but the system of accounting for privy-purse funds was not standardized. Any crown minister, royal treasurer, or king's servant who handled large amounts of money or revenue was expected to account for his stewardship sooner or later, but these special cases were heard by royal commissions, which not infrequently were required to audit accounts years after they had been closed. Since these personal agents of the king

---

[105] The earliest discovered warrant for this purpose was drawn on the Exchequer and is dated April 27, 1550, shortly after the reorganization of the privy chamber. Darcy, Dudley, Wroth, and Gates received £300 for " necessarie paymentes to be made out of the Kinges Majesties Purse." Dasent (ed.), *Acts of the Privy Council,* III, 18.

[106] As the warrant to pay Andrew Dudley, one of the principal gentlemen of the privy chamber, " for divers and soundrie paymentes for thordinarie and extraordinarie chardges and allowances of divers necessaries apperteynenge to his Highnes Pallays at Westminster, and other places therunto belongenge, due . . . , according to a book of particulars sent herewith." *Ibid.,* II, 165. Dudley had succeeded Denny as keeper of the palace at Westminster.

[107] *Ibid.,* III, 175.

[108] *Ibid.,* 198, 243, 289, 320, 346, 372, 386, 438, 503; IV, 81, 91, 101, 157, 185, 228 *passim.*

[109] *Ibid.,* IV, 154.

were never bonded, there was no particular reason for a commission audit in the event of a man's account not being declared before his death.[110] It was to avoid such contingencies, apparently, that it was decided to call the gentlemen of the privy chamber to account, although there seems to have been no ground for suspicion concerning any of them. A council letter of December, 1551, required one of the crown auditors to take the account of " the Kinges Majesties Purse " of all money paid into the hands of the gentlemen of the privy chamber and " to gyve them allowaunce of all suche parcelles of monny as they have payed owt of the same." [111] If the account were actually made, there is no record of either a declaration or an acquittal.

By 1551 governmental expenditures were far exceeding the normal incoming revenues. Among the various expedients employed to meet this increasing annual deficiency was the well-established practice of calling in old debts, which were estimated at the time to be about £100,000.[112] Accordingly, in early February of that year all the financial courts of the realm were ordered to call in their debts and pay whatever sums they collected to a crown treasurer especially appointed to receive them. Five warrants, directed to the Courts of the Exchequer, the First Fruits and Tenths, the Duchy of Lancaster, the Wards and Liveries, and the Augmentations, authorized those institutions to pay weekly to Peter Osborne " all such sommes of money as shall comme and be payd to the said Courtes, being arrerages, and certified by the severall officers of the same, indenting with him wekely for the receiptes of such sommes as shalbe payd to his handes." [113]

An important indenture of February, 1552, between Osborne and John Williams, treasurer of the Augmentations, gives a long itemized list of that Court's deliveries to the king's privy chamber, as " commaunded to be paid to the said Peter." The arrearages of debts in the Augmentations thus received by Osborne, officially styled " Clerke to the foure knightes [in] attendaunce vpon the kinges maiesties person,"

[110] As noted earlier, the accounts of the king's servant, James Rufforth, were never audited. After his death, however, he and his executors were pardoned and released from liability for all his expenditures. See note 99.

[111] Thomas Lord Darcy of Chiche, chamberlain; John Gates, vice-chamberlain; and three chief gentlemen of the privy chamber, i. e., Sidney, Wroth, and Dudley, are named in this letter as having received money for the king. The auditor's name is not given. Dasent (ed.), *Acts of the Privy Council*, III, 437.

[112] P. 183, *supra*. In May, 1552, it was resolved to sell enough chantry land to pay off all the obligations of the crown, which were said to be £251,000 "at the least." Nichols (ed.), *Literary Remains*, II, 414.

[113] Dasent (ed.), *Acts of the Privy Council*, III, 475. See also *ibid.*, 501, 502, 503.

amounted to a total of £16,667 12s. 11d.[114] Other miscellaneous warrants by the council disclose that Osborne also received various sums, ranging from £500 to £2,000 each, from the other financial institutions, including the mint, and an additional £500 from the Augmentations.[115] Total receipts of Osborne from the various sources tapped for the king's "own purposes" are uncertain, but it is a matter of record that the Augmentations delivered to him another £1,800 before its ultimate dissolution.[116]

The exact position occupied by Osborne during the reign of Edward VI is not clear beyond the fact that he was acting as "clerk" to the four principal gentlemen of the privy chamber. There is no doubt that he served as a special royal treasurer for certain funds paid into the king's personal coffers, though he functioned chiefly as receiver rather than as royal paymaster. Most of his receipts were, in fact, turned over to the principal gentlemen. Nevertheless, whatever his title, he was in fact if not in office a keeper of the privy purse, entrusted with the important financial duties contingent thereon.[117] Shortly after he was delegated to receive arrears of revenues for the crown, he was appointed clerk of dispensations and faculties in the chancery to succeed Stephen Vaughan in that office.[118] In September of the following year he was granted the office of remembrancer to the treasurer of the Exchequer, a position which he retained throughout the ensuing reign.[119] He apparently began his financial duties early in 1551, for a number of his warrants are extant for the years 1551–1553.[120] In any event, he continued to be engaged in financial affairs during the remainder of Edward's reign [121] and subsequently enjoyed the confidence of both Mary and Elizabeth.

When the commissions of 1551 and 1552 called in arrears of revenue and old debts, the money collected was paid to Osborne, who in turn

[114] The indenture is dated February 14, 1552, although all the payments listed are by the authority of a warrant of February 6, 1551. Augm. Office, Miscellanea, 314/19.

[115] Dasent (ed.), *Acts of the Privy Council*, III, 502; IV, 96, 221.

[116] Augm. Office, Treas. Rolls of Accts., No. 8, fol. 84d.

[117] In the *D. N. B.* his biographer, W. A. J. Archbold, calls him the keeper of the privy purse. However, I have found no specific reference to Osborne as "keeper" of the king's purse.

[118] Appointment of July 18, 1551. *Cal. Pat. Rolls, Edward VI,* IV, 153.

[119] *Ibid.*, 312.

[120] A file of warrants and other documents subsidiary to the accounts of Peter Osborne, in charge of the king's debts. Exch., Accounts Various, 546/19; see also *ibid.*, 625/4; Augm. Office, Misc. Books 261, fol. 69.

[121] Osborne may have risen in favor at the court through the influence of his friend, Sir John Cheke, tutor to Prince Edward and later secretary of state. See Thompson Cooper, "Sir John Cheke," in *D. N. B.*

distributed it to various departments and crown ministers as authorized by king and council.[122]

In order to replenish the privy purse, from time to time certain funds were set aside. The "relief" granted by parliament in 1547–1548 was separately reserved for "service of His Majesties";[123] at the same time, another fund known as the "sales money" was set up for the proceeds arising from the sale of chantry and college lands. Paid to Edmund Peckham, cofferer of the household and head of the mint, the latter was used as a reserve of surplus revenue, to be employed in cases of emergency wherever it was needed. Most of it was distributed among the departments of government, including the Augmentations, the admiralty, and the chamber, or sent to financial agents like Thomas Gresham to be used for purchases in Antwerp and for the repayment of loans contracted there.[124] Now and then money from this source would also be transferred directly to royal agents, "to be imploide aboute the Kinges Maiesties affayeres [*sic*] w[th]in thir seuerall Offices by vertue of a warraunte."[125]

Despite the natural secrecy that surrounded privy-purse expenditures, numerous warrants from the council to Osborne indicate how he spent the money entrusted to his keeping. In 1551 and 1552 approximately £7,000 was paid to the lord admiral and sundry noblemen for wages of bands of horsemen,[126] and over £3,000 advanced to the king's chamber, for which Osborne was to be reimbursed later.[127] During the same

[122] Dasent (ed.), *Acts of the Privy Council*, IV, 64; Nichols (ed.), *Literary Remains*, I, 56, 58; II, 500.

[123] These receipts normally were paid into the Exchequer, but large sums were transferred from that department to the king's coffers. Of the money "brought in for the Relief," Osborne received regular payments for the king's "speciall service and affayres." Dasent (ed.), *Acts of the Privy Council*, IV, 27, 28, 31.

[124] Loans were also occasionally made from this fund which were repaid to Peckham, who was required to make weekly reports to the council of the state of the sales money "so as ordre may be taken for the same, and to call for the repayment thereof from weeke to weeke." *Ibid.*, 123, 134, 135, 145–46, 149, 161, 162, 167, 183. The practice of juggling finances by shifting money from one department of the government to another reached absurdity when Peckham was required to pay £1,052 8s. 4d. to Gresham with the proviso that he was to receive it back again from the Exchequer whenever he next went up to London. *Ibid.*, 128.

[125] At various dates in October and November of 1548 money from the sale of colleges and chantries was advanced to John Rither, cofferer of the household; Robert Legge; George Maxey; Sir William Cavendish, treasurer of the chamber; and Anthony Anthony. Augm. Office, Misc. Books 257, fol. 78d.

[126] Dasent (ed.), *Acts of the Privy Council*, IV, 95, 132–33.

[127] The £3,037 18s. 8d. actually delivered to the chamber by Osborne was earmarked for specific purposes, such as victualing and equipping the king's ships. The payment was by order of a warrant of March 11, 1551, which specified that "the said Peter shall receive agayn shortly" as much money as he had paid out. The advance was fully repaid as follows: £1,000 from the Exchequer, £1,000 from

period £8,000 was delivered to the household for wages and for payments " towardes the diffrayment of thinges within his [the cofferer's] charge this Progresse tyme," £7,000 forwarded to Thomas Gresham for the repayment of a loan in Antwerp, and £827 6*s.* 8*d.* delivered to the receiver of the Augmentations for expenses of fortifications in Essex and Suffolk.[128] Lesser amounts were spent on rewards, personal loans, wages for the household, ambassadorial expenses, and incidental expenditures by governmental agents.[129]

A few of Osborne's warrants are of particular interest, revealing not only the use made of such funds but also the source of privy-purse moneys. On one occasion he was ordered to turn over various amounts to " our right trustie and welbeloued seruant Sir Andrewe Dudley . . . one of the cheife gentlemen of our priuie chamber to be kept in our priuie cofers "; specified in this warrant was £216 11*s.* of " the remayne of tharrerages of our debtes " still retained by him, £100 received from " Mr. Kellaway " in payment for his promotion as serjeant-at-law,[130] £100 in gold received of " Mr. Losse," [131] and £1,231 8*s.* 2*d.* as part of a larger advance from the undertreasurer of the mint.[132]

Just before the end of the reign in May, 1553, Osborne was called to account for money received by him since January 10, 1552. However, of all that total which had been kept in the king's chamber at Westminster Palace " wheare we most accustomabley do heare the sermondes," £600 had been stolen on May 2, 1552. Since to hold him accountable for such a great loss would have resulted in his " utter undoing," Osborne was discharged of the said theft by royal command. During the month of June he appeared several times before the commissioners of audit, Thomas Mildmay and William Berners, who presented to the privy council a perfect declaration of the account " fayre written in parchement," which represented the receipts, bills, and warrants examined by them. Osborne was charged with having received and spent in

---

the Court of Wards and Liveries, £500 from the Court of Augmentations, and the remainder, £537 18*s.* 8*d.*, from the duchy of Lancaster. *Ibid.*, III, 501–503.

[128] *Ibid.*, IV, 58, 89, 94, 130.

[129] *Ibid.*, 110, 113, 188, 202, 237; Exch., Accounts Various, 546/19.

[130] Robert Keilwey, surveyor of liveries, who was elevated to the rank of serjeant-at-law in September, 1552, under penalty of £1,000. *Cal. Pat. Rolls, Edward VI,* I, 238; IV, 355. On Keilwey see p. 174, *supra.*

[131] Probably Hugh Losse, a bailiff and collector for the Augmentations in London who, in August, 1552, had purchased crown lands for £1,125 1*s.* 8*d.*, which had been paid into the Court in ready money, with the exception of £100 in cash paid directly to the king's own hands. *Ibid.*, IV, 457.

[132] This warrant was dated May 14, 1553. A separate indenture between Osborne and Dudley is also included in this file. Exch., Accounts Various, 546/19.

the king's service £39,948 ⅛d. for which he was given a pardon and final quittance.[133]

Already a general plan for financial reorganization had been instituted. The commission for an examination of the state of the national revenues, in March, 1552, raised the question of possibly creating a permanent state fund to be used as a perpetual endowment for the privy purse. The recommendation concluded:

ffinallie aftre ordre taken in the premisses It were conveniente to devise vppon a certayne yerelie Revenue mete for thonorable main-tenaunce of the kinges maiesties Estate so as his necessarie chardges and none other being borne owte of the same ther might remayne yerelie to his highnes Coffers suche an overplus in Thesaurus as might suffice honorablie his Extraordenarie occasions ffor the con-tinuance therof it were mete so to considre the kinges maiesties landes and Revenues as his howses Castles mannours fforestes parkes Chaces and other statelie possessions being knowen and sorted from the rest the same might be so annexed in perpetuitie to thimperiall Crowne of this Realme as then might remayne inviolable vntouched and vndismembred for ever And libertie to encroche or increase the same further or more then necessitie sholde requier.[134]

There is no indication, however, that the suggestion was ever given consideration. With the accession of Mary the office of the privy purse seems to have fallen into complete disuse.

The chief interest of the historian in Augmentations finance is largely in the variety and extent of its payments. Beginning in 1548 the major business of the Edwardian council was the issuance and distribution of warrants to all the treasuries for the disbursement of national funds, which generally were spent as rapidly as they could be raised.[135] Of this total Augmentations disbursements were the largest, reaching a high point of £184,475 3s. 9d. in 1548. Its greatest rival among the other revenue courts was the Exchequer where annual expenditures, however,

---

[133] *Cal. Pat. Rolls, Edward VI*, V, 85, 185.

[134] Part III of the Commission Report, Harl. MS. 7383, fol. 72. Even before this report a note in the king's handwriting had indicated the desirability of acquiring a new surplus of £50,000 " of treasure money for all events." Nichols (ed.), *Literary Remains*, II, 543.

[135] During the first five years of the Edwardian period the government spent £1,356,687 for war purposes, direct or indirect, in addition to the regular current expenses of governmental administration. Dietz, *Finances of Edward VI and Mary*, 81. In addition to the treasurer's accounts, the payments of the Augmen-tations can be traced in Exch., Accounts Various (E. 101), 60/14, 76/12, 30–31, 35–36; Augm. Office, Misc. Books 256–262; Miscellanea, E. 413/19, 21, 23–24.

averaged considerably less. In only one year, 1551, did the total annual payments of the Exchequer exceed those of the Augmentations.[136]

As principal paymaster of the realm and receiver of special revenues, the treasurer of the Court naturally came under the close surveillance of the privy council, which retained the same control over irregular receipts as it did over expenditures. In 1547 the commissioners for the sale of alum and fustians, Sir John Gresham and Andrew Judd, were required to account before the chancellor and auditors of the Augmentations and to pay the balance of their receipts into the treasury of the Court.[137] Special fines were also channeled into the Augmentations, as that of £2,000 imposed on Lord William Paget in 1552 for malversation as chancellor of the duchy of Lancaster.[138] Similarly, surpluses from the mints were turned over to it.[139] Although preserved as a separate fund and paid immediately to a special treasurer, part of the proceeds from the sale of land and property of colleges and chantries ultimately found its way into the Augmentations.[140] When conciliar control of all governmental revenues was tightened in 1552, a systematic review of all departments was instituted.[141] Among other developments this led to

[136] The Exchequer disbursements for that year, £86,058 14s. 3d., were considerably higher than usual. Dietz, *Finances of Edward VI and Mary*, Appendix, 123. Augm. Office, Treas. Rolls of Accts., No. 4, fol. 104.

[137] Failing to dispose of the consignment of Augmentations lead shipped to him in Flanders, the king's agent Stephen Vaughan had finally contrived to exchange a part of it for 30,000 hundredweight of alum; shortly thereafter he was forced to buy 314 bales of fustians at £19 per bale in order to raise a loan of £30,000 Flemish from the Fuggers. Gresham and Judd were commissioned to receive these commodities and sell them to the king's profit. *Cal. Pat. Rolls, Edward VI*, I, 136, 140; II, 67. They paid in a total of £669 17s. 10d. remaining in their hands on October 16, 1548. Augm. Office, Misc. Books 342, fol. 29d.

[138] His original fine was £6,000, in addition to the confiscation of his lands and personal property, but he was subsequently permitted to compound for the fine. *Cal. Pat. Rolls, Edward VI*, V, 49. Sir William was created Baron Paget of Beaudesert, Staffordshire, in December, 1549. The case of Paget, as well as that of John Beaumont, receiver-general of the Court of Wards, is presented in some detail in Strype, *Ecclesiastical Memorials*, II, pt. 2, 44 ff. On the more notorious defalcations of Beaumont, see especially Joel Hurstfield, "Corruption and Reform under Edward VI and Mary: The Example of Wardship," *E. H. R.*, LXVIII (January, 1953), 24–27.

[139] *Cal. Pat. Rolls, Edward VI*, V, 398.

[140] Many warrants from the king's council to the treasurer of the Court for special payments relating to the king's affairs, "to be taken of his highnes treasure comming of the sales" or simply to be paid from "the sale money in your custody," have been preserved. If regular funds were low, a postscript would be added: "this warraunt you shalle pay of the sales money." Of course, Peckham also made payments directly from this fund. See especially Documents subsidiary to the Accounts of the Treasurer of the Augmentations, Augm. Office, Miscellanea, and Exch., Accounts Various, 76/35.

[141] *Cal. Pat. Rolls, Edward VI*, IV, 278, 353, 354–56, 391–92, 397–98.

an investigation of minor irregularities in the Court and to the temporary arrest of its treasurer, as mentioned earlier.[142] Nevertheless, despite intermittent restrictions the Court was singularly free from outside interference. The established procedure of collecting revenue was proverbially slow, but of the operational efficiency of the treasurer's department of the Augmentations, there was little occasion for government censure.

As chief financial officer the treasurer was generally under the authority of the Court's executive council, but his relationship with the superior members of that body, including the chancellor, was one of complete equality. By constitutional provision he was responsible for all receipts and issues of the Court, for which he rendered an annual account to the executive board, composed of the chancellor, two general surveyors, and two assigned auditors. No payments could be made without order, the warrant itself constituting his discharge; conversely, the acquittance of the treasurer was required for all revenues and miscellaneous sums received by the Augmentations. Since the treasurer's position was one of great responsibility, he was supposed to be bonded and sworn to the faithful performance of his office. It was probably because these safeguards were not always enforced that the later treasurers were negligent in their duty. Be this as it may, the government seems seldom to have questioned the integrity of the senior officers of the Court.

Regular declarations of accounts by the principal treasurers of the realm was a practice of long standing, particularly helpful to the privy council in determining the approximate amount of cash available at any given time. However, the frequency of reports on the state of the revenue depended on the national situation; during periods of war emergency the need for constant financial reckonings was, of course, much greater. During the last years of Henry VIII the treasurers were expected to bring their declarations to the lord treasurer every Saturday.[143] This system of turning in " parfaict bookes of the states of their offices " was continued under Edward VI, the council urging each treasurer to keep his surplus cash " in a redines, so as it be forth cumming " when needed. On one occasion in 1552, as previously stated, the chancellor and treasurer of the Augmentations were peremptorily ordered to appeal before the council to state how much balance they had on hand to meet any forthcoming emergency.[144] Indeed, such declarations were even more important to the institution itself, its own financial obligations being always quite heavy; otherwise, when funds were low, royal warrants

---

[142] See Chapter Six, pp. 196–97.

[143] *L. and P.*, XXI, pt. 1, no. 437.

[144] Tytler, *England under the Reigns of Edward VI and Mary,* I, 274. Dasent (ed.), *Acts of the Privy Council,* II, 345–46; IV, 12, 37. P. 196, *supra.*

could not be honored promptly, since payments would have to be deferred until additional revenues were forthcoming. Conversely, when the treasurer was faced with the alternative of deciding which should take priority, the king's demands or those of the Court, he was tempted to choose the former. Normal administrative charges—pensions, annuities, salaries, reparations, and special expenditures by Court warrant— however important to operational efficiency, could always be postponed. In fact, this was quite likely to happen when royal warrants were presented to the treasurer with insistence on immediate payment.

Under normal circumstances the treasurer was reasonably prompt in his payments unless he was short of funds, which often happened when he had been faced with a long run on Augmentations reserves. Sometimes the situation was forced upon him by the council, as in March, 1544, when he was directed to turn over to the chief treasurer of war not only all the surplus remaining in his hands at that time but also any other revenue which might come in during the ensuing quarter. He was ordered to keep back no more cash than was necessary for the ordinary charges of the Court.[145] If a particular payment was urgent, a note would be added to the warrant that it should be paid immediately or " w^{t}out delay." Such orders could not be ignored, even if the treasurer had to borrow the money for the payment, or advance it himself. In July, 1549, Somerset commanded the treasurer of the Augmentations to send £100 in prest to Sir William Grey, to which warrant he added the following directive: " And if at the deliuerye of the same warraunt to your handes yow shall not have redy payment to make the [same] we preye you to take some order w^t such your frendes by your bonde or otherwise that in no wise he [Lord Grey] be destitute of the said some." [146]

It was to avoid such embarrassments as this that emergency funds, " sale money," " relief money," and " arrerages " were set up within the Court and earmarked for special use. In June, 1552, Williams was directed to advance £1,000 to the warden-general in the north as part of a larger allocation. Not having that much available, he was instructed to take what he needed from " tharrearages within his custody," apprising the council of how much he had used from the fund in order that " the same may be repayed to his handes againe." The following month he was required " to delyver of the debtes " another £1,000 for

---

[145] Augm. Office, Treas. Rolls of Accts., No. 2B, pt. 1; *L. and P.*, XVIII, pt. 2, no. 231, p. 131.

[146] This advance was made to Grey (Baron Grey of Wilton) for his expenses in restoring order in Oxfordshire during July of that year. Exch., Accounts Various, 76/35, fol. 98.

the payment of a band of soldiers, with directions to reimburse the fund for that amount as regular revenues came in. Sometimes irregular proceeds, such as money due from attainders or the sale of special property might even be spent by direct warrant before it ever reached the Court's treasury. In September, 1552, the chancellor of the Augmentations was ordered to pay a local steward £75 13s. 4d. for repairs to a crown building from money he had collected through the sale of the property of Sir Michael Stanhope, recently attainted. Suspecting that the money had already been spent, Williams was ordered to make the payment out of the ordinary revenues of the Court in case there were no funds left in his possession. In one instance Williams was told to raise the money for a payment " by the best meanes " he could find.[147] In this respect the government never attempted to regulate Court procedure. It was interested in results only.

In the beginning the treasurer of the Court had spent a great deal of time in administrative matters related to the Dissolution, especially field work and specific assignments. Later, as his revenue responsibilities increased, his duties were chiefly those of financial officer. It is true that he retained his membership on the excutive council, but under the second Court most of the administrative and judicial work was handled by the chancellor and two general surveyors. Whereas the other officers could, and did, transact Augmentations business from their homes, the treasurer was kept constantly at the Westminster office. There he and his small group of clerks and servants served as the nucleus of the permanent Augmentations staff, which carried on routine work in the absence of one or more of the senior executives.

The salary of the treasurer has been criticized as being too high; though when compared with contemporary values and in relation to the responsibilities of the position, it does not appear excessive. The increase of the original £120 per year to £300, prior to the time of the reorganization in 1547, was due in part at least to the general increase in the cost of living. The later raise of £20, which incidentally gave him a higher salary than the chancellor of the Court, may have been secured because the office carried fewer perquisites than many of the other administrative offices.[148] The treasurer seldom got extra fees except when

---

[147] Dasent (ed.), *Acts of the Privy Council*, IV, 68, 97, 99, 103, 119.

[148] If to the chancellor's salary of £300 per year was added his regular allowance of £40 for diets during the annual auditing period plus certain other fees, he received more than the treasurer. The two general surveyors of the Court each received £200 and £20 for diets. The salaries for the treasurer of the Court of First Fruits and Tenths and for the receiver-general of the Court of Wards and Liveries were £279 6s. 8d. and £123 6s. 8d. respectively; that for the treasurer of the chamber, £200, plus £40 extra in various allowances. Add. MS. 30198, fols. 21, 28, 29, 31d.

called on for special service, as when ocacsionally he would be required personally to deliver large cash assignments to the royal coffers.[149] Normally transfers of money were by royal messengers or specified agents, but in cases involving safety and secrecy the treasurer or one of his personal servants might be called to make the delivery. However, these and other incidental charges on the treasurer's office were not excessive. In addition to the usual fees and rewards for the annual audit, the chief extra allowances were for office expenses and storage facilities.

[149] Manchester Papers, 15/89, 105–108.

CHAPTER ELEVEN

THE AUGMENTATIONS AS A
COURT OF LAW

N THE ORIGINAL ACT OF CREATION OF THE COURT OF AUG-
mentations its judicial functions were not clearly defined.
Vague references were made to "appearances" of litigants
summoned before the chancellor and to "acts, decrees, and
orders" made by the Court, but nowhere was either the scope or the
limitations of its jurisdiction clearly set forth. In fact, Cromwell and
the king were so much concerned with establishing an efficient organization for revenue administration that they gave practically no consideration to its judicial powers. As a tribunal of justice the Augmentations,
like the Court of General Surveyors, was a court of record for the
adjudication of disputes concerning property and revenues controlled
by it. Various types of cases were suggested by the statute as being
subject to its jurisdiction, but it would appear that originally the Court
was expected to handle only those suits in which the crown had a
primary interest. This included especially controversial claims, debts,
and revenues growing out of Dissolution property. However, legal
disputes between private parties over ownership or title were not excluded, except in cases of alienated land in which the crown had failed
to retain the fee simple. Such matters were reserved for the older courts
of common law, as were all cases involving the use of a jury. In such
cases the pertinent records were delivered to the Court of King's Bench,

where judgment was given. Money awarded the crown as a result of the judgment was returnable in the Augmentations.[1]

Section Eleven of the act defined in very broad terms the sphere of authority in the determination of causes:

> Also that the said Chauncellor for the tyme beyng shall have full power and auctoritie to awarde, under the Privie seale appoynted to the said Courte, in the Kinges name, suche processe and preceptes with reasonable peynes to be therin lymyted as be nowe commonly used in the Courte of the Kinges Duchie Chambre of Lancastre beyng at Westmynstre, agaynst every persone or personnes what so ever they be, for and concernyng the interest right and title of the Kinges Majestie his heires and successours, of in or to any of the premisses lymyted to the survey and governaunce of the said Courte, or of or for any rente accompte receyte or services in any wise touching or concernyng the same premisses or any parte of theym for and on the behalffe of our said Soveraigne Lorde the King, or of or for any dette risinge or growyng by occasion of the same.[2]

While the phraseology of this section of the statute is not very clear, it obviously was intended to empower the Court to hear cases concerning the king's revenue and the collection of debts due the crown. Chief among these were concealments of rents; by extension, cases of embezzlement or other misdemeanors on the part of the Court's officials were also included.

In endowing the Augmentations with a jurisdiction comparable to that " commonly used in the Courte of the Kinges Duchie Chambre of Lancastre beyng at Westmynstre " [3] no ambiguity or misunderstanding was anticipated. Historically, proceedings in the Duchy Chamber were " as in a court of chancery for lands, etc. within the survey of that court by English bill, etc. and decree; but this chancery court is not a mixt court as the chancery of England is, partly of the common law,

---

[1] An Acte establisshinge the Courte of Augmentacions, 27 Henry VIII, c. 27, secs. x and xi, *S. R.*, III, 572–73. In 1542 the jurisdiction of the Augmentations is again set forth in " The Byll for thestablishment of the Courte of Surveyors," 33 Henry VIII, c. 39, especially sec. xxxvii and following sections. *Ibid.*, 886 ff.
[2] *Ibid.*, 572–73.
[3] The same phraseology was used in the statutes erecting the Court of First Fruits and Tenths and the Court of Wards and Liveries, which were likewise given jurisdictional and administrative functions similar to those exercised by the Duchy Chamber. 32 Henry VIII, c. 45, sec. v; 32 Henry VIII, c. 46, sec. xiii. See also Bell, *The Court of Wards and Liveries*, 91; Coke, *Institutes of the Laws of England*, Part IV, 188.

and partly of equity." [4] Like the Augmentations it could, and sometimes did, transcend the inflexibility of the common law, both in procedure and decision, informality of practice enabling it to render speedier justice than litigants could expect in the course of the common law. Moreover, the Duchy Chamber possessed extensive jurisdiction within its own territory, not only over cases concerning lands, but also over people residing therein.[5] As authorized by parliament the Duchy Court and the Augmentations could hear and determine:

> . . . all and almaner of dettes detynues trespasses accomptes rec-
> coynynges waastes disceytes negligences defaultes contemptes com-
> playntes riottes quarreles sutes striffes controversies forfaitures
> offences and other thinges whatsoever they shalbe, . . . whiche may
> or shall towche or in any wise concerne the same wheryn the King
> shalbe onlie partie, and also almaner of states for terme of yeres
> betwene partie and parties concernyng the premysses; and to cor-
> recte and punysshe by their discrescions [i. e., the judges'] all and
> every person and persons whiche before them shalbe convicted of
> eny of the premysses according to the nature qualitie and quantitie
> of his or their offence or offences cause or causes matier or matiers;
> All and almaner of treasons murders felonyes estates rightes titles
> and interestes, aswell of inheritaunce as of frehold other thenne
> joynters for terme of life, oonly excepted and always reserved.

Consequently, the Augmentations had statutory authority over a wide variety of causes which, in anticipation of subsequent development, included future disputes emerging from or related to " eny matier cause or other thing assigned commytted or appoynted, or herafter to be assigned " to its governance.[6]

When the Court was reconstituted in 1547 few changes were made in the matter of jurisdiction. Whereas the range of its authority was laid down in broad general terms, specific regulations and particularities of procedure were conveniently left to the discretion of the judges of the Court. In view of the fact that there was little change among the officials, this operative principle was a logical one, since the chancellor and council were both familiar with the normal course of proceedings and past

---

[4] As interpreted by Coke; like the chancery, "process is by privy seal, attachment, etc." Coke, *Institutes*, Part IV, 206.

[5] Robert Somerville, *The Duchy of Lancaster* (London, 1946), 7; "The Duchy of Lancaster Council and Court of Duchy Chamber," *Transactions of the Royal Historical Society*, Fourth Series, XXIII (June, 1940), 159–77; *History of the Duchy of Lancaster*, I, 123–25, 247–48, 283–84. On duchy procedure, see D. L. 5/6.

[6] From a clause in the statute 33 Henry VIII, c. 39, defining the authority of the new revenue courts and the Duchy Chamber, *S. R.*, III, 887, sec. xxxvii.

practices. It was provided that the Court " during the foure vsuall termes shall sitte at Westminster or at suche places where the same terme shalbe kepte to here and determyne the matters and causes touching this Courte or the revenues of the same." As in the first Augmentations the administrative council, presided over by the chancellor, was also the court of law in which the principal officials acted as judges.

> And where dyuers and sondry auctorities by these presentes are made prouyded and to the Chauncellour and generall surveyours of this Courte of the Augmentacions and reuenues of the Kinges Crowne for the tyme being ioyntlye [jointly] by theym to be doon and executed fforasmoche as we mynde and determyne that the matters causes affayres and busynes of the same Courte aswell towching [touching] ourselfe . . . as touching any of our louyng subiectes shulde not in any wise be hyndered or delayed by reason of absence of the saide two generall surveyours of this Courte for the tyme being but that the same maters causes affayres and busynes shulde haue good successe and spede at all conuenyent tymes appoynted for the same aswell in the absence of any of the same two generall surveyours as in the presence of bothe of theym be it therfore prouyded . . . that when and as often as any of the same two generall surveyours of this Courte for the tyme being shalbe absent frome London at suche tyme as this Courte shalbe holden at London or at Westminster and whan [*sic*] and as often as any of the same two generall surveyours shalbe absent frome any other place where this Courte shalbe appoynted to be kepte within this Realme that then the Chauncellour and thother of the saide two generall surveyours of this Courte for the tyme being withe the Attorney and Solicitour of this Courte or withe one of theym shall and maye make and graunte leases for terme of one and twentie yeres And shall and maye make orders rules decrees and iudgementes and shall and maye here and determyne accomptes and other maters and causes being within the iurisdiccon order rule and direccon of this Courte And shall and maye execute and doo all and euery other thinge and thinges whiche the Chauncellour and two generall surueyours . . . shall or maye doo . . . And that the same orders rules decrees iudgementes and determynacions and other thing and thinges as to be hadd doon made or executed by the Chauncellour and one of the generall surveyours of this Courte withe the Attorney and Solicitour of this Courte or with one of theym in the absence of thother of the same generall surveyours . . . shalbe as good and effectuall in the lawe to all intentes and purposes as if the same hadd been made

doon or executed by the Chauncellour and two generall surveyours of this Courte.[7]

Since the Court had become a basic revenue institution, special attention was given to the comprehensive jurisdiction laid down for financial matters. Like the Exchequer before it, the Augmentations had full cognizance over not only revenues and problems arising therefrom but also over cases affecting its own accountants. Such powers encompassed disputes over " almanner of accomptes reconynges debtes dueties trespasses wastes deceytes negligences defaultes contemptes causes suytes strifes controuersies forfaytures offences and all other thinges whatsoeuer " wherein the crown was a party or was in a position to suffer damages or loss of revenue. In all other matters " betwene partie and partie wherin wee our heires or successours shall and maye not be in daunger and likelehod to lose any parte of our enheritaunce," cases were remitted to the common law.[8] Accordingly, the judges of the Court were granted authority to correct and punish, at their discretion, any person brought before them. In cases involving the collection of crown revenues or debts the Court could award process by *scire facias* privy seal of attachment against any one who refused to pay and " commite to warde " those found guilty of default or contempt. When its own accountants were involved the Court exercised practically unlimited freedom of discretion in both examination and final decision, assessing such fines and penalties as were considered just and convenient.[9]

Essentially the Augmentations was a court of special causes, concerned primarily with the administration of crown lands and the revenues derived therefrom. In this respect it was like the earlier franchisal courts, an honorial court writ large, without specific reference to either common law or equity in the traditional sense. As between prerogative rights and common law, it supported either or both as the occasion demanded. While not unsympathetic to the common law, the Augmentations judges were not members of the bench and were, therefore, more inclined to think in terms of justice as opposed to " law." Free from the obstinacy of the common-law judges in the support of an established system, they resorted indifferently to common law or to equitable forms and procedures. Although the Augmentations was, as were all the other revenue

---

[7] Pat. Rolls, 38 Henry VIII, pt. 5, mems. 21–22.

[8] *Ibid.*, mem. 21.

[9] *Ibid.*, mems. 18, 19, 20. Such powers were similar to those granted by the original act. See Section x of the act. When the colleges and chantries were dissolved and turned over to the Augmentations, similar rights of jurisdiction were reconfirmed. 37 Henry VIII, c. 4 and 1 Edward VI, c. 14, *S. R.*, III, 991 ff.; IV, 29 ff.

courts, always appreciative of the need for maintaining prerogative power, cases involving the rights of the crown might be, and oftentimes were, determinable in any of the regular tribunals, common-law courts, or otherwise. The great increase of Tudor crown revenue multiplied prerogative business without creating a corresponding body of court precedent and legal principle. Consequently, the conciliar organs of administration were peculiarly influential in molding the developing law of *prerogativa regis,* especially such powerful courts as the Star Chamber and the council proper. As contrasted to the courts of common law the royal prerogative courts emanated from the king's council and represented historically an extension of conciliar jurisdiction. Whereas with the former the procedure had become stereotyped and conventional, the newer tribunals continued to retain something of the flexibility of the council itself, which could modify its proceedings to meet the exigencies of particular cases. Unbound by the technicalities and assumptions of the common law, the prerogative courts were free to formulate principles and institute more practical techniques. Encroachments on the common-law courts there were indeed, but the real threat to them was from the rival Chancery, Star Chamber, and Requests and not from the administrative institutions where judicial functions were always of secondary importance. In any event, the needs of a strong government justified an enhanced prerogative, and under the guidance of such vigorous leaders as Wolsey, More, and Wriothesley, the Court of Chancery was bound to leave its imprint on both law and procedure.[10] The Augmentations, on the other hand, had no such leadership, and like the other revenue courts of the period drew its inspiration from king and council. It was a royal prerogative court only inasmuch as it was under close control of the crown. In spirit and judicial interpretation it continued the common-law tradition, though it was bound to come in conflict with the established courts of common law. It was quite natural that the latter should be jealous of the tribunals to whom they were progressively losing more and more practice. There was also some professional resentment by the justices of the Exchequer, the King's Bench, and the Com-

---

[10] Professor Plucknett calls all the Tudor financial courts common-law courts, with the intent of emphasizing their use of common-law forms. Theodore F. T. Plucknett, *A Concise History of the Common Law* (4th ed., London, 1948), 166. On the problem of the incompatibility between the prerogative courts and the common law, see Franklin Le Van Baumer, *The Early Tudor Theory of Kingship* (New Haven, 1940), 177–80. This resentment against the conciliar courts and the Court of Chancery continued into the early seventeenth century. Lawrence Stone, *An Elizabethan: Sir Horatio Palavicino* (Oxford, 1956), xvi, 227. Coke's definition of a court of record reveals an interesting sidelight on the question of rivalry. Samuel E. Thorne, " Courts of Record and Sir Edward Coke," *Toronto Law Journal,* II (1937–38), 24–49.

mon Pleas against the principal officials of the revenue courts, who though functioning judicially were still more administrators than judges. On the other hand, the feeling of rivalry was never intense. Within the several courts they all administered English law, however different the newer courts might be in formality and procedure. Co-operation among them was customary and spontaneous. Whatever their innovations in practice, the Court of Augmentations and the Court of General Surveyors constituted no threat to the common law.

In procedure there was a close similarity to the Chancery and the conciliar courts, especially the Star Chamber and the Court of Requests. Like judges in a court of equity those of the Augmentations proceeded according to their own wisdom and discretion, allowing the same latitude in pleading as that practiced in the Chancery and the duchy of Lancaster. As in all the revenue courts, pleadings were written and in English. In this respect the Augmentations followed the pattern used in the Duchy Chamber. When written pleadings were in English, the suit was commonly referred to as one by " English Bill," a term originally used in the Chancery to distinguish it from proceedings used in ordinary jurisdiction.[11] As exhibited by the plaintiff, the bill was a petition presented to the Court in cases where it was assumed that he had the right of recovery of possessions or lands detained from him or debts due him by the defendant, or of remedy for some other wrong. In such cases it was assumed that the plaintiff had " noe evidence nor specialty to shew forth nor can make any such proofe as is required by the strict course of the Common Law to recover or have remedy for the same, but supposeth that it lyeth in the defendants owne knowledge and that he will confesse the same in his answere." Though by suit in common law sufficient defense was impossible, the aggrieved party " in equity and good conscience ought to be relieved and get either wholly discharged or the extremity mitigated and moderated.[12] The procedure was similar, whether the disputes were between subjects or were suits wherein the king was a party. When the day of the hearing had been set, the defendant was served with process, *ad audientum judicium*, returnable at the time of the trial. Answer having been made at the pleadings, the case proceeded through the various steps, including the presentation of testimony and documentary evidence, to the final decision. The judg-

---

[11] The practice of preferring suits by English bill was begun during the reign of Richard III. Giuseppi, *A Guide to the Manuscripts Preserved in the Public Record Office*, I, 6. The use of Latin for writs, court proceedings, and in all public documents was abolished by act of parliament in 1731 (4 George II, c. 26). Cf. H. C. Maxwell-Lyte, *Historical Notes on the Use of the Great Seal of England* (London, 1926), 239.

[12] Thomas Fanshawe, *The Practice of the Exchequer Court* (London, 1658), 137.

ment was embodied in a formal court decree which reviewed the main points in the case.

Though modern scholarship has refuted the notion that the common-law courts suffered greatly at the hands of the rival courts and councils during the first half of the sixteenth century, yet the fact remains that the challenge was keenly felt by many contemporary legalists, as well as by those who had occasion to suffer the consequences of more arbitrary decrees handed down from the Chancery, Admiralty, Requests, or Star Chamber. This fear for the continuance of their own supremacy was doubtless accentuated by two prevailing factors which discerning observers could not continue to ignore: the perceptible decline in business of the common-law courts and the corresponding growth of jurisdiction in the revenue courts as well as in the prerogative tribunals. Officials in the Exchequer, King's Bench, and Common Pleas must have watched with considerable trepidation the enormous expansion of the revenue courts, which were undermining them in both litigation and fees.[13] Their resentment, when not selfishly motivated by reduction in income, personal animosity, or sheer jealousy, was usually based on a twofold indictment of what Wolsey had once exultantly referred to as the " new law." [14] On one hand, unorthodox practice and informal procedure had grievously deviated from the traditional pattern of the common law; on the other, so argued the common lawyers, perversion of the law was due not only to the establishing of unwarrantable precedents but also to dubious judgments handed down by untrained administrators and officials, " unlearned " in the law.

In spite of the fact that the Augmentations was a statutory court of record and not a prerogative innovation, it did not entirely escape contemporary censure. Since it used equitable forms comparable to those of the royal courts, it came in for a fair share of the attacks leveled against the chancery and all those like institutions engaged in the so-called subversion of the " good laws " and practices of the realm. None

---

[13] William S. Holdsworth shows that the decline of the common-law courts during the reign of Henry VIII was accompanied by a slow and cumbersome procedure which had become a scandal to the age. However, this by no means represented a permanent trend, since there was a decided increase in business under Elizabeth. The effect on the Exchequer was particularly noticeable after its absorption of the Court of Augmentations and the Court of First Fruits and Tenths. W. S. Holdsworth, *A History of English Law* (London, 1903–1952), IV, 253–54, 258–59. Hereinafter cited as *H. E. L.*

[14] Wolsey to Henry VIII, August, 1517, *L. and P.*, II, pt. 2, Appendix no. 38. Wolsey boasted that the country was never in such perfect peace and tranquility: " for all this summer I have had nother of reyut [riot], felony, ne forcible entry, but that your laws be in every place indifferently ministered without leaning of any manner."

the less, such unpopularity as the Court had, though never pronounced, was largely occasioned by its close association with the Dissolution.

The chancery was a common target for criticism, especially for those who, for one reason or another, disliked the lord chancellor; moreover, since that official, as keeper of the great seal, had been a major offender in exalting the prerogative powers of the crown, the indignation of the authors of the complaint of 1547 concerning " the manifold abuses in the Courte of Chancerye contrary to the Commen Lawes of the realme " was doubtless shared by others. The " supplicacion " in question was presented to Somerset and the council by students of the common law and directed against Thomas Wriothesley, then lord chancellor of England. The immediate occasion for this unusual reform petition was a recent commission of the lord chancellor authorizing certain ministers to try chancery cases in his absence. The result had been an " amplyfyeng and inlarging of the jurisdiction of the saide Courte of Chauncery," which had brought about not only a great increase in business but also " the great hindraunce, prejudyce and decaye of the saide Commen Lawes." According to the petitioners the common law of England had not undergone any appreciable change since the Conquest until a series of encroachments had been launched by the chancery, whereby " the good governance " of the realm was endangered. The indictment, at once vigorous and specific, doubtless appealed to the landowners who looked to the common-law courts for protection of their property rights. The magnitude of the problem was thus emphasized:

. . . now of late this Commen Lawes of this realme, partely by Injunctions, aswel before verdictes, jugementes and execucions as after, and partely by Writtes of *Sub Pena* issuing owte of the Kinges Courte of Chauncery, hath nat been only stayed of their directe course, but also many tymes altrid and violated by reason of Decrees made in the saide Courte of Chauncery, moste grounded upon the Lawe Civile, and apon matter depending in the conscience and discrecion of the hearers thereof, who, being Civilians and nat lerned in the Comen Lawes, setting aside the saide Commen Lawes, determyne the waighty causes of this realme according either to the saide Lawe Civile or to their owne conscience; which Lawe Civile is to the subjectes of this realme unknowne, and they nat bounden ne inheritable to the same Lawe, and which Jugementes and Decrees grownded apon conscience ar nat grownded ne made apon any rule certaine or lawe written. By occasion of which impedimentes . . . there ryseth nat only a wonderfull losse unto the Kinges Majeste, aswel of the proffites of his Seale, fynes, issues, amerciamentes and otherwise, but also such an incertainte aswel unto your Lordships as to all other the Kinges subjectes both of their landes, goods, cattalles and other thinges, as neyther your Lordships ne any other the Kinges Subjectes can ne may be certaine of any thing they have by any prescribed lawes. By occasion whereof the Kinges Subjectes be put aswell from their directe tryal as also from divers other advauntages whereunto they be inheritable, and which they ought to have by the due order of the saide Commen Lawes.[15]

The implication was clear, but the council had no recollection of the commission referred to by the lawyers. Eventually, however, it was found among the chancery records, though there was no warrant for such issuance under the great seal. A committee of learned judges and ministers appointed by the council to determine the legality and significance of the unauthorized commission returned a verdict unfavorable to the chancellor, which led to his dismissal from office and subsequent downfall. The committee report substantiated the bill of complaint; the " stowte and arrogant " Wriothesley, unable to produce any warrant for his actions " nor other pretence for his doing, then that he ment none evill in the geving owte of the saide Commission," was found guilty of the abuses which in " sundry wayes " had contributed to the " uttre decaye of the Commen Lawes of this realme." [16]

Actually the commission which lay behind this inquiry was not nearly as objectionable as alleged, for it simply delegated judicial authority to a few men, officiating as deputies in chancery, to receive petitions and hear cases during the absence of the lord chancellor. Their decrees, when ratified by him, were accorded the same validity as if he personally had awarded them. Earlier precedent during Wolsey's tenure in office existed for such a step, and Wriothesley himself had issued a similar commission three years earlier by warrant of Henry VIII.[17] Dated

---

[15] This " supplicacion " presented to the council at Westminster on Sunday, March 5, 1547, is given in full, including a copy of the chancellor's commission referred to in the petition. Dasent (ed.), *Acts of the Privy Council*, II, 48–57. The problem of the supremacy of the system of common law continued throughout the century. By the beginning of the Stuart period the Chancery was considered to be a prerogative court and, consequently, hostile to the common-law system. Plucknett, *A Concise History of the Common Law*, 282–83.

[16] Submitting to the mercy of the council, Wriothesley was, by unanimous consent, dismissed from office and imprisoned, subject to such penalties as should later be agreed on. His degradation followed on March 7, 1547. The actual amount of his fine is not recorded, but in June of the same year he was bound in a recognizance for £4,000 to pay whatever sum was decreed by the council. Dasent (ed.), *Acts of the Privy Council*, II, 56–57, 58–59, 103.

[17] Wolsey's special commission for hearing causes in chancery seems to have been the earliest instance of this practice (*L. and P.*, IV, pt. 3, no. 5666) ; al-

February 18, 1547, the unauthorized mandate was directed to the master of the rolls, Sir Robert Southwell, and two masters of chancery, John Tregonwell and Anthony Bellais,[18] whose activities, according to the bill of complaint, had greatly stimulated business in the chancery where cases " do daily more and more encrease " to the detriment of the nation:

> ... insomuch as very fewe matters be now depending at the Comen Lawes, or if any happen to be there commensid they can nat be permitted there to take any ende or perfection, but apon every light surmise they be called from the saide Commen Lawes into the saide Courte of the Chauncery. And by reason thereof there hath of late growne suche a discorage unto the studentes of the saide Commen Lawes, and the saide Commen Lawes have been of late so litle estemed and had in experience, that fewe have or do regarde to take paynes of the profownde and sincere knolege of the same Lawe, by reason whereof there are now very few, and it is to be doubted

---

though Elton suggests that Cromwell, as master of the rolls, may occasionally have served as a judge in chancery, such a possibility is remote. Elton, *The Tudor Revolution in Government*, 132. Wriothesley's first commission, by warrant of the king, was issued on October 17, 1544, to Sir Robert Southwell, master of the rolls, and several others to hear cases in his absence. *L. and P.*, XIX, pt. 2, no. 527(24). Like Chancellor Rich later, Wriothesley was a greater administrator than judge and gave most of his time to political affairs. At any rate, he seems thereafter to have sat infrequently as chancery judge. Rich, on the contrary, personally presided in chancery during the early part of his tenure in office, devoting all his time to chancery business. Perhaps taking note of the criticism of his predecessor in that respect, he ordered that no clerk or other official serving in the chancery " shall hereafter write to the seale or make any cerciorari or corpus cum causa of any sort or kind but only suche as shall be consigned with the hand of the Lord Chauncelor," under penalty of arbitrary fines to be imposed. George William Sanders, *Orders of the High Court of Chancery* (2 parts, London, 1845), 10. According to Campbell, he later found his job " so irksome " that he grew gradually very remiss in office, delegating all his judicial work to others, though no evidence is presented to substantiate the allegation. Campbell, *The Lives of the Lord Chancellors and Keepers of the Great Seal of England*, II, 13–14. In any event, he issued commissions in 1550 and 1551 to the master of the rolls and others to hear cases in chancery during his illness and thus relieve him of a part of his official business. *Cal. Pat. Rolls, Edward VI*, III, 346–47; IV, 113–14. Rich's successor, Thomas Goodrich, bishop of Ely, who was too occupied with duties of state to give his undivided attention to chancery business, followed the same practice. *Ibid.*, IV, 184.

[18] The fourth member of the commission was John Oliver, clerk in chancery. Far from being " Civilians nat learned in the saide Lawes," appointees were all responsible ministers, with definite legal training. Southwell, a barrister, had begun his legal career as a solicitor in the Augmentations; Tregonwell alone, as a judge in the Court of Admiralty, could possibly be considered unversed in the English tradition. With the exception of Southwell, they were all doctors of law.

that within fewe yeares there shall nat be sufficient of lerned men within this realme to serve the King in that facultie.[19]

Whatever the true status of the common law in 1547, there is little evidence of decline in the number of qualified lawyers during the first half of the century. The Inns of Court flourished; indeed their social prestige was such that many a young man spent some time there as a part of his general education. Consequently a great number of administrators, while not trained lawyers, enjoyed liberal acquaintance with the principles of common law which was reflected in all reaches of the civil service.[20] The " discorage " of the law students of the period, if discouragement had developed, was more probably a result of the keen competition offered to them by the rival governmental administration, which technically at least required no legal training. Nevertheless, the general growth in prerogative law and jurisdiction must have stimulated interest in legal studies.

Certainly in the revenue courts there was no prejudice against the common law. On the contrary, their major officers themselves were usually men of some legal training or experience and were often reputable lawyers, well trained in the common law. In this category may be listed such outstanding ministers as William Paulet, William Cecil, John Baker, Richard Rich, Edmund Peckham, Francis Englefield, and Walter Mildmay. The three chancellors of the Augmentations, Rich, North, and Sackville, were trained legalists. Pope and Williams, as treasurers of the Court, were men of both legal and administrative experience; the legal officers of the Court, of whom there were in succession four attorneys and four solicitors,[21] all were able lawyers, selected because of their proficiency in the law. Two of them, Richard Goodrich and Nicholas Bacon, also served as attorneys for the Court of Wards and Liveries, the latter becoming lord keeper in 1558. Thus, as a result of background and training, officers of the revenue courts were more likely to be sympathetic than antagonistic to the common law.

Likewise, counsels employed by litigants were usually trained in the common law, since by virtue of their study in the Inns they were more conversant with the legal principles and practices encountered in the

[19] Dasent (ed.), *Acts of the Privy Council*, II, 50.

[20] The decline of the system of legal education came later, beginning during the Elizabethan period and reaching a culmination under the Commonwealth. According to Holdsworth, the first half of the sixteenth century was " the golden age " in the development of legal training in the Inns of Court. Holdsworth, *H. E. L.*, IV, 268–70; VI, 481–83.

[21] Two of them were duplications, inasmuch as Robert Southwell and Walter Henley served the Court in both capacities. See Appendix A.

revenue courts. This custom was finally legalized in 1546 when it was ordered that no one could plead in any of the central courts at Westminster, including the Augmentations, who had not previously been a reader at the Inns of Court. Such exceptions as were permitted required the sanction of the benchers of the several Inns,[22] clearly indicating that the king and council recognized the extreme usefulness of this trend. Courts dominated by advocates of the common law were unlikely to institute radical changes in the very law which they administered. On the other hand, if the courts became unduly stereotyped and reluctant to change, it was the bench that was responsible and not the pleaders. In all cases where questionable legal interpretation arose, whether in court or council, common lawyers and judges from the outside were freely consulted.

It is easy to forget this aspect of jurisdiction when considering the diverse duties of the leading officials of the Augmentations. Fundamentally the Court was an administrative institution of which the treasury constituted a principal revenue department of the government; only secondarily was it a court of law, its judicial functions originally growing out of administrative needs and problems. Not the least of these was the executive authority necessary for the proper enforcement of its own orders and regulations, particularly governing the prompt collection of rents, debts, and revenue due the crown. First and foremost, the chief responsibility of the Court was to guarantee the full and speedy payment of revenues under its supervision; consequently, the rules and disciplines imposed upon crown tenants and other inhabitants of Augmentations lands, as well as restrictions imposed upon its own numerous personnel, were largely designed to that end. Penal jurisdiction was therefore a prerequisite of efficient administration, and many of the cases coming before the council of the Court were disciplinary in nature, related in some way to negligent behavior on the part of Augmentations officials or other ministers engaged in the supervision or collection of the king's revenue. Failure to pay crown debts brought reprisals upon the offenders, and an administrative court required powers both to enforce writs and processes and to impose punishment.

Actually the bulk of litigation was directly or indirectly concerned with either revenue matters or disputes growing out of rights in Augmentations property and land tenure, in which instance the crown was

---

[22] Proclamation of June 28, 1546, to become effective at the beginning of the Michaelmas term. Specified were the Chancery, Star Chamber, King's Bench, Common Pleas, Exchequer, Duchy Chamber, General Surveyors, First Fruits and Tenths, Wards and Liveries, and the Augmentations. *L. and P.*, XXI, pt. 1, no. 1145.

apt to be a party to the controversy or at least an interested agent behind the suit. As in all the revenue courts, action for debt was a primary concern, but the crown was not necessarily the plaintiff in such cases. The basic principle that the subject should of right be entitled to redress of grievance against the crown was recognized by statute,[23] and process for the recovery of debts or money by the subject was a common occurrence in the Augmentations. In fact, the acknowledged right of the subject to secure this redress sprang from precedents in that Court, which came to be accepted in the next century as the basis of established Exchequer practice.[24] Such suits in the Augmentations usually pertained to debts which had been contracted by the monasteries before their dissolution, surplusage of payments on audited accounts, and transactions involving the sale, exchange, or purchase of land wherein the subject claimed compensation from the crown. As earlier indicated, the Court was empowered by the original constitution to make all such payments out of its own issues.[25]

In practice, the different functions of the Court were so closely integrated that oftentimes it is difficult to distinguish between its administrative and judicial business. For example, the coercive powers to punish persons for " contempte disobedience or negligence " might result simply in executive orders for discipline of wayward officials grown careless in the performance of their duties, or it might be used against any litigant for contempt of court or for failure to comply with the provisions of a court decision. Since the executive officials of the Court were also its judges, no distinction was made between the council sitting in one capacity or the other. Although varying somewhat from time to time in both size and composition, it always consisted of the principal officers. Under the first Augmentations the chief work of the main office was done by the chancellor and treasurer, as top ranking members. These two, together with the attorney and solicitor, constituted the council. The attendance of the latter, " for the hering and ordering of matters and causes," however, was required by the constitution only when their presence was considered necessary. Nevertheless, records indicate that they were present at most of the important sessions.

After the reorganization of 1547 the council was enlarged to include not only the same four officers but also three others, making a total

---

[23] " An Acte towchinge the findinge of Offices before the Echeator, 2 and 3 Edward VI, c. 8, *S. R.*, IV, 47–48. On the evolution of this principle, cf. Holdsworth, *H. E. L.*, IX, 25–26, 29. The right of the subject to sue the crown was also guaranteed in the statutes erecting the revenue courts.

[24] This point is discussed at some length in Chapter Thirteen, pp. 468–72.

[25] See p. 152 and n. 113, *supra*.

membership of seven officials.[26] Similarly, the respective positions of the first four officers changed, the treasurer stepping down from second to third place in the official hierarchy, while the attorney and solicitor were reduced to fifth and sixth positions respectively. The second office on the council was that of the two general surveyors who acted jointly as one officer. This office was, of course, borrowed from the late Court of Survey, in which the general surveyors had officiated as " the fyrst & pryncypall offycer." [27] Sir Thomas Moyle and Walter Mildmay, who had served in that capacity, were continued in the Augmentations for the period of its entire history. Thus the chancellor as head of the Court and the general surveyors acted collectively as the executive, although in the absence of one of the surveyors either the attorney or the solicitor could serve as substitute. Thus, a full session of the Court consisted of three to seven members or judges, in which the chancellor and one of the general surveyors at least were always present. The signatures on the decrees and orders of the Court show that four members of the council were present at a normal session, usually the chancellor, general surveyors, and one of the legal officers, although three constituted a quorum. While the presence of the chancellor and one of the general surveyors was necessary for any formal decision, judicial or otherwise, it was still possible for the former, as chief executive, to dispatch much of the daily routine business of the Court on his own responsibility. Most of the executive orders and directives were, therefore, issued by him, sometimes under his sole signature and sometimes on the advice of the proper official concerned. On the other hand, by legal requirement, certain powers could be exercised only with the consent of the general surveyors. For instance, the chancellor and at least one of them had to be present during a trial. Accordingly, judicial decisions were awarded under their signatures, or in the absence of one of the general surveyors either the attorney or the solicitor signed in his stead.

The other members of the council attended meetings when their presence was required, but they did not act as judges. The two legal advisers, attorney and solicitor, " shalbe attendaunt vpon the Chauncellour and generall Surueyours . . . or eny of theym from tyme to tyme when and as often as they shall call theym aswell for the prosecutinge

---

[26] It should be noted that only seven officers were represented on the council of the Court, since the two general surveyors, the two masters of woods, and the two survyors of woods jointly constituted the second, fourth, and seventh offices. These offices were also functionally undivided, for in each case either incumbent was empowered to act alone, as if both officers were present. P. 141, *supra.*

[27] Thus the general surveyors constituted " one entyre officer " in their original court as they later did in the Augmentations. 33 Henry VIII, c. 39, sec. ii, *S. R.,* III, 880.

and settinge furthe of accions sutes and proces . . . as also for thexamy-
nacyon of maters to be examyned herde or determyned in this Courte." [28]
Actually they were in common attendance, and as business increased
during the years, their court duties obviously became heavier. Under
Edward VI neither Goodrich nor Gosnold had much opportunity for
other things, spending most of their time on Augmentations business.
With the treasurer, however, the situation was somewhat different. Primarily a financial officer, he was less concerned with judicial and administrative affairs and after 1547 devoted himself largely to treasury
business. John Williams sat in on the council's deliberations only when
questions of receipts and payments were involved.

When peculiar problems dealing with controversial points of law,
common-law precedents, or matters of jurisdiction arose, the Court
could and did rely on outside assistance. Difficult cases were referred
to the privy council or to other courts in whose province the suit might
normally lie. If the legal officers of the Augmentations were in doubt as
to the issue involved, the attorney general or solicitor general for the
crown, or even common-law judges, might be consulted. Conversely, the
other courts of law used the officers and judges of the Augmentations
for similar advice and co-operation. In this way correlation of interpretation and continuity of development was assured. The principles of
common law permeated the Augmentations also through those lawyers
who, as counsels for litigants, undoubtedly influenced the interpretation
of the law enforced. Such modification in practice and theory as emerged
represented a curious combination of the old and the new. Whatever the
impact of the justice developing in the revenue institutions, it did not
emanate from any deliberate intent, nor even from a conscious policy,
on the part of their judges and directors.

The precise relationship that existed among the revenue courts themselves and the closeness with which they co-operated with the older
common-law courts are by no means clear. Nor can the extent and
nature of that interdependence be fully disclosed so long as the history
of any of these tribunals remains unwritten. No institution exists in
a vacuum, independent of the larger operative forces around it, nor can
the ministers of any particular agency remain oblivious to the dominant
trends of the day. The judges of all these courts were fully aware of the
common problems facing them and the logical necessity of arriving at

---

[28] Pat. Rolls, 38 Henry VIII, pt. 5, mem. 23. The oath of office for the attorney
and solicitor also bound them to be " diligentlye attendante " upon the chancellor
and general surveyors, assisting them " withe your aduyse and counsell in the
hering and determynacion of suche matters and causes as shall depende before
. . . this Courte." *Ibid.*, mem. 16.

common, or at least similar, solutions. In suits concerning revenues and properties under their jurisdiction they sought, by the introduction of modern procedures, to eliminate the waste and shorten the delays of justice that characterized the older establishments. It is true that these courts were fashioned in the same general mold; there was also a remarkable similarity among them all in practical operation, especially in new procedural techniques. The Court of Survey, the Court of Augmentations, and the Court of Wards and Liveries, although completely independent of each other, developed almost identical practices. In the case of the Court of First Fruits and Tenths there is at present no adequate study on which to base a generalization, but on the evidence available there is every reason to assume that it conformed basically to the same pattern.

From the very beginning the Court of Augmentations not only drew upon representatives from the central common-law courts for assistance in arriving at difficult verdicts, but it also maintained an Augmentations official in the Court of the Exchequer, as likewise did the Court of General Surveyors and the Court of Duchy Chamber. During the Hilary term of 1545 an office of attorney for the Court of General Surveyors in the Court of the Exchequer was instituted and awarded to Alexander Chapman and Christopher Smyth, to hold jointly at an annual salary of £5 each. The fact that both men were already clerks in the Exchequer and without formal legal education suggests that they were expected to serve the Court of Survey more as special guardians of jurisdictional rights and privileges than as legal officers.

Indeed, a memorandum among the records of the court substantiates this surmise. Inasmuch " as heretofore of long tyme past many of thaccomptes ffermes ffeefermes and other sundery revenues now accoumptable in the said Courte of Generall Surveyours was and hath been accoumptable in the Kinges Exchecquyer," the explanation runs; because of the resultant state of confusion of the Exchequer records wherein many accountants were not fully discharged, it is all but impossible to ascertain just " what belongeth to thone Courte and what to thother to execute." In order, therefore, that the respective jurisdictions of the two courts might be fully and impartially preserved, it was decided:

> . . . that some apte and expert person or persons clerk or clerkes of the sayd Court of Theschecquier to be deputed and named to be attorney to solicite and attend all such affaires of this Courte of generall surveyours as now depend . . . or be in the said Courte of Theschecquier as euery of the Courtes of the Duchie of Lancastre and the Courte of Thaugmentacion . . . hath done and deputed . . . .

thoffice of Attorneye [to have] full power and auctoritie to solicite clayme and do all and euery thing belonging to attornays to do in the said Courte of theschecquier from tyme to tyme And to make relacion of their said doinges from tyme to tyme to the said general surveyours and Counsaile [of the court] in such wyse that the said Courte may be accerteyned by them of all such matters depending in the said Courte of Theschecquier So that the Kinges Majestie . . . may spedelie and truelie be aunswered of his revenues according to righte and equyte.[29]

The revenue courts seem simply to have followed the precedents established by the Duchy Chamber in this and in other particulars, as in the practice of referring mooted questions of law to the attorney general and solicitor general of the crown, and of seeking the advice of judges from the Courts of Common Pleas and King's Bench. Perhaps, like the Court of General Surveyors, the other revenue courts had resorted to such expedients from the very beginning, or at least from long before the practice became a matter of court record.

In the case of the Court of Survey neither the attorney general for the crown nor the chief justice was put on a fixed salary until 1544, although their legal services had been used frequently before that year. Heretofore they had been paid for such extra consultation by special order of the council of the court, but strictly on a temporary basis. On June 20, 1544, the court decreed that a regular fee of £5 per year for advising on the king's affairs should be allocated to Sir Edward Montague, chief justice of Common Pleas, to be paid from the revenues of the court. The decree explained that as yet there had been no fee provided the chief justice " for his labour and travayll in that behalf repayring many and often tymes to consult w^t the Counseill of the saide Courte." The phraseology itself is informative; the action was " requisite and very neadfull," the decree continued, since Montague was many times required to " repayr and consult " with the council or judges on certain " weightie causes and affayres and other comen matters that be doubtful rising and chaunsing in the saide Courte." [30]

Within a few months similar steps were taken to put the king's

[29] Decrees of the Court of General Surveyors, 34–38 Henry VIII. Augm. Office, Misc. Books 106, fols. 84–85. The salary of the office was paid by the receiver-general of the Court of Survey, i. e., by the treasurer of the king's chamber. A calendar of this volume is printed in the *Thirtieth Report of the Deputy Keeper of the Public Records* (London, 1869), Appendix, 166–96.

[30] Augm. Office, Misc. Books 106, fol. 71*d*. The decree itself warranted the payment of the annual fee by the treasurer of the chamber. Montague had held the chief justiceship of the King's Bench since January, 1539. He was transferred to the Court of Common Pleas on November 6, 1545.

attorney general, William Whorwood, on the permanent payroll of the court, and again the reasons given were the same. Although the court previously had paid him for his services by special orders, no regular salary had been appointed. Henceforth Whorwood was to be paid a fee of £6 13s. 4d. yearly for advising the council and Court of General Surveyors on questionable principles of law.[31] It is worth noting that Whorwood was performing comparable services for the Augmentations during the same period.[32]

The Augmentations practice of calling on outside consultation and assistance paralleled that of the Court of Survey, except that its demands became much greater as the volume of work increased. In the beginning these advisers were paid by Court warrant, but it was soon found easier to retain a number of " assistants " on a regular salary. The treasurer's payments show both the king's solicitor general and attorney general to have been compensated for their attendance at London in assisting the Court during term time. This assistance, however, was not necessarily confined to judicial advice. Aid was sometimes solicited in the making of surveys, exchanges of land, and drawing up of indentures. In March, 1540, the attorney general, Sir John Baker, received £20 for his diets while " assisting the Counsaille of the courte of augmentacions aboute the Kinges affayres onely concerning the said Courte." [33]

Again in 1546 Baker was allowed two years payment for reviewing petitions, giving advice, and surveying chantries. During October of the same year dinners were provided for the great master of the household and others whose services had been called on. At the time of the attainder of Protector Somerset the sum of 17s. 6d. was spent on a special dinner at Westminster, where " certeyne of the kynges Counsell Learned were appoynted to sit and attende in and aboute his graces busynes and

[31] *Ibid.*, fols. 67. By the same decree Whorwood was also allowed an annuity of £1 6s. 8d. out of the revenues of the court, payable from the issues of Chippenham manor in Wiltshire as formerly granted him by Sir Walter Hungerford (late Lord Hungerford), attainted. See p. 85, *supra*. The comparable fee paid by the Court of Wards to the chief justice of the Common Pleas was £10 and £4 paid to the attorney general for the crown. Bell, *The Court of Wards and Liveries*, 98.

[32] Whorwood was solicitor general from April 13, 1536, until November 8, 1540, and attorney general from that date until his death in May, 1545. He was succeeded in both offices by Henry Bradshaw, who in turn was replaced as solicitor general by Edward Griffin, from June 18, 1545, until September 30, 1553. Whorwood was preceded in the attorney general's office by Sir John Baker, who became chancellor of the First Fruits and Tenths and chancellor of the Exchequer in 1540.

[33] His clerks were also allowed additional fees of £3 6s. 8d. for writing and engrossing indentures of exchange. At the same time solicitor general Whorwood was paid £26 13s. 4d. for attendance on the Augmentations council from the beginning of the Hilary term until Palm Sunday. Augm. Office, Misc. Books 249, fols. 36, 38.

affaires in his highnes Courte of Augmentacions and revenues of his Crowne," [34] Moreover, the king's serjeant-at-law and the master of rolls were also in frequent consultation with the Court, each regularly retained of counsel " in divers causes " at a fixed salary of £6 13s. 4d.[35] Eventually Augmentations business necessitating conference with other judges increased sufficiently to warrant putting justices from the Court of Common Pleas and the Court of King's Bench on the regular payroll. Decrees " by thaduice of the Justices of either Benche " were not uncommon occurrences.

The Court also maintained an attorney for the duchy of Cornwall and a representative in the Exchequer. No definite time can be given for the beginning of this office in the Exchequer, although it appears to have been established shortly after the erection of the Court in 1536. While the date of his original appointment is uncertain, Thomas Andrews undoubtedly had served in that capacity for a number of years before his death in 1549, receiving an annual fee of £5.[36] Temporary appointees may have been employed as need arose, but the first definite trace of a permanent assignment is found in an annotation recorded among the decrees for the Easter term, 1544. " Forasmuche as it is thought very necessary and expedient that an Attorney shulde be appoynted in the courte of the kinges eschequyre for suche clames maters and busynes as touche and concerne the courte of thaugmentaccions," the memorandum explains, the council decided on a life appointment. The post was awarded to Andrews, a " very mete " person, who as a minor official in the Exchequer was already conversant with its business.[37] When the office was voided by Andrews' death, it was agreed that a successor should be named immediately. Accordingly, another experienced official, John Forster, a clerk in the Exchequer, was designated as his successor at the same salary.[38] He retained the office until the dissolution of the Court in 1554.

[34] *Ibid.* 255, fols. 107, 108; Augm. Office, Miscellanea, 23.

[35] Sir Christopher Hales, Sir Robert Southwell, John Beaumont, Robert Bowes, and Nicholas Hare were successively masters of the rolls during the period of the Court's history.

[36] Augm. Office, Misc. Books 253, fol. 51; 255, fol. 81d. Andrews received an additional compensation of £6 13s. 4d. when the new Court was established in 1547. The item for his first payment, March 12, 1547, detailed this amount paid to him "aswell for his paines takin in writing of a boke deliuered in the courte of thaugmentacions asallso for certeine monye as he hathe disbursed and laide out for certeine serches made by him in thexchequer as be mencioned in a bill remayninge wth thacquittaunce." Payments by warrant of the Court, *ibid.* 256, fol. 100d.

[37] *Ibid.* 104, fol. 14. The office was always referred to as that of the attorney to the Augmentations in the Exchequer.

[38] This memorandum of November 4, 1549, is found in Augm. Office, Miscellanea,

Among the Court's other consultants the services of one of the masters of the Court of Requests or even of the king's " lerned councell " would be solicited. As in the Court of Survey, Augmentations proceedings usually indicate when a decision was awarded on the " good advyse " of others or a case heard in " the presence of diuerse other of the kinges mooste honorable Councell." [39] In some instances the warrants for the payment of their fees give a clear explanation of a practice that had gradually emerged. The order of November 3, 1550, to John Williams authorizing the regular payment of an assistant to the Court is revealing:

Master Treasourer—Wher for the better resolucion of suche doutfull causes and matters as depend in the kynges Court of thaugmentacions and revenues of his graces crowne it hath ben vsed from tyme to tyme to call for assistaunce to the same Courte one of the Justices of comen place And accordyng to the same custom and vse we haue often called and must hereafter call vnto vs our lovyng frynd Sir Jamys hales [40] knyght one of theseid Justices whom at all tymes we fynd wyllyng to assist vs for the kynges maiesties seruyce in that behalf/ffor that it is requysite that for his paynes taken and to be taken in theseid causes he shuld haue of the kynges maiestie some honeste recompence as to other in lyke case hath ben gyven/ We therfore requyer you in consideracion of the premysses that of suche the kynges treasure as frome tyme to tyme shall remayne in your handes ye doo content and pay to the same Sir Jamys hales one ffee of sixe poundes thirtene shelynges and fower pence yerely from Michelmes last past at iiij termes of the yere vsuall by evyn por-[cions] vntill ye shall haue other order to the contrary/And thes our letters shalbe [your] sufficient warrant and discharge in that behalf/ Thus fare ye hartely well from Westminster.[41]

For the remainder of the Court's existence the fees of the three assistants were standardized at £6 13s. 4d. per year.[42]

35/13; E. 321/44 (Proceedings of the Augmentations, Package III, no. 73) ; and Misc. Books 105, fols. 114d.–15.

[39] Augm. Office, E. 321/45/12; Misc. Books 105, fols. 54d.–55d., 109–109d.; 106, fols. 74–81.

[40] Sir James Hales was a judge in the Court of Common Pleas from May, 1549, until shortly before his death in 1554. His services in the Augmentations were continued until its final merger with the Exchequer. Augm. Office, Misc. Books 261, fol. 59; 262, fol. 39.

[41] The warrant was signed " Yo^r louynge friende Ry. Sakevyle " and attested by Walter Mildmay, one of the two general surveyors, and John Gosnold as solicitor of the Court. Augm. Office, Miscellanea, 314/24.

[42] The justice of the King's Bench and the master of the rolls were paid the same amount. The attorney in the Exchequer always received £5 and the attorney

This practice of frequent consultation with other justices tended to accentuate the informality of procedure that was rapidly developing. Unfettered by custom or tradition, its very elasticity of organization encouraged informal conference. The object of a decision was to establish a fact or resolve a controversy, not to reinforce precedent or perpetuate legal principle. When complex questions of interpretation were involved, as oftentimes was the case, the judges had no backlog to draw on. Their decisions were apt to be based on common sense, more akin to equity than to common law. If they felt unsure of their ground, they could call in any number of legal experts to substantiate or modify an opinion. Such judicial deliberations might include as many as four or more legalists in addition to the regular judges of the court and an indefinite number of " the kinges lernyd Counsaile." [43]

Whatever resentment the lawyers and judges of the common-law courts may have felt toward the newer tribunals, their hostility seems to have been directed exclusively against the prerogative rather than the statutory courts. Indeed, if any serious opposition to the Augmentations ever developed, it has not become a matter of record. Naturally, overlapping jurisdiction led to occasional friction, but normally the relations between them were friendly and straightforward. The privy council and prerogative courts like the Star Chamber were, in a sense, potential rivals, whereas, as royal agencies, the statutory courts supplemented rather than undermined their judicial authority. The king in council received or even encouraged petitions from the subject for redress of grievance in order to counteract the slowness, formality, and technical defects of common law. Land disputes and complaints against crown ministers were particularly numerous, since aggrieved parties sought to save time and money by avoiding the protracted litigation so frequently encountered in the older courts. Bills of complaint were addressed to the council, the king in council, one of the lords in council, or simply " To the kyng our souereign lord," to be considered by them at the Table for final determination, remitted to a commission for arbitration, or parceled out to other tribunals, usually accompanied by letters of instruc-

---

for the duchy of Cornwall £20. Add. MS. 30198, fols. 19, 21, 45*d*. Sloane MS. 1520, fols. 5*d*.–14.

[43] In a case involving the interpretation of a grant of land by the king to Sir Richard Southwell in January, 1545, the Court of General Surveyors summoned for special deliberation, "aswell theffect of the said lres. patentes as of the said particlers and the circumstaunces of euery of the same," not only two legal representatives of the crown, the chief justices of both the King's Bench and Common Pleas, but also "other of the kinges lernyd Counsaile." Augm. Office, Misc. Books 106, fols. 74–81. In view of the fact that Southwell, himself a general surveyor, was a judge of that court, the case may have been given special consideration.

tion. In other words, the privy council was a clearinghouse for all business that came before it, and supplications which it did not care to entertain were transferred to whichever court seemed most appropriate. In some instances complainants would appeal to the privy council in disputes obviously under the jurisdiction of the Augmentations, presumably in the hope of securing speedier hearings. Sometimes, too, parties would begin suits in the wrong court, either through preference or ignorance; in such cases the revenue courts worked together harmoniously, honoring previous decisions submitted to them or, when desirable, referring litigants from one to another as circumstance required.[44] There was enough business for all and little cause for jealousy. As one contemporary shrewdly observed, the judges as well as the law were against the people. No remedy was available, he concluded, except from the crown, and there was no reason to believe " that the King should stop the course of his common laws." [45] Nevertheless, in spite of occasional complaints from disgruntled suitors, the only pronounced criticism of the Court came from Brinkelow, who bitterly denounced its officials for subversion and endless delays of justice.[46]

In matters of litigation the privy council appears to have made no attempt to influence the Court, either in favor of the crown or in support of particular petitioners in whom some powerful councillor might have had a personal interest. Even Cromwell abstained from interference in judicial proceedings. At most, the chancellor of the Augmentations would be asked to give an opinion on some point or to honor the claim of a pension or debt of a supplicant whose appeal had already been under conciliar review. Such cases when referred to him would be accompanied by a covering letter: " This shalbe to requyre you vpon dewe examynaccon of the matter to take such order w^t him [that is, the plaintiff] as shalbe consonant w^t iustice and equytie." [47]

[44] Such was the case of *Leak* v. *Woodward* which came before the judges in the Augmentations in June, 1546. In remitting the case to the Court of General Surveyors, the following explanation was entered into the Augmentations records: " M^d that the matter in variance betwene Wodward & Leake w^t all the circumstances of & wrytynges concernyng the same matter by thassent of bothe the said parties be remyttyd vnto the Court of Survey & the said wrytynges delyueryd to [Richard] Jenour clerke of the Counsell of the said Courte." Augm. Office, Misc. Books 3, fol. 16.

[45] John Husee, servant, to Lord Lisle, July 7, 1538. *L. and P.*, XIII, pt. 1, no. 1333.

[46] Brinkelow, *Complaynt of Roderyck Mors*, Chap. X. In speaking of the " cruelnesse and suttyltes " of the ministers of the Augmentations and Exchequer, Brinkelow, who criticized almost everything, affirms that they subverted the law to their own advantage, making " many tymes the king to robbe his subiectys, and thei robb the kyng agayne."

[47] Augm. Office, Miscellanea, 40/90–91. In other instances, requests that cases be decided in the Augmentations would be much more informal. Cf. *ibid.*, 39.

Fuller instructions were sometimes provided, as in the lawsuit between Sir Ralph Bagnali, plaintiff, and Thomas More and William Stanford, defendants, over the title and right to the property of the late deanery of Stafford. The Court was ordered to hear the case as speedily as possible and, with the assistance of the king's serjeant-at-law, to examine the allegations of both parties as presented by their counsels, with the intent of arriving at an immediate decision. In their judgment the chancellor and his council were directed to award title " to the one or thother as by law and conscience showld appere mete and conuienient so as they consume not furder theyr money at the law but soche of theym to receiue indelaid possession of the thing in controuersie as to whome the said Chauncellour and Councell shuld in forme aforesaid allot the same in reason." Accordingly, since the plaintiff had enjoyed the use of a large portion of the premises during the period of controversy, the Court tentatively decided that it was " moost consonant & agreable to law & equitie " to award temporary possession to the defendants for the time being. However, the final decree was postponed for a later hearing, either in the Augmentations or " by any other the kinges Courtes." The reason for deferment was logical enough. Finding " the matier and cawse sumwhat dowtfull or difficill in the lawe," the judges " thought it good to take a furder advice therein." [48]

Less frequently, cases were transferred from the Court of Chancery to the Augmentations if the disputes in question concerned Dissolution or chantry property.[49] When two different matters were involved, as for example a dispute over a rent accompanied by a riot, it made little difference to the council where the suit was tried.[50]

Obviously, in a great many controversies it was not always easy to determine which court should have cognizance over them, especially when the king was an interested party. It not infrequently happened, therefore, that a suit might progress almost to a hearing before the

---

[48] This case was referred to the Augmentations by Protector Somerset, March 20, 1549. The two assisting serjeants-at-law referred to were Sir Edmund Molyneux and Sir James Hales. Augm. Office, E. 321/44/69 (Package III). For similar examples, see Augm. Office, Miscellanea, and Volume IV of *Acts of the Privy Council.*

[49] The reasons given for such transferences were usually indefinite, as " vppon good causes and consideracions " or that justice might be the better expedited. Augm. Office, Miscellanea, 35.

[50] A case in the Star Chamber referred to the Court of Augmentations: *Peter Currington* v. *Richard Buller*, June 7, 1546. " Md that the matter dependyng in varyance before the Lordes in Stare Chamber betwene Curryngton and buller . . . shalbe deliuered in this Court by the comaundement of the said Lordes as bothe the said parties haue made reporte to this Courte." Augm. Office, Misc. Books 3, fols. 16*d.*, 17*d.*, 30.

court discovered that technically it had no jurisdiction over it. Usually there was close co-operation in such instances. Cases were referred to the proper tribunal immediately, with a full record of the previous proceedings. Where delinquent crown debtors were involved, two courts would sometimes unite in a joint effort to collect the debt. However, the executives of one court were careful not to offend those of another, previous consultation frequently preceding the action taken. When a receiver of the Augmentations submitted a list of delinquent debtors to the Council of the Marches of Wales, the latter recommended a commission to investigate and try the offenders locally but advised the Court that " we thought we mought not addresse furthe any suche Commissions frome hense w^{t}out your advise first had in that [respect]." The council, therefore, suspended action, forwarded to the Augmentations the list of defaulters appearing before them, and requested further directions. As an added gesture of good faith, a selected panel of names of local persons appropriate for the proposed commission was submitted.[51]

Writs restraining waste or ordering possession, until the respective rights of the parties could be determined, were common enough. Breaches of such injunctions, duly served, brought attachments. Less frequent, but not unusual, were injunctions issued to stay proceedings or to prevent prosecution in some other court. The claimant would be enjoined to proceed no further at the common law in the matter at issue, " but to abyde thordre of this Courte for the same." Specific penalties for noncompliance were detailed in the privy seal: " It is ordyrd . . . that he shall not prosecute his matter concernynge the variance for the tythes betwene hym & Sir Roland Hill & Sir Thomas Holcrofte knightes in eny other courte then this vntill the matter be determyned vpon payne of one hundred poundes." [52]

---

[51] The Council of Wales to the chancellor and general surveyors of the Court, July 16, 1548. Augm. Office, Miscellanea, 24. For a similar suit, involving the destruction and sale of timber, in which the case was transferred to the Augmentations, see Augm. Office, Misc. Books 115, fol. 21 ff.

[52] *Hodgkins* v. *Watson*; *Robert Mannering* v. *Sir Roland Hill and Sir Thomas Holcroft.* Augm. Office, Misc. Books 3, fols. 16*d.*, 47*d.* In another suit it was ordered "that the matter in variance betwene Myller and Jasper Blake shalbe dismyssed to the Comen Lawe." *Ibid.*, fol. 40.

CHAPTER TWELVE

JUDICIAL PROCEDURE IN THE AUGMENTATIONS: LITIGATION

HE OBVIOUS DIFFICULTY ENCOUNTERED IN RECONSTRUCTING the judicial work of the Augmentations is the lack, originally, of any logical arrangement for the preservation of the records of the Court's proceedings. As courts of record both the first and the second Augmentations were required to keep enrollments of all gifts, grants, leases, commissions, and other documents issued under the two seals of the Court and to preserve in " Appearance Books " a permanent record of all persons who were summoned to appear before the Court.[1] In regard to court sessions, however, the constitution of 1547 was more specific:

> And all examinacions of witnesses vacates vpon recognisaunces and all orders and decrees to be made or passed in the same Courte shalbe written and ingrossed by the Clerke of the same Courte for the tyme beinge or by his deputie or deputies.[2]

---

[1] The Court of General Surveyors also kept Appearance Books and Books of Decrees which were inherited by the Augmentations. 33 Henry VIII, c. 39, sec. vii.

[2] Pat. Rolls, 38 Henry VIII, pt. 5, mem. 23. The patent further provided that the clerk of Augmentations should " kepe a boke or registre of all maters that shall passe or be determyned in this Court and shall kepe suche other boke or Regestre as the Chauncellour and general Surveyours of this Courte shall appoynt for any matters or causes concerninge the same Courte . . . shall yerelye enrolle all leases lettres patentes recognisaunces orders decrees and other thinges whiche shall passe and be apponyted or ought to be enrolled in the same Courte before the feast of Easter yerelye."

Nevertheless, the Augmentations kept no formal plea rolls, nor did it develop anything like a systematic file of written pleadings as did some of the conciliar courts. Records it did keep, however, and in great abundance, including all the legal instruments used in the various stages of procedure. These were preserved as separate documents—bills, answers, interrogations, depositions, replications, rejoinders, etc. to the final decrees—but they were not brought together so as to constitute a single unit upon completion of a case. Consequently, it is usually impossible to reconstruct fully all the individual steps in any particular suit. For an age before law reporting became methodical, there are no contemporary collections of cases to guide the modern historian through the maze of court records.

Although the bulk of Augmentations records relates to its administrative and financial business, there is still a wealth of judicial evidence available. Unfortunately, with the exception of one volume, the Appearance Books have been lost,[3] but the entry books of decrees and orders present a fair picture of the Court's activity. While enlightening glimpses of procedural practice may be gleaned from various categories of records, such as commissions, documents under the privy seal, debts, and recognizances, most of the judicial business is brought together under the general classification of " Proceedings of the Court of Augmentations." These originals include bills, answers, depositions, injunctions, memoranda, draft orders, decrees, and miscellaneous proceedings, covering all aspects of its work.[4] Documents of the office, and later Court, of General Surveyors that have found their way into these collections show the procedure in both courts to have been practically the same. In fact, it is often impossible to identify isolated bills or depositions as belonging to the one or the other, since similar types of suits might be entertained in either institution. After 1547 especially, when the Augmentations absorbed the Court of Survey, the records of the two courts became so intermixed as sometimes to be indistinguishable. This

---

[3] The sole surviving Appearance Book for 38 Henry VIII is found among the 524 volumes of Miscellaneous Books of the Court (P. R. O., E. 315) Augm. Office, Misc. Books 3.

[4] Proceedings of the Court have been collected in three groupings of documents in the Public Record Office: unrelated miscellaneous proceedings (E. 321), 46 bundles; Miscellanea (E. 314), 42 bundles, containing scattered documents; and a number of bound volumes listed among the Augmentation Office, Miscellaneous Books. Of these, the last series of 54 volumes is the most important: Augm. Office, Misc. Books 20, 23, 91–105, 108–34, 165, 328, 436, and 516–22. Some of these are calendared and indexed in the unpublished series of (P. R. O.) Calendars and Indexes. A list of the Miscellaneous Books is given in Giuseppi, *A Guide to the Manuscripts Preserved in the Public Record Office*, I, 144–59. On the records of the Augmentations, see Chapter Fourteen.

confusion in the identity of their records has led not infrequently to misinterpretation of the sources.[5] It has been assumed by scholars that most of the records of the Court of Survey have been destroyed, but this is not entirely true. A surprising amount of unclassified material among the Augmentations documents deals with the work of both the office and the Court of General Surveyors.

As observed in the previous chapter, Augmentations procedure was similar to that of other revenue and prerogative courts. In general, chancery forms were observed, but in virtually every detail of procedure the usages and practices that had developed in the Court of Duchy Chamber of Lancaster were adopted.[6] By statutory provision even the fees chargeable in both courts were supposed to be identical, though an increase in the scale of Augmentations fees eventually was achieved. In course of time precedents were established, and modifications in existing techniques emerged; fundamentally, however, the procedural pattern of the Court did not change appreciably during its entire history.

Cases in the Court of Survey, like those in the Augmentations, were commonly administrative in nature, especially when concerned with such routine matters as destruction or theft of crown property and woods, debts, uncollected revenues, and injustices suffered by complainants at the hands of royal officials. Typical of administrative controversies likely to emerge in any royal demesne was the long dispute in 1523 between the recorder or clerk of rolls of the lordship of Denbigh in North Wales, Robert Dolben, and the king's tenants, who not only accused him of negligence and various misdemeanors in the performance of his duties but charged him as well with trespass, extortion, and felony. Although an earlier commission had reported the accusations to be malicious and untrue, the court had no record of their returns, so the recorder found himself facing a serious indictment.[7]

---

[5] Many of the bundles of Miscellanea contain bills, answers, depositions, orders, decrees, and other documents of both courts. Similarly, a number of the Augm. Office, Misc. Books are mislabeled, their contents having been classified as appertaining to the wrong court. For example, Misc. Books 516–22 are incorrectly entitled " Proceedings of the Court of Augmentations," when in fact only part of them are related exclusively to that court.

[6] Somerville, " The Duchy of Lancaster Council and Court of Duchy Chamber," *loc. cit.*, 159–77. On procedure in the Duchy Chamber under Henry VIII, see for example D. L. 5/6.

[7] Augm. Office, Misc. Books 518, fols. 6, 8, 8*d.*, 11, 31, 40, 42, 78. This case is presented in full in E. A. Lewis and J. Conway Davies (eds.), *Records of the Court of Augmentations Relating to Wales and Monmouthshire* (University of Wales, Board of Celtic Studies, History and Law Series, XIII [Cardiff, 1954]), 90–92. Similarly, the chaplain of Montgomery chapel in North Wales brought suit in the Court of Survey against the receiver of the lordship of Montgomery for the recovery of £25 due him in fees from the profits of the lordship by grant of

In the collection of debts due the crown both the Court of Augmentations and the Court of General Surveyors were quite active. As defined by law, the process of recovery was " by Capias, extendi facias, subpena, attachment and proclamacions of allegaunce if neede shall require, or eny of them." Moreover, under normal conditions the recovery of such royal debts was given preference over private suits. In describing the circumstances of the debt, informal pleading was allowed: " And that the same matter so to be shewed alleged or declared in a generalitie, w^tout shewing and declaring the circumstance therof, shalbe as of good force and effect in the lawe to all intentes constructions and purposes as if the hole matter therof had ben or were alleged and declared at large in every point, according to the due order of the comon lawes of this Realme." [8]

Not all controversies, however, were so easily adjudicated as actions for debt. When in November, 1545, the foreign merchants of Tenby, Pembrokeshire, refused payment of customs duties on imported goods and appealed to the Court of General Surveyors " to abyde & stand to suche ordre and dyreccion as by the said Courte should be considered," they presented a problem not of fact but of legal interpretation. Were the merchants in question covered, as they claimed, by the royal proclamation of 1539 which had exempted the citizens of the town from certain customs on both imports and exports? After debating the point with the king's justices and other members of the privy council, the court decided in favor of the plaintiffs and ordered their recognizances canceled.[9] If for various reasons decisions could not be reached, cases could be deferred to the king's council.

When the Augmentations absorbed the Court of Survey in 1547, it inherited a number of cases from the latter, not only suits pending, but also new ones involving earlier decisions of the General Surveyors.[10] In particular they were related to debts, arrears of rents, assigned revenues, and questions of land rights and titles.

Augmentations cases covered the whole range of controversies grow-

---

Henry VII, which for five years had been withheld by the receiver. Augm. Office, Misc. Books 518, fol. 7.

[8] 33 Henry VIII, c. 39, secs. xxxvii, 1, and li. In fact, all suits "shalbe made & tryed by due examynacion of witnes writinges proofes, or by suche other wayes or meanes" as by the Court should be thought expedient. Sec. xxxix. Items extracted from this act are given in Lansd. MS. 171, fol. 286d.

[9] Augm. Office, Misc. Books 106, fols. 100–100d. The proclamation referred to was that of February 26, 1539, dealing with the customs. L. and P., XIV, pt. 1, no. 373.

[10] A full sampling of the judicial activity and procedure of the Court of General Surveyors can be obtained from the Augm. Office, Miscellanea, 314/37, 38, 39, 40; Proceedings, 321/8, 42, 44; and the book of decrees, Misc. Books 106.

ing out of, or related to, the land, property, and revenues under its administration, particularly those suits in which the crown had an interest. Farms, meadows, commons, glebe lands, private tenements, chapels, churches, parsonages, manorial buildings, woods, rents, tithes, and growing crops were common subjects of litigation. Indeed, any matter pertaining to the former possessions of the late religious houses and of attainted persons or connected with their erstwhile rights, privileges, and obligations properly fell within its jurisdiction. This last category encompassed such things as leases, titles, advowsons, patronage, pensions, annuities, fines, debts and loans, and all kinds of tenurial rights, as well as any form of agreement contracted by the previous owner of the property. Fulfillment or breach of contract usually dealt with sales, arrearages, claims of offices, folk customs, and local rights of fishing, hunting, mining, or other privileges and obligations of land tenure. To the list must be added boundary disputes, illegal detentions, intrusions, concealments, enclosures, disseisins, destruction of crown property, and compensation for loss of revenue, lands, pensions, and offices.

Primarily the causes thus recited centered around things rather than people, their settlement hinging more upon property law than upon the rights of the subject. Still it must be kept in mind that other types of cases were also brought within the province of the Court. Though essentially a revenue and administrative body, the Augmentations like the Duchy Chamber assumed equity jurisdiction over all lands and possessions under it, which included not only portions of every county in England but also in Wales and the Marches, Jersey, the Isle of Man, the Isle of Wight, and the Scillies. Consequently, suits between subjects were common enough, even when the controversy had no immediate relationship to Augmentations land or property. When no better justification was at hand, the old legal fiction that the plaintiff was a debtor to the crown was resorted to by counsel. It was argued that the plaintiff, as a tenant of the king, was unable to pay his rent unless he in turn could recover his debt or property from the defendant. Likewise, since the Court exercised authority over its own ministers, the revenue collectors, and local administrative personnel under them, all complaints against irresponsible officials came under the review of the chancellor and his council; many of them, of course, involved little more than routine investigation. Nevertheless, full consideration of all petitions, however minor they might be, guaranteed just administration.

When a tenant was reported delinquent in his rents, he could present extenuating circumstances. If, as did the farmer of the chapel of St. Andrews at St. Albans, he could show that his own profits had declined unduly, he might secure an adjustment.[11] Not infrequently complaints against Augmentations ministers were received by the king's council, but they were usually sent on to the Court for final determination.[12]

While almost exclusively a court for civil causes the Augmentations could also hear cases involving misdemeanors and criminal negligence. Theft, forceable entry, destruction of property, embezzlement, fraud, forgery, or actions of violence were prosecuted, but jury trials were, by statutory requirement, turned over to the Court of King's Bench. The chancellor and council were permitted to inflict penalties for contempt or for refusal to obey court orders, and in matters of debt they were specifically empowered to award writs of *scire facias* under the great seal of the Court. In short, pleas were heard and execution awarded " to all intentes & purposes as is used and accustomed to be don in the Kinges high Courte of Chauncerie." [13]

As observed earlier, procedure in all the revenue courts was similar to that of the Duchy Chamber and the conciliar courts.[14] Formal written pleadings began with a bill or information, usually ending with a request that process be initiated. Normally the petition was allowed, after which the clerk was instructed to issue a privy seal to the defendant commanding him to appear in court at a specified time to answer the complaint. The allegation was seldom contained in the privy seal, but later a copy of it was presented to the defendant in order that he might study it in the preparation of his defense. Once begun, the trial proceeded through the sworn answer, replication, and rejoinder, to which demurrers, rebuttals, interrogatories, or documentary evidence were often added. If in doubt about the facts of the case, a commission of inquiry would be appointed to investigate and return a report before a final decision was rendered.

---

[11] The farmer complained to the privy council that he was unable to pay his rent because the profits of the chapel had fallen into great decay since the Dissolution. The case was referred to the Augmentations, which determined by means of a commission of investigation that the plaintiff's explanation was correct. Remedy was accordingly given. Proceedings, November, 1550, E. 321/44, Package IV, no. 17. The interrogatories for the investigation are found in *ibid.* 321/46.

[12] When Lord Hungerford in 1539 personally appealed to Cromwell for satisfaction against Sir Thomas Arundell, receiver of the Court, for alleged injuries, the case was referred to the Augmentations " bicause the mater apper[tei]neth to that [cour]t to thentent he may procede t[herin] as the ca[se sh]all require." Merriman (ed.), *Life and Letters of Thomas Cromwell*, II, no. 318. Abstracted in *L. and P.*, XIV, pt. 1, no. 1258.

[13] 27 Henry VIII, c. 27, sec. x.

[14] This idea seems to have been part of a preconceived plan of Cromwell's. When the Court of Wards was organized in 1540, he was in some doubt as to whether the patent of appointment for the receiver-general of the court should follow the design used in the duchy or in the Augmentations. Actually the duchy model was finally used. *L. and P.*, XV, no. 438 (1, 2).

Sometimes, too, with the consent of both parties, disputes were settled out of court by special commissions of arbitration.

The principal officers of the Court gave the final verdict, embodied in the form of a decree, although it might actually be little more than an executive order. In the first Court, decisions were made by the " chancellor and council," whereas in the second, the phrase " chancellor and general surveyors " is continually recurrent. Most decisions were arrived at independently by these three officials and signed by them only, without the aid of the Court's " assistants," though the latter as well as common-law consultants were available when needed. The two legal officers were present at the discretion of the chancellor, but latterly they normally signed decrees only when substituting for one of the general surveyors. In all cases where damages or compensation from the crown were awarded, the decree in effect constituted a warrant to the treasurer of the Court for payment.[15] Conversely, when a crown tenant or collector was acquitted of rent or arrears of revenue, the court decree served as a discharge.

Rex was plaintiff in a great many cases, especially when Augmentations revenues were at stake or crown property in jeopardy. Suits for collection of debts or arrears of rent, felons' goods, goods of deceased persons claimed for the crown, questions of rights in tolls, markets, and ferries, the upkeep of bridges, theft or destruction of crown property, and the sale of timber normally came within this category. Nor was the king always the prosecutor, for the subject frequently sued the crown for redress of grievance or damages sustained in a given transaction. By far the greater number of such complaints were financial claims in which compensation was demanded in some form. It might involve the repayment of loans, the refunding of rents or revenues unlawfully collected, or " recompence " for land sold but for one reason or another never delivered; in other instances suits were for unfulfilled agreements such as promises or contracts for pensions, annuities, the sale of property, or grants of offices that had since been abolished or filled by somebody else. In a large proportion of these cases the decision was against the crown for the simple reason that those who sued the crown usually had legitimate cases. Certainly there is no evidence to indicate that the Court was influenced in the king's favor. The objective of the judges was to render justice to all parties involved, and in most instances that ideal seems to have been realized. Such cases of bribery or govern-

---

[15] " And this decree shalbe to the said Treasorer suffycient warrant and discharge in that behalfe." An award of £400 in compensation for a loan and the arrears of an annuity paid by the treasurer of the Court. Augm. Office, Misc. Books 94, fols. 23*d*.–24.

mental interference as there were have not found their way into the records.

A number of suits grew out of the confusion caused by justifiable mistakes of royal officials. When the crown first took over monastic and chantry possessions, the exact size and value of particular estates were not always known. Oftentimes conflicting claims could only be determined after titles had been carefully checked and accurate surveys made. Occasionally, when land had been leased to one party, it was discovered later that it actually belonged to another. Such mistakes were usually rectified by petition to the Court. When Robert Broke, recorder of London, sued for possession of four acres of land presumed to belong to the crown in Dartford, Kent, which property was already leased to William Thynne, his claim was honored. Upon being required to surrender title in order that the previous contract might be substantiated, he was fully compensated for his loss.[16] Two years later he again won a victory in a suit concerning profits alleged to have been received from a fishing weir in the River Severn, claimed by the state as property of the dissolved Wenlock priory in Shropshire. Commission investigation revealed the fact that the weir had been torn down by royal order some sixteen years previously and that the defendant's patent or purchase of the site was valid in the law. The Court therefore decreed that " accordinge to Justice and equytie," Broke should be discharged of all arrears of rent and that he and his heirs might henceforth enjoy all the fishing rights appertaining to the late weir.[17]

Since many cases against the crown were simple and direct, subject to elementary proof, it is somewhat surprising that subjects were sometimes dilatory in seeking remedy. This may have been due to the fact that Augmentations justice was reputed to be both slow and expensive. Sir Thomas Cheyney permitted one of his buildings in London to be used as a storage house for the king's tents for five years before suing for rental.[18] More complicated claims, although processed immediately, might occasionally entail prolonged deliberation by numerous justices. Such was the case in 1551 between the king and the City of London concerning the possession of the guild or fraternity of the Principal Parish Clerks [19] there claimed by the crown. The dispute, " long

[16] July 1, 1548, *Rex* v. *Robert Broke*. E. 321/44, Package II, no. 34.

[17] *Ibid.*, Package IV, no. 16; Augm. Office, Misc. Books 522, fols. 34–35. On a similar case in Derbyshire concerning " freefysshinge " in the " ferye water " of the king's Willington ferry on the River Trent, see E. 321/5/36.

[18] Cheyney was awarded a rental of £5 yearly, plus arrears, for the period 1545–50. *Ibid.*, Package IV, no. 38.

[19] The guild was called Masters and Governors, Brothers and Sisters of the Fraternity, Mystery, and Craft of the Parish Church of the City of London.

dependynge in variaunce in the Courte of thaugmentacions," hinged upon the question as to whether or not the craft was a legal corporation and therefore composed of freemen of the City. If so, was it exempt from the Chantry Act of 1547? The matter was not only "sondery tymes solemnly debated" by the chancellor and general surveyors in the presence of the justices of King's Bench and Common Pleas, but a special hearing was held in the Council Chamber at Westminster before the lord chancellor of England, the justices of both benches, and the king's "counsell learned." After "due examynacion and delyberate aduyce hadd of and vppon the premysses," the Court decreed that the fraternity was incorporated under the name given but that it was covered by the chantry legislation. Accordingly, the property was awarded to the crown, together with the Clerk's Hall and all the land and possessions appropriated for the support of two guild chaplains. The premises were to be turned over immediately, and all issues and profits collected since Easter, 1548, paid to the district receiver of the Augmentations. Finally, the defendants were further enjoined by the Court "to performe obey and fulfyll this order and decree in and by all thynges vpon payne of forfeyture of one thowsande markes to be levied of their goodes and cattalles to the Kinges Maiesties vse and vpon payne to suffer Imprysonment of their bodies at the kinges will and pleasure." [20]

But more often than not the crown was the loser, as when £28 11s. 6d. annually, plus arrears, was awarded to St. Paul's in compensation for rents and annuities claimed by the church, owing to the confiscation of certain of its chantries.[21] In a typical suit over a chantership in Cardiganshire, Wales, the Court ruled against the crown, since "no good matter of proof" was presented to indicate any right to the office. Similarly, the archbishop of Canterbury recovered church property in 1552, of which he had been disseised by the crown during the Dissolution. Despite the fact that the Augmentations had "taken the issues and proffittes therof by space of many yeres," the land was restored to the archbishopric, and the collected revenues for the period refunded. Sometimes, too, the Court reversed its own judgments, if it was later proved that its original decision had been based on false evidence. Of course a large number of crown prosecutions were for the recovery of debts, long lists of which might be turned over to the Augmentations

---

[20] Easter term, 1551, *Rex* v. *parish clerks of the City of London.* A full bench, consisting of the chancellor, the two general surveyors, the attorney, and the solicitor, was present for the decision. E. 321/45. The decrees in this bundle of proceedings are unnumbered.

[21] November, 1550, *The warden and twelve petitioners of St. Paul's* v. *Rex.* The "bill of complaint," first presented to the privy council, was referred to the Augmentations. E. 321/44, Package IV, no. 18.

for collection, though essentially most of them were unrelated to its administration. Even in those cases the Court appears to have shown no untoward zeal in pressing what was often little more than a purely legal advantage. Many debts were discovered to be unjust or obsolete; others had been paid years earlier, though bonds remained uncanceled, while still others had been nullified by royal pardon. In one instance a debtor was cleared because his obligation had " lost its force and effect and is clearly void in law inasmuch as one of the seals is clean pulled and taken from the same." [22]

For the most part, cases in the Court of Augmentations were ordinary enough, representing routine litigation. The large majority was civil suits and conforms to pattern, but the unusual nature of a few suggests that the judicial business of the Court covered widely divergent matters indeed. Prior to 1547 certain types of questions concerning the collection of customs were decided in the Court of Survey and after that date in the Augmentations, as were also innumerable problems inherited from attainted persons whose property had reverted to the crown. All claims against these estates, of which some certainly represented collusive action to defraud, had to be settled. Valid contracts or oral agreements entered into by the previous owner, whether monastery, priory, or private citizen, were respected even though the obvious intent had been to salvage as much as possible from the property before the king took over. When they were disallowed, it was considered only fair to compensate plaintiffs for their trouble. Petitions by villagers or parishioners cover a miscellaneous number of complaints and requests, such as the support of a parish church, the distribution of alms, the feeding of the poor, and the refusal of a curate to sing Evensong. True, many were petty suits to be settled informally by the chancellor and council without formal hearings; discreet handling of them could keep the inhabitants contented under Augmentations rule.

Obviously, when the rights and privileges of a whole town were in question, the issue was one of more than ordinary significance. Franchisal rights often depended on the interpretation of old charters or the justice of ancient privileges. A controversy of this kind emerged in 1541 between the towns of Old Carmarthen and New Carmarthen in South Wales concerning the use of the quay and trading privileges in the latter port. The older town claimed " dyuers and sondry liberties and francheses " in the newer settlement, dating back to the reign of Henry VI, which had been reconfirmed by a charter of 1485. Other contested rights included the payment of tolls, the control of a local church, and

[22] Lewis and Davies (eds.), *Records of the Court of Augmentations Relating to Wales and Monmouthshire*, 35, 40; E. 321/45, nos. 4, 15.

the conflicting jurisdiction over citizens having common access to the two areas. As revealed by the testimony, incidents had occurred to disturb the peace of the district and further arouse public opinion. Cognizant of the force of usage, the Court ruled that the customs should be upheld. The ancient privileges of the charter of Old Carmarthen were guaranteed, mutual rights of extradition recognized, and freedom of trade at the quay without toll extended to her citizens. By court order, New Carmarthen was required to surrender to her rival all confiscated goods and chattels seized by her in an effort to enforce the payment of customs duties.[23]

Purely private cases embrace such varied subjects as damages for nonfulfillment of contract and suits for enforcement of dower rights. Where crown revenues were affected, no matter was too trivial to merit court action, as the case against a competitor of a crown ferry across the Thames testifies.[24]

The average process moved forward in three major stages. The suit was initiated by a complaint or petition in which grievances were set forth formally by the plaintiff, and court action to remove or alleviate the alleged wrongs was requested. The defendant then responded with a denial in the form of a detailed answer to the allegations against him. Finally, after the usual number of intervening preliminaries, the Court proceeded to the hearing which consisted of evidence presented through interrogatories and depositions. There were, of course, obvious deviations from this pattern, but they did not fundamentally alter the main course of development. The substitution of written forms for oral indictments, answers, and evidence was a characteristic feature of all Augmentations procedure.

Expressing an injury suffered by the petitioner at the hands of a specified party, the declaration in writing was in substance the formal " complaint " directed to the Court, requesting legal intervention for redress of grievance. The defendant replied by writing an answer to the allegations presented against him, thus instituting an exchange of written pleadings clarifying the issue, whether of law or fact, upon which the final decree was based. The initial petition was couched in the form of either a bill or an information, depending on the nature of the suit. The bill was normally used when the plaintiff was a private person whose

[23] E. 321/13/75, 37/6; Augm. Office, Misc. Books 93, fols. 223–23d.

[24] November 25, 1552, *John Bere, farmer of the king's ferry* v. *James Harrison.* The competition was between the royal Greenheath Ferry and Harrison's ferry between Purfleet, Essex, and Dartford, Kent, two miles down the river. The decision was in favor of the plaintiff. Augm. Office, Misc. Books 105, fols. 254d.–55; E. 321/45, no. 46; E. 321/46 (unnumbered interrogatories).

declaration was a personal petition to the chancellor and general surveyors, in which he prayed for relief of his alleged injury.[25]

The information, on the other hand, was introduced by law officers of the Court or by royal ministers on behalf of the crown, this being the form commonly employed when the king was directly or indirectly the plaintiff in the suit. In common-law development, *informatio pro rege* embraced many kinds of accusations against the subject for violations of the law or for wrongs committed on royal land and property. When this was extended to embrace " common informers " for the crown and professionals informing for profit, it led to the excessive abuses experienced during the second half of the sixteenth and early seventeenth centuries.[26] In the Court of Augmentations, however, the practice was never systematized; there the most usual informations were for intrusion and debt.

Despite legal forms ordinarily used, theoretical distinction between the bill and the information was not always followed. In fact, very few hard and fast rules were observed in the informal procedure of the Court; neither were litigants denied justice nor suits thrown out simply because they failed to meet the prescribed standards. Normally, when the crown was the plaintiff, the information was presented in the name of the king by the Court's attorney or, in his absence, by the solicitor; however, the " informer " might be anyone giving information regarding an injury done to the crown by the person or persons mentioned in the indictment, in which case the informant became the plaintiff. In most instances he was a minister of the crown—normally a steward, surveyor, or receiver of the Augmentations—reporting arrears of rent, repudiated debts, or other offenses contributing to the damage or loss of crown property. An informer begged process because the accused party " hath entred and intruded in and to the premysses," which rightly belonged to the king, " and will in no wise permytte and suffer " the king's officers to levy the profits thereof, " contrarie to all right and conscience." The deputy of the surveyor of woods south of the River Trent presented " An Information " of woods illegally seized and crown timber cut and sold; in West Riding, Yorkshire, the particular surveyor exhibited to the Court " Informacione of wronges done vnto the kinges maiestie " by willful marauders who had stripped a parish chapel within the jurisdiction of

[25] Hence, it was usually referred to as a " bill of complaint " or a " bill of petition," the plaintiff being called " complainant," " petitioner," " beseecher," or " orator."

[26] On the criminal information, see Holdsworth, *H. E. L.*, IX, 236–45; more recently, M. W. Beresford, " The Common Informer, the Penal Statutes and Economic Regulations," *Economic History Review*, Second Series, X (December, 1957), 221–37, and G. R. Elton, " Informing for Profit: A Sidelight on Tudor Methods of Law-Enforcement," *Cambridge Historical Journal*, XI (1954), 149–67.

the Augmentations of lead, iron, bells, and valuable timber.[27] The term
billa was often used in its generic sense and might be called in the
same document the bill of complaint or the information, or later referred
to in the demurrer as " the said bill or ynformacon for dyuers causes." [28]

The bill, usually written and signed by the attorney for the plaintiff,
was always engrossed in parchment by the clerk, to be filed with other
documents in the case among the Court's permanent records. It was
addressed to the judges, either to the chancellor and Court, the chancellor and council, " the right worshipfull the Chauncellor and generall
surveyors," or simply to the chancellor alone as the presiding officer
and chief justice of " the kinges highe Courte of Augmentacions of the
Revenues of his gracis crowne." Since the king's council also entertained suits similar to those heard in the Augmentations, it not infrequently happened that complaints addressed to the privy council would
be referred to the latter court for settlement. Such was the case of
the parishioners of Stone, in Staffordshire, against William Crompton;
indeed this particular claim might even have been heard by the Court
of Requests, except that it was concerned with Augmentations property.
At the time of the Dissolution the parishioners had been granted a continuation of their rights in the local church, formerly belonging to Stone
priory and spared for their especial benefit. Since then, however, the
defendant, a London merchant, had taken possession of the premises,
despoiled the church, and sold the lead for his own profit to the " vtter
vndoyng " of the local inhabitants. The plaintiffs pointed out that, if
Crompton were permitted to pursue " his ungodly purpose " further, it
would not only injure the entire community but would also serve as a
" most pernicious and wicked example of all such lyke offendours yf your
graces charitable helpe be not shortly extendid in this behalfe." [29] If the
chancellor of the Augmentations were present in the privy council when
such petitions or bills were received, they were doubtless handed over
to him with oral instructions, if such were necessary. If he were not
present, the complaint would be forwarded to the Court by the clerk of
the privy council with a brief directive on the back of the document:

[27] Augm. Office, Misc. Books 130, fol. 33; 132, fols. 29, 31; Miscellanea, 314/37.
[28] *Ibid.*, Misc. Books 517, fols. 6–7. Bell also found that this theoretical distinction
in the Court of Wards, as in the Augmentations, broke down in ordinary usage.
Bell, *The Court of Wards and Liveries*, 91.
[29] The bill of complaint of Robert Coliar *et al* was directed " To the ryght high
and myghtie prince the Lorde protectours most noble grace." Augm. Office,
Misc. Books 519, fols. 84–86. See also the complaint of the inhabitants of St.
Pancras, Middlesex, which was addressed to the privy council but transferred to
the Augmentations for settlement. *Ibid.* 519, fols. 17–20.

" To the Chauncellour and courte of Augmentacions to be considered and ansuered according to right and equitie." [30]

Normally both bills and answers were quite long, recounting in some detail the background circumstances of the case; with the exception of the headings, they varied appreciably in style and content. Despite the usual predilection for repetition and legal verbiage, the charge was sometimes succinctly, if informally, stated in nontechnical language. The shorter ones were frequently plain statements of arrears of rent or uncollected revenues and were occasionally directed to the treasurer of the Court instead of to the council.

The preferred bill, being in the nature of a petition and presented " most humble wyse," ordinarily contained three particulars : a statement of the complaint, an estimate of the damages alleged to have been sustained, and a request for relief or redress of grievance in the form of process against the defendant. When composed by the plaintiff personally rather than by counsel, the first part might also contain further amplification, in which his great need was stressed in an attempt to enlist the sympathy of the judges. Many petitions, however, were quite brief, containing mere recitals of the facts at issue and pleas for justice. Bills of this type required little more than informal hearings to determine the accuracy of their allegations. Once the facts had been established the court proceeded to a direct administrative order. Typical of such appeals was that for the restoration of land unlawfully disseised, concluding as follows :

In consideracion wherof & forasmuche as your pore orator is a pore lame man not hable to contend & stryue neither in the Lawe nor otherwise w^t the said [Bourman] being the kynges seruant & greatly fryndyd & mayntayned in those parties yt may therfore pleas your mastershippes to send for the said Bourman to appere before yow at a certeyn day by your mastershippes to be lymyted & vpon the examinacion of the hole matter to take suche order & dirreccion therin as shall appertayne to lawe equytie & consciens And your said poore orator shall pray to god for your mastershippes wurshipfull estate longe to contynue.[31]

When the collection of rent or arrears of revenue were involved, which receivers may " many tymes & often haue demaunded," an information would normally conclude with a request for immediate payment by court

[30] *Ibid.* 516, fol. 9.
[31] Augm. Office, Miscellanea, 314/24. The miscellaneous papers and documents in this bundle are unnumbered.

order. " Wherfore may it please the courte to direct privie seale to the saide parties to pay the revenues," the request would read, " or els to appere at a day certeyn to answer to the premisses as shall apperteyne." [32] Not uncommonly a number of writs were required, as when some " obstinate and peruers " parishioners of Curstock parish in Shropshire refused to pay their tithes and obligations to the plaintiff who, as crown tenant of the parsonage, was " not able of the reuenves of the same to paye the kyng hys rent." The usual formula concluded the complaint: " In consideracion wherof it may please your good mastershyp the premysses consyderyd to dyrect on the kynges behalff his most gracious letters of pryuye seale " to the parishioners, " commaundyng them to appere before your mastershyp and the counsell of the sayd Courte at Westm. in a certen day and vppon a certen payne by your mastershyp to be lymytyd." [33]

The privy seals requested were generally of three types: those summoning parties to the Court, those ordering attachment of the body or goods of the person concerned, and those authorizing execution of court orders. The first, if awarded, brought the defendant into the Court to answer the charges presented against him. The second, commanding the sheriff or some other crown minister to seize and hold the property of an individual until such time as he had fulfilled certain requirements, was used primarily in cases of debt or delinquent revenues. The third type was commonly sought for the restitution of land or belongings alleged to have been unjustly seized. Such court actions frequently served to supplement or support the administrative positions of local Augmentations estate officials. The interesting petition of Stephen Boorde, bailiff of the royal manor of Baddeshurst, Sussex, probably presented quite a common situation, one in which the authority of an estate minister was flaunted by the local inhabitants. In this particular instance a freehold tenant of the crown had refused to pay the ordinary fee assessed for the inheritance of the holding, despite the fact that the ancient customs of the manor entitled the king, as lord of the manor, to have " the best beast for & in the name of a heriot." Accordingly, the bailiff had seized a fine ox, valued at £1 13s. 4d. with the intent of protecting the interests of the crown, only to find himself finally checkmated when the tenant actually stole back the ox, remaining adamant to all reason in open defiance of right and custom. Thus defeated, the

---

[32] *Ibid.*, 314/24. In such revenue cases a list of the rents due might be included, or if too long, appended to the complaint as a report.

[33] The complaint of Richard Mody, gentleman, against the parishioners of Curstock parish which belonged to the late priory of Chirbury in Shropshire. (Undated.) Augm. Office, Misc. Books 165, fol. 57.

frustrated bailiff appealed to the chancellor of the Augmentations for assistance, astutely observing that a continuation of such invidious practices would obviously lead " to the detriment & decay of his maiesties seid songnory [seigniory] there and to the evill example of other to do the like." [34]

All privy seals were issued by the clerk of the Court upon receipt of an order, written or oral, from the chancellor or some member of the Augmentations council. When Rich was head of the Augmentations, he directed a great deal of business from his house at Leighs, necessitating an active messenger service between there and Westminster. Court officials conserved their time by scribbling informal directives on either the face or *dorso* of bills presented to them. A brief order " to start processe " or " make a privie seale " against a defendant, or a similar command, can be found on many a bill; [35] in fact, all the available space on some documents is covered with signatures, orders, instructions, or odd bits of explanation. However, a more formal order to the clerk might be forthcoming:

> To my ffrende Mr Duke, d^el. [deliver] this, with spede [36]
> Duke this shalbe to requyre you forwith to make out a privie seall for thapparaunce of one Christoffer Stokdale at the begynnyng of this nexte terme, And that he doo not faile so to doo vpon payne of one hundreth poundes, not omytting to receyve thordynari ffees therfor and to sende me the same to be seallid with spede/ Thus fare ye well. ffrom Leighes this present Satturdaye
>
> your ffrende
>
> Rychard Ryche

Such an order began court action, which proceeded with the privy seal of appearance issued in the name of the king. The typical ones varied little either in length or style.

By the King

We woll and charge you that ymmediatly vppon the sight hereof

---

[34] Complaint of Stephen Boorde against the widow of John Morten, tenant of the crown. Temp. Edward VI; undated. Augm. Office, Miscellanea, 314/24.

[35] The general surveyor or attorney would write an order to the clerk at the bottom of an information that it was the chancellor's pleasure that " you shall make a commission." If separate from the document, the order was more formal: " M [aster] Duke So it is that Master Chauncellors pleasure is that you shall make one prevye Seale for the late priory of Whiteby to be directed to Nicholas Daxtor of Newcastell vppon Tyne merchaunte accordyng to the tenour of this byll. Walter Hendle." Augm. Office, Miscellanea, 314/39.

[36] The letter is undated. Augm. Office, Misc. Books 165, fol. 36.

ye content and paie to the handes of our receivour of the reuenues
of the Augmentacions of our Crowne in our Citie of London the
some of money hereaftre mencioned due vnto vs by you in man[our]
and forme hereaftre expressed orells that ye be and personally
appere before our chauncellour and Counsaill of our Courte of Augmentacions of the reuenues of our Crowne at Westm. in the twenty
day of June next commyng there to shewe sufficient mater or cause
whye ye ought not so to doo not failing hereof vppon payne of oon
hundred poundes yeuen at Westm. vndre the privie seale of our
saide courte the xx^th daie of Aprill in the xxxiij yere of oure reign.[37]

Duke

The extent of jurisdiction can in part be gauged by the expenses incurred in the serving of process and the delivery of privy seals. In
June, 1549, messengers were allowed £20 19s. 5d. for riding costs
" by the commaundement of the Chauncellour generall Surveyours and
of the counsell of Thaugmentacion courte," in addition to their recompense for other types of service.[38] Sometimes writs were made out in
advance to be held in abeyance for execution when required. In the
summer of 1548 the surveyor of woods requested twenty-one privy seals
dated the first day of Trinity term, to be directed against various parties
for having committed " certen spoyles " of crown woods in Surrey. At
the same time he petitioned the chancellor for another batch of twenty
more privy seals to be held " in a redynes," since there were many other
bills of information for similar offenses already before him but " depending at this present unordred." This precaution he considered to be
necessary under the circumstances, in order to preserve his majesty's
timber. " And for lakk of proces," he complained, " the offenders ar
vnpunysshed." [39] It was that kind of forehandedness that won for the
Court a reputation for order and sound management in the administration of the royal demesne.

In view of the fact that no contemporary descriptions of Augmentations procedure have survived, it is not always possible to uncover every
variation in court practice. After a writ had been issued, it would appear
to have been served by court messenger, pursuivant, or even occasionally
by the plaintiff himself. When numerous summonses fell within the same

[37] *Ibid.* 331, fol. 3.
[38] *Ibid.* 258, fols. 64, 65.
[39] Thomas Pope to Richard Sackville, chancellor of Augmentations. Nor was
such procedure at all unusual. The auditor in South Wales was indented for the
receipt of eight blank privy seals to be made out " ayenst suche persons being
indetted to the kinges maiestie as I the saide Auditor shall thinke conuenyent."
Augm. Office, Miscellanea, 314/24.

vicinity, an open proclamation in some public place was legally considered sufficient notification.[40] For more serious matters, such as contempt of court, the county sheriff would be called on to execute the writ, which might enjoin appropriate disciplinary measures. Although excessive penalties were rare, temporary imprisonment was not uncommonly imposed on those who openly defied court orders.

In cases of contempt the nature of the offense was usually specified in the writs of attachment served by the sheriffs in the districts where the persons resided. When, in December of 1542, two parties in Cheshire ignored a summons to appear in court and answer the charges against them, they were held " in manyfest contempt of vs and our lawes." The authority of the Court was in question; justice was being obstructed. The sheriff, therefore, subject himself to reprisals for delay or lack of co-operation, was ordered to attach the bodies of the two offenders; " fayle ye not as ye will aunswer at your perill " was the customary warning given. " Wherefore we willyng the same contempt to be condyngly punysshed do charge and commaund youe that ye attache by the bodyes the said [defendants] . . . and kepe them safely so that ye may haue theyr bodyes before our Chauncellour and Counsell of our seid courte of Augmentacions " at the appointed time. Failure to execute the process might involve the sheriff in serious difficulties. When the culprit had flown and could not be found anywhere within the county, the sheriff returned the writ with a note of explanation on the reverse side, stating why he had been unable to carry out the commandment.[41]

The summons was customarily brief and to the point: " We woll and charge youe that ye be and personallie appere before our Chauncellour and Counsell of Augmentacions . . . in the morowe of tholy Trynytie next commyng to here Judgment in the matter in variaunce depending . . . betwene yow and John Plane of Dover not failing hereof at your vttermost perill." [42] Old age, infirmity, illness, royal service, and other reasonable excuses for nonappearance were accepted, in which case sub-

---

[40] The announcement would be instigated by a letter from Duke, the clerk of the Court, to the local sheriff authorizing him to make " open proclamacion " in the market towns and other public places that certain persons were required to appear before the Augmentations at a specified date. Augm. Office, Misc. Books 516, fol. 12.

[41] Privy seals of attachments, Augm. Office, Misc. Books 103, fol. 46.

[42] Privy seal of May 13, 1545. Augm. Office, Miscellanea, 314/40. The amount of the penalty, though not always stipulated in the privy seal, varied appreciably. When, in May, 1547, Richard Southwell was called to account for the goods and chattels of the late duke of Norfolk which had been in his custody since the duke's attainder, the penalty for nonattendance was £500. Augm. Office, Miscellanea, 314/38. If the sheriff failed to return an attachment, then he, too, was subject to amercement.

stitutes, having power of attorney, might be permitted. The returns of the sheriffs indicate that a large proportion of the writs were never served at all, or not on the first attempt. Many persons named in the schedules could not be located; some were dead, while others had moved to a different locality. Evasion or ignorance of a summons was not uncommon, though actual resistance to court orders was rare. None the less, violence was occasionally encountered. It is recorded that one defendant, upon receiving the privy seal, had " loked vppon yt and caste it vnder feet & badde hym that serued it take it uppe." Not content with this, he then collected a group of armed followers, pursued the server with threats of his life, and finally besieged him in his own house. In extreme situations the sheriff was ordered to " attache the body," of the offender, " committing hym in to sure custody without libertie " until sufficient sureties were found. When prolonged illness caused undue delay of justice, the Court would grant a writ of *dedimus potestatem* permitting the defendant to make answer locally by commission.[43]

A writ of injunction was often used as a temporary solution while the case was pending in court. It provided different types of remedy, such as re-entry into premises that had been seized, restitution of disputed property, cessation of injurious actions, and redress of particular grievances until final settlement could be reached. Refusal to obey an injunction could lead to a second bill of complaint which might incur immediate arrest and imprisonment.

When the time set for the defendant's appearance arrived, he presented to the Court the written reply, or defense, officially known as the " answer." Drawn up in prescribed form it included his denial of guilt, with a detailed refutation of each point in the indictment, and usually a full explanation or excuse for any unseemly behavior that might militate against him. When an individual admitted the charges, which was rarely the case, he entered a plea of guilty and surrendered to the mercy of the Court. In questions of ownership the defendant merely submitted his title for examination; likewise, the exhibition of a receipt was adequate to clear him of an obligation for debt. However, the title might be of questionable legality and require further investigation, as when Margaret Blithman sued for her dower rights in Hiliary term, 1545.[44] If the plaintiff was in error and the land was shown to be held of a private person and not of the crown, the case was dismissed without a hearing.

Once in a while, perhaps, the defendant may have submitted his

---

[43] Augm. Office, Misc. Books 3, fols. 5d., 35, 38, 41d.; Miscellanea, 314/35, 38; 314/39, nos. 5, 6, 7, 9, 72, 74, 76.

[44] P. 57, n. 68, *supra*.

answer without having had a chance to study the complaint and compose an appropriate refutation, but ordinarily he was given a copy of the complaint well in advance of the time limit set for his reply. Failure to answer the bill exhibited against him often brought a reprisal in the form of an attachment, but under average circumstances the defense proceeded with a plea, disclaimer, demurrer, or the acceptance of the allegations as presented. This last type of defense necessitated a court judgment on the entire case as presented by both parties.

In the event of a demurrer being recognized, the case would proceed no further; otherwise the pleadings might be drawn out by a replication from the plaintiff and, in turn, a rejoinder to the replication by the defendant, a surrejoinder, and so on. Under such conditions the case assumed the characteristics of a debate in which a series of rebuttals to the main argument were permitted. The replication reaffirmed the particulars set forth in the original complaint, modified only in the light of the defendant's denial. Allegations contained in the answer were refuted by the " complainant," who continued with a request for a decision in his favor and costs to cover all inconveniences and charges sustained. The rejoinder, as the name implies, was the second reply of the defendant. Additional arguments and new evidence could thus be introduced as the case developed, insuring a fair trial for both parties. Orders permitting litigants to amend bills and answers, bring in counsels, present new evidence, or show causes for demurrers in law, all testify to the general elasticity of procedure.

The quickest and easiest way for the defendant to meet the charges, but also the least likely of success, was to deny the jurisdiction of the Court over the case. The bill is " deuysed onely of malyce to thentent to prick thesaid defendaunt to great vexacion charges and expences of hys goodes "; moreover, it " is vncertein & insufficient in the lawe to be answered vnto " because " the matter ther in comprysed is matter determynable at the comen lawe and not in this honourable court/ wherunto thesaid defendaunt prayeth to be remitted," with costs and charges in his favor.[45] More to the point was the contention of another defendant that the controversy in question was within the province of the local court of the lordship, " by the due course of the comen lawe after the custume of the seid manor ther vsed," and should be remitted to that tribunal.[46] A demurrer in law might be entered, however, in which a claim of insufficiency or inaccuracy in the complaint or information was argued. " Wherunto no law compellith the said defendauntes

---

[45] Augm. Office, Misc. Books 131, fol. 35. Cf. *ibid.* 520, fols. 1–4; 521, fols. 11, 34; 519, fol. 69; 131, fol. 33; 522, fol. 2.
[46] Augm. Office, Miscellanea, 37.

or any of them to make any answer nor by the lawes of the realme byn bounden to answer." [47] In like manner the plaintiff could demur at the inadequacy of the defendant's answer or rejoinder.

The exchange of written pleadings between the two parties continued until the Court arrived at an issue of law or of fact. An important aspect of the case was the examination of witnesses whose testimony was presented in court either orally or by written depositions taken in answer to questions prepared by the litigant or his counsel. A time limit was usually set for the defendant to bring in his witnesses; if exceeded, then the plaintiff would be awarded a commission " vpon his owne interogatories." If, as not infrequently happened, witnesses were so intimidated that they would not " dare depose the truthe for feare and dread," then upon request " processe compulsory " was directed against them commanding their appearance in court to give testimony.[48] Moreover, either party in a suit might give evidence under corporal oath. When a defendant was required to prove his right of possession to certain premises, it was customary for him, " beyng sworne and examynid," to answer certain interrogatories administered to him.[49] When a point of evidence had to be substantiated, many " honest and indyfferent persons " were called in at the discretion of the Court to give sworn testimony; nevertheless, extant records indicate that most evidence was introduced in the form of sworn depositions by witnesses who never appeared in court at all. Nor was personal appearance really necessary until after the device of cross-examination came into use. The numberless interrogatories and depositions that have been preserved show most of the witnesses to have been examined outside the Court either by official representatives or by Augmentations commissioners.

The commission, a favorite medium of all the royal courts, was used extensively by the Augmentations during the reigns of both Henry VIII and Edward VI. It was at once practical and time-saving, having the obvious advantage of transferring much routine business to responsible agents residing in local communities. Typical of Tudor administration by commission, this practice was still another of the many responsibilities imposed on the county gentry. Already overburdened with such tasks, this addition was doubtless onerous to many a local resident, little interested in either Augmentations affairs or in his neighbors' contro-

---

[47] In this case the defendants pleaded that they lived in the marches of Wales, at a great distance, and begged to be discharged. *Ibid.* 517, fol. 7.

[48] Augm. Office, Miscellanea, 314/37. The privy seal called the " compulsory " was also used to require witnesses to appear and give testimony before commissioners. E. 321/27, no. 81.

[49] Augm. Office, Misc. Books 93, fol. 234*d.*; 516, fol. 12.

versies. Yet he was used to accepting such obligations without manifest complaint and usually executed them efficiently and with dispatch. These commissions were appointed for three purposes: to investigate particular questions in suits and to establish the facts, to take depositions of witnesses who lived too far from Westminster to appear personally in court, and to serve as committees of arbitration empowered to settle cases out of court without formal hearings.[50] Frequently, of course, they were all embodied in one commission, though powers of arbitration were only authorized with the mutual consent of the parties to a suit. Two types of documents reveal the work done: the original commission appointment, always in Latin, under the great seal of the Court, and the report in English, presented to the chancellor and council after the assignment had been completed, both of which were filed by the clerk of the Court as records. Upon receipt of the report, the Court proceeded with the case.

The commissions varied appreciably in size, depending largely on the work required of them. Though often quite small, consisting in some instances of only two members, they normally numbered four to six individuals. When the original complaint requested a commission investigation of the matter in dispute, the chancellor or general surveyors would decide whether this was desirable,[51] or if legal judgment were necessary, the bill would be referred to the Augmentations attorney with informal instructions to " examyn this and if you think met draw articles for Commission." [52] One of the Court's officials might sit as an appointed member if neither party in the suit voiced objection. In certain types of cases it is difficult to determine whether the commissioners were acting judicially or in a strictly administrative capacity. For example, in the collection of debts the commissioners might examine

[50] Arbitral commissions were used regularly throughout the sixteenth century, not only in the statutory courts, but also in the Court of Chancery and the prerogative courts of Star Chamber and Requests. Such practical settlements by laymen, based on common-sense principles, have been called by a modern scholar "a kind of popular equity," which was in general conformity with the ethical standards of Tudor society. John P. Dawson, " The Privy Council and Private Law in the Tudor and Stuart Periods," 48 *Michigan Law Review*, Part I (February, 1950), 425.

[51] " And for asmoch as your said oratoures ben men not expert in the englisshe tonge by reason wherof they cannot seek redress by thorder of the lawe," a petition reads, " yt may therfor like your good mastershippes to graunte the kinges most gracious lettres of commyssyon . . . to here and examyn the circumstances of the premisses." Augm. Office, Misc. Books 128, fol. 67. Arbitral commissioners were agents of the Court, with full powers of attachment against those who refused to appear before them. " Stubborn desobedience " on the part of those summoned was not unknown, as the commission reports show. Augm. Office, Miscellanea, 35.

[52] Augm. Office, Misc. Books 131, fol. 21. Such a note would usually be written on the bottom of the bill of complaint.

witnesses, take depositions upon written interrogatories, make inventories of the debtor's property, and so on, even though the party was not formally prosecuted by the crown. In either instance the procedure was the same.

Once the report of the commissioners was in and all depositions before the Court, a day for final hearing was fixed. Further evidence might be called for at this time—deeds, letters patent, grants, bills of sale, indentures, obligations, agreements, or any written records pertinent to the case—and additional witnesses examined. When the documents in question were lost, as in the case of two pensions to Sir Thomas Heneage out of the issues of St. Mary's monastery in Yorkshire, the Court accepted as proof of his claim the oath of the late abbot of the monastery and " the othes of other credible persons." Upon further evidence that Heneage's annuities had been paid regularly prior to the Dissolution, the justice of his plea for continuation of payments was recognized, and judgment awarded in his favor.[53]

In many instances suits were more in the nature of common-sense settlements than court adjudications in which significant interpretation of the law was handed down; " ffor quietnesse of all which vary-aunce the saide parties haue put them selffes to the order and determynacon of the saide Chauncellour and Counsell for an ende to be had in the premisses," many entries read. The disputants having submitted voluntarily to the discretion of the Court, the judges then proceeded to a practical examination of the case, " hering all and euery thynge that coude or myght be shewed or alledged by either of the same parties in the premisses." [54]

The hearing, unless complicated by some difficult point of law, was generally straightforward. No attempt was made to coerce crown tenants or to browbeat other litigants. In suits between subjects it was partly a poor man's court in which ordinary disputes could be settled legally at a minimum of expense. Administratively, if not always judicially, it was in the interest of the Court to satisfy petitioners who had legitimate grievances with as little difficulty as possible. Throughout its history the summary methods used were in striking contrast to the costly and more complicated procedure of the older common-law courts. Arbitration actually appears to have found favor with the chancellor and general surveyors, not only because it relieved them of some judicial

---

[53] July 10, 1540, the case of *Sir Thomas Heneage* v. *the crown*. The suit hinged on the validity of the original grant by the prior of the monastery, " which writinges by chaunce are loste." The sums involved were five marks and £5 per year. Augm. Office, Misc. Books 95, fols. 229–29d.

[54] *Ibid.* 98, fol. 70; 101, fol. 10d.

business, but also because it offered a saving of time and money to litigants. However, suits settled out of court or by arbitral commission were reported back to the Court, where the decisions were promulgated in decrees. Thus the records of the Court became an important source of evidence in cases concerning the territorial demesne of the crown, and its decisions served as precedents in later land disputes.

The skeletal outline of court procedure explained above belies somewhat the real extent of judicial operations. Extenuating circumstances and the human element, always present in litigation, could intervene to render rapid judgment extremely difficult. Death, illness, loss of evidence, procrastination on the part of commissions, failure to comply with court orders, or negligence of attorneys offered unexpected difficulties and delays. During term time the Court was constantly busy with warnings, court orders, injunctions, and attachments designed to speed up the process of justice. Despite this vigilance, however, cases might still drag on for weeks or months before being finally terminated by court decree. Of course many cases were dropped because of inconclusive proof or judgment awarded by default or arbitration, all of which tended to lighten the Court's calendar; but average cases were quite prolonged. Miscellaneous entries in the Books of Memoranda, however brief they may be, fully reveal the practical character of the Court; a commission was commanded to certify what it had done without further ado, a plaintiff required to " shew better matter " in support of his suit or the case would be dismissed, and a time limit fixed for the defendant's answer under penalty of immediate attachment. The suit might be dropped at any time on the grounds of insufficient evidence or, in certain circumstances, " the matter in variance . . . dismyssed to the comen lawe." Conversely, the litigants might be ordered to " precede no further at the comon lawe . . . but to abyde thorder of this courte for the same." A new issue sometimes emerged during a hearing, necessitating the review of a related dispute; when in disagreement on a judgment, the council of the Court might seek the opinion of other judges.[55] Whatever the weaknesses of the Augmentations, inattention to detail was not among them.

Although no two suits were ever quite the same, cases in the Augmentations can be divided conveniently into about a dozen categories, according to their subject matter.[56] The first four were the most numer-

---

[55] *Ibid.* 3, fols. 9, 14, 16, 22, 22d., 24d., 27, 30, 40d., 47d.

[56] Since its jurisdiction included all suits in any way related to crown land and revenue and not to law, this classification of the various types of Augmentations cases is purely arbitrary and is so presented for the sake of convenience. The divisions are: (1) land cases, (2) debts, (3) pensions, (4) rents and delinquent

ous—cases concerning land, debts, pensions, and delinquent revenues—
although problems of compensation for financial loss or for surrender
of office were quite recurrent. Controversies arising from the Dissolution were mostly settled by 1549, but by that time the administration of
crown woods and the sale of timber were important enough to give
rise to considerable litigation. Suits over rights to offices and complaints of crown tenants were common in both the first and second
Augmentations, whereas other types of cases were more infrequent and
scattered. However, a large bulk of the petitions presented to the Court
was of a miscellaneous character, not falling within any particular classification. Probably some were disallowed at the very outset while others,
for one reason or another, failed to develop. Nevertheless, the numerous isolated interrogatories, depositions, and decrees illustrate the
variegated pattern of litigation.[57]

In the absence of any records of plea rolls it is seldom possible to
reconstruct a case fully, since at least one step in its development is
invariably missing. Still this deficiency does not necessarily destroy the
value of the over-all picture which becomes clear in all essentials. Literally hundreds of interesting examples could be presented from among
those extant, but only a few can be included in this study. Because case
studies of the Court's jurisdiction and procedure have heretofore not
been available, a selection of typical instances will reveal far more clearly
than narrative description the judicial Augmentations in daily operation.

The majority of cases heard was concerned with either land disputes
or related controversies pertaining to crown possessions under the
Court's supervision. A major governmental agency for land administration, the Augmentations was for many years preoccupied with questions
of title, boundaries, and rights and obligations of tenure. As might
be expected, particularly in the beginning, much of the litigation was
concerned with its jurisdiction. Immediately after the Dissolution the
control of some of the monastic property was contested by the duchy of
Lancaster, for example, which necessitated legal decisions on the various
conflicting claims. Such was the situation in Warwickshire when both
courts sought possession of Alcester priory. During the trial the prior,
Christopher Bradwey, exhibited " wrytynges euydencye escriptes &

---

revenues, (5) woods and timber, (6) Dissolution controversies, (7) compensations,
(8) disputed offices, (9) trespass, (10) grievances of tenants, (11) destruction of
crown property, and (12) miscellaneous disputes. A brief glance at the manuscript volumes of Calendars and Indexes of Proceedings of the Court (5/43A and
5/43B) will indicate the wide variety of cases adjudicated.

[57] Depositions of the Court have been collected in Misc. Books 108–29, 134;
in addition to these, innumerable interrogatories and blind depositions are scattered
among the Proceedings and Miscellanea.

munymentes " proving to the satisfaction of the court that the house was a part of the foundation of the duchy and that its lands, therefore, did not come under the jurisdiction of the Augmentations. William Coningsby, attorney for the Duchy Chamber, was present and agreed to the decision.[58]

In Gloucestershire certain priories which were assumed to be dependent cells of St. Peter's monastery were given up temporarily on the grounds that the evidence examined was inconclusive. Accordingly, a commission of " indifferent persones " was appointed to investigate the titles further and report to the Court. Meanwhile the case was dismissed " tyll such tyme as better matter can be shewed for the kynges highnes to prove his title in and to the same celle or priory and the possessions thereof." [59] In like manner, when grants by religious houses made before their surrender to the crown were in dispute, the plaintiff presented his indenture of sale or lease for verification by the Court. If recognized as bona fide, the grant was confirmed; but if it was decreed void, a court order would command the plaintiff to vacate the premises immediately and " in nowise fromhensforth entermedle in the same." [60]

Not infrequently the crown sued for possession of Dissolution property, in which instances the attorney or solicitor of the Court acted as plaintiff, but more often the litigation for clearance of title was between two individuals. Questions of disseisin and encroachment were also common enough in the sixteenth century, and the Augmentations had its share of them. In one petition the plaintiff, a crown tenant, blamed his predicament on the fact that he had received no written lease and was not sure of the exact extent or boundaries of his lands. Consequently, " evill dysposyde persons dwellyng nyghe " continually encroached and trespassed upon his property, " by reason wherof yf remedie shall not shortely be provydyde your supplyant shall nott onely be vnable to pay his seide rent but also the kyng shalbe lyke to be dyshenrytyde [disinherited] contrarie to all right and goode consience." He begged that his land be surveyed and a commission set up to investigate his right to certain pastures on which the nearby villagers had encroached. A

---

[58] Bradwey (Bradway, Bradewaye) alleged his house to be a cell of the abbey of Evesham, Worcestershire. *L. and P.*, X, no. 1191. As in parallel cases, the cell eventually came to the Augmentations with the fall of its parent house.

[59] Both these cases occurred in 29 Henry VIII, the former being heard on April 26, 1537. Augm. Office, Misc. Books 91, fols. 49, 84d.–85. In the case of *Rex* v. *the inhabitants of the village of Gravenhurst, Bedfordshire*, Michaelmas term, 1550, the town chapel with its tithes and lands was restored when it was proved that it was originally a chapel of ease. Augm. Office, Proceedings 321/44, Package IV, no. 6.

[60] Augm. Office, Misc. Books 93, fol. 234d.; 97, fols. 34d.–35d.

commission of five was duly appointed, which certified to the Court that, upon the deposition of local witnesses, it had found the defendants in the wrong. Full rights in the use and occupancy of the premises were then awarded to the plaintiff.[61]

Justice, however, was entirely relative, and it occasionally happened that a person found himself caught inadvertently in a chain of circumstances over which he had little or no control. In July, 1533, James Lawson, a merchant of Newcastle, was granted the manor of Byker in Northumberland on a twenty-two years' purchase. At that time the property was rated at £19 16s. 8d. per year, but fifteen years later, by which time it had come under the administration of the Augmentations, the land had increased somewhat in value because certain fishing preserves on the premises had not been considered in the original evaluation. Having been informed that the crown had been deceived regarding the value of the manor, the Court made an attempt to cancel the grant. During the progress of the suit Lawson died and his son, Edmond, was forced to proceed with it. Deeds were examined, land records checked, and auditors questioned, but it could not be shown that either the crown or the previous owner of the manor had ever received any special profit from the fishing privileges which had always been enjoyed by the local bailiff as part of his regular fee.[62] Thus the Court decreed the grant " good and avayleable in the lawe "; nevertheless, " for thavoydyng of suche sute vexacion and trouble as myght in anywise hereafter be attemptid," the defendant, " of his owne ffree and good will," was bound in a recognizance for the payment of £100 " for quieting the possession." [63]

Cases between subjects covered a very wide range of controversies indeed, from those over rights, rents, and revenues to those of title and tenure. Those of a more trivial nature were settled informally by court order or referred to the land steward appropriate to that particular vicinity. " Where varyance stryfe and debate hathe long tyme depended " between two parties, they " commytted theym selfes to the ordre and direccon of the Chancellour and Counsell of the Kinges Courte of

[61] Augm. Office, Misc. Books 100, fols. 108–10.

[62] William Bowman, bailiff of Byker, had certain fishing rights in the manor and in the River Tyne, since the lands had come under the control of the crown by the death of the earl of Northumberland. Augm. Office, Misc. Books 232, pt. 2, fol. 42; Dasent (ed.), *Acts of the Privy Council*, II, 456.

[63] The case was finally heard in Easter term, 1548. Augm. Office, Misc. Books 105, fols. 51d.–52. The payment of such " overplus " by decree of the Court was not at all exceptional. In November, 1551, George Tresham paid an additional £153 3s. 4d. for his manor and lordship of Preston in Northamptonshire, it being proved in court that the survey and evaluation for the original sale was of " uncertain & imperfect making." *Ibid.*, fols. 164–65.

Augmentacions," the official memoranda record; whereupon the Court, having " thoroughly pounderid and considerid " the same and " preceyvyng the trouthe therof in euery behallff haue orderyd and decreyd in and vppon the premysses in the terme of Ester " a settlement. The decision, of course, aimed to establish " a contynuall quyetnes " between the disputants and was awarded upon the mutual consent of both.[64]

In accordance with ancient practice copyhold claims were decided by customs of the manor and turned over to the steward for execution in the manorial court. Parishioners petitioned support for their parish church or begged that a local priest be appointed to serve them.[65] When a disgruntled suitor had failed to get possession of his property by other means, because some influential person in the community had opposed him, he resorted to the Augmentations for an injunction to permit occupancy until the validity of his right was determined. Sometimes the case was well under way before it was discovered that the land in question was not held by the crown at all or that it had been sold out of the king's hands; in other instances it was dismissed without a decision " for asmouche as the matter is put in arbitrament . . . for the endyng therof." [66]

Crown officials no doubt welcomed suits which clarified manorial custom and settled troublesome problems of enclosures or rights in the common land. Bailiffs, stewards, surveyors, and receivers alike must have encouraged tenants to appeal for redress in all matters which would expedite their own work and lighten the burden of local administration. Many such controversies were long standing, certain ones inherited from the Star Chamber and Requests having been pending in those courts

[64] Augm. Office, Misc. Books 93, fol. 210; 101, fols. 10d.-11.

[65] See the interesting suit of the parishioners of Dynham, Norfolk, where by virtue of the dissolution of the priory there the king had become the patron of the local church. The parishioners sued " for ayde helpe and sucours towardes the charges in that behalff so that some rosonable order may be taken and hade for the maytenaunce of the said Churche." In a lengthy decision the Court awarded the parish a continuation of their church, including the premises and adjacent chapel (the king's chancel excepted), with the free use of lumber and other materials for the repair of the buildings, the " said parysheners and inhabitantes beyng pore people." Then the Court went on to remit an ancient workservice with cart and plow—" plough byndes and cartebyndes "—which by custom was due from all the tenants on the demesne lands of the late priory. The decree provided that henceforth all farmers and inhabitants of the parish would be " clerly discharged and acquyted ayenste our Soveraign lord the kyng " for such services. (May 20, 1538.) Augm. Office, Misc. Books 95, fols. 100-101.

[66] The case of Edward Stanley, earl of Derby, in November of 1546. The arbitrators were Sir John Paulet and Sir Richard Phillips. Augm. Office, Misc. Books 3, fol. 41. On cases similar to those mentioned in this paragraph, consult Bills, Answers, and Miscellaneous Proceedings in Augm. Office, Misc. Books 20, 23, especially 20, fols. 2-3, 8, 16 *passim*.

when the Augmentations acquired jurisdiction over them. The following altercation will illustrate. It concerned " the right title & interest of the tythe corne grayne haye calf lands and wolle and all other tythes commyng growyng & encreassing in & vppon the graunge callid harnage graunge " in Shropshire, which had formerly belonged to the dissolved Cistercian monastery of Buildwas. Both the late abbot of the monastery, Stephen Green, and David Egerley, clerk and parson of the parish church of Counde, claimed the tithes of Harnage grange, which had come under the survey of the Augmentations in 1537 when the monastery surrendered. At that time the case was already before the Court of Star Chamber, where it had progressed through the preliminary stage; but before a final decision was reached, the Augmentations had acquired " the order & determynacyon of the sayd matter." By authority of the privy council the " hole processe," including the pertinent records, was sent to the latter court for settlement. The trial was held on May 10, 1537, and judgment awarded to the defendant, Egerley. A commission of six " of the moste substancyall and honest persones of the sayde paryshe " was appointed by the Court to assess the value of the arrears in tithe rent due him during the four-year period of litigation.[67]

Debts to the crown were as aggravating to the officials of the Court as they were to the king and council, though they seldom entailed litigation. Periodically the revenue courts were commanded to call in all outstanding debts and revenues within their jurisdiction and to serve process on those who refused to pay; the government, too, periodically turned over to the Augmentations batches of obligations and lists of debtors with instructions for collection, which greatly increased its business. In addition, there was also a constant flow of petitions requesting judgment against the crown. When financial liability was established, the debt to the plaintiff was settled by an order to the treasurer for immediate payment. The bulk of these suits sprang from the multitudinous claims, legitimate or otherwise, against former owners of crown land and property. All such debts, gifts, arrears of officials' salaries, and other forms of contractual obligation were allowed following proof that they had been entered into in good faith and represented no intent to defraud. Most of the debts were small sums, insignificant as isolated payments, but which in the aggregate amounted to an appreciable drain on the incoming revenue.

[67] *Ibid.* 91, fols. 63–63d. *L. and P.*, XII, pt. 2, no. 411(13). In a similar case in June, 1546, between Richard Buller and Peter Currington over right of possession, the transfer from Star Chamber to Augmentations was likewise made by order of the king's council. A commission was also appointed to determine the " ouerplus of rente " since the time the land came into the possession of the crown. *Ibid.* 3, fols. 16d.–17d.

Such was the case of £15 4s. 8d. paid, in this instance, by the court receiver rather than the treasurer to John Mede and Robert Newman of Mocke Eston, Essex, "in full satisfacon and payment" of a debt contracted earlier by a royal minister. In 1536, after the dissolution of Tiltey abbey, Essex, they had been authorized by Richard Cromwell, as supression commissioner in Essex, to furnish the late abbot, John Palmer, with six quarters of wheat, sixteen quarters of malt, and £4 6s. 8d. "in redy money" for "and towardes the necessary fyndynges and expensys of the said late Abbot and Convent" during part of that year. In addition to that obligation Palmer was also indebted to Mede for £55 which he had borrowed before the abbey's dissolution, for which the latter had already secured a judgment in the Court of Common Pleas. The following year he sued the crown in the Court of Augmentations for recompense of both sums, a total of £70 4s. 8d. By personal oath and "by dyvers & other ways and meanes" the debt was shown to be valid, and full compensation was awarded.[68] About the same time, February, 1538, William Gifford was allowed £100 for the bargain and sale of wood and underwood from the forest of Whitewood in Northumberland. The previous owner, Lord Harrowdon,[69] had sold the timber before the property was acquired by the crown, and the Augmentations was required "by his graces express commoundyment" to give justice to the plaintiff. After examining the evidence the Court called for cancellation "all suche wrytynges" as pertained to the sale before awarding payment.[70]

[68] (November 20, 1536) *L. and P.*, X, no. 408. Augm. Office, Misc. Books 92, fol. 24d.; 91, fol. 5d. Frequently previous judgments for recovery of monastic debts had not been executed when the Augmentations took over the property and, hence, assumed liability for payment. See the case of Richard Gervis, citizen and mercer, who in Hilary term, 1541, sued for payment of the remainder of an old debt of £300 5s. against the late abbot of St. Peter's, Westminster. By two separate actions in the Court of Common Pleas he had collected only £166 13s. 4d. of the sum due him. *Ibid.* 97, fol. 40d.

[69] Sir Thomas Vaux, second baron Vaux of Harrowden, the poet, had no political significance during the period. He seems to have held but one public office, that of Captain of the Isle of Jersey, for a short while prior to the Dissolution.

[70] Augm. Office, Misc. Books 92, fol. 24d. Less self-evident was the claim of the chief mason of the Augmentations, Robert Sylvester, for stone valued at £10, which he had bought under royal commission of 1544-45, of one Culpepper of Kent, probably Thomas Culpepper, the elder. The stone had been delivered to Thomas Lark, the paymaster of Calais, for reparations of the fortifications there, but neither party had ever been paid for the materials thus accepted and used by the king's agent. Eventually, after Culpepper had begun legal action in London for payment of the debt and Sylvester had been arrested, the case was brought to the Augmentations. Sylvester petitioned that Lark be compelled to settle the claim, since it was quite likely that he had already received allowance for the same, for otherwise he would be held personally responsible for negligence that was

Many religious houses were heavily in debt at the time of their surrender, either for small sums borrowed to meet temporary emergencies
or for larger amounts, for which the claimants usually held indentures,
the legality of which was beyond question. Some of the obligations were
of long standing and provide interesting sidelights on monastic management. In December, 1531, the abbot of Cleeve abbey in Somersetshire,
William Dowell, sold a thousand wethers and two hundred ewes to
Richard Smith, but instead of delivering the sheep according to contract
he was permitted to retain the use of them for five years, paying an
annual rental of one half the profit in wool and lambs, estimated at
£12 13s. 4d. Breach of contract or failure of ultimate delivery entailed
a forfeiture of £108. On January 24, 1537, after the dissolution of the
monastery, Smith presented his claim for the £108 plus an additional
amount " for the moytie of the proffytes of the same shepe for the said
two last yeres." Upon exhibition of the various contracts involved, the
claim was allowed in full and paid by the treasurer of the Court.[71]

When indentures, recognizances, and " bills of debt " sealed with the
authentic seals of the monasteries in question were forthcoming, the
investigation usually presented few difficulties.[72] It was often much
harder to prove cases for the crown, since the evidence was likely to be
indefinite. Procedure for the payment of a debt or arrears of rent due
the crown customarily began with a report by a court bailiff or receiver;
less frequently it grew out of the annual court audit of accounts. Auditors and receivers especially were summoned to appear in order that
the Court might " here what can be said for the kinge." When a debtor
was sent to the Augmentations by the king's council, he was cursorily
examined and ordered to present proof at a given date. If he failed to
offer adequate discharge, he was required to pay the debt according to
the council's orders: " Wherefore we haue thought mete the Lordes
ordre to stand." Moreover, persons in no way connected with the Court
often informed the Augmentations or some one of its officials of a rent
due, a debt unpaid, or some leakage in revenue whereby the crown was
the loser. In most instances brief memoranda reminded the judges that
certain parties, usually identified, were scheduled to come before the
Court " to enforme the king." [73]

Ordinarily a privy seal directed to the debtor through the medium of

---

obviousy not of his doing. He, therefore, prayed discharge from the payment
thereof " as iustice and equytie requyreth because thesame ought to be paid by
the kinges Maiestie " and not by himself. Augm. Office, Miscellanea, 314/24.

[71] Augm. Office, Misc. Books 91, fols. 26–27.

[72] *Ibid.*, fols. 34d.–35; 96, fols. 21d.–22, 43–43d., 47, 47d., 54, 54d., 82d.–83d.

[73] Augm. Office, Miscellanea, 15/109, p. 90 ff.

the local receiver, enjoining prompt payment or " ells that yᵉ be and personally appere before . . . our Courte of Augmentacions . . . to shewe sufficient matter or cause whie ye ought not so do " upon pain of a fine of £ 100 or more, was a sufficient threat, but with stubborn tenants stronger measures were employed. In 1539 William Bolles, receiver for the twelfth district, " dyd arreste and restrayne by lerened Counsaill " certain goods of William Parker, a crown tenant in Cheshire, only to face a *replevin* for their recovery by the sheriff of the county. Appealing for a " reformacion " therein, the receiver obtained a court summons for the sheriff's appearance before the Court to answer for his conduct.[74] The most difficult of all debts to collect, however, were those of crown receivers who died while in office. Practically all revenue officials carried from year to year a large accumulation of arrears, part of which was a genuine deficit, and part of which oftentimes represented a sizable amount of revenue collected but not paid into the royal treasury. This unpaid balance they had retained for their own use, not usually with any intention of actual theft but as a personal convenience. Such temporary " borrowings " were generally repaid within a reasonable period as part of the arrears that were always dribbling in, however slowly.[75] None the less, unexpected death found the estates of many royal officials inadequate to meet the claims against them. When ministers were not bonded, it was especially desirable for the crown to establish prior claims to their property before any steps could be taken by the family or other interested parties to evade the natural course of the law.

A commission of investigation generally afforded the best solution for safeguarding the rights of the crown. In all instances where the commissioners' instructions have been preserved, they show the same consideration given by the Court for the protection of the king's interests. When William Thompson, the crown receiver of the possessions in Cumberland of the late attainted earl of Northumberland, died, a commission of three men was appointed to investigate his estate and take the necessary steps to establish the crown's right to various sums

[74] *Ibid.*, 314/20; Augm. Office, Misc. Books 165, fols. 12, 25, 37, 49, 56.

[75] See p. 164 f., *supra*. Even legislation against this abuse does not seem to have checked the practice. In " An Acte concerning Collectoures and Receyvoures," 1542–43, receivers were required to pay in all money collected within three months after it was due, under penalty of forfeiting 4s. in every pound " so reteyned kepte or layde out for gaine." Great losses had been incurred, it was alleged, because receivers and collectors in all the revenue courts had been in the habit of using the money collected for their own profit. Instead of paying in their collections when due, they " reteyned occupied and converted the same to theyre owne singuler proffite and commoditie, as in loning or laying out the same for gaynes, in purchasing landes of greate value, and in bying of wolles and other merchaundyse." *S. R.*, III, 898–99.

still due from the office. They were charged to go to Thompson's house and there determine by search and the examination of credible witnesses : (1) the value and extent of the personal property of the deceased at the time of death, (2) how much cash was available, (3) the value of his lands and to whom leased, (4) what debts and unpaid revenues from his office were still due, and (5) the total of all outstanding sums owing to the estate. An inventory of all possessions was made, and the movable property impounded and put under the custody of Thompson's widow. Since, according to public report, the widow and her brother had secreted certain goods and were under suspicion, all "redy money" was turned over to one of the commissioners. The inquiry disclosed further that revenues totaling over £150, due from the royal manor of Cockermouth within Thompson's jurisdiction, remained uncollected. These were secured and delivered to a crown agent to be paid over to the treasurer of the Augmentations. The commissioners completed their assigned work and submitted a full report within a week.[76]

Almost all Augmentations lands were legally encumbered with rentals and revenue assignments dating from some earlier period when a completely different set of circumstances had prevailed. During the course of years some of these grants had expired or their recipients had died, yet inattentive officials had failed to record such changes in their accounts, so that the customary payments might have been continued indefinitely unless terminated by court order. When the Court was established, it began a systematic check on such commitments which brought a whole new series of problems before it. As cases came under review, each had to be judged on its own merits, pensions in particular being investigated most carefully.

Upon the presentation of documentary proof of the original grant, corodies and annuities were usually permitted to continue unaltered, often with arrears, when payments had been suspended pending the decision of the Court.[77] Nevertheless, review of innumerable cases was

---

[76] The commission was issued under the great seal of the Court on January 6, 1544, and began work on March 6 following. The certificate of returns was submitted on March 12 of the same year. Augm. Office, Misc. Books 131, fol. 34 ff.

[77] It is difficult in some cases to determine whether the decreased amount allowed by the Court represents a deliberate cut in the stipend or merely an error in recording the sum. For example, when Gray's Inn sued for the continuance of an annuity of £7 13s. 4d. for the support of their chaplain out of the revenues of the late priory of Bartholomew in Smithfield, which for "tyme out of mynde before the dissolucon" had borne that charge, they were awarded but £6 13s. 4d. yearly. The usual arrears were also included in the decree. Augm. Office, Misc. Books 93, fols. 47d., 194d. Frequently a single annuity was granted in lieu of various allowances stipulated in the original indenture, as when a servant of the late prioress of St. Mary Magdalen of Icklington, Cambridgeshire,

bound to uncover instances of deception and fraud. Curiously enough many claims were brought to life which heretofore had lain dormant. In November, 1537, John Marshall sued for a pension of £4 per year granted to him from the late Bermondsey abbey in Surrey but actually paid indirectly by Chepstow priory in the marches of Wales, where he had once been prior. As such he had received an annuity of £6, which the house had transferred to Bermondsey when Marshall resigned his position to go there. Despite this generous arrangement, the latter monastery gave him only £4 in addition to food and shelter, presumably without divulging how much was being received from the Welsh priory. Since the dissolution of Chepstow, however, no payments had been made at all, and the poor pensioner, " a verey aged blynde and impotent person," was forced to appeal to the mercy of the crown. He was awarded £6 per year from the Augmentations revenues with separate compensation for the arrearages due him.[78]

Even more complicated was the claim of the suffragan bishop of Dover, Richard Bishop, who demanded and secured an annuity of £6 13s. 4d. from Dorothy Verney, defendant and tenant of the crown. In this case the annuity extended back as far as July, 1532, being stipulated in the will of Ralph Verney. The widow, Dorothy, was unable to disprove the claim, so she was ordered to pay the annuity for Bishop's lifetime and " after his deathe to our seide Sovereigne Lord . . . as hertofore it hathe ben accustomyd to be payde." [79]

Despite the fact that many of these encumbrances had been carried " time out of mind," they failed to stand up under close investigation. Some were disallowed, others adjusted according to merit. On the other hand, a worthy recipient might suffer grave injustice because a minister refused to pay his allotted stipend. Various explanations would be given, such as lack of available funds or that his grant was invalid or had been cancelled. Sometimes this was true, but on occasion a dishonest minister collected the pension himself and, by persuasion or intimidation, tried to prevent the injured pensioner from taking his complaint to court. If the

---

was given £4 annually, plus 40s. for arrears. He had received from the priory not only a subsidy but also a house and maintenance for life. The latter included annually a load of wood and two quarts of coal for fuel, twenty candles or twenty pounds of " white lightes " for his chamber, livery, the services of a domestic during illness, and " meate and drynke sufficient and convenyent for a gentilman." *Ibid.* 91, fols. 7–8.

[78] *Ibid.*, fols. 4-4d.

[79] *Richard Bishop* v. *Dorothy Verney*, widow of Ralph Verney, February 8, 1541. Both parties were tenants of the crown in Hertfordshire, the former by an Augmentations grant of February 7, 1540. It was decreed that the defendant should also pay the Court £6 13s. 4d. for the first of the three years for which the annuity was due. *Ibid.* 97, fols. 32d.–33.

minister was at fault, an order for prompt payment directed to him with the alternative of appearing before the chancellor and council to " aduertise us of the cause of the deteynyng " was usually sufficient warning. Abuses of this kind undoubtedly constituted one reason for imposing restrictions on the system of local payments by receivers. Although the effect was greatly to increase the number of pensions paid from the central treasury, the fact remains that the majority of the pensioned religious continued to be paid at the source of collection, from the local revenues.[80]

In addition to the existing burdens already carried there were, of course, all the pensions to ex-religious contingent upon the Dissolution. These newer grants always carried the proviso that they would be discontinued whenever recipients obtained other emoluments or ecclesiastical preferments commensurate with them. Only occasionally was a charitable appropriation established by decree of the Court, as when in July, 1540, forty-seven " poore bedfolkes," being " verie olde and dyuerce of them blinde and lame," were granted £1 6s. 8d. yearly in alms from the revenues of the dissolved Yorkshire monastery or hospital of St. Leonard's.[81] Besides all these, there were the innumerable pensions and annuities, established from year to year by the crown, in compensation for losses sustained by governmental action or in reward for faithful service. Long before the abolition of the Augmentations the increased outlay in that direction had become a serious problem.

Under the acts of the Dissolution all churches, priories, and smaller religious establishments specifically attached to larger monasteries as subsidiary cells were considered as dependent units, their status being the same as that of the house governing them.[82] Although the law was explicit enough on this point, a number of houses claimed exemption on the grounds that they were, by foundation charter, independent institutions and not dependent cells. If they failed to establish legal proof thereof, surrender was taken by court order. All back issues and profits of the houses in question, lost to the crown during the period of litigation, were turned over to the Augmentations as legitimate revenues of the Court.[83]

[80] See p. 228, *supra.*
[81] Augm. Office, Misc. Books 95, fol. 145.
[82] Legally a cell owed " obedyence " to some superior house and could neither " sue or be sued by the Lawes of this Realme." 27 Henry VIII, c. 28, sec. xv, *S. R.,* III, 577.
[83] Augm. Office, Misc. Books 91, fol. 85; 100, fols. 20–20d., 41; 102, fol. 154d.; 516, fol. 57. When in Hilary term, 1538, a priory in Hertfordshire claimed to be attached to St. Albans, the heads of both houses were called before the Augmentations to submit evidence. Since " no pregnaunt metter coulde be founde nor

The many references to damages against the crown awarded by the Court tend to refute the earlier conclusion of some writers that the Augmentations favored the royal position. True, it was careful to assert every possible claim to lands or revenues in which the crown had an interest, but if any attempt was made by the chancellor and council to divert the course of justice, it is not evidenced in the proceedings. When, for example, the inhabitants of the town of Mount Sorrell, Leicestershire, complained that the crown was entitled to only one of the dozen cottages which royal officials had taken over, the Court found for the plaintiffs and returned the property to the town. More than once in cases of this kind restraints were imposed upon over-zealous ministers.[84] In fact, if any prejudice at all was shown, it was more apt to be in favor of one of the Court's central officials or of some influential noble of the realm.

As so often true in litigation where the motives of individuals are open to suspicion, it is seldom possible to prove either favoritism or corruption. In 1546 the Court ruled against Sir Thomas Pope in voiding a grant of the church and parsonage of North Leigh, Oxfordshire, sold to him the preceding year, when it was disclosed by an indenture duly exhibited that the premises had been alienated by an earlier grant. Pope gave possession but demanded compensation for his loss. He was awarded £144, plus an additional £4 to cover the profit on the property sacrificed by him for a period of over half a year.[85] In certain instances where the decision on the basis of the principles involved was obviously fair, the amount of compensation may have been excessive. Usually, however, this was not the case. When Sir Robert Southwell, formerly legal officer of the Augmentations, was awarded £16 in recompense, it was for payment of a strip of land which had been excluded from a grant of property in Essex at the time of its purchase. The judgment was perfectly valid since it was shown that the six and one-half acres under dispute were " parcell of the rente of assize of the said manor "; nor

shewyde " to prove the priory a cell under the monastery, the Court ruled it to be independent and, having possessions under the clear annual value of £200 per year, as stipulated in the first act of Dissolution, ordered its suppression. Proof of independence was indirect; the priory had possessed a seal for as long as men could remember, could grant land, collect its own taxes, and sue in all national courts. " And also dyuers other causys and consyderacions beynge evydent," no further proof was required. *Ibid.* 92, fols. 43–43d. Many cases were dismissed until such time as the king " should be able to prove his Title thereto." *Ibid.* 1, fols. 48d., 49, 84d., 85.

[84] Augm. Office, Proceedings, 321/45.

[85] The property in Pope's grant, dated March 20, 1545, was valued at £7 4s. annually; the previous sale was made on August 28, 1544. For the original grant, see *L. and P.*, XIX, pt. 2, no. 166(44). Augm. Office, Misc. Books 104, pt. 2, fols. 121–21d.

was the amount allowed padded in any way. The land was sold at twenty years' purchase, with an assessed yearly value of 16*s.* for the exempted portion. The judges merely accepted the surveyor's evaluation in determining the worth of the land.[86]

Compensation was awarded for a variety of reasons, often occasioned by circumstances for which no one party was entirely responsible. Money already paid to the crown was refunded for unfulfilled contracts, for reversions of land, and for breach of royal agreement.[87] An interesting case came up under Sackville in 1551 in relation to a contract entered into with John Hartford and son, officers in the royal stables, for the pasturage of the king's horses in Yarnewood Park, Shropshire, which they held for life. Later the park was granted to Sir George Blount for term of years, without mention of the former agreement, and the question of who should enjoy the rights of herbage and pannage arose. The Court decreed that the payment of £8 per year as originally contracted should go to the Hartfords for life, to be paid by the district receiver, with the proviso " that yf the kinges ma[tes] said horsses be hereafter had from thens whereby the said Sir George may take the preffectes [profits] of therbaege and pannage of the said parke then to cause the said Sir George to dyscharge the kinges Ma[tie] against the said John Hartford . . . of the said annyal rent." [88]

Typical of prosecutions by the crown were suits against tenants who had either defaulted in the payment of their rents or been guilty of destruction of crown property. However, the tenant was not always to blame. Sometimes he had been overcharged by the receiver and therefore given a refund of the overplus, or surplus, paid on his account. On rare occasions he might successfully refute the crown's claim to arrears by proof of enclosures that more than equaled his own debt.[89]

---

[86] Decree of Easter term, 1546; the original grant was made on February 8, 1545. *Ibid.* 104, pt. 2, fols. 124–24*d.* In such cases a suitor was never paid for the expense and personal inconvenience incurred. When Richard Southwell, in 1539, surrendered Westacre manor in Rowdham, Norfolk, which he had bought of the prior of Westacre monastery in December, 1537, he was reimbursed exactly what he had paid for it, £280. *Ibid.* 100, fol. 270*d.*

[87] By a decree of February, 1544, Thomas Mildmay was paid £40 for a Norfolk mill which was granted to him through the Augmentations under letters patent of March 11, 1539, at twenty years' purchase. The property was sold in good faith, despite the fact that, unknown to the Court's officials at the time, the mill had been torn down by the authority of a royal commission. The £40 represented the full value of the property, reckoned at 40*s.* rental per year. Augm. Office, Misc. Books 104, pt. 1, fol. 131.

[88] Augm. Office, Miscellanea, 314/17.

[89] See the case of Sir William Finch who was sued for £30 8*s.* 9½*d.* in rent and arrears in 1547. He showed that part of his land had been enclosed for a park, which put the crown in his debt £7 15*s.* 5*d.* more than he himself owed. Augm. Office, Misc. Books 105, fols. 6*d.*–7.

The Court shared with the Star Chamber, the Court of Requests, and the Council of Wales suits concerning enclosures and encroachment of commons, especially by the overstocking of sheep. Many cases concerned the imparking of crown lands, but more generally complaints came from resentful tenants whose rights in the commons were endangered. A large flock of sheep turned out on the commons, contrary to custom, was sure to produce an immediate objection. Nor was the outcry against those who " wrongfully w^{th}out ayther right or colour of title " had ditched and enclosed commons and wastes any less pronounced.[90] Agrarian discontent mounted during the period of the second Augmentations, and the Court did little or nothing to allay it.

Perhaps less significant but equally necessary were decisions handed down on matters of disputed offices and conflicting jurisdiction. Although administrative in nature, judgments of this kind seldom established policy or laid down ethical principles which might have become precedents for future administrators to follow, but they did serve to promote a feeling of security and confidence among Augmentations personnel. Every official, high and low alike, could present his problems to the Court and, given a legitimate grievance, expect a full and impartial hearing. Trivial issues were settled quickly by arbitration or fact-finding commission; more complicated disputes, however, might run the entire gamut of procedural development from initial complaint to concluding decree. Appeals were made for nonpayment of salaries, for insubordination or malfeasance of subalterns, or for special authority to treat with recalcitrant tenants. When two or more parties claimed the same office, possession was decided on the basis of merit; if a job was abolished or surrendered upon the request of the crown, compensation was awarded; when disciplinary action was called for, the Court furnished the necessary injunction.

Ordinarily cases between subjects were heard in the common-law courts unless it could be shown that the crown had a tangible interest in the matter, but Augmentations ministers freely sued in their own court despite the frequent contentions of defendants that private suits for debt or recovery of personal property were matters for the common law only. Such was the argument of Martin Cowdrey when he was sued by Richard Paulet, receiver of the Augmentations in the third district, for the recovery of various sums of money illegally appropriated. Cowdrey had served Paulet continuously as deputy from 1536 to 1547, during which time he had kept the full salary of the receivership as well as the other profits of the office. In spite of this, he had pocketed

[90] *Ibid.* 520, fols. 42–44.

£20 from wood sales, £6 13*s.* 4*d.* in rent, and " dyverse greate sommes " received for bells and lead. His crowning mistake had been in
obtaining an advance of 400 marks for the upkeep of royal garrisons
within his district which he had not repaid. As the official receiver
Paulet was, of course, held responsible for all revenues received as well
as the sum borrowed, but the deputy ignored his demands for the
settlement of both the money misappropriated and a share of the salary.
Cowdrey maintained unsuccessfully that the case " ought to be deter-
mynyd at the common lawe and not yn this honorable Courte," that
Paulet should seek his remedy by an " accion of desceyte " or an " accion of accompt," under which process justice could be obtained " apon
his ease at the common lawe." Further, he reasoned that the charges
presented in the bill of complaint contained nothing " that towchyth the
king our soueraygn but that the same are pryuate matyers only betwene
the sayd complaynaunt and the sayd def[endaunt] whyche are not determynable yn this honorable Courte." [91]

Close relation between the administrative and judicial functions of
the Augmentations accounted in part for the diverse character of its
decisions. Interspersed between weighty judgments on forceable ejec-
tion or concealment of lands are found judicial orders relating exclusively to administration. Since the same officers issued executive directives as proclaimed judicial decrees, little or no distinction was made
between them. After deliberation, decisions were rendered on all kinds
of question, whatever their nature: a grant of relief to poor tenants,
an invalidation of an obligation, an adjustment in rent, a discharge of
a debt, an abolition of an office, or a preliminary opinion pronounced
on some matter at the request of the king's council. Indeed, so varied
are they that no sampling of cases, however selective, can present more
than a limited insight into the business that came before the Court.

As already observed, when the payment of money was embodied in
a judgment, the decree itself acted as a warrant to the treasurer of the
Court, and a large number of the " payments by decree " recorded in his
official rolls of account were the direct result of court action. In most
instances complete records are not preserved, making it impossible to
explain either the reasons for, or the circumstances leading to, particular
payments. Occasionally, however, a brief memorandum indicates that

[91] *Richard Paulet* v. *Martin Cowdrey.* The documents in this case, viz., the
complaint, answer, replications, etc., are undated. Neither the decree of the Court
nor other related evidence has been discovered, but it would appear that the trial
was heard early in the reign of Edward VI. Augm. Office, Misc. Books 522, fols.
15–18. Meanwhile, in July, 1546, Cowdrey had been appointed general woodward
in Hampshire, holding his office jointly with Edmund Clerk. *Ibid.* 236, fol. 243.

considerable investigation had been necessary before judgment could be pronounced. In fact, when old customs were perpetuated, as sometimes they were, the judges were in effect establishing court policy that could not easily be broken. Before the Dissolution many voluntary and curious obligations had been assumed by the monasteries which the Court of Augmentations was expected to continue. Both Bury St. Edmunds in Suffolk and Ramsay monastery in Huntingdonshire, for example, by ancient practice had borne " all the costys and charges " of the common-law justices when sitting on commissions for gaol delivery, oyer and terminer, and assize in their neighborhoods. These special allowances were reassigned by the Court, with an additional allotment of £2 per year out of the Ramsay revenues for the expenses of executing assize commissions in Huntingdonshire.[92] In like manner the officers and clerks of the Court of Common Pleas were awarded £2 13s. 4d. annually out of the revenues of the late possessions of St. Peter's, Westminster, in compensation for the ink formerly furnished by the monastery for the making of their writs and records.[93] In the aggregate, recurrent payments of this kind bore hardly upon crown revenues already heavily encumbered with debts, annuities, and other contractual obligations.

Such was the judicial business of a court, whose official motto implied truth and equity and for whom the fleet greyhound engraved upon its great seal symbolized, ironically, the speed of justice.

[92] By decree of the Court, Michaelmas term, November 20, 1540. *Ibid.* 98, fols. 46d.–47.

[93] Decree of January 23, 1545. *Ibid.* 104, pt. 2, fol. 99.

CHAPTER THIRTEEN

THE RENOVATED EXCHEQUER

HEN THE Augmentations and First Fruits were united to the Exchequer by letters patent of January 24, 1554, each became a " membre and parcell " of that court; by the same authority lands and revenues so annexed were to be governed and administered according to articles set forth in two appended schedules. Under fifty-one detailed items the basic principles of the enlarged Exchequer administration were laid down, not so much as an exposition of required Exchequer practices as a guarantee against Augmentations innovations. Changes were frowned on in the older system; it was assumed that henceforth Exchequer development would proceed " according to the auncient course and custome " of the past.[1]

The schedules outlined the problems presented by the amalgamation and provided that all records, leases, decrees, and other court actions of the late dissolved institutions should have the same force and legality as formerly. That for the dissolved Court of Augmentations was inclusive, covering the whole range of administrative practices and procedures. In effect, the enumerated articles present a fair picture of the Exchequer system as it was supposed to operate after the reforms of 1554. That in

---

[1] Letters patent of annexation of the Court of Augmentations and the Court of First Fruits and Tenths to the Exchequer, Close Rolls, 1 Mary, pt. 7 (C. 54/500), mems. 3–6. There are thirty-seven articles in the schedule for the former and fourteen articles for the latter. The original patent is preserved among the valuable miscellaneous documents of the Exchequer. Exchequer of Receipt, Miscellanea, 13/2. Copies, made in the eighteenth century by the clerk of the rolls, are also available in the Duchy of Lancaster, Miscellanea, 12/26.

fact it never actually adhered to the theoretical course prescribed is a tribute to the progressive faction in the changing administration. Almost immediately Exchequer procedure began to be influenced by new personnel and the use of new revenue techniques. Many of the methods formerly used in the defunct revenue courts were now found convenient. As the century progressed, the more efficient forms and practices of the late Augmentations tended to prevail. In other words, the dominant Elizabethan developments in revenue administration were always " augmentation-wise."

In the administration of Augmentations revenue the proposals were quite definite. The system of twelve districts, each with its own particular receiver, was to be abandoned in favor of the traditional Exchequer method in which all revenues flowed through the same channel and were collected by the sheriff or other collectors of the county. Welsh revenues were gathered in by the chamberlain there and paid into the receipt annually, as anciently provided. Sheriffs and all other accountants were paid yearly, in proportion to their total collections.[2] As a guarantee of uniformity rules and regulations laid down for the payment of receipts and for the final settlement of accounts closely followed the accepted Exchequer pattern.

In brief the procedure was as follows: all rents, issues, and profits for each fiscal year were charged against the sheriffs or other designated accountants, as set forth in their yearly accounts from Michaelmas to Michaelmas. The preliminary audits, known as views of accounts, were held annually sometime before the feast of the Ascension,[3] the sums in the accounts due at Michaelmas and St. Martin's being payable at the receipt of the Exchequer not later than Christmas and February 20, respectively. In default of such payments the accountants were required to submit warrants sufficient to account for any disbursement of the issues charged against them. The final declaration or audit was held during Hilary term and concluded before the twenty-fourth of February. On this occasion the accountant was required to appear in person, or by authorized agent, and under oath submit to the examination of the Exchequer board " according to thauncient vsage."[4] The account, duly engrossed in parchment and subscribed by the treasurer, undertreasurer, chancellor, and barons, or any three or more of them including the first

---

[2] Article 3 of the schedule. They were " to haue a taile of rewarde yerely according to the rate of their seuerall charges if it shalbe thought convenyent." These " tallies of reward " were allowances paid as a recompense for their services.

[3] A movable feast falling on the Thursday forty days after Easter.

[4] Written authorization for the use of a deputy had to be obtained, the necessary warrant being filed with the treasurer's remembrancer for purposes of permanent record. Article 8.

two, was signed by the auditor and delivered by him into the Pipe Office by March 20 following, there to await further process in case it was required. Normally, the declarations of account were taken by officers of the Exchequer board only, but they might at their own discretion call in any auditors or other officers of the court to assist them in the hearings.[5]

All this was considerably more complicated, and aside from the obvious advantage of consolidation, it is hard to see any improvement over the less involved schedule of the Augmentations. As might be expected, special safeguards were laid down for both the jurisdiction and fees of various officers; writs of attachment or distress for debts, as well as commissions for wood sales and for surveys, came under the control of the Office of Treasurer's Remembrancer; conversely, all recognizances were to be enrolled in the Office of King's Remembrancer.[6] Indirectly, several points of difference between Exchequer and Augmentations practices were emphasized. Heretofore pensions had been paid from the central treasury as well as by district receivers; now they were to be paid locally by the revenue collectors in the county " oneles they shall haue speciall commaundement by the Courte to the contrary "; wood sales could be conducted under commissions of the court but not by local officials; reparations could be made only by court warrant; and tellers and auditors must attend to their office in person and not by deputy. Similarly, special provision was made for strengthening county administration. Each year, before the annual audit of his accounts, every steward was required to submit to the Exchequer a duplicate copy of his court rolls, signed by himself and certified by the receiver of the shire. Thus, information pertinent to fines, heriots, amercements, wood sales, and other casualties, as well as lists of recommended reparations to be made, were available to the Exchequer board during the accounting period. For practical reasons the original roll was kept in the manor or lordship where the local court was held.

Finally, two series of provisions, each representing a basic aspect of Augmentations development, must be noted: namely, those governing the disposition of the voluminous records of the dissolved Court and the important work of its specialized auditors. In view of the sheer bulk of its records, if for no other reason, the first was a matter of as much

---

[5] Articles 4–11 inclusive. The penalty for failure to comply with these regulations was the seizure of the accountant's lands and property, as was previously the custom in the Exchequer.

[6] Profits of the clerk of the pipe, which had decayed as a result of loss of fees since the erection of the Augmentations, were protected in Article 17. All yearly leases of land under the annual value of 40s. were made by the clerk of the pipe and enrolled separately in his office.

concern to Exchequer officials as it was of major significance to posterity. In addition to its vast collection of land grants, pensions and annuities, surveys, and Dissolution materials, the Augmentations Court had compiled a series of Precedent Books unparalleled among the courts of record of the sixteenth century, all of which were essential to the future operation of the Exchequer. Storage space and an official custodian had to be provided for these muniments, as well as for the less bulky records of the Court of First Fruits and Tenths. Formally authorized by royal writ, the transfer of documents was completed by February 12.[7] Warrants, enrollments of leases, accounts, and declarations of accounts, as well as all unfinished business, were retained by the clerk of the pipe, but all the other records of the former Court were to be kept in a " Tresourie house " to be chosen for that purpose.[8] Such a repository was duly appointed, known as the Augmentation Office, so that the accounts of the former Augmentations revenues remained " severed from thauncient Recordes of thexchequier." [9] Similarly, a new Office of First Fruits and Tenths was set up in the Exchequer to supervise the records and administer the business of that former court. Though its director was styled a remembrancer of first fruits and tenths, the position actually was held jointly, being filled by two former officials of the dissolved court.[10]

The Augmentation Office was under the general jurisdiction of the clerk of the pipe, who came to appoint its keeper or clerk. Christopher Smyth was in charge of the Pipe Office at the time the Augmentations records were acquired and apparently became the first custodian of these archives. He was assisted in that position by a deputy of his own appointment, who probably performed the routine work of the office. No

[7] Exchequer of Receipt, Miscellanea, 13/2. The Exchequer received the records of the Court of First Fruits and Tenths on January 25, those of the Augmentations on February 12. Close Rolls, 1 Mary, pt. 7 (C. 54/500), mem. 5*d*.

[8] A ledger of specialties was prepared by Augmentations officials and submitted to the Exchequer. Article 36.

[9] Articles 21, 23, 24, and 25 of the schedule. Among the important documents specifically to be kept in the Pipe Office, readily available to the court at all times, were the accounts of the receivers. Though the intention of the schedule in this respect was clear, persistent violation of the rule by the auditors later became the subject of violent controversy.

[10] The third article of the schedule for the annexation of the Court of First Fruits and Tenths to the Exchequer stipulated that the office should be filled the first time by two men, but thereafter by one person only. This was done to accomodate two officials of the former court, Thomas Godfrey, clerk, and Thomas Argall, keeper of the records. They were appointed in February, 1554, to hold office jointly for life at a salary of £80 per year. *Cal. Pat. Rolls, Mary*, I, 6; Lansd. MS. 171, fol. 322. The office was abolished in 1838 by act of parliament (1 and 2 Victoria, c. 20). Giuseppi, *A Guide to the Manuscripts preserved in the Public Record Office*, I, 163.

formal appointments seem to have been made, but by the beginning of 1558, Smyth and Thomas Reve were officiating as keepers of the records of the late Court of Augmentations.[11]

From 1554 until its ultimate absorption by the Public Record Office in the mid-nineteenth century, the Augmentation Office had a continuous existence. As a records division rather than an administrative department, it was headed by a succession of minor Exchequer officials who were, in their archival capacity at least, obscure and undistinguished.[12] Until his death around 1590, Smyth, as clerk of the pipe, retained the custodianship without grant or patent, but only by informal appointment of the treasurer and barons. Although united in the same person, the clerkship and keepership were considered as separate positions, being " in law distinct offices " to which reversionary rights were obtainable. Beginning with the keepership of William Mintern, 1602–1619, the Augmentation Office had its own independent director and deputies solely responsible for what was commonly called " the Records of the Augmentacion Court of the Exchequer in Westminster." [13] These records remained under the general control of the Pipe Office until its abolition in 1833, during which period the long term of the antiquary John Caley, 1787–1834, was the most important.[14] The sorting, binding, calendaring, and modern classification of Augmentations materials was begun under his direction.

Meanwhile, the growing volume of business inherited from the defunct Court necessitated constant reference to its records. Consequently Exchequer officials found it desirable to draw up lists of fees, annuities, and pensions, extract pertinent information from documents commonly consulted, and prepare exemplifications of patents, decrees, and proceedings which would expedite their work. Externally, the records were accessible to the public by means of official copies furnished by the Office staff or through deliveries of documents to courts, other government departments, or even to private individuals. Lent only by warrant of the lord treasurer, these records and evidences were supposed to be

---

[11] Dasent (ed.), *Acts of the Privy Council*, VII, 48; *Cal. Pat. Rolls, Edward VI*, II, 8–9. Earlier, Smyth had served the Court of General Surveyors as an attorney, representing the court in the Exchequer. Augm. Office, Misc. Books 106, fol. 84 f.

[12] The history of the office in evolution is presented in the following chapter.

[13] *Cal. State Papers, Domestic, Elizabeth, 1595–1597*, 184; warrants for the delivery of records, E. 324/46, 48, 49, 51.

[14] Appointed by Lord William Bentinck, clerk of the pipe, in 1787, Caley held office until his death in April, 1834. After October, 1833, when the Pipe Office was abolished, the Augmentations records were put under the administration of the king's remembrancer of the Exchequer.

returned; nevertheless, to the detriment of the Augmentation Office, many valuable items were lost in this manner.[15]

More significant than these minor changes was the recommended modification of the department of audit. Traditionally there were six Exchequer auditors, but long before the Marian reform that number had been reduced to five.[16] In contrast, there had been eight regular ones in the Augmentations, plus two special auditors of prests and foreign accounts, while at the time of its dissolution the Court of First Fruits and Tenths had maintained only two. Obviously an addition to the Exchequer staff was necessary, though the innovatory Augmentations arrangement of special auditorships for prests and foreign accounts was to be avoided at all costs. The schedule was quite definite in this respect. Two auditors were to be added to the Exchequer, making seven altogether, each of whom was to receive a salary of £20 per year, executing his office in person and without deputy. More specifically, all accounts were to be returned to the ancient course of the Exchequer, " as heretofore they haue ben accustomed before the ereccion of the Courtes of Survey and Augmentacions of the Revenue." Certain accounts were stipulated, namely the accounts of the hanaper, the butlerage, the customers of the ports of Chester, Berwick, and Calais, the great wardrobe, the mints, the revenues and staple of Calais, and the prests. This last item, of course, referred to the two special auditorships of prests and foreign accounts which had grown out of the original Court of General Surveyors.[17] Clearly these were not to be continued.

The two new auditorships for the Exchequer as provided for in the patent were instituted almost immediately, with the appointment of John Thompson on February 16, 1554, and John Swift on March 30 of the same year.[18] But even the increased number proved insufficient for the additional revenue burden, so an eighth auditor was added by Elizabeth in July, 1560.[19] Meanwhile, further relief was accorded them by

[15] Mostly the indentures and warrants for the delivery of records out of the Augmentation Office are collected in two series: Augm. Office (E. 324), warrants for the delivery of records, 82 pieces; and various lists and memoranda of records delivered from the Augmentation Office and the Augmentations Court, Henry VIII —Elizabeth, Exch., K. R., Miscellanea, 12/9, 31 pieces.

[16] " Item Where in tyme past there hath ben contynuallye six Auditours seruyng in thesaid Courte of Thexchequier Wherof at this daie and of longe tyme hath remayned but five having x li euery oone by yere for his fee." Article 30 of the schedule of annexation.

[17] Article 29 of the schedule. On the origin and evolution of the earlier auditorship of the prests, see p. 146 ff., *supra.*

[18] *Cal. Pat. Rolls, Mary,* I, 6, 229. Both patents specified an annual fee of £20 to be paid from the previous Michaelmas.

[19] The appointment of Thomas Neale was dated July 30, 1560, although he had been exercising the office since the previous Lady Day, March 25. The in-

a step in a different direction when the convenient prests office was reconstituted as part of the expanding program. Duplicating the dual auditorship of prests in the Augmentations, the two Exchequer auditors of "lez prestes" and foreign accounts carried a salary of 100 marks annually, a considerable advance over the fees of the regular auditors.[20] Nevertheless, their work was heavier than that of their fellow auditors since the accounts of the first fruits and tenths were now included among the foreign accounts. By appointments of January 19, 1560, the offices were awarded to John Hanby and Henry Coddenham, already professionally trained.[21] Formerly auditor of the Augmentations, Hanby, since May, 1554, had been drawing 200 marks per year in compensation for the loss of that office. However, he was persuaded to surrender his annuity in exchange for the Exchequer appointment. Coddenham also had served as auditor of the mint accounts, previously separate but now absorbed by the new auditorship. The prests office continued until 1785, when these auditors were succeeded by the commissioners for auditing public accounts.[22]

Thus the initial effort of conservative officials to restore the prests accounts permanently to the Pipe Office, where they would be audited by the regular Exchequer auditors, had failed. The weight of experience in favor of a practice dating back to the reign of Henry VII was too strong to be overthrown. As a matter of fact the authorized plan was never followed, even during the interim period when there were no auditors of the prests. Large sums were prested to royal agents as before, and the accounts of the special departments enumerated in the twenty-ninth article of the schedule, including the chamber, were processed as formerly.

If there were any complaints at this disregard of regulations, there is no record of them; Exchequer officials were probably only too glad to get rid of part of their extra burden. The council continued to supervise special accountants, whose accounts were examined by royal commissioners appointed for that purpose, a system inaugurated at the beginning of the century. The final accounts of the treasurers of Augmentations, First Fruits and Tenths, and the chamber were taken in this manner.

---

creased work resulting from the transfer of all the Augmentations business to the Exchequer was given as the reason for the creation of another auditorship. *Ibid.*, *Elizabeth*, I, 323.

[20] The regular auditors still received £20 annually as contrasted with the 100 marks, or £66 13s. 4d., paid to the new appointees.

[21] *Cal. Pat. Rolls, Elizabeth*, I, 295, 299.

[22] *Ibid.*, 250, 326. An Act for Auditing the Public Accounts (1785), 25 George III, c. 52, W. C. Costin and J. Steven Watson (eds.), *The Law and Working of the Constitution: Documents, 1660–1914* (London, 1952), II, 1–2.

Former auditors of the Augmentations were often called on to assist in this work, preparing the accounts for final declaration before the larger commission. Bonds, receipts, specialties of obligations, and other agreements were then delivered to the Office of Queen's Remembrancer. Finally, as later became the establishd practice under Elizabeth, one copy of the former Declaration of Account was preserved in the Exchequer, while another parchment copy, signed by the commissioners or a specified number of them, was presented to the accountant as proof of his discharge.[23] After the auditors of the prests and foreign accounts were appointed, the audited accounts were also signed by them.

Despite the regulations and precautions laid down in the schedule to preserve old forms and methods, the traditional pattern was never fully realized. In fact, it is doubtful if the more progressive wing of the Exchequer staff—men like Winchester and Mildmay—ever intended the program to be followed literally. Article thirty-two of the schedule furnished the necessary excuse for evasion, if indeed such authority were required. In delegating to the court power to alter its own constitution, the proviso was indeed quite unprecedented.

Item for that thorder establisshement and vniting of this cannot perfectlie be establisshed without exercise proof and experience of thesame The Quenes highnes is pleased that the lorde Treasourer and thesaid Courte of Exchequier shall haue full power and auctoritie from tyme to tyme to amende refourme and correcte any clause or article aforsaid and to add to or diminisshe any thing that shalbe founde necessarie for thamendement of thesame And to make suche furder order from tyme to tyme as to the Courte shalbe thought expedient.

This permissive item appears to have been inserted deliberately in the hope that a more tolerant opinion soon would prevail; and in fact an order, far different from that proposed, gradually emerged. At least someone had had the foresight to provide a loophole. Those familiar with both Exchequer and Augmentations forms of administration must have realized that some measure of compromise was not only desirable but almost inevitable. Fortunately for the court the forces at work were not radical and caused no serious departure from the broader program already projected.

[23] *Cal. Pat. Rolls, Mary,* I, 76–78, 176, 194–96, 265–66, 300, 301, 302, 506–507; *Philip and Mary,* II, 104, 343–44; III, 23–24, 313–14, 316–17; IV, 11–12, 14, 72–74, 193. The Exchequer was usually represented on these commissions of audit, frequently by the treasurer and chancellor. In his study of the later period, Professor Dietz found that the lord treasurer, the undertreasurer, and one of the Exchequer barons were always included. Dietz, *The Exchequer in Elizabeth's Reign,* 109.

With the exception of these supplementary offices, the most significant changes were in the procedure of collection and audit. The details of that development are described later, but it should be observed in passing that it brought about a simplification and shortening of both processes. The newer revenues actually were never returned to the sheriff's farm nor were their accounts channeled through the traditional Exchequer grooves. That the older procedures were not followed was the result of two contributing factors, each supporting the other and both acceptable to the council, which welcomed progressive reforms. The problem was at once one of ideas and personalties. Under the practical impact of cold logic in the approach to suggested reform, it was soon discovered that the methods which had been developed by the Augmentations administration were easier and more efficient. When measured by pragmatic standards, most of the recent improvisations proved acceptable; moreover, this position was strongly supported by a number of Exchequer officials, especially those who had seen service in the dissolved revenue courts and had been trained under Cromwell's rigorous regime. Of course, conservative opinion argued bitterly for the old ways, but to no avail. When the heat of controversy had abated, the queen's council was always there, ready to give governmental sanction to a reform policy already implemented in fact.

In the administration of the revenues from the first fruits and tenths the changes were fewer and less involved. The Office of First Fruits and Tenths was an administrative department as well as an official repository for the records of the court. Unlike the head of the Augmentation Office, its director, a remembrancer by title, was a leading official of the renovated Exchequer, fully responsible for the revenues, debts, obligations, and other business under his charge. This division of the Exchequer kept no official rolls, but like the older remembrancers' departments, it retained writings and muniments related to its special category of revenues and could issue process necessary for the assessment, collection, and discharge of all issues assigned to it. The remembrancer was authorized to take compositions for first fruits, draw up obligations and indentures for future payments, and give acquittances or other discharges for cash receipts. In practice he appointed commissions and received their returns in his office and, upon request, prepared " true values " of spiritual promotions and benefices. He personally collected first fruits, but the tenths and subsidies, gathered regionally by the clergy, were paid directly into the receipt, although these collectors were accountable in his office. Annually a detailed ledger of compositions of first fruits was presented to the Exchequer. In all respects, therefore, the office was a self-sufficient and virtually independent unit. With only a few minor modifications this procedure remained essentially unchanged until the nineteenth century. At the beginning of Victoria's reign it was abolished when its revenues were transferred to the Queen Anne's Bounty Office. Shortly thereafter all the records in the Exchequer pertaining to first fruits and tenths were transferred to the Public Record Office, where they still remain.[24]

Economy in administration and decay of revenue had been the only reasons given for Exchequer amalgamation. There was perhaps some justification for the former in view of the fact that personnel costs were somewhat cut down, but the facts do not support the implication that, in relation to the broader national administration, either of the two instiutions was in a state of great decay at the time of its dissolution. Revenues of the Court of First Fruits and Tenths had never been extensive, even including subsidies, debts to the crown, and other miscellaneous foreign receipts assigned to it, but there had been no appreciable decrease in revenues during the thirteen years of its history. Receipts averaged over £71,000 yearly, exceeding that figure during the later years.[25] The total in 1550–1551 was £23,564 4s. 3d., or £15,042 5s. 8d. for certainties and £8,521 18s. 7d. for casualties. Receipts in the Court of Augmentations for the same year were £159,295 10s. 4d., or more than four times that of the Exchequer.[26] On the basis of size and financial significance, therefore, there was more reason to annex the Exchequer to the Augmentations than the reverse.

The assumption that wholesale alienation of crown lands had greatly reduced the revenues of the Court is again not borne out by facts.[27] The second Augmentations had increased its holdings when the lands of the Court of Survey were joined to it; to this acreage were added the possessions of the colleges and chantries, plus piecemeal acquisitions from time to time by purchase, exchange, and attainder. Occasionally

[24] Statutes 1 and 2 Victoria, c. 20, and 1 and 2 Victoria, c. 94. Cf. Giuseppi, *A Guide to the Manuscripts preserved in the Public Record Office*, I, 163, 336.

[25] Richardson, *Tudor Chamber Administration, 1485–1547*, 344–45; Dietz, *English Government Finance, 1485–1558*, 139, 222–24. Receipts for the Court of First Fruits and Tenths varied appreciably, depending on the amount of extra revenue allocated to it from time to time. For the earlier period, 1535–40, they averaged something over £60,000 per year, but the total for these years included £130,711 16s. assigned to the treasurer by royal order. *L. and P.*, XVI, no. 352 (iii).

[26] Add. MS. 30198, fol. 35. The comparative receipts for the Exchequer were £39,348 16s. 10d.

[27] The patent of dissolution states the case pointedly for the Exchequer. The alienation of Augmentations lands, "aswell by giftes and grauntes of our said late father as of our said dere brother dispersed cutawaye and greately dismembred from thorder and survey of our seid Courte." Close Rolls, 1 Mary, pt. 7 (C. 54/500), mem. 3.

also crown land was acquired by gift, forfeiture, escheat, or debts taken in lieu of cash payment. Thus, in spite of alienations, the Augmentations revenues derived primarily from land, certainties as they were called in the treasurer's accounts, were not so greatly diminished. The receivers' accounts show the total receipts from crown lands under the survey of the Court to have remained fairly constant during the reign of Edward VI. For the sixteen months previous to its dissolution, Augmentations lands yielded a clear profit of £26,883 9s. 10d. out of a total receipt of £124,462 17s. 4d. for the period. By the careful husbanding of resources, primarily through higher rents and larger fines for entry, this land revenue increased under Mary rather than diminished. The Excequer accounts near the end of the reign show that receipts from former Augmentations lands stood at £47,723 12s. 2d.[28]

Signs of decay were, of course, apparent in both courts by 1554, but they were common to all revenue institutions. Breakdown of morale, lack of discipline, petty offenses, superfluous offices, and increases both in salaries and personnel were as much manifestations of a changing order as they were weaknesses of any single departmen. The problem was rather one of thoroughly reforming a top-heavy bureaucracy than that of renovating or abolishng a few units of it, which at best would have been only a temporary solution. The criticisms in the commission report of 1552 pinpointed most of the particular evils which faced the government, but few of them could be eliminated by amalgamation. General demoralization had pervaded the entire administration, affecting directors and subordinate officials, high and low alike. In the Court of First Fruits and Tenths the chancellor had found it convenient to delegate part of his official duties to a clerk, whose work was improperly checked; the certificates on which the tenths were assessed were found to be old and uncertain, while more significantly the auditors had grown negligent in the examination of accounts. As in other courts, increases in officers' salaries had passed unnoticed, in this case to the tune of over £490 without legal permission, and yet, despite specific regulations to the contrary, ministers sometimes remained unbonded. This last was a pernicious evil, often augmented by the carelessness of the central authorities. Longstanding debts and arrears presented no new problem, but in many instances revenues remained uncollected through negligence or indifference, and debts " for lack of calling on in time grow utterly desperate." [29]

---

[28] Augm. Office, Treas. Rolls of Accts., No. 8, fol. 31d. Michaelmas to Michaelmas, 1556–57; there appears to have been a like increase during Mary's reign, though less pronounced, for the revenues of the Duchy of Lancaster. Dietz, *Finances of Edward VI and Mary*, 107, 119, 124.

[29] According to the constitution of the court the bishops were supposed to bring

If the Augmentations had had considerable criticism, it was mainly because of the size of its staff and the extent of its possessions. Incidentally, it should be noted that the judicial activities of the Court had for the most part escaped censure, though this may have been less by virtue of their merits than because of the inordinate emphasis placed on revenue affairs by the government. As observed in an earlier chapter, the Court had been investigated thoroughly by the commission of 1552, with somewhat damaging results. Nevertheless, most of the bad practices uncovered at that time were due to maladministration rather than to any imperfections inherent in the Court itself. In fact a strict enforcement of regulations already established by constitutional provision or court order would have prevented most of the corruption from developing in the first place. Even the unnecessary fees and superfluous offices were evils no less attendant upon the Exchequer. Then as now, the success of any system, however sound, depended to a large degree on the integrity of its ministers. Unbonded and irresponsible officials, no longer required to account annually, had reduced all the financial courts to a state of " great Confusion." The recommendations that they " be reduced to the old form again " simply meant that the earlier dsiciplines should be restored.[30]

It is hard to see how any of the defects of the Augmentations organization could have been reduced, much less eradicated, by fusion with the Exchequer. Such abuses as delay in revenue collection, collusion in relation to pension grants, payments made without written warrant, and negligence of local officials were serious problems, but all of them could have been expected to continue under Exchequer administration, awaiting further remedial measures. Moreover, a number of the charges concerned questions of policy, which in reality transcended the Court's jurisdiction. Superfluous offices, excessive fees, irregular audits, and costs of home garrisons and fortifications were perennial problems. That an annual outlay of over £4,000 for governmental pensions and annuities was borne by the Augmentations was certainly not its fault, nor was there any fairness in the accusation that they had been illegally paid by the treasurer instead of by the particular receivers.[31] Moreover,

---

in the tenths they collected by April 1 of each year, yet almost none of them did so; in fact many of them were far behind in their payments. The commission's criticisms of the Court of First Fruits and Tenths were itemized under nine headings. Add. MS. 30198, fols. 50–50d.

[30] *Ibid.*, fol. 47.

[31] *Ibid.*, fol. 45d. The twenty-fourth of fifty items (unnumbered) in the Report, suggesting improvement in Augmentations administration. As a matter of fact, payments of Augmentations annuities had always been by both treasurer and receivers except when restrictions were imposed by the privy council.

the advisability of regular land surveys by the several courts and a special investigation of arrears of revenues due from the sale of plate, lead, and bell metal was apparent enough to the council. These and other abuses were duly dealt with by Mary and Elizabeth. Exchequer reform was part of the general retrenchment policy, but the program was by no means restricted to that institution. There is every indication that the Court of Wards and the Court of Duchy Chamber, which were not included in the amalgamation, were as much in need of reformation as either the Augmentations or the Court of First Fruits and Tenths.[32]

In many respects the oldest revenue institution was the one most in need of improvement. More impervious to new ideas than its rivals the Exchequer had gone its own way, largely unaffected by the administrative changes of the sixteenth century. In procedures of collection and audit it still followed a pattern essentially medieval, reflecting the general condition of the times only in being beset by the current abuses of the Edwardian period. In common with other departments, however, the breakdown of Exchequer administration was due less to corrupt officials than to inadequate supervision. As elsewhere, petty dishonesty, multiplication of offices, minor neglect of official responsibilities, and even gross inefficiency had gone unchallenged. Sloth and negligence were widespread, revenues belatedly collected or lost altogether to the crown through deceit and mismanagement. Instead of giving personal attendance at the Exchequer during term time the auditors had drifted into the habit of delegating deputies to represent them, which no doubt often led to improper audit of the collectors' accounts and hence decay in the court's revenues.

In their report on Exchequer maladministration the commissioners of 1552 instanced several examples of diminished revenues resulting from irresponsibility. In some cases the sheriffs were suspected of withholding receipts, especially when the sole check on their honesty was their own confession. It was noted, for example, that the annual profits from felons' goods amounted to only £41 6d. for all the realm, which was very little and " evill answered "; yet the court maintained no effective control over these collections since " the Sheriffs are charged therewith upon their own Confession." Serious losses, too, were sustained among other casualties, such as goods of waifs, strays, and outlawed persons which were also " very slenderly answered." A more significant criticism pertained to the department of receipt, where the tellers continued to go

[32] *Ibid.*, fols. 49, 51–52; Somerville, *History of the Duchy of Lancaster*, I, 319–21. A general decay of the revenues and increased charges by all departments had imposed an intolerable burden on the government. Harl. MS. 7383, fols. 67–72.

unbonded, despite the fact that they were in charge of all the revenues of the court.[33]

Sheriffs were slow in serving process for debts, the commissioners discovered, especially writs of extent and attachment " wherein is daily used much Corrupcion & affeccion & therefore worthy of Reformacion." Other deficiencies in official procedure were reported, particular attention being focused on recognizances and court judgments for debts to the crown. It was recommended that a book of such judgments be kept conveniently accessible to the Exchequer during court sessions to facilitate speedier process and collection.

Curiously enough, among all the contemporary critcisms of the Exchequer there was no suggestion of any untoward increase in officers' salaries. It seems strange that it should have been the exception in this respect when so many other institutions were charged with such increments. The integrity of Exchequer ministers appears even more exceptional in the face of salary raises for officials of the ordnance, admiralty, and customs, all of which were subsidiary departments accounting at the Exchequer. In the last department the customers and controllers were accused of having obtained as much as £1,237 5s. yearly " above their old ffees." [34]

The Exchequer was characteristically slow in putting its own house in order, though a change to more modern methods, especially in the cumbersome system of audit, was long overdue. The accounting division had been somewhat improved by Henry VII, but little had been done to stir the lower division of receipt from its medieval lethargy. Delays, slowness in procedure, and inattention to detail had combined to produce " terrors and ghosts of unlaid accountants " to haunt the public for generations to come. Edmund Burke's celebrated speech of 1780 on the gross corruption of administration included a strong indictment of the inefficient Exchequer of his own time. It might have been penned in 1554 by any of the former Augmentations ministers who were arguing for the superiority of modern techniques. Undue strictness and regularity of form were as true then as later : " They have in the exchequer brought rigour and formalism to their ultimate perfection. The process against accountants is so rigorous, and in a manner so unjust, that correctives must, from time to time, be applied to it. . . . delays are produced ; and thus the extreme of rigour in office (as usual in all human affairs) leads to the extreme of laxity." [35]

---

[33] Add. MS. 30198, fols. 40–41*d*. Thirty-one unnumbered items on the abuses in the Exchequer system are presented.

[34] *Ibid.*, fol. 40*d*.

[35] Henry G. Bohn (ed.), *The Works of the Right Honourable Edmund Burke*

The Marian Exchequer was a combination of old and new, with medieval practices somewhat overshadowing modern ones, but before the end of the century the forces of change had effected what was tantamount to revolutionary improvements. All this was accomplished gradually within the existing framework and without too great an increase in personnel. With the exception of county officials, the new auditors of the prests, and the heads of the Augmentation Office and the Office of First Fruits and Tenths, the reforms of 1554 had created no new offices in the Exchequer. If the central organization was larger than that of the other revenue courts, it was partly because of its traditional division into the two departments of audit and receipt. Principal officials in the upper Exchequer, or Exchequer of Account, constituted a board not unlike the executive council of the Augmentations, in effect shaping the policies and controlling the finances of the court. These seven ministers—the treasurer, chancellor, undertreasurer, and four barons— also acted as judges for cases that came before them, rendering judgment *per considerationem baronum*. Also in this division were the two chamberlains, the attorney, the solicitor, the queen's remembrancer, the treasurer's remembrancer, the foreign apposer, and four major clerks of special offices. These principal clerks, as heads of the Pipe, Estreats, Nichils, and Pleas, were in addition to the minor clerks and numerous assistant staff members.

In the lower division, Exchequer of Receipt, the undertreasurer, the four tellers, the two underchamberlains, the clerk and two controllers of the Pells, and the writer of the tallies were the most important, but the receipt department also included a marshal, two parcel makers, a tally cutter, appraisers, tally joiners, a keeper of the court seal, five ushers, and four messengers. Seven auditors, together with more than thirty clerks and minor officials, completed the central organization which totaled over eighty-three members. Beyond London, of course, Exchequer officials in the field were even more numerous.

It is not always easy to determine when each innovation was introduced, since many of them are not described for a generation or more after the change began. Even more difficult is the task of reconstrucing a full list of all the officials at the court during the second half of the century when the renovated Exchequer was taking shape. It is quite clear that some of the earlier Tudor officials were of paramount importance in designing the program. In contrast to the Exchequer of Henry VII, that of Elizabeth showed a marked change in the status of treasurer, under-

---

(London, 1846–62), II, 93–94. On the changelessness of Exchequer procedure, see Anthony Steel, *The Receipt of the Exchequer, 1377–1485* (Cambridge, 1954), 368–69.

treasurer, and chancellor. By Mary's reign the political influence of the undertreasurer was waning, and his decline witnessed the corresponding rise in position of both the treasurer and the chancellor of the court.

The office of undertreasurer has a curious history, its significance being due to the honorific position occupied by the lord treasurer as nominal head of the Exchequer. Originally a clerk of the treasurer, by 1485 the undertreasurer had become the chief official in the lower division.[36] According to an early authority he chested up the money in the receipt, took it to the king's treasury in the Tower, and performed other similar menial duties in the lower Exchequer for his master. Such work was " too mean a thing for his Lordship to be troubled with, and yet fit to be done by some meaner person of trust and great secrecie." The writer was speaking of the late fifteenth century when the first official of the court, the treasurer, had ceased to be its real administrative head, though nominally remaining its director.[37] By the early Tudor period the treasurership had become a great office of state which brought honor and position to its holders without the corresponding obligations of office. The Henrician treasurers, from Audley to Somerset, were all prominent noblemen and councillors, too busy with affairs of state to give much attention to Exchequer business.[38] It was therefore necessary to have competent deputies to act for them in supervising the work of the Exchequer. However, the rapid ascendancy of first the chamber and then the Augmentations brought new leadership to the national revenue administration; as a result, none of the treasurers or undertreasurers of Henry VIII's reign became important administrators or financiers. In fact, down to the death of Sackville the political standing of the undertreasurers might almost be taken as a measure of the relative importance of the Exchequer at any given period.

Thomas Fanshawe's observation that the office originated with Henry VII is incorrect, but he may have been right in assuming that the earliest incumbents held office by word of mouth appointment rather

[36] The only modern investigation of the office is limited to a study of its early development in the fifteenth century. J. L. Kirby, " The Rise of the Under-Treasurer of the Exchequer," *E. H. R.*, LXXII (October, 1957), 666–77.

[37] Fanshawe, *The Practice of the Exchequer Court*, 22; Francis Watt, " Thomas Fanshawe," *D. N. B.* Fanshawe was an Elizabethan remembrancer of the Exchequer; the treatise was written for Burghley when he became lord treasurer in 1572. The original version can be consulted in the Lansd. MSS. 171. Cf. his answer to articles concerning the lord treasurer's office, in *ibid.* 253, art. 33.

[38] Under the first two Tudors the office was held successively by Sir John Audley (1484–86), Sir John Dynham (1486–1501), Thomas Howard, earl of Surrey (1501–22), Thomas Howard (son of Surrey), duke of Norfolk (1522–47), and Edward Seymour, earl of Hertford and duke of Somerset (1547–50). The appointment of Winchester in early February, 1550, began a long period of revival.

than by patent.[39] Apparently the post first became prominent under Edward IV who filled it with trained civil servants possessing all the skills of professionals. During the Wars of the Roses the treasurership had degenerated into a nominal position, held by political appointees who were indisposed as well as inadequately equipped for the routine business of the office. Henry Bourchier, the earl of Essex, had no second-in-command during the early years of his long tenure in office under Edward IV, but Sir John Wood was acting in that capacity by 1482. He was followed by a number of able undertreasurers who became, in every respect, the real heads of the Exchequer. Under Henry VII the office was held successively by Sir Reginald Bray, Alfred Corneburg, Robert Litton, and Sir John Cutt, the latter continuing in his post for more than a decade of the next reign. None of these ministers held a patent appointment, nor did Sir Thomas More, who appears to have succeeded Cutt about 1521. Neither More nor his two immediate successors, Sir William Compton and Sir Richard Weston, left much imprint upon the office; certainly they failed to measure up to the high standards set by Cutt, who was the most outstanding of the undertreasurers of this period.

With the privy seal appointment of Sir John Baker in June, 1543, however, the status of the office was changed. Baker had assumed the chancellorship of the Exchequer three years earlier and now joined the two positions in one person,[40] having simultaneous authority in both its upper and lower divisions. In the former department his duties were nominal, but in the receipt he was the dominant member, supervising with the tellers and chamberlains the important work of revenue dis-

---

[39] Fanshawe assumed that Sir Robert Litton, also remembrancer of the lord treasurer and keeper of the great wardrobe, was the first undertreasurer of the Exchequer but that John Baker was the first person to hold the office by patent appointment. He also stated that it was uncertain who controlled the nomination, the lord treasurer or the king. Fanshawe, *The Practice of the Exchequer Court*, 21. The earlier undertreasurers had been criticized for being inexperienced and "vnlearned in the Lawes," a criticism which did not apply to Baker and his successors in office. Baker's appointment was for life at a salary of £100 per year. Cotton. MS., Titus B. iv, fol. 76.

[40] *L. and P.*, XV, nos. 1027(33) ; XVIII, pt. 1, no. 802(84) ; D. L. 42/133, fol. 233d. Lists of undertreasurers are included in Lansd. MSS. 168, fol. 282, and 171, fol. 343. Baker succeeded Cromwell in the chancellor's office in August, 1540. During the same year he was made chancellor of the newly created Court of First Fruits and Tenths after surrendering the office of attorney general. *L. and P.*, XVI, no. 305(11, 18). This combination of offices gave him an influential position in the government. The Declarations of the State of the Treasury by Baker began in 1542. *Second Report of the Deputy Keeper of the Public Records*, Appendix II, 198.

bursement and presenting annually to the crown and council the official Declarations of the State of the Treasury.[41]

Beyond lending prestige to the Exchequer Baker seems to have done little to advance either office, possibly because his time was largely consumed by the chancellorship of the Court of First Fruits and Tenths. He must have realized that his success would be measured largely by his achievements in the latter institution. At any rate, he failed to profit from the strong precedents established by Cromwell, who had given to the Exchequer chancellorship something of the significance that it was to assume later.[42] It was not until Elizabeth's reign, under Sir Walter Mildmay, that the office became an important one, with actual administrative duties to be performed. Still the nominal keeper of the court seal,[43] the chancellor rose from third to second position in the reformed Exchequer, assuming many of the functions formerly belonging to the treasurer's office. After the annexation of the dissolved courts his duties had been greatly increased, partly by extra work delegated to him by the lord treasurer, who henceforth came to be more generally occupied with matters of policy. As the two head officers of the court the treasurer and chancellor had similar responsibilities, such as issuing warrants, commissions, decrees, injunctions, and executive orders. However, as the treasurer became more and more a major financial officer in the ministerial sense, he permitted his colleague to take over a great deal of this work in both departments of the court. At the turn of the century Fanshawe could write that the chancellor had " the proper place of the Bench above the Lord Treasurer " and commonly did what the latter " useth to do." He acted for the treasurer in his absence and upon his death; particularly during an interregnum when a new appointment was under consideration, he " doth all things which the Lord Treasuror both in the Exchequer and Receipt doth use to do." Likewise, he was accustomed " in great causes of the Court, to make the Lord Treasuror privie, and to confer with his Lordship about the same." [44] After the

---

[41] These yearly Declarations were introduced under Richard III in 1484 and continued until 1552, when they were superseded by the less adequate Declaration Books, made up half-yearly by the clerk of the pells. Giuseppi, *A Guide to the Manuscripts preserved in the Public Record Office*, I, 193.

[42] Elton, *The Tudor Revolution in Government*, 107–108, 113–17, 118. Elton has brought together enough new evidence to prove conclusively that the Exchequer chancellorship under Cromwell was certainly no mere sinecure.

[43] The actual work of the Exchequer seal was performed by a clerk who was officially known as the keeper of the seal. Fanshawe, *The Practice of the Exchequer Court*, 102–103.

[44] *Ibid.*, 19–20. A sixteenth century account, "touchinge the Places and Authorities" of the chancellor and undertreasurer, pointed out that Mildmay sat upon the first bench as Cromwell had, "but by what aucthoritie or reason the

death of Sackville in 1566 the duties of the undertreasurer's office were mostly taken over by the chancellor. An appreciation of this increased responsibility was reflected in the salary increase granted to Mildmay in 1559.[45]

The death of John Baker in late December, 1558, created a dual vacancy in the Exchequer, for he had united the offices of chancellor and undertreasurer in one and the same person, though by separate appointments. He was succeeded almost immediately by Mildmay in the first and Sackville in the second office, the latter being retained until his death in 1566.[46] At that time Mildmay also took over the duties of undertreasurer, thus uniting once again the two positions, a practice continued by the next three chancellors, Sir John Fortescue, Sir George Home, and Sir Julius Caesar.[47]

More important to the administration at large was the transformation in the position of lord treasurer. Under Winchester and Burghley it ceased to be an honorary office and became a major administrative post in the government. Obviously the change was greatly accelerated in

---

Chauncellor hathe sitten in theise seuerall places appeareth not." Cotton MS., Titus B. iv, fol. 55d.

[45] Conflicting figures on Exchequer salaries are often given, even among official records. The discrepancy arises from the fact that basic fees were supplemented by diets, liveries of clothing out of the great wardrobe, and special allowances. The fee, exclusive of liveries, for the chancellor under Henry VII was £26 13s. 4d. per annum. Although there had been no increase in basic salary during the ensuing reigns, Mildmay's increment for diets and special allowances for attendance at the court during vacations gave him an extra £140 yearly, bringing the total to £166 13s. 4d. for the year. Primarily the adjustment was made because the supervision of first fruits had added greatly to his regular duties. The corresponding salaries for the lord treasurer and undertreasurer at that time were £365 and £173 6s. 8d. respectively. William Campbell (ed.), *Materials for a History of the Reign of Henry VII* (London, 1877), II, 100, 500; Add. MS. 30198, fol. 8d.; Lansd. MSS. 168, fol. 174; 171, fols. 344, 413d.; Society of Antiquaries of London, MS. 209, fols. 3–30.

[46] Both grants were for life and executed the same day, February 5, 1559. *Cal. Pat. Rolls, Elizabeth*, I, 56, 57. Mildmay owed his appointment to Winchester's influence. *Cal. State Papers, Domestic, 1547–1580*, 42, p. 118.

[47] It has been commonly assumed by most scholars that Sackville was chancellor of the Exchequer instead of undertreasurer and that Mildmay succeeded Baker in the latter post. Sidney Lee, in his article on Mildmay, states, without authority, that Mildmay succeeded Sackville as chancellor; James Tait, in the article on Sir William Paulet, also refers to Sackville as chancellor of the Exchequer instead of the Augmentations. Writing on Sackville, W. A. J. Archbold is correct on this point, but he is wrong on the date of Sackville's appointment as undertreasurer. On these articles, see *D. N. B.* The same error is found in the more recent works on Tudor administration—in particular, Frederick C. Dietz, *English Public Finance, 1558–1641* (New York, 1932), 2, and Elton, *The Tudor Revolution in Government*, 23, 254, 256–57. There is likewise an error in the patent rolls where Sackville is referred to as the treasurer of the Exchequer. *Cal. Pat. Rolls, Elizabeth*, II, 523.

1554 by the amalgamation of the two dissolved courts and the subsequent increase in Exchequer business, both in scope and volume. As a result of the union, questions regarding institutional practice and policy were arising continually which necessitated frequent consultations among the court's officials. Formerly, the treasurer had seldom sat in the Exchequer and had given little attention to the daily operation of the court, " but left all there belonging to him, to be ordered by the Chancellor, Vice-treasurer, and Barons." Fanshawe's description is explicit on this point:

> Hee hath used before the uniting of the sayd Court of augmentation, and the first fruits and tenths in all great matters of the Courts, sometimes to confer with the Chancellor and under Treasurer alone, and sometimes with them and the Barons, and sometimes with them and the King's learned Councill, and some times with them all, and the two Remembrancers and Clerke of the Pipe about the same, what was best to be done. But since the uniting of the sayd Court, according to the Articles of uniting the same, he hath used much to conferre and joyne with the Chancellor and Vice-Treasurer, upon all forraine matters, Causes and Actions of the Court, that stand not in plea, Suits or Judgement before the Court, but come in question, order, and determination by the sayd union, and shall call such Officers as shall please them to consider and determine upon the same.[48]

The lord treasurer was the director of the Exchequer as well as the finance minister of the state, although his two capacities were by no means clearly differentiated until a much later period. Under Elizabeth, Burghley was both, in every sense of the word, though Winchester had found time to devote himself more wholeheartedly to the internal operation of the Exchequer than had his successor. As chief officer of the court the treasurer's official powers were extensive, though his influence on the government was variable, depending on personality and ability. Most of his powers were subject to the advice of his major colleagues in the Exchequer, but usually this restriction was more nominal than real. He issued orders and executive decrees for pensions, allowances, payments, and fees; under his patronage privileges he nominated customs officials, controllers, searchers, and escheators, and had a principal voice in the selection of the sheriffs; moreover, he granted leases of crown property, made commissions for land surveys, wood sales, and other administrative affairs, and directed warrants for the control of

---

[48] Fanshawe, *The Practice of the Exchequer Court*, 13, 15.

revenue matters, sometimes on his sole authority. Particularly in personnel supervision his authority over the large corps of subordinate Exchequer officials was quite adequate. With an eye to greater efficiency Lord Burghley, it should be noted, introduced the practice of ordering a serjeant-at-arms to go out into the counties and bring negligent ministers into the central office for questioning or punishment. Finally, he might officiate as a judge in Exchequer chamber. According to Fanshawe he sat with the barons only when it pleased him to do so, but frequent attendance was always desirable.[49]

The power of the purse was as great in the second half of the century as it had been in the first, and the influence of one who directed the nation's finances was apt to be considerable. In addition to specific duties the lord treasurers of Mary and Elizabeth acted generally as chief paymasters of the crown. Leading members of the privy council, they also advised the government on all financial problems; in effect they exercised the same types of ministerial responsibility later entrusted to the new treasury commission of James I in 1612.[50] But an energetic statesman was too much concerned with general administrative and conciliar policy to concentrate on the actual routine of the Exchequer. Thus gradually the treasury emerged as a distinct department of state. When the treasury board took over the financial duties of the lord treasurer, the practical direction of the Exchequer fell to its chancellor, who in turn became an important minister of the cabinet. Charles Talbot, earl of Shrewsbury, was the last lord treasurer of England.[51] The treasury board, in commission regularly after 1714, was headed by the chancellor of the Exchequer, as first lord, throughout the remainder of the eighteenth century.

No institution could have had better guidance through a crucial period in its history than did the Elizabethan Exchequer under the direction of Winchester, Burghley, and Mildmay. Unquestionably, Winchester was the ablest of the revenue administrators turned out by the Tudor system

[49] Fanshawe gives a complete description of the office under twenty-six headings, couched in the form of question and answer. *Ibid.*, 1–18.

[50] In the renovated Exchequer the treasurers were: William Paulet, marquis of Winchester, 1550–72; William Cecil, Lord Burghley, 1572–98; Thomas Sackville, only son of Sir Richard Sackville, Lord Buckhurst and earl of Dorset, 1599–1608; and Robert Cecil, earl of Salisbury, 1608–12. Upon the death of Salisbury in 1612, the treasurer's office was put in commission under Henry Howard, earl of Northampton, and other commissioners, of whom Sir Julius Caesar was a prominent member. During the ensuing Stuart period, the treasurer sometimes served alone and sometimes with a board of commissioners. However, after Queen Anne's reign the office was always in commission.

[51] Appointed at the end of Anne's reign, he held office but a short while, from August to October, 1714. The succeeding commission of the treasury was always headed by a first commissioner.

and one who had profited immeasurably from the fundamental Cromwellian precepts of efficiency and loyalty. Having once rescued the Exchequer from its half-century of eclipse, he was careful to see that the immediate gains were not swallowed up by a blind return to the evils of the earlier routine. Assisted by the chancellor, Mildmay, he was faced with the task of modernizing a cumbersome organization without destroying its essential worth. As in the days of Cromwell the administration once more had capable leadership. The support of a sovereign who was interested in both economy and financial reform was all that was necessary for the initial impulse, and once begun the reform movement was pushed forward by the very force of its own momentum.

During his twenty-two years in the lord treasurer's office Winchester left an indelible impression on the Exchequer. Until the accession of Elizabeth, however, he had little opportunity to do more than inaugurate and put through the reform program of 1554, which paved the way for further improvements. An overhauling of the administrative system was not Mary's first concern, and his real talents were reserved for Elizabeth.[52] Nevertheless, financial difficulty was an ever recurring problem of the Tudors, and as in previous reigns the treasurer was always concerned vitally with the state of the revenue. Some attention, indeed, had been given by Mary to the expedition of revenue collection and to the declaration of Exchequer payments. In the autumn of 1558, just before the close of the reign, tellers were ordered to deliver immediately " a perfect note " of all money in their custody and henceforth not to pay out anything without authorization from the council. At the same time a " perfect certifycat " of all receipts and expenditures was required weekly.[53] Whereas Mary was willing to subscribe to a policy of retrenchment, Elizabeth was insistent on more positive economy measures. Under her and Burghley, efficiency was again the guiding principle, and Paulet, though already well over seventy years of age at the beginning of the reign, was still energetic enough to implement her revenue program.[54]

Any comprehensive account of the Elizabethan Exchequer is beyond the scope of this study, although many of its improvements grew out

[52] Paulet's work as a financial adviser of the government under Mary was chiefly through special commissions, on which he served either as director or prominent member. Most of these special assignments concerned finances or revenue matters; on those which were related more closely to Exchequer affairs Paulet was assisted by the chancellor and undertreasurer of the Exchequer, Mildmay and Sackville.

[53] Dasent (ed.), *Acts of the Privy Council*, VI, 416–17; V, 323.

[54] Paulet was vigorous and active in the administration until his death at Basing House on March 10, 1572, at almost ninety. On the controversial date of his birth, see *D. N. B.*

of the earlier experimentation. That the expedients used were effective—foreign loans, stabilization of the currency, successful resumption of Mary's wilfull grants to the church, and above all, complete overhauling of the customs administration—is shown by the augmentation of revenues flowing into the treasury.[55] Within the Exchequer proper reforms proceeded along two lines: a tightening up of the administration in all branches of revenue collection and audit, and internal changes in the basic procedures of the court. For each program able leadership was available in the Exchequer itself. By training and character Winchester was as much appalled by negligence and waste as he was by disloyalty and incompetence. The administration badly needed a restoration of personal incentive and official discipline which only a conscientious executive could accomplish. Gradually this was attained by the lord treasurer's insistence on more effective supervision of each official and by personal recognition of superior achievement. Mildmay and Burghley, accepting these principles, had simply to continue basic policies which had already been laid down.

At the beginning of Elizabeth's reign the high cost of the war with Scotland and France necessitated an examination of the financial resources of the country, that the potential revenue might be estimated. Long before he succeeded Paulet in the treasurer's office, William Cecil, Lord Burghley after 1571, was busying himself with all sorts of financial matters, advising the council on national expenditures and working closely with Exchequer officials who kept him constantly informed on the current state of the revenues. Among the many investigating bodies organized to assist in this survey was the standing committee of the council which was charged with an examination of the total national revenue and how it might be increased. This commission of June 19, 1561, was composed of Cecil himself as principal secretary, the chancellor, the treasurer, the steward of the household, William Herbert, earl of Pembroke, and the chancellor and undertreasurer of the Exchequer; with the exception of Walter Mildmay they were all leading councillors. Under the guidance of Winchester they were to render periodic reports on the state of the revenue to Elizabeth, remaining active until their

---

[55] Brief interpretations of the financial and administrative reforms of Elizabeth are presented in Rowse, *The England of Elizabeth*, especially Chap. VIII; Read, *Mr. Secretary Cecil and Queen Elizabeth*, Chap. IX; and in Dietz, *English Public Finance, 1558–1641*, especially Chaps. XIII, XIV. Particularized accounts of the important reformation of the customs system are found in A. P. Newton, "The Establishment of the Great Farm of the English Customs," *Transactions of the Royal Historical Society*, Fourth Series, I (May, 1918), 129–55; and Frederick C. Dietz, "Elizabethan Customs Administration," *E.H.R.*, XLV (January, 1930), 35–58.

commission was terminated by writ of *supersedeas* or signed bill.[56] The survey gave a full financial report on the treasuries under four heads: (1) a comparative estimate of the revenue due the crown in 1547, 1553, 1558, and 1561, both ordinary and casual, (2) debts and arrears that remained outstanding, including those that were doubtful as well as those which were sure of payment, and the dates they were contracted, (3) liabilities of the government, such as fees, annuities, pensions, wages, and money borrowed, the latter being based on obligations originating mostly in the reigns of Edward VI and Mary, and (4) actual cash remaining on hand in the Tower or other treasuries, together with all sums due at the time the report was tendered. At about the same time, the three Exchequer officials were supervising a program for the increase of tillage and the restoration of decayed castles in the northern counties and Wales.[57]

As the treasurer of the Exchequer under Elizabeth gradually assumed the duties of a " lord high treasurer " of England, he ceased to be exclusively the head of a single division of revenue administration. Like a modern minister of finance he was responsible for the national revenues, not just in the Exchequer alone, but in all financial departments. Moreover, to him was delegated the obligation of providing the necessary annual revenues required for the expenses of the government. Consequently, the chancellor of the Exchequer more and more took over the actual direction of his own department. He was given general control over first fruits and tenths; and in other ways, too, he was more heavily burdened with additional duties, both in and out of term time, than

---

[56] Pat. Rolls, 3 Elizabeth, pt. 5, mems. 12*d.*–13*d.* Already the council had instituted numerous measures to increase the revenues. The customary *mises* were collected in Wales, grants of crown lands made during the last reign were re-examined, immediate returns were made of debts due in the revenue courts, and the chancellor of the Exchequer, Mildmay, was ordered to check on the payment of revenues due from crown tenants. Dasent (ed.), *Acts of the Privy Council*, VII, 11, 16, 22–27, 28, 60, 64 *passim*. On all revenue matters Mildmay, being " well versed in accounts," played a prominent part. Strype, *Annals*, I, pt. I, 18, 19, 21, 35–36, 149.

[57] Pat. Rolls, 3 Elizabeth, pt. 10, mem. 31*d.*; 4 Elizabeth, pt. 3, mems. 1*d.*–2*d.* Similar commissions to the treasurer, chancellor, and undertreasurer of the Exchequer for the more profitable leasing of the crown lands often yielded an increase in the yearly rents. Due to continued neglect by former officials, some crown possessions were in a state of great decay. In Denbighshire, Wales, the disorder was such that most of the tenants claimed to hold their lands in various uncertain ways, " some by copy of court roll for terms of years, some for lives, some for the time until the lands can be better let for the lord (allowing in this case the tenant's charge) and others claim to hold to them and their heirs in the name of a tenant right, for proof of which they have alleged charters and other writings which have often been considered and cannot be found allowable, notwithstanding the great charges sustained about the trial thereof." *Ibid.*, 4 Elizabeth, pt. 3, mem. 5*d.*; *Cal. Pat. Rolls, Elizabeth*, I, 119, 444–45; II, 169, 274–76, 278–79, 623–24.

formerly had been customary. After the lord high treasurer's office was placed in commission by the Stuarts, the chancellor became an official of increased importance and responsibility.

Within the Exchequer proper reforms came more slowly, largely because of the strong concentrated opposition to change by the older and more conservative officials. Each of them was jealous of the rights and privileges of his own office, fearful lest the very novelty of the new ways might destroy respect for the old. Despite such resistance, however, the need for greater efficiency prevailed. Winchester himself initiated most of the improvements, though he had the full support of Sackville and Mildmay, both of whom were sympathetic to further change. Furthermore, Winchester's position on the council was a strong one, his administrative skill and unquestioned loyalty having won for him the personal confidence of the queen. A successful career behind him, he no longer labored for advancement or recognition. On the other hand, the crown owed Paulet a great deal of money and that indebtedness alone caused him anxiety. Thus, heavily involved himself in the public financial difficulties of the times, he was not completely a free agent. This involvement in the royal service probably made him reluctant to push the reform program too far. As a public servant he was an administrative perfectionist, unwilling to compromise on a single particular wherein ultimate efficiency and progress might be retarded. With money so urgently needed he could count on the backing of the queen and Burghley in anything that promised results. In the end he had his way on most points, but altercation over the newer techniques and procedures continued long after his death, even into the Stuart period.

While all the reforms of the Elizabethan Exchequer were not occasioned directly by the Marian reorganization, nevertheless, many of them did grow out of the 1554 annexations. These in particular were resented by the Exchequer staff as representing the more practical procedures of the rival revenue courts, especially the former Augmentations which for so long had been their chief competitor. Actually, from the very beginning, the demands of the technicians had prevailed, and the Exchequer had proceeded, by well-established Augmentations methods, in the administration of all the annexed revenues.

A threefold series of changes was achieved fundamentally altering the system. It concerned the collection and administration of land revenues, modifications in the accounting procedure in keeping with the more advanced Augmentations methods, and certain alterations in the Exchequer of Receipt, designed to increase the efficiency of that department. Winchester's capable judgment and sense of compromise are reflected in each of these innovations.

The bulk of revenues administered by the renovated Exchequer, all of which were paid into the department of receipt, fell roughly into four main categories: (1) those derived from the ancient demesne, still the most substantial portion of th sheriffs' farms, and accountable in the Pipe Office, (2) the customs revenues which in themselves necessitated a special reform program, (3) the receipts from first fruits and tenths, and finally (4) the revenues and profits acquired from the former Court of Augmentations at the time of annexation. The only revenues excluded were those of the duchy of Lancaster and the Court of Wards which had remained unaffected by the recent merger.[58] Of these groupings it was in the third and fourth that immediate changes in administration were made. The first constituted chiefly the fixed revenues from the counties, which comprised not only the collections of the sheriffs but also those of the bailiffs and escheators; they continued to be processed in the traditional Exchequer manner. Nor was there any basic modification in the customs system where stricter supervision was more important; such changes as resulted from the reform of the customs were chiefly in the declarations of accounts. In the office of first fruits and tenths the major alterations were embodied in the articles of annexation and modified but slightly in the years to come.[59] The recommendations set forth for the administration of the Augmentations revenues were, on the contrary, not followed at all.

In the upper Exchequer the ancient *firma comitatus* and other fixed revenues generally fell within the division of the lord treasurer's remembrancer, which also controlled the Foreign Roll, Subsidy Roll, and Customs Roll, as well as the Pipe Roll. Conversely, the queen's remembrancer was traditionally responsible for the casual revenues, which included the chief spending departments of government, the household, the wardrobe, the ordnance, the king's ships, public works, and the mint. Nevertheless, the gradual breakup during the latter fifteenth and sixteenth centuries of this system, whereby all accounts passed through the divisions of the two remembrancers, rendered these offices less important. Furthermore, the hereditary revenues of the crown had declined

[58] At the beginning of Elizabeth's reign these revenues totaled slightly over £33,000 annually, being £20,290 net for the Court of Wards and £12,828 for the Lancastrian revenues, of which some £2,460 net represented issues and profits from the Dissolution. Surplus funds from both these institutions might sometimes be paid into the Exchequer. Bell, *The Court of Wards and Liveries*, 48, Table A, 192–93; Somerville, *History of the Duchy of Lancaster*, I, 304, 318. Dietz, however, gives the duchy total for the year as £12,871. Dietz, *Finances of Edward VI and Mary*, 124.

[59] Fanshawe alludes to a late Elizabethan decree altering the regulations governing the Office of First Fruits and Tenths but does not explain the change. Fanshawe, *The Practice of the Exchequer Court*, 84.

in relation to the newer revenues of the Tudors, which, independently administered, had proved the validity of modern accounting procedures. In part, therefore, the preservation of the "ancient course" so much under discussion was only stubborn insistence on perpetuating anti-quated machinery.

Under the second Augmentations England and Wales had been divided into twelve revenue districts—thirteen when the duchy of Corn-wall is included—each administered by a receiver-general and an auditor. Later, upon the dissolution of the Augmentations, the hope of the Ex-chequer had been to bring all the estates thus annexed within the survey of the sheriffs, but Winchester sought to avoid such a reactionary step.

A way out was found by providing for a period of experimentation and review, which in the end brought victory to the proponents of the Aug-mentations system. The previous arrangement continued with the twelve original districts giving way to seven, thus affording a modest reduction in personnel.[60] Of the five Exchequer auditors at the time of amalgama-tion, three of them—John Hornyold, William Rigges, and Brian Taylor —were also auditors in the Augmentations. Moreover, the appointees of 1554, as required by the statute of annexation, had been former audi-tors in the dissolved Court, while still another of the seven, Francis Southwell, had held the auditorship of prests in the Court of General Surveyors.[61] Thus six of them had served earlier in one or the other of the defunct revenue courts and were thoroughly familiar with Augmen-tations practices and procedures.[62] In 1707 the seven auditors were

[60] The revenue districts in the Exchequer were similar to those set up by the Augmentations: first district—the bishopric of Durham, Northumberland, the archdeaconry of Richmond and Yorkshire; second district—Cambridgeshire, Essex, Hertfordshire, Huntingdonshire, London, Middlesex, Norfolk, and Suffolk; third district—Cumberland, Herefordshire, Lancashire, Leicestershire, Northamptonshire, Rutland, Shropshire, Staffordshire, Warwickshire, Westmoreland, and Worcester-shire; fourth district—Cheshire, Derbyshire, Lincolnshire, and Nottinghamshire; fifth district—Bedfordshire, Berkshire, Buckinghamshire, Kent, Oxfordshire, Sur-rey, Sussex, and the honor and castle of Windsor; sixth district—Cornwall, duchy of Cornwall, Devonshire, Dorsetshire, Gloucestershire, Hampshire, Somer-setshire, and Wiltshire; seventh district—Monmouthshire, North Wales, and South Wales. Dietz, *English Public Finance, 1558–1641,* 293; Sidney J. Madge, *The Domesday of Crown Lands* (London, 1938), 38.

[61] P. 148, *supra.* Southwell also had held an auditorship in South Wales under the general surveyors. *L. and P.,* XIV, pt. 1, no. 403(2).

[62] To the original five auditors, John Hornyold, Brian Taylor, William Rigges, Francis Southwell, and John Osborne, Mary added the two former Augmenta-tions auditors, John Thompson and John Swift. With the exception of Taylor, who was succeeded by Valentine Brown, these men all continued in office during Mary's reign. The Elizabethan appointment of Thomas Neale in 1560 was only a tem-porary addition apparently; with the death of Rigges, sometime during the follow-ing year, the number of permanent auditorships was again reduced to seven. In 1558 another former Augmentations auditor, Anthony Rone, was granted a sur-

reduced to three in number, and their offices eventually abolished altogether. Their duties were transferred in 1832 to audit commissioners, at which time the Office of Land Revenue Records and Enrollments was created to take charge of the land records.[63]

Within the auditors' districts particular Exchequer receivers were appointed to collect the land revenues in each county. They all received life tenure, with salaries ranging from £20 to £100 annually, plus additional portage fees of twenty shillings for each £100 of collected revenue paid into the court, in accordance with recent Augmentations practice. Their number varied appreciably, depending on how many counties and towns were assigned to each, but the receivers were always numerous; at the beginning of the seventeenth century there were twenty-three.[64] As formerly under the Augmentations, crown holdings were separated into categories such as lands acquired by the Dissolution, chantry lands, queen's lands, exchanged lands, and possessions acquired from private individuals; within each district local receivers and special collectors continued as before. Moreover, under this arrangement the county surveyors and stewards were retained with practically no change in duties. These officials served a twofold function, which in fact had been the principal reason for the creation of their positions. Locally, they took over a great deal of the supervisory work of the auditors and receivers, thus eliminating a considerable part of the field travel of those officials and reducing appreciably the riding costs of the court. But, still more important to the crown, they conducted surveys, reported concealed lands and rents, and brought to the attention of the Exchequer stray items of revenue that otherwise might have been overlooked.[65] Nevertheless it is doubtful if any absolute saving resulted from the amalgamation. The renovated Exchequer, including as it did the whole customs service, still had a larger personnel than that of the three revenue courts put together.

In the much-needed reformation of the customs an excellent opportunity for extending centralized control over all revenues presented itself. Indeed, the plan of the lord treasurer provided for just that type

---

vivorship to Southwell's office. *Cal. Pat. Rolls, Edward VI*, IV, 267; *Mary*, I, 495; *Philip and Mary*, III, 457; IV, 401, 419; *Elizabeth*, I, 322, 323; II, 217. The basic salary of the auditor's office remained £20 per year, although it was supplemented substantially by extra traveling allowances.

[63] Giuseppi, *A Guide to the Manuscripts preserved in the Public Record Office*, I, 169; II, 114.

[64] Lansd. MS. 171, fol. 35*d*.

[65] In the 1552 study of Exchequer practices it had been pointed out that a loss of revenue had resulted from lands held *in capite* which had been alienated without license. It was then suggested that special offices be set up to report such alienations. Add. MS. 30198, fol. 40.

of unified supervision under the direction of customs surveyors and sur-veyors-general. This idea had been incorporated in his general pro-posals for the improvement of the customs, but the scheme was never fully developed. Lord Burghley, on the other hand, favored the system of farming out the customs, apparently with the conviction that fixed annual payments, assurable in advance, were in the long run more profitable. In the end, the latter policy was adopted, but only after considerable experimentation in the use of royal surveyors.[66]

Among the significant changes introduced, the greatest departure from Exchequer practice came in the adoption of Augmentations techniques in the accounting process. Double entry bookkeeping, accounts in Eng-lish and on paper rather than parchment, and the hearing of accounts privately by the auditors without swearing in the accountants were all devices new to Exchequer procedure. Furthermore, the auditors de-veloped the habit of retaining in their own possession the accounts of the receivers and other collectors of revenues instead of processing them through the offices of the two remembrancers, so that any deficit in the final balance of the year's reckoning could easily remain a secret between the auditor and the accountant. There is no evidence that open dis-honesty resulted, but the possibility was there. However much the ele-ment of simplicity may have recommended it, such a practice would seem certainly to have facilitated concealment and fraud.

At any rate protests were not slow in forthcoming. An " infinite charge to the crown " would be saved, it was alleged, if only a return to the true course of the Exchequer were required, for all " mischeifes " had been caused by the departure from the old order. Formerly the auditors had received only £10 for their services; with but one clerk each in regular attendance, they had no liveries and took no allowances nor special fees. But " contrarywise yt is vsed at this daie: "

> And to th'effect of their offices touching the revenewes . . . , and
> in what sort they vse their offices at this present noe perfect
> declaracion can be made well thereof, for that they vse not the
> same according to the course of th'Exchequer but Augmentation
> like and not to the meaning of the vniting of the Courtes, for
> why they charge what they list, and discharge what they list, often-
> tymes w^{th}out record of þe same, and put in *super* what they list,
> and vpon whom they list, make what allowance for what they list,
> and to whom they list. And they haue the generall & perticuler

[66] Winchester may have been responsible for the new book of rates in 1558 and the subsequent appointment of Sir Francis Englefield to the position of surveyor-general of the customs of London in July of the same year. Lansd. MS. 3, fol. 145; *Cal. Pat. Rolls, Philip and Mary,* IV, 13–14, 75–76.

Receivors accompt of long tyme alwaies remayning in their custodies, so as from tyme to tyme they may change & alter the same as they list. And vpon change of any of the said officers by death or otherwise, the said accomptes so remayning in their custodies oftentymes be altered, ymbeselled & lost, and so by reason of mischarge, & discharge and other the causes afore said, Non concordat Psalterium cum Cythera to the losse of the Prince, damage of the subiectes, and great slaunder of the Court, their fees augmented from £10 to £20 by yeare, and the guift of them is in the Prince.[67]

Other abuses likewise were recorded, including excessive fees, delays in accounting, informal oral instructions issued to ministers without written warrant, and an undue number of county officials. Particularly detrimental was the confusion resulting from the unsorted Augmentations records, which "are so intermingled that one officer knoweth not in effect what apperteineth to another, so as oftentymes if þe Court call for them for the service of the Prince, they cannot tell directly to what officer to call for the same." The cause of disorder was obvious; since the union with the Exchequer "there hath bene noe good order for sorting the Recordes thereof into the offices certaine, . . . wch causeth no small evill speech of the Court." Locally conditions were equally lax because stewards, surveyors, and woodwards were no longer skilled or conscientious in the execution of their offices.[68] As for the audits of the land revenue, there was no further record nor enrollment of the ministers' accounts save the declarations of the auditors presented to the treasurer and other officials of the Exchequer upon the yearly completion of their circuits.

Winchester and his supporters in the Exchequer, particularly Mildmay and Sackville, withstood all attempts to force the new revenues through the ancient channels of the Pipe Office, but some concessions were granted later, after their restraining influence was removed. In the late nineties Burghley required the audited accounts of Exchequer payments to be turned over to the clerk of the pells for enrollment and record. The Declaration Books of receipts and issues compiled half-yearly by the pells office, together with the tellers' Views of Account replaced

[67] Cotton. MS., Titus B. iv, fols. 12*d.*–13, 18*d.*; "A Declaracion of the Old and Auncient Duties of th'Officers and Clarkes seruing in th'Offices," Lansd. MS. 171, fols. 321–21*d.* Similar charges against the auditors are presented in Add. MS. 12504, fols. 181*d.*–91.

[68] Seven "Causes of euill Reportes" of the Exchequer, Lansd. MS. 171, fols. 323–24; "A discours touching þe Survey of his Maiesties landes" (July, 1606), *ibid.*, fols. 394*d.*–96*d.* The county surveyors of the Augmentations who were not reappointed were given a life pension for the surrender of their offices.

earlier Declarations of the State of the Treasury which had been discontinued in 1552 shortly before the Exchequer merger.[69]

With reference to the foreign accounts in the Exchequer the conservative position of the diehards in 1554 had been adamant. These accounts were to be " yearlie taken and engrossed by thauditours of Thexchequier " in the traditional manner, as customary in the court before the emergence of the auditorship of prests.[70] So strong was the feeling within the Exchequer against this particular innovation that, despite the protests of the reformers, the provision was carried out literally. Thus an office which, for more than a decade, had rendered yeoman service to the crown was allowed to lapse because of the prejudice of a rival department. This concession had been granted in order to procure the acceptance of the merger, but Winchester seems to have had no intention of enforcing it. In effect, the conciliar system of hearing accounts through royal commissions, unsatisfactory as it was, continued unchanged. This situation was at length remedied when the office of the two auditors of the prests and foreign accounts was re-established. This extra office, whose Declared Accounts, in the colorful language of Fanshawe, " be never entred in the Court of Exchequer, nor examined nor written upon there as they had wont to be " but declared only before the lord treasurer, chancellor, and undertreasurer, remained a separate and independent department in the reformed Exchequer.[71]

After the amalgamation of 1554 the receipt department of the Exchequer emerged as a central treasury for the greater part of the revenues of the kingdom. Obviously its custodians acquired increased

---

[69] A detailed description of the changing auditing practices in the Exchequer is too long and involved for inclusion here. It is fully explained in the *Reports of the Deputy Keeper of the Public Records,* especially *Second Report,* Appendix II, 195–99, and *Fourth Report,* 179–80; Giuseppi, *A Guide to the Manuscripts preserved in the Public Record Office,* I, 180, 188, 189, 193; and Fanshawe, *The Practice of the Exchequer Court.* See also the statutes 1 James I, c. 26, " An Acte for the continuance and due observation of certaine Orders for the Exchequer, first set downe and established by vertue of a Privie Seale from the late Queene Elizabeth," and 8 and 9 William III, c. 28, " An Act for the better Observation of the Course anciently used in the Receipt of Exchequer," *S. R.,* IV, pt. 2, 1052–55; VII, 275–79. Manuscript sources giving full accounts of Elizabethan changes, although controversial and repetitious, are found in numerous collections, especially (B. M.) Lansd. MSS. 106, 166, 168, 171; Cotton. MS., Titus B. iv; (P. R. O.) Exch. of Receipt, Miscellanea, 71, 396; and Exch., L. T. R., Misc. Books 117. Scattered material on the renovated Exchequer is also included among the State Papers, as in *Cal. State Papers, Domestic, James I, 1611–1618,* pp. 109, 371, 388, 421, 486; elsewhere a few contemporary treatises have been published, as in *Political Tracts, 1661–65,* XIX, 1–25.

[70] Item 29 of the Articles of Annexation.

[71] Fanshawe, *The Practice of the Exchequer Court,* 83–84. Cf. George, " Notes on the Origin of the Declared Account," *loc. cit.,* 41–58.

prestige, though their influence was somewhat minimized by the division of responsibility. At the beginning the four tellers were the most essen-tial officers of this department, taking charge of all revenue as it came in and making payments on the authority of the lord treasurer and chan-cellor as directed by warrants of the crown or council. But later under Elizabeth a modified procedure in the regulation of the tellers' receipts and expenditures was initiated, which ultimately had the effect of elevat-ing the clerk of the tallies, *scriptor talliarum*, to a position of control.

Anciently, clerical work of the receipt had been in the hands of two principal officers—the clerk of the pells, who kept the receipt rolls and issue rolls of money taken in and paid out by the tellers, and the clerk of the tallies, who had charge of the writing of the tallies of receipt. How-ever, the issue roll, which was always referred to as the *pellis exitus*, or pell of issue, was discontinued at the end of the reign of Edward IV and not resumed until 1597, along with other measures introduced by Burgh-ley just before his death. During the intervening years the writer of the tallies, who retained sole custody of the tellers' vouchers and accounts as well as the enrollment books of privy seals and warrants for their disbursement, was the only person who could properly supervise the work of the tellers and check the certificates of payments. Actually he took over a great deal of the responsibility once exercised by the under-treasurer as real head of the lower Exchequer and in time became the auditor of the receipt. It was he who kept a " fair book " of each teller's receipts and certified weekly to the lord treasurer and the court just how much money was taken in and spent. Without his official debenture no money could be expended, and regularly twice a year he received the tellers' counter books and took their accounts; occasionally he might even order the tellers to correct or revise their original accounts, from which he calculated the balance. When the receipt was moved to St. Stephen's in the new Palace of Westminster, he was entrusted with the safekeeping of the money in the treasury, which he guarded under lock and key for the treasurer.[72]

With his having finally risen to such a dominant position, it is little wonder that " Mr. Auditor " would object to any encroachment on his authority. When finally the clerk of the pells was allowed to share his responsibility, he could with some justification expostulate bitterly to

[72] Details of the transition here described emerged in the long quarrel waged between the two Elizabethan clerks of the pells, Robert Hare and Chidiock Wardour, and the clerks, or writers, of the tallies, Robert Peter and Sir Vincent Skinner. About a hundred items concerning this dispute have been collected in the Exch. of Receipt, Miscellanea (E. 407), 71. In particular, see nos. 13, 15, 34, 63, 65, 81, 82, 92, 93, 94, and 104. Nos. 68, 96, and 100 give lists of the holders of these offices with the increases in fees.

Lord Burghley: " If this Pell shall be revived in my time, that so long hath discontinued, I must think myself an unhappy man, having served for this twenty years past and more painfully and as uprightly as any that hath preceded me in that place: the world will judge and say that the same could not take effect without some great fault committed by me, the which would shorten the few days I have to live." [73] As in all progress those who oppose new measures usually have a tangible interest in preserving the old.

Somewhat different in impact was the effect of Augmentations practices upon the judicial work of the court; involving as it did the broader concepts of equity jurisdiction, it was destined both to affect public interest and to influence the emergence of modern principles of law. In addition to being a revenue department the Exchequer was also a court of law, possessing an equity as well as a common-law jurisdiction. In this respect it was similar to the Augmentations, its immediate objective having always been to collect the crown revenues and initiate process against delinquent debtors. Consequently, while common-law jurisdiction developed early, equitable functions were not assumed to any degree by the court until after the reorganization of 1554. People living in the areas originally administered by the Augmentations, in Wales as in England, now looked to the Exchequer for protection and relief. With the increase in the number of cases there was a gradual assumption of equitable jurisdiction during the latter half of the sixteenth century, which was in part at least an inheritance from the defunct Augmentations.[74]

The most pronounced influence on procedure was twofold, effect on the power of the court to order payments out of the issues of the receipt of the Exchequer and on the recognition of the right of the subject to equitable relief against the crown. In numerous instances of Exchequer litigation the decision hinged on one or the other of these points, final judgment resting upon precedents drawn from Augmenta-

---

[73] H. M. C., *Cal. of Cecil Manuscripts*, pt. 4, 455–56.

[74] The Exchequer had developed a threefold jurisdiction—as a court of revenue, a court of common law, and a court of equity, in which practices, such as the writ of subpoena, were used long before the reign of Elizabeth. Although equitable functions were claimed earlier, they were not commonly applied until her day. Holdsworth, *H. E. L.*, I (7th edit. revised, under the general editorship of A. L. Goodhart and H. G. Hanbury, London, 1956), 234 ff.; IX, 29 ff. In Wales the great number of suits transferred from the Court of the Council of the Marches to the Elizabethan Exchequer, where there was a better chance of a fair trial, suggests that after the abolition of the Augmentations the Welsh people at least looked on that tribunal as a court of appeals. Emyr Gwynne Jones, *Exchequer Proceedings (Equity) Concerning Wales: Henry VIII—Elizabeth* (Board of Celtic Studies, University of Wales History and Law Series, No. IV [Cardiff, 1939]), Preface, ix-x.

tions decrees. It was repeatedly pointed out that the court's authority to order the treasurer and chamberlains to pay out money from the receipt was inherited from the Augmentations by virtue of its annexation to the Exchequer. Nevertheless, it was assumed by some judges that since the court was one of justice and not of equity no money could be issued out of the receipt except by warrant of the queen under the great seal or the privy seal. The Exchequer, therefore, could act only by rule and not according to discretion, as had been the custom in the Augmentations.

The power exercised by the Court of Augmentations was, of course, grounded upon fact, for the treasurer had been empowered by statute to expend money, not only by the authority of royal warrant, but also to honor " any bill assigned & subscribed with the handes of the said Chauncellor Attorney & Solicitor or two of them, upon suche consideracions as shalbe thought convenient by their discrecions." [75] The question was debated in Michaelmas term, 1596, in the case of Sir Walter Mildmay, who had been paid a larger fee in consideration of the heavier duties contingent upon his office after the annexation of the two revenue courts.[76] Although Augmentations practices employed in the authorization for treasury payments had crept into Exchequer usage, it was resolved in this case that Exchequer officials could not, either individually or collectively, " dispose of the king's treasure ex officio, though it be for his [the king's] honour or profit, unless by warrant from himself." The decision even ruled out warrants by royal sign manual or orders by word of mouth, so commonly resorted to in the earlier period.[77]

Far more important than the issue of the court's payments, though closely associated with it, was the broader one of the subject's right to redress of grievance against the crown which grew out of the acquired equity jurisdiction of the Exchequer. Under certain conditions this privilege was, of course, recognized by Tudor statute in 1548; [78] but more to the point, in practical application the Court of General Surveyors and the Court of Augmentations had both commonly extended

[75] 27 Henry VIII, c. 27, sec. xxi. Similar powers were conferred on the second Augmentations by the letters patent of erection. Pat. Rolls, 38 Henry VIII, pt. 5, mems. 19–20, 22.

[76] See p. 454, *supra.*

[77] Sir Edward Coke, 11 *Reports*, 91a–91b; William Cobbett, T. B. Howell, *et al.* (eds.), *A Complete Collection of State Trials* (London, 1816–98), XIV, 68, 92, 102. Hereinafter cited as Cobbett (ed.), *State Trials.* The quote is from a seventeenth-century interpretation. 77 *English Reports—Full Reprint*, 1268–69, hereinafter cited as *Eng. Rep.*

[78] An act concerning the finding of offices before the escheators, 2 and 3 Edward VI, c. 8, *S. R.*, IV, 47–48. By means of the traverse and *monstrans de droit* the older remedy of petition of right was considerably supplemented.

such rights to the subject as a matter of course. Among the numerous
cases of this nature which came before the Elizabethan Exchequer those
of *Neville* and *Wroth* are of greater interest because they were used
as important precedents in the decisions of the next century.

In the first case the facts were definite and clear cut. Shortly before
his attainder in 1538, Sir Edward Neville had been granted in survivorship with his son, Henry, the keepership of Aldington Park, in Kent,
with a fee of £3 10d. yearly, payable from issues of the manor of the
same name. Subsequently the property came into the possession of
the crown, and jurisdiction over it was acquired by the Exchequer from
the Augmentations. In time, payments were allowed to lapse, whereupon
Sir Henry Neville brought suit for the accumulated arrears due him. In
the procedure by English bill the petition was directed to the court rather
than to the queen. In 1570, some nine years later, judgment was accorded the plaintiff in accordance with established Augmentations procedures by which it was decided to honor the petition and award payment as requested. Payment was made, however, not by royal warrant
but by judicial writ of the court, the formal decree thus being accepted
by the treasurer and chamberlain of the Exchequer as sufficient warrant
for the payment.[79] Had the Court of Augmentations continued, the case
would have been adjudicated by it. Clearly this was an example of inherited jurisdiction.

The second precedent was parallel to the first, inasmuch as it hinged
on the transfer of legal obligations and responsibilities from the Augmentations to the Exchequer. In October, 1541, Rich's son-in-law, Sir
Thomas Wroth, had received a life appointment as gentleman usher of
the privy chamber of Prince Edward, with an accompanying annuity of
£20 as a fee. This grant was under the seal of the Augmentations, and
from the beginning the fees were payable from its revenues. Although
the recipient had assumed the duties of his office, serving Edward until
his death, the annuity had never been collected. Nor had the original
grant been cancelled by Mary, for it was proved that subsequently, in
1561, payments had been allowed by the Exchequer for several years.
Upon Wroth's death in October, 1573, his executors brought suit in the
Exchequer for the arrears of salary due, which were granted. The
decree was implemented by a court writ directed to the treasurer and

---

[79] Edmund Plowden, *An Exact Abridgment in English of the Commentaries
or Reports . . .* (London, 1650), 221–24. The manor and park of Aldington were
included in an exchange between the king and the archbishop of Canterbury, the
original deed of sale, dated February, 1541, being enrolled in the Augmentations.
Augm. Office, Misc. Books 249, fols. 36, 38. 1 Plowden, 376a–83; 75 *Eng. Rep.*,
572–82. In effect such payments by judicial writ were ruled out by the decision of
1596. See page 469.

chamberlains of the receipt authorizing the required expenditure. Several points were debated at the time, but a major issue was that of whether or not the annuity terminated at the death of Edward VI, since the grant of appointment to office had not contained the legal words of limitation, *pro nobis heredibus et successoribus nostris*. The judges supported the contention of the petitioners that the fee was terminated only by the death of the annuitant, that is, that discharge had come as an " act of God." Both cases, therefore, involved the problem of expending government funds without royal warrant, but in neither instance was the more important question of the nature and manner of the suit raised.[80]

Some century and a quarter later it was argued in the famous *Bankers' Case* that Exchequer proceedings were grounded upon particular reason and not upon common law, and further, that all annuities, pensions, and other like payments founded upon Augmentations revenues were equally binding on the Exchequer by virtue of the provisions of the letters patent of union of 1554. Contrarily, it was forcefully maintained that there could be no accession of power by the Exchequer, since the patent of January 24 uniting the courts " came too late and was utterly void." This new twist to the argument was based on the fact that the patent of the previous day had dissolved the Augmentations. There could, consequently, be no annexation of a court which did not legally exist; such an implied union, it was reasoned quite groundlessly, was therefore *quasi absurdum et impossibile*, in spite of the empowering act of parliament to the contrary.[81] It was during this long and complicated trial that the whole problem of equitable justice on the part of the subject was brought under review and thoroughly analyzed for the first time.

While the principle of the right of relief against the crown had been slow in evolving, it appears to have been given explicit recognition as early as 1668 in the case of *Pawlett* v. *the Attorney General*, which became the starting point for the discussion of the right of petition in the *Bankers' Case*. During the former trial it was admitted that the plaintiff, a mortgagee, had the right of petition by a bill in the Exchequer for restoration of property which had been seized by the crown. Again, as

---

[80] Plowden, *Commentaries or Reports*, 20–23. *Neville's Case* and *Wroth's Case* are both fully discussed in *State Trials*, in relation to the *Bankers' Case*. Cobbett (ed.), *State Trials*, XIV, 36–37, 83 ff. 2 Plowden, 452–59; 75 *Eng. Rep.*, 678–88.

[81] Cobbett (ed.), *State Trials*, XIV, 36, 89–90. An act of parliament, 1 Mary, St. 2, c. 10, empowering the sovereign to dissolve any of her revenue courts by letters patent and to erect new courts by similar process. *S. R.*, IV, 208–209, sec. v. Coke had suggested the same approach: " and the next day following by other letters patents united the same to the exchequer, which was utterly void, because she had dissolved the same before: so as she pursued not her authority." Coke, *Institutes*, Part IV, 118, 121–22. On this point cf. John Reeves, *History of English Law*, ed. by W. F. Finlason (Philadelphia, 1880), IV, 390.

previously, the judges harkened back to the equitable powers which the court had inherited from the Augmentations. Redemption, it was noted, " was Natural Justice; and that an Act of Parliament, that should take it away, would be void in it self; . . . And no more than the King can deny Justice in his own case, no more can he deny Common Equity; and Common Equity is as due to the Subject against the King as Justice is." Sir Matthew Hale, chief baron of the Exchequer, pointed out that the principle involved was one of great consideration, that relief in equity did lie against the king, and ruled that in natural justice redemption of a mortgage was desirable. Baron Robert Atkyns in his supporting argument emphasized the notion that " the King is the Fountain and Head of Justice and Equity; and it shall not be presumed that he will be defective in either." [82]

The implications of the whole controversy are perfectly clear, for the issue was an important one of acquired jurisdiction. It mattered little whether or not the Exchequer secured additional equity powers from the accession of the Augmentations. It did exercise them and probably would have assumed them in any event, even if the merger of 1554 had not occurred.

In this case, as in several others, the court cited the sixteenth century statute creating the Court of General Surveyors, which plainly had guaranteed " Relief in equity against the King." Specifically, the act also had enlarged the powers of the Court of Augmentations by authorizing the chancellor and council of the Court to entertain such suits and " by wyttnes prosses and other waies and meanes by their discrecions, to heare and determyn the same." Such extended jurisdiction was, moreover, a departure from the common law. Indeed, argued Lord John Somers in the *Bankers' Case*, nothing was further from the intentions of the founders of the Augmentations than to fashion it after the model of the Exchequer; on the contrary it was created a court of equity, and from it the barons of the Exchequer received their inspiration for judicial innovation. [83]

It would seem that for a long time the Exchequer officials had assumed the position that equitable relief should, as of right, be given upon proper petition to the barons, and this course of action was one which had been acquired from the Augmentations. The point was forced by Somers that " the whole tenor of the proceedings of the court of Exchequer, in rela-

---

[82] Thomas Hardres, *Reports of Cases Adjudged in the Court of Exchequer* (London, 1693), 465–69. 145 *Eng. Rep.*, 550–52.

[83] Cobbett (ed.), *State Trials*, XIV, 94–96, 98. Sections xxxvii and xxxviii of 33 Henry VIII, c. 39, had extended the powers of the Augmentations, *S.R.*, III, 386–87.

tion to cases which were before of the jurisdiction of the court of Augmentations," was similar to the summary methods practiced in the earlier court, representing " a great variation made from the ancient manner of proceedings in the Exchequer." This principle of direct procedure, by petition to the barons of the Exchequer as a proper means by which the subject might obtain equitable relief, was reaffirmed in the decision of the *Bankers' Case*. In effect, it simply added to the older correctives of petition of right and *monstrans de droit* a third remedy against the crown. The case concerned a suit in the Exchequer for arrears of payments to the goldsmiths or bankers for money lent to the king, which had grown out of the earlier stop of the Exchequer in 1672. The bankers proceeded by the usual petition, to which the attorney general for the crown demurred on the grounds that a petition was not the proper remedy. However, the judges upheld the plea of the plaintiff that their procedure was valid and gave judgment in 1690 for the bankers. A writ of error appealed the matter to the Court of Exchequer Chamber, where the decision was reversed. It was there held that a petition was not the correct procedure because the barons of the Exchequer had no legal way of authorizing payment. The case dragged on until 1700 when it was carried to the high court of parliament where the house of lords restored the original judgment of the Exchequer.

The real significance of the case, of course, lay in its broader application to the question of remedial rights of the subject against the crown, but for the Exchequer it meant a vindication of practices already well established. Substantially, the various decisions supported the claim of the Exchequer that a petition to the barons, while not the only possible recourse available to subjects, was at least " a proper and legal remedy " and that payments out of the receipt, as in the former Augmentations, were allowable under certain circumstances, upon court direction, in which a judicial decree " would be a good warrant in point of law." In the concluding arguments in the house of lords it was clearly demonstrated that these equity developments in the Exchequer emerged after the absorption of the Court of Augmentations and the Court of First Fruits and Tenths, from which certain powers " by that annexation subsist in that court to this day." [84]

As the judicial work of the Exchequer increased, its judges, the four barons, gave increasingly more attention to their judicial duties and less

---

[84] The *Bankers' Case* is fully presented in Cobbett (ed.), *State Trials*, XIV (Case no. 414), 1–114. On quotations from arguments, see pages 34, 93, 101, 111. For the equitable implications of the principles involved, see Holdsworth, *H. E. L.*, IX, 27–39; Costin and Watson (eds.), *The Law and Working of the Constitution: Documents, 1660–1914*, I, 271–78. Coke, 11 *Reports*, 89a–93a; 77 *Eng. Rep.*, 1266–71.

time to purely administrative detail. The barons, who from 1579 onward were always chosen from the legal profession, often required information on the proper procedure to follow, especially in relation to Augmentations techniques developing after 1554. Instruction of this kind on technical procedure became the peculiar function of the fourth or cursitor baron, who was usually selected by the clerks in the Offices of the Remembrancers and the Pipe. Among his special duties he was responsible for informing the other barons and the king's learned council from time to time, both in court and out of court, what the correct course, or " cursus," of the Exchequer was, why it was so directed, and wherein it might or might not be amended. Above all, he was expected to uphold the old order by maintaining " the preservation of the same." [85]

In conclusion, it may be observed that the cumbersome Exchequer, while to a large degree preserving its historical continuity, was forced to put its own house in order. Yet in view of all the significant changes during the sixteenth century, from the reforms of Henry VII to those of Elizabeth, it is amazing how tenaciously stubborn officials clung to established customs. Conservative habits, particularly when they have become institutionalized, are slow to be put away. On the other hand, though modernization came slowly and painfully, a competent government could, and did, insist on the necessary modifications and improvements in age-old techniques that could not be discarded completely, even in the interests of administrative efficiency. Thus was the national Exchequer of the later Stuarts reformed, though in organization and routine it was still committed, and almost irrevocably so, to the " ancient practices " and forms of the fifteenth century.

[85] Fanshawe, *The Practice of the Exchequer Court*, 34–36. The number of barons in the Exchequer had been reduced to four in the reign of Edward IV. On the rise of the cursitor baron, see Giuseppi, *A Guide to the Manuscripts preserved in the Public Record Office*, I, 73, 134, 167; Holdsworth, *H. E. L.*, I (7th ed. revised), 235–37.

CHAPTER FOURTEEN

RECORDS OF THE AUGMENTATIONS

NY HISTORY OF THE COURT OF AUGMENTATIONS IS INCOM-
plete without some interpretation of the records and literature upon which it is based. An analysis of sources is particularly desirable when it is remembered that nothing has
been written concerning either the Court itself or that vast collection of
land and revenue records which eventually found lodgment within the
Augmentation Office of the Exchequer. Since the two institutions, Court
and Office, were distinctly separate, though historically related, it is
important to note that a large part of the manuscripts classified by the
Public Record Office as "Augmentation Office" documents has no
direct relation to the earlier Court. Indeed a great many of them ante-
date the sixteenth century, while others cover the subsequent years
down to the Restoration, with even a few items in certain series as late
as the Georgian period. This classification is meaningful to the specialist,
familiar as he is with the checkered history of interrelated governmental
institutions, but is mystifying to the searcher, who logically expects the
label of a document to indicate the nature of its source. In fact, these
miscellaneous records are only rendered intelligible in the light of circumstances attendant on the origin and development of the Augmentations
Office.[1]

When the second Court of Augmentations was annexed to the Ex-

---

[1] This chapter appeared in essentially this form as a published article in 1957.
W. C. Richardson, "Records of the Court of Augmentations," *Journal of the
Society of Archivists*, I, (October, 1957), 159–68.

chequer in 1554, all its records were likewise transferred to that department. Even then the Augmentations archives were very comprehensive, embracing not only the combined records of the Court of Augmentations and the earlier office and Court of General Surveyors, which had been joined to it in 1547, but also surveys, monastic records, and numerous categories of documents and manuscripts relating to the Dissolution and to the various units of crown lands formerly under the jurisdiction of the two courts.[2] Within the latter class are found the records of such large divisions of property as monastic possessions, chantry lands, the ancient crown demesne, attainted lands, purchased and exchanged lands, and the extensive estates of the principality of Wales and the duchy of Cornwall.[3] The records of these crown possessions, as well as all the miscellaneous documents and materials acquired by the Augmentations prior to its abolition, also came to the Exchequer. In order to accommodate them, a new division of Exchequer records was created, which became known as the Augmentation Office. This office remained as the repository of a large section of Exchequer records until its abolition in 1834.

From time to time other documents were deposited in the Augmentation Office when they appeared to be related to the records already retained there. Such was the acquisition in 1620 of a register book of the monastery of Pershore, in Worcestershire, consisting of entries of deeds and other legal instruments, all prior to the thirteenth century. When discovered, the book was sent to the chancellor of the Exchequer, who immediately turned it over to the keeper of the records in the Augmentation Office.[4] Documents in this office were also occasionally transferred to other departments or storage centers, but more frequently Augmentations records " escaped " into other hands and were lost by the Exchequer as a result of carelessness or inadequate supervision. It was

[2] Article 35 of the schedule attached to the patent of annexation provided " that all Recordes late beyng in thesaid Courtes dissolued and belongyng to thesame Courtes shalbe Recordes in thesaide Courte of thexchequier and of the sameforce and strength as they were in thesaid late Courtes dissolued." Close Rolls, 1 Mary, pt. 7, mem. 5. Since not a few Augmentations documents were originally nothing more than personal notes or letters of officials, many private manuscripts and memoranda were thus raised to the dignity of public records.

[3] The records of the duchy of Cornwall and the duchy of Lancaster were transferred from the Augmentation Office to the respective duchy offices in July, 1800. At the same time over 4,000 rolls of Ministers' Accounts in the Offices of the Auditors of the Land Revenue were brought into the Augmentation Office. However, there are still scattered accounts for the duchy of Cornwall and a few records for the duchy of Lancaster classified as Augmentation Office documents. *Report from the Commissioners appointed to execute the Measures Recommended by a Select Committee of the House of Commons respecting the Public Records of the Kingdom* (London, 1812), 17, 19, 45.

[4] *Reports from a Select Committee of the House of Commons respecting the Public Records, 1800–1819* (London, 1820), Second Report, Appendix V, 518.

a common practice for manuscripts or documents from the Augmentation Office to be requisitioned by auditors and other officials having need of them or to be exhibited as evidence in the law courts. Many of them, of course, were not returned to their original home. Similarly, deeds, evidences, accounts, court rolls, and various types of muniments related to crown property were often sent to purchasers of crown lands. Needless to say, a great number were never recovered. Many were destroyed, some remained in private hands, while still others strayed into foreign collections or were eventually acquired by public libraries.[5] The *Reports* of the Historical Manuscripts Commission reveal numerous instances of isolated manuscripts which can be traced back to Augmentation origins.

The Augmentation Office repository was placed under the general administration of the Pipe Office in the Exchequer, but more specifically it was controlled by a clerk, or keeper, who was appointed by the clerk of the pipe.[6] Originally the records were housed in an "ancient and inconvenient" brick building in St. Margaret's Lane, near New Palace Yard, Westminster, adjacent to the Exchequer. Upon its demolition in 1793, however, they were removed to a more substantial structure known as the Stone Tower near Westminster Hall, where they were arranged in five large rooms, just over the records of the King's Bench Treasury; there they remained until the fire of October 16, 1834, which destroyed both houses of parliament and imperiled all the nearby buildings. In the confusion that ensued frantic attempts were made to protect the threatened Augmentation Office records from any possible damage. The extent to which the archives were endangered remains a moot question, though the building in which they were stored actually adjoined the old house of commons. The fact remains that their keeper, Sir Henry Cole, thought that they were in great jeopardy and had all of them carried to the safety of an adjacent church. These exciting events are recorded in his own words:

> The fire broke out about 7 p. m.: it was caused by the over-heating of flues, in burning the wooden tallies of many centuries belonging to the Exchequer, when, as Jack Cade says, "our forefathers had no other books than the score and the tally." I was fetched by Peter Paul, a workman engaged in the repair of the

---

[5] Warrants, lists, and memoranda concerning the delivery of records from the Augmentation Office. Exch., K. R., Miscellanea, 12/9; Augm. Office, Misc. Books 472, fol. 78; Augm. Office (E. 324), Warrants for the Delivery of Records.

[6] Sometimes the clerk of the Pipe Office retained the keepership of the Augmentation Office in his own hands. Beginning in 1554 with Christopher Smyth, the latter had a long list of keepers of whom Thomas Madox, John Caley, and Sir Henry Cole were the most prominent. On the earlier keepers, see p. 440, *supra*.

records, who was attached to the Augmentation Office, and I found that the office was threatened by the fire. With the aid of the Guards and policemen, I moved the whole of the Records into St. Margaret's Church during the night, and in a few months they were sorted, re-arranged, and placed in safer circumstances than they had been before in the memory of man.[7]

Nevertheless, overzealous hands can be responsible sometimes for what otherwise would pass as wanton destruction. During that hurried removal to the choir loft of St. Margaret's Church nearby some documents were lost or destroyed, while others were torn, watermarked, or even trodden under foot in the excitement of the moment. It was reported in parliament that the records " were all thrown out of the windows, to be preserved from the ravages of fire by the mire of Palace-yard, and soaked by water from the fire-mains." [8] Still, the damage was not irreparable; after weeks of drying, cleaning, and repairing the documents, the Augmentation Office was restored to its normal order. Prior to that time, however, when the office of clerk of the pipe was abolished in 1833,[9] the records of the sub-department had been put under the jurisdiction of the Office of King's Remembrancer. With the death of the last keeper, John Caley, in April, 1834, the Augmentation Office was officially declared defunct.[10] Thereafter the keepership was under the appointment of the king's remembrancer, being in fact exercised by a deputy keeper. The office remained unchanged in status until its final absorption into the Public Record Office in the 1850's.

The circumstances attending Caley's death gave rise to a bitter altercation between the record commissioners and the king's remembrancer of the Exchequer, Henry William Vincent. When the keepership was thus vacated, the question of its status immediately arose since there was no longer a clerk of the pipe to appoint a successor.[11] C. P. Cooper,

[7] Henry Cole, *Fifty Years of Public Work* (London, 1884), I, 8.

[8] The speech of Charles Buller in the house of commons on the condition of the public records, 1836. Buller went on to remark that records made admirable rat-traps. " It was astonishing the quantity of remains of rats which were found amongst the records," he explained. " On one occasion the skeleton of a cat had been found amongst them." *Ibid.*, II, Appendix I, 85.

[9] (August 29, 1833) " An Act for facilitating the Appointment of Sheriffs, and the more effectual Audit and passing of their Accounts; . . . and to abolish certain Offices in the Court of Exchequer." 3 and 4 William IV, c. 99, secs. xli and xlv, *Statutes at Large*, XIII, 505–12. This act became effective in October, 1833.

[10] *Report of the Select Committee of the House of Commons on the Record Commission* (London, 1836), 29, 447.

[11] The control of the Augmentation Office by the clerk of the pipe had ended the previous year, with the abolition of that office, but the parliamentary act failed to mention specifically either the keepership or the records of the Augmentation Office.

the secretary to the board of commissioners then engaged in an investigation of the public records, took upon himself to appoint Henry Cole as overseer of the Augmentation Office, though the appointment proved to be of short duration. An ensuing quarrel between the two men led to Cole's dismissal, at which time the keys to the office were turned over to the king's remembrancer. Vincent, in turn, had designated Thomas Adlington as the new keeper on the grounds that the Augmentation Office records had the same status as the other documents of the Pipe. The board refused to yield its claim, however, until it was ruled that the custody of the office lay in the Remembrancer's Division of the Exchequer.[12]

Some ten years later, on February 8, 1843, the master of the rolls ordered the Augmentation Office records to be removed from their previous quarters in St. Margaret's Church, where they had been in temporary storage since the fire of 1834. During the following spring the transfer to a new home in Carlton Ride was accomplished under the supervision of Joseph Hunter, who as assistant keeper of the Public Records Office had been in charge of those records since November of 1841.[13] Carlton Ride, formerly a riding academy attached to Carlton House, had nothing to recommend it as a storage building, save its spaciousness and possibly the fact that it was already half empty.[14] Nevertheless, this huge shell was soon converted into what was really a makeshift clearinghouse, pending the erection of a permanent building. Thus it was that Carlton Ride became at once a storage depot and repair shop where blocks of records were mended, classified, and bound, preparatory to transference elsewhere.

Actually, the parliamentary provision that all public records should

---

Consequently, these records were not immediately absorbed by the Office of the King's Remembrancer, as were those of the Pipe and other Exchequer departments abolished by the act, but were left under Caley's direction pending a legal clarification of their future custodianship.

[12] *Report of the Select Committee of the House of Commons on the Record Commission* (presented in August, 1836), xvii, 10, 29, 30, 133–35.

[13] *Third Report of the Deputy Keeper of the Public Records*, pt. 1, p. 4; pt. 2, p. 6; *Fourth Report*, 11–12; *Fifth Report*, 2. At that time the group of records known as "Topographica" were transferred from the Augmentation Office to the Office of Queen's Remembrancer. This removal to Carlton Ride, in effect, marked the termination of the Augmentation Office as a separate repository. *Fifth Report*, Appendix I, 1. Upon receipt of the records in 1841, Hunter reported them to be "generally in very good condition."

[14] The building was used for the storage of old Carlton House furniture, which was subsequently put in the loft, together with an old stove constituting the only heat in the place. Eventually the furniture was taken away, but only after protest had been lodged against the quite obvious fire hazards. Cf. Cole, *Fifty Years of Public Work*, I, 19–22.

be brought together at some definite place under the jurisdiction of the master of the rolls had already been passed, in August, 1838, but various delays had postponed the implementation of the act.[15] Work on the new repository finally began in 1851, though the first unit of the structure was not completed until 1856. Nominally under the master of the rolls, the Public Record Office was staffed by a deputy keeper of the records and a number of assistant keepers, each of whom was given jurisdiction over certain categories of records. Among the many scattered divisions of records to be centralized in the new national archives building was the Augmentation Office series, which having been kept intact as a distinct collection was finally moved from Carlton Ride in 1856 and 1857 and taken to the repository in Chancery Lane.[16] With the abandonment of its old premises the Office henceforth continued in name only as one of the several important categories of Exchequer documents.

In spite of the vicissitudes of three centuries of abuse, the Augmentations records were surprisingly well preserved when acquired by the Public Record Office.[17] Indeed they had fared far better than many of the other great collections, though this was due more to luck than to design.[18] Reporting in 1836 Charles Buller's select committee of the house of commons found the conditions in the Stone Tower—the old Augmentation Office building—rather worse than they had been during

---

[15] "An Act for keeping safely the Public Records," 1 and 2 Victoria, c. 94, *Statutes at Large*, XIV, pt. 3, 883–86. The act was subsequently amended by 40 and 41 Victoria, c. 55, and 61 and 62 Victoria, c. 12.

[16] *First Report of the Deputy Keeper of the Public Records*, I, 27b, 107a. A list of Augmentation Office records removed from Carlton Ride and Stone Tower to the new repository, showing their place of deposit on December 31, 1858, is presented in the *Twentieth Report*, Appendix, 77–92.

[17] The excellent condition of the Augmentations records was in part the result of the earlier care given them by conscientious custodians like the legalist and anti-quarian, Thomas Madox, and Henry Cole; this was especially true of the latter, who gave special attention to the mending, sorting, and classification of those records. Madox himself bears testimony to the condition of the Office in 1718: "The most useful Records of this Office are in tolerable Order, but there are many others which were never yet Digested and Methodized. Several small Necessaries are wanting to wit, Parchment Covers for many of the Records; Canvas to make New Bags instead of the Old ones, most of which are rotted; New Bindings of several Parchment Books of Enrollments, Wooden Boxes, and other small Things." Report of Thomas Madox, presented February 14, 1718. *The Report of the Lords Committee appointed to View the Public Records* (London, 1719), 56.

[18] During the previous century when considerable attention had been given to the cleaning, sorting, and arranging of the records of the department of receipt in the Exchequer, the Augmentation Office records seem to have been ignored completely. See *Calendar of Treasury Books and Papers, 1729–1730*, I, 348, 401–402, 458. The several reports of John Lawson and Richard Morley, successively appointed to digest and classify the Exchequer documents, are presented in this and later volumes.

the previous century. Reliable witnesses testified that the rooms were dark and dirty, subject to ridiculous fire hazards, and inadequately secured. In the absence of any required attendance of the custodians, no one lived near the repository nor was any particular interest shown in the preservation of its valuable contents. That searchers were not permitted to enter the premises to inspect documents, for which privilege they had already liberally paid, is quite understandable for an archives " as dirty as a chimney-sweeper's room." One informant pointed out that the Office " had long been in a filthy state; it is possible that when the operation of cleansing the Records commenced, the rooms may have been so encumbered as to render order and neatness scarcely attainable; but it has long been unnecessary to leave the Records on the floor, or to permit the workmen to tread them underfoot when engaged in picking out those which might merit repair; and it was slovenly to leave heaps of dirt in the chimnies, to be blown over the bound books and cleansed Records every time the doors were opened." [19]

Left to his own devices, John Caley probably contributed more to the deplorable neglect of the Augmentation Office than did all of his predecessors put together. During his tenure in office the records were in complete disorder, being in such confusion that hours were wasted in the locating of documents. Manuscripts were bound together with regard neither to date nor content, inaccurately labeled, and separated from their seals, which were used to make wax reproductions for his private collection.[20] Still more reprehensible was Caley's assumption that the records entrusted to his care could be used as personal property, to be exploited for his own gain. Since his clerk performed the work of the office, he seldom put in an appearance there, preferring instead the profitable use of the records in his own home at Spa Fields. The occasion for this peculiar arrangement was the practice, prevalent at the time, of requiring regular fees for the examination or transcription of all public documents, irrespective of the reliability of the investigator or the nature of the search. Considering the excessive costs of private research, it is not at all surprising that original sources were seldom consulted except by corporations, public departments, and the legal profession.

A modern scholar, accustomed to the courtesies of public officials and to the generous regulations established by national archives, would be

---

[19] *Report of the Select Committee of the House of Commons on the Record Commission*, viii, xvi, xvii.

[20] In addition to accumulating a large library, Caley also acquired a valuable collection of casts of seals. The original seals, detached from conventual leases and other Augmentations documents, were retained by him for convenience in copying and making casts. Gordon Goodwin, " John Caley," in *D. N. B.*

appalled by the obstacles imposed on an early nineteenth century investigator. The fees were excessive, and the difficulties encountered were sometimes almost insurmountable. Having applied for permission to examine a particular Augmentation Office document, a petitioner would then have to await the convenience of the keeper, who meantime would have ordered all the volumes, rolls, and bags most likely to contain the manuscript to be brought to his house. This was, in fact, not only a help to Caley but a necessity, since all indexes and other research aids were retained at Spa Fields in his own library. Other hindrances might arise, as when an untrained servant fetched the wrong lot of records and had to go back for another, which entailed still further delay before the search could begin. Finally, the reference located, the applicant had to content himself with the keeper's findings, for he had played no part in the quest; nor was he usually permitted to do more than examine the originals. If abstracts or transcriptions were required, they were furnished by the keeper for what amounted practically to discretionary charges.[21]

Although the cleansing and repair work on the records was halted for a short period after Caley's death, most of the abuses in the office were eradicated under the new regime. Under the supervision of competent, responsible Public Record Office officials the exploitation of what had become virtually a sinecural office ceased,[22] and the indexing and

[21] There had always been charges for the examination or copying of records in the Augmentation Office, based on the schedule of rates allowable in the chancery, but Caley charged fees *ad libitum*, beyond all reason. The scale was a variable one, ranging from 1*s.* 6*d.* per folio of seventy-two words for a copy or extract from the records up to £1 1*s.* for any one day, but not less than 8*s.* 8*d.* was charged for any one search regardless of the time consumed. For the examination or re-examination of a document, as certified by the keeper, the charges fluctuated from 2*s.* to 13*s.* 4*d.* When the applicant was only permitted to look at a document the fee was still 8*s.* 8*d.* In some instances the fees for cases concerning peerages were quite unreasonable; later, on good authority, it was reported that single fees were not infrequently a guinea or two, irrespective of the time wasted during the transaction. Nevertheless, despite excessive charges, Caley took in an average of £199 9*s.* 5⅓*d.* per annum for a three-year period shortly before his death. *General Report to the King in Council from the Honourable Board of Commissioners on the Public Records* (London, 1831), Appendix, 209–10; *Report of the Select Committee of the House of Commons on the Record Commission*, 59.

[22] Ostensibly Caley had received no regular salary for the Augmentation Office keepership beyond the normal profits derived from fees nor for the custodianship of the records in the ancient treasury at Westminster (formerly the Chapter House records), which he had enjoyed since 1818. Moreover, in addition to these two lucrative positions, he was also given a special assignment as sub-commissioner of superintending the repair and binding of the records under his charge. His fixed salary was only £200 per year, but there was an understanding with the commission that it should be made up in one way or another to not less than 500 guineas. *Ibid.*, 33.

calendaring of Augmentations materials proceeded anew. No longer were calendars considered to be the personal property of their custodians, nor was departmental time consumed in personal undertakings.[23] Fees for the use of original materials, once a major concern of custodians of records, came to be less important than the preservation and accessibility of the documents themselves. In this, as in other respects, the Augmentations records profited from the general policy of the Public Record Office. A few changes in the earlier regulations were introduced before the end of the century, but free and unrestricted access to the records did not come until 1909, when the present system of issuing " student tickets " or research permits to readers was inaugurated.[24] The public response was manifest almost immediately. The policy went into effect on the first of March; within ten months 733 student tickets had been issued. By 1949 the total of " Literary students " working at the Public Record Office had mounted to over 12,700.[25]

There is no record of the number of people using the Augmentations documents during the earlier periods, but they were probably as much in demand as the other categories of records. Actually, the testimony of those in a position to know the facts varied appreciably. Caley reported in 1800 that the Office was used by the public only occasionally, whereas some thirty years later the deputy keeper of the records in the Tower could observe quite differently on the use of Augmentations documents. In the light of his own experience with public records he wrote : " there is no Record Office, excepting the Rolls Chapel, to which such continual resort is had for Searches and Copies of Records; and these on subjects of the greatest importance, as connected with Tithe Suits, and

[23] Caley had refused to release the Augmentation calendars on the grounds that they were the personal property of the keeper. The board of commissioners negotiated with him for the purchase of the volumes but failed to reach a satisfactory agreement. When his library was finally liquidated, the twenty-five volumes of manuscript indexes sold for £225; his special collection of approximately 1,500 drawings of seals of English, Welsh, Scottish, and Norman monasteries brought £290. The impressions of those seals, made from Augmentations originals, were sold separately. " The Obituary of John Caley, Esq.," in *Gentleman's Magazine*, New Series, II (July-December, 1834), 320–21.

[24] *Seventy-first Report of the Deputy Keeper of the Public Records* (London, 1910), 2. Free research for literary purposes was tried in 1860, with "cards of admission," but soon discontinued. Again in 1866 fees were abolished for certain classes of documents but were reinstated in 1887. Although fees may still be charged in a few departments, most records prior to 1842 are now open to the public.

[25] *Guide to the Public Records* (London, 1949), Part I, 48–50. The original distinction between "literary" and "non-literary" research had become purely fictional.

where Parties derive their Titles, through the Crown, to possessions parcel of a dissolved religious House, or an attainted Person." [26]

Whatever the truth regarding the use of these records, the total amount of fees collected for any given year gives some indication of their popularity. In spite of the fact that the Office was in a disgraceful condition, " dirty and dark, and anything but what it should be," the profits from it increased from an average of £130 per year in 1778 to more than £199 in 1830.[27] The larger part of such fees came from the legal profession, by whom Augmentations materials were used as evidence in court or in the determination of land abstracts and titles. It was not until more recent times when interest in the Reformation stimulated intensive researches in the Dissolution activities that the records of the Augmentation Office became better known to historical students.

During the long years of peregrination, the contents of the Office were subjected from time to time to numerous changes, and in the arrangement and reclassification at the hands of many custodians, both individual items and entire categories of documents have been added to or withdrawn from the original nucleus bequeathed to the Exchequer in 1554. However, the acquisitions were much more numerous than the losses, for most of the land and revenue records pertaining to the crown demesne, formerly administered by the Court of Augmentations, were retained by the Exchequer as long as the reconstituted department of Receipt continued to function " augmentation-wise." [28] Thereafter, new materials, often foreign to the nature of the collection, were added continually; such additions were accepted through inadvertence or because they formed a logical part of a larger series already acquired. Nevertheless, curious examples of inconsistency occasionally occur, and isolated cases of completely irrelevant matter may be found.

Of the thirty classes of the Public Records Office manuscripts and documents presently classified as records of the Augmentation Office,[29]

---

[26] *Privately Printed Tracts on the Record Commission,* of which the first is a tract by William Illingworth, deputy keeper of the public records in the Tower, written in May, 1831: " Observations on the Public Records of the Four Courts at Westminster . . . ," 1–67. On the Augmentation Office, see pp. 55–61, especially 58. Caley was apparently trying to minimize the extent of his profits derived from searches among the Augmentations records. His report in September, 1832, showed that for attendance with a document at the Exchequer he received £1, 1s. per day. For a search of over three hours in the Augmentation Office, a similar fee was charged. *General Report to the King in Council from the Honourable Board of Commissioners on the Public Records,* Appendix (G. 19), 207–10.

[27] *Ibid.,* 210–12.

[28] Chapter Thirteen, pp. 437–39, *supra.*

[29] (P. R. O.) Class List of Records of the Court of Augmentations (Literary Search Room; unpublished), E. 301 to E. 330. The calendars and indexes for the

only a few series strictly appertain to the work of the original Court. Those categories most closely related to its history are the forty-six bundles of the Proceedings in the Court of Augmentations (E. 321), the Treasurers' Rolls of Accounts (E. 323), the mass of uncalendared and unclassified materials known as Miscellanea (42 bundles or boxes, E. 314),[30] and the series of bound volumes now labeled Miscellaneous Books (E. 315). Further, a number are directly concerned with the varied activities of the Court, such as Accounts of Wood Sales (E. 325), Deeds of Surrender of religious houses and chantries (E. 322; 278 vols.), Particulars for Grants of Lands and Offices (E. 316),[31] Enrollments and Particulars for Leases (E. 309 and E. 310), Conveyances of Crown Lands (E. 304), and Particulars for Grants (E. 318 and E. 319).

These series, however, constitute only a small portion of the total extant records of the institution. Augmentations warrants, commissions, administrative orders and directives, ministers' accounts, surveys, indentures, recognizances, receipts, decrees, interrogatories, depositions, memoranda, and other items of court procedure are widely scattered among other collections of documents, often entirely unrelated to the history of the Court itself. Such important items as commission returns, special surveys, letters of officials, or even accounts of the treasurer may turn up in the most unexpected places.[32] Whereas one would expect to find all the accounts of the collectors and receivers of the Augmentations among the Miscellaneous Books where some of them are preserved, many are found in the general series of Ministers' Accounts (S. C. 6) and in the third series of the Exchequer, L. R., Receivers' Accounts (L. R. 12).

More significant to the history of the Court than all of these, however, is the series of bound volumes classified as the Augmentation Office,

---

group comprise forty-three large manuscript volumes, some of which individually extend into several books or "parts."

[30] Like most of the other classes, the Miscellanea contain many sections unrelated to the history of the Court. Unfortunately the material in the last two boxes of this series, entirely Augmentations documents, is so decayed and pulverized as to be of little value. In one of these boxes, 314/38, there are a number of privy seals for the Court of Wards and Liveries.

[31] This series is mislabeled as Particulars for Grants of Offices, though many of the earlier ones are particulars for leases. Covering the period from Henry VIII to Charles II, in 23 boxes, they still remain unindexed and unclassified. Those rolls for the reigns of Henry VIII, Edward VI, and Mary are leases by the Court of Augmentations.

[32] Among the Miscellaneous Enrolled Accounts of the lord treasurer's remembrancer of the Exchequer is a long account of the treasurer of the Augmentations for the end of Edward VI's reign (E. 358/22), 35 membranes. Similarly, the State Paper Office occasionally acquired the treasurer's Declarations of Account (S. P. 10/18, no. 14 and S. P. 11/1, no. 13).

Miscellaneous Books. Classification and binding in book form of related materials in the Augmentation Office was begun early in the nineteenth century under the direction of the record commission of the house of commons.[33] Nevertheless, the first attempts in that direction by John Caley were not altogether successful, since miscellaneous documents and manuscripts were sometimes brought together without reference to date or character; but in the expert hands of Public Record Office officials many of the original errors in indexing and classifying were in time corrected. The 524 volumes of Miscellaneous Books, still inadequately indexed and calendared, now constitute the largest and most important single collection of all the Augmentations records.[34]

A number of these volumes have been indexed and calendared, making certain classes of documents more serviceable to the scholar. Thus, useful indexes are now available for enrollments of letters patent and indentures, monastic pensions, inventories of church goods, rentals and surveys, particulars for the sale of colleges and chantries, and *cartae miscellaneae*.[35] A great many, such as books of inventories, leases, pen-

---

[33] This commission was renewed six times and sat continuously from 1800 to 1831, expiring finally in 1837. It reported over fifty species of records in the Augmentation Office in 1800, arranged only alphabetically, for which about twenty volumes of indexes already had been made at governmental expense, in addition to the private indexes retained by Caley for his own use. In some two hundred bags, miscellaneous records of many different kinds were thrown together without any pretense at logical arrangement. Once under way, reparation and binding proceeded rapidly after 1819; as many as 397 volumes of bound documents were available by 1832, principally charters, surveys, rentals, court rolls, inventories, certificates, and ministers' accounts, including approximately 5,000 ancient charters and deeds. *Reports from the Select Committee Appointed to Inquire into the State of the Public Records of the Kingdom* (July 4, 1800), Appendix (G. 19a), 210–12; a report on the Augmentation Office submitted by John Caley on September 15, 1832, in the *General Report to the King in Council from the Honourable Board of Commissioners on the Public Records*, Appendix (G. 19), 207–10.

[34] (P. R. O.) *Lists and Indexes*, 42/3 (Literary Search Room; London, 1892–) A complete list of the Miscellaneous Books, inadequately described and often mislabeled, is given in Giuseppi, *A Guide to the Manuscripts preserved in the Public Record Office*, I, 144–59. Volumes 209–18, 232–36, 248–55, 331, 442, and 456 are calendared in *L. and P.*

[35] Misc. Books 29–54 form part of a large collection within the Augmentation Office, earlier classified as *Cartae Antiquae, Cartae Miscellaneae*, and *Cartae Selectae*. These deeds were formerly scattered in several repositories before they were acquired by the Augmentation Office, many of them being originally records of the Court of Augmentations. They are chiefly conveyances of land, some dating back to the Norman period, but the collection also includes agreements, wills, bonds, acquittances, and other instruments related to private transactions from the twelfth to the sixteenth centuries. Most of these deeds concern either monastic possessions or the ancient estates of the crown, though many relate to claims presented in the Augmentations and other courts of law as evidences of title. The volumes of this series are listed and analyzed in Calendars and Prescriptive Catalogues. See Press 5/43C to 5/43L in the Literary Search Room.

sions, surveys, warrants, and ministers' accounts, as well as records of wood sales and rentals, illustrate the activities of the Court, while other volumes deal more specifically with internal Augmentations problems and court procedure. The Enrollment Books of leases, bills, indentures, and grants of offices, pensions, and annuities (volumes 209–25, 232–36, and 238–42), Recognizances and Obligations (volumes 327, 352), the Books of Payments (volumes 249–62),[36] and the nine volumes of Miscellaneous Letters and Papers (volumes 472–80)[37] all relate directly to administrative or financial matters. The voluminous judicial Proceedings of the Augmentations are mostly records of orders and decrees, commissions, interrogatories, complaints, answers, and depositions (volumes 20, 23, 91–105, 108–34, 165, 328, 436, and 516–22) which are intermixed with numerous legal instruments of a similar nature for the Court of General Surveyors. Finally, a few additional volumes yield further information on isolated aspects of Augmentations activities.[38]

Owing to the close relation between the Court of General Surveyors and the Court of Augmentations, the records of the two institutions have been hopelessly mixed up by custodians who had little knowledge of the original jurisdiction of the two courts. Nor was the confusion due as much to carelessness as to the striking similarity of their records, since frequently the only possible differentiation between them depended on a minute acquaintance with the revenues and personnel of each or with minor differences in administrative technique. Obviously, the various steps in the procedure of hearing cases were practically identical in both courts, so that comparable records are all but indistinguishable. Isolated documents of the Court of General Surveyors turn up repeatedly among the records of the Augmentations, and most of the extant records of the former court are found within the Augmentation Office classification. Besides innumerable other classes of documents, twenty odd of the Mis-

---

[36] Misc. Books 248, the first of the series of fifteen volumes described in Giuseppi as Books of Payments, is an account book by Tristram Teshe for attainted lands in the Court of General Surveyors. Giuseppi, *A Guide to the Manuscripts preserved in the Public Record Office*, I, 151.

[37] These miscellaneous papers are chiefly reports of auditors and other officials in the Augmentations and Exchequer, together with original warrants, bills, receipts, and memoranda covering the reigns of Henry VIII, Edward VI, Mary, and Elizabeth. Some relate to the work of the Augmentation Office under Christopher Smyth (volumes 477–78). Volume 476 contains documents as late as 1698.

[38] Especially grants of local offices (volumes 157–58), memoranda concerning accounts (volumes 264–67), bills of acquittances (volume 1), an appearance book (volume 3), and copies of acts of parliament relating to the work of the Court (volume 2). A copy of the letters patent creating the second Court of Augmentations in 1547 is contained in volume 17. Privy seals of the Court are collected in volume 331, and volumes 336–39, 341–44, 346, and 348–49 contain the ledgers of receipts of the treasurer of the Augmentations.

cellaneous Books are materials which at one time belonged to the Court of General Surveyors.[39]

As in other series of Augmentation Office records a large number of the Miscellaneous Books are only remotely connected with the main theme of the class, namely accounts of crown lands and revenues and subsidiary documents relating thereto. However, such items as household books, chamber payments, army and navy accounts, and presentments of concealed lands are found there probably because of the earlier links between the institutions they belonged to and the Court of General Surveyors or the Court of Augmentations. Less explicable is the presence of accounts of the stannary courts in Devon and Cornwall, customs accounts, declarations of the revenues of Queen Anne of Denmark, certificates of musters, royal charters, and miscellaneous Exchequer documents for the late sixteenth and seventeenth centuries. Not illogically the Parliamentary Surveys for the period of the Restoration were transferred to this Office by the clerk of the pipe, where they were calendared in 1764. Wholly irrelevant are certain manuscripts which have inadvertently found their way into this series, including the interesting fifteenth-century treatise on conveyancing and an inquiry into the fees and allowances of English courts in 1634.[40] Since the Augmentations acquired the muniments as well as the estates of the dissolved monasteries, valuable collections of title deeds and other records were preserved virtually intact. Notable among such unique collections is that of the famous Sion abbey in Middlesex, suppressed by Cromwell in 1540.[41]

More interesting to students of administrative history are the three volumes of navy accounts for the reigns of Henry VII and Henry VIII, which include two early account books of the keeper or clerk of the king's ships. These not only yield valuable material on such royal vessels as the *Sovereign*, the *Regent*, the *Sweepstake*, and the *Mary Fortune*, but they

---

[39] Proceedings and decrees in the Court of General Surveyors, Misc. Books 19, 21–22, 106, 516–22 (miscellaneous examples); leases, *ibid.* 230; and records of attainted lands, *ibid.* 7–13, 248, 288, 298–99, 304, 307, and 384. Two minute books of the Court have survived in *ibid.* 313A and 313B; also, a Calendar of decrees for 34–38 Henry VIII is available in the *Thirtieth Report of the Deputy Keeper of the Public Records*, Appendix, 166–96. Cf. Chapter Eleven, n. 29. Many of the E. 321 series, which are classified as Proceedings in the Court of Augmentations, and the Augmentation Office, Miscellanea (E. 314) are in reality documents relating to the office or Court of General Surveyors.

[40] Augm. Office, Misc. Books 329 and 330.

[41] The Augmentation Office records of the abbey were noted in Thomas Tanner, *Notitia Monastica* (London, 1744) and in Dugdale, *Monasticon Anglicanum*. Accounts of Sion lands and property prior to the Dissolution are found among the Ministers' Accounts (S. C. 6/7177–7236). See also Auditors of Land Revenue, Misc. Books 112; Exch. of Receipt, Misc. Books 152; and Augm. Office, Misc. Books 436.

also reveal that a total of £2,061 18s. 7d. was spent on the construction of a dry dock at Portsmouth.[42]

As already indicated, the combined land and revenue records of the Court of General Surveyors and the Court of Augmentations bridge much of the Middle Ages, especially in the complete series of monastic cartularies, title deeds, court rolls, and accounts of land and land revenues under the survey of the crown. However, just as the Augmentation Office became a convenient catchall for miscellaneous documents of a much later period dealing with similar matters, so many portions of what were once properly Augmentations archives have been widely dispersed. Large sections of Exchequer records, Ministers' Accounts, Ancient Deeds, and various classes of records now classified as belonging to the Office of the Land Revenue are examples, to mention only a few.[43] Equally important for the sixteenth century is the series of enrollments of leases, particulars for grants of crown lands, accounts of attainted lands, particulars for the sale of colleges and chantries, accounts of wood sales, and grants of pensions and annuities. Even within the scope of the Court's jurisdiction the large collections of land surveys, surveys of woods, and commission returns by Augmentations ministers present a full cross section of the Tudor demesne.

Although the surviving records are largely centralized in one place, a number of Augmentation Office volumes and many individual documents and manuscripts have strayed into other national and private collections.[44] Most of these are records of the Office rather than of the Court, yet a few are related to aspects of Augmentations development. In the Ex-

---

[42] Augm. Office, Misc. Books 315–317. The second of these, "parcells of thaccompts of Robert Brygandyne" for the period May, 1495, to December, 1497, has been printed in Michael Oppenheim (ed.), *Naval Accounts and Inventories of the Reign of Henry VII* (London, 1896).

[43] For particulars of such categories of dispersed Augmentation Office records, see Lewis and Davies (eds.), *Records of the Court of Augmentations Relating to Wales and Monmouthshire*, Introduction, x–xi.

[44] Among the valuable Manchester Manuscripts, three or four thousand in number (G. D. 15), acquired by the Public Record Office in 1880, are 112 items relating to the first Court of Augmentations, covering the years 1536 to 1539. These particular manuscripts, originally in the private possession of Sir Richard Rich, the first chancellor of the Augmentations, were retained by the Rich family and passed on to the dukes of Manchester through subsequent marriage. The documents are of a varied nature, being principally warrants and orders of the Court, declarations of monastic plate delivered to the mint for coinage, charges for surveys of woods, receipts, miscellaneous accounts, copies of court decrees, and itemized expense accounts of Augmentations ministers. The latter are of especial interest, since they contain an abundance of material on sixteenth century prices. The entire collection has been fully described in the *Eighth Report of the Royal Commission on Historical Manuscripts*, Appendix, Part II, especially pp. 20a–27a.

chequer, Accounts Various,[45] Miscellaneous Books (K. R.), Miscellanea
(K. R.), Memoranda Rolls (K. R.), and Duchy of Lancaster Division
all have materials pertinent to the Court, while other odd volumes have
been acquired by the British Museum. Among the latter should be mentioned Harleian Manuscripts 433, 605–608, and 1509–1511, Additional
Manuscripts 5063–5103, 21481, and 32469,[46] Royal Manuscripts 14. B.
XI, and scores of isolated manuscripts found within the Stowe, Arundel,
Lansdowne, and Cottonian collections.[47] Indeed a few documents have
strayed far afield, one to Wales [48] and two across the Atlantic to American libraries. The Widener Library acquired by purchase an isolated
Augmentations manuscript from a private collection relating to the
plunder of Abingdon abbey, which probably represents an account origi-
ally delivered from the Augmentation Office to a purchaser of monastic
lands.[49] Of more interest but greater uncertainty as to origin is the
Augmentations item found among the early sixteenth century manuscripts of the Folger Shakespeare Library in Washington, D. C. Prior
to its acquisition by the late H. C. Folger in 1923 there seems to be no
trace of the earlier history of the document. It is a bound manuscript
copy, made near the end of Elizabeth's reign, of the original letters patent
erecting the second Augmentations in January, 1547.[50]

More widely scattered and too numerous to list are the occasional
references to court procedure and court personnel hidden away in unsuspected places. Land surveys and wood sales of both the Court of

[45] Originally part of the "Ancient Miscellanea" of the Office of King's Remembrancer, the Accounts Various were sorted and reclassified during the period
1886–94. Large sections of them are really Augmentation Office documents, as those
relating to pensions, payments, and transcripts of accounts of the treasurer of the
Augmentations, warrants, receipts, and accounts of woodwards and wood sales.
For these and innumerable other items, see *Lists and Indexes*, XXXV (Press
7/117A).

[46] This rare volume is an evaluation of crown lands and revenues for 1541–42
under the survey of the Court of General Surveyors.

[47] Among the Additional Manuscripts are the Scudamore Papers (19 volumes),
of which Add. MS. 11041 consisting of the correspondence of John Scudamore,
receiver in the Court of Augmentations, is particularly revealing. Most of these
letters from Augmentations officials relate to the sale and exportation of the
"king's lead."

[48] A register of fees due to the crown for leases and patents out of the Court
of Augmentations. National Library of Wales, Aberystwyth, Peniarth MS. 34.
Likewise, the notebooks and memoranda books of the Floyd Collection contain
some materials relating to Wales, extracted from the Augmentation Office records.

[49] Harvard University, MS. Lat. 101. *Compotus Edmundi Powel*; paper, 26
folios, 1538.

[50] The Folger Shakespeare Library, 1174.4 (58 folios). See Seymour de Ricci,
Census of Medieval and Renaissance Manuscripts in the United States and Canada
(N. Y., 1935–40), I, 378. There are also several items in the Folger Library
relating to various officers of the Court.

General Surveyors and the Court of Augmentations are dispersed generally among the various series of Exchequer records; stray warrants and receipts of the Court or excerpts from original accounts may turn up in any of a number of unrelated collections.[51] The Patent Rolls and Close Rolls contain scores of grants and commissions pertaining to the Court, while odd rent rolls, ministers' accounts, and isolated receipts are discoverable in almost all the land and revenue record series for the period. Moreover, miscellaneous data on Augmentations personnel are almost inexhaustible. Excluding purely local and minor officials, many of the dozen or so leading officers of the Court were influential ministers, active in other governmental service or in court life. With respect to them the problem is one of overabundance rather than paucity of material. In fact it is sometimes hard to determine in just what capacity the individual minister was officiating, so varied were his many activities. A great deal of information on the work and career of most of the principal officials is available in the Acts and Proceedings of the Privy Council, Ministers' Accounts, the State Papers, and in the collections of manuscripts in the British Museum. With the exception of the treasurer, Sir Thomas Pope, biographies of none of the officials of the Augmentations have been written, though men like Sir Richard Rich, Sir Edward North, Sir Richard Sackville, and Sir Walter Mildmay ranked among the leading administrators of the period.[52]

A full section on the Augmentation Office records is being prepared for the forthcoming *Guide to the Public Records*,[53] by Professor J. Conway Davies, who has included as Augmentation Office materials several important classes of documents incorrectly classified in Giuseppi's *Guide*. Among other additions a large number of records of a miscellaneous character, heretofore unknown to the public, have been added to the existing collection.

[51] An Elizabethan list of officers in the Augmentations is held by the Library of the Society of Antiquaries of London, 205/7; and in addition to several general documents concerning the Court, the Bodleian Library, Oxford, has three interesting Augmentations items, viz.: extracts from ministers' accounts, extracts from deeds in the Court, and pensions payable out of the renovated Exchequer " to the late Incumbents of Religious Houses," 1553. Bodleian Library, Misc. MSS. 30694c., fol. 60; 5005, fol. 78d.; and 27657. Likewise, the Cambridge University Library has a manuscript copy of the articles of annexation of the Augmentations to the Exchequer, extracted from Mary's patent of January 24, 1554. MS. G. g. II. 7. A few isolated Augmentations items are also found among the Cecil Manuscripts preserved at Hatfield House.

[52] Thomas Warton, *The Life of Sir Thomas Pope, Founder of Trinity College, Oxford* (London, 1772). An inaccurate and highly colored biography, but withal a comprehensive account of his career, based on original sources. Cf. Herbert E. D. Blakiston, " Thomas Warton and Machyn's Diary," *E. H. R.*, XI (April, 1896), 282–300.

[53] The introductory volume of this new *Guide* appeared in 1949. Cf. p. 483, n. 25.

Appendix A

Officers of the Original Court of Augmentations at Westminster

		Annual Salary
1. Chancellor and principal officer	Sir Richard Rich Jointly { Sir Richard Rich Sir Edward North Sir Edward North	£300
2. Treasurer and second officer	Sir Thomas Pope Sir Edward North Jointly { Sir Edward North Sir John Williams Sir John Williams	£120 £300
3. Attorney and third officer	John Onley Robert Southwell (Fee increased £50 in March, 1540) Walter Henley	£ 40 £ 90
4. Solicitor and fourth officer	Robert Southwell Walter Henley (Fee increased £50 in March, 1540) Nicholas Bacon	£ 20 £ 70
5. Master of Woods (Office instituted in 1543)	Sir Thomas Pope	

APPENDIX A (Continued)

Officers of the Original Court of Augmentations at Westminster

No.	Office	Officer	Salary
6.	Surveyor of Woods (Office instituted in 1537)	William Cowper	£ 20
		Jointly { William Cowper, David Clayton, David Clayton, Geoffrey Gates	
7.	Clerk of the Court	Richard Duke	£ 10 Increased to £ 40
8.	Keeper of the records	Walter Farr (4d. per day)	£ 6 1s. 8d.
		Edward Stradbury (Permanent appointment for life, 18 May, 1547)	£ 10
9.	Usher of the Court	James Johnson (2d. per day)	£ 3 10d.
10.	Messengers of the Court	Original—Walter Skinner (4d. per day)	£ 6 1s. 8d.
		Later appointments { John Ward, pursuivant; Robert Makerell; Jasper Pounte; Henry Atkinson; Thomas Tyrrell, pursuivant	
11.	Chief mason of the Court	Robert Sylvester	£ 6 1s. 8d.
12.	Chief carpenter of the Court	John Parker	£ 6 1s. 8d.
13.	Surveyor and receiver-general of purchased lands	Geoffrey Chamber, George Wright	£ 20

Appendix A (Continued)

Officers of the Original Court of Augmentations at Westminster

14. Auditor of purchased lands	John Ashton	£ 20
	Richard Mody	
15. Receiver of wood sales	Walter Farr	£ 20
(Office instituted in 1543)	Richard Tyrrell	
16. Auditor of wood sales	Griffin Tyndale	£ 20
(Office instituted in 1543)	John Perte	
17. Seventeen particular receivers		£ 20 plus profits
18. Ten auditors of the court		£ 20 plus profits
19. Chief steward south of the River Trent	Thomas Howard, duke of Norfolk	£100
(Office instituted in May, 1536)	Nicholas Hare, deputy	£ 20
20. Chief steward north of the River Trent	Thomas Cromwell	£100
(Office instituted in February, 1538)	Henry Polsted, deputy	£ 20
	Thomas Audley, lord of Walden	£100
	John Lucas, deputy	£ 20
	Charles Brandon, duke of Suffolk	£100
	George St. Pole, deputy	£ 20
21. Office of auditor of the accounts of the treasurer of the Court	Two regular auditors appointed by the Court. Always William Berners, assisted by either John Wiseman or Robert Burgoyne	£ 40 (£20 each)
22. Attorney for the Augmentations in the Court of the Exchequer	Thomas Andrews	£ 5

Appendix B

FIELD OFFICERS OF THE SECOND COURT OF AUGMENTATIONS

---

1. Twelve county receivers.

2. Receiver-general of the duchy of Cornwall.

3. Twelve circuit auditors.

4. Auditor of the duchy of Cornwall.

5. Forty-four particular surveyors.

6. Thirty-six local woodwards.

7. Stewards and keepers of courts.

8. High steward, comptroller of the stannary, attorney, and other officers in the duchy of Cornwall.

9. Bailiffs, reeves, local receivers, and collectors of revenues.

10. Keepers of houses, castles, parks, forests, and chases.

BIBLIOGRAPHY

PUBLISHED WORKS

Arber, Edward (ed.). *Seven Sermons before Edward VI, on each Friday in Lent* (1549). (English Reprints, no. 2.) London, 1869.

Arber, Edward (ed.). *Thomas Lever's Sermons* (1550). (English Reprints, no. 25.) London, 1871.

Baker, Agnes C. *Abingdon Abbey: Some Notes on its History and Buildings*. Published by the Friends of Abingdon, 1949.

Baskerville, Geoffrey. *English Monks and the Suppression of the Monasteries*. London, 1937.

Batho, A. R. "The Finances of an Elizabethan Nobleman: Henry Percy, Ninth Earl of Northumberland," *Economic History Review*, Second Series, IX (April, 1957), 433–50.

Baumer, Franklin Le Van. *The Early Tudor Theory of Kingship*. New Haven, 1940.

Bell, H. E. *An Introduction to the History and Records of the Court of Wards and Liveries*. Cambridge, 1953.

Beresford, M. W. "The Common Informer, the Penal Statutes and Economic Regulations," *Economic History Review*, Second Series, X (December, 1957), 221–37.

Bickley, W. B. (tr.). *Survey of the Borough and Manor or Demesne Foreign of Birmingham*, with notes and introduction by Joseph Hill. C. Cooper and Co., undated.

Bickley, W. B. (tr.). *Abstract of Bailiffs' Accounts of Monastic and other Estates in the County of Warwick under the supervision of the Court of Augmentation for the year ending Michaelmas, 1547,* with an introduction by William Fowler Carter. Publications of the Dugdale Society, 1923.

Bindoff, S. T. *Tudor England.* (The Pelican History of England, Vol. V.) London, 1950.

Blakiston, Herbert E. D. " Thomas Warton and Machyn's Diary," *E. H. R.,* XI (April, 1896), 282–300.

Bohn, Henry G. (ed.). *The Works of the Right Honourable Edmund Burke.* 8 vols. (Bohn's British Classics.) London, 1846–62.

Borlase, William. *Observations on the Ancient and Present State of the Islands of Scilly.* Oxford, 1756.

Bowley, E. L. *The Fortunate Islands.* St. Mary's, Isles of Scilly, Cornwall, 1945.

Brinklow [Brinkelow], Henry. *Complaynt of Roderyck Mors, Somtyme a Gray Fryre, unto the Parliament Howse of England his Natural Cuntry: For the Redresse of Certen Wicked Lawes, Euel Customs, and Cruel Decreys* (1545), ed. J. M. Cowper. (Early English Text Society, Extra Series, no. 22.) London, 1874.

Brooks, F. W. *The Council of the North.* (The Historical Association, General Series: G. 25.) London, 1953.

Burnet, Gilbert. *The History of the Reformation of the Church of England.* A new revised edition by Nicholas Pocock. 7 vols. Oxford, 1865.

Bushby, Frances. *Three Men of the Tudor Time.* London, 1911.

Calendar of the Cecil Manuscripts Preserved at Hatfield House, ed. M. S. Giuseppi. 18 vols. or " Parts." London, 1883–1940; in progress.

Calendar of the Patent Rolls Preserved in the Public Record Office, Edward VI, 1547–1553, ed. R. H. Brodie. 5 vols. London, 1924–26. *Index,* 1929.

Calendar of the Patent Rolls Preserved in the Public Record Office, Philip and Mary, 1553–1558, ed. M. S. Giuseppi. 4 vols. London, 1936–39.

Calendar of the Patent Rolls Preserved in the Public Record Office, Elizabeth, 1558–1563, ed. J. H. Collingridge and R. B. Wernham. 2 vols. London, 1939–48; in progress.

Calendar of State Papers, Domestic Series, of the Reigns of Edward VI, Mary, Elizabeth, James I, Preserved in the State Paper Department of Her Majesty's Public Record Office, 1547–1625, ed. Robert Lemon and M. A. E. Green. 12 vols. London, 1856–72.

Calendar of State Papers, Domestic Series, of the Reign of Charles II,

Preserved in the State Paper Department of Her Majesty's Public Record Office, ed. M. A. E. Green, *et al.* (Vol. I, 1660–61; IV, 1664–65.) 28 vols. London, 1860–1939 [1947].

Calendar of Treasury Books and Papers Preserved in Her Majesty's Public Record Office, 1729–1745, ed. William A. Shaw. 5 vols. London, 1897–1903. Preceded by Joseph Redington (ed.), *Calendar of Treasury Papers, 1557–1728.* 6 vols.

Camden, William. *Britannica or a Chorographical Description of Great Britain and Ireland.* London, 1586. Trans. from the Latin, 1722 ed., 2 vols.

Campbell, John. *The Lives of the Lord Chancellors and Keepers of the Great Seal of England.* 8 vols. London, 1845–69.

Campbell, William (ed.). *Materials for a History of the Reign of Henry VII.* 2 vols. (Rolls Series, no. 60.) London, 1873, 1877.

Challenor, Bromley (ed.). *Selections from the Municipal Chronicles of the Borough of Abingdon, 1555–1897.* London, 1898.

Chambers, R. W. *Thomas More.* (Bedford Historical Series, Vol. II.) London, 1938.

Cheyney, Edward P. " The Court of Star Chamber," *A. H. R.,* XVIII (July, 1913), 727–50.

Clark, G. N. *The Wealth of England.* First pub., 1946. Home University Library. London, 1954.

Coate, Mary. " The Duchy of Cornwall: Its History and Administration, 1640–1660," *Transactions of the Royal Historical Society,* Fourth Series, X (April, 1927), 135–69.

Cobbett, William, T. B. Howell, *et al.* (eds.). *A Complete Collection of State Trials and Proceedings for High Treason and Other Crimes and Misdemeanors.* 42 vols. London, 1816–98.

Coke, Sir Edward. *Institutes of the Laws of England.* In four Parts or Institutes. London, 1628–44; 16th ed., London, 1809.

Coke, Sir Edward. *Law Reports. The English Reports.* 176 vols. Edinburgh, London, 1900–30.

Cole, Sir Henry. *Fifty Years of Public Work.* 2 vols. London, 1884.

Constant, G. *The Reformation in England.* Vol. I. *The English Schism: Henry VIII (1509–1547),* tr. the Rev. R. E. Scantlebury. London, 1934.

Constant, G. *The Reformation in England.* Vol. II. *Introduction of the Reformation into England: Edward VI (1547–1553),* tr. E. I. Watkin. London, 1942.

Cooper, J. P. " The Counting of Manors," *Economic History Review,* Second Series, VIII (April, 1956), 377–89.

Corrie, George Elwes (ed.). *Sermons and Remains of Hugh Latimer.*

2 vols. (The Parker Society Publications, Vols. XVI, XIX.) Cambridge, 1844–45.

Costin, W. C. and J. Steven Watson (eds.). *The Law and Working of the Constitution: Documents, 1660–1914.* 2 vols. London, 1952.

Cowper, J. M. (ed.). *The Select Works of Robert Crowley.* (Early English Text Society, Extra Series, no. 15.) London, 1872.

Cuttino, G. P. *English Diplomatic Administration, 1259–1339.* Oxford, 1940.

Dasent, Arthur Irwin. *The Speakers of the House of Commons.* London, 1911.

Dasent, Sir John R. (ed.). *Acts of the Privy Council of England.* New Series, 37 vols. London, 1890–1930.

Dawson, John P. "The Privy Council and Private Law in the Tudor and Stuart Periods," 48 *Michigan Law Review*, Part I (February, 1950), 393–428; Part II (March, 1950), 627–56.

Deputy Keeper of the Public Records, *Reports* [Annual]. London, 1840– .

Dickens, A. G. "The Edwardian Arrears in Augmentations Payments and the Problem of the Ex-Religious," *E. H. R.*, LV (July, 1940), 384–418.

Dictionary of National Biography, eds. Sir Leslie Stephen and Sir Sidney Lee. 63 vols. London, 1885–1900. *Supplement*, 3 vols., 1901; *Index and Epitome*, 1903; *Errata*, 1904; later *Supplements* for the twentieth century have been added.

Dietz, Frederick C. *Finances of Edward VI and Mary.* (Smith College Studies in History, Vol. III, no. 2.) Northampton, Mass., 1918.

Dietz, Frederick C. *English Government Finance, 1485–1558.* (University of Illinois Studies in the Social Sciences, Vol. IX, no. 3.) Urbana, Ill., 1920.

Dietz, Frederick C. *The Exchequer in Elizabeth's Reign.* (Smith College Studies in History, Vol. VIII, no. 2.) Northampton, Mass., 1923.

Dietz, Frederick C. *English Public Finance, 1558–1641.* New York, 1932.

Dietz, Frederick C. "Elizabethan Customs Administration," *E. H. R.*, XLV (January, 1930), 35–58.

Ditchfield, P. H. and William Page (eds.). *A History of Berkshire.* 4 vols. (The Victoria History of the Counties of England, ed. William Page.) London, 1906–24.

Dixon, Richard W. *History of the Church of England from the Abolition of the Roman Jurisdiction.* 6 vols. Oxford, 1895–1903.

Doddridge, John. *The History of the Ancient and Modern Estate of* the Principality of Wales, Duchy of Cornwall, and Earldom of Chester. London, 1630.

Dodds, Madeleine Hope and Ruth Dodds. *The Pilgrimage of Grace, 1536–1537, and the Exeter Conspiracy, 1538.* 2 vols. Cambridge, 1915.

Dugdale, Sir William. *Monasticon Anglicanum.* New ed. by John Caley, Henry Ellis, and Bulkeley Bandinel. 6 vols. London, 1817–30.

Dunham, William H. " Henry VIII's Whole Council and Its Parts," *Huntington Library Quarterly,* VII (November, 1943), 7–46.

Dyer, Sir James. *Reports of Cases.* Dublin, 1794.

Elton, G. R. " Informing for Profit: A Sidelight on Tudor Methods of Law-Enforcement," *Cambridge Historical Journal,* XI (1954), 149–67. The *Cambridge Historical Journal* became the *Historical Journal* in 1958.

Elton, G. R. *The Tudor Revolution in Government: Administrative Changes in the Reign of Henry VIII.* Cambridge, 1953.

Emmison, F. G. " A Plan of Edward VI and Secretary Petre for Reorganizing the Privy Council's Work, 1552–1553," *Bulletin of the Institute of Historical Research,* XXXI (November, 1958), 203–10.

English Reports: Full Reprint. 176 vols. Edinburgh, 1900–30. *Index,* 2 vols. London, 1932.

Fanshawe, Sir Thomas. *The Practice of the Exchequer Court with its Severall Offices and Officers.* London, 1658.

Finberg, H. P. R. *Tavistock Abbey.* Cambridge, 1951.

Finch, Mary E. *The Wealth of Five Northamptonshire Families, 1540–1640.* (Northamptonshire Record Society Publications, Vol. XIX.) Oxford, 1956.

Fisher, H. A. L. *The History of England from the Accession of Henry VII to the Death of Henry VIII, 1485–1547.* (Political History of England Series, eds. William Hunt and R. L. Poole, Vol. V.) London, 1906. New Impression, London, 1928.

Foss, Edward. *Judges of England, with Sketches of their Lives and Notices connected with the Courts at Westminster, 1066–1864.* 9 vols. London, 1848–64.

Foss, Edward. *Tabulae Curiales: or Tables of the Superior Courts of Westminster Hall, Showing the Judges who sat in them from 1066 to 1864; with Attorney- and Solicitor-generals for each Reign, an Alphabetical List.* London, 1865.

Foxe, John. *Actes and Monuments.* (Better known as *The Book of Martyrs.*) London, 1563. George Townsend ed., 8 vols. London, 1843–49.

Friedman, Paul. *Anne Boleyn, a Chapter of English History, 1527–1536.* 2 vols. London, 1884.

Froude, James Anthony. *History of England from the Fall of Wolsey to the Defeat of the Spanish Armada.* 12 vols. London, 1856–70. Am. ed., 12 vols. New York, 1875.

Fuller, Thomas. *The Church History of Britain.* London, 1655. 3 vols. London, 1837.

Gasquet, Francis Aiden. *The Eve of the Reformation.* London, 1900.

Gasquet, Francis Aiden. *Henry VIII and the English Monasteries.* 6th ed., 2 vols. London, 1902.

George, M. Dorothy. " Notes on the Origin of the Declared Account," *E. H. R.,* XXXI (January, 1916), 41–58.

Gibson, Alexander G. and Herbert J. Gibson. *The Isles of Scilly.* London, 1925.

Gilbert, Sir Geoffrey. *A Treatise on the Court of the Exchequer.* London, 1758.

Giuseppi, M. S. *A Guide to the Manuscripts preserved in the Public Record Office.* 2 vols. London, 1923–24.

Goff, Cecilie. *A Woman of the Tudor Age.* London, 1930.

Goldsmid, E. M. *Ten Scarce Books in English Literature.* Edinburgh, 1886.

Grigson, Geoffrey. *The Scilly Isles.* London, 1949.

Guide to the Public Records, Part I. London, 1949.

Habakkuk, H. J. " The Market for Monastic Property, 1539–1603," *Economic History Review,* Second Series (April, 1958), 362–80.

Hall, Edward. *Chronicle; Containing the History of England during the Reign of Henry the Fourth, and the Succeeding Monarchs to the end of the Reign of Henry the Eighth,* ed. Henry Ellis. London, 1809.

Hall, Edward. *Henry VIII,* edited with an Introduction by Charles Whibley. 2 vols. London, 1904.

Hammersley, G. " The Crown Woods and their Exploitation in the Sixteenth and Seventeenth Centuries," *Bulletin of the Institute of Historical Research,* XXX (November, 1957), 136–61.

Hardres, Sir Thomas. *Reports of Cases Adjudged in the Court of Exchequer, in the Years 1655, 1656, 1657, 1658, 1659, and 1660.* London, 1693.

Historical Manuscripts Commission. *Reports.* London, 1870 on.

Hitchcock, Elsie Vaughan (ed.). *The Lyfe of Sir Thomas Moore, knighte, written by William Roper, Esquire.* (Early English Text Society, Original Series, no. 197.) London, 1935.

Holdsworth, Sir William S. *A History of English Law.* 14 vols. London, 1903–52. Vol. XIV has not appeared. Various editions. Vols. XIII and XIV edited by A. L. Goodhart and H. G. Hanbury. Seventh ed. of Vol. I revised and edited by A. L. Goodhart and H. G. Hanbury, with an Introduction and additions by S. B. Crimes. London, 1956.

Hughes, Philip. *The Reformation in England.* 3 vols. London, 1950–54.

Hurstfield, Joel. "Lord Burghley as Master of the Court of Wards, 1561–98," *Transactions of the Royal Historical Society,* Fourth Series, XXXI (October, 1948), 95–114. London, 1949.

Hurstfield, Joel. "Corruption and Reform under Edward VI and Mary: The Example of Wardship," *E. H. R.,* LXVIII (January, 1953), 22–36.

Hurstfield, Joel. "The Profits of Fiscal Feudalism, 1541–1602," *Economic History Review,* Second Series, VIII (August, 1955), 53–61.

Hurstfield, Joel. "William Cecil: Minister of Elizabeth I, 1520–1598," *History Today* (December, 1956), 791–99.

Hurstfield, Joel. *The Queen's Wards: Wardship and Marriage under Elizabeth I.* London, 1958.

Jones, Emyr Gwynne. *Exchequer Proceedings (Equity) Concerning Wales: Henry VIII-Elizabeth.* (University of Wales, Board of Celtic Studies, History and Law Series, no. 4.) Cardiff, 1939.

Jordan, W. K. *Philanthropy in England, 1480–1660.* London, 1959.

Journals of the House of Lords. London, 1767–   . The *Journals* began in 1509; Vols. I and II cover the sixteenth century.

Kemble, J. M. (ed.). *Knights Hospitallers in England: Historical Introduction.* (Camden Society Publications, no. 65.) London, 1857.

Kerridge, Eric. "The Movement of Rents, 1540–1640," *Economic History Review,* Second Series, VI (August, 1953), 16–34.

Kirby, J. L. "The Rise of the Under-Treasurer of the Exchequer," *E. H. R.,* LXXII (October, 1957), 666–77.

Knowles, Dom David. *The Religious Orders in England.* 3 vols. Cambridge, 1948–59. Vol. III: *The Tudor Age.*

Lambarde, William. *Archeion or a Discourse upon the High Courts of Justice in England,* eds. Charles H. McIlwain and Paul L. Ward. Cambridge, Mass., 1957.

Lander, J. R. "Council, Administration and Councillors, 1461–1485," *Bulletin of the Institute of Historical Research,* XXXII (November, 1959), 138–80.

Lapsley, Gaillard Thomas. *The County Palatine of Durham, A Study in Constitutional History.* (Harvard Historical Studies, Vol. VIII.) Boston, 1900.

Leach, A. F. *English Schools at the Reformation, 1546–1548.* Westminster, 1896.

Letters and Papers, Foreign and Domestic, of the Reign of Henry VIII, 1509–1547. 21 vols. in 33 parts. Eds. J. S. Brewer, James Gairdner, and R. H. Brodie. London, 1862–1910. Vol. I, 2d ed., in 3 parts, London, 1920; *Addenda* to Vol. I, 2d ed., London, 1929–32.

Lewis, E. A. and J. Conway Davies (eds.). *Records of the Court of Augmentations Relating to Wales and Monmouthshire.* (University of Wales, Board of Celtic Studies, History and Law Series, no. 13.) Cardiff, 1954.

Liljegren, S. B. *The Fall of the Monasteries and the Social Changes in England.* Leipzig, 1924.

Lipson, Ephraim. *The Economic History of England.* 3 vols. London, 1929–31. [Vol. I has title: *An Introduction to the Economic History of England.*]

Lists and Indexes. (Public Record Office series.) London, 1892–   .

Lloyd, David. *The Statesmen and Favourites of England since the Reformation.* London, 1665. Later, a reprint under the title *State Worthies,* edited by Charles Whitworth, appeared. 2 vols. London, 1766.

Mackie, J. D. *The Earlier Tudors, 1485–1558.* (Oxford History of England Series, ed. G. N. Clark, Vol. VII.) Oxford, 1952.

Mackintosh, Sir James. *Miscellaneous Works.* 3 vols. London, 1846. The eulogistic " Life of Sir Thomas More " is contained in Vol. I, 391–99.

Madge, Sidney J. *The Domesday of Crown Lands.* London, 1938.

Maxwell-Lyte, Sir H. C. *Historical Notes on the Use of the Great Seal of England.* London, 1926.

Merriman, Roger Bigelow (ed.). *Life and Letters of Thomas Cromwell.* 2 vols. Oxford, 1902.

Naunton, Sir Robert. *Fragmenta Regalia: or Observations on the Late Queen Elizabeth, her Times and Favourites.* London, 1641; Edward Arber (ed.), London, 1895. The Harleian Miscellany, Vol. V. London, 1810.

Newton, A. P. " The Establishment of the Great Farm of the English Customs," *Transactions of the Royal Historical Society,* Fourth Series, I (May, 1918), 129–55.

Nichols, John G. (ed.). *Autographs of Royal, Noble, Learned, and Remarkable Personages Conspicuous in English History.* London, 1829.

Nichols, John G. (ed.). *The Diary of Henry Machyn, Citizen and*

Merchant of London, 1550–1563. (Camden Society Publications, no. 42.) London, 1848.

Nichols, John G. (ed.). *Literary Remains of King Edward VI.* 2 vols. Roxburghe Club, 1857. Vol. II contains the whole of Edward's Journal, together with his essays on political subjects and such state papers as are extant in his own autograph.

Nicolas, Sir N. H. (ed.). *Proceedings and Ordinances of the Privy Council of England, 1386–1542.* 7 vols. London, 1834–37. Vol. VII covers the period from August 10, 1540, to April 8, 1542.

North, Dudley. *Some Notes Concerning the Life of Edward Lord North, Baron of Kirtling.* First published, 1658. London, 1682.

" The Obituary of John Caley, Esq.," *Gentlemen's Magazine,* New Series, II (July-December, 1834).

Oman, Sir C. W. C. " The Tudors and the Currency, 1526–1560," *Transactions of the Royal Historical Society,* New Series, IX (1895), 167–88.

Oppenheim, Michael (ed.). *Naval Accounts and Inventories of the Reign of Henry VII, 1485–88, 1495–97.* (Navy Records Society Publications, Vol. VIII.) London, 1896.

Phillips, Charles J. *A History of the Sackville Family.* 2 vols. London, 1930.

Pickthorn, Kenneth. *Early Tudor Government.* 2 vols. Cambridge, 1934.

Plowden, Edmund. *An Exact Abridgment in English of the Commentaries or Reports of the Learned and Famous Lawyer, Edmond Plowden, by F[abian] H[icks].* London, 1650.

Plucknett, Theodore F. T. *A Concise History of the Common Law.* 4th ed., London, 1948.

Pocock, Nicholas. " The Condition of Morals and Religious Belief in the Reign of Edward VI," *E. H. R.,* X (July, 1895), 417–44.

Pollard, A. F. *England Under Protector Somerset.* London, 1900.

Pollard, A. F. " Council, Star Chamber, and Privy Council under the Tudors," *E. H. R.,* XXXVII (July, 1922), 337–60.

Pollard, A. F. *Wolsey.* Second impression, London, 1929.

Powell, Thomas. *Directions for Search of Records in the Chancerie, Tower, and Exchequer.* London, 1622.

Powicke, Sir F. M. *The Reformation in England.* London, 1941; 3d impression, 1949.

Preston, Arthur E. *The Church and Parish of St. Nicholas, Abingdon.* Oxford Historical Society Publications, Vol. 99.) Oxford, 1935.

Price, George. *A Treatise on the Law of the Exchequer.* London, 1830. Cover title: *Revenue Exchequer Practice.*

Privately Printed Tracts on the Record Commission. London [undated], c. 1833.

Read, Conyers. *Mr. Secretary Cecil and Queen Elizabeth.* London, 1955.

Read, Conyers. *Lord Burghley and Queen Elizabeth.* London, 1960.

Reeves, John. *History of English Law.* A new Am. ed. by W. F. Finlason. 5 vols. Philadelphia, 1880.

Reid, R. R. *The King's Council in the North.* London, 1921.

Record Commission. *Reports or Publications.* 92 vols. London, 1802–69.

Ricci, Seymour de. *Census of Medieval and Renaissance Manuscripts in the United States and Canada.* 3 vols. New York, 1935–40.

Richardson, W. C. *Tudor Chamber Administration, 1485–1547.* Baton Rouge, 1952.

Richardson, W. C. *Stephen Vaughan: Financial Agent of Henry VIII.* Baton Rouge, 1953.

Richardson, W. C. " Some Financial Expedients of Henry VIII," *Economic History Review,* New Series, VII (August, 1954), 33–48.

Richardson, W. C. " Records of the Court of Augmentations," *Journal of the Society of Archivists,* I (October, 1957), 159–68.

Roper, William. *The Life of More,* ed. S. W. Singer. Chiswick, 1817.

Rowse, A. L. " The Duchy of Cornwall," *Nineteenth Century,* CXXI (January, 1937), 43–56.

Rowse, A. L. *Tudor Cornwall, Portrait of a Society.* London, 1941.

Rowse, A. L. *The England of Elizabeth.* London, 1950.

Sackville-West, V. *Knole and the Sackvilles.* London, 1948.

Sanders, George William. *Orders of the High Court of Chancery.* 2 parts. London, 1845.

Sargeaunt, John. *A History of Felsted School, with Some Account of the Founder and his Decendants.* London, 1889.

Savine, Alexander N. *English Monasteries on the Eve of the Dissolution.* (Oxford Studies in Social and Legal History, ed. Sir Paul Vinogradoff, Vol. I.) Oxford, 1909.

Savine, Alexander N. " Bondmen under the Tudors," *Transactions of the Royal Historical Society,* New Series, XVII (January, 1903), 235–89. London, 1917.

Simon, Joan. " A F. Leach on the Reformation: I and II," *British Journal of Educational Studies,* III (May, 1955), 128–43; IV (November, 1955), 32–48.

Smith, H. M. *Henry VIII and the Reformation.* London, 1948.

Smith, Lacey Baldwin. *Tudor Prelates and Politics*. Princeton, N. J., 1953.

Snell, Lawrence S. *Documents Towards a History of the Reformation in Cornwall. No. 1: The Chantry Certificates for Cornwall*. Exeter, 1953. *No. 2: The Edwardian Inventories of Church Goods for Cornwall*. Exeter, 1955.

Somerville, Robert. " The Duchy of Lancaster Council and Court of Duchy Chamber," *Transactions of the Royal Historical Society*, Fourth Series, XXIII (June, 1940), 159–77. London, 1941.

Somerville, Robert. *The Duchy of Lancaster*. London, 1946. Printed by the Council of the Duchy.

Somerville, Robert. " The Duchy of Lancaster Records," *Transactions of the Royal Historical Society*, Fourth Series, XXIX (November, 1945), 1–17. London, 1947.

Somerville, Robert. *History of the Duchy of Lancaster*. 2 vols. London, 1953–   . Only the first vol. published.

Stanway, the Rev. Oscar. *The Story of Okewood Church*. Dorking, 1940.

Statutes at Large, ed. Danby Pickering, *et al*. 105 vols. Cambridge, 1762–65. Followed by *The Public General Statutes*.

Statutes of the Realm, eds. A. Luders, T. E. Tomlins, J. Raithby, *et al*. 9 vols.; *Index*, 2 vols. London, 1810–28.

Steel, Anthony. *The Receipt of the Exchequer, 1377–1485*. Cambridge, 1954.

Stenton, Sir F. M. *The First Century of English Feudalism, 1066–1166*. Oxford, 1932.

Stone, Lawrence. " The Political Program of Thomas Cromwell," *Bulletin of the Institute of Historical Research*, XXIV (May, 1951), 1–18.

Stone, Lawrence. *An Elizabethan: Sir Horatio Palavicino*. Oxford, 1956.

Stow, John. *Survey of the Cities of London and Westminster*. London, 1720.

Strype, John. *Historical Works*. New ed., 21 vols. in 27 parts. Oxford, 1920–40.

Tanner, J. R. (ed.). *Tudor Constitutional Documents*. Cambridge, 1940.

Tanner, Thomas. *Notitia Monastica: an Account of all Abbeys, etc. in England and Wales*. London, 1744. Later ed., with notes by J. Nasmith, Cambridge, 1787.

Tawney, R. H. *The Agrarian Problem in the Sixteenth Century.* London, 1912.

Thomas, F. S. *Note of Materials for the History of Public Departments.* London, 1846.

Thorne, Samuel E. " Courts of Record and Sir Edward Coke," *Toronto Law Journal,* II (1937–38), 24–49.

Thorne, Samuel E. (ed.). *Prerogativa Regis: Tertia Lectura Roberti Constable De Lyncolnis Inne Anno 11 H. 7.* New Haven, 1949.

Tout, T. F. *Chapters in the Administrative History of Mediaeval England.* 6 vols. Manchester, 1920–33.

Trevelyan Papers, eds. J. Payne Collier (Parts I–II), Sir Walter Calverley Trevelyan and Sir Charles Edward Trevelyan (Part III). (Camden Society Publications, Old Series, nos. 67, 84, 105.) London, 1857, 1863, 1872.

Troutbeck, John. *A Survey of the Ancient and Present State of the Scilly Islands.* London, 1794.

Tytler, Patrick Fraser. *England under the Reigns of Edward VI and Mary.* 2 vols. Illustrated by a series of original letters. London, 1839.

Vyvyan, C. C. *The Scilly Isles.* (The Regional Book Series, ed. Brian Vesey-Vitzgerald.) London, 1953.

Walcott, M. E. S. " Inventories and Valuations of Religious Houses at the Time of the Dissolution," *Archaeologia,* XLIII (1771), 210–49.

Warton, Thomas. *The Life of Sir Thomas Pope, Founder of Trinity College, Oxford.* London, 1772; 2d ed., enlarged, London, 1780.

Wheeler-Holohan, V. *The History of the King's Messengers.* London, 1935.

Williams, Penry. *The Council of the Marches of Wales under Elizabeth I.* Cardiff, 1958.

Wolffe, B. P. " The Management of English Royal Estates under the Yorkist Kings," *E. H. R.,* LXXI (January, 1956), 1–27.

Wright, Thomas. *History of the County of Essex.* 2 vols. London, 1836.

Wright, Thomas (ed.). *Letters relating to the Suppression of Monasteries.* (Camden Society Publications, no. 26.) London, 1843.

Youings, Joyce A. " The Disposal of Monastic Property in Land in the County of Devon," a thesis summary, *Bulletin of the Institute of Historical Research,* XXIV (November, 1951), 198–202.

Youings, Joyce A. " The Terms of the Disposal of the Devon Monastic Lands, 1536–58," *E. H. R.,* LXIX (January, 1954), 18–38.

Youings, Joyce A. (ed.). *Devon Monastic Lands: Calendar of Particulars for Grants, 1536–1558.* (Devon and Cornwall Records Society Publications, New Series, I.) 1955.

Youings, Joyce A. "The Council of the West," *Transactions of the Royal Historical Society,* Fifth Series, X (March, 1959), 41-59. London, 1960.

INDEX